FREUD AND JUNG

FREUD AND JUNG
Conflicts of interpretation

Robert S. Steele

With consulting editor
Susan V. Swinney

Routledge & Kegan Paul
London, Boston, Melbourne & Henley

First published in 1982
by Routledge & Kegan Paul Ltd
39 Store Street, London WC1E 7DD,
9 Park Street, Boston Mass. 02108, USA
296 Beaconsfield Parade, Middle Park,
Melbourne 3206, Australia and
Broadway House, Newtown Road,
Henley-on-Thames, Oxon RG9 1EN
Printed in Great Britain by Billing & Sons Ltd
Guildford, London, Oxford and Worcester
Copyright © Robert S. Steele 1982

Library of Congress Cataloging in Publication Data

Steele, Robert S.
Freud and Jung, conflicts of interpretation.

Bibliography: p.
Includes index.
1. Freud, Sigmund, 1856–1939. 2. Jung,
C.G. (Carl Gustav), 1875–1961. 3. Psycho-
analysis. I. Swinney, Susan V. (Susan
Virginia) II. Title. III. Title: Conflicts
of interpretation. [DNLM: Psychoanalysis.
2. Psychoanalytic interpretation. WM 460.7
S814f]
BF175.S647   150.19'52   81-22699
ISBN 0-7100-9067-6   AACR2

CONTENTS

v

FOREWORD

Hermeneutics is the art or science of interpretation and it provides the best criteria with which to evaluate the works of Freud and Jung. For too long psychoanalysis and analytical psychology have been judged by the standards of the natural sciences or experimentally oriented social sciences when these theories should be assessed on an entirely different basis. Both are hermeneutic systems and should be evaluated using interpretative criteria: how open in his work is each man to the people and texts he is analyzing, what are the organizing principles used by each theory to construct historical portraits of humankind, and how does each man understand his own life and use this vision of himself in his work?

That Freud's and Jung's lives shaped their theories is obvious and well known, but the degree to which each man used his psychological insights to order his own life and his description of his past is explored for the first time in this book. Freud's recounting of his childhood, especially his emphasis on conflicts with his father, is a model psychoanalytic narrative and Jung's autobiography, which emphasizes his mystical experiences, has clearly been shaped by his theories.

Each man's account of their collaboration and bitter separation must be carefully examined because the events of those years between 1906 and 1914 have been obscured by the tendentious distortions of both men and their biographers. The two men were very close for several years and then, within a year, they separated because of a massive alienation of affections, administrative squabbles, theoretical disagreements, and because each man's questioning of the other's views called into doubt the other's explanation of his whole life.

Freud saw his life and the lives of other people as determined by biological drives and the residues of difficulties in early childhood. However, I show that his biological determinism is a fiction which he uses to create models for constructing individual biographies. Freud, constantly searching for real events by which to explain adult suffering, created these 'actual' occurrences in the infantile past and human phylogenetic history. Jung saw life as the unfolding of a spiritual destiny and saw in human development the recapitulation of archetypal fictions. His work was devoted to explicating the role these guiding fictions played in his and others' spiritual quests.

After the break Freud and Jung did not agree on many things and their differences are canonized in their interpretative dis-

agreements about science, religion, mythology, and the forces
operating in individual's lives. Their antithetical positions on
many issues can be traced to one central philosophical divergence. They did not agree on what reality was. I show how each
transformed the unknown into the known through interpretation
and why, given their views on reality, Freud's case studies are
better than Jung's and Jung's textual analyses are superior to
Freud's.

This book provides a re-orientation and new direction for the
study of psychology. It finds in psychoanalysis and analytical
psychology two model hermeneutic systems which in their conflicts provide complementary schemata which can both be used
to restory human lives. By stressing the role that interpretation
plays in constructing biographical histories, in showing how
Freud and Jung built their own life stories through interpretation, and in providing hermeneutic guidelines for psychology
'Conflicts of Interpretation' should open a new way of doing
research in psychology; provide a manifesto, based on the work
of the human sciences, which legitimates therapy as a form of
investigation; and alert each reader to the ways in which both
fiction and fact are used by people in understanding their lives.

Many people make a book; I would like to thank the two people
who have contributed the most to this work. My thanks first to
Susan V. Swinney, who taught me how to write the English
language and how to think analytically. Her constant question,
'What are you really trying to say here?' was with me through
every stage of this work. Without her ability to formulate a
question clearly and develop an orderly answer, plus her endless
perseverance in discussing everything from commas to cathexes,
this book would not have taken the form it did, and without the
stimulation of her critical intelligence I might not have written
it at all.

Thanks, also, to Paul B. Jacobsen, a good friend and co-
worker, whose discussions with me helped to change how I think
about psychoanalysis.

ACKNOWLEDGMENTS

Grateful acknowledgment is made to: Basic Books, Inc. Publishers, New York for permission to quote from 'Studies on Hysteria' by Josef Breuer and Sigmund Freud, translated from the German and edited by James Strachey in collaboration with Anna Freud, assisted by Alix Strachey and Alan Tyson, published in the United States by Basic Books, Inc. by arrangement with The Hogarth Press, Ltd; and from 'The Origins of Psycho-Analysis: Letters to Wilhelm Fliess, Drafts and Notes: 1887-1902' by Sigmund Freud, edited by Marie Bonaparte, Anna Freud, and Ernst Kris, authorized translation by Eric Mosbacher and James Strachey. Introduction by Ernst Kris, introductory Essay by Stephen Marcus, Copyright © 1954 by Basic Books, Inc. Introductory Essay Copyright © 1977 by Stephen Marcus; Basic Books, Inc. Publishers, New York and George Allen & Unwin Ltd to quote from 'The Interpretation of Dreams' by Sigmund Freud, translated from the German and edited by James Strachey; Collins Publishers and Pantheon Books, a Division of Random House, Inc., for permission to use excerpts from 'Memories, Dreams, Reflections' by C.G. Jung, recorded and edited by Aniela Jaffé, translated by Richard and Clara Winston, Copyright © 1961, 1962, 1963 by Random House, Inc.; Alfred A. Knopf, Inc. for permission to quote from 'Opus Posthumous,' by Wallace Stevens, edited by Samuel French Morse, New York: Knopf, 1975; Princeton University Press, Routledge & Kegan Paul Ltd, Sigmund Freud Copyrights Ltd, and The Hogarth Press Ltd. for permission to reprint excerpts from 'The Freud/Jung Letters: The Correspondence between Sigmund Freud and C.G. Jung,' edited by William McGuire, translated by Ralph Mannheim and R.F.C. Hull, Bollingen Series XCIV. Copyright © 1974 by Sigmund Freud Copyrights Ltd and Erbengemeinschaft Prof. Dr C.G. Jung; Princeton University Press to quote from the following volumes of 'The Collected Works of C.G. Jung,' translated by R.F.C. Hull, Bollingen Series XX: vol. 1: 'Psychiatric Studies,' copyright © 1957, 1970 by Princeton University Press, vol. 2: 'Experimental Researches,' copyright © 1973 by Princeton University Press, vol. 4: 'Freud and Psychoanalysis,' copyright © 1961 by Princeton University Press, vol. 5: 'Symbols of Transformation,' copyright © 1956 by Princeton University Press, vol. 6: 'Psychological Types,' copyright © 1971 by Princeton University Press, vol. 7: 'Two Essays on Analytical Psychology,' copyright 1953, © 1966 by Princeton University Press, vol. 8: 'The Structure and Dynamics of the

Psyche,' copyright © 1960, 1969 by Princeton University Press, vol. 9.1: 'The Archetypes and the Collective Unconscious,' copyright © 1959, 1969 by Princeton University Press, vol. 9.2: 'Aion: Researches into the Phenomenology of the Self,' copyright © 1959 by Princeton University Press, vol. 10: 'Civilization in Transition,' copyright © 1964, 1970 by Princeton University Press, vol. 11: 'Psychology and Religion: West and East,' copyright © 1958, 1969 by Princeton University Press, vol. 12: 'Psychology and Alchemy,' copyright 1953, © 1968 by Princeton University Press, vol. 14: 'Mysterium Coniunctionis,' copyright © 1965, 1970 by Princeton University Press, vol. 15: 'The Spirit in Man, Art, and Literature,' copyright © 1966 by Princeton University Press, vol. 16: 'The Practice of Psychotherapy,' copyright 1954, © 1966 by Princeton University Press, vol. 17: 'The Development of Personality,' copyright © 1954 by Princeton University Press, vol. 18: 'The Symbolic Life,' copyright 1950, 1953, © 1955, 1958, 1959, 1963, 1968, 1969, 1970, 1973, 1976 by Princeton University Press; Routledge & Kegan Paul Ltd for permission to quote from 'The Collected Works of C.G. Jung,' translated by R.F.C. Hull; Sigmund Freud Copyrights Ltd, The Institute of Psycho-Analysis, and The Hogarth Press Ltd, for permission to quote from 'The Standard Edition of the Complete Psychological Works of Sigmund Freud' translated and edited by James Strachey.

1 HERMENEUTICS, HISTORY AND BIOGRAPHICAL STORIES

Interpretations answer questions; questions confront us. They block the flow of experience and set reflection in motion. Reflection is also experience, but of a different kind. It diverts our interest from involvement in the world and turns it on ourselves, our pasts, and our relations with others and the world. When the child begins to ask who, what, how and why we know she or he has left a world which from then on will remain but a dream. From that point we know beyond a doubt that another member of our species is conscious. Perhaps the origin of our species lay in the first question the first person ever asked. This primal question, this moment of doubt and wonder, would have provided the spark which has been the light of consciousness.

Each time a question is asked, a halt in experience is being called. One asks for an answer which requires a reordering, rerouting, and rethinking of existence. In short, one must reflect before one re-enters the unreflective flow of experience. Periodically through the land we hear the cry: 'Return to experience,' as if we had left our homeland. For us, the departure took place a long time ago in our infancies and the birth of our race. The challenge to return to experience is in itself a questioning of questioning. We are asking ourselves what reflection really achieves, and calling into doubt human powers of recreating a unity which has been lost.

With the questioning of the questioner, with the doubt about our conscious ability to restore unity, with the fear that consciousness itself may be the problem, and with the problem of consciousness - which is the question for philosophy and psychology - we entered the modern age. The Age of Enlightenment brought doubt for it asked self-referential questions - we began questioning ourselves: who are we, what is our place in the world, and how do we answer such questions? The history of human thought is the chronicle of questions that individuals have put to themselves and others and the responses which have been given, answers which have in turn raised questions. The question sets the dialectic of question and answer in motion. It engenders the dialogue which is at the heart of individual and collective consciousness.

For us today, existence lies in the dialectic; it is situated between outside and inside, between the world and ourselves, between reality and imagination, between objective and subjective, and in the gulf that magically links the signified to the signifier. It lies in the chasm separating the world-views of

Freud and Jung - between Sigmund Freud, who located the core
of being in the vicissitudes of sexuality, anchoring his interpretative system to material reality, the body, and social interaction; and C.G. Jung, who located the essence of experience
in the transformations of the imagination, tying his hermeneutic
to psychological reality, spiritual being, and mythology. The
Weltanschauungen of these two men are as different as those of
Aristotle and Plato, Origen and Tertullian, positivists and ideal-
ists, physics and metaphysics, the sciences and the humanities.

To question and compare systems which themselves question
the very nature of experience, and to weigh fairly the answers
given by such systems, one must locate oneself within a context
of inquiry which can do justice to antithetical positions, to
world-views in collision. Our position must take an *a priori* stand
of neutrality on fundamental questions about the nature of reality and experience if we are to successfully inquire into the
conflicts of interpretation which arise between psychoanalysis,
committed as it is to a positivist materialist view, and analytical
psychology which is equally committed to an idealist spiritual
position. It is in hermeneutics that we will ground ourselves, for
it recognizes the necessity of such antitheses; only in the dialectic is the dialogue which is essential to human existence maintained.

Freud and Jung asked questions and our concern is to question
them, to keep the dialogue which they helped to foster at the
beginning of this century alive and vital. Orthodoxy and faith
are antithetical to inquiry for they restrict questioning. On the
Continent psychoanalysis has been revived by the 'return to
Freud' in the writings of Lacan, Laplanche, and Ricoeur and
revitalized by the works of Gadamer, Habermas and Radnitzky.
In America psychoanalysis survives but does not excite. One
asks, why? Because we, with our devotion to science, misread
Freud. We follow his own misunderstanding of his work as being
a natural science. We then require of Jung, because we expect
psychology to be a science and he calls himself a psychologist,
that his work be verifiable by natural scientific methods.

This book will not examine in depth the natural scientific
paradigm which psychology has almost without question adopted,
but will point the way, following Freud and Jung, to another
conception of psychology. This is psychology as a member of the
Geisteswissenschaften, as a human not a natural science. 'As an
extension of biology, psychology is a science in the most rigorous
and demanding sense of that term,' but 'psychology as a field of
enquiry connects as easily to biography as to biology' (Scheibe,
1978, p. 880). If we put aside our competitive comparisons we
see that neither the sciences nor the humanities 'should be
regarded as superior - their relationship should be conceived
horizontally rather than vertically' (p. 881). Psychology as a
humanistic discipline needs an intellectual and methodological
revival so that it will survive as an equal to psychology as a
science. For only if this humanistic side is healthy can psychology

maintain that dynamic tension which locates it on the point of division between the sciences and humanities.

Freud and Jung were scientific visionaries. Both men went beyond their natural scientific educations to found new sciences - human sciences - thereby organizing their own often deeply moving experiences and the experiences of others within two interpretative frameworks. We will here show that these two systems are hermeneutic, historical, and biographical, and that both systems are best understood when evaluated in the light of hermeneutics.

HERMENEUTICS

Hermeneutics is the art or science of interpretation. Its traditional concern has been with textual interpretation and methodological issues in such work. Hermeneutics in its modern form is the dominant method of the human sciences; it is used in the law, history, and criticism, and by those social sciences which are not conceived on the model of the natural sciences.

The paradigmatic hermeneutic situation is the reader questioning a text. The core of hermeneutics is the question. For with the question a dialogue - the model method of interpretative inquiry - between the text and reader is instigated. The interpreter - for any reader who asks questions becomes an interpreter - tries to find within the text answers to her or his questions: what does that mean, why was that said, how does that relate to what was said earlier? The questions we ask of the printed word are asked of the author who is present in the text and are the same questions which we ask of others and of ourselves. Hermeneutics has expanded beyond its origins in textual interpretation and become a discipline concerned with the interpretation of human products and experiences. There would be no need of hermeneutics if we did not ask questions about ourselves, but we do. We put questions to anything: paintings, novels, political essays, cosmological theories and other people. Modern hermeneutics provides methodological guidelines for asking and answering questions.

The hermeneutic method is not hard to understand, but it is damnably difficult to practice. The method is dialogue. Questions are answered through the give and take of discussion, through the dialectics of exchange between two subjects. What makes interpretation hard is granting the other the status of subject, seeing that the text, painting, or other person is a carrier of meaning, and letting their meanings question our own understandings. We learn nothing if we do not question. If we do not let others or ourselves question us then we remain forever unchanged. To let the other speak and try our best to hear is the difficult task that hermeneutics sets for us.

The goal of hermeneutics is to increase human understanding by questioning how we come to misconstrue, misunderstand,

disagree, agree, understand and reach consensus. Freud and
Jung were not only two of the great questioners and answer-
givers of our century, but they were also partners in creating
one of the twentieth century's great intellectual battles. An
investigation of their monumental mutual misunderstanding will
be a central concern of ours. We will try to fathom how two men
could work closely with each other for six years and then within
a year sever all personal relations. Each man, of course, has
his explanation for the break, but neither answer, nor the
answers of each man's followers, is satisfactory. This is because
once the dialogue between Freud and Jung was terminated, two
competing schools of interpretation, carried forward to our day
by Freudians and Jungians, were founded. As both Freud and
Jung denied the validity of each other's work and questioned
each other's sanity, so each school often denies the world-view
of the other.

To understand the break we must return to it and immerse
ourselves in these two men's works and lives. In chapters 7 and
8 we will do this. Chapter 7, 'Binding ties,' explores the bonds
of personal, intellectual, and administrative co-operation which
led Freud to designate Jung his 'son and heir' and Jung to
address Freud as 'father.' 'The break and its ramifications,'
chapter 8, seeks through interpretation to reach an understanding of why Freud came to call Jung 'brutal and sanctimonious'
and why Jung challenged Freud to analyze himself. There we will
begin to explore the essential theoretical disagreements which
divide psychoanalysis from analytical psychology.

There is an irony in the break between Freud and Jung. Two
men who devoted their lives to helping others understand themselves could not, in the end, understand or tolerate each other.
In founding psychoanalysis, Freud established a method of
therapeutics which is hermeneutic, but neither he nor Jung, who
followed him into hermeneutic therapy, could save their friendship, because in the end they disagreed about how one does
interpretation. The dialogue between analyst and analysand is,
in ideal form, a model for hermeneutic inquiry. It is an interaction which is relatively free of restrictions on questions which
can be asked and answers which can be given, of conjectures
which can be advanced and responses which can be made, and
it is a place where the analysand is free to tell his or her story.
The relations between Freud and Jung came nowhere near this
ideal, and in this we will find the basic fault in their association.

In the last chapter, 'Hermeneutics and interpretative psychology,' we will return to an investigation of the close bond between
hermeneutics and psychoanalysis. There is another irony here,
for to do so we will have to uncover through interpretation something in Freud's work which in some places he denies, at others
ignores, and in still others admits. This is that psychoanalysis
is an interpretative science and that interpretation lies at the
core of psychoanalysis. An examination of Jung's ties to hermeneutics will not be as difficult; soon after he broke with Freud

he declared his work to be hermeneutic and saw it as increasing understanding through interpretation. In chapter 11 we will also formulate a hermeneutic methodology for psychology which establishes a foundation for it as an interpretative discipline.

Such a model denies the possibility of one answer. It celebrates the power of individuals to inquire and to construct replies which, within a context, answer their questions. In the penultimate chapter, 'Conflicts of interpretation,' we will see how Freud's and Jung's answers to the questions they asked about myth, science, religion, art, and reality, about the structure of the psyche, about men and women, and about the history of consciousness were quite different because the assumptions they made about interpreting human communications - texts, fantasies, dreams, and stories - were radically different. Freud assumed a position of doubt, questioning the manifest content of human expression in order to find by interpretation the real latent meaning. Where Freud saw disguise and distortion, Jung saw a failure to understand. He did not decode, but worked by explication to bring out meanings which had not been realized.

If we take up the position that theoretical conflicts can be resolved by some scientific observation, or that a theoretical statement is useless if it is not testable scientifically, we lose far too much. The disagreements over theory and the different positions which Freud and Jung arrived at through interpretation will not be resolved by an experiment or set of experiments. Attempts have been made to conjure away their work by calling it unscientific, but this is only the condemnation of someone who feels that all psychological inquiry must ape the methods of natural science. People happen to disagree about a great many things. Hermeneutics accepts this as a starting point. The questions become on what issues do individuals disagree and how did their methods lead them to different answers? For Freud and Jung these are central questions which we address throughout this work, especially in chapters 7, 8, 10 and 11. We have here in chapter 1 established our context of inquiry on the most neutral ground we can find. We have located ourselves within hermeneutics.

HISTORY

Some of the disagreements between Freud and Jung can, of course, be traced to their life experiences. Chapter 2, 'Recollections,' is a brief history of each man's life until he committed himself to his lifelong vocation. 'Josef Breuer: Freud's last father,' chapter 3, is about Freud's relations with the man he once called the discoverer of psychoanalysis and about the beginnings of narrative therapy in Breuer's treatment of Anna O. Freud's break with Breuer as well as his relations with Wilhelm Fliess were prototypical for his later problems with Jung and were in part responsible for his undertaking his self-analysis.

In chapter 4, 'The immaculate analysis,' we will explore in depth
the origins of psychoanalysis in Freud's own self-analytic
investigation.

'The whole lost story: the psychoanalytic narrative,' chapter
5, examines Freud's psychoanalytic works and uncovers in them
a systematic methodology for constructing life histories. We will
find in 'The Interpretation of Dreams' the work, not of a natural
scientist, but of an interpreter. At the core of this foundational
work is Freud's fundamental misconception of his own work. It
is the misconstrual of his task as scientific, when that work is
actually hermeneutic and historical.

History provides us with a retrospective understanding of
experience. Historical studies are non-deterministic and apredic-
tive, because the meaning of a past event is always provisional,
awaiting future developments and interpretations. Collingwood's
view in 'The Idea of History,' which is here adopted, is that in
historical explanation 'earlier terms are *retrospectively and only
retrospectively* both necessary and sufficient' (Mink, 1972,
p. 175). An event is given meaning by constructing a context of
prior and subsequent occurrences, thereby locating it in a causal
narrative which gives it significance.

Natural science has built itself upon the hypothetical-deductive
model – the if-then paradigm. Its power lies in the prediction of
outcomes and its explanatory system is causal. Neither psychoanalysis nor analytical psychology is predictive, although both
use causal explanation to create understanding. They operate
retrospectively, trying to delineate those events and transformations which were necessary to produce what is observed.
The predictive causality of natural science is replaced in them by
narrative causality. Looking backwards from the present to the
past, they construct by interpretation of reminiscences a causally
linked sequence which explains the present. Chapter 5 demonstrates that this is fundamental in psychoanalytical explanation,
and chapters 8 and 9 develop its centrality for analytical psychology. In chapter 7's analysis of the Rat Man case and chapter 8's
analyses of 'Totem and Taboo' and the Wolf Man case we will
further show the historical hermeneutic nature of analytic inquiry.
Such a view recognizes that all accounts of the past are shaped
and ordered by the historian-interpreter's position in the present. In chapter 8 we will see that disagreement over this point
was an issue which divided Freud and Jung, and that Jung's
claim that patients retrospectively sexualized their childhood
experiences was rejected by Freud.

To see that the present shapes one's view of the past is vital
in understanding the confluence of the works and lives of both
men. It is their works which have made their lives so interesting,
and it is the importance of their works and questions arising
from them which have led to the great proliferation of biographies
of these two men. The biographers rely on Freud's and Jung's
own histories of their lives, especially for information about their
childhoods. The point most biographers miss is that what is

known of Freud's and Jung's childhoods has been shaped by each
man's psychological theories. Most chronicles of their lives point
with varying degrees of astonishment at how perfectly their
childhood experiences predestined them to create the systems
that they did. What is lost in this amazement is that Freud's
reports of what happened to him as a child were shaped by
memories which he sought to understand through his own analysis. His childhood has been retrospectively colored by his ordering of his life in analytic terms. Jung's autobiography, 'Memories,
Dreams, Reflections,' makes this point even clearer. Written when
Jung was in his eighties, it is obvious that his past was being
reconstructed and that his view of the past and the events which
were significant in his life had been shaped by his life's work.
In chapter 4 on Freud's self-analysis, and chapter 9 'Archetypal
visions' in which we examine Jung's self-analysis and the founding of analytical psychology, we will see how each man's understanding of his past and the life histories of people in general
was shaped by the radical change in consciousness his own
analysis created.

   While it is important to realize how much a person's adult life
experiences shape his or her recollections of the past, the conventional view that one's life experiences affect one's work is
also true, and we will find that a profound difference between
the lives of Freud and Jung was that Jung's ideas, as is shown
in chapter 6, were shaped by studying under Freud, while
Freud had already committed himself to a system of interpretation before he ever heard of Jung.

BIOGRAPHICAL STORIES

Histories of individuals who have actually lived are biographies.
Freud and Jung shaped a genre of biography - the case history.
Case studies, along with the interpretation of novels, myths,
and works of art, were the proofs which both men used for their
theories. The case history is the story of a patient's life told
from a theoretical perspective. Such stories are narratives which
retrospectively order a person's experience in an attempt to
explain his or her suffering. They do not provide scientific
proofs following the hypothetical-deductive model of predictive
causality. The narrative causality of a story is ideally suited
for presenting interpretative evidence. Such an approach combines the particulars of an individual life, the idiographic, with
general theoretical presuppositions about human nature, the
nomothetic, to present evidence which orders a life in terms of
a theory.

   The case history has a second advantage. It easily incorpor-
ates changes over long periods of time into a coherent story. It
integrates incidents by establishing amongst them a matrix of
interconnections. Narrative brings together the synchronic and
diachronic dimensions of the temporal. Whereas science's main

focus is on the synchronic dimension, what is observed in the
present or at a particular point in time, and history's main
focus is the diachronic, what happened in the past, the biographical account produced by analysis integrates the two. What
is observed in the ongoing present of the analytic session is
incorporated with the recollections of the analysand to provide
a coherent life history which makes sense of the present in terms
of the past.

While Freud's strength lay in the case study, Jung's lay in
textual interpretation. In 'Case and text,' the last section of
chapter 10, we will examine this difference and the reasons for
it more closely. Freud's cases masterfully weave together a
story; Jung's, however, fail to bring the analysand as a person
to life. But Jung's textual analyses, especially of myths, are
hermeneutically far superior to Freud's.

Facts in the form of dates, documents, and trustworthy observations are the warp around which the weft of interpretation is
woven to produce the fabric of a historical narrative. Like social
historical explanations, our explanations of our own pasts are
always being modified by present circumstances and future
expectations. However, an individual life is rarely as well documented as a social event and an individual's recollections of the
past are, perhaps, more shaped by the intervention of time and
experience than are social histories. Social history can return to
the documents as a foundation upon which to weave its stories.
Individual lives are rarely well documented, and one must weave
one's speculations around reminiscences - copies of events which
change with the passage of time and are retrospectively modified
by intervening experiences. Often it takes a great deal of interpretation to establish a fact of any interest about an individual
life. Herein lies another way in which the consideration of stories
enters into our study. Both Freud and Jung were acutely aware
of their own life histories and concerned about the presentation
of their stories to their followers and readers. Both men created
tales of mythic proportions about themselves. We will try to find
them behind their myths, not in order to denigrate, but to ask
why each man presented his story as he did. Our goal will be to
understand, for this is the task of interpretation.

2   RECOLLECTIONS

Two stories capture the differences between the childhoods of Freud and Jung. A Christian knocks a Jew's cap off into the mud. God defecates on a church. The first event has occurred countless times: the second is more unusual. Although the first shaped the life of Sigmund Freud and the second was vital in Jung's development, neither occurrence was a physical reality in the life it influenced. The first took place in a story, the second in a fantasy.

When he was over forty, Freud recalled that at age ten or twelve his father Jakob told him:

> When I was a young man...I went for a walk one Saturday in the streets of your birthplace [Freiberg, Moravia]. I was well dressed, and had a new fur cap on my head. A Christian came up to me and with a single blow knocked off my cap into the mud and shouted: 'Jew! Get off the pavement!'

Young Sigmund asked, 'And what did you do?'
Jakob quietly replied, 'I went into the roadway and picked up my cap....' (1900, p. 197)

In his eighties, Carl Jung recalls that at age twelve while walking home from school in Basel he saw the new brightly glazed tiles of the cathedral.

> I was overwhelmed by the beauty of the sight, and thought: 'The world is so beautiful and the church is beautiful, and God made all of this and sits above it far away in the blue sky on a golden throne and...' Here came a great hole in my thoughts, and a choking sensation. (1973b, p. 36)

Jung felt numbed and knew he could not go on thinking for if he did something terrible would happen. He was in agony for three days. A thought he did not want to think was being forced on him. But by whom? Not by his parents. His father was a pious, if uninspired, Protestant minister and in his mother's family there were eight parsons. His mother asked what was troubling him. Carl would not tell her, for to confess he would have to think the terrible thought. On the third night his torment became unbearable. The idea was forcing itself upon him against his conscious will. He resolved to discover the force behind the unthinkable thought. It did not lie in his family. He mentally ran through his ancestors including Adam and Eve and came to the

conclusion that God had placed before the first man and woman
the opportunity to sin. Jung at an early age was being tested;
his faith and courage were on trial. God was the force behind
the terrible thought:

> I gathered all my courage, as though I were about to leap
> forthwith into hell-fire, and let the thought come. I saw
> before me the cathedral, the blue sky. God sits on His golden
> throne, high above the world - and from the throne an enor-
> mous turd falls upon the sparkling new roof, shatters it, and
> breaks the walls of the cathedral asunder (p. 39).[1]

Out of the multitude of physical events, stories, fantasies,
and dreams Freud and Jung experienced as children the Jew's
cap and God's defecation, along with others, were used respectively by each man retrospectively to create an understanding
of his life for himself and others. In both these vignettes are
two themes, religion and the father-son relationship, which will
recur again in our study of these two men's lives and works.
The two stories also highlight an important point. Each man in
his childhood recollections found and told us about very different
types of events. While their childhoods must have shaped their
adult lives and works, we should not lose sight of the point that
each man's work shaped what we know about his childhood.

CHILDHOOD

There is a problem in writing about Freud's childhood. Our
information comes almost entirely from Freud himself. In his
reminiscences he has told the incidents which he could remember
and the events he wanted others to know about. 'The Interpretation of Dreams' is not only the cornerstone of his work, it was,
until the publication of Freud's correspondence with Wilhelm
Fliess, also the richest source of biographical details about
Freud's childhood. Robert charges, too strongly, that in it
Freud 'deliberately omitted the figures of his parents' (1966,
p. 21). Freud told what was necessary from his life in order to
make his method of dream-interpretation understandable. What
we know of his early years has also been dictated by the direction of his self-analysis. From a mass of analytic material he
used those events of which he could make sense. We know those
incidents around which he could, by using his simultaneously
developing psychoanalytic theories, weave a coherent explanation
- construct a consistent story. Psychoanalytic theory in turn
has had such a great impact that it has shaped all subsequent
accounts of Freud's life. The Fliess correspondence has been
edited highlighting Freud's progressive deepening of his own
self-understanding, and the major biographies of Freud - for
example Jones (1953) and Schur (1972) - have been written from
a psychoanalytic perspective. With its emphasis on familial

relations - ambivalence towards the father, love for the mother, early sexual experience, rivalry with siblings, and the origins of adult character in childhood - Freud's account of his youth was the first life history constructed following the narrative guidelines of psychoanalysis. It remains the prototypical analytic story.

Jakob Freud was a wool merchant. Three years after Sigmund's birth on 6 May 1856, the family moved to Vienna because of Jakob's financial troubles. Although forty when Sigmund - the first child by his third wife - was born, Jakob had not yet managed, according to Sigmund's adult recollections, to provide a very secure household. Of the early years in Vienna Freud says they were 'long and difficult' not 'worth remembering' (1899, p. 312). There is in Freud's memories of his father the presence of two antithetical currents. Jakob is both aggrandized and denigrated.

Jakob is elevated as the man whose words - 'The boy will come to nothing' - haunted his son into middle age, goading him on to success after success in order to prove that he had 'come to something' (Freud, 1900, p. 216). The essence of success for Freud was to do better than one's father, and yet it seemed to him that to excel one's father was forbidden (1936). To succeed where the father has failed is to put oneself higher than that being which psychoanalysis equates with God.

Yet Freud's portrait of Jakob is of a man who was powerless. Freud once described him as much like the Dickens character Mr Micawber, 'always hopefully expecting something to turn up' (Jones, 1953, p. 2). From Jones's biography and Freud's accounts, Jakob emerges as an ineffectual man. His worldly success was minimal, not much to overcome. He was neither a strong forceful patriarch nor a tyrant in the home. He was kind, gentle, and impressed by his son's academic brilliance. He provided little direction in helping Sigmund make decisions about his education and placed few restrictions on his son. He was neither ambitious nor a fighter; he was a man who would simply go into the road and pick up his cap.

Jakob does not seem like a man who could fulfill what his son came to see as the strongest of childhood needs: 'the need for a father's protection' (1930, p. 72). There is a problem here and Freud's own work highlights the difficulty of assessing what the actual nature of any important emotional relation was. Memory is retrospectively altered by the passage of time; the past is refracted by the medium of the intervening years and shaped by interpretative frameworks. To understand Freud's portrait of Jakob and subsequent psychoanalytic accounts of this relationship one must understand Freud's ideas on the Oedipus complex. In an essay with many personal references Freud speaks of 'organic necessity' introducing 'into a man's relation to his father an emotional ambivalence which we have found most strikingly expressed in the Greek myth of King Oedipus' (1914e, p. 243). The boy first loves and admires his father, but because the

father thwarts the son's instinctual sexual longing for the mother
the son also comes to hate his father. After age six the son finds
that his father is not really 'the mightiest, wisest, and richest
of beings' (p. 244). He begins to criticize him and replaces his
earlier childish overvaluation with an equally strong undervaluation.

In making this an 'organic necessity' Freud dismisses the possibility that simultaneously held feelings of love and hate, overvaluation and undervaluation, are idiosyncratic in his relations
to Jakob and universalizes the condition by biologizing it. His
life becomes prototypical, not atypical. Freud's self-analysis,
undertaken in his forties, was instrumental in his discovery of
Oedipal emotions and as we will see in chapter 4 was a way of
making reparations to Jakob for Sigmund's low opinion of him.
Jakob died in October 1896, just as Freud was beginning his
analysis, and Jakob's death stirred long forgotten memories in
his son. His death transformed him in his son's eyes. He became
a man of 'deep wisdom,' and the loss of the father was described
by Freud as the most poignant in a man's life (1954, p. 170). The
paternal apotheosis followed as the father became a central figure
in the Oedipal drama. Freud repaid the insult of having once
undervalued his father by elevating all fathers to the majestic
position of the all-powerful, a position Jakob had not held since
Sigmund was a very young child.

To complete an Oedipal interpretation one must know about
Freud's early relations with his mother. Amalie Nathansohn was
nineteen years old and twenty years younger than Jakob, who
was already a grandfather, when they were married. Sigmund
was Amalie's firstborn, and he was his mother's pride and joy.
In his public recollections of childhood Freud said very little
about his mother and almost nothing bad. In his private correspondence with Fliess he recalls that at age three 'libido
towards *matrem* was aroused' when they spent a night together
and he 'must have had the opportunity of seeing her *nudam*'
(1954, p. 219). Freud's reserve in the use of Latin is a good
example of the hesitation he displayed in discussing his feelings
for his mother.

It was not until late in his psychoanalytic work that Freud discussed in detail the importance of the mother-child relationship.
He says that in analysis the initial sexual attachment of female
patients to their mothers was difficult for him to discover because
this first infantile love had been buried by a strong repression
and was hidden behind these women's strong emotional trans-
ferences to him as a father-figure (1931). We can find in Freud's
own analysis this same difficulty. Under the recent influence of
his father's death, and suffering through a bitter separation
from his last father-figure Josef Breuer, the emotional thrust of
Freud's self-discoveries was towards understanding his relations
with men. The ambivalence in his ties to Amalie was never extensively analyzed by him, because the forces which made his
excavations of the past necessary directed his concerns away

from women. He seemed satisfied with discovering his hate for Jakob and protected his mother and mothers in general with the simple expedient of making them universal objects of adoration.

Lacking information about the actual relationship between Sigmund and Amalie we can turn to Freud's writings to gain some idea about what this relation might have meant to him and what he thought it meant to Amalie. In more than one place (for example, 1900; 1917a) Freud expresses the following idea.

> I have found that people who know that they are preferred or favored by their mother give evidence in their lives of peculiar self-reliance and an unshakeable optimism which often seem like heroic attributes and bring actual success to their possessors. (1900, p. 398)

In the story of his life, we will see that Freud stresses the theme of his own heroic self-reliance.

The mother, also, greatly benefits from her tie to the son. In several places Freud expresses the sentiment that the bond between mother and son is unrivaled in goodness:

> A mother is only brought unlimited satisfaction by her relation to a son; this is altogether the most perfect, the most free from ambivalence of all human relationships. A mother can transfer to her son the ambition which she has been obliged to suppress in herself. (1933a, p. 133)

Relations are usually free from conscious ambivalence when they have been idealized and not analyzed.

The letter to Fliess in which Freud tells of his infantile sexual excitement towards his mother has as its primary concern memories about 'a woman, ugly, elderly, but clever, who told me a great deal about God Almighty and Hell and who gave me a high opinion of my own capacities' (Freud, 1950a, p. 261). The woman was Freud's childhood nurse. She was a Catholic and used to take Sigmund to church services in Freiberg. The old nurse is blamed for a great deal by Freud and in his recollections she is as bad as his mother is good; a sign perhaps that in memory she is protecting Freud's mother from his scorn. Freud, in his published work, says that based on inferences from his dreams the nurse's treatment of him was not always amiable and her words were often harsh (1900). Privately to Fliess this idea is expanded. In a somewhat obscure passage Freud reports the results of a dream analysis; neither the dream nor his associations are given: 'She was my teacher in sexual matters and scolded me for being clumsy and not being able to do anything' (1950a, p. 262). We do not know, and perhaps neither did Freud, if his nurse had actually introduced him to sex. We will see that the question of the reality of infantile sexual experience became important in Freud's work and was a central issue in his disagreements with Jung.

We have briefly reviewed Freud's recounting of his emotional ties to his father, mother, and mother-surrogate - his nurse. To complete the picture we need to examine his relations to siblings. Again to Fliess, he recalls that at about one-and-a-half he greeted his brother Julius' birth 'with ill-wishes and genuine childish jealousy, and that his death [six months later] left the germ of self-reproaches in me' (1950a, p. 262). This recollection is followed by memories of his nephew, John. A year older than Sigmund, John was Sigmund's half-brother Emmanuel's first child. Emmanuel, Jakob's first son by his first wife, and his family lived next door to the Jakob Freuds, so John and Sigmund were constant companions and very close friends. Because of the similarity in age, their relationship was more like that of brothers than like that of uncle and nephew.

After the story of the Jew's cap, in 'The Interpretation of Dreams', Freud says that at age ten or twelve his father's behaviour in this incident struck him as unheroic for such a strong man. He contrasted this with his own defiance and courage in his relations with John, who as the older and stronger tried to dominate Sigmund. Freud speaks of having 'shown courage in the face of my tyrant' and in conjunction with the recollection of his father's capitulation to the Christian this is obviously an avowal that he, unlike his father, is a fighter and always has been (1900, p. 424). Defiance in the face of superior force is one of the traits which Freud cherished most in himself.

In looking back after forty years on this relationship of closeness, love, rivalry, and competition with John, Freud says, 'All my friends have in a certain sense been re-incarnations of this figure....My emotional life has always insisted that I should have an intimate friend and a hated enemy' (p. 483). Such relations with men could always be established anew by Freud and often, just as in childhood, friend and enemy came together in a single person. In his adult years hate would usually follow love, while with John love and hate were in continual oscillation. In Freud's friendships with Breuer, Fliess, and Jung there was definitely a recapitulation, with some variations, of this pattern.

Although Freud had six younger siblings - five sisters and a brother - they remain on the periphery of his analytic autobiography. Anna, who was born when Sigmund was two-and-a-half, is mentioned as an early sibling rival, but his sisters, like his mother, were protected, at least in print and perhaps also in memory, from Freud's exhumations of the past. His sisters and his brother, who was ten years younger than Sigmund, may not in fact have been significant rivals. As the eldest son Freud had certain privileges. He had a room of his own in which to study, he to some extent directed his sisters' educations, and commented on their boyfriends. He was even given the honor of naming his baby brother. As the oldest he was in a position of authority, and as a male in Victorian days his duty was to guard his sisters' mental and moral virtue. To have deeply analyzed his relations to his mother or his sisters would have been a

violation of a societal trust. Even though through psychoanalysis
he did much to usher in the modern age, as a child of the Victorian age he was particularly blind to the sexism produced by
the idealization of women and to the restrictions engendered by
an attitude of paternalistic protection. It is relations to males
which dominated Freud's recounting of his past for men were
unprotected by a code of chivalry and were then, as they still
are today, felt to be the significant sex.

The focus of psychoanalysis is on the past, locating the origins
of adult character in infantile and childhood conflicts. Our
review of Freud's childhood has found in it those events which
typify an analytic narrative: ambivalence towards the father,
Oedipal conflicts, love for the mother, infantile sexuality, and
sibling rivalry. This is, of course, the information we are given
because Freud's childhood was recovered by him in the course
of the first extensive psychoanalytic investigation – his own
self-analysis. However objective one tries to be, no one could
possibly analyze every memory of an entire childhood; Freud had
to select for analysis what seemed to be meaningful memories,
and in doing so he was guided by his theories (see chapter 4).
The contrast with Jung's childhood recollections is sharp and
introduces us to the divergence between their respective methods
of recounting what is important in human affairs.

In contrast to Freud's concern with childhood conflicts, Jung's
position – overstated by himself – was that 'when normal the
child has no real problems of its own' (1931b, p. 392). By this
criterion, Jung did not have a normal childhood. Jung's recollections involve solitude, fantasies, troubled relations between
his parents, and feelings of being an outsider among his peers.
In advising others on child-rearing he advocated letting children
give free rein to their imaginations and as a child he certainly
had a vivid imagination.

The movement away from the analysis of intrafamilial conflicts
to the investigation of universal patterns of human experience
which is characteristic of analytical psychology is found in Jung's
accounts of his childhood. We have seen in his story of God's
defecation his questions: 'Who wants to force me to think something I don't know and don't want to know? Where does this
terrible will come from?' (1973b, p. 37). His schoolboy answer,
that it was not his parents but God, came to be replaced after
years of research, study, and self-analysis with a similar but
more sophisticated response: it is certainly not the actual parents
or necessarily any real events which produce life's most important conflicts and solaces, but typical modes of human fantasy
arising from the interplay of conscious and unconscious forces.
Jung's interest was in establishing a concordance between the
imaginative products of modern individuals and the mythologems
of diverse cultures. His goal was to anchor modern oneiric
activities to the heritage of images and motifs which have
characterized human thought through the ages.

The first marked contrast in the life histories of Freud and

Jung is that while little is known about Freud's ancestors, Jung's
progenitors were individuals of some renown in Switzerland.
Freud in this respect is modern, while Jung is traditional. To
find out about who he was, Freud was limited to information from
his extended family; Jung could ruminate on stories about his
grandparents, looking beyond his parents to his ancestors in
an attempt to understand what it meant to be Carl Jung. There
was a family legend that Jung's great-grandmother had had an
affair with Goethe and that Jung's German-born grandfather,
Carl Gustav Jung, was Goethe's illegitimate son. Evidence does
not support the legend and although Jung often found the story
annoying he at times thought that as a legend, a psychic reality,
it might explain his fascination with Goethe's 'Faust.' Great-
grandfather Franz Jung was a successful doctor and his son Carl
Gustav was also a doctor. Carl Gustav settled in Basel and became locally famous as a Professor of Medicine at the University
of Basel where his son and grandson both studied. In the first
half of the nineteenth century he was active in founding the
Institute of Good Hope for mentally disturbed children and in
one speech he talked of trying to 'heal them by psychic methods'
(Hannah, 1976, p. 20). He was a legendary figure in Basel and
Jung did not find it easy being in a town where he had to live
up to his grandfather's name.

Paul Jung, Carl Gustav's son and Carl's father, was not as
successful as either his father or his son. He earned a PhD as
a philologist, but his father's death forced him to give up his
dream of an academic career because of the family's financial
difficulties. To escape debt, Paul took up the study of theology
and was ordained. He became a minister in the Basel Reform
Church. He married Emilie Preiswerk, a daughter of his former
Hebrew teacher. The Reverend Jung got on well with his parish-
ioners; he had a friendly disposition and enjoyed talking to
everyone. However, he left all of his academic interests behind
in school and let his considerable intellectual talents go to waste
in the trivialities of daily life (Jung, 1973b).

Samuel Preiswerk, Jung's maternal grandfather, was a distinguished theologian and Hebrew scholar. In the Basel Church
he rose to the position of president of the company of pastors.
He wrote poetry, hymns, and a Hebrew grammar. He had strong
pro-Jewish sentiments and 'was convinced that Palestine should
be given back to the Jews...so that today he is considered a
precursor of Zionism' (Ellenberger, 1970, p. 661). He had second
sight, experienced entire dramatic scenes in which he talked with
ghosts, and believed he was surrounded by the dead. His second
wife, Augusta Faber, was Carl's grandmother. She, too, had
second sight, saw spirits, and many members of her family had
parapsychological abilities (Jaffé, 1968).

Emilie Preiswerk, like her parents and her son, was interested
in the supernatural. She kept a diary of premonitions, 'spookish'
phenomena, and strange occurrences (Jaffé, 1968). Emilie was
a well-educated woman for her day and was at home in the

intellectual circles of Basel. After marrying Paul Jung, she found life as the wife of a country parson rather difficult and Jung thought that she must have been 'terribly bored' in her marriage (Bennet, 1961). Paul and Emilie's marriage had difficulties from the beginning; one son, Paul Jr, died in infancy before Carl was born.

Carl Gustav Jung was born on 26 July 1875, at Kesswil, Switzerland. His early childhood recollections are numerous and his 'Memories, Dreams, Reflections' provides vivid pictures of his boyhood concerns: love of the country, fascination with death and funerals, and fear of Jesuits dressed in black. Of interest to us is what Jung tells us of his childhood and how he orders these events, for in this we will see a sharp contrast with Freud's recollections. We know the story about God's defecation, which Jung calls his third great secret. He felt his entire youth could be understood in terms of his three secrets and the story of his early years is developed around these and his relations to his parents.

Jung's first secret was a dream he had at around age four. The dream is made additionally significant by Jung's conviction as a psychologist that 'the earliest remembered dream as a rule contains the pattern of the future fate and personality' (Hannah, 1976, p. 24). The dream, vividly retold by Jung (1973b), was of entering an underground vault and seeing sitting upon a throne a huge tree trunk of a curious composition. It was made of skin and at the very top was a single eye. Above it the room was lit by an aura of brightness. Afraid the thing would creep towards him, and hearing his mother say, 'That is the man-eater,' Jung awoke terribly frightened. He did not understand the dream at the time, but he did experience it and the experience stayed with him all his life.

Jung says as a child he associated the dream with death, burial, and an impression he got from a prayer that Jesus ate the dead in order to protect them from Satan. The dream made it hard for him to accept the Christian platitudes which his father and uncles uttered; experience had put him beyond their words. His dream introduced him to the dark side of religion. Jung came to an understanding of the dream fifty years later and his explanation, which is a typical Jungian interpretation, connects his childhood experience to age-old ceremonies of initiation. Light is brought into the underground darkness by the ceremonial phallus, a symbol of creativity and generativity. The 'man-eater' expresses the idea that the renewal of life associated with initiation is intimately connected with death. The dream, Jung says, 'was an initiation into the realm of darkness. My intellectual life had its unconscious beginnings at that time' (p. 15).

Jung's second secret comes from his tenth year. He carved a little manikin, painted it black and put it, along with an oblong stone which he colored to look as if it were divided in half, into a pencil case which he hid in the attic. He wrote his favorite sayings on scraps of paper and with great ceremony gave them

to the manikin to read. He conquered his anxieties by either
sneaking up to the attic or merely thinking about his stone and
manikin.

Jung says that as an adult his recollection of the stone and
manikin gave him 'for the first time, the conviction that there
are archaic components which have entered the individual psyche
without any direct line of tradition' (p. 23). At thirty-five when
he was doing research for his book, 'Wandlungen und Symbole
der Libido' (1911-12), a work which contributed to the break
with Freud, he read about sacred stones and recalled his boyhood ritual. The stone, painted to look as though it were divided
in half, is strikingly similar to the Australian aborigines'
'churingas,' sacred stones; to soul-stones found at Roman ruins
near Arles, France; and to the 'lapis,' the philosophers' stone
of alchemists. These stones, along with Jung's, are all symbols
of the soul, the life force. No wonder Carl felt the stone had to
be protected. The manikin is like a god of the ancient world, 'a
Telesphoros such as stands on the monuments of Asklepios and
reads to him from a scroll' (Jung, 1973b, p. 23). He checked his
father's library to see if as a child he might have read about
these things, but not one book spoke of these matters and neither
of his parents had transmitted such information to him. Carl was
spontaneously producing ritual objects with great similarities to
those used by the ancients. At age ten Jung understood none of
this. He simply performed the ritual and gained a feeling of
security from his actions. Such security was very necessary, for
his parents did not provide a very stable emotional atmosphere.

The position of a country parson and his wife is not an easy
one. They must, or at least they feel they should, lead exemplary
lives. Paul and Emilie in public lived above reproach, but this
led to many private differences and angry scenes. When Carl
was two, his parents were temporarily separated. His mother
spent several months in a Basel hospital because of some illness
apparently connected to her marital difficulties. Jung felt abandoned by her. At six, after they had moved from Laufen to
Klein-Hüningen near Basel, his parents were sleeping apart and
Jung had anxiety dreams about his mother. There was something
uncanny and unpredictable about her; his father was powerless
in dealing with her.

On the surface Emilie Jung was a very conventional woman.
She tried to live the life of the good wife of a pastor. Like all
mothers she scolded her son about his dress and reminded him
of his manners. However, she was at times alienated from the
conventional role of the minister's wife; remember her diary of
premonitions and strange occurrences. Jung says there was a
very natural, rather uncivilized side to his mother, an unconscious side, to which he felt a strong and reassuring tie. Torn
between convention and her own sense of the world, she often
produced diametrically opposed views on the same question.
Carl learned not to challenge her conventional views with her
unconventional utterances, which were nearly unconscious to her.

He came to quietly accept the insight, approval, and support his mother provided through such assurances.

Emilie came to rely more and more on her son as her marital relations grew increasingly difficult. She assumed he was very intelligent; she treated him like an adult and talked with him about problems that she could not speak about to her husband. Jung took such conversations very seriously and yet had to learn the difference between his mother's emotional over-reactions to a problem and the actual situation. By age ten he was acting as the family arbitrator in quarrels between his parents. This position made him feel very grown-up, but it further diminished his sense of confidence in his parents and increased his feelings of emotional insecurity.

Jung's relations with his mother produced a sense of mistrust in her and in the world, 'I always wanted to know at the start to what and to whom I was entrusting myself. Was this perhaps connected with my mother, who had abandoned me [at age two] for several months?' (p. 30). In a psychological work Jung wrote poetically about one type of universal mother-image, the image of a being who is unreliable, a source of both strength and mystery; 'Intimately known and yet strange like Nature, lovingly tender and yet cruel like fate, joyous and untiring giver of life....Mother is mother-love, *my* experience and *my* secret' (1954b, p. 92). There can be no doubt that this passage in Jung's work was drawn, in part, from his experience with Emilie.

Paul Jung was reliable, but powerless. His views about the world were completely predictable, and yet inwardly his life was in turmoil. He was often irritable and Jung attributes his father's emotional problems to religious doubts. Carl never spoke with his father about the phallus dream or the stone and manikin. He knew the Reverend Jung would neither understand nor approve of them. Jung's third great secret, the fantasy of God's defecating on the cathedral could certainly not have been told to his father. The fantasy was a condemnation of the church and all his father stood for. Carl felt he had directly experienced the will of God and His grace, something his father had never known. Paul Jung believed in God, but had never had a religious experience. He went into the ministry for financial reasons. Out of the deepest faith and for good reasons he surrounded himself with Protestant ritual and dogma so as to protect himself from God (Jung, 1973b).

An incident just after the time of the defecation fantasy illustrates well the profound alienation that Carl felt from his father and traditional Protestant Christianity. Carl had hopes that his first communion would bring an experience of the mysteries of religion. After all, it is an initiation and they say, 'Take, eat, this is my body.' Communion was a negatively numinous experience. Absolutely nothing mysterious happened. He knew the bakery where the wafers came from and the tavern where the wine was bought. Everyone went through the ritual motions,

but no one cared. Jung came to feel that church was not a place
alive with mystery, but was simply dead. Because of this experience he says he, 'was seized with the most vehement pity for
my father. All at once I understood the tragedy of his profession and his life. He was struggling with a death whose existence
he could not admit' (p. 55). His father had been kind to him in
many ways and had for the most part let him go his own way.
For example, after his first communion Carl very seldom went to
church and his father said nothing about this. Carl was powerless to help his father. He felt that only a truly religious
experience, a direct experience of God, like his own, could help.
This type of experience, however, had been avoided by Reverend
Jung.

Conflicts over theological questions surrounded Carl Jung all
his life. At fifteen he began having violent arguments with his
father about religion. In his relations with Freud, Jung's defence
of religious experience was a cause of friction. In his work he
also caused theologians some distress. They saw in him a scientist who talked about God, sympathetically investigated religious
experience, and criticized materialism; this they liked. They
disliked his position that Christianity is a myth and the fact
that he was often critical of organized religion, saying that it
kept people from experiencing God directly.

Jung was hardly a well-adjusted child. He had the world of
his secrets and these experiences, which he would never deny,
separated him from his father, his peers, and to some extent
from his mother. Afflicted or gifted with a vivid imagination,
he found playing by himself and developing his own thoughts
far more rewarding than playing with other children. Speaking
of the fantasy of God's defecation - and this could just as easily
have been said about the phallus dream or the manikin and the
stone - Jung says, with the hindsight of seventy years:

> My entire youth can be understood in terms of this secret.
> It induced in me an almost unendurable loneliness. My one
> great achievement during those years was that I resisted
> the temptation to talk about it with anyone. Thus the pat-
> tern of my relationship to the world was already prefigured;
> today as then I am a solitary, because I know things and
> must hint at things which other people do not know, and
> usually do not even want to know. (pp. 41-2)

The three secrets were not only the guiding lines of Jung's
entire life, but were used retrospectively by Jung to understand
himself and create an image through which he wished to be
understood. As we have seen his adult work helped him both in
recovering these memories and in creating a context of explanation for these profound experiences. Bennet says, 'Perhaps in
these boyhood experiences lie the germs of his theory of the
collective unconscious, for the mind, like the body, has its
ancestry' (1961, p. 13). Jung, in his work, found an answer to

the boyhood question: 'Who caused me to think this?' The explanation lies in our human heritage, in the spontaneous appearance
of similar symbols in different times and places to express certain fundamental ideas and emotions. Bennet is correct in saying
that in Jung's childhood were the experiential seeds for his
later work, but we should also remember that what we know of
Jung's childhood, like what we know of Freud's, was greatly
shaped by his work. Jung spent his adult life developing his
ideas about human psychology; such theories mold our perception of our own and other people's behavior. Jung's work has
shaped what he has told us, if not what he remembered, of his
childhood.

We can find in both Freud's and Jung's childhoods the origins
of their theories, but without the self-exploration they did as
adults and the theories they developed, we would not have found
their childhoods so fascinating. Nor would they have been so
interested in their own pasts. Their memories and experiences
of childhood increased in value for them when they began to need
material out of which to develop their psychological theories. As
Freud says of his own self-analysis, 'Since I have started
studying the unconscious I have become so interesting to myself' (1950a, p. 236). Freud's and Jung's studies of the unconscious led to their formulating two theories or narrative formats,
psychoanalysis and analytical psychology, by which they framed
the stories of their childhoods. We have seen how very different
these two childhoods were. Their boyhood years were no doubt
quite dissimilar and the differences between their youths have
been magnified by how they, as adults, because of their psychological investigations, came to remember, selectively present,
and structure their childhood experiences. While Freud championed the effects of childhood on adult character and psychoanalysis focuses on intrafamilial conflict, it was in Jung's life
that we found actual family turmoil. In reaction to Freud's focus
on the causal significance of childhood, Jung eschews psychoanalytic explanations. Although the phallus dream and God's
defecation call out for psychosexual interpretations, Jung gives
us none. While he recaptured his ambivalent feelings about his
mother, something Freud failed to do in his own case, and
recognized his devaluation of his father, Jung makes no Oedipal
interpretations. When he rejected psychoanalysis as an explanatory system, he rejected such an understanding for his own
life. He created in its stead a psychology which seeks self-
understanding by linking individual experiences to the spiritual
experiences of our ancestors, and therein Jung found and
presented an explanation of his life. Freud's childhood history
does not cry out for a Jungian explanation because his early
life seems to have been bereft of numinous experience.

EDUCATION AND VOCATION

While in school one is often faced with the questions: 'What shall I study?' 'What will I become?' Freud and Jung both agonized over these questions. We will find, not surprisingly, that each made the correct decisions. When we know how a life has turned out, we can, if we have any gift for story-telling, construct a chain of sensible actions that have, almost with the force of causes, led to this or that ending. This is the advantage that the historian has over the scientist. Science deals in prediction, foresight; history deals in retrospective analysis, hindsight. In telling stories, in making sense out of life, hindsight is usually much better than foresight. Looking forward, there are many possibilities in life; looking back, those occurrences are selectively stressed which best explain the present and one's hopes for the future.

From the time he entered school until he committed himself to a vocation, Jung's alienation from his father continued and his feelings of being an outcast grew as he felt himself to be misunderstood by his peers and teachers. Such difficulties forged in him a dedication to self-directed study and a determination to fulfill his vision of combining the study of the spiritual and natural sides of humanity in his life's work. Ambition, worship of certain teachers, and a commitment to introspection are the features of Freud's personality which in retrospect emerge from his school years as the salient traits of the man who founded psychoanalysis. And in founding it he found his vocation, uniting his interests in the humanities and the sciences. There is also in the maturing Freud a penchant, which will be even better developed in his later life, for seeing any opposition to him as complete rejection. Before psychoanalysis was even invented or had met with opposition, Freud had a tendency to cast himself in the role of a crusader being attacked by others.

It is fortunate that Freud was intellectually gifted, for his dreams of success were great. Academic honors came early to him and flamed his fantasies of fame. He entered the gymnasium at age nine and within two years he was at the head of his class. He remained Primus for six years and at seventeen he graduated summa cum laude. His final examinations included a translation from the Greek of a passage from Sophocles' 'Oedipus Rex,' and for a composition on the subject, 'Considerations Involved in a Choice of Profession,' a problem which was to occupy Freud for many years, he earned high praise. Encouraged by this, Freud wrote to a friend - Emil Fluss - that he, Emil, had probably been unaware that he was 'exchanging letters with a German stylist. And now I advise you as a friend, not as an interested party, to preserve them - have them bound - take good care of them - one never knows' (1960, p. 4). Emil saved the letters.

Twelve years later his dreams of fame were even stronger but his course of action was different. He wrote to his fiancee, Martha Bernays, that he had burnt his old notes, manuscripts of published papers and correspondence because they were piling up. He says, again with some humor, that this drastic action taken in 1885 would disappoint his future biographers, but let them worry for he had no desire to make their job easy: 'Each one of them will be right in his opinion of "the development of the Hero," and I am looking forward to seeing them go astray' (p. 141). Freud's longing for fame and drive to succeed almost led 'the Hero' astray when he thought research on cocaine would establish his name in medical circles. We will take up this research after examining Freud's relations with his teachers, his love for Martha Bernays, and his dedication to introspection, three areas in which several facets of Freud's style come together.

To their young charges teachers are often individuals of great reputation and Freud found in his gymnasium instructors men whom he could emulate. Looking back on these men, Freud, with years of psychoanalytic work behind him, says, 'We transferred on to them the respect and expectations attaching to the omniscient father of our childhood' (1914e, p. 244). Freud's own experiences are the source from which this generalization is drawn. He found, on going to school and comparing his father to the fathers of other boys and to his teachers, that Jakob was not 'omniscient,' but relatively poor and uneducated. Sigmund found in his teachers powerful figures, men to be admired in his father's stead.

In a paper entitled 'Family Romances' (1909b) Freud tells us that during adolescence a boy's ambition often leads him to fantasize that he is the son of a man other than his father. The boy's own father, whom he has come to undervalue, is replaced in fantasy by a more powerful adult male. In his own fantasies Freud replaced Jakob with other men; the first was his older half-brother, Emmanuel, who upon emigrating to England had become successful in business. He was followed by a succession of Sigmund's teachers. These men came to occupy the idealized father's position of model, advisor, and benevolent authority. At the university Ernst Brücke came to fill this position perfectly.

Having no predilection for the career of medicine, either at seventeen or for that matter at any time in his life, Freud entered the University of Vienna in 1873 intent on studying natural science. The decision to study science was a momentous one for him. At the gymnasium his interests had been in literature and languages. He had a talent for translation, a field to which he would later compare psychoanalysis, and a love of Shakespeare, of whom he remained fond because of Shakespeare's keen insights into human character. He had plans of becoming a lawyer, but a few months before graduation he wrote to Fluss that in a coming letter he would 'report what is perhaps the most important news in my miserable life.' The news was that, 'I have decided to be a Natural Scientist....I shall gain insight into the age-old dossiers of Nature, perhaps even eavesdrop on her eternal processes, and share my findings with anyone who wants to learn' (1969, pp. 423-4).

Why the change from an interest in law to natural science? In 1925(b) Freud says that, 'it was hearing Goethe's beautiful essay on Nature read aloud at a popular lecture by Professor Carl Brühl just before I left school that decided me to become a medical student' (p. 8).[2] The essay is a fine expression of roman-tic nature philosophy (Goethe, 1893 [1780]):

> She [nature] speaks to us unceasingly and betrays not her secret (p. 207).
> She rejoices in illusion (p. 209).
> Man obeys her laws even in opposing them: he works with her even when he wants to work against her (p. 211).
> In her everything is always present. Past and Future she knows not. The Present is her Eternity (p. 212).

These few lines from the essay express some of its powerful sentiments.[3] They are quite similar to statements which Freud later made about the most natural part of the human psyche – the unconscious. Psychoanalysis with its emphasis on psychic forces, the unconscious, and its concern with history and cul-ture in many ways revived, in a new form, Naturphilosophie, and Jung's work is almost a direct descendant of this late eighteenth and early nineteenth-century outgrowth of German Romanticism.

During his first three years at the University Freud kept his interest in the humanities alive by attending some of Franz Brentano's lectures and seminars. Brentano's philosophical work is concerned with the intentional nature of consciousness and is a forerunner of modern phenomenology. His courses may have helped to mitigate the strong materialistic bias of Freud's science courses, but any such effects did not show up until Freud's later psychological works. The anti-philosophical indoctrination which Freud received from Brücke is evidenced by a motto which Freud hung in his room (Jones, 1953, p. 66): 'Travailler sans raisonner' ('Let us work without philosophizing').

Of Brücke Freud says he 'carried more weight with me than anyone else in my whole life' (1926, p. 253). Here was a famous man, a respected scientist, and someone who took a benevolent interest in Freud's studies and in his future; here was a father who could be admired. Brücke was a physiologist and a leading advocate of materialist physiology. Emil DuBois-Reymond, Carl Ludwig, Hermann von Helmholtz and Brücke were joined together in a crusade for materialism and in their lifetimes helped to transform German physiology from a vitalist orientation to mechan-istic and physicalistic determinism. The philosophy that joined these four men together, and which Freud took up with a passion, is summarized by DuBois-Reymond:

> Brücke and I pledged a solemn oath to put in power this truth: 'No other forces than the common physical chemical ones are active within the organism. In those cases which cannot at the

time be explained by these forces one has either to find the
specific way or form of their action by means of the physical
mathematical method, or to assume new forces equal in dignity
to the chemical physical forces inherent in matter, reducible
to the force of attraction and repulsion. (quoted in Bernfeld,
1944, p. 348)

Brücke's views were diametrically opposed to Naturphilosophie,
which held that there was a spiritual force uniting humans with
nature. This force penetrated the organic and inorganic and
bound together the entire universe. The philosopher's job was
to investigate this rather mystical and certainly metaphysical
force. When Freud came under the influence of Brücke he
completely rejected Naturphilosophie and became a crusading
radical materialist. Although psychoanalysis, as we will see, can
be seen as undermining a strict materialist position, Freud
remained throughout his life a materialist and a devout determinist. 'Project for a Scientific Psychology,' written in 1895, was
one of Freud's first attempts to explain systematically psychological phenomena and a forerunner of psychoanalytic theoretical
formulations. The goal of this work is the materialist's dream
of representing 'psychical processes as quantitative states of
specifiable material particles' (Freud, 1950b, p. 295).

Not only was Freud's philosophical outlook shaped by Brücke,
his entire university career was centered on work with the
German physiologist. Brücke focused Freud's considerable talents
on specific projects, providing him with guidance and yet freedom to explore questions on his own. Brücke also represented
a cause; the cause of science working against vitalism, mysticism,
and speculative philosophy. Freud devoted himself to both
Brücke and the crusade of science. 'Like most adolescents Freud
had the need to "believe in something" and in his case the something was Science with a capital' (Jones, 1953, p. 40). Freud in
his later years transformed his adolescent belief into an unshakeable dogma. Science moved beyond belief for him; it was True
with a capital.

Freud was appointed a research scholar at Brücke's Institute
for Physiology in 1876 and the next year his first paper, 'On
the Origin of the Posterior Nerve-Roots in the Spinal Cord of
Ammocoetes (Petromyzon plancri),' was published. Within the
next seven years seven more papers concerned with the study of
nerves followed. This work pointed towards a unitary conception
of the nerve cell and its processes - the essence of the neuron
theory which made Waldeyer famous (Jones, 1953). Freud had
established himself as a competent physiological biologist, but
no special accolades - except for Brücke's favor - came to him
for this work.

Freud received his MD degree in 1881; it took him eight years
to get it, three years longer than average. Why, if Freud was
both poor and ambitious, did it take him so long? One reason
is that he simply never wanted to become a doctor. He wanted to

be a researcher (Jones, 1953; Freud, 1926). Another is that
he had dreams of a well-paid academic appointment at the university. Such dreams were exceedingly unrealistic: first,
because two of Brücke's assistants, Exner and Fleischl, would
receive any such appointment before Freud, and second because
Freud was a Jew. At the University of Vienna, Freud had already
met with anti-Semitism as a student and in professional appoint-
ments such prejudice was even stronger. Yet another reason for
the delay can be attributed to his work with Brücke. Freud says
that at the Institute he had 'spent the happiest hours of my
student life, free from all other desires' (1900, p. 206).

The association with Brücke was a vital part of Freud's life,
and it was difficult for Freud to leave his home in the laboratory.
Brücke, however, had Freud's welfare in mind, and it was on his
advice that Freud completed his university work. It was Brücke
who, Freud says, 'corrected my father's generous improvidence
by strongly advising me, in view of my bad financial position,
to abandon my theoretical career' (1925b, p. 10). Brücke was
the ideal, not the improvident, father. He retained a warm
interest in Freud's career, and they remained close friends for
several years.

Freud's idealization of Brücke was a manifestation of a general
tendency of his towards infatuation. As a teenager he was
enamoured on first seeing Emil Fluss's sister, and ten years
later in 1882 at his first meeting with Martha Bernays he once
again fell in love. Such adoration, in sublimated form, was
repeatedly being expressed by Freud towards men. While at
Brücke's laboratory, Freud developed a close friendship with a
colleague, Ernst Fleischl von Marxow, and came to idealize him.
Later Freud would form similar attachments to Breuer, Fliess,
and Jung.

The object of such devotion had to pay a price for Freud's
strong attachment. Freud expected his sentiments to be reciprocated. This attitude is vividly displayed in Sigmund's relations
with Martha. He wanted her exclusively in both large and small
matters. On one occasion he accused her of placing her mother's
interests before his: 'If that is so you are my enemy: if we don't
get over this obstacle we shall founder. You have only an Either-
Or. If you can't be fond enough of me to renounce for my sake
your family, then you must lose me, wreck my life, and get not
much yourself out of your family' (Jones, 1953, p. 130). We will
see Freud's 'Either-Or' attitude again and again. His devotion
to both people and ideas was uncompromising, and so he created
a great many crises by demanding of others the same allegiance
that he gave to them. Martha avoided crises by waiting out the
storm and compromising; Breuer, Fliess and Jung fueled the
strife when they failed to capitulate.

Freud's love was demanding. One of his demands was that his
friends should promptly answer letters. Nothing angered Freud
more than violation of his rather strict rules of correspondence.
If he didn't get a letter that he was expecting he felt both

slighted and abandoned. Fluss, Bernays, Fliess, and Jung were
each chastised by Freud for failing to write. Jung was at times
quite negligent about replying to Freud's letters and this played
a part in their separation.

The four-and-a-half-year courtship of Freud and Bernays,
although never written about by Freud, has been partially preserved in over 900 letters that he wrote to Martha. The letters,
ninety of which have been published (Freud, 1960), provide
valuable insights about Freud's views on religion, science and
literature. These are the opinions of a man in his twenties and
are the presuppositions on which later psychoanalytic positions
were formulated. Every system of interpretation is founded
upon an unexamined set of assumptions, and we will seek to
articulate these in order to understand the base upon which
psychoanalytic theory was to be constructed.

Martha Bernays was raised in an orthodox Jewish household
and was quite religious. Freud, the atheist, called on Martha
to renounce her 'religious prejudices' and promised to make a
heathen of her. He did not, however, renounce Jewish culture
or his identity as a Jew. He promised Martha that 'something of
the core, of the essence of this meaningful and life-affirming
Judaism will not be absent from our home' (1960, p. 22).

Better than any verbal proclamation of being a Jew is to
fight against anti-Semitism itself. Freud wrote to Martha that
while on a train he had opened the window and a dispute arose
when a man near him insisted he shut it. From the back of the
car came the shout, '"He's a dirty Jew!"' and then the man near
him 'turned anti-Semitic and declared: "We Christians consider
other people, you'd better think less of your precious self."'
Freud defended his rights telling the man in the back to keep
his 'empty phrases' to himself and offering to fight the Christian.
He says, 'I was quite prepared to kill him, but he did not step
up.' Freud concludes, 'I held my own quite well;' the Christian
'mob' 'must have noticed that I wasn't afraid, and I didn't allow
this experience to dampen my spirits' (pp. 78-9). How very different this is from Jakob's retrieving his cap from the mud. A
mixture of a heroic defense of himself as a Jew and a condemnation of all religious belief remained Freud's position on religion
throughout his life.

Regarding science, Freud's feelings were not mixed; to Martha
he wrote, 'I think brain anatomy is the only legitimate rival you
have or will ever have' (p. 145). Science and Martha were Freud's
future.

In 1885 Freud thought that brain anatomy would be his scientific field, but in his letters to Martha there is evidence of the
talents and interests that would lead him beyond neuroanatomy
to found his own science. Gedo and Wolf (1970) note that in his
letters to Fluss Freud took pleasure in telling stories and demonstrated skill in doing so. In one letter he designates his description of an incident a 'small novel.' These adolescent letters show
a love of metaphor and a talent for writing. The same is true of

the correspondence a decade later with Martha. In introducing
a detailed description of a colleague's suicide, Freud writes,
'his life was as though composed by a writer of fiction, and this
catastrophe was the inevitable end' (1960, p. 60). A six-page
case history follows. It is a narrative worthy of an accomplished
writer of fiction. The man's life was full of strange events which
Freud, by skillful interpretation, weaves into a smooth and
coherent tale. He concludes the case story, 'Thus his death was
like his life, cut to a pattern: he all but screams for the novelist
to preserve him for memory' (p. 65). Freud, the novelist, has
achieved this. He would later immortalize others - Dora, Rat Man,
and Wolf Man - in his psychoanalytic case studies.

Freud said to Martha, 'I have a talent for interpreting' (Jones,
1953, p. 127). This talent, combined with a rigorous training in
observation, a solid education in and love for the humanities,
and a gift for writing, was the foundation on which Freud was
to later build psychoanalysis. An additional stone in this foundation was Freud's knowledge that fiction conveys truth. From
France he wrote to Martha, 'To understand Paris this is the
novel [Victor Hugo's 'Notre-Dame'] you must read; although
everything in it is fiction, one is convinced of its truth' (1960,
p. 188).

There is one other essential in psychoanalysis: a conviction
that introspection, self-analysis, is essential. In his teens,
Freud wrote to Fluss about the need for self-examination and
said if one practices 'self-dissection' 'you will see how little
about yourself you are sure of' (p. 5). Twelve years later, in
1886, his dissection had improved, and he sent to Martha a brilliant and perceptive character sketch of himself. He complained
of his tiredness, which he identified as a minor illness, neuraes-
thenia - a rather fashionable malady thought to be caused by
stress and overwork. He pointed out that he was not a genius
nor perhaps even gifted; he felt that his capacity for work
sprang from his character and from the absence of any outstand-
ing intellectual weaknesses - a combination which 'is very con-
ducive to slow success' (p. 202). Freud was almost fifty before
he received wide recognition for his discoveries, so his prediction was borne out.

The letter continues with Freud's recognition that since his
school days he 'was always the bold oppositionist' willing to
defend an extreme position and take the consequences. He closes
saying he was greatly moved when Josef Breuer, his older friend
and colleague,

> told me he had discovered that hidden under the surface of
> [my] timidity there lay in me an extremely daring and fearless
> human being. I had always thought so, but never dared tell
> anyone. I have often felt as though I had inherited all the
> defiance and all the passions with which our ancestors defended
> their Temple and could gladly sacrifice my life for one great
> moment in history. And at the same time I always felt so help-

less and incapable of expressing these ardent passions even
by a word or a poem. (pp. 202-3)

Intellectual courage, being in the opposition, 'all the defiance
and all the passions': these are the traits of a revolutionary,
but Freud did not yet have either revolutionary ideas or a means
of expressing them. At this time his thoughts and his writings
were restrained by materialistic notions, the limited subject matter acceptable to scientific investigation, and the stylistic limitations of causal scientific prose. Freud became a revolutionary,
a member of the opposition, because of his radical new ideas and
his creation of a new mode of expressing them. The psychoanalytic revolution broadened the boundaries of scientific inquiry,
transformed causality into narrative interpretation, and dealt a
blow to materialism, from which it has yet to recover.

Freud's engagement, along with his giving up his dreams of a
research career, led him to do pioneering work on cocaine. We
can see in retrospect that Freud's methods in this first piece of
research done on his own anticipate in many ways his later style
in psychoanalytic investigation. He announced to Martha in 1884
that he was going to try experiments on cocaine because not
much work had been done by others in this area, and he hoped
to make a major therapeutic discovery which would perhaps
facilitate their getting married. He cautioned her not to expect
too much, noting that 'an explorer's temperament requires two
basic qualities: optimism in attempt, criticism in work' (1960,
p. 108).

Freud used the cocaine himself and reported on its subjective
effects: one experiences exhilaration and feelings of lightness,
psychically there is a lasting euphoria which does not differ
from normal euphoria, and one feels an increase in self-control
and more capable of doing work (1884). In this paper, his first
publication on cocaine, Freud is using self-observation of psychic
states. This method with great modifications would become a
central feature of psychoanalysis.

Freud's friend and colleague from Brücke's laboratory, Fleischl
von Marxow, also became involved in Freud's cocaine work.
Fleischl had been taking morphine for a painful nerve illness
and had developed an addiction. Freud gave Fleischl cocaine to
both combat the morphine addiction and relieve his pain. There
was early success:

Prof. Fleischl of Vienna, confirms the fact that...cocaine is
invaluable, subcutaneously injected in *morphinism*...a gradual
withdrawal of morphine requires a gradual increase of cocaine
....It is evident that there is a direct antagonism between
morphine and cocaine. (Freud, 1885b, p. 31)

There is an obscuring of the line between researcher and patient
in this passage. Fleischl is presented as the investigator, not as
both co-investigator and patient. The clear distinction between

observer and observed, so fundamental to natural science, is broken down both here and in Freud's own self-observations on the use of cocaine. We will find this same blurring of the line between investigator and subject of investigation in the psychological works of both Freud and Jung.

Freud's and Fleischl's optimism about using cocaine in curing morphine addiction was premature. Fleischl developed a great dependence on cocaine and took massive doses; his morphine addiction was cured by an addiction to cocaine. His nerve condition worsened and Freud expected him to die within six months. After he first tried cocaine, Freud gave it to his friends, colleagues and patients, his sisters and Martha. Fleischl's difficulties led Freud to caution Martha to use cocaine in moderation and not acquire a habit. Freud found that reports of addiction to cocaine occurred only in cases where it was used in the treatment of morphine addiction and that cocaine, alone, especially if not injected, had never caused addiction. Freud reports he had taken the drug himself for many months and had not had 'any desire for continued use of cocaine. On the contrary, there occurred more frequently than I should have liked, an aversion to the drug, which was sufficient cause for curtailing its use' (1887, p. 59).

We will find this tendency throughout Freud's later work in psychoanalysis: if he found, based on careful self-observation, that something was true of him he assumed that it was true of other people. A finding was confirmed on the basis of self-observation and the observation of a handful of other people. The cocaine episode is the first example of this very characteristic way in which Freud worked. Gone is the reserve and caution which were so evident under Brücke. Freud always remained a careful meticulous observer (Brücke taught him well), but he came to generalize on the basis of really very few observations. Perhaps this tendency can also be traced back to his early work in physiology. After all, there is not much variation in the nerve cells of Ammocoetes; if you've seen a few fish you've seen them all. In the work on cocaine Freud (1887) recognized the importance of individual differences in people's reactions, but there always remained in his work the conviction that if something were true of him it was true of a great many other people.

The cocaine work also reveals another important point about Freud's method of working. The only experimental study he ever published concerned cocaine's effects on muscular strength and reaction time (Freud, 1885a). This study in 'its rather dillettante presentation shows that this [experimentation] was not his real field' (Jones, 1953, p. 92). While a student, Freud had done two experimental studies on animals, but they lead to nothing. He had little talent for experimentation; he preferred observation to manipulation. In his psychoanalytic work he never did an experiment, although he would cite experimental studies that confirmed psychoanalytic findings. He maintained vigorously that the validity of psychoanalytic findings was firmly based on observation. While experimental validation was fine, it was in no way necessary for establishing the truth of psychoanalytic propositions (Shakow and Rapaport, 1964).

Cocaine served a function that psychoanalysis would come to perform for Freud. It relieved some of his mildly neurotic symptoms. Freud suffered from periodic depressions, apathy, and fatigue, symptoms which were exacerbated by his anxieties over his engagement to Martha. Cocaine relieved his distress.

Anti-cocaine forces lead by Erlenmeyer, who called cocaine 'the third scourge of humanity' (the other two were alcohol and morphine) began marshalling evidence against Freud's findings. The opposition prevailed and by 1887 Freud's hopes of becoming famous through cocaine research turned into recognition that this work had harmed his professional reputation in Vienna. He says the work lead to 'serious reproaches' (1900, p. 111).

From 1885-6 Freud published studies on the histology of the acoustic nerve; in 1885, because of Brücke's support and his own fine work, he was appointed a Privatdozent (lecturer) in neurology at the University of Vienna; he was in charge of the nervous diseases department for a few months; and by 1886 he had gained a local reputation as an expert in nervous diseases. In short, Freud was on his way to becoming a highly respected neurologist. Upon his return from visiting Paris Freud opened a private practice in neuropathology on Easter Sunday, 25 April 1886. He had committed himself to the treatment of nervous disorders, but he had not yet found his vocation, in the sense of his calling. He had to create it.

Except for his courses with Brentano, Freud had been immersed in an organic and materialistic approach to inquiry ever since he entered the university. After twelve years of intensive materialism, Freud found in Charcot's work a different approach. Brücke's support helped Freud win a post-doctoral traveling fellowship. He used the money to go to Paris in order to, as he wrote to Martha, 'become a great scholar and then come back to Vienna with a huge, enormous halo, and then we will soon be married, and I will cure all the incurable nervous cases' (1960, p. 154). Freud dreamed of fame and in Paris he met and studied under a famous man - Jean-Martin Charcot. Charcot was at this time, 1885-6, the most renowned neurologist in the world. He had succeeded, because of the greatness of his work, in reintroducing the discredited topic of hypnotism to scientific study in France and was making hysteria a respectable disease. It was thought that all hysterics were women and women suffering from hysteria were, before Charcot's work, thought to be malingerers, sympathy-hunters, fakers of physical disorders, and undeserving of medical attention. Charcot changed this. A man of his fame investigating hysteria gave the disease and its sufferers a right to exist. In his work he was demonstrating that hysterical symptoms could be understood: they could be simulated by hypnotized subjects and hysterical symptoms could be relieved by hypnosis. In addition, different types of hysteria could be reliably

diagnosed and classified. According to Charcot, men as well as
women could develop hysteria. He theorized that the primary
cause of the disease was hereditary degeneracy. Hysterics were
physiologically predisposed to develop hypnoid states, reduced
states of consciousness in which hysterical paralysis and symptoms could be produced by suggestion. For Charcot, then, the
primary cause of hysteria was organic. The symptoms of hysteria
were secondary manifestations of the disease and were dyna-
mically (psychologically) caused by suggestion (Ellenberger,
1970; Freud, 1893b).

The above is what Freud learned from Charcot. The four
months in Paris were 'the turning point in his career, for it was
during this period that his interest shifted from neuropathology
to psychopathology – from physical science to psychology'
(Strachey, 1962, p. 9). In Charcot, Freud found another powerful teacher, a man of great fame, who, as Brücke did, altered
Freud's life. About his reactions to Charcot, Freud wrote to
Martha:

> Charcot...is simply wrecking all my aims and opinions. I
> sometimes come out of his lectures...with an entirely new
> idea of perfection....Whether the seed will ever bear any
> fruit, I don't know; but what I do know is that no other
> human being has ever affected me in this way. (1960,
> pp. 184–5)

Freud had once again been enchanted by a teacher.

Charcot was a great observer. He would look and look again
until a pattern emerged which allowed him to classify into types,
and variations of types, symptom groupings that had never
been seen before.

> He might be heard to say that the greatest satisfaction a man
> could have was to see something new – that is, to recognize
> it as new; and he remarked again and again on the difficulty
> and value of this kind of 'seeing.' He would ask why it was
> that in medicine people only see what they have already
> learned to see. He would say that it was wonderful how one
> was suddenly able to see new things – new states of illness –
> which must probably be as old as the human race. (Freud,
> 1893b, p. 12)

From Brücke, the physical scientist, Freud learned meticulous
observation and from Charcot, the 'visual,' Freud learned to see
in new ways and to dare to see something new. What better
teachers for a scientific visionary, who changed our view of the
world?

Charcot was a champion of clinical observation, of seeing and
ordering. Freud, too, in his defense of psychoanalysis, championed the rights of observation. Freud tells the story of a
group of German physiologists who were trying Charcot's

patience with their theoretical doubts about his clinical observations, '"But that can't be true," one of us objected, "it contradicts the Young-Helmholtz theory."' Charcot replied, '"Theory is good, but it doesn't prevent things from existing"' (p. 13). The objector was Freud himself, and Charcot's reply became one of Freud's favorite quotations. In addition, Freud said of Charcot that he could not rest until he had correctly described and classified some phenomenon, 'but that he can sleep quite soundly without having arrived at the physiological explanation of that phenomenon' (1956 [1886], p. 13). We will find that in his psychoanalytic work Freud, too, could rest long before any physiological explanation was found. But what a wrenching of his Brückean materialistic ideals Charcot's approach must have caused.

Freud went to Paris to study the new and exciting work that Charcot was doing in hysteria and hypnotism. When he returned to Vienna he thought the French work would have a definite impact on Viennese medical circles, and his prestige would be raised by having introduced these ideas. He wrote to Martha that his lecture in May 1886, on hypnotism to the Physiological Club 'went off very well and received general applause.' He continued, saying more talks were scheduled and 'the battle of Vienna is in full swing' (1960, p. 218). Freud was over-optimistic about the outcome of the battle and his optimism led him to take the rather tepid Viennese reaction to Charcot's work as a defeat. In October Freud lectured to the Society of Physicians; his paper was provocatively titled 'On Male Hysteria.' He reviewed Charcot's ideas: hysteria has regular diagnostic features and there is a clearly defined ordering of hysterical symptoms; hysterics are not malingerers; and, hysteria in males is common (Bernfeld and Bernfeld, 1952). Freud, departing from Charcot, also argued that hysteria in males could be caused by a traumatic event; hereditary degeneracy was not, in all cases, a necessary cause (Ellenberger, 1970). Freud says his talk 'met with a bad reception' (1925b, p. 15). The reception might have been cool, but, on the basis of the notes of the meeting, Jones (1953) contests Freud's very negative assessment. Freud's extreme account has it that the chairman, 'declared that what I said was incredible' (1925b, p. 15). Jones, more realistically and moderately, says that the older physicians attempted to minimize the novelty of Freud's claims by pointing out that male hysteria was, in fact, known to them. Also, at these meetings the senior physicians greeted all papers critically. The society expected true originality, and they were probably disappointed by Freud's report on the investigations of the French researcher.

Challenged to demonstrate a case of male hysteria, Freud says that when he tried to find such a patient his efforts were blocked by senior physicians, 'who refused to allow me to observe them or to work at them' (1925b, p. 15). 'At length,' Freud concludes, 'outside the hospital' he found a male hysteric with classic symptoms. Jones notes that the words 'at length' indicate Freud's

impatience, for it took him only a week to find this case. Freud
(1886) demonstrated the case showing that although the patient
reported complete anesthesia on the left side of his body actually
various regions were sensitive to stimulation. He attempted to
demonstrate, by way of a brief case history, the traumatic origin
of the symptoms. The etiological evidence in the case was ambiguous and as with his paper 'On Male Hysteria' it was again difficult in a single case to demonstrate that only environmental,
and not also hereditary, factors played a determining role in
symptom formation (Ellenberger, 1970). Freud ends his account
saying that for his demonstration of the male hysteric he

> was applauded, but no further interest was taken in me. The
> impression that the high authorities had rejected my innova-
> tions remained unshaken; and, with my hysteria in men and
> my production of hysterical paralyses by suggestion, I found
> myself forced into the Opposition. (1925b, pp. 15-16)

It would be more correct to say 'put myself' into the Opposition. In his reconstruction of the incident forty years later,
Freud continues the story of the alien in opposition saying he
was soon after excluded from Meynert's laboratory, had no place
to deliver his papers, and 'withdrew from academic life and
ceased to attend learned societies' (p. 16). Freud is constructing a story about the isolation of the revolutionary originator
of psychoanalysis, about his having had to overcome great
obstacles, and about his intellectual integrity and perseverance.
It is the story of a hero, a moving story and one that Freud used
to make sense out of his life, but it is only marginally based in
reality. In fact, Freud was elected as a member to the Society
of Physicians in 1887, less than a year after presenting his two
papers on hysteria. He continued to attend medical meetings,
read papers at medical societies until 1904, and lectured at the
University of Vienna until 1917. He was not immediately excluded
from Meynert's laboratory, although because of Meynert's opposition to Charcot's work (he thought it unscientific), Freud's
and Meynert's relationship did become acrimonious (Jones, 1953).
    Freud has represented his strong feelings of rejection with a
story of actual rejection. He had been bitterly disappointed when
older physicians did not openly applaud his new and foreign
ideas; his great expectations of fame were dashed when his
views met with indifference or criticism, to which he was over-
sensitive. Senior colleagues are not prone to change their views
on a subject given one or even many presentations by a junior
worker in a field. Freud expected too much from his seniors,
as he expected too much from his father, and got too little. A
few years earlier he had told Martha, 'to teach an old teacher
something is a pure, unmitigated satisfaction' (1960, p. 73). He
had been denied this satisfaction and he was resentful. His
feelings of rejection are understandable, and his distortion of
the events in retelling the story forty years later is a testimony

to his disappointment and to our thesis that a life story is not merely a document of actual events, but is a mental reconstruction, based on events and their psychological concomitants, that allows one to make sense out of one's experience.

Accounts of being rejected because of his ideas will be used again by Freud in telling of the reception of psychoanalysis at the turn of the century. Jones (1955) accepts and fosters the story of the heroic first years of psychoanalysis; we will see, however, that this story, like the one just recounted, is only marginally true. The story of being the rebel in opposition will also be used by Freud in explaining Jung's leaving the psychoanalytic movement. Freud will tell us that Jung, in de-emphasizing the importance of infantile sexuality and questioning the reality of the Oedipal situation, was capitulating to the critics of psychoanalysis. He, Freud, the defender of the truth, had to reject Jung's deviant ideas, and so once again he found himself in the opposition. We will find this account to be an accurate description of Freud's psychological reactions to the break with Jung, but it is not an entirely true representation of the actual situation.

Jung was also fond of seeing himself as an outsider, who was misunderstood because he refused to renounce his views and experiences in order to be accepted by his peers. It was Freud's radical ideas that drew Jung to psychoanalysis, and it was each man's insistence that his views were original, could not be compromised, and were based on observation that drove them apart. We will now consider Jung's education and vocational choice, emphasizing those events which in retrospect we can see as having been vital for the development of his later work and recounting his story, which, like Freud, he exaggerates, of being an outcast forced into the opposition.

Jung's grammar-school days went well; he was at the head of his class and was respected because of his father's position in the village, but when the family moved to Basel this all changed. At eleven, on entering the gymnasium, the school for classical education, Carl found himself alienated from his classmates, many of whom were the sons of rich businessmen. No longer was he the son of the well-educated and socially prominent Reverend Jung, he was now the child of a relatively poor minister. Doubts assailed him, not only about his father's religious views but also about his father's standing in the community.

Because of difficulties in his classes, boredom, and feelings of social inferiority, school became intolerable for Jung. When he was twelve he found a temporary solution to his problem. A classmate pushed Carl, and he fell, striking his head. He almost lost consciousness and was dazed for half an hour. 'At the moment I felt the blow the thought flashed through my mind: "Now you won't have to go to school any more"' (Jung, 1973b, p. 30). For about the next six months he had fainting spells whenever he was told to go to school or do homework. This was initially a great relief to him, for he no longer had to go to the

gymnasium. He had time to carry on his own explorations: to
play in fields, draw, build, dream, and read in his father's
library. After a while, all this became rather empty and unsatis-
fying; feelings that he was avoiding the real world and being
untrue to himself began to overtake him. His parents were very
worried and took him from doctor to doctor, but there was nothing organically wrong. The turning point came when Carl heard
his father saying to a visitor: 'The doctors no longer know what
is wrong with him....It would be dreadful if he were incurable.
I have lost what little I had, and what will become of the boy
if he cannot earn his own living?'
'I was thunderstruck. This was the collision with reality. "Why,
then, I must get to work!" I thought suddenly' (p. 31).

Carl immediately took up his books and in the course of an
hour fought off three fainting attacks. After this no more attacks
occurred. He studied hard for several weeks and returned to
school.

Retrospectively, Jung says that this incident 'was when I
learned what a neurosis is' (p. 32). The concussion meant that
he would not have to return to school, but during the course of
his difficulties he says 'I forgot completely how all this came
about' (p. 31). A forgotten wish, a wish that brought on a rather
disgraceful situation and so had been denied, lay at the bottom
of his problems. He felt that he had tricked himself and was
ashamed of his cowardly behavior. The neurosis became a shame-
ful secret; it had been motivated by Jung's distaste for school
and his delight in solitude.

He had immersed himself in his own world and in nature in
order to avoid the human world of school. With great determination, he vowed not to trick himself ever again. He dedicated himself to his studies. But his problem of alienation from the world
was not solved forever at age twelve. In his life there was the
recurrent problem of balancing the demands of nature, his own
being and his own perceptions with the everyday world of
schools, colleagues, and a career. In his work we will find this
same issue: the necessity for the individual to find a balance
between the demands of one's inner, timeless, and natural
experiences with the outer, transient reality of contemporary
culture. Jung's work and his life are two overlapping stories
sharing this theme: denying either inner experience or the
outer world causes serious problems, and yet living a life that
combines the two in ideal harmony is very difficult. Only through
critical self-examination of one's relations to oneself, others,
and the world can one hope to achieve a balance. Any balance
is only temporary; one learns to live in perpetual imbalance,
always seeking balance.

Jung adjusted to school, even becoming first in his class. But
when he found his classmates were envious of him for being first,
he purposely did a little less well in order to be second. He
disliked competition and found it hard to cope with the additional
alienation that his peers' jealousy caused him.

Jung's adjustment was by no means perfect; 'collisions with reality' continued to occur. Within a year after the fainting spells Jung had the fantasy of God's defecation; a decision to stick to the straight and narrow does not eliminate an active imagination. His classmates must have sensed Jung's feelings of a connection with the past, his rather other-worldly nature, and his profound religious experiences because they gave him the nickname 'Father Abraham' (Jung, 1973b). This name hit the mark and made the part of Jung that was trying to adjust to urban reality and adolescent social relationships cringe.

His teachers also made Jung's attempts at finding a place in the world difficult. One teacher accused him of plagiarism simply because Jung turned in an excellent essay when he felt Jung was not capable of such work. A few years later, Jung wrote a superior paper on philosophy. His teacher called it brilliant, but because of its carefully polished untortured style, which had cost Jung great pains to achieve, condemned it as being 'tossed off...carelessly.' The teacher warned him that he would get nowhere in life with such a 'slap-dash attitude' (p. 71).

For Freud there were memories of praise while at the gymnasium; for Jung hard work and good writing earned him contempt. Cautious enquiries after this second teacher's scolding revealed to Jung what he had done wrong. He knew more than he should have known. He found that many of his peers felt he was 'a braggart, a poseur, and a humbug' because he pretended to know about Kant and Schopenhauer. He had read these men in attempting to find answers to the burning questions raised by his own experiences, but such questions were of little interest to his teenage classmates. Philosophy, for a time, became a private interest and like his three great secrets was not to be talked about in public.

Fortunately for Jung, these negative experiences did not extinguish his interest in finding answers to questions because he had to have an answer for himself. Jung continued to read philosophy all of his life and, unlike Freud, who at times claimed a distaste for philosophy, he found in it an anchorage for his own speculations. In his work on analytical psychology he took care to mention how his ideas were similar to the thoughts of Heraclitus, Plato, Eckhardt, Goethe, Kant and Schopenhauer - all men he began reading while at the gymnasium or at college. Curiously enough he was at times criticized by his former psychoanalytic colleagues for his wide reading in philosophy.

Jung had tried his best to cope with the world of the gymnasium and achieved, between his eleventh and seventeenth years, a minimal adjustment, but, like many of us, he was ultimately saved from high school and a rather poor adjustment to adolescent life by nothing more miraculous than graduation. Having to rely completely on Jung's retrospective account of these years has probably created an overly negative impression of his gymnasium days. There are no other sources by which to correct Jung's slanting of his life history during these years towards

a portrait of himself as a misunderstood loner trying bravely to
follow the dictates of his own being while still adjusting to the
demands of others. His accounts of his college experiences are
similar, but fortunately there are other sources which provide
a corrective to Jung's bias.

Typically, Jung presents his decision on what career to pursue
in terms of a series of vocational revelations. Just before entering the University of Basel in 1895 at age nineteen, Jung says
three dreams helped him to decide on the study of medicine.
While Jung's dreams and fantasies as a child took him away from
the everyday world and drew him into a timeless realm of mystery, darkness, and power, his dreams, or at least his interpretations of them, were now leading him back to the realities of
contemporary life: money, a profession, and getting along with
his teachers and classmates. The third dream climaxed this
trend. Jung dreamt he was in an unknown place, the wind was
blowing and the fog was thick and swirling. He was making slow
progress. His hands were cupped around a tiny light; everything depended on his keeping the light alive, although it seemed
that the light might go out at any moment. He felt something
behind him. Looking back, he saw a gigantic black figure following him. Terrified, he knew that he must keep the light burning.
Jung says of this dream: 'I knew...that this light was my consciousness, the only light I had. My own understanding is the
sole treasure I possess, and the greatest. Though infinitely
small and fragile in comparison with the powers of darkness, it
is still a light, my only light' (p. 88).

The realm of darkness, of the shadow, of the unconscious, is
created by the light of consciousness, and yet consciousness
feels the ominous threat of the darkness. Jung knew of the
darkness: of death, the underground phallus, the ritual manikin,
and God's defecation. This was an obscure realm unknown to
most, but Carl knew it almost too well, and this knowledge had
alienated him from his father and his peers. Jung, in retrospect,
says his task was clear: he had to commit himself to finding a
place in the world, he had to carry consciousness, the light,
forward - 'into study, moneymaking, responsibilities, entanglements, confusions, errors, submissions, defeats' (p. 88) - without denying to himself that he knew of the darkness, of another
world that was timeless and also exacted a price if one failed to
adjust to it. The price of denying the unconscious, the immense
shadow, was a fear of the unknown, a clinging to conventional
opinion and an estrangement from oneself and one's inner nature.
Jung fulfilled his task. He made a place for himself at the
university and in the secular world and yet, he never denied
the dark and magnificent world he came to know as a child. His
greatest success was in bringing these two worlds together in
his work, for analytical psychology holds as a central principle
that adaptation to the modern world needs to be combined with
an integration of the timeless experiences of the unconscious.

While in college, Jung successfully began his task of making a place for himself in the world: he established independence from his family, was successful in his classes and popular with his peers. He also committed himself to the vocation he would practice for the rest of his life.

During Jung's final years at the gymnasium he and his father had violent quarrels over theological issues. In the face of the then fashionable materialist attack on religion, Paul Jung's religious doubts grew more severe and he more strongly stressed the need for belief in God. Exposed to the psychiatric materialism of the day in both his work as a chaplain at a mental hospital and as a patient in sanatoriums, Reverend Jung was trying to defend his faith from the materialist position that God's existence could not be proved, therefore, God did not exist; and from psychiatry's reduction of both mind and spirit to brain physiology. He besought his son that if he studied medicine he 'should in Heaven's name not become a materialist' (p. 94). Carl was in little danger of this. He argued with his father that what was needed to stem doubt was not blind faith, but the experience of God and that the arch sin of faith was that it forestalled experience.

In arguing for experience and against belief Jung was taking up a position which he would use later in his disputes with Freud - a man whom he came to call father. It was during this period of crisis in his father's life that Jung was first exposed to the name of Freud. Paul Jung rarely read anything but novels and travel books, yet - obviously searching for some explanation of the increasing severity of his depressive moods and apparent hypochondria - he read Freud's (1888) translation of Bernheim's book on 'Hypnotism and Suggestion.'

Paul Jung's condition worsened and he died in 1896. The immediate cause of death seems to have been cancer, but Jung later maintained that his father's religious doubts had in part been responsible for his death (Hannah, 1976). While mourning Paul Jung's death, Carl's mother mysteriously said to him, 'He died in time for you' (Jung, 1973b, p. 96). He took this to mean that since he and his father did not understand each other his father's death had removed a hindrance from his path. His mother's words made Jung feel guilty, but he also realized their truth. His father's death meant that he was now free to follow his own path without worrying about his father's opinion. Jung took up the position of head of the family; he moved into his father's room and took over the management of the household finances. Years later, Freud was to accuse Jung of harboring death wishes towards him and the parallels between Jung's relations to his father and Freud add credence to Freud's interpretation. Both Paul Jung and Freud insisted that Carl adhere to certain orthodoxies; Jung would not do so. His father's death cleared Jung's path allowing him to take his own course and direct the household; Freud's death would have given Jung freedom to remain within the psychoanalytic movement and to direct its development.

Paul Jung had changed his career plans because of his family's difficulties after his father's death. After Paul's death, Carl defied his relatives' advice, refusing to give up the future he had planned for himself. He worked to put himself through college, and completed his medical studies in the autumn of 1900, passing his exams with distinction. It took him five years to earn his degree. Unlike Freud, Jung made a decision on what he was going to study and concentrated his energies and resources on achieving his goal. Also in contrast to Freud, Jung, by graduation, had settled his mind on the vocation he would pursue as his only calling for the rest of his life.

Consistent with the story of his life, Jung (1973b) tells us that his decision to go into psychiatry was a revelation. He had taken two courses in psychiatry in his final year of medical school but found them boring. To prepare for the state medical examinations he needed to review psychiatry so he decided to read Krafft-Ebing's 'Lehrbuch der Psychiatrie.' Krafft-Ebing, one of the precursors of modern dynamic psychiatry, was a recognized expert in the field, but Jung did not expect much from the book. Upon opening it he saw the phrases 'psychiatric textbooks are stamped with a more or less subjective character' and psychoses are 'diseases of the personality.' His heart began to pound; he stood up to catch his breath; his excitement was intense. Jung says,

> it had become clear to me, in a flash of illumination, that for me the only possible goal was psychiatry. Here alone the two currents of my interest could flow together and in a united stream dig their own bed. Here was the empirical field common to biological and spiritual facts, which I had everywhere sought and nowhere found. Here at last was the place where the collision of nature and spirit became a reality. (pp. 108-9)

Jung's grandfather had talked of psychic treatment, Paul Jung had had contact with psychiatrists, and Carl had taken two courses in psychiatry at the university; how could a decision to go into psychiatry have been a revelation? First, Jung had a motto: 'Only don't imitate;' this may have made him think twice about entering a field in which his grandfather had done some pioneering work. Second, Jung formed a low opinion of psychiatry because of his father's experiences. Third, his courses in psychiatry probably taught the standard materialistic psychiatry of the day: (1) all mental illness has an organic cause; (2) although the physical cause of most illnesses is not known the psychiatrist's job as a scientist is to carefully observe and classify mental diseases; and (3) treatment consists of custodial care and physical therapy. Such views would hardly inspire Jung. But Krafft-Ebing was not, at least in the passages that Jung quotes, talking about an exclusively materialist psychiatry. He used the word 'subjective' and the phrase 'diseases of the personality.' The personality is not the brain, and the admission

that psychiatry was subjective must have been reassuring to
Jung. Jung's revelation was a vision of a new psychiatry, a
psychiatry not based solely on biological causation but on considerations of the psyche and human spirit.

Jung was living in an age of change. It was hard for him or
anybody else to see what was coming. The then dominant materialist orientation of psychiatry was to be greatly altered. Jung
would join the forces of change helping to found and foster a
new dynamic psychiatry based on a psychological viewpoint and
a non-materialist philosophy. The psychiatry of the latter
decades of the nineteenth century, which he was taught in college and which his father feared, held little interest for Jung.
His interests were in areas which were anathema to materialism,
but which were the foundations of the revolution in psychiatry
which was to come. Nietzsche's work along with the investigation
of spiritism and hypnotism were the forerunners of the psychiatric revolution. While in college Jung did not see his passion for
Nietzsche or his interest in spiritism as related to psychiatry.
They weren't related to the old psychiatry; but Nietzsche,
spiritism, and hypnotism would be seen by historians of the
future as precursors of Freud's and Jung's revolutionary work
on the unconscious (Ellenberger, 1970). In nineteenth-century
psychiatry there was no way in which Jung could integrate his
interests in science, philosophy, theology, and the objective
investigation of spiritualistic phenomena. His illumination was in
seeing a new psychiatry, one that investigated both the biological and spiritual sides of human beings; he committed himself
to that vision. With hindsight we can say that in 1900, while
reading Krafft-Ebing, Jung glimpsed the direction of twentieth-
century psychiatry.

Spiritism - the communication with the dead through mediums
at seances - had its origins in America and spread through
Europe in the 1850s and 1860s. It was an event of major importance in the history of dynamic psychiatry, for it provided
psychologists and psychopathologists with a way of exploring
the poorly understood processes of the human mind. Jung, in his
doctoral dissertation, produced a major work in the scientific
study of spiritism.

During his second term at the University, Jung began reading
books on spiritualistic phenomena. He read Crookes, Zollner,
Kant's 'Dreams of a Spirit Seer,' and everything else he could
find on the subject. He also continued reading philosophy.
Nietzsche was the focus of his interest.

To use Ellenberger's phrase, Nietzsche was 'the prophet of a
New Era' (1970, p. 271). A brilliant philologist, Nietzsche was
a professor at the University of Basel, and the town was full of
stories about this eccentric genius. Jung grew up hearing his
name. Nietzsche's 'Zarathustra,' the mythic story of the super-
man and man's eternal responsibility for the life he leads, had a
powerful effect on Jung. Nietzsche, using his philological exper-
tise, allegory, aphorism, and myth, began in 'The Birth of

Tragedy' (1872) to forge a philosophy which stressed the importance of artistic perception, self-examination, self-realization,
and individual transformation. He asserted, however, that one's
true nature is difficult to discern and at base man is driven by
the will to power. These ideas were coupled with a strong criticism of modern culture: its barrenness, alienation, and the
renunciation of instinct which makes it possible. He also attacked
the emptiness of the reigning scientific, materialistic, and
mechanistic philosophies. In contrast to objectivity, Nietzsche
saw that the individual's story is central to human understanding:

> 'The Life' as the Proceeds of Life.
> A man may stretch himself out ever so far with his knowledge;
> he may seem to himself ever so objective, but eventually he
> realises nothing therefrom but his own biography. (1878,
> p. 361)

His readings in Nietzsche and spiritism helped Jung develop
his arguments against the materialist position that the mind was
equal to the brain and that the human spirit did not exist. Jung
held that materialism was a very limited viewpoint; a dogma that
not only ignored transcendent aspects of human experience, but
also denied the psychological side of existence. He had ample
opportunities to discuss his views with his friends and fraternity
brothers. Jung says his peers did not understand his view that
spiritism could be objectively studied; he 'came up against the
steel of people's prejudice and their utter incapacity to admit
unconventional possibilities. I found this even with my closest
friends. To them all of this was far worse than my preoccupation
with theology' (1973b, p. 100). He goes on to say that his views
caused derision, incredulity, anxiety and even dread among his
peers.

Two accounts of this time, one by Jung's close friend Oeri
(1935) and the other by a fraternity brother, Gustav Steiner
(1965), do not agree with Jung's story of alienation because of
his interests in spiritual phenomena and advocacy of an anti-
materialist philosophy. Jung was by choice an outsider in his
fraternity. Oeri says, however, that Jung truly enjoyed attending the weekly presentations and discussions of scholarly papers
at the Zofingia. Carl came to command both the attention and
the respect of his fraternity because of his participation at these
meetings. Beginning in November, 1896, Jung gave a series of
talks to the Basel Zofingia. The first, 'On the Limits of the Exact
Sciences,' was an attack on contemporary materialist views in
science, stressing that instead of rejecting outright both hypnotic and spiritualistic phenomena, a true science should encourage
the objective investigation of these poorly understood areas.
Systematic research, he asserted, could be done on questions
involving non-material mental events. The presentation was so
successful that his fraternity unanimously recommended Jung's

talk for publication in the central journal of the International
Zofingia. In addition to this talk, he presented at least three
other papers: one criticized a popular theologian for his historical view of Christ and for trying to deny mystical elements
in religion; another was entitled 'Some Reflections on the Nature
and Value of Speculative Research;' and the third, 'A Few
Thoughts about Psychology,' deplored the current lack of interest in metaphysics. Presaging his later work, Jung argued that
one task of psychology should be the investigation of the soul.
The soul was not material; it existed independently of space
and time. In addition, he proposed that psychology's narrow
concern with consciousness should be expanded by investigating
somnambulistic and hypnotic states. The debates over Jung's
views were lively and Oeri says Jung had no trouble in leading
his peers 'into highly speculative areas of thought, which to the
majority...were an alien wonderland' (1935, p. 8).

The Zofingia, according to Steiner (1965) gave Jung an opportunity to test out his ideas in intense discussions with other
students. Jung, unlike Freud, must have enjoyed such debate,
for throughout his life he encouraged discussion and questions
after he presented papers. Since Jung did not participate in the
social outings of the fraternity, it must be that his abilities as
a speaker were appreciated because he was elected president
of the Basel Zofingia for the winter term of 1897. The president's
position is usually not given to someone who has little in common
with the other members of an organization or whose ideas they
view with derision.

Jung, further developing his story of intellectual alienation
from his classmates, says only two people among his friends
declared themselves adherents of Nietzsche. Both were homosexuals and led tragic lives. 'The rest of my friends were not so
much dumbfounded by the phenomenon of *Zarathustra* as simply
immune to its appeal' (1973b, p. 104). Jung's friends must have
been particularly unfashionable, for between 1890 and 1910 there
was a wave of enthusiasm for Nietzsche on university campuses
(Ellenberger, 1970). Jung was not unusual in reading and being
enthusiastic about 'Zarathustra;' most college students were doing
the same thing.

Why is Jung trying to convince us that he was an outcast, an
obscurantist, and a highly unusual person in his circle for
championing research into spiritism, admiring Nietzsche, and
attacking materialism when the accounts we have from Oeri and
Steiner maintain that Jung was respected by, and quite popular
with, his peers? In his eighties, Jung, in recalling his college
days, is telling us a story. It resembles Freud's tale about being
in the opposition and has elements of the classic myths about
the young and lonely hero overcoming great obstacles, both
internal and external, to make his way in the world. It is the
'myth of the hero,' a recurrent narrative in Jung's work and a
universal mythic theme (Campbell, 1956; Steele and Swinney,
1978). Oeri and Steiner provide evidence for doubting Jung's

account, just as Jones gave reasons for doubting Freud's emphasis on being in the opposition. We can doubt any story, any
myth. Our doubt leads us usually to overreaction: 'If what he
says here is not the absolute truth, then how can I trust anything he says?' Stories are not mathematics problems, they are
not either right or wrong. In the 'Prologue' to his autobiography,
Jung says:

> Thus it is that I have now undertaken, in my eighty-third
> year, to tell my personal myth. I can only make direct state-
> ments, only 'tell stories.' Whether or not the stories are 'true'
> is not the problem. The only question is whether what I tell
> is *my* fable, *my* truth. (1973b, p. 3)

Until now, we have relied on Jung's story taking it as both
the actual and the psychic truth. For Freud there were sources
other than his professional publications by which to check his
rather selective presentation of the events of his childhood and
adolescence. We have seen that although those sources are
structured psychoanalytically, they do shed additional light on
the events of his early life. For Jung, the alternative sources
are not available. The research simply has not been done. Jung,
by writing an extensive autobiography, although admittedly
focused on his internal and not external life, has probably
assured that such a biography will not be written in the near
future or that any such biography will be largely shaped around
his own memories, dreams and reflections. For Jung's childhood
and early adolescence, then, we have relied on his story and
that story is centered in Jung's vivid fantasy life and his own
reported alienation from people. Beginning with his college
studies and throughout his adulthood we have other accounts of
his life and these narratives will allow us, as we have done with
Freud, to correct, amend, and see from slightly different perspectives Jung's story.

It is clear that Jung, like Freud, took opposition to mean
rejection. Jung at twenty-one had strong convictions that his
views were correct, and he had read widely enough in philosophy
to convince himself that many renowned thinkers were in agreement with him. He knew he was right, so how could anyone disagree? If they did so, it must be out of some prejudice on their
part. In addition, Jung felt he had been rebuffed by his peers
at the gymnasium and so probably overreacted to any sign that
his college classmates might think him odd. Let us not forget,
also, that Jung is telling a story fifty years after it occurred,
and it is always nice to see oneself as having overcome the
prejudices of one's peers, maintaining one's views against great
odds and triumphing in the end.

Although we have seen that Jung's views on spiritism did not
cause his fraternity brothers to loathe and despise him, he says
that his inability to sway their opinions and change their doubts
about his position led him to realize that arguments don't con-

vince people - only facts do. Nietzsche, for all his brilliance
in his stand against materialism, had only philosophical arguments and so convinced very few people; he, Jung, became
determined to set out on the quest for facts. Jung found his first
facts at home. He was studying; there was a loud explosion. The
oak dining table had split nearly in half. The fissure ran right
through solid wood and not along any joint. Jung was impressed
and his mother intimated that there was a meaning behind the
event. Two weeks later he came home and found his family greatly agitated. An hour earlier there had been another loud report,
not from the dining table, but from the sideboard. The sideboard
was intact and after some searching Jung found what had ex-
ploded. A breadknife had shattered into four pieces, one piece
resting in each corner of the drawer. Jung could find no plausible physical explanation for either event. Why had they occurred?

A few weeks later he found out that a younger teenage cousin,
Helene Preiswerk, a granddaughter of Samuel, was conducting
seances with some relatives. Jung thought the table and knife
explosions might be connected with these gatherings. His cur-
iosity piqued by his reading, the events in his house, and his
wish to study spiritism objectively, he began regularly to attend
the Saturday night seances.

At the seances Helene would go into a somnambulistic state,
a condition of greatly reduced conscious awareness, and a wide
variety of events would follow. While in a trance, Helene incar-
nated the spirits of deceased relatives. The first was Samuel
Preiswerk, and he remained a central figure throughout the
seances. Like Carl, Helene had never known her grandfather,
but her imitations of him and other dead relatives were uncanny.
Jung says, 'she copied' them in a remarkable way 'with all their
foibles, so that she made a lasting impression even on persons
not easily influenced' (1902, p. 19). She began acting out whole
dramatic scenes, she served as a medium for conversations with
the departed, and she engaged in automatic writing and had
vivid hallucinations. After Helene produced an elaborate cosmological vision in March of 1900 her powers began to diminish.
Her trance performances became redundant and artificial. She
became unsure of herself and tried harder to please her audience,
'So that the impression of willful deception became ever stronger'
(p. 43). At this time Jung stopped attending the seances, and
six months later Helene 'was caught cheating *in flagrante*' (p. 43).
Jung's observations, which he recorded in detail even before
he decided to go into psychiatry, formed the core of his doctoral
dissertation 'On the Psychology and Pathology of So-Called
Occult Phenomena' (1902). It was his first publication. We will
return to it when we discuss Jung's early psychiatric work.

Our discussion of Jung's school years would be incomplete if
we did not speak of his infatuations. Unlike Freud, Jung does
not mention having idealized any of his teachers and only speaks
of once having formed a strong tie to another male. In a confes-

sion to Freud, Jung wrote 'as a boy I was the victim of a sexual
assault by a man I once worshipped' (McGuire, 1974, p. 95).
He uses this memory to explain why he has since feared intimacy
with males and why he is troubled by the increasing closeness
of his friendship with Freud.

Even more than Freud, Jung was prone to infatuations with
women. At sixteen he was strongly drawn to a girl he met while
on vacation, and at twenty-one there was a second fateful
encounter. He visited Frau Rauschenbach who had taken him
for walks when he was a boy, and during the call he saw a girl
in her teens go up the stairs. He 'knew in a flash, beyond all
doubt, that he was looking at his future wife' (Hannah, 1976,
p. 83). The girl, who was just fourteen, was Emma Rauschenbach; she and Jung were married seven years later. This story
of fated lovers is balanced by a more mundane tale. Oeri tells
us that at a fraternity dance Jung fell hopelessly in love with a
young woman. He took all his money and went to buy engagement
rings. He was many francs short of the necessary funds, the
jeweler would not let him have the rings, and Jung thereupon
dropped his plans of marriage. This incident provides a nice
counter to the rather too spiritual accounts which Jung, and
Jungians, have created of a life composed entirely of meaningful
experiences.

There were other strong emotional involvements with women in
Jung's life. The most important one besides his marriage came
during his break with Freud, when Jung formed a lasting relationship with Antonia Wolff, a woman who was a patient of his
and who aided him with his own analysis and who remained very
close to him throughout her life.

The close friendships in Jung's life seem to have been primarily with women, whereas Freud's were with men. In chapter 10
we will see how this difference is manifest in their work. Jung's
emphasis on the feminine nature of a man's unconscious and the
projection of a man's feminine side - the anima - on to women
thereby creating infatuations is a central feature of analytical
psychology. Freud's focus on Oedipal conflicts and rivalry
between men gives a more masculine focus to his theory.

IN RETROSPECT

Jaffé (1968) finds in Jung's observations of Helene Preiswerk
and his exposition of this case 'the germs of some of Jung's later
concepts which are of basic importance' (p. 4). Ellenberger
(1970), likewise, finds in this work and in Jung's talks to the
Zofingia the 'germinal cell of Jung's analytical psychology'
(p. 687). Bennet (1961), as we have seen, and Hannah (1976)
find the impetus to much of Jung's later work in his childhood
experience. The origin of Jung's work is both in his experiences
at college and his childhood. It would be foolish to try to say
that this or that event was the seed from which Jung's work

developed. His work developed from his life and in a person's life it is hard to locate any specific first causes.

In physical explanations we can simplify a problem and say with confidence 'a' caused 'b': 'the nail puncture caused the tire blow-out.' We can ignore for convenience the age of the tire, our foolishness in running over the nail, and countless other variables which are not as immediate as the nail being in the tire. The strength of natural scientific explanation lies in this very simplification, focusing on one or two factors and allowing other less important events to recede into the background.

Causal explanation on the model of the natural sciences can also be used to explain human lives. Focusing on certain events, we construct chains of linked experiences that simplify the complexity of existence. With Ellenberger we say Jung's work had its origins at the Zofingia or with Bennet we find our first causes in Jung's childhood. Jones provides an excellent example of finding first causes:

It has often been assumed that Freud's psychological theories date from his contact with Charcot or Breuer or even later. On the contrary, it can be shown that the principles on which he constructed his theories were those he had acquired as a medical student under Brücke's influence. (1953, p. 45)

Certainly, under Brücke Freud learned exacting observation, developed a commitment to materialistic explanation, and acquired his ideas on energy dynamics. Yet, why stop at Brücke? In Freud's schooldays we found him already speaking of the need for, and difficulties in, self-analysis. We can go even further back.

Jones recognizes that 'Freud has taught us that the essential foundations of character are laid down by the age of three' (p. 13). Certainly Freud's character, with his ambivalence towards close male friends, which he traces back to his relations to his nephew John; with his passion for fame, which he traces back to his childhood; and with his comfort at being in the opposition, the manifestations of which we found in his child-hood and in his university years, had much to do with his later psychoanalytic formulations.

The point is that there are no unambiguous first causes or points of origin in which we can locate the beginning of either Freud's or Jung's work. One might say, 'Well, certainly it all began with their births.' Freud and Jung, however, both talk about how individuals recapitulate in their lives aspects of archaic human experience. So our lives are linked to the lives of our ancestors. Also, Freud and Jung, like all of us, were born into an already existing culture and much of their work can be traced to the pre-existing cultural matrix. The spirit of the times, the Zeitgeist, is used by both Boring (1950) and Decker (1977) in locating the origins of Freud's work. For both Freud and Jung, Ellenberger (1970) in his 'The Discovery of the

Unconscious' traces the intellectual and social backgrounds of their ideas.

If our commitment is to telling a story causally, linking 'a' to 'b' and making sure that 'c' follows, we will tell clear unambiguous stories that sound very scientific. A causal narrative leads us to say: 'Brücke's work was the origin of Freud's ideas on psychic energy;' 'Jung's reading of Nietzsche lead him to reject materialism.' Both contain some truth, although in their gross oversimplification they create much that is false. Causal narratives simplify experience. This is their power and their weakness. Freud, in his work, committed himself to a narrative modeled on scientific causality. He tried to tell stories where 'a' led to 'b' and 'b' to 'c.' But, as we will see, Freud was more committed to understanding human experience than he was to purely scientific explanation. So the psychoanalytic narrative, although it has its roots in causal analysis, is infinitely more complex. Freud's explanations of a case read more like a novel than a scientific treatise. Jung could never fully commit himself to a causal analysis of phenomena and this will be one of the problems in his disputes with Freud. The narrative of analytical psychology creates life stories that are more mythical than scientific.

In retrospect it is easy to find causes and a causal analysis is seductive in its simplicity. We will see that Freud, unknowingly, and Jung, deliberately, so greatly modified the causal natural scientific explanation of behavior that each created his own new way of analyzing human experience. In psychoanalysis and analytical psychology causal explanation is transformed into interpretation and with this shift both leave the realm of natural science and become hermeneutic disciplines. They are alternative systems, with much in common and yet significant differences, for constructing meaningful life stories through interpretation. Each system has its origins in the life of its creator, not in some one event, and we have found and will continue to find that each man's life is best seen from the perspective of his own interpretative system. It would indeed be a sad commentary on psychoanalysis if it did not help us understand Freud's life and on analytical psychology if it did not help us understand Jung.

Biography is double-edged. While it draws us closer to great individuals by showing us their human side, it can also alienate us from them. Many of us live in doubt about our futures and the meaning of our pasts - so the well-ordered retrospective history of another's life often distances that individual from us. For those of us who are not sure what the future holds remember that Freud did not found psychoanalysis until he was in his forties and Jung did not christen his work analytical psychology until he was in his late thirties. It was only with great effort and in restrospect that Freud and Jung made sense of their lives. And it is only retrospectively through interpretation that each of us will understand his or her life. Each man's legacy to us was an interpretative framework by which to order experience, and we betray their bequest if we do not question ourselves, each other, them and the theories they have given us.

The next three chapters will be devoted to following the development of psychoanalysis in the 1890s: Freud's working with and liberation from Josef Breuer, his emotional dependence on his analytic investigations and on Wilhelm Fliess which lead to Freud's self-analysis, and an examination of the psychological works which founded psychoanalysis as an interpretive science. Chapter 6 will explore Jung's early psychiatric work which lead him to support Freud's ideas and chapter 7 will discuss these two men's joint efforts in founding depth psychology.

3   JOSEF BREUER: FREUD'S LAST FATHER

We left the story of Freud's work in 1886-7 with his setting up
practice in the treatment of nervous disorders, with his disappointment over his colleagues' reception of his Charcotian ideas,
and with his early researches in hysteria. In order to understand the evolution of his thought from the 1880s to the 1890s,
and to begin to understand the emotional problems which drove
him to self-analysis in 1897, we must return to 1882, the year
in which Freud came under the influence of the last man who was
to be a teacher to him - Josef Breuer.

Breuer, by the time Freud met him, was one of the most successful physicians in Vienna, and although his services were in
demand, he also managed to do scientific research. Early in his
career he had won recognition for his researches on the semi-
circular canal. He was appointed Privatdozent in 1868, began
his private practice in 1871, and was given an honor rarely
accorded to a non-academic when he was elected Corresponding
Member of the Vienna Academy of Science in 1894.

Freud and Breuer met in Brücke's laboratory and both were
faithful members of the school of Helmholtz. The friendship
became closer in 1882 when Freud left the university and Breuer
took him under his wing. For Freud, Breuer was a professional
role model, advisor, teacher, and financial patron; in the language of psychoanalysis he was a father-figure. Their relations
became intimate; for Freud, Breuer was a 'friend and helper in
difficult circumstances' (1925b, p. 19). Breuer had told Sigmund
that few things interested him more than Freud's work. He had
also pleased Freud by telling him that although he, Sigmund,
had a timid demeanor, underneath he was a daring and fearless
human being. Sigmund was grateful for the esteem in which
Josef held him and he owed much to Breuer.

A not insubstantial debt was purely financial. In accord with
an old Jewish custom of wealthy members of the community helping promising scholars, Breuer made regular loans to Freud.
The debt carried obligations. Freud was afraid of being a
'Schnorrer' (sponger), one who pays back his debt by his wit
and loveability (Robert, 1966). For the loans to be justified,
he had to amount to something. As Freud felt he had to prove
himself to his father, so these loans obligated Freud to demonstrate his worthiness. Freud disliked this indebtedness, which in
the end was 2300 florins (almost one thousand dollars), and it
played a part in alienating Freud from Breuer; it created an
obligation to him which Freud could not tolerate. We will see that

debt and friendship were an important issue in Freud's personal
analysis.

In addition to money, Freud owed Breuer an intellectual debt.
In telling Freud about the case of Bertha Pappenheim (Anna O.),
Breuer radically influenced Freud's thought. Breuer treated
Miss Pappenheim from late in 1880 to June 1882, and described
his work in full to Freud several months later. The case was so
far outside Freud's experience 'that it made a deep impression
on him, and he would discuss the details of it with Breuer over
and over again' (Jones, 1953, p. 226). Breuer's work with
Pappenheim merits attention because: it was one of the earliest
recorded cases of narrative therapy; it captured Freud's imagination in the eighties and influenced his formulations on theory
and treatment in the nineties; and it became the focal point of
Freud's published criticisms of Breuer.

Bertha Pappenheim was from a prominent Jewish family; she
had an excellent education, read Italian and French, and spoke
English perfectly. Her parents were puritanical and her home
life was very limited. To relieve the monotony of needlework and
socials she escaped into daydreams which she called her private
theater. At age twenty, while nursing her dying father, she
became ill.

More than twelve years after Breuer had finished treating
Miss Pappenheim he recorded her story as the case of Anna O.
(Breuer and Freud, 1895). This study is our source for what
Breuer told Freud about Bertha. Anna's illness went through
four overlapping phases. In July 1880, her father, of whom she
was passionately fond, fell ill and Anna nursed him, using all her
energy. She became physically exhausted and Breuer was called
to examine her. A pattern had developed from the sleep-wakeful-
ness cycle established while Anna was nursing her father: she
began to crave rest in the afternoons; in the evenings she fell
into a sleep-like state and upon waking became highly excited.
For her later illness, the period from July to December 1880,
was the period of 'latent incubation' (p. 22). It was the point of
origin for psychic traumas which were later elaborated into a
host of physical difficulties and mental terrors.

The second period, from December 1880 to April 1881, was
marked by the appearance of a museum of hysterical symptoms:
paralytic contractures of the right arm and both legs, visual
disturbances in which she complained that the walls of the house
were falling, and linguistic disorganization marked by her speaking an agrammatical jargon composed of words from four or five
languages. In March her normal ability to speak returned, but
while she still understood German, she only spoke English. She
was bedridden for the greater part of this time. Her psychic life
was dominated by two states of consciousness which alternated
frequently and without warning and became increasingly differentiated as her illness progressed. In her normal state, she
recognized her surroundings, was melancholy and anxious. In
her other state 'she hallucinated and was "naughty" - that is to

say, she was abusive, used to throw cushions at people, so far as the contractures at various times allowed, tore buttons off her bedclothes and linen with those fingers she could move' (p. 24). In March, despite efforts to speak, she was dumb for two weeks, and this made the psychical mechanism of her illness clear to Breuer. He knew she had been offended by something and that she was determined not to say anything about it. He says, 'When I guessed this I obliged her to talk about it, the inhibition, which had made any other kind of utterance impossible as well, disappeared' (p. 25).

Here was the key, and it was used by Anna O. and Breuer to open the way to a cure. By talking to Breuer about what was troubling her, Anna was relieved of her symptoms. A regular pattern for the treatment was formed: if during her auto-hypnotic sleep-like state in the evenings 'she was able to narrate the hallucinations she had had in the course of the day, she would wake up clear in mind, calm and cheerful' (p. 27). Breuer visited Anna nightly and as long as she could tell him her stories, which began as basically sad, very imaginative tales modeled after those of Hans Christian Andersen, she felt better. The central situation of these fables was usually a girl nursing her father and from this she built elaborate fictions. If she did not tell Breuer her story she would be agitated all night. Before she could be calmed the next night, she had to tell him two stories - yesterday's and today's.

On 1 April 1881, she got out of bed for the first time in many months, but on 5 April her father died. With his death the third and most severe stage of her illness set in. She was violently excited for several days and then fell into a two-day stupor. After emerging from this she was calmer. The contractures in her right arm and leg persisted, but most disturbing was a progressive limiting of her visual field. Breuer became the only person she could recognize, and she was calm only while speaking with him. She now spoke only English and could not understand German.

During this period the division between her two states of consciousness was exacerbated. Normal states were diminished and her 'condition seconde,' her 'absenses,' became more terrifying. Her evening narratives, told to Breuer while in a state of auto-hypnosis, 'ceased to have the character of more or less freely-created poetical compositions and changed into a string of frightful and terrifying hallucinations' (p. 29). The hallucinations recapitulated the terrors she experienced during her afternoon somnolent state. Her mind was completely relieved if she could tell her doctor about these frightening episodes. If for some reason Breuer could not see her for several days, Anna daily became progressively more agitated. This summing of psychical excitation was only relieved if she could discharge the accumulated tension of her untold tales by telling them to Breuer. She called the procedure her '"talking cure"' and referred to it jokingly as '"chimney-sweeping"' (p. 30). Narrative therapy was

born. We should not forget this. In their work Freud and Jung
wrote a great deal about therapy and the nature of the therapeutic relationship, but at base they were both practicing the
'talking-cure.' They listened to and made sense of the stories
their patients told them.

In December 1881, the fourth phase of Anna O.'s illness
began. A year had passed since the onset of the worst of her
difficulties and almost as a memorium she deteriorated. Around
Christmas her evening sessions were entirely taken up with
complaints about her troubles the previous Christmas. Her
alternating states of consciousness took a most unusual turn.
The initial difference was that the first state was normal,
although a bit melancholic; the second was abnormal, marked by
childishness, fears, anxieties, and alienation from herself and
others. Now her normal consciousness lived in the present, the
winter of 1881-2, while her second consciousness lived a year
earlier in the winter of 1880-1. The change from her normal state
to her 'condition seconde' could either occur spontaneously or
be caused by a sense impression which recalled the previous
year. The transfer to the past was always precise; 'she lived
through the previous winter day by day' (p. 33). While in an
'absense' she had no knowledge of any events which had occurred during 1881, except her father's death. Her mother had
moved to a new house and Anna's hallucinations were so vivid
that she bumped into a stove that was positioned where a door
had been in her old room. Psychical states from the year before
also altered Anna's emotions during her normal state. The reliving of the previous year in her 'condition seconde' continued
for seven months, until June 1882, when Anna's illness came to
an end.

Her evening hypnosis during the fourth phase was taken up
with three sets of complaints: her imaginations and troubles
from the current day, her vexations from the same day a year
ago (fortunately Breuer had listened to her imaginative stories
from that day a year ago and so did not have to relieve her of
them) and a third set of disturbances. These were the psychical
events from the period of incubation, July to December of 1880.
It was these events 'that had produced the whole of the hysterical phenomena, and when they were brought to verbal utterance
the symptoms disappeared' (p. 34).

For example, throughout her illness she had been troubled
by hallucinations of black snakes. These visions were traced
back to a time when she was nursing her father and had fallen
into a 'waking dream' and imagined that she saw a black snake
coming toward him: she 'tried to keep the snake off, but it was
as though she was paralyzed. Her right arm...had gone to sleep
and had become anaesthetic and paretic; and when she looked
at it the fingers turned into little snakes with death heads [the
nails]' (p. 38). The snakes vanished and in her terror she had
tried to pray but language failed her. She finally said some
children's verses in English and came to pray in that language.

In this episode were the origins of the snake hallucination, the paralysis of the right arm, and being able to speak only in English. Once Anna O. had described all the incidents in which a particular symptom had played a part, ending with a description of the origin of the symptom at some point during the incubation period, the problem vanished. This descriptive procedure had to be exhaustive.

Breuer said of his treatment procedure that it 'left nothing to be desired in its logical consistency and systematic application' (p. 35). Here, if Anna's case is typical, is a standardized procedure for treating hysteria. While the patient is hypnotized, she or he narrates every event, beginning with the most recent and moving back into the past, which is associatively related to a symptom. Once the earliest event connected with the symptom is told the symptom is permanently removed. Anna's case was not entirely typical. The reliving, in the fourth phase, of the previous year day by day was unique as was the necessity of telling in reverse order every thought and deed connected with a symptom. What is typical, in light of developments in psychotherapy, is reconstructing the history of mental disturbances by uncovering their origins, discharging bottled-up emotions, expressing psychical difficulties in bodily symptoms, and revealing fantasies associated with life problems. With modifications, Freud's psychoanalytic work was to be concerned in case after case with these issues. The search for causes in the past and the idea that the patient must recall and relive the past - regress - were to become essentials of psychoanalysis. In his attempts to find causes, Freud was to take analyses farther back than Breuer had. As Freud's researches progressed, he moved the cause of neurosis ever farther backwards from present-day adult events towards infantile experiences.

Breuer probably told Freud more about the case than he published, both because the case had to be disguised for publication and because Breuer wrote the case from incomplete notes many years after the treatment of Bertha Pappenheim. One can see, however, why Freud - trained in Brücke's laboratory and not yet having studied under Charcot - would have been struck by what Breuer told him. Here was a woman's body at the mercy of her mind; mental events dominated physical space.

Freud's interest in the case was not purely scientific; it was also aroused because Bertha was a friend of his fiancee Martha Bernays. There is another interesting connection between Pappenheim and the Bernays family, and it shows that the origins of analytic therapy are to be found in the arts as well as science. Martha's uncle, Jacob Bernays, had published a book on the Aristotelian concept of catharsis in 1880. Because of this book 'catharsis was one of the most discussed subjects among scholars and was a current topic of conversation in Viennese salons' (Ellenberger, 1970, p. 484). It is not too much to suppose that the well-educated, socially prominent Pappenheim might have taken as her therapeutic model Aristotle's notion of catharsis:

a 'psychological purgation which relieves us of unwanted feelings
through contemplating their projection in a work of art' (Dodds,
1968, p. 48). Bertha relieved herself of unwanted emotions and
affectively determined physical symptoms by purging herself in
her nightly narratives. Breuer used the term catharsis to denote
a discharge of affect and his method, Anna O.'s talking cure,
became known as the cathartic method.

Ellenberger gives Bertha credit for designing her own treatment:

> She had unique symptoms, directed her cure, [and] explained
> it to the physician....Because she chose for her self-directed
> therapy the procedure of catharsis (which a recent book had
> made fashionable), Breuer believed that he had discovered
> the key to the psychogenesis and treatment of hysteria. (1970,
> p. 892)

Breuer, with the help of Anna O., or Anna O. with the help of
Breuer, had found that words heal, that talking can cure. We
will return to Anna O. shortly, for it is around this case that
many of the troubles originated which led to Freud's first bitter
separation from a colleague.

Besides his financial and intellectual debt to Breuer, Freud
also owed him a professional debt. When Freud opened his
private practice the majority of his cases were referred to him
by Breuer. Breuer's opinion was also respected in medical circles,
and his support of Freud must have been quite valuable in the
early years of Sigmund's practice. Breuer gave his advice on
professional matters and this was not always supportive. He was
not impressed by Freud's work on cocaine and advised Freud to
be cautious in his researches. And, although his wife, Mathilde,
was excited about Sigmund's marriage to Martha, Josef dis-
approved, advising that Freud should wait another two years
until his medical practice was better established. Freud was not
deterred by either piece of cautionary advice (Jones, 1953).

Until the beginning of their collaborative work on hysteria in
the early 1890s, Freud viewed Breuer as an ideal father. He was
a suitable substitute for Brücke, a respected guide in professional matters, and a man worthy of respect. In 1885 Freud
wrote to Martha about Breuer, 'By saying only good things
about him one doesn't give a proper picture of his character.
One ought to emphasize the absence of so many bad things'
(1960, p. 149). Radical changes in Freud's opinion of Breuer
were to come. In the 1880s, Breuer could do no wrong; in the
1890s he could do no right. To set the stage for this reversal of
affection we need to consider Freud's historical account of his
first years in private practice.

Freud's investigations had been steadily progressing since
he began his private practice. In the beginning his therapeutic
arsenal 'contained only two weapons, electrotherapy and
hypnotism' (Freud, 1925b, p. 16). Electrotherapy involved

passing a small current through the patient's body and Erb's textbook gave detailed directions for the treatment of all the symptoms of nervous diseases. Years later Freud said about this therapy:

> Unluckily I was soon driven to see that following these instructions was of no help whatever and that what I had taken for the epitome of exact observations was merely the construction of fantasy. The realization that the work of the greatest name in German neuropathology had no more relation to reality than some 'Egyptian' dream-book, such as is sold in cheap book shops, was painful, but it helped to rid me of another shred of innocent faith in authority from which I was not yet free. So I put the electrical apparatus aside. (1925b, p. 16)

Here it sounds as though Freud had no success with the technique. However, he wrote to Fliess about a woman who was steadily improving under electrical treatment and Bernfeld and Bernfeld (1952) have the testimony of one man whom Freud had treated for a traumatic hysteria by farradization and cured. There must have been other successes, but Freud never recorded these. In the late 1880s he was escaping the authority of physiologically oriented neuro-psychiatry. Thirty-five years later, in the passage quoted above, he was taking pleasure in his triumph. His 'Interpretation of Dreams' had been seen by a few neurologists as a cheap dream book advocating old wives' psychiatry and Freud, never one to forget a slight, was reminding psychiatry of one of its dubious treatment fads.

The last fourteen years of the nineteenth century were, for Freud, a time of freeing himself from all those authorities who restricted his thought: neurology, psychiatry, Charcot, Breuer, Jakob Freud, and Fliess. His self-analysis was central in this liberation process and the freer Freud became, the more his thought was his own. Charcot and Breuer had taught Freud about hypnotism, and he used it from 1886 into the early 1890s in treating patients. Hypnotic suggestion was used by him to relieve patients of their symptoms, and while patients were hypnotized, he questioned them about the origins of their problems. This suggestion technique for symptom cure was popularized by Bernheim and Liebault. In 1889 Freud met with Bernheim and this consultation was important to the development of Freud's work for several reasons. The first was that Bernheim advocated a psychological view of hypnotism; he disputed Charcot's claim that hypnotizability was dependent on physiological factors. Although Freud remained for a time faithful to Charcot's views, Bernheim's ideas helped Freud to take another step away from physiological determinism. Second, Bernheim taught Freud that his problems with hypnotism - not being able to hypnotize every patient and a frequent inability to achieve a deep state of hypnosis - were problems that all therapists had. Third, he demonstrated to Freud that patients who had been in a somnolent

state did not lose their memories for what had happened while
they were 'asleep.' Upon waking they claimed no memory, but if
the therapist while pressing his hands to their foreheads insisted
that they knew what had happened they gradually began talking
about what they had experienced. Eventually memory would
return 'in a flood and with complete clarity' (Freud, 1925b,
p. 28). They knew all along what had happened while they were
in a state of reduced consciousness, and yet they didn't know
that they knew.

Although hypnotism might have been more efficient at getting
at what people knew but did not know, Freud felt that with more
encouragement on his part, patients could be helped to remember
events vital to their illnesses which they had forgotten. He concluded, 'My expectations were fulfilled; I was set free from
hypnotism' (p. 29). He no longer had to depend on hypnosis,
which he wasn't very good at, for assistance in helping his
patients to remember the forgotten histories of their difficulties.
In Anna O.'s treatment, Breuer had been completely dependent
on her auto-hypnotic states in tracking down the origin of her
symptoms. Freud was now free of hypnosis and so was liberated
from Breuer's method. In telling the history of his abandonment
of electrotherapy and hypnotism Freud is also telling us about
freeing himself from neuropsychiatry and from a dependence on
what Charcot and Breuer had taught him. The outcome of this
liberation of therapeutic technique was free association, the
method Freud used in his own self-analysis to understand his
past and thereby gain some freedom from it.

The intellectual, professional, and financial debts to Josef
Breuer which Freud had incurred in the 1880s became an unbearable obligation to him in the 1890s. In 1889, in response to a
letter containing some criticisms of his character, Freud addres-
ses Breuer as his 'Dearest Friend and best beloved of men'
(1960, p. 226). He agreed with Breuer's criticisms and only
chastised his old friend for not addressing him with the familiar
'du' instead of 'Sie'. After the turn of the decade, however, the
relationship deteriorated. In 1891 Freud wrote to Minna Bernays,
Martha's sister, that 'the breach' between Breuer and himself
'is widening all the time, and my efforts to patch things up with
the dedication [to Breuer in Freud's book on aphasia] have probably had the opposite effect' (1960, p. 229).

The problems arose over Freud's attempts to have Breuer
collaborate with him on an article and a book about hysteria.
Ever since Anna O. they had often consulted about the treatment
of hysterical patients. It was their co-operation in the case of
Frau Cäcilie that led to the publication of their 'Preliminary
Communication' (1893) on hysteria. Freud announced to Fliess
in June 1892, that Breuer had agreed to joint publication, but
in December he said that the detailed 'Preliminary Communication'
'has meant a long battle with my collaborator' (1954, p. 64). This
battle which culminated in 'the development of psycho-analysis,'
Freud says, 'cost me his [Breuer's] friendship. It was not easy

for me to pay such a price, but I could not escape it' (1925b,
p. 19).
   Why was Breuer lost as a friend? Freud (1914d) tells us it was
not because they had two different theories about the psychical
mechanism underlying hysteria. Indeed, in the preface to 'Studies
on Hysteria' (1895) they say that their opinions diverge at points
and this is to be expected when two observers who agree on
the facts are not at one in their interpretations. Breuer maintained that 'the basis of hysteria is an idiosyncracy of the whole
nervous system' upon which psychically determined symptoms
are elaborated (p. 244). Overlying these secondary ideogenic
complexes, which are charged with undischarged affect, is a
tertiary tendency to hypnoid states or auto-hypnosis. This is a
condition of decreased consciousness in which reveries are elaborated. Innate and experiential factors play a part in the
development of hypnoid states. They arise, as we have seen in
Anna O., as the result of the monotony of sick-nursing. Breuer
felt that

> apart from sick-nursing, no psychical factor is so well-
> calculated to produce reveries charged with affect as are
> the longings of a person in love. And over and above this
> the sexual orgasm itself, with its wealth of affect and its
> restriction of consciousness, is closely akin to hypnoid
> states. (p. 248)

   Freud maintained that he 'had never in my own experience
met with a genuine hypnoid hysteria. Any that I took in hand
turned into a defense hysteria' (p. 286). Freud's explanation
of the psychical mechanism of hysteria was the theory of defense.
That is, 'hysteria originates through the repression of an
incompatible idea from a motive of defense' (p. 285). In another
place Freud says, 'before hysteria can be acquired for the first
time one essential condition must be fulfilled: an idea must be
intentionally repressed from consciousness and excluded from
associative modification' (p. 116). Intentional does not mean with
conscious awareness, but having a clear and defineable motive
for not being aware of the idea. The person is unaware of the
repression, but the therapist can specify why the individual
would not want to know the thought. The repressed idea persists
as a memory trace, but the strong affective intensity of the idea
which led to the defense against it 'is torn from it' and converted
into a somatic innervation (p. 285). The defense against the idea,
the repression of an emotionally laden thought, 'becomes the
cause of morbid symptoms' (p. 285). 'In so far as one can speak
of determining causes which lead to the acquisition of neurosis,'
Freud said, 'their aetiology is to be looked for in *sexual* factors'
(p. 257). Defense against ideas of a sexual nature is, then,
the cause of hysteria. Such ideas are charged with affect, and
they are unacceptable to consciousness. Therefore, they are
repressed. Once repressed, the affect is diverted into bodily

excitation, converted into the various physical symptoms of hysteria, and the idea persists as a memory trace outside of consciousness.

The break, then, was not over Breuer's opting for an explanatory model that was at base physiological, while taking into account psychological issues, and Freud's more purely psychological explanation. Freud says the battle between them was focused on the sexual etiology of the neuroses:

> When I...began more and more resolutely to put forward the significance of sexuality in the etiology of neuroses, he [Breuer] was the first to show the reaction of distaste and repudiation which was later to become so familiar to me, but which at that time I had not learned to recognize as my inevitable fate. (1914d, p. 12)

Freud wanted Breuer to join him in battle, to give his support entirely to the notion that the cause of the psychoneuroses lay in sexuality. While Breuer and Freud were working on 'Studies,' Freud announced that in all cases of obsessional neurosis he had analyzed 'it was the subject's *sexual life* that had given rise to a distressing affect of precisely the same quality as that attaching to his obsession' (1894, p. 52). Freud says that the connection between obsessional neuroses and sexuality is not always obvious. About one specific case he admits, 'If anyone less mono-ideistic than I am had looked for it, he would have overlooked it' (p. 57). Soon the cause of *all* acquired neuroses - obsessional, hysterical, and anxiety - was found in 'influences from *sexual life*' (Freud, 1895, p. 99). From 1894 to 1895, just as his relations with Breuer were becoming more difficult, Freud was setting out on a crusade that would last a lifetime and he was looking for allies. Breuer would not give Freud unconditional support for the sexual crusade, so Josef became Sigmund's enemy.

We have seen Freud's 'either-or' attitude in his letter to Martha, where he insisted on her allegiance; he was now confronting Breuer with the same choice. Either support me totally or we are no longer friends or collaborators. Freud had transformed his intellectual and professional debt to Breuer into a demand: back me or I owe you nothing. Breuer was no longer the ideal father of the 1880s, providing instruction and advice; he had become weak and vacillating in Sigmund's eyes because he would not fight for the cause of sexuality. When Breuer showed unconditional support for the theory, he was Freud's friend. Freud wrote to Fliess, the man who replaced Breuer in Sigmund's affections, 'Breuer...is a new man. One cannot help liking him again without any reservations....He has become fully converted to my theory of sexuality' (1954, p. 121). Six months later in November 1895, when Breuer did not evince total support, Freud was alienated from him and angry:

> Not long ago Breuer made a big speech to the physician's
> society about me, putting himself forward as a convert to
> belief in sexual aetiology. When I thanked him privately
> for this, he spoiled my pleasure by saying: 'But all the
> same I don't believe it!' Can you make head or tail of that?
> I cannot. (p. 134)

Four months later he found it impossible to get along with Breuer
and was finding it hard to reconcile himself to Josef's being out
of his life. A year later he announced to Fliess that he was glad
he never saw Breuer, as the mere sight of him would have led
Freud to think about emigration (Jones, 1953). The estrangement
was complete. Freud even avoided walking down the street on
which Breuer lived. Attempting to sever all ties with Breuer,
Freud began paying off his debt in 1898. Breuer resisted the
repayment, but Freud insisted. Two years later the debt was
still not paid, and Freud resented this because it kept him from
being completely free of his old teacher (Jones, 1953).

Breuer was an unassuming and non-combative person and
does not seem to have reciprocated Freud's ill feelings. In 1900
when a patient whom Breuer had referred to Freud told Breuer
of her extraordinary improvement he clapped his hands and
exclaimed again and again, 'So he is right after all!' (Freud,
1954, p. 320). Breuer was acknowledging that Freud's diagnosis
of a sexual etiology in the case was correct. As a memento of
their collaboration, Breuer, in 1909, sent Freud early drafts
which Sigmund had penned for their first joint publication.

Freud was far more bitter. Breuer's daughter-in-law recalls
walking with Josef when he was quite old and passing Freud in
the street. Breuer opened his arms to Freud; Freud passed by,
pretending not to see (Roazen, 1971). In celebration of Breuer's
seventieth birthday a fund awarding prizes for scientific research
was established in his name. 'The list of subscribers included
the names of the foremost Viennese scientists, writers, and
artists. The name of Freud, however, is not to be found on this
list' (Ellenberger, 1970, p. 809).

Freud wrote to Fliess in March 1896, the time when he was
completing the break with Breuer, 'I believe he has never for-
given me for having lured him into writing the *Studies* with me
and so committed him to something definite, when he always knows
of three candidates for one truth and abominates every generalization as a piece of arrogance' (Jones, 1953, p. 312). On the
contrary, it seems that Freud never forgave Breuer for his caution and inability to totally commit himself to Freud's one truth -
sexuality.

We have seen that Freud could not understand at the time it
happened why Breuer would support the sexual theory in a public speech and yet deny his belief in private. Psychoanalysis
later provided a tool by which Freud could explain Breuer's
inconsistent behavior. In 1914, in an essay which also condemns
Jung for giving up the psychoanalytic cause, Freud gives the

real reasons for the breach in his relations with Breuer. He says, 'at first I did not understand' why the friendship fell apart and that 'it was only later that I learnt from many clear indications how to interpret it' (1914d, p. 11). Here is the essence of psychoanalysis. It is a method that through inter-pretation from various clues allows one to come to an understand-ing of that which was not previously understood. Freud's explan-ation of Breuer's inability to support Freud's views whole-heartedly was that Breuer had to deny that Anna O. had been sexually attracted to him. Breuer explicitly states, 'The element of sexuality was astonishingly undeveloped in her' (1895, p. 21). More than thirty years after the treatment Freud says that one can hardly miss the importance of sexuality in the case, for example: the phallic symbolism of the snakes, the stiffening paralysis of her arm, and the nursing of her father at his bed-side with her passionate devotion to him. During the hundreds of sessions involved in her treatment she transferred her love from her father to Breuer. Freud in two places in his published writings (1914d; 1925b) says he suspected that Breuer terminated the treatment for reasons having to do with the sexual nature of the transference, but over the 'final stage of this hypnotic treat-ment there rested a veil of obscurity, which Breuer never raised for me' (1925b, p. 21). To put it kindly, Freud is being discreet here. In his private correspondence with Stefan Zweig, Freud wrote:

> On the evening of the day when all her [Anna O.'s] symp-toms had been disposed of, he [Breuer] was summoned to the patient again, found her confused and writhing with abdominal cramps. Asked what was wrong with her, she replied: 'Now Dr. B.'s child is coming!'...Seized by conven-tional horror he took flight and abandoned the patient to a colleague. [letter of 1932] (1960, p. 266)

Freud says long after the break in his relations with Breuer he had remembered Josef telling him this incident; he must have had it in mind when, right after speaking about the Anna O. case, he wrote 'the emergence of the transference in its crudely sexual form...has always seemed to me the irrefragible proof that the source of the driving forces of neurosis lies in sexual life' (1914d, p. 12). In retrospect, Freud has attributed his problems with Breuer to one cause; Breuer would not recognize and cope with transference love, and, therefore, could not accept Freud's sexual theories. Freud's analysis seems convincing, especially with the additional piece of evidence about Dr Breuer's baby, but there is a fault in the analysis. Freud has not been entirely honest with himself or the reader. Psychoanalysis has not been used in a noble search for greater understanding, but to publicly absolve Freud of any responsibility in the break with Breuer. Although Freud was fond of saying that he was not a tendentious person and that psychoanalysis was devoted to finding the truth, he too often used analysis to condemn others and uphold himself. Breuer was victimized in this way and so was Jung. Freud has abused analysis by using it in the service of self-justification. Even in his obituary for Breuer he uses the transference interpretation as an explanation for Breuer's not pursuing work on the neuroses (Freud, 1925c). Freud is probably correct in what he says about Breuer's relationship with Anna O.[1] But he has still abused the science he founded, because he has left out two important points. First, Breuer continued to work with hysterical patients after the Anna O. case and second, it was Freud who could not tolerate Breuer. There were four reasons for this. First, we have seen that Freud resented Breuer's lack of total support for the sexual theory. Second, he also resented the obligation that owing Breuer money put him under. Third, Breuer's inability to admit that Anna O. had fallen in love with him must have been intolerable to Freud (Schlessinger et al., 1967); twenty years after the break, this event remained so important that it became Freud's explanation for the end of the friendship.

Fourth, their relationship deteriorated because Freud had projected on to Breuer ambivalent feelings that he had towards his own father and brothers (Grinstein, 1968). Like Jacob Freud, Josef Breuer was not combative; he simply was not a fighter. Ellenberger (1970) contrasts Breuer's and Freud's attitudes towards anti-Semitism. Breuer was for assimilation and attempted in every situation to avoid or smooth over problems arising from his being a Jew; he was very successful in doing this. Freud, as we have seen, resented his father's not defending his rights as a Jew, and Sigmund himself gloried in his defense of himself as a Jew in the incident on the train. Freud had mixed emotions about assimilation to Gentile culture. He wanted its recognition, and he occasionally attributed rejection of his ideas, sometimes incorrectly, to anti-Semitism. He had disavowed Judaism as a religion and did not idealize his ancestors or their accomplishments. Yet, he defended his Jewish identity and felt that he had found in the B'nai B'rith, which he joined in 1895, people with whom he shared a mutual understanding because he and they were Jews. Freud resented both Breuer's success as an assimilated Jew and his lack of courage in defending his heritage.

The connection between Josef and Jakob is an important one. Sigmund's childhood overvaluation of Jakob Freud was followed by an equally strong undervaluation. His overvaluation of Breuer was followed by a definite and bitter undervaluation. Neither Jakob nor Josef would fight for the causes which Sigmund championed and for this he came to despise them. In his self-analysis, which Freud began just as his relations with Breuer disintegrated, he uncovered many of his hitherto unconscious feelings of hatred for Jakob. He might have been aided in this excavation by the current hatred he was feeling for Josef. Rank boldly suggests that Freud, in emphasizing the dramatic effect that Jakob's death had in releasing his long buried animosities towards his father, might have been deceiving himself (Roazen, 1971). Jakob died in 1896, the same year that Freud's estrangement from Breuer became complete. Freud may have been projecting into the past of his childhood and on to his now dead father the hatred aroused by his contemporary problems with Breuer. It might have been easier for Freud to relive his childhood angers against his father than to admit that at forty he was being childish in his relations to Josef Breuer.

Breuer was the only one of Freud's mentors with whom he collaborated, and their partnership transformed Freud's emotional relationship with Josef. The collaboration put them on an equal footing; Breuer in the 1890s was no longer in a position that demanded respect. Freud could now find fault; his mentor, his ideal father, had now become an equal - a brother. Freud wrote to Fliess,

> As far as Breuer is concerned, you are certainly quite right in calling him *the* brother. However, I do not share your contempt for friendship between men, probably because I am to a high degree a party to it. As you well know, in my life a woman has never been a substitute for a comrade, a friend. If Breuer's masculine inclination were not so odd, so faint-hearted, so contradictory, as is everything emotional in him, he would be a beautiful example of the kinds of achievements to which the androphile current in man can be sublimated. (letter of 8/7/1901 quoted in Schur, 1972, pp. 216-17)

If Breuer had been more of a man, more willing to fight on Freud's behalf, then Freud could have easily invested in him his sublimated homosexual love. Breuer, however, failed him and all that love turned to hate. From chapter 2 remember Freud saying that his ambivalent childhood relations with his cousin, John, had been revived in his adult male friendships. He had the dream that lead him to this revelation in 1898, so the recent transformation of love for Breuer into hate probably helped Freud to recover memories of John. The prototypical love-hate bond to John found its first clear adult expression in Freud's relations to Breuer and this pattern was to be repeated again.

There is little evidence that in his self-analysis Freud successfully dealt with his feelings towards Breuer. If he had done so, he might have been willing to admit that there were many more reasons for his break with Josef than Breuer's inability to recognize sexual transference in the case of Anna O. He might also have been able to more consistently evaluate the importance of Breuer's work in the creation of psychoanalysis and to have more accurately represented what he and Breuer wrote in 'Studies on Hysteria.'

Just a year after the appearance of 'Studies,' in 'Further Remarks on the Neuro-psychoses of Defense,' Freud said that 'Breuer and I' had expressed the opinion that the cause of hysterical symptoms was a psychic trauma originating in 'the

patient's sexual life' (1896b, p. 162). This perhaps slightly
over-represents Breuer's support for the sexual theory, but not
by much. Less than a month later, in 'The Aetiology of Hysteria,'
Freud maintained that the hypothesis of the sexual etiology of
hysteria was entirely his own and that 'the two investigators as
whose pupil I began my studies in hysteria, Charcot and Breuer,
were far from having any such presupposition; in fact, they had
a personal disinclination to it which I originally shared' (1896c,
p. 199). Only extensive observation of patients, Freud said,
convinced him that the cause of hysteria lay in sexuality. By
1895 Breuer's 'personal disinclination' must have vanished, or
he must not have meant it when he wrote, in italics, *'the great
majority of severe neuroses have their origin in the marriage
bed'* (p. 246). This quote, other quotes from 'Studies,' and
Freud's statement in the 'Further remarks...' essay make it
difficult to understand Freud's 1925(b) statement: 'It would have
been difficult to guess from the *Studies on Hysteria* what importance sexuality has in the etiology of the neuroses' (p. 22). No
guessing is necessary; both Breuer and Freud, as we have seen,
express the conviction that difficulties surrounding sex are
either a cause, or the cause, of hysteria. One might argue that
after thirty years of investigating the sexual causes of neurosis,
Freud had simply underestimated what Breuer and he had accomplished. This is no doubt true, but such a gross misrepresenta-
tion of Breuer's emphasis on sexuality in 'Studies,' combined
in the same essay with Freud's emphasis on Breuer's failure to
deal with Anna O.'s sexual transference, can only be aimed at
representing Breuer as completely naive or perhaps willfully set
against recognizing the sexual theory.

Another essay, 'On the History of the Psycho-Analytic Movement,' confirms this interpretation. Freud in this essay declares
psychoanalysis to be his invention. He says that in a 1909 lecture
on psychoanalysis (1910a, p. 9) he had been overgenerous when
he gave Breuer credit for inventing psychoanalysis.[2] Now, in
1914, he is going to take full credit for this invention since
critics attack him and not Breuer.

Revising history again, Freud now reverses the statement he
made in 'The Aetiology of Hysteria' that he had no preconceived
notions about sexuality. He says Breuer, Charcot, and a famous
Viennese gynecologist, Chrobak, had each given him clues, during the early years of his practice, that sex played a vital role
in the neuroses. Breuer had said, '"These things are always
secrets d'alcove [marriage bed]!"' (1914d, p. 13). He had overheard Charcot say, '"But in this sort of case it's always a question of the genitals - always, always, always"' (p. 14). Chrobak
had taken him aside and said the prescription for a woman patient
whose husband was impotent was repeated doses of a normal
penis (p. 15). When he heard these three maxims, Freud says
he was astounded, but he feels they must have influenced his
later researches. He adds that both Chrobak and Breuer denied
ever saying such things. Why would Breuer have denied saying

it, when in fact he wrote the same thing in 1895? Freud is trying
in his two works on the history of psychoanalysis to make the
discovery of the sexual etiology of the neuroses all his own. He
knows that history is retrospectively reconstructed and that by
representing Breuer as having only hinted about sex, and Charcot as having known about it but not pursued the issue, he can
claim sole credit for the sexual theory. Freud is retrospectively
freeing himself from his teachers, saying that Breuer did not
invent psychoanalysis, and neither Charcot nor Breuer was
really committed to the idea that the neuroses had a sexual cause.

With the break in his relations with Breuer, Freud was freed
from his last teacher, and he became the father of psychoanalysis.
Freud deserves full credit for founding psychoanalysis, but not
for discovering the sexual causation of neurosis. His historical
fictions sometimes leave the realm of fact too far behind. Ellenberger has pointed out that Richer, a disciple of Charcot, had
in 1881, four years before Freud's visit to Paris, written that
in hysterical attacks there is a re-enactment of a psychic, often
sexual, trauma; 'Had he read it [Richer's book], Freud would
not have been so surprised when he heard Charcot mentioning
the role of sexuality in neurotic disturbances' (1970, p. 753).
Some would have us believe, including Freud and Ernest Jones,
that Freud singlehandedly rediscovered sex just before the turn
of the century. Decker (1977) and Ellenberger have shown that
this is simply not true. Numerous researchers were involved in
the scientific exploration of sexuality and artists, novelists and
playwrights, many of whom Freud read, were composing works
in which sexual conflicts and perversions were a central theme.

Freud's power lay in synthesizing diverse trends of thought
and giving them the trademark: Made by Freud. In the 1890s
Freud not only founded psychoanalysis - he gave birth to a
legend. The Freudian legend has two main features:

> The first is the theme of the solitary hero struggling against
> a host of enemies, suffering 'the slings and arrows of out-
> rageous fortune' but triumphing in the end. The legend con-
> siderably exaggerates the extent and role of anti-Semitism,
> of the hostility of the academic world, and of alleged Victorian
> prejudices. The second feature of the Freudian legend is the
> blotting out of the greatest part of the scientific and cultural
> context in which psychoanalysis developed, hence the theme
> of the absolute originality of the achievements, in which the
> hero is credited with the achievements of his predecessors,
> associates, disciples, rivals, and contemporaries. (Ellenber-
> ger, 1970, p. 547)

An excellent example of this is the story of the reaction to
Breuer and Freud's joint publications. Freud sets the first stones
for the building of the legend in his two historical works.

There was some consolation for the bad reception accorded to
my contention of a sexual aetiology in the neuroses even by
my most intimate circle of friends – for a vacuum rapidly
formed itself about my person – in the thought that I was taking up the fight for a new and original idea. (1914d, pp. 12-13)

In 1925(b) Freud says Breuer's self-confidence and powers of
resistance were not well developed and that when 'Studies' met
with a bad reception in Germany and Vienna, and Adolf von
Strümpell, a well-known neurologist, wrote a very critical review
'Breuer felt hurt and discouraged' (p. 23). Freud says he, himself, laughed at the lack of comprehension that Strümpell's review showed.
    'Oh, the myth-forming power of mankind!' (Freud, 1960,
p. 19). In the above passages, which were buttressed by many
others, Freud has managed to take full credit for arriving at
the 'new' and 'original' idea of the sexual etiology of the neuroses, eliminate Breuer as a weakling for bending to foolish
criticism, and elevate himself as a lone crusader. Stories to be
effective must be told, and in founding the psychoanalytic movement Freud ensured that his tales would be retold again and
again. Jones is so taken by Freud's story of the reception of
'Studies' that he doesn't even see he is contradicting it. First
he says, 'The book was not well received in the medical world'
(1953, p. 252). His sole piece of evidence for this assertion is to
quote Freud on Strümpell's review. He then cites three favorable
reviews by prominent medical men: Mitchell Clark, Havelock
Ellis, and Eugen Bleuler! He goes on to say that the book was
widely reviewed outside of medicine and quotes an extremely
favorable review which appeared in Vienna's leading newspaper.
Robert (1966) and other popular biographers of Freud spread
the story by depending on Jones and Freud for their information. Repeating the story more vividly and not bothering to cite
any evidence, Erikson – an expert on psychohistory – says that
Freud in his collaboration with Breuer 'had committed himself to
theories so unpopular and, in fact, so universally disturbing
that the senior co-author had disengaged himself from the junior
one' (1954, p. 133). Passed on from one author to another, a
legend has grown and been sustained. Freud says the book was
not well received in Germany and Vienna, Jones expands this
to the medical world, and Erikson grandly extends it to universal
unpopularity.
    If we return to the records of the past, as Freud taught us
to do, we can rectify the historical amnesia which sustains a
legend. Returning to the critical notices of Breuer and Freud's
work, Ellenberger and Decker both conclude that on the whole
their writings were fairly and positively reviewed. The 'Preliminary Communication' was favorably received by European medical
men, Ellenberger says, and supports this point by mentioning
five good reviews and one negative notice (1970). Summarizing
the reaction in Germany to the 'Preliminary Communication,' one

of the many papers in the early 1890s about hysteria, Decker says: 'The German medical reaction was limited but it was interested and appreciative. Two of the three commentaries were by well-known authorities. There was no hostile reaction' (1977, p. 87). 'The traditional belief that *Studies in Hysteria* met no success is definitely contradicted by the facts' (Ellenberger, 1970, p. 771). In support of his point, Ellenberger cites passages from four positive, two mixed but generally favorable notices and only one negative review. According to this noted historian of depth psychology, the book was also successful in literary circles. Decker found two reviews by physicians that were quite positive while other reviews by German critics were mixed.

Freud and Jones maintain that Strümpell's review of 'Studies' was ill-informed and very critical. Ellenberger, quoting from this review, presents it as mixed but generally positive. Decker sees Strümpell's piece as having correctly restated the cathartic method and as 'not entirely negative,' but she faults him for questioning the propriety of Breuer and Freud's investigations into the sexual lives of their patients.

The centerpiece of the story about the bad and uncomprehending reception of Breuer and Freud's work is this review by Strümpell. The review began by saying that the Viennese physicians had a '"correct and sharp conception of *many* cases of severe hysteria and that under some conditions "their method could produce" a certain therapeutic success"' (Decker, 1977, p. 159 quoting Strümpell, 1895). This comment is at least mildly positive. Strümpell wondered '"whether what is learned from patients under hypnosis corresponds precisely to reality";' he feared that patients may let their fantasies roam and invent stories (Decker, 1977, p. 159). He concluded that hypnosis could be done away with and replaced by direct psychic treatment. Freud no doubt resented the comment about patients inventing stories, but he was to discover shortly after Strümpell's review was published that patients did exactly this. They mixed fantasy with reality in retelling their life histories. Freud, of course, treated this discovery as his own, and it played an important part in his self-analysis and in the origins of psychoanalysis. Strümpell in advocating direct psychic treatment was simply championing something that Freud was already doing. By 1895 Freud had given up hypnosis, and, as we have seen, maintained that he had discovered, with no help from his teachers, that he could obtain information by a more direct method. Perhaps it was disconcerting to his sense of originality to have Strümpell advocating this same method.

Freud's relations with Josef Breuer have taken us through several different psychoanalytic stories: the origins of narrative therapy in the case of Anna O., Freud's accounts of Breuer's weakness and his own strength, and the legend of the early rejection of their work. We have seen Freud in his historical reconstruction of this relationship simplify his problems with

Breuer in order to absolve himself of any responsibility for the deterioration of their friendship, a technique which we will see him use again. It was difficult for Freud to free himself from his last mentor, because he owed him so much. Freud repaid his debt by demeaning his creditor. The man who had been an intellectual, professional and financial benefactor to Freud was in the end reduced to the doctor who could not cope with a female patient's love. The internal inconsistencies in Freud's story and the degree to which his accounts of the reactions to his early work depart from reality alert us to the mythic realm Freud has entered. If the purpose of a psychoanalysis is to help an individual to put his or her life story in order and to connect this story to the real world, then we must conclude that Freud never successfully dealt with the issue of Josef Breuer. If, on the other hand, analysis provides a myth by which a person can go on living, then Freud handled Breuer brilliantly; he buried his last father behind stories of his own heroic struggles. Breuer was the first to be sacrificed in building the monumental legend of psychoanalysis. He was not the last.

4   THE IMMACULATE ANALYSIS

Psychoanalytic doctrine maintains that every analyst must be
analyzed by a trained psychoanalyst: it is his safeguard against
self-deception. But who - the bright schoolchild will ask -
analyzed the first analyst? Without that fertilization of thought
made possible by two minds how could psychoanalysis be born?
Parthenogenetically, a great mind, through introspection, fer-
tilized itself. In finding himself, Freud founded psychoanalysis;
in this borning was a miracle; in this immaculate analysis Freud
freed himself from self-deception, the original sin of rational
man. When one person is freed, then we can all be saved. Freud's
feat was miraculous, or so Jones (1953), Schur (1972) and
others would have us believe. By the methods he used in putting
an end to, or at least diminishing, his own self-deception, Freud
created psychoanalysis with its promise that we can all be disillusioned: that through analysis we can give up our self-deceits,
our lives will be changed, and we will come to reside closer to
the truth. Of course, this assumes that Freud was not deceived
in his own analysis, for if he had been, then psychoanalysis
would have been born in deception and not truth. Freud's truth-
finding fused his life and work, changing both. In this act he
found his vocation and modified the ever-changing course of
Western thought.
    As befits such a monumental achievement, this first analysis
has had monuments erected to it: Grinstein calls it a 'Herculean
task' (1968, p. 20); Robert talks of Freud's heroic journey into
the 'dark regions in which he long struggled, aided only by his
intense thirst for knowledge' (1966, p. 101); and Marcus regards
it 'as a culmination of the particular tradition of introspection
which began with the adjuration of the oracle at Delphi "Know
thyself"' (1977, p. vii). Analysts and scholars return to the
records of Freud's self-interpretations, endlessly reinterpreting
them in order better to understand the beginning and the
founder. They ask questions which must be answered by interpretation and so carry forward the work of Freud. To ask if
Freud was deceived in his self-analysis, or, more precisely,
about which aspects of his life he was deceived, is to pay homage
to Freud by asking the question he taught us how to ask. As
with any beginning, the origin of psychoanalysis has been
sanctified in a disciple's words. The apostle Jones writes:

    In the summer of 1897 the spell began to break, and Freud
    undertook his most heroic feat - a psychoanalysis of his own

unconscious. It is hard for us nowadays to imagine how
momentous this achievement was, that difficulty being the
fate of most pioneering exploits. Yet the uniqueness of the
feat remains. Once done it is done forever. For no one
again can be the first to explore those depths. (1953, p. 319)

Every beginning has its history: no achievement is difficult
to imagine if we immerse ourselves in its story. The struggle of
the Titans and Olympians, the 'big bang' theory, the origin of
the species, 'Genesis', and 'The Birth of a Nation' are all stories
of origins. When we speak of beginnings - our births, the first
humans, the first gods, the first minutes of the universe - our
narrative becomes numinous. The stories of our distant past
attempt to locate us in history, to give an event to which we feel
tied a special importance. Beginnings are not shrouded in darkness; they are too important to remain unknown. They are
illuminated by words. Stories about the early days are told and
retold. For in the word the beginning is re-experienced now,
the past is made present, and we find out who we are by exploring who we were.
A journey back into the past is always a movement forward in
consciousness. A story usually begins at the beginning; and so
in telling about Freud's and Jung's lives we began with their
births. Although their lives began with their births, the significance of their lives to themselves and others was established
much later. If Freud had not become the founder of psychoanalysis and Jung had not split with Freud and established
analytical psychology we probably would not be interested in
their stories. Freud's story, or at least the story which insures
his place in history, began in the 1890s and was first told in
one book - 'The Interpretation of Dreams.' This text records
Freud's journey back into his adolescence and childhood, an
excursion which preoccupied him for many years and which
expanded his vision of who he was. Through his self-analysis,
the public record of which is the dream book, Freud by exploring
his past and coming to understand who he was made his present
more liveable and assured his place in history.
Origins are recreated in rituals and reproductions which recapture the activities of the past: 4 July has its militarism, nativity
scenes always have cows along with the baby Jesus, laboratory
simulations of the beginnings of life try to create the living from
collections of chemicals, Passover has its unleavened bread,
and college homecoming has beer and fellowship. The beginnings
of psychoanalysis are also celebrated by the activity which best
characterizes psychoanalysis - interpretation. 'The Interpretation
of Dreams' is celebrated by the reinterpretation of Freud's
dreams and stories. In the interminable analysis which characterizes every hermeneutic system psychoanalysis celebrates its
past and thereby comes to better understand its founder and
itself as a movement.
Freud (1954, p. 233), with his eye on history, erected in

words a monument to the beginning of psychoanalysis:

> In this house on July 24th, 1895
> the Secret of Dreams was revealed
>   to Dr. Sigmund Freud

Dates serve to anchor history in time. They provide points of
reference by which to organize a story. 24 July 1895, is for
Freud, and for us, a punctuation point in time. We will work
backwards and forwards from this date in retelling, which is
always reinterpreting, the story of the origins of psychoanalysis.
In his teens, in the letters to Fluss, and in his twenties, in the
Bernays correspondence, we have found early attempts by Freud
to understand himself. This self-dissection matured in the 1890s
and a new species of introspection, psychoanalysis, was born.
Six interwoven episodes form the fabric of this chapter: Freud's
relations with Fliess, his finding his vocation, the formulation
and renunciation of the seduction theory, the dream of Irma's
injection on 24 July 1895, Freud's self-analysis and its outcome.

WILHELM FLIESS

In 1887, the year following his marriage to Martha, Sigmund met
Wilhelm Fliess. Freud was giving lectures on neurological topics
at the university and Breuer encouraged Fliess to attend these
talks. For Freud, the meeting with Fliess must have been friendship at first sight. In his initial letter to Fliess (there were at
least 283 more), Freud opened, 'I have a strictly business motive
for writing you to-day, but I must start with the confession that
I hope to remain in contact with you, and that you left a deep
impression on me' (1954, p. 51). The friendship became closer
over the next eight years, becoming most intimate in the middle
years of the 1890s when Freud was breaking away from Breuer
and beginning his self-analysis. As troubles with Breuer increased, Wilhelm came to take Josef's place in Freud's life. He became
a teacher, a friend, and an ally in the sexual crusade. As Freud
began to explore his emotional difficulties, his dreams, and his
past Fliess became a confessor. The letters to Fliess are a document of Freud's self-analysis. They are an incomplete document,
as is 'The Interpretation of Dreams,' of Freud's attempt to free
himself from self-deception. Living in Freud's legacy, however,
we see that every document of human experience is incomplete;
every text has become a pretext for interpretation. There is
always more to find out; the hermeneutic task is never finished.
The Fliess letters, 'The Interpretation of Dreams' and numerous
commentaries on Freud's life will be used to explore what led up
to Freud's self-analysis, the problems he dealt with in the
analysis, and the benefits he gained by coming to know himself.
We will also venture into a more obscure area, speculating on
ways in which Freud deceived himself and on areas of his life

which remained opaque to him.

Sociologically the close friendship between Freud and Fliess is understandable. They were both doctors starting out their practices; they shared a scientific commitment to materialist explanation; and they both had classical educations and shared an interest in the humanities. Freud's letters to Fliess[1] are filled with allusions to and quotes from the classics and modern literature. They also contain Jewish stories by which Freud delivers telling, and often humorous, accounts of his difficulties. Fliess was a Jew and with him Freud commiserated about anti-Semitism. Freud complained of Viennese conservatism and envied Fliess's residence in progressive Berlin.

The geographic separation was bridged by letters and occasional visits, which Freud called 'Congresses.' At these Freud and Fliess shared their new, and they felt revolutionary, scientific ideas. Both men were convinced that their scientific contemporaries did not understand or sympathize with their radical notions and so each man found an audience in the other. We know why Freud felt he was an outcast, and to understand why he found a fellow traveler in Fliess, it is necessary to briefly review Fliess's researches.

Fliess, unlike Breuer, shared Freud's determination to convince science that sexuality played a fundamental biological role in human health and sickness. Fliess was a nose and throat specialist and had a successful practice in Berlin. His medical and scientific interests were very broad. He had a wealth of biological knowledge and a talent for mathematics. He was imaginative, fond of speculation, and somewhat dogmatic in his pronouncements.

At Freud's urging, Fliess published a paper on the nasal reflex neurosis. The diffuse somatic symptoms of this unusual syndrome were linked together because '"one can bring them temporarily to an end by anaesthetising with cocaine the responsible area in the nose"' (Fliess quoted in Kris, 1954, p. 5). Fliess held that neurosis with a sexual causation often assumed the form of the nasal reflex neurosis because there was a special connection between the genitals and the nose; for example, the turbinate bones of the nose swell during menstruation. Fliess's nasal-sexual hypothesis attracted early support in Germany, but then fell under attack and has not survived.

From the nose and its ties with menstruation Fliess elaborated a theory of great scope. In 1897 he began formulating his ideas on periodicity. He held that the twenty-eight-day period of female menstruation is present before puberty and that there is a male period of twenty-three days. Both periods, but with a different emphasis, are present in men and women because of the human 'bisexual constitution.' The recognition of this fundamental periodicity in life led Fliess to assert that: human development takes place in fits and starts dependent on the sexual periods; the days of a person's birth, death, and illnesses can be predicted by periodic calculations; periodic rhythms are inherited by the child from the mother and the same rhythm is passed on from generation to generation; and finally such rhythms extend into the animal world and probably throughout the organic world. Fliess's definitive work on this subject was 'Der Ablauf des Lebens' ('The Course of Life') published in 1906.

Fliess was a whiz at arithmetic and by adding, subtracting, multiplying and dividing he used his two numbers, 23 and 28, to predict headaches, death dates, and the outcomes of meetings with Freud. If the prediction was not correct, Fliess would recalculate, finding a reason to add or subtract something so that his period theory would be confirmed (Jones, 1953). Jones, Brome (1968) and others treat Fliess's periodicity theory as sheer number mysticism. They note that although it aroused interest in the early part of this century it has failed to stand the test of time. Fliess's work has not been totally forgotten and is in fact being revived in current work on biorhythms; he is often treated as the father of this new area of pop-psychology (Gittelson, 1976).

Freud for a time took Fliess's ideas on the nasal reflex neurosis and periodicity seriously. He kept track of the dates and times of his, his family's and his patients' problems for Fliess. Using the period theory Fliess predicted that Freud would die at age fifty-one, a calculation about which Freud was quite concerned. We will see that part of Freud's neurosis was his fear that he would die before his work was complete and Fliess's prediction helped to both confirm and fuel this fear. There was in Fliess's number game a particular attraction for Freud. To Jung, Freud said that under his fascination with the numerical prediction of events lay the influence of Fliess and 'the specifically Jewish nature of my mysticism' (McGuire, 1974, p. 220). After their break in 1901, Freud renounced Fliess's theory, but as late as 1920 this work was still important enough to Freud to warrant his writing, 'doubts must be cast upon the rigidity of Fliess' [periodicity] formulas or at least upon whether the laws laid down by him are the sole determining factors [of life events]' (p. 45). Two of Fliess's ideas were incorporated into psychoanalysis. These were the notions of latency and bisexuality. Freud's annexation of the bisexuality hypothesis was to play a part in the dissolution of his friendship with Fliess.

Champions of Freud feel compelled to explain how this man of genius became involved with Fliess, whose scientific theories are highly suspect (see Jones, 1953; Kris, 1954; Brome, 1968). Instead of defending our hero or condemning him for poor judgment in picking his friends, let us follow this relationship and place it within the context of Freud's life.

In the early stage of their friendship Freud, downcast by not being able to visit Wilhelm, wrote to Fliess about the importance of their talks:

Though otherwise quite satisfied...I feel very isolated, scientifically blunted, stagnant and resigned. When I talked

to you, and saw you thought something of me, I actually
started thinking something of myself and the picture of
confident energy you offered was not without its effect.
(letter of 8/1/90, 1954, p. 60)

He continues, saying that their talks are professionally beneficial 'because for years now I have been without anyone who
could teach me anything...' (p. 60). Four years before Freud
announced the sexual theory that supposedly made him a scientific outcast he was already feeling isolated. This theme of isolation recurs throughout the letters to Fliess as one of Freud's
prime complaints in the 1890s. This time was later romanticized
by Freud as a 'glorious heroic age,' his years of 'splendid
isolation' in which he thought and worked at his own speed
(1914d, p. 22). However, in the 1890s he felt cut off from his
colleagues, teacherless, and without support. The isolation was
later attributed by Freud to his scientific colleagues' unreasonable, prejudiced, and unthinking rejection of his theories about
the sexual etiology of neuroses and the interpretation of dreams.
This leitmotif is expanded, as we will see, to mythic proportions
by Freud's followers. To bring some perspective to the 'heroic'
1890s, to stay at least within reach of the evidence, and to
absolve Freud's scientific colleagues of the sole responsibility
for making him an outcast we must keep in mind, in the face of
Freudian propaganda, these few words - 'I feel isolated' - written
to Fliess in 1890 years before Freud ever published a word about
sex, dreams, or psychoanalysis.

Fliess became important to Freud as an audience for his speculative ideas. Because of his previous contact with Charcot and
Breuer in the 1880s, his therapeutic use of hypnotism, and his
daily treatment of neurotics, Freud, in the 1890s, was breaking
away from mainstream materialistic views of nervous illnesses.
Fliess, too, was forging a similar path and almost like children
in the woods, each of them urged the other forward into unexplored territory. They led and followed one another into the
unknown area of sexuality. Freud sent Fliess drafts of his
thoughts on the sexual etiology of the neuroses, the meaning
and interpretation of dreams, and models of the mental apparatus. Included in the fifteen drafts which have been preserved
is 'The Project for a Scientific Psychology,' written in 1895, a
one-hundred-page essay in which Freud, using the terms of
the neurology of his day, first systematically set forth ideas
that would be expanded and modified over the course of forty-
three years in his psychoanalytic writings.

The first draft, sent to Fliess late in 1892, presents the thesis
that 'No neurasthenia or analogous neurosis exists without a
disturbance in the sexual function' (1950a, p. 178). The next
draft presents in more detail Freud's views on sexuality and
neurosis; it opens 'You will of course keep the draft away from
your young wife' (p. 179). The area was a sensitive one; Freud
was venturing into new territory in these papers. His energies

in these pages were focused on his sexual hypotheses and many of his complaints arose because he felt his colleagues would not understand his views. Much of his determination to go forward with his sexual theories, to be 'impudent' and to take pleasure in the 'arrogance' of proposing such ideas was predicated on Fliess's being pleased with and approving them (Freud, 1954, p. 132).

As the story of Freud's intellectual and personal discovery further unfolds, Fliess will come forward again and again. Having introduced him we now move closer to the center of Freud's scientific and self-discoveries by taking up in turn his commitment to a vocation, his views on sexuality, and his solution of the puzzle of dreams.

THE VOCATIONAL 'PROJECT'

In July 1895, Breuer wrote to Fliess 'Freud's intellect is soaring at its highest. I gaze after him as a hen at a hawk.' Fliess passed the compliment on to Freud, but Freud was at the moment neither fond of Breuer nor his opinions and replied, 'Despite Breuer I am not a bird' (Jones, 1953, p. 242). Breuer was correct, Freud's imagination had taken flight. In 1895 he discovered his vocation, psychology, and this helped to release his genius from the confines of neurology. In May he wrote to Fliess:

a man like me cannot live without a hobby-horse, a consuming passion - in Schiller's words a tyrant. I have found my tyrant, and in his service I know no limits. My tyrant is psychology; it has always been my distant, beckoning goal and now, since I have hit on the neuroses, it has come so much nearer. (1954, p. 119)

After completing 'Studies' earlier in the year, Freud became obsessed with his 'Psychology for Neurologists' ['Project for a Scientific Psychology' (1950b)]. He said, 'I have never been so intensely preoccupied with anything' and he hoped that something would come of all his effort (1954, p. 118). The 'Psychology' had as its goal the explanation of mental phenomena in physiological terms. Working with the recent discovery that the neuron was the elemental structure of the nervous system and the assumption that information transfer between neurons was carried out by an exchange of a quantity of charge, Freud tried to explain consciousness, primary and secondary process (that is the difference between primitive, alogical thought and ordered, logical thought), dreams, neurosis, defense against unacceptable ideas, repression, memory, and perception. By tracing the path of a quantity of energy through three types of neurons and cataloguing the modifications in each neuron group, Freud hoped to explain by using an economics of the nervous system, that is a systematic accounting of energy transfer, all psychological phenomena. Still battling with this project in August after having proclaimed an earlier victory, Freud wrote to Fliess:

> I came up against new difficulties....I threw the whole thing aside and persuaded myself that I took no interest in it at all....
>   This psychology is really an incubus....All I was trying to do was to explain defence, but I found myself explaining something from the heart of nature. I found myself wrestling with...the whole of psychology. (p. 123)

Freud's emotional life was completely invested in this work. He had found an all-consuming profession - a vocation.

A visit with Fliess in September during which Freud intensively discussed the brain model produced a breakthrough. Fliess had served in his vital role as an inspirational consultant and on the train ride home Freud finished the 'Project.' His announcement of the feat was joyful.

On 8 October, however, he was again depressed over his 'Psychology.' The mechanics of it appeared good, but the machine would not explain repression. He felt apathetic and despaired that 'it does not hang together yet and perhaps never will' (p. 126). Although this theoretical, model-constructing side of his work was going badly, he took solace in his clinical findings. In this October letter was the first hint of the seduction theory which explained the etiology of the psychoneuroses and, as we will see, this piece of clinical insight gave him satisfaction.

On 20 October he was triumphant:

> One strenuous night last week, when I was in the state of painful discomfort in which my brain works best, the barriers suddenly lifted, the veil was dropped, and it was possible to see from the details of the neurosis all the way to the very conditioning of consciousness. Everything fell into place, the cogs meshed, the thing really seemed to be a machine which in moment would run by itself. (1954, p. 129)

Freud had had a scientific vision, he had realized the mechanist's dream; his brain machine - in which mind had been captured in the energy transfers between neurons and the structural modifications of neurons - ran by itself. He concluded 'The whole thing held together, and still does. I can hardly contain myself with delight' (p. 129).

Twenty-two years after beginning his work with Brücke, Freud had lived up to the Brücke-Reymond pledge: he had explained mental functioning by using 'No other forces than the common physical chemical ones [which] are active in the organism.' In the words of the 'Project' he had represented 'physical processes as quantitative states of specifiable material particles' (1950b, p. 295). This was a triumph of mechanistic explanation and materialistic science. His teachers had undertaken similar projects

and in the work of Brücke, Meynert, Breuer, and Exner one
can see mechanisms which are very similar to those in Freud's
'Psychology' (Amacher, 1965). Going back beyond Brücke,
Ellenberger (1970) has traced concepts used by Freud to the
associationist psychology of Herbart and the work of Fechner.
As German neurology became increasingly materialistic and
mechanistic, ever more ambitious attempts were made to explain
all mental functioning in terms of brain physiology. This led to
a number of speculative works by the very men who, like Brücke,
disavowed speculation in favor of facts, which Ellenberger calls
'Hirnmythologie' (brain mythology) (1970, p. 478). The brain
structures and functions which were known to neurologists were
used in works of vast speculation to explain all of mental life.
Freud's 'Project' was a piece of 'Hirnmythologie.' This work is
a monument to Freud's quantitative, materialistic, mechanistic,
scientific training. It was his last attempt to explain human
psychology by using, in an unmodified form, the philosophical
framework inherited from his teachers.

Freud's triumph was short-lived. On the last day of October
he expressed doubts about this work and one month later it had
completely fallen apart: 'I no longer understand the state of
mind in which I concocted the "Psychology"; I cannot conceive
how I came to inflict it on you [Fliess]. I think you are too
polite; it seems to me to have been a kind of aberration' (Freud,
1954, p. 134). But Freud had difficulty abandoning this work
which had become the center of his emotional and intellectual life.
On 1 January 1896, he sent Fliess a short revision dealing with
neuronal interactions and 'with this the *Project* disappears from
view' (Strachey, 1966, p. 286).

All through 1895 Freud had been writing to and talking with
Fliess about the 'Project.' This was the time during which Freud's
intellectual and emotional dependence on Fliess's judgment was at
its height. Sigmund had ventured into broad biological speculation and Fliess, with his knowledge of biology was to have supplied the facts by which Freud would correct his work. Fliess
also, in part, supplied the inspiration for Freud to pursue the
work. On reading some of Fliess's work, Freud wrote to him, in
a letter in which he was finding problems with his own work,
'My first impression was of amazement at the existence of someone
who was an even greater visionary than I, and that he should be
my friend Wilhelm' (1954, p. 130). With the speculation in the
'Project,' Freud was on the verge of becoming a scientific visionary. It was a comfort to him to think that Fliess, whom he
respected, was one, too. However, Freud's vision was still
restricted by his attempts to see psychology entirely within the
framework of brain physiology. The 'Project' served to overcome
this tie to the bio-mechanical world view of his teachers. For
when the machine did not run, when the brain apparatus of the
'Project' failed, Freud was freed from an old obligation to the
Helmholtz school. He had tried to explain the mental in materialist
terms and he had both integrity and intelligence enough to see

that he had failed. The ideas - primary and secondary process, experience of satisfaction, cathexis, and many more - which Freud formulated and tried to explain in terms of brain physiology were to play a central explanatory role in psychoanalysis. In one year he had attempted to explain in the limited language of neurobiology processes which he would, over the course of the next forty years, try to explain again and again in the language of psychoanalysis. In the 'Project' Freud found his vocation and its failure freed him to become a visionary, to construct a world-view of his own which revolutionized science. But before this was possible he had to change his view of himself and to do this he had to turn inward and make himself the object of his studies.

The three essential elements of Freud's life work became: clinical practice, psychological explanation of abnormal and normal phenomena, and metapsychological speculation - the theoretical model-building which was to organize all psychological knowledge. These three tasks remain the major occupations of psychoanalysts. Few today do all three well and most have become solely clinical practitioners. Freud was never happy with clinical practice alone. His life work became in 1895 the development of a science of the mind.

THE SEDUCTION THEORY

Freud first introduced the word 'psychoanalysis' in a paper written in French, 'Heredity and the Aetiology of the Neuroses' (1896a). The paper set forth systematically for the first time the sexual hypothesis which dominated Freud's work in the 1890s - the seduction theory of the psychoneuroses. In 1893 there were early hints of this theory, and a restricted version of it was used to explain hysteria due to sexual traumas in 'Studies' (1895, p. 133). The theory as presented in this 1896 paper was based on the observation of thirteen hysterical and six obsessive cases; it held that the specific cause of hysteria was 'A *passive sexual experience before puberty*.' The traumatic event was the '*actual excitement of the genitals, resulting from sexual abuse committed by another person*' (p. 152). The seduction is not understood by the child at the time, but the event is retained as an unconscious memory. The unconscious memory of the childhood seduction acts as a mental scar and after puberty even the mildest of sexual excitements inflames this old wound. If, at eighteen, a person who had been seduced at four overheard a conversation about sex, this contemporary and innocuous event might produce all the emotions of an actual sexual experience. The post-pubertal hysteric represses both the memory of the original childhood seduction and the strong emotions caused by contemporary sexual experiences. These sexual effects are converted into the various bodily symptoms of hysteria. Obsessional neurosis, the other psychoneurosis, is also caused by a

child's being seduced, although the developmental scenario differs from that of hysteria (see Freud, 1896b).

The formulation of this theory was a triumph for Freud. He
wrote to Fliess in October 1895 that he had 'solved the riddle of
hysteria and obsessional neurosis with the formula of infantile
sexual shock and sexual pleasure' (1954, p. 128). He felt he
could now cure the psychoneuroses by bringing to consciousness
the repressed memories of the sexual trauma. He felt satisfied
that he had 'not lived some forty years in vain,' but was still
troubled because there were 'psychological gaps' in his explanation (p. 128). Confirmation for this theory poured in from his
analyses; by the end of 1895 he was confident in his treatment
method and had a great many patients. At this time the metapsychological explanations (which were really biological explanations) of mental functioning in the 'Project' were dissolving,
but Freud's psychological and clinical work helped to relieve his
despair.

On 1 January 1896, he sent Fliess a draft of a paper titled
'The Neuroses of Defence (A Christmas Fairy Tale)' (1950a). In
it he tried to fill in the psychological gaps in his theory of the
sexual etiology of hysteria and obsessions. This 'Fairy Tale'
contained many of the ideas later expressed in a lecture Freud
gave in April 1896 to the Society for Psychiatry and Neurology
in Vienna. In this talk he presented his seduction theory of
hysteria, this time based on eighteen cases, and said of his work,
'I believe that this is an important finding, the discovery of a
caput Nili [head of the Nile] in neuropathology' (1896c, p. 203).
His colleagues did not share Freud's opinion; Freud wrote to
Fliess that his lecture 'met with an icy reception from the asses,
and from Krafft-Ebing [the chairman] the peculiar evaluation:
"it sounds like a scientific fairy tale"' (quoted in Schur, 1972,
p. 104). Four months earlier Freud had called similar ideas a
'Christmas Fairy Tale,' but criticism from others meant the same
to him in 1896 as it had ten years earlier - rejection. His colleagues were fools for not recognizing his great discovery. The
paper contained many new ideas and Wolf maintains that stylis-
tically the paper was brilliant: 'this work of science did have the
beauty of a fairy tale and, to that audience, beauty in a work
of science was suspect and unscientific' (1971, p. 226). Freud
was both formulating new theories and forging new literary
standards for scientific writing. He was becoming a revolutionary.
But he wanted what the true revolutionary can never have -
immediate acceptance of his ideas. In 1914 Freud, in his 'History
of the Psycho-Analytic Movement,' wove this incident into the
story of the early rejection of psychoanalysis and his heroic
battle with scientific prejudice against sexual research. However,
there is little evidence, for example, that Krafft-Ebing was prejudiced either against sex or Freud. His 'Psychopathia Sexualis'
published in 1886 was a pioneering work on the sexual perversions and a year after Freud's lecture Krafft-Ebing was one
of Freud's chief supporters in his attempts to be appointed

professor extraordinarius.

Moreover, Freud soon came to share some of his colleagues' doubts. Less than seven months after his lecture, Freud wrote to Fliess that he had still not got to the bottom of a single psychoneurotic case and he felt 'an essential piece is missing' (1954, p. 182). By February 1897 he was 'beset by riddles and doubts' about the seduction theory and seventeen months after declaring his colleagues 'asses' for not applauding his great discovery Freud declared to Fliess, 'I no longer believe in my *neurotica*' (1950a, p. 259).

This letter to Fliess continued with Freud enumerating his reasons for giving up the theory: (1) it failed to bring complete therapeutic successes; (2) it meant that perversity would be improbably widespread; and (3) the seduction theory failed to articulate with his emerging ideas about the unconscious. Commenting on his emotional state Freud says, 'I have more of the feeling of a victory than of a defeat' (p. 260). He was proud that after spending so much time developing the theory and committing himself to it that he still retained his power of self-criticism and hoped that the incident merely represented 'an episode in the advance towards further knowledge' (p. 260). At that time he was determined to go on working and actually found some joy in the discovery of his error.

In his two historical works the story is more heroic; the error becomes a nearly fatal mistake. Looking back on his abandonment of the seduction theory he says, 'I would have gladly given up the whole work....Perhaps I persevered only because I no longer had any choice' (1914d, p. 17); 'I was for some time completely at a loss. My confidence...suffered a severe blow' (1925b, p. 34). He speaks of his despair and finally pulling himself together to go on with his investigations of sexuality.

The contemporary account written in 1897 is radically different from the historical ones written well after the turn of the century. It is doubtful that this discrepancy occurs because Freud was putting on an air of confidence for Fliess; his other letters, as we have seen, were often filled with doubt and loss of hope. It is more likely that Freud has, after the passage of time and his elevation to the leadership of a movement, constructed a moving historical narrative that, like romantic fictions, dash the hero into despair so that he may rise up to greater glory.

There is some evidence that Freud's historical account of events surrounding his renunciation of the seduction theory are more fictional than factual. In 1896 he takes full credit for formulating the seduction theory and specifically says that Charcot's teachings did not predispose him to this theory; in his 1914(d) history, when he was trying to make excuses for his error, he said,

Influenced by Charcot's view of the traumatic origin of hysteria, one was really inclined to accept as true and aetiologically significant the statements made by patients in which they

ascribed their symptoms to passive sexual experiences in the
first years of childhood - to put it bluntly, to seduction.
(p. 17)

In the face of Freud's scapegoating, it is useful to recall that
Charcot stressed the importance of hereditary determinants in
hysteria and gave traumatic factors a secondary position. More
importantly, in this quote Freud blames his patients for his
error. He does the same in his 1925(b) essay when he says,
'I believed these stories' of seduction my patients told me (p. 34).
He had believed them because he was 'intentionally keeping [his]
critical faculty in abeyance' so as to be open to the novelties he
was discovering. He continues saying he was at a loss when he
was 'Obliged to recognize that these scenes of seduction had
never taken place, and that they were only phantasies which my
patients had made up or which I had perhaps forced on them'
(p. 34). Eight years later Freud says about these traumas,
'Almost all my women patients told me that they had been seduced
by their fathers' (1933a, p. 120). He no longer admits he may
have 'forced' the stories on them.
    It is curious that in these historical accounts Freud credits
his patients with telling him seduction stories, while in his 1896
papers presenting the seduction theory Freud specifically states
that his patients never told him any stories of childhood seduction! He makes this statement explicitly in each of the three
papers on the seduction theory (1896a, p. 153; 1896b, pp. 165-6;
1896c, p. 204). The last cited summarizes his views. He rhetorically asks if it is not possible that docile patients are telling
the physician what he wants to hear and are simply making up
stories of childhood seduction. He dismisses doubts about the
genuineness of these scenes by arguing that before coming to
analysis patients know nothing of them and are indignant when
he suggests that such things may emerge in treatment; he says,
'Only the strongest compulsion of the treatment can induce them
to embark on a reproduction of them' (p. 204). When recalling
the seductions, patients suffer violent emotions which they are
ashamed of and try to conceal. Even when they have relived the
scenes more than once, 'they still attempt to withhold belief from
them, by emphasizing the fact that, unlike what happens in the
case of other forgotten material, they have no feeling of remembering the scenes. This latter piece of behavior seems to provide conclusive proof' (p. 204). Freud continues asking why
patients would deny the reality of such scenes if in fact they
had, as his opponents suggest, invented such scenes.
    There is simply no statement in these 1896 papers, as Freud
asserts later in 1914, 1925 and 1933, that his patients told him
stories of seduction. At this time he thought the importance of
his new psychoanalytic technique was that it helped him piece
together from the patient's symptoms, associations, and stories
a childhood seduction scene. Patients resisted admitting that
such events ever occurred, so Freud did have to force these

stories on his patients. But in his historical accounts when Freud wishes to discredit the seduction theory his patients are given the responsibility for having invented the scenes.

Such discrepancies in Freud's presentation of his own ideas leads to serious questions about the effects of his self-analysis. Supposedly after an analysis one comes to distort the past less and to put greater store in historical truth. One also supposedly stops attributing blame for one's errors to others. In 1896 Freud had not yet undergone his self-analysis. His analysis began a year later and was pursued until about 1900; thereafter he renewed it whenever he felt the need to do so. By the time he wrote the first history of psychoanalysis, in 1914, Freud should have gained a good deal of insight into himself and put an end to at least gross self-deception. If Freud is not deceiving himself in these historical accounts by blaming his patients for telling him seduction stories, when in fact in 1896 he was constructing such scenes while his patients were denying their occurrence, then he is purposely deceiving his readers in order to absolve himself of the responsibility for making an error. Either way, he is creating a pleasing fiction about his overcoming the influences of his hysterical patients and Charcot to go on and formulate a better theory of the psychoneuroses. In his histories Freud is the hero and other people, Breuer, Charcot, and psychoneurotics, are blamed for his mistakes. Analyzed or not, we all want to be heroes and Freud's self-analysis certainly did not free him from using the common deception of blaming others in making a hero of himself. Of course, the best way to deceive others is to deceive oneself by believing one's own stories; we will see that Freud's self-analysis played a large part in his mastery of this technique.

In the works on seduction there is an omission that is significant in terms of Freud's own self-analysis. In his three 1896 papers on the theory, and in the case of Katharina in 'Studies,' the father is never identified as the seducer of his own children. Katharina's uncle is identified as her seducer until 1924, when in a footnote Freud corrects this falsification by saying that the girl fell ill 'as a result of sexual attempts on the part of her father' (1895, p. 134). Another case in 'Studies,' that of Fraulein Rosalia H., is falsified and corrected in the same way. In the seduction theory papers of 1896 Freud names brothers, governesses, servants, nursemaids, teachers, tutors, and close relatives as seducers, but never the father. The corrections nearly thirty years later in the Katharina and Rosalia H. cases prove that Freud was aware that fathers were sometimes the seducers of their own daughters. But before the death of his own father and Freud's subsequent self-examination fathers were protected in print from the charge of being perverts. Even in his 1905(b) and 1906(a) partial retractions and modifications of the seduction theory fathers are not mentioned as seducers. Only when the Oedipus complex became central to psychoanalysis did Freud admit that fathers played a vital role in seduction stories.

In his physiological studies and his work on cocaine Freud
was not faced with the problem of his own emotional life being
tied to his scientific investigation. His relations with his own
father or his friends had little effect on his investigations of
nerve cell structures. In the 1890s Freud's life became inextricably tied to his scientific investigations and in this confluence
lay the origins of psychoanalysis and the founding of a science
where objectivity was no longer a given. Informed subjectivity
with its goal of knowing oneself as completely as possible and
thereby limiting self-deception had to take the place of objectivity
in analytic investigations. In the spring of 1894 Freud saw this
problem. He wrote to Fliess, 'It is painful for a medical man,
who spends all the hours of the day struggling to gain an understanding of the neuroses, not to know whether he is himself
suffering from a reasonable or a hypochondriachal depression'
(1954, p. 82).

BLAMING OTHERS

The first dream Freud analyzed completely, the dream to which
he erected the written monument, provides a fine summary of
issues raised so far and takes us a step further in Freud's self-
discoveries. While on vacation on the night of 23-4 July 1895,
Freud had a dream that has come to be known as 'Irma's Injection' (1900, p. 107). The central figure in the dream, besides
Freud himself, was a patient, to whom Freud gave the name Irma.
Freud dreamt that he and his wife were receiving guests. Among
them was Irma. Sigmund took Irma aside *'to reproach her for
not having accepted my "solution" yet.'* He said it was her fault
if she still had pains and she replied complaining of severe pains
in her throat and stomach. He was alarmed, looked at her and
felt he might be missing *'some organic trouble.'* He examined her
mouth and among other problems found scabs on some curly
structures *'which were evidently modeled on the turbinal bones
of the nose.'* He immediately called in Dr M., who confirmed the
diagnosis. Dr M., however, looked quite different from usual.
He limped and was beardless.[2] Sigmund's friend Otto was standing beside Irma and another friend Leopold was percussing her
through her dress. Leopold indicated that *'a portion of the skin
on the left shoulder was infiltrated.'* M. said that there was an
infection. They were aware of its origins: Otto had given Irma
'an injection of a preparation of... trimethylamin (and I [Freud]
*saw before me the formula for this printed in heavy type)....
Injections of that sort ought not to be made so thoughtlessly....
And probably the syringe had not been clean.'*
    This dream was given the honor of being the first to be inter-
preted in 'The Interpretation of Dreams' and has been further
honored by many reinterpretations. Although 'Irma's Injection'
occupies just under a page in print, Freud's associations to and
interpretations of it take up just over ten pages of text; and

even then he says he could have spent much more time over it.
Herein lies the first lesson of dreams - they are condensed.
Interpretation elaborates the dream text in order to connect elements of the dream with the dreamer's life. This is probably the
first dream which Freud submitted to a process of systematic
expansion and his discovery was that: *'when the work of interpretation has been completed, we perceive that a dream is the
fulfillment of a wish'* (p. 121). As early as 1894 Freud suspected
that dreams were wish-fulfillments. Now he knew that if one
associated to each element of the dream and submitted both the
dream and associations to interpretation one would find that
wishes had been satisfied by the dream. The wish fulfilled in
'Irma's Injection' was that Freud 'was not responsible for the
persistence of Irma's pain, but that Otto was' (p. 118). Blaming
others for what might be considered his own errors is the dream's
central theme and is an important unexplored aspect of Freud's
analysis.

Avoiding for now Freud's mechanics of dream-interpretation,
since we will take this up in a new way in the next chapter, let
us examine what Freud tells us and does not tell us about his
life by telling us this dream. First and foremost, dreams are
stories or fragments of stories and an uninterpreted dream
beckons, like an unopened book, to be read, interpreted, and
understood. When a dream is transposed from a private night-
fantasy to the light of day by being retold to oneself and others
it becomes a verbal product and opens itself to interpretation.
Freud tells us he has not fully recorded his interpretations of
this dream, and how much he knew and didn't know about it or
any other dream he analyzed is hard to determine. Freud knew a
great deal about 'Irma's Injection' and he has recorded much of
this in the ten pages of interpretation in the dream book. However, these interpretative pages must be reinterpreted, for in
them Freud has disguised the identities of people in the dream
and has omitted many important details.

Who was Irma? Robert (1976), following Anzieu (1959), argues
that Irma was Anna Hammerschlag, the daughter of Samuel, the
man who taught Freud Hebrew and the Scriptures at the gymnasium. Sigmund greatly respected Professor Hammerschlag. He
was one of the first to recognize Freud's promise and, although
poor, had lent Sigmund money to help him pursue his studies.
Curing Anna would have meant repaying a debt to his old teacher
and fulfilling the promise he had shown as a student and the
promise implicit in medical treatment. This is an important issue
which emerged from Freud's analysis of his dreams. In the Irma
dream the concern is a contemporary one phrased in terms of
professional responsibilities. In subsequent dreams as Freud
carried his analyses further back into his past this theme of living up to one's promise and promises came to be a central topic
of Freud's life story. In the chapter on Freud's childhood and
adolescence we followed this narrative thread, but it is important
to realize that the Irma dream perhaps gave Freud his first

insights into a problem, which on reflection, he found as a
central issue in his life.

Irma (Anna), unfortunately, had not been cured by Freud's
treatment. Otto, Dr Oskar Rie, one of Sigmund's closest friends
and the family pediatrician, had seen Irma recently and said to
Freud, '"She's better, but not quite well"' (1900, p. 106). In
Oskar's tone Sigmund heard a reproach that he had promised
the patient too much. This reproach was called to mind the night
before the dream when Freud was writing up the case with the
idea of giving it to Dr M. (Josef Breuer). The dream absolves
Freud of Irma's lingering illness. Her problems were her own
fault because she had not accepted his solution. He recalls that
he may have told her this in waking life, and continues saying
that he felt that his task was fulfilled when he informed a patient
'of the hidden meaning of his symptoms' (p. 108). Freud does
not tell the solution he proposed to Irma. We know, however,
that Irma had been diagnosed by Freud as an hysteric and in
1895 he was operating under the notion that hysterias were
often caused by a sexual seduction in childhood and that the
father of the patient was often the seducer. Had Freud proposed
to Irma (Anna) that her father, his much respected friend and
teacher, was a pervert? This is a possibility to which Cioffi
(1974) alludes and during this period, as we have seen from
Freud's 1896 papers on seduction, he repeatedly faced the problem of patients not accepting the seduction-scene solution, so
perhaps Irma too was protesting against this radical idea.

Connecting the dream to other areas of Freud's life, we see
that Dr M. is called in and confirms Freud's diagnosis. M. then
says that Irma had an infection, but that dysentery will follow
and the toxins will be eliminated. Freud, in his analysis, says
he was making fun of Dr M. (Breuer) by putting this silly speech
about dysentery into his mouth. In addition, Erikson (1954) sees
that by giving M. a limp and making him beardless Freud is
turning Breuer into a castrated old fool. This is sweet revenge
on Freud's former collaborator, who would not fully support
Sigmund's sexual theories. The dream, when interpreted, protests that Breuer and not Freud is the incompetent doctor.

Otto, however, is the real incompetent; he gives Irma an
injection with an unclean syringe. Oskar Rie, who set the dream
in motion with his comment that Irma was not completely cured,
has been made the culprit. Freud is not to be blamed for Irma's
problems. It is Otto (Oskar) who has created them in real life
by questioning Freud's therapeutic success and in the dream by
the injection. In the German text Otto uses a 'Spritze' - syringe,
or, more colloquially, 'squirter' - to make the injection. Con-
notatively, and the interpretation of dreams depends on con-
notation, Otto is a dirty squirter or a little squirt 'not just a
careless physician' (Erikson, 1954, p. 147). 'Squirter' makes the
sexual significance of the injection more obvious as well as the
condemnation of Otto.

In Freud's associations the theme of injections leads him to

memories of medical irresponsibility and to thoughts about
Fleischl von Marxow's tragic death which Freud connects with
Fleischl's having injected cocaine to cure his morphine addiction.
In his interpretation of 'Irma's Injection' Freud says that in 1885
he had been the first to recommend the use of cocaine (1900,
p. 111). This is an interesting error, for Freud had first recommended the oral use of cocaine in 1884; it was in 1885(b, p. 31)
that he, along with Fleischl, recommended injecting the drug.
However, in 1900 Freud asserts that, 'I had never contemplated
the drug being given by injection' (p. 117). This is not a distortion in the dream, but an error in Freud's telling about his
past. It was not just his dreams that were wish-fulfillments; in
the recounting of his life Freud also fulfilled his wishes. Historically, Freud is trying to absolve himself of any responsibility in
his friend's death by making the cocaine injections Fleischl's sole
responsibility. Stories about the past serve the purpose of self-
absolution for Freud. Four times now we have seen him shift the
blame for failings which were at least in part his responsibility
on to other people: Breuer, Charcot, Freud's own patients, and
now Fleischl.

In writing about the dream, Freud also protects his friend
Fliess, for behind Irma's injection is the figure of Fliess. In
Freud's associations to 'trimethylamin' there is Fliess, who
believed this chemical was one of the products of sexual metabolism. Boldly printed in the dream, the chemical formula for
trimethylamin stands for the 'immensely powerful factor of sexuality' (1900, p. 117), a factor left largely untouched in Freud's
interpretation of this dream. Freud wants to lead his readers
slowly, step by step, to this central theme in dreams, seduce
them - so to speak. In this first dream sex is introduced, but
not elaborated on; that will come later.

Fliess, Freud tells us, had examined Irma to see if her gastric
pains might have had a nasal origin. Sex and Fliess were also
associated in the turbinal bones of the nose which Fliess maintained swell during sexual excitement. Fliess is, however, much
more deeply implicated in the dream than Freud admits. Freud in
interpreting the dream fails to tell us about another patient of
his and Fliess's, Emma, who has much in common with Irma.

Like Irma, Emma had been examined by Fliess to ascertain if
there was an organic cause underlying her complaints. Fliess
came to Vienna, recommended surgery, and in late February
1895 operated on her; he then returned home. The surgery probably was on the turbinate bone and sinuses. After the operation Emma had a massive hemorrhage, the nasal area was badly
swollen, and she complained of great pain. Freud wrote to Fliess
informing him of Emma's condition and asking his advice. Freud's
next letter to Fliess on 8 March tells that on the sixth he and
Dr R. examined Emma. R. was cleaning the 'foetid' nasal cavity
'and suddenly pulled on a thread. He kept right on pulling, and
before either of us had time to think, at least half a meter of
gauze had been removed from the cavity' (quoted in Schur,

1966, p. 56). Freud nearly fainted when this happened and left the room. Emma's complaints after Fliess had operated on her had not been hysterical; Freud and Fliess had done her an injustice by thinking so: 'she had not been abnormal at all, but a piece of iodoform gauze had gotten torn off when you [Fliess] removed the rest, and stayed in for fourteen days' (p. 57). Notice the passive construction 'had gotten torn off,' almost as if it hadn't been Fliess's fault. In this letter Freud also says he was not clear-headed enough to reproach Dr R. for what he had done. In concluding the letter Freud expresses sympathy for Fliess, apologizes for torturing him with the news, and says 'Of course no one blames you in any way, nor do I know why they should' (p. 58). One might blame R. or the gauze, but not Wilhelm. Twenty days later he wrote to Fliess that Emma did not blame either of them for the whole affair.

This did not end the case. A year after the gauze incident and ten months after the Irma dream Freud succeeded in making the hemorrhages Emma's fault. In an April 1896 letter he called the bleeding 'hysterical' and said it was 'brought on by *longing*, probably at the "sexual period"' (p. 80). The half meter of gauze which Fliess left in the nasal cavity had been forgotten. The original event was buried by at least four letters in which Freud used psychological interpretation and Fliess's period theory to convince himself and his friend that Emma's troubles had an hysterical origin and were thus no fault of theirs. It had taken Freud only a year in rewriting the history of this event to absolve himself and Fliess of any blame.

Freud does not mention Emma or this incident as having had any influence on the Irma dream or his associations to and interpretations of it. Schur (1966) has shown that the Emma incident provides many additional points of clarification about 'Irma's Injection.' For example, the distress over Emma's problems probably influenced the dream's concern over the question of whether or not Irma was suffering from an organic illness, and in the dream Freud seeing the turbinate bones connects to Fliess's operation on Emma. The central theme of the dream, medical irresponsibility, is of course a central issue in the Emma episode.

In the Irma dream Freud's wish to be cleared of all responsibility for her illness was fulfilled by means of interpretation, finding that: Otto was the culprit, Breuer was a fool, and Irma was a bad patient for not accepting Freud's solution. He and Fliess, 'whose agreement I recalled with satisfaction whenever I felt isolated in my opinions' (1900, p. 117), were conscientious; it was the others, the ones who questioned Freud's ideas and treatment, who were in the wrong.

Fliess was in the mid-1890s the prototype of the healer; he had operated on Freud's nose, Freud consulted him about his heart, and he was Freud's supporter in the exploration of sexuality. He had to be protected for the time being from any criticism. The distortions in the Emma episode and the omissions in the analysis of the Irma dream show how far Freud would go in this

defense. Jones's (1953) failure to tell about Emma, when he had
access to letters concerning her, and the failure of the editors
of the Fliess correspondence to publish these letters demonstrate
the length to which the keepers of Freudian history will go in
defense of their hero's story.

Much has been made of Freud's honesty in divulging so many
details of his life and his own villainy in 'The Interpretation of
Dreams.' Freud tells us

> There is some natural hesitation about revealing so many
> intimate facts about one's mental life....But it must be pos-
> sible to overcome such hesitations. 'Every psychologist,'
> writes Delboeuf, 'is under an obligation to confess even his
> own weaknesses, if he thinks that it may throw light upon
> some obscure problem.' (1900, p. 105)

In concluding his analysis of the Irma dream, Freud says more
time could be spent analyzing it and he knows 'the points from
which further trains of thought could be followed' (1900, p. 121).
Perhaps by the time he wrote up the analysis of the Irma dream
he was aware of the importance the Emma episode had as a
determinant of the dream and simply chose not to include the
material. If this is the case, then he has certainly not followed
Delboeuf's advice. The evidence uncovered by Schur from the
Fliess correspondence leads to a different conclusion. Freud,
following the example afforded him by the Irma dream and its
analysis in 1895, disposed of Emma's problems in 1896 in a similar
fashion. As he had dreamt of doing with Irma, he did with Emma;
he made her problems her fault and not his or Fliess's. Dreams
tell stories in distorted and disguised forms, and stories themselves can serve to distort events in order to produce a satisfying narrative. Freud's self-analysis and love of truth were no
antidote for his wish to be blameless and his fulfillment of this
wish in telling his life story.

In the middle years of the 1890s we have seen Freud find his
vocation while writing the 'Project' and then abandon the 'Project,' formulate the seduction theory and lose faith in it, and
begin his self-analysis in the interpretation of 'Irma's Injection.'
He never gave up his method of interpreting dreams or his
insight that dreams, when interpreted, fulfilled wishes. Fortunately for Freud's emotional life, which was so invested in his
work, the demise of the 'Project' in late 1895 was marked by
his rising confidence that he had discovered the cause of the
psychoneuroses in the seduction of children. By September 1897
when he no longer believed in the seduction theory he felt he
had mastered the psychological theory of defense. He had also
begun rebuilding his metapsychology and knew that his work on
dreams was secure. He wrote to Fliess, 'It is a pity one cannot
live by dream interpretation' (1954, p. 218).

SELF-ANALYSIS

Freud did come to renew his life by dream-interpretation. The interpretation of his own dreams was central in his self-analysis, for he could treat a dream text and his associations to it with some objectivity and thereby he became an analyst to himself. He became his own healer and his creative illness and cure became a model for all future psychoanalytic treatment.

In 1896 the seduction theory of the psychoneuroses, dream-interpretation, and the concept of defense were the three pillars of Freud's work. The first breakthrough in his self-analysis was marked by his loss of faith in the seduction theory and his coming to emphasize infantile sexuality and the role of Oedipal feelings in the place of childhood sexual traumas. The interpretation of his own dreams and the analysis of his relations with Jakob Freud were vital in the demise of the notion that hysterics and obsessives had been seduced in their childhoods by an older person, often by their own fathers. Freud might have been able to tell even friends like Anna Hammerschlag that their fathers had been seducers, but once Freud began his self-analysis, the seduction theory would have implicated Jakob in the neurotic difficulties of his children. Could Freud's own father be a pervert?

In Freud's reconstructions of his childhood we have seen that he saw himself as initially overvaluing and then undervaluing his father. Jakob was pictured as a father who did not provide much guidance for his son and as an ineffectual man who did not defend his rights as a Jew. A letter to Martha, written when Sigmund was 28, confirms this historic portrait of his father. Freud says that Jakob, now in his sixties, was still hoping that some project would work out and was in need of financial help from his sons.

In another letter to Martha, written just two years later, Freud implicates his father as being partly responsible for his and his sister's neurasthenia because, according to Sigmund, the Freud lineage shows definite signs of hereditary mental problems. For Freud, being Jakob's son was being the offspring of an incompetent dreamer and a Jew with poor heredity.

We next hear of Jakob in 1895 when Freud mentions to Fliess that he is responsible for the care of his mother and father. In June 1896 Jakob at age eighty-one was very ill; he was suffering from heart trouble, bladder weakness and other difficulties. Facing his father's death Freud became more dependent on Fliess. He wrote that he was 'looking forward to our congress as to a slaking of hunger and thirst' (1954, p. 169).

In October 1896 Jakob died and Freud wrote to Fliess, 'He bore himself bravely up to the end, like the remarkable man he was.' November brought a letter that announced the importance of Jakob's death to Sigmund's emotional life:

By one of the obscure routes behind official consciousness
the old man's death affected me deeply. I valued him highly
and understood him very well indeed, and with his peculiar
mixture of deep wisdom and imaginative light-heartedness
he meant a great deal in my life....at a death the whole past
stirs within one.
I feel now as if I had been torn up by the roots. (p. 170)

Jakob's death brought his resurrection. The incompetent, ineffectual dreamer has become, at his death, a remarkable man,
full of wisdom and highly imaginative. Jakob has been reinstated
to the position he held during Sigmund's youngest years and
from which he fell when Sigmund began school. The sentiments
expressed may be those of a son who is carrying out his duty
towards his dead father by closing his eyes to his father's faults.
Subsequent developments in Freud's life and theory, however,
argue that Jakob's death did bring his re-elevation to a position
of vital importance in Sigmund's life.

After Jakob's death fathers were, for awhile, still held to be
responsible for their children's hysterias. In a letter written
late in 1896 the question of poor heredity (remember Freud's
doubts concerning his own lineage) was cast in terms of the
seduction theory: 'It seems to me more and more that the essential point of hysteria is that it results from perversions on the
part of the seducer, and more and more that heredity is seduction
by the father' (1950a, pp. 238-9). Perverted fathers cause hysteria in their children by seducing them. Was Jakob such a
father? This doubt was one of two concerning his heritage which
haunted Freud.

The other centers on being Jewish. In February 1897 Freud
was nominated for the title of professor extraordinarius at the
University of Vienna and he feared that being a Jew would hurt
his chances of obtaining the appointment. In analyzing a dream
related to these fears, Freud found the roots of his ambitious
strivings. He discovered in his childhood two prophesies of his
greatness: a peasant woman's prediction that he would be a
great man and a poet's prediction that he would be a cabinet
minister. He remembered too that when he was young his father
had brought home pictures of successful Jewish politicians and
'we had illuminated the house in their honour' (1900, p. 193).
The roots of Freud's ambition, then, lay in his childhood; this
ambition was fostered by his father. But his father had also made
him a Jew, and therein lay a major obstacle to Sigmund's ambition and his chances of gaining the professorship. Freud would
not deny that he was a Jew, but saw his heritage as an obstacle
to his wish for advancement.

Jakob was doubly condemned as a Jew and a father, but Sigmund, too, was both a father and a Jew. On 31 May 1897, Freud
wrote to Fliess about a dream of 'having over-affectionate feelings towards Mathilde [Freud's eldest daughter].' The dream
when analyzed expressed the wish 'to catch a father as the

originator of neurosis, and so put an end to my doubts about
this which still persist' (1950a, pp. 253-4). The father's role
in seduction was uncertain to Freud in waking life, but his
dreams provided the wished for confirmation.

Fathers and mothers, or mother-substitutes (nurses), now
became the center of Freud's self-analytic concerns. With the
letter of 31 May there was enclosed a draft of some theoretical
thoughts. In these Freud mentions for the first time, without
labeling them as such, the child's Oedipal feelings: 'it seems as
though this death wish is directed in sons against their father
and in daughters against their mother' (p. 255). This insight
about the son's hate for the father was crucial for Freud's own
analysis.

The very next letter to Fliess, dated 12 June 1897, announced:

> I have never yet imagined anything like my present spell of
> intellectual paralysis. Every line I write is torture....Inci-
> dentally I have been through some kind of neurotic experi-
> ence, with odd states of mind not intelligible to conscious-
> ness - cloudy thoughts and veiled doubts, with barely here
> and there a ray of light....I believe I am in a cocoon, and
> heaven knows what sort of creature will emerge from it. (1954,
> pp. 210-11)

He hoped that Fliess would help him by revealing to him secrets
from the 'world of children,' but Fliess was little help. Only as
the man to whom Freud could write about his troubles - an act
which was made difficult by the troubles themselves - was Fliess
of assistance. Fliess's presence was really the presence of the
blank piece of stationery waiting for thoughts to be illuminated
by words. Freud had not yet seen that his inability to write,
think, and create was a resistance on his part to self-insight.
Within six months he would see this, but first he had to turn to
the analysis of his own life in order to release himself from the
cocoon of neurotic doubts.

In August things were fermenting inside of Freud and he had
not yet got the better of his turbulent thoughts and feelings. He
said he was 'tormented with grave doubts about my [seduction]
theory of the neuroses.' He announced: 'The chief patient I am
concerned with is myself....[My] analysis is more difficult than
any other. It, too, is what paralyzes my psychical strength for
describing and communicating what I have achieved so far. But
I think it must be done, and is a necessary intermediate stage
in my work' (1950a, p. 259).

In September of 1897 Freud wrote to Fliess exclaiming that he
no longer believed in the seduction theory. A reason for giving
up the theory was 'the fact that in every case the father, not
excluding my own, had to be blamed as a pervert' (p. 259). If
Jakob were to be a pervert, then the seduction theory had to be
wrong. Remember that in all of his 1896 publications about the
seduction theory Freud had said that his patients had no memory

of the seduction and had vigorously denied that such an event took place. Freud's confidence in his reconstructive methodology lay in the fact that his patients did *not* recall incidents in their childhood of genital manipulation by their elders, but that psychoanalysis provided a means of unearthing and elaborating these supposedly repressed memories. In his own case Freud could not find seduction by the father and less than two weeks later wrote with relief '*der Alte* (my father) played no active part in my case' (p. 261). Using his own method on himself, Freud found no evidence that his father was implicated in his own neurotic suffering. Of course, when his patients denied the reality of seduction Freud took this as confirmation of his theory, but he did not do this with himself. There was no analyst, outside himself, to insist that even though he could not remember, admit, or confirm a seduction story that such a seduction took place. There was no analyst to insist that his failure to remember a paternal perversion was simply a resistance which was at the heart of his troubles.

Robert maintains that Freud believed the seduction stories told to him by his patients because he needed them 'to justify his animosity toward Jakob and to help him misrepresent his fits of jealousy' toward him (1976, p. 120). Although Robert ignores the important publications in which Freud maintains that his patients never told him seduction stories, her point would be stronger if she had taken them into account. Freud in many cases (it is hard to tell in how many cases seduction occurred or did not occur) invented seduction stories which fulfilled his wish that fathers were perverts, thereby unconsciously justifying his hatred of Jakob. Increasing doubts about the seduction theory were tied to Freud's self-analysis because questions about the theory led to his relations with his own father and every doubt about seduction meant that Freud's as yet unacknowledged hate for his father was not to be justified by Jakob's actions.

When Jakob was cleared of the accusation of seduction another culprit was instantly found; 'the "prime originator" [of my troubles] was a woman, ugly, elderly, but clever' (1950a, p. 261). This woman was Freud's childhood nurse from the days in Freiberg. Freud felt his memories about her, including the recollection that she was his 'teacher in sexual matters and scolded [him] for being clumsy,' were memories of actual experiences (p. 262). However, he recognized the possibility that a 'severe critic might say of all this that it was retrogressively phantasied and not progressively determined' (p. 263). This foreshadows Jung's claim made when he was breaking away from psychoanalysis that adult neurotics retrospectively sexualize memories from their childhoods, eroticizing previously innocent experiences.

All the evidence that Freud had seemed to him to convict his Catholic nurse as his seductress and therefore as the cause of his current problems. The evidence is, however, not very good. In a detailed reanalysis of Freud's memories about his nurse, Schur (1972), who is by no means a severe critic of Freud's, has convincingly shown that these recollections were fantasies constructed from the fusion of other memories and not recollections of actual events. Schur's analysis calls into question the initial insights on which Freud's self-analysis was based. Events which Freud took as fact may have been fantasy and so the narrative he constructed in freeing his father and convicting his nurse may have been a pleasing fiction, more a story that fulfilled his wishes than a causal etiological history of his problems. There are, in the end, few crucial experiments which decide either for or against the validity of an analytic construction. Schur's reinterpretation is more persuasive than Freud's account. Freud was looking for evidence by which he could anchor his method of using memories in reconstructing life histories to reality. His claim that he found what really happened is understandable, but given Schur's work we must recognize the distinct possibility that retrospective fantasy determined the 'reality' of the original events.

In his October 1897 letter Freud cleared his father of seduction and proclaimed that he no longer believed in the seduction theory, and yet his nurse was made his seductress. In fact, Freud never totally gave up the seduction theory and although the etiological significance of actual sexual molestation was greatly diminished, Freud continued for forty years to use the seduction hypothesis whenever it was necessary in his psychoanalytic explanations (Jacobsen and Steele, 1979). The month after his renunciation of this theory Freud was using it again and seems to have forgotten his criticisms of it.

A letter written in mid-October opened with Freud saying that his self-analysis was the 'most essential thing I have at present and it promises to become of the greatest value to me if it reaches its end' (1950a, p. 263). He continued

> To be completely honest with oneself is good practice. One single thought of general value has been revealed to me. I have found, in my case too, falling in love with the mother and jealousy of the father, and I now regard it as a universal event of early childhood. (p. 265)

The first hint of the Oedipal triangle had been in a letter written in May; by October Freud regarded it as universal mainly because he had found evidence of it in himself. He could not have analyzed very many cases in the intervening five months, but Freud's arguments of universality were not based on induction from observation. His argument was based on self-observation and on what he supposed were people's reactions to the play 'Oedipus Rex.' The Greek legend has its power, Freud asserted, because it 'seizes on a compulsion which everyone recognizes because he feels its existence within himself' (p. 265). Every audience member was once 'in phantasy just such an Oedipus' and each recoils in horror from seeing his repressed infantile wishes fulfilled on the stage.

If Freud were an Oedipus, then Jakob was a Laius. As of 3-4 October, Jakob had been acquitted of perversion, but he was still a Jew and so was his son. Eleven days later Freud's problems were no longer those of a Jew with poor heredity, but problems faced by all men and celebrated in the fates of a Sophoclean king and a Shakespearean prince. No longer was Jakob guilty of perversion and no longer was Sigmund the only son who had feelings of jealousy and hatred for his father. All men were Oedipus; Freud was no longer alone in his filial furor. Gentiles and Jews alike were father-killers and mother-fuckers in their unconsciousness. Universalizing one's guilt makes it easier to bear, since there are so many other sinners with whom to commiserate.

With this insight Freud made a significant advance in his own analysis. He had discovered the role that children's fantasies play in neurotic suffering. One's elders were not responsible for all of one's feelings towards them because the child actually generates strong ambivalent emotions towards his or her parents. Freud came to invest a great deal in this idea. It formed the core of his self-understanding and became the centerpiece of psychoanalysis. The Oedipal insight had to be true for it absolved Jakob of the charge of perversion, elevating him to the position of the prototypical father, and it connected Freud to all humanity, including the Gentile world, making his fits of jealousy and lust at age forty-one understandable. These emotions were revivals of memories long ago repressed of feelings he had had in his childhood. Through his self-analysis he had unearthed - some would say created - these infantile unconscious affects and thereby explained the long lost origin of his difficulties. He was behaving childishly as an adult because the child still lives on in the adult.

The first published account concerning Oedipal feelings was in 'The Interpretation of Dreams.' Freud said 'Being in love with one parent and hating the other' is one of the essential constituents laid down in childhood for later neurotic suffering (1900, p. 260). Such emotions are present in people who remain normal; in neurotics, however, the emotions of love and hate are magnified. As he did in the letter to Fliess, he asserted that this discovery was confirmed by the story of King Oedipus. He then summarizes the Sophoclean drama providing proof for his assertion. For additional support he goes on to analyze 'Hamlet.' For a scientist, using literary works as evidence for psychological assertions is a bold tactic.

Freud warns us that, like Oedipus, we all live in ignorance of these wishes which have been forced upon us by our natures. We deny our lust and hate for our parents because these emotions are repugnant to morality and after the revelation of these feelings 'we may all of us well seek to close our eyes to the scenes of our childhood' (1900, p. 263). Just as Freud told of his patients' denying the reality of seduction, so four years later he said we will all deny the reality of our Oedipal feelings.

To the passage quoted above are attached archaeological strata of footnotes by which we can trace the history of Freud's thought about the Oedipus complex.[3] In a 1914 note Freud says that the conception of the Oedipus complex has provoked more bitter denials and fierce opposition than any other psychoanalytic proposition. 'An attempt has even been made recently to make out, in the face of all experience,' Freud incredulously says, 'that incest should only be taken as symbolic' (1900, p. 263). Freud is referring to Jung's (1911-12) charge that children's supposed incestuous wishes toward the opposite sex parent and aggressive feelings toward the same sex parent are really retrospective fantasies of adult neurotics. These people transposed imaginings from their later years back into their childhoods in order to make sense of their adult difficulties. Jung linked his criticism of the reality of children's Oedipal feelings to Freud's error in calling seduction stories real events. This was too much for Freud and was an important issue in the break between the two men.

In a 1919 footnote Freud says that recent studies have shown that the Oedipus complex 'throws a light of undreamt of importance on the history of the human race and the evolution of religion and morality' (1900, p. 263). In just two decades Freud's private revelation, born from his self-analysis, has become a scientific vision providing insight into the psychological dynamics of human cultural evolution.

Returning to 1897 we go back to the significance of Freud's loss of faith in the seduction theory. Sadow et al. (1968) see Freud's self analysis as being vital to the modifications of the seduction theory. What Freud was previously projecting on to parents, that is, seduction of their children, he now internalized and saw as emanating from the child itself. This change in attribution of forbidden acts from others to oneself is a characteristic movement in all psychoanalytic insight. The analysand learns to see in him or herself what he or she has only been willing to attribute to others. With this insight Freud had taken an important step in the exploration of the psyche, for he transformed extrapsychic projections into intrapsychic realities. However, in absolving Jakob and Amalie of sexual misconduct, he had not yet freed himself of projections, for now his nurse was his seductress. Nothing came of this indictment, however, and the only evidence we have pertaining to the charges is in Freud's October 1897 letters.

Months of suffering had been undergone before the Oedipal discovery and Freud saw that part of his trouble was that he had been resisting revelations about his past. Although part of him was longing for self-knowledge, another part of him was dead set against such knowledge. His depressions and moods, his inability to write, think and analyze, were all manifestations of his illness. They were resistances to self-understanding, ways of clinging to childish desires which had been preserved in distorted forms in his neurotic symptoms. His goal became to analyze these resistances in himself and his patients, for every resistance was a manifestation of neurotic defense. In November Freud announced a major discovery, the presentiments of which he traced back for several months and the discovery of which he credited to his own analysis. His letter outlines in four pages the idea of infantile sexuality proceeding developmentally through successive erotogenic zones – oral, then anal. The child, at the behest of socialization, renounces sexual pleasure from these areas and this denial of previous pleasures is the prototype of repression. In December, as Freud discovered repressed anal themes in his own analysis, he wrote of the internal stench of his own memory.

This discovery of infantile sexual zones momentarily interrupted Freud's analysis. He despaired of self-analysis saying that if it were truly possible there would be no neurotic illness. He felt he had to analyze himself as if he were an objective outsider and that this was difficult. In situations in which he was an objective observer, the analysis of his patients, he was still often puzzled by the same questions which held him up in his own analysis. There is no Archimedean point outside the analytic situation; there is no point outside of human interaction by which to objectively judge one's interactions, and there is no way to stand outside oneself in order to analyze oneself. To know another one must know oneself, but one's self-knowledge is based upon interactions with others and one's ability to see oneself as the other. Only by a dialectical process of using partial insights about oneself to provide insight into others and then using this insight from others to revise one's self-insight can one solve the puzzles which baffle us about ourselves. Freud's own analysis was creating a bond of common exploration between him and his patients – a union which is vital to psychoanalytic discourse. In October he wrote of experiencing in himself all that he had previously viewed as an outsider and that he was gaining an intimate understanding of his patients' moods through his own depressions and flashes of insight. By December 1897 he had learned to be resigned to his moods and not to try to force insight. He complained to Fliess of feeling stagnant and 'terribly lonely.' Continuing, he said, 'I cannot talk about it to anyone, and I cannot force myself to work, as others can. I have to wait until things move inside me and I experience them. And so I often dream whole days away' (1954, p. 236). Here, isolation is a mood tied to Freud's analysis. He had no one to talk to about his troubles and had to rely on himself and his own experience. We will return to this theme of isolation, for out of his personal feelings of being separated from his fellows, Freud and his followers have created a story that Freud was in fact cast out socially by his colleagues. The typical movement in a successful analysis, the dissolving of projections onto others, was in this instance reversed: others were blamed for Freud's own sense of alienation.

Along with his complaints of isolation Freud spoke about another

problem: his 'deeply neurotic' longing to visit Rome. He said it
was connected with his schoolboy worship of the Semitic Hannibal,
a conquerer who never reached Rome. But Rome stood for more;
it was a nodal point for a network of associations having to do
with Freud's position in both Gentile and Jewish culture and with
conflicts going back to his childhood relations with his father.
A series of dreams involving Rome is reported in 'The Interpretation of Dreams.' Each of the dreams brings Freud closer to the
Eternal City and in the last one Freud is in Rome. In his associations to it he remembered that on his last visit to Italy a quotation had occurred to him: '"Which of the two, it may be debated,
walked up and down his study with greater impatience after he
had formed his plan of going to Rome - Winckelmann...or Hannibal...?"' (1900, p. 196). Freud's associations follow Hannibal
and he recalls the incident of his father's cap being knocked into
the gutter by the barbaric Christian. As a youth, Freud says,
he contrasted his father's timid response to the bold actions of
Hannibal's father, 'who made his boy swear before the household
altar to take vengence on the Romans' (p. 197). To Sigmund's
youthful mind, Hannibal and Rome symbolized the conflict between
'the tenacity of Jewry and the organization of the Catholic church'
(p. 196).

Judaism meant persecution, but also strength. Rome, as the
center of Catholicism, meant anti-Semitism, but it also represented classical culture, which Freud loved. For Freud, Judaism
was not a religion, but the experience of an invisible and indivis-
ible bond with other Jews built upon a heritage of events and
stories. Freud collected and told funny, and yet strength-giving,
anecdotes about Jews in order to illustrate and ameliorate his own
trials. Deeply enmeshed in the dream book and unsure of his
course or what he was saying, Freud sent a chapter to Fliess
along with the following: '[This chapter] was all written by the
unconscious, on the well-known principle of Itzig, the Sunday
horseman. "Itzig, where are you going?" "Don't ask me, ask the
horse!"' (1954, p. 258).

While Judaism was in Freud's blood, classical culture with its
artifacts, literature, and history was acquired by him through
formal education. He revered the classics and he collected
Egyptian, Roman and Greek antiquities, in part because he
needed real objects to reassure him of the existence of ancient
times. Freud could not give up Rome or the beauties of Gentile
history because of a pre-adolescent fantasy of avenging his
father. They were too important to him. Psychoanalysis, itself,
was often ennobled by Freud's comparing it to archaeology. Both
were concerned with unearthing the remains of former times:
the archaeologist digs up artifacts and uses them to construct a
picture of ancient civilization; the analyst searches for lost
memories of childhood and uses them to reconstruct a life story.
Freud also used his knowledge of ancient culture and the classics, like 'Oedipus Rex,' to validate and universalize his psychoanalytic findings. His classicism and love of antiquity also

brought him 'as much consolation as anything else in the struggles of life' (Freud, 1914e, p. 241).

Following Hannibal, being unconsciously ruled by childish
dreams of revenge, meant never seeing Rome and Freud's 'Rome
neurosis' was the fulfillment of adolescent commitments. But, as
an adult Freud longed for Rome. Winckelmann or Hannibal? The
first lived in Rome. Although Freud followed his Hannibal associations back to childhood, the course of his life paralleled that
of Winckelmann. Winckelmann was born poor, studied theology,
then medicine, and had a deep love for ancient literature and
art. He converted from Protestantism to Catholicism in order to
pursue his passion for antiquity as a Vatican librarian. He wrote,
'It is the love of science and it alone that can move me to the
proposal [to convert] suggested to me' (quoted in Schorske,
1973, p. 338). Science triumphed over religion and Winckelmann
became one of the founders of antiquarian studies. Young Sigmund, with Hannibal as his hero, would not compromise; the
middle-aged Freud, however, was more like Winckelmann. Freud's
self-analysis allowed him to give up the remnants of his pledge
of revenge and to found his science which was his mediation
between Jewish and Gentile culture. Insight came to replace
fantasies of political action; the way to Rome was via his dreams.

Schorske (1973) in a fine reanalysis of 'Count Thun, or the
Revolutionary Dream' (Freud, 1900, pp. 209-11), finds in it a
further elaboration of Freud's renunciation of political action in
favor of psychological insight. Reviewing the manifest dream
Schorske sees in its unfolding a condensation of Freud's political
life history. From a political encounter (Freud's youthful commitment to politics and pledge to revenge anti-Semitism), the dream
moves to a flight into academia (Freud's renunciation of the
study of law for a career in science) and concludes with Freud's
nursing his aging father. The dream was set in motion by Freud's
having seen Count Thun, a cabinet minister, on a railway platform and Freud's whistling subversively 'If the Count wants to
dance, I'll call the tune.' The dream ends with Freud on the
platform caring for his father. As the Prime Minister's place was
taken by Jakob in the dream so in Freud's life dreams of social
revolution were transformed by analysis into fantasies of overthrowing the father. About the dream, Freud concludes, 'the
whole rebellious content..., with its *lèse majesté* and its derision of the higher authorities, went back to rebellion against
my father' (p. 217). Goaded all his life by his father's reprimand,
'"The boy will come to nothing,"' Freud has had his revenge.
The 'Count Thun' dream not only fulfills a wish, but is testimony
to an actual accomplishment. Freud has fulfilled his youthful
promise not by becoming a cabinet minister, but a minister to the
sick (in the dream his own father), and the founder of a revolutionary science.

Jakob's death in 1896 precipitated Freud's analysis because it
was only through such an effort that Sigmund could bury, with
honor, the memory of his father. Jakob's spirit was laid to rest

by a dream that Freud had early in 1899. He dreamed that his
father played a political part among the Magyars, and how 'like
Garibaldi' his father 'had looked on his death-bed, and felt glad
that that promise had come true' (p. 428). Freud's analysis of
the dream expresses some derogatory sentiments towards his
father's loss of excretory control, but the central theme of the
dream is an expression of the wish that a father should '"stand
before [his] children's eyes, after [his] death, great and
unsullied"' (p. 429). Freud honored his father by making him a
political ruler. This paternal apotheosis was safe, for Jakob no
longer ruled his son's life; the oneiric tribute was a posthumous
one for the king was dead.

   An additional dream during this period dealt with another father
in Freud's life. The theme of this 'Self-Dissection' dream was a
surgical operation Freud performed on himself in order to satisfy
'Old Brücke' (1900, p. 452). After a detailed reanalysis of the
dream, Grinstein (1968) concludes that Freud felt guilty because
his work on dreams had so divorced him from Brücke's teachings.
Freud's analysis was his way of breaking his emotional bonds to
both his father and past father-figures and of paying penance
for doing so through the suffering his self-dissection cost him.
With the completion of the dream book, Freud had freed himself
from Brücke and finally from Jakob. We have also seen his
attempts to free himself from Breuer. His one hero, his one god
became science; he became the father of psychoanalysis; and
'The Interpretation of Dreams' has become a revered text. Breuer's book had been 'Studies on Hysteria,' perhaps Brücke had
been honored by the 'Project,' but Jakob's book was the most
important, for it was to his memory that Freud credits 'The
Interpretation of Dreams.' In the 1908 'Preface to the Second
Edition' Freud honors his father with the words

   This book has a...subjective significance for me personally -
   a significance which I only grasped after I had completed it.
   It was, I found, a portion of my own self-analysis, my reaction to my father's death - that is to say, to the most important event, the most poignant loss, of a man's life. (p. xxvi)

   Freud makes a curious statement about the dream book in his
history of psychoanalysis, 'The Interpretation of Dreams...was
finished in all essentials at the beginning of 1896 but was not
written out until the summer of 1899' (1914d, p. 22). This dating
of the book came just after Freud said he could work slowly
before the turn of the century because there was no worry about
'priority'; no one was challenging him in a race to publish. With
this dating, however, Freud is obviously worried about priority
for he is claiming the dream book was finished more than three
years prior to its publication, over a full year before he first
mentions to Fliess in May 1897 that he will write something about
dreams, and months before he began his self-analysis. Issues
concerning priority troubled Freud throughout his life and we

will see that an argument over priority contributed to the final break with Fliess. Before discussing the falling out with Fliess, who was the last barrier holding Freud back from Rome, let us sketch the course of Freud's composition of the dream book, for his work on it, as he said, was part of his self-analysis. Freud's analysis was preceded by his intense involvement in writing the 'Project' and was gradually replaced by his ever-growing dedication to 'The Interpretation of Dreams.' In his letters to Fliess the central issue from May to December 1897 was his own analysis. A letter of February 1898 marks an important change. Freud announced, 'I am deep in writing the dream book' and 'Self-analysis has been dropped in favour of the dream book' (1954, pp. 244-5).

Freud's progress on the book was steady. The only parts that gave him real trouble were the first and last chapters. The literature review was difficult because he hated plowing through the thought of other authors. The seventh - 'philosophical' - chapter was continually being revised by him; he said one draft of it 'was written as if in a dream' (p. 257).

May 1899 brought word that the dream book had suddenly taken shape for good. Freud decided that any efforts at disguising the sensitive material would not do, but that giving up the book would not do either. He says this was because, 'I cannot afford to keep to myself the finest - and probably the only lasting - discovery that I have made' (p. 281).

Freud, in fact, did manage to leave much sensitive material out of the book and successfully disguised other material. Ellenberger (1970) calls the book a disguised autobiography. In explicating his dreams, Freud revealed important incidents from his life, but by presenting fragments of his life history, Freud avoided a unified revelatory personal narrative. By partially analyzing his dreams and analyzing segments of the same dream at different places in the text he distorts the continuity of his analyses and thereby shields himself by making it harder for his readers to form a coherent picture of the man behind the work. Although he maintained that Oedipal feelings were central in one's emotional conflicts and vital to understanding the human psyche, Freud did not provide any complete Oedipal interpretations of his own dreams in 'The Interpretation of Dreams.' In fact, where material was present which pointed to both sides of the Oedipal conflict, love for the mother and hate for the father, Freud broke off the analysis short of complete disclosure. Freud spoke in the Fliess correspondence and the dream book about it being necessary to both distort and censor his presentations and interpretations of dreams in order not to offend his public; 'It is a pity that one always keeps one's mouth shut about the most intimate things' (1954, p. 236). He was fond of quoting Goethe, '"After all, the best of what you know may not be told to boys"' (1900, p. 142). The founding text of psychoanalysis is a curious scientific document because the evidence for Freud's hypotheses was not objectively and openly presented. The text of the dream book

is much like a dream itself; it has been censored by its author.
It is full of things which must remain unsaid and can only be
hinted at.

In September he was still working on the last, seventh chapter
and said about the book, 'If only someone could tell me the real
worth of the whole thing' (1954, p. 295). By his analysis and
his work on dreams Freud had advanced beyond the judgment of
his former teachers and had freed himself from his dependence
on Fliess's opinion. Wilhelm helped Sigmund work on the book by
discussing with him the best way to present his ideas and by
providing stylistic criticisms. He was, however, no longer elevated in Freud's eyes as a teacher or as a judge of Freud's
thought. The price of being a revolutionary thinker is that no
contemporary can adequately judge one's thought. Unfortunately,
the delusion of many thinkers is that their thought is so revolutionary that their peers do not understand it.

In late October Freud sent a copy of the book to Fliess as
a birthday present and said, 'I have long since made my peace
with the thing, and I am awaiting its fate with - resigned curios-
ity' (p. 301). The book came out in early November 1899,
although its publication date was 1900. 'The Interpretation of
Dreams' became a dominant force in twentieth-century thought
and it is fitting that the publisher dated it with the imprint of
the new century.

The completion of the book brought Freud a new sense of
time; he felt he was 'terribly far ahead' of his time and was 'ten
to fifteen years in advance' of the people to whom his book was
addressed (1954, pp. 306-7). Erikson (1955) points out that one
of the features of Freud's neurotic difficulties was a feeling that
he was behind schedule. Subjectively time had contracted for
Freud and he felt he would not accomplish what he wanted to do.
With the impending death of Jakob, Freud wrote to Fliess expressing the wish that he 'would hold out until that famous age limit
of approximately 51' (quoted in Schur, 1972, p. 106). As Freud's
time horizon expanded with the completion of the dream book,
his dread of dying was greatly diminished.

Freud's neurotic difficulties had also produced a contraction of
his sense of space. At the height of his suffering in 1897 he
complained of being in a cocoon, of being paralyzed, of waiting
for things to move inside him. His gaze was turned inward and
his focus was on himself. Space had imploded on him and all he
could see was his own suffering. By December 1897 his horizons
had widened, but his mobility was still limited. He had got the
better of his railway anxieties, which had troubled him for ten
years, and was now longing to visit Rome.

This limitation of vistas was also present in Freud's approach
to his profession. Instead of actively pursuing the appointment
of professor extraordinarius in February 1897 he resigned himself to fate. In June of that year the university professors voted
positively on the appointment, but the Ministry of Education
delayed final approval. At that time Freud did not take any

active steps to obtain the title. It was only after his temporal
horizon was expanded with the completion of the dream book and
his spatial horizon was broadened by seeing Rome that his professional ambition reasserted itself and he actively pursued the
professorship.

The tie to Fliess was holding him back. Fliess had been his
audience throughout the 1890s and their 'congresses' had satisfied Freud's needs for academic fellowship. Fliess was Freud's
solace in his isolation; as late as May 1900 Freud wrote to him,
'I should have no objection to the fact of splendid isolation, if it
were not carried too far and did not come between me and you'
(1954, p. 318). After the turn of the century, however, the
relationship was much less close than it had been in the middle
1890s.

As Freud's self-insight grew and his work on the book progressed, there was a steady decline in his dependence on Fliess.
At the height of his self-analysis Freud told Fliess about his
ideas on Oedipus. Fliess failed to respond to these thoughts and
Freud was annoyed by this. A month later, in December 1897,
there was a congress in Breslau at which Fliess talked of his
work on bilaterality and reasserted his thoughts about bisexuality. Bisexuality held that human beings were inherently both
male and female; bilaterality maintained that in every person the
right half was male, the left was female. After the Breslau meeting Freud expressed doubts about bilaterality and wrote that
this was the first time in many years that he and Fliess had
disagreed. Fliess thought Freud was rejecting both bisexuality
and bilaterality, but Freud assured him that he thought bisexuality was a great discovery and he was sure Fliess was right
about it. This crediting of Fliess with the discovery of the
importance of bisexuality was to change radically as their relationship fell apart.

Another problem was added to the difficulties in the relationship. As Freud's confidence in his psychological explanation of
neurotic disturbances increased, as he became more certain that
life experiences and defense against them were determining
factors in psychic difficulties, his questioning of the strict
biological determinacy of Fliess's period theory increased. The
conflict between his dynamic explanations and Fliess's physiological causality had been ignored by Freud as long as he felt
his own system would someday be anchored in biology. While
working on the dream book, however, Freud declared, 'I must
behave as if I were confronted by psychological factors only'
(1954, p. 264). He said he had no desire to leave the psychology
'hanging in the air with no organic basis,' but beyond the conviction that there must be an organic foundation, he had neither
any therapeutic nor theoretical material by which to connect his
work to biology. He ended by saying, 'I have no idea yet why I
cannot fit it together [the psychological and the organic]' (1954,
p. 264). In this statement Freud's philosophical naivety or
perhaps confidence in his own intellect is astounding; he had no

idea why he could not solve the mind-body problem which has challenged thinkers for millennia. For the next forty years Freud hoped, dreamed, and wished that biological bedrock would one day be found for psychoanalytic theory. The wish still lives on in the fantasies of many, for example Holt (1965) and Pribram (Pribram and Gill, 1976), but to this day the organic foundation remains a materialist's dream. This letter of September 1898 dates the beginning of a change. Freud had seen that much could be done with a purely psychological theory and, realist that he was, he founded his work as a science of the psyche.

This declaration meant that conflict with Fliess was imminent. It came in January 1899. Freud asked Fliess if some place must not be left for mental influences, so that dynamic determinants were not entirely ruled out by biological periodicity. The relationship was floundering over disputes about periodic and psychological determinacy and bilaterality-bisexuality. Freud was chastising Fliess for not writing and was desperately trying to rekindle the friendship. Upon receiving a letter from Fliess after three weeks' hiatus in the correspondence, Freud wrote in March 1900, that he was delighted to hear from Wilhelm because he felt they would both be sorry if their correspondence dried up and their meetings came to an end. The letter also contained the complaint that because Breuer's daughter was marrying a close friend of Wilhelm's and his wife Ida's, Fliess would be further separated from Freud by this '"Breuerization"' (quoted in Schur, 1972, p. 204). With this, the specter of Breuer entered to hasten the disintegration of their friendship. A year later Breuer along with Ida was again accused of coming between Wilhelm and Sigmund. Many years before, Breuer had said to Mrs Fliess that it was good that she and her husband were living in Berlin, because this meant that Wilhelm would not be so influenced by Freud. Freud attributed his current difficulties with Fliess to Ida's 'working out, under a dark compulsion' Breuer's old suggestion that Wilhelm and Sigmund should be separated (p. 216).

Although in characteristic fashion Freud was trying to blame others for his difficulties, the friendship with Fliess had hardly gone bad because of Ida and Breuer. It deteriorated because of disagreements over theoretical issues and Freud's slowly freeing himself, over the course of ten years, from an over-high estimate of Wilhelm. In 1896 Freud's confidence in Fliess had been challenged by the error in surgery on the patient Emma's nose. By 1900 because of the insights which Freud gained from his analysis he no longer had a clinging emotional dependence on Fliess. Wilhelm had been many things to Sigmund, physician, counsellor, co-conspirator, brother, and at times even a father. Their relationship had recapitulated many aspects of Freud's first close friendship with his nephew John. As Freud buried the ghosts of his past, the unconscious projections that he invested in Fliess were withdrawn and Fliess's power over him was diminished.

In March 1900 Freud told Fliess that although he was touched by his proposal for a congress at Easter, he felt the necessity to avoid him. He thanked Fliess for all of his work on the dream book and assured him of his importance in his life, but said seeing Fliess would revive too many old problems with which he was struggling. Freud said that many of his castles in the air had been demolished and that he had conquered the recent collapse by a 'special intellectual diet' which was bringing about a healing. He concluded, 'No one can help me in the least with what oppresses me; it is my cross, I must bear it; and heaven knows in the process of adaptation my back has become noticeably bent' (quoted in Schur, 1972, pp. 205-6). This was a declaration of independence from Fliess; he was no longer the healer to whom Freud entrusted himself. Freud's analysis had shown him the wisdom of combining the Delphic 'know thyself' with Luke's biblical admonition 'Physician, heal thyself.'

The relationship continued to die slowly throughout 1901. In a magnificent understatement Freud said, 'there is no concealing the fact that we have drawn somewhat apart from each other.' He continued by saying that Fliess had taken sides against him when Fliess had said, '"the thought-reader merely reads his own thoughts into other people."' Freud concludes correctly that this statement 'deprives my work of all its value' (1954, p. 334). The letter went on with Freud announcing that his 'Every-day Life' book was finished and that it was 'a testimonial to the role you have hitherto played in my life' (p. 334). Books were fast becoming monuments of Freud's dead relationships: Breuer's gravestone was 'Studies,' Jakob's marker was 'The Interpretation of Dreams,' and Fliess's was to be 'The Psychopathology of Everyday Life.'

The letter concluded with Freud's proposing a book on 'Bisexuality in Man.' He said the idea was Fliess's and he wanted to develop the psychological side of it while Fliess handled biological issues concerning bisexuality. He hoped that Fliess would co-author the book with him and that it would satisfactorily unite them again in scientific matters. A September letter shows that Fliess took the proposal amiss and viewed Freud's proposition as an attempt to steal his ideas. For his part, Freud was still troubled by the 'thought-reader' accusation. He said that if Fliess really believed this, then he was no longer Freud's audience.

THE OUTCOME OF THE SELF-ANALYSIS

In this letter of September 1901 there is good news; Freud had visited Rome. Three years of being obsessed with Rome and much hard work at analyzing his conflicts about the city had come to an end. As we all meet ourselves wherever we go so Freud found in Rome a reflection of himself. The classical humanist, the antiquarian, the archaeologist in Freud predictably loved ancient Rome. The rationalist and the Jew was disturbed by Christian Rome with its aura of mysticism and salvationism. This Rome was

not for Jews, who were sinners in the eyes of fervent Christians
and scapegoats for religious hate. Modern Rome with its easy
going Southern ways and warm hospitable people was probably a
welcome relief to a man who worked too hard.

With the visit to Rome, Freud's horizon had been considerably
expanded and his professional ambition was renewed. Telling
about how he had finally received the appointment to the position
of professor extraordinarius, Freud said:

> When I got back from Rome, my zest for life had somewhat
> grown and my zest for martyrdom had somewhat diminished
> ....I reflected that waiting for recognition might take up a
> good portion of the remainder of my life...so I made up my
> mind to break with my strict scruples and take appropriate
> steps, as others do after all. One must look somewhere for
> one's salvation, and the salvation I chose was the title of
> professor. (1954, p. 342)

There has been some debate about how Freud obtained the
appointment for which he had waited four years (see Ellenberger,
1970). The important point for us is that as Freud took an
interest in his future, he obtained what he desired. In 1897 he
left his future to fate because his neurotic difficulties meant he
had to focus his attention on himself and his past. By 1901 he
had laid his past to rest and so could attend to his fate and
thereby influence his future. In less than one half-year, by
March 1902, he obtained the long-desired appointment. The
appointment meant an end to his sense of isolation. Freud, in high
spirits, wrote that the title had brought congratulations from all
quarters and instant recognition of his work. Jokingly, he said,
it was as if the king had recognized sexuality, the Cabinet had
confirmed the interpretation of dreams, and his work on hysteria
had been approved by parliament (1954). Psychoanalysis triumphed in Vienna, and it would not be long before Freud's name
would be known throughout the western world.

Freud's analysis freed him from many of his problems. As we
have seen it helped him to define his position in respect to
Gentile and Jewish culture. By realizing that many of his conflicts about the university appointment and travel to Rome originated in his childhood relations to his father and a wish to take
revenge on Christians for his father's disgrace, Freud was able
to overcome archaic hatreds which were blocking his adult
desires.

Recognizing that his feelings of hatred for his father and
extreme aggressiveness towards Jakob were remnants of childhood emotions, Freud, by reexperiencing these negative affects,
was able to work through his lingering resentment towards his
father. As Freud did this, Jakob assumed greater importance in
his life. In 1897 Jakob was elevated from the status of pervert
to the position of the universal paternal prototype as the Oedipal
father. By 1909 the death of one's father had become for Freud

the most poignant event in a man's life. For Freud this was
certainly true. His father's death had stirred the past within him
and in his past he found the explanation for his current malaise.

Moving backward in time by way of his dreams, Freud found
that his moods, writing paralyses, travel anxieties, depressions,
and feelings of isolation were revivals of infantile and youthful
conflicts. His self-analysis brought these conflicts, which had
long been repressed, to the surface and by facing his demons
he was able to disarm them of much of their power.

Dreams provided a perfect vehicle for this analysis because he
could objectify them. By writing out a dream he could externalize
his subjective reactions and thereby partially step outside himself in order to analyze himself. There was no analyst to whom
Freud could turn for insight; he had to see in himself what he
could not see. Dreams allowed him to put his subjectivity at arm's
length and thereby to recognize what might otherwise have
remained hidden from him forever. No wonder dream-interpretation became the center of psychoanalysis, for it was by following
his own dreams - *'the royal road to a knowledge of the unconscious activities of the mind'* - that Freud found himself (1900,
p. 608). He found that the suffering man in his forties was but
a child still trying to live out the wishes of his youth. This discovery was his salvation, for when the wish was avowed its power
was dissipated.

Psychoanalytic followers of Freud have been overflowing in
their praise of Freud's self-analysis. Jones says that this analysis
was the final phase in the evolution of Freud's character and
from his suffering there 'emerged the serene and benign Freud,
henceforth free to pursue his work in imperturbable composure'
(1953, p. 320). Kohut proclaims that Freud's analysis was truly
awe-inspiring because Freud was able 'to turn each personal
insight into a suprapersonal scientifically valid psychological
discovery' (1976, p. 392). We are entering the realm of myth-
making here. The picture is of the wise man who in himself
discovered the secrets of all humanity. Eissler sees in Freud's
life story those elements which are so often encountered in the
biographies of cultural heros: the prophesy of greatness in
childhood, 'great isolation and seclusion,' the creative outburst,
'the great persecution, the great endurance in the face of in-
human suffering,' the exile at the end of his life, 'and the rise
of a myth after death' (1951, p. 321). The portions from Eissler
that I have left in quotation are precisely those parts by which
the story of a man who found his way in life and helped others
to find theirs has been transformed into a hero myth. Jones,
Kohut, Eissler and others have all helped to foster this myth.

Myths are very useful, but when myth is treated as fact it
obscures the story of a person's life. Freud's life story, filled
with conflicts, is too good to be shrouded in myth. The fact is
that Freud did not emerge 'serene, benign, and imperturbable,'
from his analysis. Evidence against Jones's claim is very easy to
find even in Jones's biography of Freud. The end of the relation-

ship with Fliess which came in 1904, at least two years after
Freud's self-analysis was completed, shows Freud being as self-
interested and defensive as he was in the break-up with Breuer
in 1895.

Fliess was outraged when he saw his ideas about bisexuality
published in a popular book, 'Sex and Character' (1903), by Otto
Weininger. From a citation in the work he saw that a pupil-patient
of Freud's had been in contact with Weininger and so he asked
Freud if he had been responsible for Weininger's pirating of his
ideas. Freud, in his own defense, tried first to lie to Fliess,
saying he didn't know Weininger, but Freud in fact had read the
manuscript of 'Sex and Character.' Fliess confronted Freud with
this accusation and Freud used psychoanalysis to defend himself
saying he had forgotten having read the manuscript and that he
had long felt guilty about being over-generous in sharing Fliess's
ideas with others. He then tried to demean Fliess's concern by
calling the whole dispute over priority trivial, and finally he
argued that the notion of bisexuality was very old and that Fliess
could not claim priority in its discovery. This last position is in
clear contradiction to everything Freud had told Fliess in the
1890s. These are hardly the actions of a benign, imperturbable
man.

Jones passes the whole matter off as a case of Fliess having
developed 'persecutory ideas' about Freud's actions towards him
(1953, p. 316). This piece of psychoanalytic character assassina-
tion is unfortunate. Fliess did feel betrayed and lied to by Freud.
Fliess might have overreacted, but his actions originated as
reactions to actual offenses that Freud had committed against
him; that is, they were not paranoid.

Freud had not achieved by way of his analysis that insight
spoken of by Shakespeare:

> This above all: to thine own self be true,
> And it must follow, as the night the day,
> Thou canst not then be false to any man.
> ('Hamlet,' Act I, Scene 3, line 75)

To believe Jones's account of the calm, wise, analyzed Freud is
to condemn all the men with whom Freud battled after 1900 to
being in the wrong. Freud, before and after his analysis, had
been false to Breuer; immediately after the analysis he was false
to Fliess; and we will see that he was not completely blameless
in the bitter dispute with Jung. Freud would never have claimed
that his analysis turned him into a saint. His 1899 verdict on
his self-cure was that: 'All this has done a lot of good to my
mental life. I am obviously much more normal than I was four or
five years ago' (1954, p. 280). To achieve normality was for
Freud a heroic task, but being normal does not make a person a
hero.

Let us now take up Kohut's immortalization of Freud. This
noted analyst maintains that Freud turned each personal insight

into 'a suprapersonal scientifically valid psychological discovery.'
This is mere self-congratulation by a follower for the master's
achievements. It also makes a claim that psychoanalytic theories
are scientifically valid; a claim widely made by analysts and
disputed by many. We will return to this issue in later chapters.
Of importance here is that Kohut is carrying forward Freud's
own representation of psychoanalysis. Remember Freud's October
1897 discovery of love for the mother and hate for the father in
himself, followed by the statement, 'I now regard it as a universal event of early childhood.' A year earlier, while still advocating the seduction theory, which no analyst today claims has
universal validity, Freud wrote to Fliess, 'I am met with hostility
and live in such isolation that one might suppose I had discovered
the greatest of truths' (1954, p. 161). If Freud's findings were
universally true, then any opposition was rejection of truth.
Rejection, in fact, became for Freud a validation of his insights.
Looking back in his history of psychoanalysis, Freud says he
was not embittered by the massive critical attacks on his work,
'for psycho-analytic theory enabled me to see it as a necessary
consequence of fundamental analytic premises' (1914d, p. 23).
If people deny those deep-seated psychic truths which upset or
frighten them, then by a leap of logic, anything which is denied
must be a deep-seated psychic truth. As Freud took his patients'
denial of seduction as proof of seduction in 1896, so he took his
colleagues' critical attacks on his theories about dreams, neuroses, and sexuality as evidence for the psychoanalytic premise
that people will resist insight into the workings of the unconscious. This is a hermetically sealed system. The idea strikes one
that if there had been wide acceptance of his work Freud would
have had to reject the idea that he had discovered 'the greatest
of truths.' Looking back to this time Freud says he understood
that from 1900 onward he was to be one of those 'who have
"disturbed the sleep of the world"...and that I could not reckon
on objectivity and tolerance' (pp. 21-2).

An interesting facet of the outcome of Freud's analysis was this
claim that his work was rejected, that his colleagues shunned
him, and that he was 'isolated.' Eissler speaks of Freud's isolation and says that 'the manner in which Freud endured persecution may make his biography exemplary for generations of scientists' (1951, p. 324). Niederland speaks of the 'massive colleagial
rebuff which Freud experienced in the early years' (1971, p. 23).
Schur (1972), Grinstein (1968) and Jones (1953) also speak of
Freud's isolation and the prejudicial criticism of his work. Kris
bemoans Freud's struggling with an environment whose rejection
of his work endangered his livelihood and his 'isolation and
estrangement from all colleagues and friends' (1954, p. 43).

In these statements the followers are echoing the leader. In
the Fliess correspondence Freud was continually complaining of
his isolation. In response to reviews of his work, Freud mostly
found what was negative and emphasized that the critics did not
understand him. He complained that 'The Interpretation of

Dreams' was being ignored and that when it was reviewed nobody
saw what was good in it. These complaints were voiced publically
in Freud's 1908 'Preface to the Second Edition' of the dream book
where he wrote, 'The attitude adopted by reviewers in scientific
periodicals could only lead one to suppose that my work was
doomed to be sunk into complete silence...'(p. xxv). 'On the
History of the Psychoanalytic Movement' contains Freud's declaration that 'my writings were not reviewed in medical journals, or,
if as an exception they *were* reviewed, they were dismissed with
expressions of scornful or pitying superiority' (pp. 22-3). In
his autobiography Freud said that, 'After the briefest acquaintance with psycho-analysis German science was united in rejecting it' (1925b, p. 49). How did ideas which were so despised
ever become the common currency of our daily psychological
exchanges?

Working from Freud's inner circle outward let us see if he was
isolated and if his ideas were rejected. Jones pointedly contradicts Kris's statements that Freud was estranged from his
friends; 'When Freud spoke of...isolation one must understand
that this referred to his scientific, not his social, life' (1953,
p. 332). Evidence from the Fliess correspondence, Freud's
maintenance of a close circle of friends with whom he met every
week, and Breuer's and Fliess's continuing to send Freud
patients well into the 1900s all argue in favor of Jones's
point.

Kris and Jones agree that in Vienna Freud's practice was
harmed by his colleagues' refusing to refer patients to him, and
patients' shying away from him because of his sexual theories.
Both points are refuted by Freud. In October 1893 he wrote to
Fliess: 'The sexual business attracts people; they all go away
impressed and convinced after exclaiming: "No one has ever
asked me that before!"' (1954, p. 77). One month later he was
complaining of a shortage of patients. In December 1895 he
boasted that he could begin to dictate his fees and that the 'town
is gradually beginning to realize that something is to be had
from me' (p. 136). Two months later he complained of his isolation. Freud's practice fluctuated in size, but in the published
correspondence with Fliess he does not attribute any decline in
the number of patients to his colleagues' prejudice against him.

Jones, who fosters the isolation story, could obviously find no
evidence that Freud's Viennese colleagues had cast him out: 'Any
ostracism, if one may use such a strong word, was passive rather
than active' (1953, p. 343). In other words, there are no documents which confirm Freud's sentiments that his colleagues were
all prejudiced against him. His practice did not suffer; Krafft-
Ebing and Nothnagel, two leading Viennese scientists, proposed
him for a professorship which was approved; and Freud never
had any trouble publishing his work.

Perhaps in the wider circle of German science there is evidence
in the reviews of Freud's work that psychoanalysis met with
'united' rejection or that his work was ignored. Even this claim

is disputed by Bry and Rifkin; 'The Interpretation of Dreams' and the shorter popularized account 'On Dreams' 'were widely and promptly reviewed in recognized journals' (1962, p. 21). Between them the two books were reviewed at least thirty times and all the reviews were respectful. After a fair summary, those reviews which were critical centered on two points: (1) Freud's interpretations, although interesting, seemed too far-fetched; and (2) his method was not scientific. These are not unreasonable criticisms.

Decker is straightforward in rejecting Freud's and his followers' claims that his work on dreams, sex, or the unconscious met with universal condemnation. She went back to the reviews of Freud's work in Germany before 1907 and found that his work was widely reviewed. Reviewers were critical of parts of his work and accepted other parts. There was never a wholesale rejection or acceptance of psychoanalysis because scientific critics did not see it as a monolithic system, but as a collection of separate hypotheses some of which they felt were supported by Freud's researches and some of which they felt were not.

Nor were Freud's sexual theories universally rejected by a repressive society. By the time - 1905 - Freud wrote his 'Three Essays on the Theory of Sexuality,' scientific works on sexuality and novels dealing with sexual themes were very popular. Freud's fear of bad reviews was nicely illustrated by an incident involving 'Three Essays.' Fliess's work on sex had received a bad review in a Viennese medical journal. Freud resigned from the editorial board in protest and in fear that his book would suffer the same fate (Grinstein, 1968). Reality is sometimes nicer than fantasy, especially when one has as low an opinion of one's critics as Freud did. The journal devoted the entire review section of one issue to an extremely positive piece on Freud's 'Three Essays.' The reviewer discussed the book as a work of genius and called it epoch-making (Bry and Rifkin, 1962).

Ellenberger concurs with Bry and Rifkin and Decker. He presents evidence against the notion that 'The Interpretation of Dreams' was badly received and says, 'There is no evidence that Freud was really isolated, and still less that he was ill-treated by his colleagues' (1970, p. 448). Ellenberger characterizes Freud's complaints of isolation by saying, 'It is as though Freud identified himself with the Byronic figure of the lonely hero struggling against a host of enemies and difficulties' (p. 465).

Freud's self-analysis helped to foster a piece of romantic self-deception. As early as 1890 he was feeling isolated from his colleagues, and as his psychic difficulties increased and his analysis became intensive, his sense of isolation was exacerbated. We have seen his equation of true originality with rejection by one's peers and so he looked for signs of rejection as reassurance that his ideas were truly revolutionary. His inner turmoils and doubts about his work were projected outward, and he took every sign of opposition as evidence that he was on the right track.

With his work on the 'Project' in 1895, Freud entered into a
period characterized by symptoms of what Ellenberger calls a
creative illness. In working on the 'Project,' Freud found his
vocation and dedicated his life to a single concern - the explanation of the human mind. With the failure of the 'Project' and
Jakob's death, Freud's interest turned inward. His own mind
was the center of his investigative work. He suffered from a
multitude of symptoms associated with giving birth to new ideas:
depression, neurotic complaints, self-doubt, and feelings of
isolation. Alternating alleviation and exacerbation of his symptoms marked the advances and set-backs in his work, but he
never gave up his dominating preoccupation. As his analysis of
his own problems put his world in order again his interest
turned outward. The intensive period of incubation was followed
by an outpouring of work. 'The Interpretation of Dreams,' the
first-born, fuses autobiography with general propositions about
dreams and the human psyche. In universalizing discoveries
from his own psychic explorations, formalizing principles of
interpretation, and outlining a methodological approach to investigation Freud provided a basis for psychoanalysis.

Freud had a conversion experience, and he was converted to
his own creation. As Freud emerged from his creative illness, he
was convinced that the truths he discovered internally were to
be seen in all other people. He became a scientific visionary. He
had developed a systematic method of observation, psychoanalysis, which could be taught to others and which allowed its
practitioner to see into the unknown. By the methods of free
association and interpretation he could make the unconscious
conscious; the unknown known. Because he had done it in himself he could lead others to avow what they had disavowed and
so connect them with their pasts which they had denied.

He had discovered 'the greatest of truths' and the whole world
became impregnated with meanings which confirmed his theories.
The resistance of patients to his interpretations became a sign
that his constructions were on the right track; colleagues' criticisms of his work became an affirmation of his ideas. There
were no longer any secrets for Freud's perception had been
renewed by a vision:

> He that has eyes to see and ears to hear may convince himself
> that no mortal can keep a secret. If his lips are silent, he
> chatters with his finger-tips; betrayal oozes out of him at
> every pore. And thus the task of making conscious the most
> hidden recesses of the mind is one which is quite possible to
> accomplish. (Freud, 1905c, pp. 77-8)

These lines, originally written in 1901 just as Freud was con-
solidating his visionary gains, demonstrate the power he felt
analytic insight provided him. Psychoanalytic technique provided
the Rosetta stone by which to translate previously unintelligible
signs and symptoms into a coherent narrative.

Looked at from a perspective of pathology, any world-ordering system, including Freud's, has certain paranoid qualities (Roazen, 1971). Everything becomes a sign confirming one's suspicions. Persecutory paranoids:

> cannot regard anything in other people as indifferent, and they...take up minute indications with which these other, unknown people present them, and use them in their delusions of reference....
> They...displace to the unconscious minds of others the attention which they have withdrawn from their own....[We] may infer that the enmity which the persecuted paranoic sees in others is the reflection of his own hostile impulses against them. (Freud, 1922, p. 226)

Compare Freud's own behavior with this description. As his psychoanalytic theories crystalized he saw himself as isolated and persecuted by his colleagues. He wanted them to embrace his work totally, and when they did not he felt rejected. In almost every review and every colleague's behavior he saw signs that other medical men disliked his work. The Fliess correspondence contains evidence that Freud despised his colleagues: they were called asses and were held up to ridicule. He projected on to his colleagues the rejection he felt for them and saw this rejection as emanating from them and not from himself. Jones admits that there was no active ostracism of Freud and we have found no evidence of others actually persecuting him. This being the case argues that Freud himself created his own rejection by expanding academic criticisms or lack of understanding into personal attacks upon himself. Talking of his estrangement from his colleagues and especially from older medical men, Freud says, 'often enough when I approached some man whom I had honored from a distance, I found myself repelled...by his lack of understanding for what had become my whole life to me' (1932, p. 224). He expected too much from Breuer and from his respected elders and got too little. This led him to undervalue and attack people whom he had overvalued; love turned to hate. He then transposed the attacks to them, transforming himself from the aggressor into the victim. He certainly did this in 1886 when he took his colleagues' treatment of his paper 'On Male Hysteria' as a total rejection of his work. In his retrospective account of the initial reception of psychoanalysis he again spoke of the total rejection of his work. The evidence from the reviews does not confirm Freud's story.

By 1905 the most dramatic period in Freud's life was coming to an end. In the ten years surrounding 1900 he had made all his important discoveries, at least in essence, and had laid the foundation for all his future work. 'The Interpretation of Dreams,' 'The Psychopathology of Everyday Life,' 'Fragment of an Analysis of a Case of Hysteria,' 'Three Essays on the Theory of Sexuality,' and 'Jokes and their Relation to the Unconscious'

were all products of Freud's intense period of suffering and
creativity around the turn of the century. They came out of
deep personal insights and for Freud they revealed heretofore
unknown truths about humanity. These were foundational works
for psychoanalysis and have become classics of both literary and
scientific thought. When the world did not instantly respond to
his genius, Freud felt rejected and consoled himself with the
thought that 'from time immemorial mankind has always been wont
to laugh at an idea to which one day it is obliged partly or entirely to submit' (1960, p. 244). Our laughter was never as loud
as Freud thought and our submission, although never as great
as he hoped, came much more quickly than he might have expected.

The discoveries which Freud made in his own analysis were to
be confirmed in countless analyses of others. Themes extracted
from his own life story were to be found in the life stories of all
humanity. In everyone's past was hatred for one parent and lust
for the other. All adults suffered because they resisted insight
into the unconscious and denied that infantile desires still fueled
their activities. Measurement always requires a reference point
and stories are always told from a perspective. Freud became his
own fixed point, for he came to rely on his judgment of others
as a measure of what others did not know of themselves. Upon a
thorough exploration of his subjectivity, Freud felt he had
transformed himself into an objective observer. In 'The Psychopathology of Everyday Life' he set forth his ideas on this:
'There thus runs through my thoughts a continuous current of
"personal reference"... It is as if I were obliged to compare
everything I hear about other people with myself' (p. 24). Freud
then confirms this statement by universalizing it: 'This cannot
be an individual peculiarity of my own: it must contain an indication of the way in which we understand "something other than
ourself" in general. I have reasons for supposing that other
people are in this respect very similar to me.' We come to know
other minds by knowing our own mind. Long before he ever
wrote a word about psychoanalysis he was aware of this in himself. In 1882 he wrote to Martha saying, 'I always find it uncanny when I can't understand someone in terms of myself' (quoted
in Jones, 1953, p. 320). To make sense of other minds through
interpretations grounded in a hermeneutic system born of his own
self-analysis became Freud's vocation.

His story became the human story. His life became psychoanalysis, for every analysis confirmed his own self-understanding. If psychoanalysis were not universally true, then Freud's
insights would have in some way been idiosyncratic. They might
have come from his being Viennese, Jewish, an eldest son or
merely self-deceived. To question the universality of psychoanalysis, or attack its fundamental principles as Jung did in
1912, was to challenge the very basis of Freud's own self-understanding, an understanding which he felt linked him to all of
humanity. Freud had been able to admit that he had been

deceived about seduction. This admission was facilitated by his self-analysis. But after 1900 he was to be deceived no longer for all truth was first discovered in himself. Just before the turn of the century Freud fused self-understanding with scientific discovery and altered our twentieth-century understanding of ourselves and science.

Before Freud, people had for millennia recognized the importance of self-knowledge. Augustine had preached 'Seek not abroad, turn back in thyself, for in the inner man dwells the truth.' Montaigne, the sixteenth-century French philosopher, advocated 'Let us only listen; we tell ourselves all we most need' (1965, p. 822). He had carried out extensive self-exploration through analyzing his fantasies and proclaimed that his book about this had made him. Gedo and Wolf (1976) have pointed out that during the Renaissance poets, historians, and philosophers felt that introspection was a vital part of their work as humanists. After the seventeenth-century Cartesian cataclysm, introspection into irrational human motives became suspect and explorations of subjectivity were buried by the growth of scientific objectivism. In Freud, two currents flowed together, an objective scientific education and a reverence for men of letters. His work combined systematic observation of others, self-observation, and a respect for the insights of the poets to forge a humanistic science - a science of people, not objects. Freud's initial evidence for Oedipal emotions is a perfect demonstration of the fusion of art and science in his work. He found confirmation in Sophocles and Shakespeare, in his own analysis, and in the systematic observation of others.

Freud's genius was to find that without a theological system or the stamp of natural scientific approval 'the story of each human life could yet be rendered into some measure of intelligibility' (Marcus, 1977, p. xviii). Freud founded a system of biographical story construction, a method for making sense out of human lives. His method was both empirical and speculative. His language was both scientific and literary. He took his inspiration from Brücke, Charcot, and Breuer as well as from Shakespeare and the Greek tragedians, whom he called 'my masters.' Freud's genius lay in his ability to synthesize and systematize, to look and see what others had ignored, and in his gift for convincing others that what he saw was there. He had a vision and his insight was close enough to our own that it has revolutionized the historical narratives which we tell about ourselves.

5 THE WHOLE LOST STORY: THE PSYCHOANALYTIC NARRATIVE

We turn now to the evolution of Freud's thought from ten years before to five years after the turn of the century. During this time Freud's work became revolutionary because he created a new science, a science of the non-material - a mental science. His thought during these years removed his psychological theories from a linkage with biology and located human malaise in the psyche, a structure with uncertain material footings. The mind, in Freud's work, evolved from an epiphenomenal emanation of physiological processes to the matrix of human self-understanding and self-deception. Brain physiology, he found, did not explain consciousness or how a person could know and not know something at the same time. What explained a person's existence was a person's life. Psychoanalysis became a radical science because Freud created a science that was historical and interpretive. Psychoanalysis became devoted to constructing life stories with the goal of telling the whole lost story of an individual's life; that is, formulating a narrative which had been denied consciously, but which unconsciously influenced a person's entire existence. Psychoanalysis is different from the sciences of nature because instead of being anchored in the material, its foundation is in words. Psychoanalytic theory is not devoted to an explanation of people as objects but to understanding the human story; it is a theory about the historical narratives that we use to both understand and misunderstand ourselves. In tracing the revolution in Freud's work and in criticizing his thought we will consider the movement from biologically based causal explanation to interpretive narrative formulations in the following works: essays from the early 1890s, 'Studies on Hysteria,' the 'Project,' the seduction theory papers, 'The Interpretation of Dreams,' 'Three Essays on the Theory of Sexuality,' and Dora's story in 'Analysis of a Fragment of a Case of Hysteria.' By 1905 psychoanalysis was firmly founded as a hermeneutic discipline - an interpretive science.

Freud formally declared his emancipation from biology in 'The Interpretation of Dreams.' He had informally proclaimed it to Fliess when in 1898, after having survived the most intense period of his analysis and in the middle of work on the dream book, he said, 'I must behave as if I were confronted by psychological factors only' (1954, p. 264). There is much evidence that throughout the 1890s Freud's thought was moving towards this proclamation. We will trace this movement showing the liberation of his thought from biology, and the concomitant development

of psychoanalysis as a systematic technique for the construction
of historical narratives in the form of individual life histories.

THE POWER OF THE WORD

The first stirrings of a revolution came with the beginning of
the new decade in 1890. In an essay on 'Psychical (or Mental)
Treatment' Freud declared that psychical therapeutics operate
upon the mind and that 'words are the essential tool of mental
treatment' (p. 283). He reviewed the great strides that medicine,
guided by natural science, had made in understanding biological
man, but held that physicians had made an error by restricting
their interest to the physical side of things. The success of
medicine led to the understandable error of seeing mental events
as exclusively 'determined by physical ones and dependent on
them' (p. 284). Freud rejected this epiphenomenalist position - a
view which, as we will see, he supported in his 1891 monograph
on aphasia - taking up a stance of interactional dualism, a view
consonant with his later psychoanalytic work. He stated:

> The relation between body and mind...is a reciprocal one,
> but in earlier times the other side of this relation, the effect
> of the mind upon the body found little favour in the eyes of
> physicians. They seemed to be afraid of granting mental life
> any independence, for fear of...implying an abandonment of
> the scientific ground on which they stood. (p. 284)

The danger of departing from the philosophical assumption that
all human existence is anchored in biological processes is that
one will cut off one's work from the moorings of scientific
materialism. Freud is, of course, perfectly correct here, for
one cannot have a natural scientific medicine if one abandons
materialist doctrines. He did not see at the time, and never saw,
that he left natural science when he began practicing mental
therapeutics.
   Freud argues that recent clinical evidence has necessitated
a modification of medicine's one-sided view on the body-mind
relationship. After exhaustive physical examinations, and in some
cases autopsies, physicians had found no organic causation for
cases of 'nervousness' (neurasthenia, hysteria, obsessions,
and delusional insanity). Freud felt that such cases provided
doctors with an opportunity to investigate that which they had
previously neglected - the effect of the mind on the body. For
in some of these patients their illnesses 'originate from nothing
other than *a change in the action of their minds upon their
bodies* and...the immediate cause of their disorder is to be looked
for in their minds' (p. 286).
   After this groundwork, in this rather radical essay, Freud
then discusses mental treatment; the focus of the essay is on
hypnosis as a method of psychic cure. Freud notes that in all

psychic treatment, including that of priests and miracle-workers, the patient's expectations and rapport with the physician are vital and that hypnosis greatly increases the power of the practitioner. He argues that hypnosis should be respected as a form of medical treatment and that it has a wide application.

The power of hypnosis and of many forms of so-called miracle cures, Freud asserts, lies in 'the "magic" of words. Words are the most important media by which one man seeks to bring his influence to bear on another; words are a good method of producing mental changes in the person to whom they are addressed' (p. 292).

Freud came less and less to depend on hypnosis, but he never abandoned his faith in words. Thirty-six years later, when his thought had undergone many important modifications, he still maintained that words had power: 'And incidentally do not let us despise the *word*. After all it is a powerful instrument; it is the means by which we convey our feelings to one another, our method of influencing other people. Words can do unspeakable good and cause terrible wounds' (1926, pp. 187-8). After thirty years of practicing the treatment he developed, a method which was his modification of Anna O.'s and Breuer's talking cure, Freud simply stated that in psychoanalysis, 'Nothing takes place between them [analyst and analysand] except that they talk to each other' (p. 187).

Until about 1892, Freud, still following Charcot and Breuer, carried on conversations with patients while they were under hypnosis. He found that, while hypnotized, patients had access to the whole of their memories, an access which was restricted in normal waking life. One woman patient made a peculiar noise, a clacking of the tongue, which intruded into her conversations. Freud asked her when and how this first originated; she answered that she didn't know, but it started a long time ago. Under hypnosis the woman told the whole story to Freud: while nursing her ill daughter, who had just fallen asleep, the woman had thought that she must be completely quiet in order not to wake her child. At this moment the clacking occurred for the first time. It passed off, but years later it returned when her coachman was having trouble controlling the horses and she thought to herself that she must not scream or the horses would bolt. At that moment the clacking returned and had lasted ever since. Once she told this story to Freud, as Anna O. had told her tales to Breuer, the disturbing noise disappeared for good. Freud says this was the first case in which he 'was able to observe the origin of hysterical symptoms through the putting into effect of a distressing antithetic idea - that is, through counter-will' (1892-3, p. 124). The woman had consciously willed herself not to speak, but outside of consciousness there was the impulse to make a sound and this idea, antithetic to consciousness, was expressed through the bodily system of tongue clacking. Once the lost story was retold the woman stopped clacking.

Freud's explanation of the case follows Breuer's notion of

hypnoid states. Hysterical symptoms arise when 'those elements of the nervous system associated with the primary consciousness' are exhausted (p. 126). Ideas outside of ego-consciousness are, however, not exhausted, and these normally suppressed ideas break through the weakened ego inhibitions, finding expression; at that moment antithetic ideas and counter-will predominate, and the hysterical disposition is formed. Freud's explanatory dynamics are interesting, because they show his thought in transition. Being faithful to his education, he speaks in very general terms about a physiological basis of hysteria - exhaustion of the nervous system - but the central terms of his formulation are psychological - ideas and will. In simplistic terms he has stated a problem which will dominate his life's work: people's bodies, behaviors, and thoughts are influenced by impulses and ideas of which they are not aware. Counter-volitions and antithetic ideas 'are stored up and enjoy an unsuspected existence in a sort of shadow kingdom, till they emerge like bad spirits and take control of the body, which is as a rule under the orders of the predominant ego-consciousness' (p. 127). This 'shadow kingdom' became the unconscious, and Freud wrote volumes detailing and modifying this simple formulation.

Treatment involved the expression of one's denied intentions and thoughts. Actions and ideas which could not be expressed consciously lived on in the dark realm and found alternative modes of expression in dreams, in the compromise formations of obsessional ideas, and in the bodily symptoms of hysteria. If dammed-up emotions are causing problems by running off in directions which could not be controlled, then treatment would tear down the dam and work to rechannel these affects by bringing them within the stream of consciousness. The most effective way to do this was through speech, for 'language serves as a substitute for action; by its help, an affect can be "abreacted" almost as effectively' (Breuer and Freud, 1893, p. 8).

Language serves as a substitute for action just as the word serves as a substitute for the thing. Language and its elements, words, are in a sense fictions for actions and their constituents, objects. They stand for them, but are not them; they are wonderfully non-material and incorporeal; they are the prime tools of the imagination, the place where we fabricate fictions; and they are the stuff from which stories are constructed.

Words are powerful, for through them we express emotions and ideas. The impulses and thoughts behind the word, if denied an outlet in speech, seek other vehicles of communication. In hysteria the mind invades the body and the soma becomes a material signifier for the psyche. Countering Charcot's thesis that there must be a physical lesion in the brain that causes hysteria, Freud states:

I, on the contrary, assert that the lesion in hysterical paralyses must be completely independent of the anatomy of the nervous system, since *in its paralyses and other manifesta-*

tions hysteria behaves as though anatomy did not exist or
as though it had no knowledge of it. (1893a, p. 169)

Hysteria is ignorant of the science of the nervous anatomy;
hysterics have fictional bodies. In hysteria the body is governed
by linguistic anatomy: any part of the body which the hysteric
thinks of as a unit - an arm or a leg for instance - may respond
as a unit regardless of its neurological structure. A hand may
become paralyzed from the wrist down - that part covered by a
glove - although this breaks the rules of nervous system functioning. Perhaps an entire arm becomes anesthetic, although no
nerve patterning would account for this and no anatomical lesions
can be found. The lesion is *'the abolition of the associative acces-*
sibility of the conception of the arm' (p. 170). Here Freud uses
lesion psychologically, transforming a term which had previously
been used anatomically and articulating a new field of meaning
for it. This shifting of a term's significance from the physiological to the psychological sphere is at the center of Freud's
creation of a science of the mind. It creates a sense of comfort
in his readers; he is still using the old words, and this non-
material mental realm appears to be ordered by the same concepts
as the physical body. Hysterics may not have brain lesions, but
they do have lesions in their minds. New ideas are often presented
in old words, and sometimes these old terms create the illusion
that nothing new is being said. Freud, in fact, is saying that
hysteria is a disease of verbal representation and that the body
need not behave by the rules of medical science, for it can be
forced to serve rebellious emotions which capture parts of the
body in order to express their will. If hysterics cannot express
their wishes in words, then they will make their bodies organs
of speech.

Freud's language forever retained its denotative ties to materialism, for psychoanalysis anchors itself to the body. Prone to
find equivalences and determined to reduce the mental to the
physical, many insist on reading Freud by equating psychological
with physical lesions, orality with mouths, and instincts with
biochemical processes. Freud, himself, is not beyond reducing
simile to identity. Here, however, where the issue is so clear let
us be explicit: a psychological lesion is like a physical lesion,
but it is not an actual rupture in a thing.

Where does one find proof that there has been a psychological
lesion, that a person is suffering from a discontinuity in his or
her associative history and that the body has been altered by
the mind? A physical examination will not do and one cannot show
slides of a psychological lesion; Freud came to depend on the
life histories of his patients as evidence for his ideas. In the
essay in which he introduces the concept of a mental lesion he
uses three stories to support his thesis. One is a comic story
about a loyal subject who would not wash his hands because the
king had touched it. The idea of the hand had been charged with
so much emotional importance by the king's touch that the sub-

ject refused to let it enter into any mundane actions. The hand
has been figuratively cut off from the rest of the man's life.

The concept of a psychological lesion is at the heart of Freud's
notion of defense. Defense is the splitting off of a content of
consciousness as the result of an act of will. Unaware of what
they are doing, individuals who develop a neurosis of defense,
hysteric or obsessional neurosis, push disturbing thoughts out
of consciousness. Freud's evidence for this thesis is presented
in several case vignettes.

In proposing the concept of defense as the origin of neuroses,
Freud was propounding an alternative thesis to Breuer's more
physiologically based concept of hypnoid hysteria and Charcot's
notion that hysteria was caused by physiological degeneracy.
Freud speaks of a disposition towards neuroses, but does not
commit himself to any physiological dynamics. His uncertainty
about leaving materialist explanation behind is clear. In this
essay, 'The Neuro-Psychoses of Defence,' in which he has
focused on purely psychological issues and illustrated his thought
with case stories, he leaves open the possibility that such processes are really physical. Perhaps, he speculates, they are
physical processes whose psychical consequences are expressed
as if a mental act of defense had actually occurred. The psyche
was not yet quite real to Freud. In epiphenomenalist terms he
has said that perhaps what he is describing is only an emanation
of real underlying physiological events. The psyche is simply a
fiction, an 'as if' construction, whose processes may be at base
physiological.

The issue of the underlying physiological bases of psychic
processes is one that Freud never resolved. We will see that in
his later work he sometimes expressed the hope that one day
neurobiology would find the physiological processes underlying
the psychic dynamics described by psychoanalysis. In other
places he asserted that the psyche was an independent realm
and psychoanalysis was independent of biological confirmation.
However, the movement of his work in the 1890s, and for that
matter the whole train of Freud's developing thought, was away
from physiology towards psychology. With one exception, the
'Project for a Scientific Psychology,' the 1890s was devoted to
an ever-increasing explanation of human functioning in terms of
psychic processes. In work after work he was elaborating the
idea of the psychological lesion and progressively removing the
notion of a 'lesion' from any grounding in physiology. Turning
lesion into defense broke one more tie to physiology.

'STUDIES' IN STORY

The notion of defense was central to Freud's explanation of the
dynamics of hysteria in 'Studies on Hysteria.' In chapter 4 we
saw that Freud and Breuer disagreed about the explanation of
this neurosis, Breuer preferring the more physiological hypothe-

sis of hypnoid states, Freud opting for the psychological thesis
of defense. 'Studies' is an important work, for in it clearly lie
the origins of the psychoanalytic narrative. Breuer's presentation of the case of Anna O. marks the recording of one of the
earliest narrative therapy treatments. When all of Anna's stories
had been told her treatment came to an end.

If psychical treatment is concerned with the untold tales of
neurotic patients - if *'Hysterics suffer mainly from reminiscences'*
(Breuer and Freud, 1893, p. 7) - then the case account, to be
true to the material, should be a telling of these stories - a retelling of reminiscences. Reminding his readers that he was a
neuropathologist and had used electrotherapy, in other words
that he was a medical scientist, Freud says:

> it still strikes me myself as strange that the case histories I
> write should read like short stories and that, as one might
> say, they lack the serious stamp of science. I must console
> myself with the reflection that the nature of the subject is
> evidently responsible for this, rather than any preference of
> my own. (1895, p. 160)

Asserting that electrical treatment leads nowhere in the study of
hysteria, Freud maintained that combining 'a detailed description
of mental processes such as we are accustomed to find in works
of imaginative writers' with a few psychological formulations
allows one to obtain some insight into this disease (p. 160). He
says his case histories are to be judged like psychiatric studies,
but have one advantage over the latter. For in his cases there
is 'an intimate connection between the story of the patient's
sufferings and the symptoms of his illness,' a connection which
does not exist in psychiatric histories (p. 161). The man who as
a teenager delighted in writing elaborate narratives, who in his
twenties told the tragic story of a colleague's suicide, and who
appreciated the insights into human nature of poets and novelists
is asserting that to understand the hysteric one must understand
her or his story.

Hysterics do not suffer from brain lesions, but from untold
stories. In fact, improvement did not occur unless a patient's
entire story had been told, and Freud 'gradually came to be able
to read from patients' faces whether they might not be concealing
an essential part of their confessions' (p. 79). Hysterics' bodies
were vehicles of communication for their denied lives, and Freud
learned how to listen to what was being said by this mute but
highly expressive object. He asserted that the bodily symptoms
of hysteria 'have an original or long-standing connection with
traumas, and stand as symbols for them in the activities of the
memory' (p. 95). The bodily symptom is but a symbol for an
event too painful for the hysteric to avow. Their bodies are
signifiers for their minds. The hysteric says my problem is my
arm's paralysis, but the paralytic arm simply stands for a deeper
psychological trauma which has been denied. The physical

symptom is connected to the trauma and plays a vital role in bringing about a cure. Freud says that during treatment symptoms make known their connection to traumas by '"joining in the conversation"' (p. 296). As the patient comes nearer to the memory of the traumatic event, the intensity of the symptom associated with it increases. The symptomatic pain reaches a climax just before the patient gives utterance to the memory, and diminishes or vanishes when he or she has finished narrating the painful episode. Body parts are not only material entities, but are also actors in the hysteric's drama; they tell part of the story.

Treating his patients, Freud found that he could not 'evade listening to [their] stories in every detail to the very end' (p. 61). Frau Emmy von N. in fact gave Freud a useful piece of technical advice. She told him to stop interrupting her and that he should let her tell her stories in her own way. Of the four major cases Freud reports in 'Studies,' Emmy von N. is the only one in which he used hypnosis. He treated her in the late 1880s and by the time he treated Lucy R. and Elisabeth von R. in 1892 he had for the most part given up hypnosis. With Elisabeth he used the concentration technique and with Lucy the pressure technique. Applying pressure with his hands to Lucy's forehead he told her that when he released his grip the memory or image they were looking for would come to her. If nothing occurred to her he would apply pressure again and usually by the third or fourth press the information came forth. Occasionally patients would say that they had the thought the first time, but they just didn't want to say it or they hoped the memory was not the one being looked for. Freud was coming up against the problem of resistance.

With Lucy the problem of her resistance came to a dramatic conclusion. Lucy complained that whenever she became agitated she smelled burnt pudding. This symptom was a symbol to which many strong emotions were attached. While cooking pudding with the children for whom she was a governess, she received a letter from her mother. The children teased her about the letter, and the pudding began to scorch. At this moment Lucy was considering leaving the employment of the childrens' father, the 'Director,' to go live with her mother. She was upset about having to leave the children, whom she loved, and she had been disturbed by the jealousy of the household servants. From these clues Freud felt that there could be only one conclusion, and he informed Lucy of his interpretation. He told her that she was in love with the Director, but that she might not even have known this herself. She responded to Freud's interpretation

in her usual laconic fashion: [Lucy] 'Yes, I think that's true.' [Freud] 'But if you knew you loved your employer why didn't you tell me?' [Lucy] 'I didn't know - or rather I didn't want to know. I wanted to drive it out of my head and not think of it again; and I believe latterly I have succeeded.' (p. 117)

To this dramatic dialogue Freud appends the following note:

> I have never managed to give a better description than this
> of the strange state of mind in which one knows and does not
> know a thing at the same time. It is clearly impossible to
> understand it unless one has been in such a state oneself.

The psychical lesion in Lucy's case was a defense against
knowing what she did not want to know. She did not want to
admit that she had fallen in love with the Director, a man well
above her station, and felt that people would laugh at her if they
knew she had committed such a folly. The idea was split off
from consciousness, denied awareness, but its affect became
attached to the smell of burnt pudding, an innocuous sensory
impression which came to stand for the tragedy of inappropriate
love. Owning up to her emotions led to a clearing up of Lucy's
sensations of smelling scorched pudding. But then she began to
smell cigar smoke; it was as though the pudding smell had simply
been masking the cigar odor. Under pressure, she remembered
an incident two months prior to the pudding episode. The Director and an old friend of his were smoking cigars. As the friend
got up to leave he tried to kiss the children goodbye. The
Director flew into a rage at the old gentleman for attempting to
kiss the children on the mouth. The cigar smoke and not the
scene lingered in Lucy's memory, but telling the story did not
eliminate the problem. There was yet another story to be told.
Several months earlier a lady friend of the Director had kissed
the children goodbye and instead of saying anything to the
woman the Director upbraided Lucy for allowing someone to kiss
the children. This had occurred when Lucy thought the Director
loved her, and his anger had dashed her hopes. The pudding
had been a mere cover for the cigar odor which had been a token
memory for this first scene. Lucy had to deny this incident,
because if she had remembered it she would have had to admit
that she loved the Director and that her love had been crushed
by his actions.

   The story has a happy ending. After the last piece of analysis
Lucy returned two days later to Freud's office; the depressive
woman Freud had known in treatment 'was as though transfigured'
(p. 121). She was cheerful and carried herself erect. She was
her normal, happy self again. She affirmed that she was still in
love with her employer, but said '"that makes no difference. After
all, I can have thoughts and feelings to myself"' (p. 121). Her
mild hysteria had been brought on by a series of minor traumas,
and her transfiguration back to health required a transformation
of consciousness, a change in her story. She had admitted what
she had previously denied and so could live a life unclouded by
the disturbances of physical hallucinations which had come to
be mnemic symbols for a disavowed drama. In denying her love
for the Director Lucy created two bodily fictions, the burnt
pudding and cigar smells, as symbols for what she knew but did

not know. When she avowed her love, the symbols were no longer
needed as mnemic markers for buried secrets. The thoughts were
admitted to consciousness, and Lucy no longer had to live out
a story which could not be told.

In the case of Elisabeth von R. Freud searched for lost memories by using the technique of concentration. At any point in her
narrative where some obscurity occurred, Freud had her con-
centrate and thereby carry the story further back into her past.
Freud says his job is 'one of clearing away pathogenic material
layer by layer' and that he 'likes to compare it with the technique
of excavating a buried city' (p. 139). This is an early statement
of one of Freud's favorite analogies: he is a psychological
archaeologist in search of his patients' lost memories from which
he will construct the stories of their lives.

We have followed one such reconstruction in the case of Lucy
R., and the other cases in 'Studies' follow similar, but more
complicated lines. In all his cases Freud had to accomplish two
things: recreate the case and present a psychological explanation
of it. In the study of Elisabeth von R. this double requirement
is clearly expressed in one sentence: 'With regard to these feelings [being in love with her brother-in-law] she was in a peculiar situation of knowing and at the same time not knowing – a
situation that is, in which a psychical group is cut off' (p. 165).
Freud used his considerable writing talents to engage his
readers in the confused world of the hysteric and to abstract
from cases general psychological principles. Experientially,
Elisabeth was in physical pain, because she had denied that
she was in love with her sister's husband; in psychological terms
a group of ideas had been split off from consciousness by a
motive of defense – not wanting to know – and their affect had
been converted by the mechanism of hysteria into somatic excitation. Freud leads his audience through his clients' disordered
worlds with a well-ordered narrative and simultaneously uses
this story to illustrate psychological theories. Freud's theories,
of course, shape his observations and treatment, and in turn
what emerged from his cases shaped his theories. In 'Studies'
there are two interconnected lines of exposition which are
characteristic of all Freud's psychoanalytic work: the case, story,
or example – the experiential narrative; and the psychological
explanation of the case – the psychic narrative. Both narratives
are intimately tied together for the first sequentially orders the
analysand's experience in time and space and the second abstract-
ly orders material from many cases into a mental model.

In the last chapter of 'Studies' Freud constructs such a model.
It closely parallels, as it should, the narratives he presented
in his case studies: the 'psychical material in such cases of
hysteria presents itself as a structure in several dimensions
which is stratified in at least three different ways' (p. 288). The
model is quite elaborate and Freud constructs it by using a
number of similies. The mind of a hysteric is like a structure
built of concentric rings around a central nucleus. The nucleus

consists of memories of events or thoughts in which the traumatic
factor or pathogenic idea has its purest manifestation. This
nucleus is deeply buried. In rings around it are strata of ideas,
those closest to the nucleus being most resistant to uncovering
and those furthest away being most accessible to consciousness.
In addition to this concentric arrangement there is a linear
ordering. Ideas arranged in a linear sequence constitute what
Freud calls themes. In uncovering a thematic thread, one exposes
the most recent thoughts first, since they are the closest to the
surface and occupy the strata of least resistance, and the oldest
thoughts last, as they are the most deeply buried, closest to the
nucleus, and occupy the strata of greatest resistance. Because
of resistance, a thematic thread cannot be followed straight to
the nucleus. A whole stratum of themes, all at an equivalent
layer of resistance, must be excavated before one can dig down
to the next stratum and pick up each thematic line again.

The arrangement is, however, more complex, for there is a
third important aspect of remembering. Ideas emerge according
to thought content and associative links. There is a connection
of material by a logical thread which cuts across strata and zig-
zags through time. Freud calls this the dynamic arrangement of
the material; it is that arrangement which makes sense out of
the data by ordering ideas from different levels of resistance and
different points in time into a coherent narrative. These lines
are the ones Freud follows in constructing his cases; for the
dynamic arrangement makes sense of a life.

Although formally we can arrange our thoughts into thematic
groups or we can try to recall superficial layers of events moving on to those harder to recall, our lives do not reveal their
meaning to us in this way. Life is a complex narrative with many
subplots, and to make sense of a disordered life a strong story
line must be woven together thereby bringing coherence to a
multitude of dynamic threads. Following a logical linkage, Freud
finds that often several dynamic threads will meet in a knot, a
nodal point, and from this point a single line will run straight
to the nucleus. 'To put this in other words, it is very remarkable
how often a symptom is determined in several ways, is "over-
determined"' (p. 290). To put it still another way, and bring us
out of the psychological model and back to life, few events have
a single cause. In order to understand any event we must weave
together several different subplots into a coherent story.

The analyst must piece together various memories, for ego-
consciousness is a narrow passage through which remembrances
emerge into awareness one at a time. This defile may easily be
blocked by resistance, and so scenes and events appear dis-
jointedly and memory arrives cut up into pieces. This, of course,
serves resistance, for the patient can make nothing of this jum-
ble. So it is 'the psychotherapist's business to put these together
once more into the organization he presumes to have existed...
[one] may think at this point of a Chinese puzzle' (p. 291).
The organization is, of course, a story modeled after the stories

Freud has constructed in other cases and is consistent with his
conceptualization of the psyche as an abstract structure organized linearly, concentrically and logically to provide a model for
constructing real-life stories. This psychic model constructed
by simile is the most elaborate mental metaphor Freud has yet
built - it goes far beyond the psychological lesion simile. It was
really the first of a series of elaborate models of the mind,
theoretical fictions, that he would construct.

With Elizabeth von R., Freud used the concentration technique,
and in the case of Katharina he depended solely on talking with
her. Freud's method of inquiry was moving away from hypnosis
towards free association. After 1896 hypnosis came to be replaced
by what Gedo and Pollock call 'directed assocation' (1976, p. 231).
Freud used this technique in the analysis of his own dreams,
and it is the method he used in analyzing Dora. A symptom or
element of a dream was the starting point for associations, and
the patient's thoughts emerged in terms of this focus. It was not
until 1907 with the case of Rat Man that free association became
the method of psychoanalysis. In free association the analyst
'no longer seeks to elicit material in which he is interested, but
permits the patient to follow his natural and spontaneous trains
of thought' (Freud, quoted in Nunberg and Federn, 1962,
p. 227). Almost twenty years after Emmy von N. had told Freud
to stop asking her questions, he announced that his technique
allowed complete freedom of recall for each person's remembrances.
Free association frees one's speech so that it may follow thought
and thus tries to eliminate a censorship that exists between idea-
tion and communication.

In moving away from hypnosis, Freud came to place greater
emphasis on his clients' participation in the therapeutic process.
In 'Studies' there is an important recognition - fundamental for
all Freud's future analytic work - of the necessary co-operation
between therapist and patient. In talking about inducing a client
to give up her or his resistances, Freud says that the therapist
must engage the client's intellectual interest in the work making
her or him into a collaborator. The subject of the investigation
must become a partner in it and must achieve a certain detachment in order to view her or himself with some objectivity.
Freud's emerging science of the mind is indeed an odd science,
for it studies objects who can think and reflect, and its findings
are dependent upon the active co-participation of its object,
the patient, in the process of discovery. No natural scientist
speaks with the object which he or she is investigating. And
yet, for psychoanalysis, dialogue is essential. Indeed, without
speech and the reflection made possible by language, without the
stories that can be constructed by words, analysis would be
impossible. Language allows us to change our position without
moving, to reflect upon ourselves, to deceive ourselves, and to
free ourselves.

Freud's involvement with patients was reflected in his intimate
case studies which read like short stories. Such stories, in turn,

had an important effect on his formulation of psychological theory.
His first major model of the psyche had a structure which paralleled his case histories. With his patients he worked to overcome
their resistances to remembering their pasts, encouraged them
to discharge the accumulated affects of unexpressed emotions by
verbalizing incidents that they had denied, and ordered their
lives into a coherent story. His model of the psyche dealt with
these same issues, but in abstract terms: resistance was conceptualized in terms of stratified layers of memory, defense was
a motive for pushing an idea out of consciousness, the mechanism
of conversion transformed psychic affects into bodily innervations, and the logical threads of memory were woven together
to provide a coherent multi-determined explanation of a case.
His psychological theory was constructed inductively, working
from experience to a general abstraction of the central dynamics
present in his cases.

In contrast to Freud's inductive method, Breuer's approach to
his theoretical chapter in 'Studies' was deductive. Although
asserting that he would deal with 'psychical processes...in the
language of psychology,' Breuer's theoretical section is filled
with references to nerve pathways, intracerebral tonic excitation,
and cortical arousal (p. 185). From neurological principles
Breuer tried to derive an explanatory model of the psychology
of hysteria. Working inductively from his case material, Freud
avoided anatomical speculation. One glaring lapse into the world
of physiology was in the final sentence of 'Studies:' 'With a
nervous system that has been restored to health you will be
better armed against...unhappiness' (p. 305). In 1925 'nervous
system' was replaced by 'mental life.' In Breuer's theoretical
essay the language of neurology kept emerging, and in Freud's
the shadow of physiology was lurking just behind the mind.

THE 'PROJECT'S' REGRESSION TO NEUROLOGY

With the completion of 'Studies' Freud devoted himself to the
'Project for a Scientific Psychology,' and in it he formulated a
speculative brain physiology which tried to reduce all mental
life to nervous system functioning. The essay, like Breuer's
work in 'Studies,' is deductive. It could hardly be inductive,
since Freud's case work involved few physical examinations and
no neurological testing. It was an attempt to order from above,
using premises borrowed from physiology and physics, the
phenomena observed in and inferred from clinical practice. In
the last chapter we traced Freud's emotional commitment to the
'Project,' and here we will briefly consider the 'Project's'
importance in terms of the emergence of the psychoanalytic narrative.

Before taking up the 'Project,' let us examine an earlier view
that Freud propounded on the relation between the mind and the
brain. In his last major theoretical work in anatomy, 'On the

Interpretation of Aphasia,' Freud clearly assumes an epiphenomenalist position: 'the psychical is a process parallel to the
physiological – "a dependent concomitant"' (1957 [1891], p. 207).
Mind does not affect body. The relationship is one-way; body
affects mind. Freud simply could not maintain this position in
the face of the evidence from hysteria, and we saw that as early
as 1890, at least in his writings dealing with 'Psychical Treatment,' he did not support such a position.

Given his clinical experiences, Freud made a bold attempt in
the 'Project' to order these within a model of brain functioning.[1]
Freud's purpose in writing this work was 'to furnish a psychology that shall be a natural science: that is, to represent psychical processes as quantitatively determinate states of specifiable material particles' (1950b, p. 295). This goal is consonant
with the epiphenomenalist position in the aphasia book: the
explication of the psychical in materialist terms making the mind
a 'dependent concomitant' of neurological states. It is also completely in step with the Helmholtzian tradition which was devoted
to a 'rigorous attempt to treat the organism as a mechanical
system' (Holt, 1965, p. 95). The mechanics of the 'Project' were
developed around two physicalist ideas: (1) activity is distinguished from rest by a quantity (Q), which is subject to the laws
of motion, and (2) neurons are material structures. The first
rule of functioning was the principle of neuronal inertia; 'neurons tend to divest themselves of Q'; that is, neurons try to
remain in a quiescent state and discharge energy as quickly as
possible (Freud, 1950b, p. 296). Q is a rather strange quantitative factor. In another essay Freud says such a quantity must
be assumed 'though we have no means of measuring it' (1894,
p. 60). This creates a formidable problem for a quantitative
psychology, but like all scientists, Freud no doubt hoped that
advances in technology would handle the problem of measurement.

The principle of neuronal inertia is immediately modified, for
under the exigencies of life and the need to cope with endogenous
stimuli – the precursor notion to instincts – the organism must
keep a store of energy in neurons large enough to carry out
specific actions. Neurons operate to keep their charge as low as
possible, guard against any increase, and maintain a minimum
but constant charge. This is the 'constancy principle,' and
when rephrased in psychological terms, it became one of Freud's
fundamental metapsychological assumptions.

Freud initially postulates two types of neurons ϕ, phi or
physiological, and Ψ, psi or psychological neurons. Φ neurons
are permeable perceptual neurons which conduct stimulation from
the outside inward to Ψ neurons, which are semi-impermeable.
At contact barriers with other Ψ neurons Ψ are resistant to
discharge and are thus able to hold a cathexis, a quantity of
energy. There are two types of Ψ neurons, those connected to
ϕ and those which receive endogenous stimulation. Ψ neurons
are 'the vehicles of memory and so probably of psychical processes in general' (Freud, 1950b, p. 300). By the facilitations and

inhibitions among Ψ neurons and their capacity for memory,
Freud constructs a neuronal 'ego' and attempts to explain
defense in neuro-anatomical terms. He was never satisfied with
his explanation of repression, but the 'Project' ran into an even
bigger problem: consciousness.

> Hitherto, nothing whatever has been said of the fact that
> every psychological theory, apart from what it achieves from
> the point of natural science, must fulfil yet another major
> requirement. It should explain to us what we are aware of,
> in the most puzzling fashion, through our 'consciousness'.
> (p. 307)

Freud argues that consciousness cannot reside in either the φ
or Ψ neurons, and so posits a third type of neuron, ω(omega).
So far Freud has stayed within the natural scientific boundaries
which he set for himself by only dealing with quantitative states
of neurons, but to cope with consciousness he recognizes that he
must consider qualities. He does this by assuming that differences in quality are reflected in the periodic or temporal nature
of stimuli. Φ transmits the period of a stimulus through Ψ to ω.
Neither φ nor Ψ respond to the period; Freud says the Ψ system
has a period, but it is 'monotonous.' Later he will say that the
unconscious is timeless. Ω responds to the temporal dimension of
stimuli and thereby produces an awareness of quality. As the
material representatives of consciousness, ω neurons are permeable and although they respond to increases in the quantitative
cathexes of Ψ neurons, they themselves do not hold a charge;
that is, they are not responsible for memory. The Ψ system does
this. Consciousness is really a very high order perceptual system whose ultimate job in Freud's brain model is to differentiate
between qualitative states and to decide whether the source of
a stimulus is external or internal.

Having introduced consciousness, Freud now rejects the stance
he took in the aphasia book and implied in his initial assumptions
in the 'Project.' He asserts that consciousness is not a dependent
appendage of physiological processes, but in fact affects neuronal
functions. Under the assumption of special consciousness neurons, ω, Freud has managed to introduce into a materialist frame
the notion that human awareness influences bodily states. It is
interesting that even in the language of neurons Freud sees
consciousness as responding to the periodic nature of stimuli;
at base consciousness is a system for recording changes in
stimuli through time. Narrative in its simplest form chronicles
changes in events across time. Kermode (1967) suggests that
when we say that a clock goes 'tick tock,' we are producing a
rudimentary narrative. Both ω and narrative record time-changes,
that is, consciousness functions as a narrative.

Freud immediately employs the ω neurons in explaining our
sensations of pleasure and unpleasure. Here he departs from
the quantitative frame and instead of equating pleasure with a

decrease in the quantitative charge of neurons and unpleasure
with an increase, he says that these quantitative changes are
transmitted from Ψ to ω and thereby we become aware of the
sensations of pleasure and its opposite. Here Freud is substituting the language of quality and sensation - psychological explanation - for the language of quantity - neurological explanation.
He does this because the former is far less cumbersome and
better describes experience. This shifting from quantitative to
qualitative explanation occurs throughout the 'Project' and carries over into all of Freud's later metapsychological works.
Although this marks a failure to stay within the boundaries of
natural science, we should not fault him too greatly for this.
After all, in experience what we are aware of is qualities and
not quantities. To be both parsimonious and true to experience,
then, a qualitative explanation makes more sense. But, a qualitative explanation does not fulfill what Freud set as his goal in
the 'Project:' to represent psychical states quantitatively in
order to make them 'perspicuous and free from contradictions'
(1950b, p. 295). When Freud introduces the ω neurons and tries
to explain consciousness in qualitative terms, he has forsaken
his goal and admits that it 'is only by means of such complicated
and far from perspicuous hypotheses that I have hitherto succeeded in introducing the phenomena of consciousness into the
structure of a quantitative psychology' (p. 311). The project
fails because of the problem of quality, which is ultimately the
problem of accounting for human consciousness in physiological
terms. In trying to explain defense, wish-fulfillment and secondary process, Freud must continually evoke ω processes and
translate the language of quality into that of quantity. Instead
of explaining psychical processes in terms of two fundamental
natural scientific propositions - that there are neurons and
energy is transformed as it flows through them - these basic
assumptions become appendages to phenomenological description.
The 'Project' fails because it does not explain; it is simply a
superstructure of neuroanatomy attached by clever translation
techniques to Freud's clinical observations. Freud slips easily
from qualitative descriptive accounts of states of consciousness
- pleasure-unpleasure, discriminations between hallucination and
reality, and experiences of pain and satisfaction - to quantitative, materialist energetics.

The 'Project' marked Freud's final attempt to frame his thoughts
within the restraints imposed upon him by the natural scientific
assumptions of his teachers. As one proceeds through it, as we
have seen, the quantitative and neuronal assumptions recede
into the background, providing a restrictive, but familiar,
language in which Freud tried to conceptualize his new discoveries; the '"Project" stands as the greatest effort Freud ever made
to force a mass of psychical facts within the framework of a
quantitative theory, and as the demonstration by way of the
absurd that the content exceeds the frame' (Ricoeur, 1970,
p. 73). It 'represents what could be called a nonhermeneutic

state of the system' (p. 69). That is the 'Project's' goal is not
to increase interpretive understanding of human experience, but
to reduce experience to neuro-mechanics.

At the end of the 'Project' there is a good example of Freud's
difficulties in this work. Freud asks, 'in what do logical faults
consist?' He answers, 'in the non-observance of the biological
rules for the passage of thought.' He then launches into a mixed
discourse, slipping easily from qualitative to quantitative terms
in describing neural functioning. He concludes the *existence of
biological rules of this kind can in fact be proved from the feeling of unpleasure at logical faults* (p. 386).' The tautology is
obvious. More important, however, is that in this one paragraph
the faults of the 'Project' are obvious. Starting from the observation that people commit errors, Freud then says these errors
occur because certain biological rules have been broken. However, it is not on the basis of any neurological experiments or
observations that we know this; we know it because people feel
bad when they make a logical error. Although this last assumption is itself highly questionable, the point is that the invocation
of biological rules and the machinery of neurological explanation
is superfluous. It adds nothing to the observation that people
feel bad when they make mistakes, and the only validation for
Freud's assertion is observation. In 1895 there was, and even
today there is, no neurological data that could be used to either
verify or falsify Freud's assertion that biological and logical
rules can be equated. Of course, science supporters, like fans
everywhere, say 'wait until next year.'

Freud could not wait. The 'Project' failed to explain experience
because neurons do not tell us very much about our lives; Freud
needed a system with which to organize his clinical observations
and bring order to his own life. After the regression to neurophysiological explanation in the 'Project,' Freud returned to the
radical approach that he first fully used in 'Studies.' The foundation for his future work was formed in 'Studies,' for in it, as
we have seen, he ordered his clinical observations by writing
psychological short stories and constructed his psychological
theory as an abstract system which captured the dynamics of
these stories.

At the base of psychoanalysis are clinical observations,
interpretations, and generalizations (Waelder, 1962). At the next
level is psychological theory followed at still a higher level of
abstraction by metapsychology. Within the narrative of a case
study, Freud presents what happened (clinical observation),
why it happened (interpretation), and what it means (generalization). Psychological theory then makes explicit the system which
Freud has used to order cases: it is a statement of the principles
he has used in constructing life histories. In 'Studies' Freud
remains on clinical and psychological ground and rarely enters
into metapsychological speculation. The 'Project,' with its biological formulations about psychical phenomena, was Freud's first
metapsychological work; there were to be many more. Meta-

psychology is, however, not the foundation of psychoanalysis.
It is nearly at the top of the edifice.

TRAVELING BACKWARD TO CHILDHOOD SEDUCTION

The principal psychological theory which Freud used to order his
clinical material in the 1890s was the seduction theory. It was
Freud's first attempt at discovering the origins of the psychoneuroses, his first try at creating a beginning for the dramatic
stories of neurotics. Prior to the seduction theory, Freud saw
the cause of hysteria and obsessions as a psychological lesion.
This evolved into the notion of the 'traumatic moment;' that point
in time when a dissociation first occurred (1894, p. 50). Any
incident which recalls the first moment exacerbates the neurosis.
When Freud introduced the notion of the traumatic moment, his
case studies became dynamic narratives for he ordered the
material according to the life movements that had led up to and
followed from this point of crisis. The 1896 seduction theory
papers transformed the traumatic moment into a scene: a prepubertal incident of actual seduction which, although it has no
effect prior to puberty, comes to be the post-pubertal cause of
neurotic suffering. The trauma has a delayed effect and is in
fact not traumatic until adolescent sexual understanding makes
the meaning of the childhood experience obvious. Post-pubertal
sexual experiences, even if quite mild, reactivate the earlier
scene. The original scene and the adolescent or adult moment
are both defended against by dissociating them from consciousness. In their place a memory marker, some innocuous symbol
or event, comes to stand for all that is lost. Hysterical symptoms
are also bodily signifiers for the lost events.

Of course, as we have seen, hysterics and obsessives never
did spontaneously tell Freud that they were seduced as children.
He constructed seduction scenes by interpreting memory fragments and the significance of symptoms. He needed a beginning
for his stories, and psychoanalytic interpretation made it possible for him to construct what he thought were the origins of
neuroses in past real-life events.

In the same paragraph in which Freud christens his work
'psychoanalysis,' he tells his readers the course which all his
future work will follow: 'Travelling backwards into the patient's
past, step by step, and guided by...symptoms...memories and
thoughts aroused, I finally reached the starting-point of the
pathological process' (1896a, p. 151). In the individual case, at
the microcosmic level, Freud pushed backward from present adult
experience to the past of childhood in search of the origins of
psychopathology; at the macrocosmic level, in speaking of human
nature, Freud was to push backward from the present - modern
day, to the past - the early history of humanity, in search of
the origins of human discontent. In this essay the origin of the
patient's problem was found in seduction. Freud continually

rewrote the beginning of the history of human difficulties and
the movement of his revisions was always retrolinear; the origin
of suffering was progressively moved further into the past.

Seduction stories turned out to be fictions and were replaced
by the fiction of the Oedipal drama. Freud in abandoning the
seduction theory wrote to Fliess 'there are no indications of
reality in the unconscious, so that one cannot distinguish between
the truth and fiction that is cathected with affect. (Thus, the
possibility remained open that sexual phantasy invariably seizes
upon the theme of the parents)' (1950a, p. 260). The Oedipal
drama is an inversion of the seduction story transposing agent
and object: in seduction the agent is the adult and the object
is the child; in Oedipal fantasies the roles are reversed. In addition to this transposition there is the recognition that the cause
of neurotic suffering need not lie in a real event, but can be
found in an individual's living as though a fantasy were a reality.
Freud, however, was not satisfied with putting to one side the
question of reality; he was searching for the empirical, verifiable origins of life's problems. He sought the real story, even if
it lay in fantasy. Within a month of stating that one cannot
distinguish between truth and fiction in the unconscious he
proclaimed that, 'I have found in my case too, falling in love
with the mother and jealousy of the father' (p. 265). Freud is
speaking of the reality of emotions. Boys really do love their
mothers and hate their fathers. The power of the tragedy of
'King Oedipus' is that this play transforms the childhood wishes
of every male into a dramatic reality. As the result of his self-
analysis Freud found that he was living out just such a dream
in his adult fantasies.

A fiction, the Oedipus myth, came to order the reality of
experience for Freud himself, and he used it in turn to order
both his patients' stories and mankind's history. Over the next
forty years it became increasingly important as an explanatory
concept in psychoanalysis. It was seen as a theme of certain
typical dreams in 1900, used to order elements of the Dora case
(1905 [1901]), and invoked as the most prevalent theme in childhood sexual fantasies in 'Three Essays' (1905). The Oedipal
drama was retold in the case of 'Little Hans' (1909a), where Freud
traced the origin of a horse phobia to a five-year-old boy's love
for his mother and fear of his father. In 'Totem and Taboo'
(1913) it was found to be a central factor in the origins of religion. After 1913 the Oedipus complex assumed mythic proportions
as an explanatory principle in psychoanalytic narratives; it was
used to order a substantial portion of each individual's life and
mankind's collective history.

The seduction theory united both mind and body in explaining
the origins of psychoneuroses. The body was involved because
the child's genitals were manipulated; the mind because the childhood experience became traumatic when adult experiences resurrected the memory of the event, and the adult retrospectively
reacted with disgust. As the Oedipal narrative took the place of

the seduction theory within the psychical sphere, so the notion of infantile erotic zones came to replace the bodily aspects of childhood seduction. The stimulation of the child's genitals by an adult was transformed into the child's manipulation of, or intense interest in gaining pleasure from, his or her own erotogenic zones. Children became sexual creatures, interested in obtaining bodily sexual pleasure from themselves, other children, and their own mothers and fathers.

The last months of 1897 produced major and lasting changes in Freud's search for the origins of the psychoneuroses. In September he lost faith in the seduction theory; October brought the announcement of the importance of Oedipal fantasies, and November was devoted to articulating the relationship between infantile sexual zones – oral and anal – and the role of repression in the adult's denial of, and yet unconscious regressive longing for, pre-genital pleasure.

Both Oedipal feelings and infantile sexual experiences were, like seduction, denied by adults, because such things were repulsive to mature consciousness. Freud asserted that these things happened, but adults, and especially neurotics, were amnesic about them because socialization, and perhaps organic factors, produce disgust for these early memories. Dreams were residues of, psychoneuroses had their origins in, and the unconscious was formed from 'the prehistoric period of life (between the ages of one and three)' which in later years cannot be remembered (Freud, 1950a, p. 274). Psychoanalysis became an interpretative science for filling in the 'whole lost story of...childhood' (p. 275); it became a system of constructing historical narratives which, like all histories, order events retrospectively and turn the prehistoric, the unnarrativized, into a story that has been told.

The lost story was constructed using all the missing pieces from a life. Adults were amnesic for portions of their lives, because early experiences had been repressively denied. Freud proposed to put lives which had become puzzling in order by constructing missing pieces of the puzzle. He interpreted the dreams, symptoms, and stories of his patients in order to replace a tale rife with amnesic gaps – 'I don't remember'; 'No, it couldn't have happened' – with a narrative that brought coherence and continuity to experience. In 1899 he wrote to Fliess about a patient who had been cured by Freud's unearthing a scene from the patient's prehistoric period which explained many later problems 'and into which all the surviving puzzles flow' (1954, p. 305). Freud remained quite fond of seeing psychoanalysis as a technique for solving puzzles, and we will see that in the case of Wolf Man (1918 [1914]) – written in part as an empirical refutation of Jung's work – he was again to find (or, as I will argue, construct) a prehistoric infantile scene which resolved all the puzzling aspects of the case.

The unconscious became for Freud a vast storehouse of untold tales; the place where lost stories were to be found. Following

Crites (1971) we can say that consciousness, being temporal,
is inherently narrative. As humans we are capable of having a
history and that history orders our lives chronologically, placing experience within a narrative frame. The unconscious is not
conscious; it is that which is not yet part of the narrative we
consciously avow as our life history. As sentient beings we
order experience in terms of past, present, and future. That
which is outside of time is outside of conscious existence; it is
in the timeless realm of the unconscious, unchanged because it
has not been experienced consciously and thereby ordered within
the unfolding story of one's life.

In 'The Interpretation of Dreams' Freud, for the first time,
articulated a model of the psyche which set forth his ideas on the
unconscious. He said 'it is a prominent feature of unconscious
processes that they are indestructible. In the unconscious
nothing can be brought to an end, nothing is past or forgotten'
(p. 557). The unconscious is continually in the present and,
therefore, timeless. A humiliation suffered thirty years ago, if
repressed into the unconscious, can, as soon as it is touched by
some current experience, re-emerge as a new trauma untouched
by time's dulling of its emotional sting. The task of psychotherapy is 'to make it possible for the unconscious processes to
be dealt with finally and be forgotten' (p. 577). First, we must
know what those unconscious processes are. We cannot forget
what we never know. Defense severs unpleasant experiences
from consciousness, and so these experiences are never modified
by the passage of time which marks the progress of our conscious
lives. If an experience is conscious, it can have an ending
because it is incorporated into the narrative of awareness. Stories come to an end, and as time passes experiences are forgotten.
Repressed experiences are not forgotten, because they are dissociated from memory and thereby saved from the natural erosion
that wears away our recollections of the distant past. Psychoanalytic therapy attempts to make the unconscious preconscious,
that is, bring what has remained encysted outside of experience
into the sphere from which it can be volitionally recalled. In
this way 'the fading of memories and the emotional weakness of
impressions which are no longer recent' can be produced by
'the effect of time upon mental memory-traces' (Freud, 1900,
p. 578).

'DIE TRAUMDEUTUNG': NARRATIVE AND INTERPRETATION

In 'The Interpretation of Dreams' Freud's concern was in showing how dreams, when interpreted, express wishes which, before
the process of interpretation, had been unconscious. He also
set forth a model of the psyche which was to explain the dynamics
of dream-formation. In this basic work of psychoanalysis Freud
proposed an interpretative science formulated in two overlapping
narratives: one - the experiential narrative - was concerned

with incorporating dreams into an individual's life story; and the
second - the psychic narrative - was concerned with the construction of a narrative model of the mind. The psychic apparatus was an abstraction from and theoretical justification for the
experiential narrative.

The recounting of experience begins with the dream one remem-
bers by retelling it either to oneself or another or by writing it
down. This is the manifest dream. It often contains gaps and
obscurities; it is an incomplete story. In order to amplify the
dream one systematically associates to each element of it. The
success of psychoanalysis depends on the client's 'noticing and
reporting whatever comes into his head and not being misled,
for instance, into suppressing an idea because it strikes him as
unimportant or irrelevant or because it seems meaningless'
(Freud, 1900, p. 101). This was christened the fundamental rule
of psychoanalysis in 1912, and it remained the foundation of
Freud's treatment method. Clients, of course, had difficulty in
adhering to the rule, because as painful, infantile, and consciously inadmissible thoughts and emotions occur to them they
will resist either acknowledging or communicating these ideas
and affects to the analyst.

Associations arise when conscious criticism has been suspended.
They are the thoughts which we usually ignore, involuntary
thoughts which have been transformed by the technique of free
association into voluntary ones. Freud calls these associational
ideas, images, and emotions the dream-thoughts and says that
although they did not appear in the manifest dream itself they
were determinants of the dream content.

Once the manifest dream is told and associations to its elements
are given, interpretation begins. Interpretation is central to all
of psychoanalysis; Laplanche and Pontalis emphasize that 'Interpretation is at the heart of the Freudian doctrine and technique.
Psychoanalysis itself might be defined in terms of it, as the
bringing out of the latent meaning of given material' (1973,
p. 222). Freud begins with the reported dream, the manifest
dream, obtains free associations to it and formulates an interpretation which he calls the latent dream. He asserts that both the
associations and the latent dream were determinants of the manifest dream and says the task of dream-interpretation is 'investigating the relations between the manifest content of dreams and
the latent dream-thoughts, and of tracing out the processes by
which the latter have been changed into the former' (1900,
p. 277). Comparing the interpretation of dreams to translation,
Freud says, 'the [manifest] dream-content seems like a trans-
cript of the [latent] dream-thoughts into another mode of expression, whose characters and syntactic laws it is our business to
discover by comparing the original [latent dream-thoughts] and
the translation [manifest dream-content]' (p. 277). Freud
immediately illustrates this distinction between manifest and
latent with an analogy to a rebus: the rebus is a pictographic
distortion of some original phrase, just as the manifest dream-

content is a systematic distortion of the original latent dream-thoughts. A phrase is translated and distorted into a puzzling picture by the rebus-maker and the latent dream-thoughts are translated and distorted by the dream-work into the manifest content.

The rebus analogy beautifully illustrates Freud's causal model of dream-formation; latent dream-thoughts modified by the dream-work determine the content of the manifest dream. This is, of course, consonant with the Breuer-Freud model of hysteria on which, Freud says, his technique for interpreting dreams is based: traumatic experiences distorted by defense are transformed into symptoms. In fact, it is the causal paradigm of Freud's thought: the prior distorted by defense is transformed into the current. Latent dream-thoughts, infantile sexuality, primary process, primary narcissism, and the unconscious are each transformed by censorship into elements of manifest thought and behavior - that is, respectively, manifest dream content, adult sexuality, secondary process, secondary narcissism, and the preconscious-conscious.

The rebus analogy unfortunately leads us astray, but in doing so it focuses our attention on an important misunderstanding of Freud's thought; a misunderstanding held by Freud, his followers, and many of his critics. In solving the rebus we can check our solution against the original phrase, but, and this is where Freud's analogy misdirects us, there is no text independent of interpretation to which we can compare our dream-solution. The original text of the dream, the latent dream, exists solely as a product of interpretation - psychoanalytic translation - performed on the reported manifest material and associations to it.

The interpretation of the manifest content leads Freud to the supposedly original latent dream-thoughts, and Freud equates the interpreted dream with the original, latent dream. Within Freud's causal scientific scheme the original, latent dream has undergone modification and distortion at the hands of the dream work and has emerged as the translated manifest dream. It would be more true to the chronology of events and illuminate the experiential narrative that Freud is producing to emphasize what Freud really does: there is a manifest dream and associations to it which he interprets. The dream-interpretation occurs after the manifest dream report. However, Freud maintains that the interpreted dream is identical to the latent dream which supposedly occurred prior to, and was a cause of, the manifest dream. The match between the interpreted dream and some antecedent original dream, Freud's latent dream, is uncertain. There is a confusion between an actual meaningful narrative explanation - the dream-interpretation which makes sense out of the manifest dream and connects it to the dreamer's life - and a hypothetical original event, the latent dream, which is treated as a causal determinant of the manifest dream. If one follows what Freud does and is not distracted by his own misunderstand-

ing of his work, it is obvious that dream-interpretation is a form
of historical explanation and not scientific analysis. His causes
are narrative, not scientific. Standing within the frame of the
present, using the manifest dream and associations to it, he
produces an account of what must have been in order to cause
what is. This account is historical, because it is retrospective;
psychoanalysis looks back from the present to the past, producing a story, articulated in causal terms, which explains present
experience. The causality is narrative; it is a string of thoughts,
events, emotions, and actions connected in an ordered sequence.
It is not scientific, however, because the cause can never be
manipulated in order to produce the effect. The power of natural
science lies in prediction, in forecasting that when X is done
then Y will follow. History and psychoanalysis are not predictive.
Their power resides in producing a story which helps us to
understand who we are by ordering and supplementing our knowledge of who we were. Both psychoanalysis and history infer
causes from effects; unlike natural science, they lack the control of events which makes possible the manipulation of causes to
produce effects.

The historical nature of Freud's inquiry into dreams is vividly
illustrated in the unfolding of 'The Interpretation of Dreams.'
The movement in the book is that retrolinear movement characteristic of all psychoanalytic investigation; it is a movement from
the present to the past. In the book 'our forward movement is
always retrospective' (Schwaber, 1976, p. 529). As psychoanalysis moves forward by increasing the client's understanding
of his or her past, so the dream book moves forward by Freud's
progressively uncovering the sources of his dreams as lying
farther and farther back in his childhood. A movement forward
in self-understanding necessarily involves a reordering of one's
understanding of the past.

The transformation of Freud's fundamental hypothesis from the
beginning to the end of the book nicely illustrates this movement
from present to past. An early statement of the hypothesis
couches it in contemporary terms: *'When the work of interpretation has been completed, we perceive that a dream is the fulfillment of a wish'* (1900, p. 121). The hypothesis has been radically
transformed in its final statement: 'Our theory of dreams regards
wishes originating in infancy as the indispensable motive force
for the formation of dreams' (p. 589). The first statement is in
accord with the chronological unfolding of Freud's method. After
a dream is interpreted, then we understand it as the fulfillment
of a wish; interpretation causes a change in our perceptions.
This clearly situates Freud's work as hermeneutic, as a job of
reaching understanding, of explicating what is given in order to
put it into the context of the analysand's life. Dreams, like other
activities, satisfy our desires.

The modification of this common-sense hypothesis clearly
demonstrates Freud's transformation of a meaningful interpretation into a causal sequence: infantile wishes are the motive force

for or necessary cause of dream-formation. Freud here makes
explicit what has been implicit in the notion of the hypothetical
original event, the latent dream; that is, a movement or regression from adulthood back to childhood. 'The deeper one carries
the analysis of a dream, the more often one comes upon the
track of experiences in childhood which have played a part
among the sources of that dream's latent content' (p. 198). But,
childhood scenes are not explicit in the manifest dream; they are
produced by an interpretative act: 'It is true that as a rule the
childhood scene is only represented in the dream's manifest content by an allusion, and has to be arrived at by an interpretation of the dream' (p. 199). One must question what the analysis
reveals and what it supplies. Can one prove that the childhood
scene was actually a causal factor in the formation of the dream,
or must one accept the empirical evidence that the childhood
scene came to mind as a result of associations to the dream and
was crystalized as meaningfully related to the dream by the process of interpretation? Freud confronts this question most clearly
and directly in an analysis of one of his own dreams - the
'Botanical Monograph': 'It may perhaps be doubted whether this
[childhood] memory really had any share in determining the form
taken by the content of the dream or whether it was not rather
that the process of analysis [interpretation] built up the connection subsequently' (p. 191). To answer the question in favor
of the former one would first have to determine whether or not
the recollected childhood scene ever occurred. Needless to say,
none of us have documents of our childhoods which would provide conclusive historical evidence. In fact, it is difficult to think
of any workable criteria for deciding in favor of the first alternative, yet Freud holds that 'the copious and intertwined associative links warrant our accepting the former alternative'
(p. 191). But remember that the associations were supplied in
response to the manifest dream and play a significant role in the
interpretation of that dream. It is hard to believe that Freud
himself was convinced; after all, he has just asserted that something which is a response - an association - is a causal and prior
agent. In no way do associations show that the childhood scene
is a cause of the manifest dream. The scenes arise as a result of
associations and interpretation which come after the reported
dream. Treating them as causes is equivalent to transforming
a response into a cause. It is to treat *post hoc* explanation as
scientific causal analysis. It is to confuse history with natural
science. Possibly sensing that he has not proved his point, Freud
adds: 'Moreover I can assure my readers that the ultimate meaning of the dream, which I have not disclosed, is intimately related
to the subject of the childhood scene' (p. 191). This statement
leaves the reader in doubt and passes beyond the bounds of
acceptable evidence.

   Freeing Freud's work on dreams from his assumed, but clearly
undemonstrated, scientific causal paradigm allows us to see more
clearly what he accomplished. At its core the dream book has two

interrelated causal sequences; simplified they are:
(1) latent dream —→ dream-work —→ manifest dream
(2) primary process —→ preconscious censorship —→ secondary
                                                  process.
Based on the previous argument and more detailed work by
Steele and Jacobsen (1978), Jacobsen and Steele (1979), and
Steele (1979), it is obvious that Freud does not uncover causes,
but instead supplies interpretations. Given this view, which
synchronizes the chronology of psychoanalytic psychotherapy
with an exposition of Freud's findings, the causal sequence can
be transformed into a diagram of the movement of Freud's
thought on two narrative planes:
(1) manifest dream —→ interpretation —→ historical experiential
                                                  narrative
(2) secondary process —→ interpretation —→ unconscious psychic
                                                  primary process.
    According to Freud, the dream-work transforms the latent
dream thoughts and residues from the previous day into the
manifest dream. Conscious wishes or problems from the past
twenty-four hours - the daily residue - can only succeed in insti-
gating a dream if they arouse an unconcious wish and thereby
receive reinforcement from it. The motive force for the dream,
the wish which is represented, *'must be an infantile one'* (Freud,
1900, p. 553). The result of the dream-work, according to
Freud, is distortion of the dream-thoughts so that infantile
wishes in them are not evident to whatever consciousness is
retained during sleep. The censorship takes place on the border
between the unconscious and the preconscious. Dreams seem
strange because the normal censorship of waking consciousness
is diminished and so unconscious wishes attached to daily residues break through, but these dream-thoughts are modified
and disguised by the remaining power of the censor.
    Freud (1923b) insists that neither the manifest content nor
latent dream-thoughts are the essence of the dream; dreams are
essentially the work they carry out. Dreams are best differentiated from other modes of thought by the dream-work whose four
mechanisms are: condensation, displacement, considerations of
representability, and secondary revision. Instead of treating
these four processes as the tools of the dream-work, let us view
them in the way in which Freud used them, as principles for
interpreting the manifest dream. Freud felt that condensation
and displacement were the two most important aspects of the
dream-work. Associations to the elements of the manifest dream
expand condensed images and relocate displaced emphasis. Condensation expresses the idea that within a single dream-image
many associations may converge. For Freud over-determination
is the work of condensation; a single image results from a combination of several latent dream-thoughts. Over-determination
speaks of multiple causality and is perhaps more easily understood within the framework of interpretation; an image may give
rise to many lines of association all of which clarify the meaning

of that image within an individual's life. One technique we use
to make any story clearer is to expand elements of the narrative,
and the work of dream-interpretation lies in enlarging that which
is unclear because it is so condensed. A second technique for
bringing clarity to a story is aimed at dealing with displacement
by supplying missing elements or changing the emphasis of the
story. At base, the two operations are the same, for leaving an
important element out is simply an exaggeration of failing to give
it the proper emphasis. By expanding the dream, free association produces images and themes not originally manifest. Associations to even minor elements of the dream may be quite elaborate and very emotional. Interpretation aims at highlighting
the differences in content and emotional tone between the manifest dream and free association, thereby bringing into relief
displacements of emphasis.

Considerations of representability and secondary revision
supplement condensation and displacement. When interpreting
a dream, we must consider what distortions arise when thought
is represented primarily in visual images. Interpretation translates these pictures into a verbal narrative. With the notion of
secondary revision, Freud explicitly recognized that in their
dreaming and their telling we attempt to make dreams into relatively consistent and comprehensible scenarios. Interpretation
points out where such scenarios are artificially joined together
and attempts to replace confused or too sudden transitions by
a more elaborate and sensible linkage.[2]

Using free association and the translation rules provided by
his notions of condensation, displacement, considerations of
representability, and secondary revision, Freud was able to
transform the distorted narratives of manifest dreams into the
more coherent and meaningful narratives of interpreted dreams.
When interpreted a dream makes more sense; it is brought into
connection with the analysand's ongoing life and helps to fill in a
life history which has been lost. Dreams provide a vehicle with
which to construct stories that have never been told. We interpret dreams in order to make sense of them, as we interpret all
of life's experiences in order to assimilate them into the unfolding narrative of our retrospectively constructed life histories.

The approach to Freud's work on dream-interpretation presented
here has attempted to outline what Freud did. We have recognized and highlighted his method: he began with the manifest
dream, obtained associations to it and from these associations -
guided by his translation rules (condensation, displacement,
etc.) - produced an interpreted dream. This interpreted dream
made sense out of the manifest dream and articulated with the
analysand's life. Dominated by the principles of nineteenth-
century natural science, he recast his interpretative methodology
into a theoretical system that was causal and mechanistic by
transforming origins into results and results into origins. He
began with the manifest dream, but labeled it an effect. He
obtained associations to this dream, but called these associations

determinants of it. Interpreting these associations, but labeling this interpretation an unraveling of a prior dream-work, he constructed the latent dream. This end point of his work was labeled a cause and seen as the origin of the manifest dream.

An aspect of this transmogrification from interpretation to natural science is clearly exemplified in the last chapter of 'The Interpretation of Dreams.' In introducing his goals for chapter 7, Freud says that in previous chapters, 'the problems of dream-interpretation have hitherto occupied the centre of the picture' and that this has led to an elucidation and fuller under-standing of dreams (p. 510). However, we are no longer going to be hermeneuts practicing the art of interpretation in order to produce a coherent experiential narrative: we are to become speculative mechanical engineers, setting up 'a number of fresh hypotheses which touch tentatively upon the structure of the apparatus of the mind and upon the play of forces operating in it' (p. 511). 'The Psychology of the Dream-Processes,' chapter 7, is the son of the 'Project' and the father of all future meta-psychology. Like the brain machine in the 'Project,' the psychic apparatus will be a mechanoenergic system and, like all meta-psychology that follows it, it is built far above the foundation of observation. These ideas come last in the dream book; they are the top of the structure, an edifice of speculation which will undergo constant revision in psychoanalytic theorizing. The psychic apparatus is a theoretical fiction abstracted from obser-vation and used by Freud to justify his system of dream-inter-pretation by demonstrating that it articulates with a model of the mind.

Taking a radical step, and totally overthrowing his goals in the 'Project,' Freud announces:

> I shall entirely disregard the fact that the mental apparatus with which we are here concerned is also known to us in the form of an anatomical preparation, and I shall carefully avoid the temptation to determine psychical locality in any anato-mical fashion. I shall remain upon psychological ground.
> (p. 536)

Just four pages later Freud mentions neurons, and they appear often enough in the text to remind us that the psychic apparatus is somehow related to the brain. Neurology, however, has been replaced by psychology: the neurons of the 'Project' become memory traces in chapter 7, Q (quantity) becomes psychic energy, and neuronal pathways are transformed into associative links among mnemic images.

The walking tour through dreamland, as Freud envisioned the step by step journey of leading his readers through the dream book, culminates in chapter 7's topographic model – a map of the mind. His decision to stay on psychological ground liberated his thought from the anatomical confines of his education and freed his language so that it became 'a *workshop for making maps*'

(Radnitzky, 1973, p. 40).

The psychic apparatus is structured as a narrative. Freud says it would be sufficient for the purposes of building this model 'if a fixed order were established by the fact that in a given psychical process the excitation passes through the systems in a particular *temporal* sequence' (1900, p. 537). He chooses to make his model a bit more elaborate by constructing a spatial order for the systems or agencies. They are areas standing in relationship to one another through which psychical impulses must pass in an orderly fashion. The order is equivalent to that postulated for the impulses in dreams, because Freud's psychic narrative necessarily parallels the developmental scenario of the dream.

In the psychical apparatus, the progressive function is from perception to motor activity passing through memory:

perception $\longrightarrow$ mnemic images $\longrightarrow$ motor.

Freud inserts an unconscious (Ucs.) followed by a preconscious (Pcs.) between the mnemic images and the motor end:

perception $\longrightarrow$ mnemic images $\longrightarrow$ Ucs. $\longrightarrow$ Pcs. $\longrightarrow$ motor.

In normal functioning, stimuli originate either exogenously, coming in through perception, or endogenously in the unconscious or mnemic images. An external stimulus may enter perception and move directly to the preconscious or may arouse previous memories or the unconscious and thereby be channeled through these systems before reaching the motor end. However, for both exogenous and endogenous stimuli, movement is progressively towards the motor end.

During sleep, however, release through motor activity is blocked and so any psychical excitation will move backwards, regressively, toward the perceptual end. This is the reason the apparatus was called into being, to explain the hallucinatory character of dreams. In this backward movement Freud identifies another type of regression in which thoughts are transformed into visual images. There is a third dimension to regression; it arouses infantile scenes which become modified in dreams by being transferred on to recent experiences. The setting of the dream is the present, but regression ensures that the motive force for the dream is an infantile one.

The notion of regression is vital for Freud. First, it serves to explain the dissolution of thoughts into images (formal regression). Second, it provides a transport mechanism, explaining the movement from the adult present to reconstructed infantile scenes from the past (temporal regression). Third, intrapsychically, the reversal of the flow of psychic energy from the motor to the perceptual end (topographical regression) provides an explanation of the previous two. Freud notes that the three types of regression are 'one at bottom and occur together as a rule; for what is older in time is more primitive in form and in psychical topography lies nearer to the perceptual end' (p. 548). The manifest dream is in pictorial form and contains hidden within it infantile scenes, because during sleep the whole flow of the psychic apparatus is reversed. The manifest dream is distorted, because on the border between the unconscious and preconscious there is a censorship, an agency through which unconscious material must pass. Infantile wishes have been repressed, because they are too painful, obscene, and unacceptable to be allowed into our preconscious awareness even while we sleep. If such wishes, or even terribly troublesome thoughts from the previous day, break through they have the power to awaken us. *'Dreams are the GUARDIANS of sleep and not its disturbers'* (p. 233). The dream-work manages to distort and muddle disturbing memories enough to allow us to remain asleep. The manifest dream, then, must truly be the resultant of the distortion of latent dream-thoughts by the censorship. Is our previous questioning of Freud's notion that infantile impulses are the motivational fuel for the formation of dreams mistaken? No! Freud is simply a fine builder of interlocking narrative systems. Remember the psychic apparatus is built upon his notions of dream-formation; it does not provide evidence that dreams must unfold in the way which Freud maintains.

This contention can best be illustrated if we go to the core of the functioning of this mental model. There are two systems of thought which in the apparatus correspond to the differences between the unconscious and preconscious; these are the primary and secondary process. Freud's problematic assumption that an interpreted event is the same as some original event - that the interpreted dream is the latent dream - is also present in his formulation that the primary psychical process precedes the secondary.

Freud observed that the adult's normal rational relations to the world degenerated into irrationality in dreams and mental illness. The differentiation between secondary and primary processes was developed by him to explain such aberrations. Why do we hallucinate in dreams and why do neurotics seem to be at odds with reality? These questions were answered by Freud in terms of his model of the psychic apparatus and in the mechanoenergic language of that machine.

The 'irrational' primary process occurs in the unconscious where psychical energy flows freely and cathexes, bonds between ideas, are easily formed and broken. In both dreams and psychopathology thoughts are subjected to an abnormal treatment, because functioning follows the primary process. Displacement and condensation are good examples of this type of operation. Unconscious primary process functioning is under the domination of the pleasure principle; it is oriented towards seeking pleasure and avoiding unpleasure. By utilizing free mobile cathexes and totally disregarding reality, the unconscious gains immediate pleasure through hallucinatory wish-fulfillments. A wish, an unfulfilled desire, an endogenous instinctual need, creates a state of tension in the psychical apparatus, but while we are asleep, motor discharge, which would gratify such impulses by locating the needed object, is blocked. Perceptions of satisfying

objects which are not present are reactivated by the primary
process of topographical regression producing a hallucinatory
satisfaction of desire. The flow of energy associated with the
mnemic image of fulfillment moves backward in the apparatus,
away from the motor, toward the perceptual end, thereby producing a hallucination that the object fulfilling desire is present.
Operating by the principle of neuronal inertia, the unconscious
works like a simple reflex apparatus to reduce all tension to zero
and produce pleasure by the shortest possible path. In dreams
this road is a regressive one to hallucination.

In a waking state, in normal functioning, the situation is different. The ego which binds energy operates by the constancy
principle. Energy is reduced to the lowest possible level once
motor discharge has taken place, but never to zero. Sufficient
energy is always maintained so that the preconscious ego can
conduct reality-testing. Operating under the reality principle the
preconscious postpones energy discharge into motor activity until
it has been ascertained that a real object which will reduce tension and produce pleasure is present.

The ego, in both sleep and neurosis, has relinquished some of
its power to check the primary process functioning of the unconscious, and so the secondary process and reality-testing are
partially overthrown. The primary process comes into ascendency
giving images and memories all the power of perceptions from
the external world. Only through the operation of dream-censor-
ship or belated neurotic defense does the weakened ego reassert
any control over the primary process.

Why has Freud labeled normal basic adult mental functioning
the secondary process and deviations from it the primary process? He assumes that the primary process, which he has built
based on his understanding of dreams and psychopathology, is
actually the mode by which infants relate to the world: 'When I
described one of the psychical processes occurring in the mental
apparatus as the "primary" one, what I had in mind was not
merely considerations of relative importance and efficiency; I
intended also to choose a name which would give an indication of
its chronological priority' (Freud, 1900, p. 603). Here again is
the central problematic assumption in Freud's methodology. A
theoretical interpretation, primary process functioning in dreams
and neuroses, is taken as an actual original occurrence; infants'
psyches operate by primary process. Actually, the primary process is a metaphoric mechanoenergic representation of operations
supposedly underlying the formation of the reported phenomena
of dreams and symptom formations. The original event of the
infantile primary process is a completely theoretical construction,
a high-level speculative metapsychological postulate. Clinically,
Freud observed that secondary process reality-testing was transformed into primary process hallucinations. Secondary preceded
primary; however, in his theoretical formulation the order is
reversed. Theoretically there is an infantile hallucinatory relation
to the world, the primary process, which evolves developmentally

into secondary process. In this formulation Freud ignores the
order of his observations.

Freud's prototype for the primary process is dream life and
the assertion that interpreted - latent - dreams are hallucinatory
wish-fulfillments: 'It is precisely from this that I am inclined to
infer *that primary wishful cathexis, too,* was of a hallucinatory
nature' (Freud, 1950b, p. 340). Freud did not observe infants,
but adults, yet using his regression formula - what is older in
time is more primitive in form and topographically lies nearer
to the perceptual end - he transported his views on a breakdown
in normal adult mental functioning back to the past and located
their origin in a hypothetical infantile state.

What proof does Freud have that in the first months of life
wishes are satisfied by hallucination? Since he did not do empirical work with infants he obviously has no observational evidence.
Laplanche correctly sees that Freud's proof of this 'is the existence of dreams, the model of the primary process, in which the
activation of ideas is accompanied by a feeling of utter reality'
(1976, p. 61). What kind of proof is this? The positing of the
infantile primary process is part of Freud's developmental explanation of mental functioning constructed to explain the occurrence
of dreams. To use the hallucinatory vividness of dreams to prove
the existence of infantile primary process, when infantile primary
process is used to explain the hallucinatory vividness of dreams,
is circular. Yet this is precisely what Freud does.

Freud has moved his theory of symptom and dream formation
back into infantile mental life where it is an unverified, and
perhaps unverifiable, hypothesis. He has equated unconscious
mental processes with infantile psychic experience; the unconscious is a primitive mental structure and so, Freud reasons,
belongs to a primitive stage of mental life, infancy. The sequence
primary-to-secondary is a parallel narrative to the chronological
unfolding that Freud hypothesized for dreams cast in the language of the psychic apparatus. Both narratives are constructed
by moving from the present to the past and then treating this
past of hypothetical events - primary process, latent dreams,
infantile mental life - as actual origins which are transformed
into present functioning. It requires no small amount of analysis
to uncover this, because Freud would rather have the actual
derivation of his concepts from the observation of adult mental
functioning forgotten and their new origin in hypothetical infantile mental processes remembered and treated as fact.

Fact or fiction? Is the primary process a theoretical fiction for
Freud or is it an actual psychic function which is developmentally
prior to all others? Freud vacillates on the factual versus fictional
status of this concept; his uncertainty is captured in a passage
from the dream book where he treats it first as a fiction, then a
fact:

> It is true that, so far as we know, no psychical apparatus
> exists which possesses a primary process only and that such

an apparatus is to that extent a theoretical fiction. But this much is fact: the primary processes are present in the mental apparatus from the first, while it is only during the course of life that the secondary processes unfold, and come to inhibit and overlay the primary ones. (1900, p. 603)

Cut off from the direct observation of our beginnings and unable to communicate either with our phylogenetic ancestors or our own infants, we create fictions to explain our origins. These fictions are always works of creation which give form to chaos. Myths take us back to the origins of the universe showing the 'demiourgos' (artificer, craftsman) forging in some past long ago a world much like the one in which we now live (Crites, 1978). As myths create the past by putting present conditions into a historical context, so Freud's narratives create a past which explains the chaotic lives and dreams of adults. Out of the memories of the past, which have been denied, Freud creates a new past which makes sense of aberrant adult psychic functioning. Neurotics are childish and in dreams we act like children because psychopathic states and oneiric fantasies are resurrections of infantile mental processes. Freud insists, like all good story-tellers, that he is giving us the facts; it is a 'fact' that primary processes exist from the beginnings of life. There is simply no proof of this. Facts are established by making observations within a theoretical framework. Freud observed that dreams are hallucinatory and that when interpreted they fulfill wishes; he observed that, when interpreted, neurotic symptoms fulfilled wishes. He never observed that infants live in a state of hallucination, first because he did not systematically observe infants, and second, because even if he had, he could not have ascertained with certainty whether or not they were hallucinating. We may infer that adults are hallucinating by the way they act, but we confirm such inferences by having them describe what they see that we do not see. This avenue of confirmation is blocked with infants and for Freud, whose entire method was founded on talking, this is a formidable obstruction.

The paucity of observations confirming the existence of infantile primary process casts doubt on its status as a fact; additional reservations are created by inconsistencies in Freud's theoretical fiction. Steele and Jacobsen (1978) detail some of these; the most important is that Freud presents formulations contradictory to the possibility that primary process is the infant's initial relation to the world. They have shown that even when Freud introduces the primary process in the 'Project,' he cannot maintain that it is the infant's first relation to the world. To engage in hallucinatory wish-fulfillment, the infant must have present in the mind something to hallucinate, an object that has previously satisfied desire. Freud sees the experience of satisfaction as prior to the operation of primary process and as supplying the needed object. An infant must be fed by a care-taker and form a mnemic image of a satisfying object before entering

the non-object-related state of primary process. To have an
experience of satisfaction, the infant, at the beginning of life,
must be in contact with reality, related to other people (objects),
and must be able to differentiate between internal and external.
These relations characterizing the experience of satisfaction have
much more in common with the secondary process than with the
primary.

In 'Instincts and Their Vicissitudes' (1915) and 'A Metapsychological Supplement to the Theory of Dreams' (1917b) Freud
recognizes that there is some form of reality-testing and object-
awareness in the first days of life. He postulates that preceding
functioning of the pleasure-ego, which operates by the primary
process according to the pleasure principle, there is an original
reality-ego. This first ego uses the 'sound objective criteria' of
muscular action to differentiate between external and internal,
and object and image (Freud, 1915, p. 136). Freud, then,
accepts that some form of reality-testing, secondary process,
must be present before the hallucinatory primary process. In a
later essay, 'Negation' (1925d), Freud reverts to his earlier
model, maintaining that the initial relation to the world is hallucinatory. The original reality-ego is abandoned in favor of the
more elegant, though implausible, idea that the primary process
and the pleasure-ego date from the beginning of life.

Primary process is a fiction about origins describing the supposed hallucinatory chaos of the infant's first days. We have
seen that it is neither supported by observations nor consistently
maintained theoretically. Remember that primary process was
originally developed to account for the disintegration of adult
secondary process which occurred in dreams and symptom formation. This sequence of secondary to primary, which Freud disguises in his work by insisting that the primary precedes the
secondary, has reasserted itself when Freud acknowledges that
the experience of satisfaction and the original reality-ego, two
states which operate by secondary process, constitute the
infant's initial relation to the world.

Primary process was used by Freud as the explanatory psychic
mechanism for latent dream-formation. His work, cast within the
framework of scientific causality, fixates our perception on the
parallel unfolding of a causal psychic sequence - primary pro-
cess $\longrightarrow$ censorship $\longrightarrow$ secondary-process - and a causal dream
sequence - latent dream-thoughts $\longrightarrow$ dream-work $\longrightarrow$ manifest
dream-content. However, scientific causation cannot be estab-
lished retrospectively. One must be able to predict an effect
from a cause. Freud did not do this, and so we must see his work
as providing an historical causality, retrospectively creating
what must have been from what is. That is, Freud presents two
intertwined narratives that are built from interpretation. He
transposes the results of interpretation from the present to the
past to serve as origins for the unfolding of two matched
sequences:

1 a psychic narrative

secondary process $\rightarrow$ interpretation $\rightarrow$ primary process

movement from present to past equates
interpretation with unraveling censorship

movement from present to past transforms
primary process into a cause

2 an experiential narrative

manifest dream $\rightarrow$ interpretation $\rightarrow$ interpreted dream

movement from present to past
equates interpretation with
decoding dream work

movement from present to past
transforms interpreted dream
into the latent dream.

Neither sequence provides evidence validating the other. They
are simply two narratives written in two different registers -
a mechanoenergic and an experiential language.

FROM PRESENT TO PAST: INFANTILE SEXUALITY

In chapter 9 we will see how in response to Jung's criticisms of
psychoanalysis Freud, again working from present to past and
transforming interpreted events into causal agents, developed
the differentiation between primary and secondary narcissism.
More important, for now, this tactic is the central methodological
tool in Freud's major work on infantile sexuality, 'Three Essays
on the Theory of Sexuality.' Before considering this text let us
return to the precursor notion of infantile sexuality, the seduction theory. Freud constructed seduction scenes from the memory
fragments of his patients by moving from reminiscences of the
past recollected in the present to what he felt were actual causal
events in the past. 'Three Essays' significantly modified Freud's
etiological focus; although never fully abandoning the seduction
theory, he came to emphasize constitutional instead of environmental factors in the causation of neurosis. Freud's thought
retained a historical and developmental approach to psychopathology by building a peculiarly psychoanalytic hereditary and
constitutional scheme which still provided an understanding of
the present in terms of the childhood past.
    In 'My Views on the Part Played by Sexuality in the Aetiology
of the Neuroses,' Freud explains how his new theory of infantile
sexuality supplants the old seduction theory. With an endogenous

theory stressing the role of constitutional factors in the unfolding of childhood sexuality, the role of environmental traumas in
creating neuroses, while not eliminated, is clearly secondary;
'"infantile sexual traumas" were in a sense replaced by the
"infantilism of sexuality"' (Freud, 1906a, p. 275).

Following Jacobsen and Steele (1979), let us turn to 'Three
Essays' to examine Freud's method of establishing the existence
of sexuality in infants. If one looks at the format of the text,
the techniques of theory construction with which Freud developed the constitutional theory of infantile sexuality become
apparent. The order of the essays shows that Freud moved from
present to past, deriving infantile sexuality from adult psychopathology. In the first essay, 'The Sexual Aberrations,' Freud
highlights the significance of erotogenic zones – sexually arous-
able areas of the body such as the mouth and anus – in the
different adult perversions and neuroses. The supposed biological constitutional basis of this view is the idea of a sexual
instinct which is initially divided into component instincts. An
area of the body is considered an erotogenic zone when it is
cathected with one of the component sexual instincts. For example, the oral instinct has its source in the mucous membrane of
the oral cavity and its aim is obtaining satisfaction through the
mouth. The different neuroses and perversions indicate con-
stitutions distinguished 'according to the innate preponderance
of one or the other erotogenic zones or of one or the other component instincts' (Freud, 1905b, p. 171). At the conclusion of
the first essay, and foreshadowing the second on 'Infantile
Sexuality,' Freud states, 'A formula begins to take shape which
lays it down that the sexuality of neurotics has remained in,
or been brought back to, an infantile state' (p. 172). In a familiar fashion, Freud has begun by interpreting adult clinical
phenomena, this time in terms of bodily zones. By the last essay
he is assuming that these interpretations are equivalent to
original occurrences, the actual unfolding of infantile sexual life:
'The innumerable peculiarities of the erotic life of human beings
...are quite unintelligible except by reference back to childhood
and as being residual effects of childhood' (p. 229). Freud's goal
is to make sense out of adult sexuality by constructing a childhood sexual past that can be used to explain causally sexual
aberrations in the adult present. This past was built from adult
memory traces, the psychic relics of the infantile prehistoric
age. Using the fragmentary memories of his patients, occluded
by infantile amnesia (a severe loss of memory for the past which
can be circumvented like hysterical amnesia by the psychoanalytic method) and patients' associations, Freud created a
replica of the past by using the interpretative tools of psychoanalysis.

'Three Essays,' and especially the essay 'Infantile Sexuality,'
are a product of psychoanalytic construction:

the beginnings of human sexual life which are here described
can only be confirmed by investigators who have enough
patience and technical skill to trace back an analysis to the
first years of a patient's childhood. (Freud, 'Preface to the
Fourth Edition,' 1920 (1905b, p. 133)

The essays are a historical, not a natural scientific, investigation. They are not the product of the observations of infants or
children; Freud explicitly states: 'If mankind had been able to
learn from a direct observation of children, these three essays
could have remained unwritten' (p. 133). Freud wishes us to see
his theory as disclosing what happened to individuals in their
pasts and psychoanalysis has been traditionally viewed as providing a causal analysis of the present in terms of the past.
Actually, Freud is telling us about what happens to individuals
in memory and how people suffer from reminiscences. Dealing
with memory, Freud's work is historical, for he reconstructs a
view of the past from memories and associations in the present.
The evaluation of a historical theory requires methods different
from the evaluation of a scientific theory, and Freud's fundamental misunderstanding of his work as scientific has led to
investigations which have tried to establish whether or not
infants actually progress through oral and anal stages of development. These studies are interesting, although often questionable on scientific methodological grounds; but strictly speaking,
Freud's work is independent of the results of actual investigation of infants. One might establish that anal difficulties in early
development did not predispose a person to neurosis, thus challenging Freud's scientific causal model. However, this finding
would not invalidate the historical explanation that when the
memories of adult neurotics are interpreted psychoanalytically
they disclose a history of anal problems.

We will return to Freud's method of constructing the past from
the present and then treating this past as a necessary cause of
the present, when in chapter 8 we consider the break between
Freud and Jung. Jung had difficulties in accepting Freud's etiological stress on the importance of infantile sexuality and Freud
could not accept Jung's argument that neurotics recreated out
of their present difficulties a past consonant with their current
suffering.

The important developments in psychoanalytic theory around
the turn of the century have for the most part been reviewed:
Freud's theory of dreams, his model of the psychic apparatus,
his differentiation between primary and secondary process, and
the work on infantile sexuality. In all of this we have stressed
the importance of interpretation and Freud's construction of
overlapping narrative explanations. Dreams when interpreted
disclose infantile wishes, behind secondary process lies primary
process, and adult neurotics' difficulties - when interpreted
psychoanalytically - present a picture of regression to earlier
infantile stages of development. Like the dream theory:

The theory of the psychoneuroses asserts as an indisputable
and invariable fact that only sexual wishful impulses from
infancy, which have undergone repression...during the developmental period of childhood, are capable of being revived
during *later* developmental periods...and are thus able to
furnish the motive force for the formation of psychoneurotic
symptoms of every kind. (Freud, 1900, pp. 605-6)

Behind the manifest dream is the latent infantile wish and behind
neurotic symptoms can be found an infantile sexual desire. In
short, behind the present is the sexual past, a past in which
Freud sees scientific causes of the present, but in which we have
found a retrospective historical narrative, created by psychoanalytic interpretations of memories, that serves to make sense
out of the present.

DORA'S STORY

In 'Dreams and Hysteria,' 'Fragment of an Analysis of a Case of
Hysteria' (1905c, [1901]), Freud brought together the theories
of dreams and neuroses in his first in-depth psychoanalytic case
study. Freud began treating 'Dora' when she was eighteen. He
wrote to Fliess that 'the case has opened smoothly to my collection of picklocks' (1954, p. 325). However, it closed quickly.
After three months Dora terminated the treatment, and Freud,
unhappy with this severance, continued the relationship by
writing up the case. He worked intensively, finishing it during
the first three weeks of January 1901. After completing it he
wrote to Fliess that he felt as if he were 'short of a drug.' His
judgment of the book was quite positive - 'it is the subtlest
thing I have so far written' - and he was sure it would 'put
people off even more than usual' (1954, p. 326). As we saw in
chapter 4, the mark of success for Freud was rejection, or at
least fantasized rejection.
    Freud's presentation of the case is complex; if in 'Studies' he
was writing short stories, then 'Fragment of an Analysis'... is
his first novel. Indeed, the case report was novel. The opening
pages are full of cautions for the reader. As Richardson did in
'Pamela,' so Freud warns us that this work is not meant for
amusement, but instruction. He finds it revolting that there 'are
many physicians who...choose to read a case history of this kind
not as a contribution to the psychopathology of neuroses, but as
a 'roman à clef' designed for their private delectation' (1905c,
p. 9). As Richardson disavowed his status as an author in that
forerunner of the English novel, so Freud declares he is not a
'man of letters' but a 'medical man' interested in advancing
science (p. 59). The work is, however, more fruitfully seen as
experiment in narration than the simple report of a scientific
investigation. With this work Freud forged a new genre, the
therapeutic biography, and in doing so he radically altered

psychiatric discourse. Psychoanalysis was concerned with the
reconstruction of fragmentary life stories, and so Freud's case
histories had to present this endeavor in all its complexity.

He wonders how the psychiatric authorities can produce 'such
smooth and precise histories in cases of hysteria' when, in fact,
'the patients are incapable of giving such reports themselves'
(p. 16). That patients tell about their illnesses haltingly, con-
fusedly and contradictorily is *a necessary correlate of their
symptoms and one which is theoretically requisite*' (p. 18).
Patients must tell of things which they have known all along, but
which have been kept back by or have not occurred to them.
Their problem is of knowing and yet not knowing, of narrating
a tale which has been made obscure by repression and denial.
One must tell the whole lost story. Psychiatry, in focusing on
the somatic and writing linear case studies, is, according to
Freud, misrepresenting and perhaps missing altogether the problems of the neuroses. Psychiatric studies either do not tell life
stories or tell them badly, and the problem in the neuroses is an
incomplete life; a badly told story containing omissions, falsifica-
tions, and confusions. Freud is asserting that a difficulty in
hysteria is the shortcomings in the neurotic's narrative and he
is implying that a coherent story is an important aspect of mental
health. Further, there is the unstated recognition that consciousness has a narrative structure and that when there are gaps
in awareness due to conscious and unconscious disingenuousness
and amnesias then an individual is not well. Marcus concurs:

> human life is, ideally, a connected and coherent story, with
> all the details in explanatory place, and with everything (or
> as close to everything as is practically possible) accounted
> for, in its proper causal or other sequence. And inversely
> illness amounts at least in part to suffering from an incoher-
> ent story or an inadequate narrative account of oneself.
> (1974, p. 92)

In this work Freud was faced with reporting how he tried to
help Dora put her life story in order, with the job of relaying
to the reader the essentials of his psychoanalytic theories, with
the scientific task of demonstrating how the case material provided evidence for the validity of psychoanalytic hypotheses,
and with the formidable literary task of putting this all within
the context of a case study and making it sound scientific. We
will consider each of these, in turn, although in Freud's essay
they are intricately interwoven.

Dora suffered from dyspnea, migraine, and periodic attacks
of nervous coughing often accompanied by loss of voice. During
the treatment Freud learned that she also suffered from other
symptoms which he related to hysteria: a feverish attack that
mimicked appendicitis, a limp that manifested itself periodically,
and a vaginal discharge. After reviewing the clinical picture
Freud states that all these symptoms have a meaning and that

he will elucidate their psychological determinants by tracing the
origin of the symptoms to affective conflicts and disturbances
in the sexual sphere.

Dora's symptoms were symbolic manifestations of a tale of
deceit, infidelity, and sexual intrigue. Her family had moved to
a health resort where her father - a strong-willed conceited
man - was being treated. A very close friendship between them
and a family named K. developed. Dora's father's dissatisfaction
with his marriage was known to all, and the K.'s were also
unhappily married. Frau K. nursed Dora's father and befriended
Dora with whom she was very intimate. Herr K. also became
friendly with Dora, sending her frequent gifts and taking walks
with her. Dora, in turn, acted like a mother to the two small
K. children. It becomes evident that Dora's father and Frau K.
have been engaged in sexual relations for many years, that
Dora knows all about this, and that Dora's father - although he
would deny such a slander - has tacitly agreed with the K.'s
that Dora is to be Herr K.'s compensation for the loss of his
wife. The three adults with whom Dora was close, separately and
together, attempted to conceal from Dora that anything improper
was happening and in fact refused to acknowledge that anything
was happening at all. Dora, too, had to deny her affection for
the three adults and especially for Frau and Herr K. In addition,
she denied any sexual knowledge.

This sounds like a plot summary of a play by Ibsen, and
indeed Freud's first full-length case study is part of the uncovering literature so often identified with the Norwegian dramatist.
Things are not what they seem on the surface; sex, deceit, and
scandal underlie the actions of even our most respected citizens.
Although Freud's case histories are within the then popular
genre of psychological works exposing the depths of human
character, they 'are a new form of literature - they are creative
narratives that include their own analysis and interpretation'
(Marcus, 1974, p. 108). Freud's purpose was not only to tell a
story, but also to present a psychological theory that could be
used to understand the story and other stories as well.

In 'Fragment of an Analysis of a Case of Hysteria' Freud's
theoretical endeavors are in transition. He is still exposing
psychical traumas as he did in 'Studies,' he has his eyes open
for childhood seduction scenes, and he is beginning to discuss
the role of infantile sexuality in the causation of neurosis. He
failed to find a convincing early childhood trauma, and his discussion of Dora's childhood sexual life is tentative. Freud comments that Dora was unusually amnesic for early events in her
life. Perhaps this was because a satisfactory analytic relationship was not established, and Dora was never sure whether
Freud, like the other people in her life, would betray her.

Dora was in treatment against her will. Her father had brought
her to Freud charging him to bring the girl to reason. Freud
predicted early in the treatment that Dora would not see the
analysis come to a natural conclusion. The prediction was fulfilled.

After only three months Dora was through with therapy. As
the narrator of Dora's story, her analyst, and another man in
Dora's life, Freud is an important character in the book. Like
so many narrators in modernist fiction, he is unreliable. Instead
of providing an objective view of events, he becomes entangled
in them and is not totally in command of his other two roles.
Although he says he knew the treatment would end prematurely,
when Dora terminated he says he was shocked and hurt: 'Her
breaking off unexpectedly, just when my hopes of a successful
termination of the treatment were at their highest, and her thus
bringing those hopes to nothing - this was an unmistakable act
of vengence on her part' (p. 109). Dora, the vengeful; Freud
tells us one of her main motives in life was revenge on all men.
Her hysterical symptoms punished her father for his affair.
She punished Herr K. with a slap in response to his overtures,
and failing to obtain sufficient revenge on him she punished
Freud by dashing his hopes for therapeutic success.

Freud came to be another man in Dora's life, and she transferred on to him feelings that she had for her father and Herr K.
Freud failed to confront this transference, and in his failure he
finds the explanation for the treatment's lack of success. In
restrospect he sees that from the beginning he was replacing her
father in Dora's imagination. He cannot, however, fathom the
connection with Herr K. He speaks of an 'unknown quantity' in
him which reminded Dora of Herr K. and says 'she took her
revenge on me as she wanted to take her revenge on him, and
deserted me as she believed herself to have been deceived and
deserted by him' (p. 119). Because Freud did not perceive that
Dora was casting him in the role of Herr K., he failed to interpret
these fantasies and so Dora was driven to acting them out instead
of discussing them.

Freud was obviously bitter about Dora's leaving treatment and
troubled by his failure to deal with the transference. Remember
that Freud's main complaint against Breuer was that he had
failed to recognize Anna O.'s transference love. Well, with Dora,
Freud failed to recognize her transference emotions. His interest
in writing up this case was, in part, an attempt to understand
what went wrong. He located the failure in not recognizing the
transference, but there was another failure. He didn't recognize
or interpret the counter-transference. He had not mastered,
because he failed to recognize, the role that his feelings about
Dora played in the analysis and this in turn distorts the objectivity of his narration. When Dora leaves treatment, Freud's
words are those of a spurned suitor: her actions are 'unexpected,' she 'deserts' him, and her prime motive is 'revenge.'

Since Freud the narrator and analyst is baffled by the
'unknown' resemblance between himself and Herr K., we do not
have many clues as to why Dora subjected both men to a similar
treatment. There is, however, a striking similarity in two
phrases Freud used in describing the relations among Dora and
the three men in her life (Swinney, 1978). The first speaks of

Dora's father having 'handed her over to me [Freud] for psychotherapeutic treatment' (p. 19). The second describes Dora as
feeling embittered by the idea 'that she had been handed over
to Herr K. as the price of his tolerating' her father's affair with
Frau K. (p. 34). Freud and Herr K. were connected, because
they were both seen by Dora as allies of her father in his
attempt to maintain his illicit affair. At sixteen Dora attempted
to destroy the affair by revealing that Herr K. had propositioned
her. Herr K. denied it and Dora's perception of reality was
questioned. Two years later Dora's fainting, a suicide note, and
her refusal to tolerate the K.'s prompted her father to bring
her to Freud with the plea 'bring her to reason.' Dora saw Freud,
too, as questioning her reality, which, of course, he did. For
Frau K., Dora's father sacrificed his own daughter; he 'handed
her over' first to Herr K., then to Freud. In focusing on Dora's
problem, at points even intimating that perhaps she should not
have rejected Herr K., Freud was in Dora's eyes serving her
father's will. Freud failed to make his position clear on this
issue, and when Dora obtained what she wanted from him she
severed the relationship.

She wanted validation of the reality that Herr K. and her father
had denied her. Freud provided this by affirming that the scene
involving the proposition at age sixteen actually occurred, and
when this was done Dora had no more need for his services.
Fifteen months after she left treatment Dora returned for one
visit and announced that she had confronted Frau K. with the
affair and that she had got Herr K. to admit his actions. Freud
calls these acts of revenge; perhaps they were, but they were
revenge in a good cause. Dora was simply trying to confirm that
she had accurately perceived reality.

Besides his discussion of transference, Freud's theoretical
presentation focuses on the psychodynamics of symptom formation in hysteria and the interpretation of dreams. There is little
new in the way of theory, but it is obvious that Freud has
become a master of interpretation. Piecing together bits and
fragments, taking hints, treating no as yes, and making assumptions, Freud weaves together theory and case material to provide a narrative that on the surface and taken as a whole is
convincing, although it is fragile when its parts are examined.

Freud theoretically maintained that bodily symptoms in hysteria
represent the interaction of psyche and soma, and that 'the
clearing-up of symptoms is achieved by looking for their psychical significance' (1905c, p. 41). More than one meaning may be
expressed by a symptom, and through the processes of condensation and displacement many elements of a life drama may be
played by a single somatic disturbance.

Let us take up the analysis of one scene to see how Freud uses
this theory to elaborate a psychoanalytic report of Dora's actions,
an account which unravels when questioned. At the age of fourteen, Dora was in Herr K.'s office with him when to her surprise
he locked the door and then seized and kissed her. Dora was

upset and disgusted. Freud assumed that such a situation would 'surely' call up distinct feelings of sexual pleasure in a girl 'who had never before been approached' (p. 28). Trapped in a room with a married man who suddenly attacks her, Dora is supposed to instantly feel sexual pleasure. Freud goes on; Dora's behavior was at this time 'clearly and completely hysterical,' for he considers a person 'hysterical in whom an occasion for sexual excitement' elicits feelings that are 'preponderantly or exclusively unpleasurable' (p. 28). After the questionable assumption that Dora should have become pleasurably aroused, Freud then says that her reaction of unpleasure was an obvious *'reversal of affect'* and that this mechanism is one of the most important, yet least understood, in the neuroses. Having named the mechanism Freud fails to explain it, but one of Dora's problems is certainly that she cannot accept Herr K.'s attentions with unmitigated pleasure. Had she been able to do so, she would have caused less trouble to the adults around her, and might never have been brought to Freud for treatment.

Freud assumes that when Herr K. embraced her, Dora – if she were like any 'healthy girl' - would have felt pleasurable sensations from her own genitals (p. 29). Dora's feeling of disgust is a response that her culture would have expected of a normal girl, but Freud sees it as unnatural and associates it with anal functioning. He later traces the development of disgust in relation to feces and notes that this association of alimentary functioning with sex is ancient. Dora's disgust for the kiss was felt because the displacement of excitement, which was transformed to a feeling of disgust, was from the genitals laterally to the anus and then upwards to the mouth.

This displacement of sensation from the lower to the upper part of the body is characteristic of hysteria, and in connection with the kiss there was another such displacement. Dora complained that she could still feel upon the upper part of her body the pressure of Herr K.'s embrace. Freud's explanation is that the 'pressure of the erect member probably led to an analogous change in the corresponding female organ, the clitoris; and the excitation of this...erotogenic zone was referred by a process of displacement to the simultaneous pressure against the thorax and became fixed there' (p. 30). Dora had to repress clitoral excitement, not acknowledging that it occurred. So this repressed memory and its affect came to be expressed in lingering feelings of the pressure of Herr K.'s embrace on her chest. A curious assumption here is that through the heavy armour of late Victorian dress Dora's clitoris was stimulated by Herr K.'s fleeting, though fervent embrace. In Freud's hands Dora's story of Herr K.'s kiss and her disgust becomes a new story; his 'reconstruction of the scene' is that, 'during the passionate embrace she felt not merely his kiss upon her lips but also the pressure of his erect member against her body' (p. 30). This is an arousing retelling, one to which Dora did not assent, but which Freud used to make sense out of the case for himself and his readers. Dora was not revolted by the kiss, but by her own pleasure. She had to deny her own lust, transforming it to disgust. Freud's theoretical exposition explains this transformation. But, let us remember the theory is called forth to buttress a very weak initial assumption: that Dora, though she repeatedly denied being so, must have been aroused by Herr K.'s attack. Just as Dora would not give in to Herr K., she would not submit to Freud's insistence on his version of events.

The above examination calls into question just a small part of Freud's analysis and highlights the general method he followed throughout the case in transforming what he tells us Dora said into a psychoanalytic account of her life story. The general conclusions he draws from a multitude of such formulations are consonant with his reconstruction of the scene involving the kiss at fourteen:

> Incapacity for meeting a *real* erotic demand is one of the most essential features of neurosis. Neurotics are dominated by the opposition between reality and phantasy. If what they long for the most intensely in their phantasies [in Dora's case, supposedly, the love of Herr K.] is presented to them in reality [Herr K.'s attack], they none the less flee from it [Dora's running away]. (p. 110)

Given a situation where reality presents no chance for erotic involvement, hysterics' fantasies become active. An actual sexual shock exacerbates the neurotic problems, and current sexual emotions can lead to new waves of sexual repression. Confronted with sexual stimulation, the neurotic must deny it, and the damming up of libidinal expression brings about libidinal flow 'back into old channels which had formerly seemed fated to run dry' (p. 51). The motive force for symptom formation is found, then, in a confluence of the repression of normal sexuality and denied remains of perverse infantile sexual impulses. 'Psychoneuroses are, so to speak, the *negative* of perversions' (p. 50). The pervert expresses infantile sexual impulses; the neurotic represses them. In neuroses, as in dreams, such infantile impulses can be uncovered by interpretation, for underlying the symptom is an infantile sexual wish.

The entire case is dominated by attempts to reconstruct traumas and to push the inquiry further and further back into Dora's childhood in a search 'for any influences or impressions which might have had an effect analogous to that of trauma' (p. 27). From remembrances of gastric pains - which 'It is well known... occur especially often in those who masturbate' (p. 78) - bedwetting, and thumb-sucking, Freud builds a highly circumstantial case for Dora's having both masturbated and been erotically attached to oral gratification. The renunciation of such activities provided a foundation for her later neurotic difficulties.

Freud warns us from the beginning that the case is fragmentary, and throughout it there are assurances that if he had had

more time additional light could have been shed on obscure
points. As a rhetorical technique, this is brilliant. It leaves the
reader certain that the author is on the right track and that all
Freud has said is pointing towards a possible, but not yet
visible, resolution.

The case is incomplete in another way. It does not resolve all
the problems of hysteria. Freud says we should not expect more
of a single case than it can offer and that anyone 'who has
hitherto been unwilling to believe that a psychosexual aetiology
holds good generally and without exception for hysteria is
scarcely likely to be convinced of the fact by taking stock of a
single case history' (p. 13). The reader is asked to 'suspend
his judgement until his own work has earned him the right to
a conviction' (p. 13). Such a conviction, of course, can only be
properly formed by thorough psychoanalytic investigation of
neurotics. Jung was to follow Freud's advice, and after several
years of psychoanalytic work he came to the conclusion that
psychosexuality did not provide a causal explanation of the neuroses. For his efforts he was to lose Freud's friendship.

This work, then, is brought forward to demonstrate the twin
theses that dreams, when interpreted, fulfill infantile wishes and
that hysteria has a psychosexual etiology. Freud speaks of his
duty towards science in publishing this work and demands his
right as a physician-scientist to openly discuss sexual matters
with patients and to freely discuss such issues in writing. He
asserts that he, as a scientist, finds the need to make such
declarations deplorable; but his work has been rejected by some
people because it deals with sexual topics, and he feels that it is
his duty to speak out against the prudery of the day which
stands in the way of serious scientific investigation. In these
opening assertions, and throughout the book, Freud assures us
he is a medical man – a man of science. Physicists and chemists
do not feel the need to make such declarations, but Freud does.
Why? Because he was worried, and would remain concerned
throughout his life, that psychoanalysis would not be considered
scientific. Science for him was the only form of inquiry that
moved towards the truth.

Early in the case he likened psychoanalysis to archaeology,
that science 'whose good fortune it is to bring to the light of
day after their long burial the priceless though mutilated relics
of antiquity' (p. 12). Freud says that in this work 'I have
restored what is missing, taking the best models known to me
from other analyses; but, like a conscientious archaeologist, I
have not omitted to mention in each case where the authentic
parts end and my constructions begin' (p. 12). Freud does not
inform us at all times where his constructions begin, that is,
where what Dora said is rendered into what Dora meant or what
must have happened. The analogy to archaeology also leads us
astray because a piece of stoneware excavated from a depth of
ten feet is not equivalent to a memory trace. Although the
archaeologist literally digs up the past, in memory we only meta-

phorically uncover lost thoughts. Freud chooses a materialist metaphor in order to suggest to us that memories and our pasts are as concrete as the extant remains of lost civilizations. This is obviously not the case, and we must be careful not to confuse a useful metaphor with actual equivalency.

As a scientific work this case is seriously flawed. Freud tells us he has 'as a rule not reproduced the process of interpretation to which the patient's associations and communications had to be subjected, but only the results of that process' (p. 12). Interpretation is the core of the psychoanalytic method and yet in a work of science, where an accurate and detailed report of one's method is compulsory, Freud has left out this information. Freud realizes that in failing to reproduce the way in which he transforms the 'raw material of the patient's associations' into the 'pure metal of unconscious thoughts' he has put the reader at a disadvantage. For the reader is 'given no opportunity of testing the correctness of my procedure in the course of this exposition of the case' (p. 112). Being able to evaluate, either by reading or reproducing, another person's work is fundamental to scientific investigation.

Freud tells us that when interpreting the two major dreams of the work he has revealed the technique of interpretation. His reports here are somewhat more detailed, but in presenting the second dream he seriously violates another central tenet of science - accurate reporting of the data: 'I shall present the material produced during the analysis of this dream in the somewhat haphazard order in which it recurs to my mind' (p. 95). Freud, here, honestly reports what he has done. We see Dora through his eyes, and her dreams and associations are not reported as Freud observed them but as they recurred to him. This tells us something about Freud and his method of working, but leaves us in doubt about what Dora actually said and the sequence of her associations.

Point of view in science is supposedly eliminated by the doctrine of objectivity which works to standardize observers' views of reality. Freud's viewpoint pervades this work as the narrator's view dominates a novel. Why has Freud failed to report his method, and why has he forsaken the task of objective reporting? He says he could not have reproduced his interpretations, for if he had 'the results would have been almost unreadable' (p. 112). Considerations of style, as any reader of scientific reports knows, are not a major concern of scientists. To reconstruct Dora's reality as it was built by him, Freud must tell the life story he constructed for Dora. An accurate reporting of what he did must include him in the report, because he was an active agent in Dora's life.

Freud attempted to compromise between accurate scientific reporting and the presentation of the story of a person who had been in psychoanalysis. Scientific method allows few compromises. Freud saw the compromises he was making and this worried him, but he would not sacrifice his vision of the case to the narrow

rigors of science. His goal was to make sense out of a person's
life and to do this he had to report the story which for him did
just that.

The manifest presentation of the work is medical and scientific.
Freud compares himself with an archaeologist, asserts that as
a doctor he should be able to discuss sex, and calls his work a
scientific case study. There are, however, indications that the
work might be something else. Freud tells us it is not a 'roman
à clef,' and he is not a man of letters. It must have crossed his
mind that he was writing a novel, since he assures us that he
was not. Although the work was published in a medical journal,
he recognizes that non-professionals may read it and, as we
have seen, he sacrificed a report of his method to considerations
of readability. Hillman says:

> The manifest material was medical; but the latent intention,
> which necessitated the transfigurative suppression of medi-
> cal, empirical methodology, was that of the poetic art. His
> case histories are...a new genre of narrative; they are...
> compromises between two irreconcilable demands, providing
> defences against awareness of what he was most deeply
> engaged in - fiction writing. Ever since him we are all in
> this field of psychotherapy, not medical empiricists, but
> workers in story. (1975, p. 129)

We have seen Freud's Richardsonian denials and, like the novels
of Austen, 'Fragment of an Analysis...' has a country setting
and is concerned with the romantic entanglements and lives of
a few characters. The chief concern of many novels is to express
the inner side of human nature, which includes 'the pure passions, that is to say the dreams, joys, sorrows, and self-com-
munings which politeness or shame prevent...[people] from
mentioning' (Alain quoted in Hillman, 1975, p. 128). For Dora,
Freud tried to do this. He attempted to make the unconscious
conscious. The case study is a revealing of all that Dora could
not say: of her dreams, passions, and sorrows.

While science and positivist history search for external causes,
in many novels almost everything is founded upon human nature.
Everything can be understood in terms of character and even
crimes and miseries have an intentional structure. Freud says of
dreams, and this is also true of neurotic symptoms, that 'After
the work of interpretation has been completed they can be
replaced by perfectly correctly constructed thoughts which can
be assigned a recognizable position in the chain of mental
events' (1905c, p. 15). Dreams and symptoms are intentional;
they express wishes. In the novel, plot reveals these human
intentions and shows how everything fits together, making sense.
Plot provides a direction - an Ariadne thread - through the
maze of experience. When Freud spoke of the dynamic organization of psychic material, he was describing a psychoanalytic
plot line through the mind which made sense of case material.

Plot is a strong feature in all of Freud's case studies, and he holds our attention by promising and delaying the dénouement. Throughout the case of Dora, Freud tells us more will be disclosed later and at the end he reminds us of what we know so far. Complications are introduced by way of his having to give us information before a coherent conclusion can be reached. At one point he says he must consider further complications to which he would give no space if he were a 'man of letters engaged upon the creation of a mental state like this for a short story, instead of being a medical man engaged upon its dissection' (p. 59). Scientists dissect what is there; artists create what is not there. Freud views himself as a scientist in that he is concerned with the world of reality which he is trying to depict. In the real world a complication, accumulation, and conjunction of motives 'in a word, overdetermination - is the rule' (p. 60). Freud's hypothetical artist ignores all such complications. But only bad writers of wooden characters avoid complications. Marcus exposes Freud's ruse: 'That hypothetical writer is nothing but a straw man; and when Freud in apparent contrast represents himself and his own activities he is truly representing how a genuine creative writer writes' (1974, p. 90).

Freud's work is full of modernist novelistic techniques. At the beginning, like Borges and Nabokov, there is the challenge to the reader. Freud tells us that if we have not read 'The Interpretation of Dreams' - and not many had in 1905 - we 'will find only bewilderment in these pages' (p. 11). Our narrator at times confesses he is confused by the material, but will try to lead us through it as best he can. The case is also framed by a preface which, upon inspection, leaves the reader questioning the very nature of the reality which she or he is entering. Freud tells us this 'record is not absolutely - phonographically - exact, but it can claim to possess a high degree of trustworthiness' (p. 10). He weaves through subtle differentiations - which he does not entirely control - between the history, the report, the case, and the record which leave one uncertain about just exactly what one is reading (Marcus, 1974). Additionally, he tells us that what he is doing is new and 'What is new has always aroused bewilderment and resistance' (1905c, p. 11). And, finally, as with all modernist endeavors, there is the admission that all of this, despite its creator's heroic attempts, is fragmentary.

It is fragmentary because in it Freud sets himself two contradictory tasks. He wants both to tell Dora's life story and to record her case history. Case histories are medical accounts of the chronology and cure of illness and fall within the realm of science; life stories are narratives with a plot and fall within the realm of biography. Freud insisted he was doing the former, but he achieved the latter. Freud hoped to bring the two together:

Whereas the practical aim of treatment is to remove all possible symptoms [the goal of medicine captured in case

histories], and to replace them by conscious thoughts, we
may regard it as a second and theoretical aim to repair all
the damages to a patient's memory [help her to recover
her life story]. These two aims are coincident. When one
is reached, so is the other; and the same path leads to both
of them. (p. 18)

With Dora he failed to relieve all her symptoms, and he did not
reconstruct with her the life story that she had lost to hysterical
amnesia. In the end Dora would not acquiesce to Freud's influence; she would not buy Freud's version of her life, and so
Freud had constructed a narrative that failed to convince his
first audience - Dora. Without her assent an important piece of
validation is missing. Freud can explain why the confirmation
was lacking - he failed to interpret the transference - but this
is only a promise that 'it would have worked, if only I....'
  Freud asserted that curing symptoms was 'coincident' with
helping people to recover their life stories, and that his goal
was not incompatible with medical science. But we have seen
that Freud's reporting of this case is incompatible with natural
scientific methodology - a methodological frame in which he
insisted his work was contained. Beyond science there is life.
In the end Freud was more true to life than to science. He was,
after all, a scientific visionary; he saw beyond the constraints
of natural scientific practice, and his first lengthy case biography moved beyond the narrow confines of factual reporting
to fictional modes of representation. The mind was no longer
reducible to neuronal connections; it was a fiction with both
a narrative structure and a plot. Symptoms could be cured by
finding their meaning and meaning was constructed by recovering and ordering the lost incidents of a person's life. Mental
illness is a disorder of one's life story and to cure it one needs
a word specialist - an interpreter - not a doctor. To report the
findings, one needs to be a writer more than a scientist. Freud
bows to the insights of men of letters, saying, 'it is [hard] for
a psychoanalyst to discover anything new that has not been
known before by some creative writer' (1901b, p. 205).

THE EMERGENCE OF AN INTERPRETATIVE SCIENCE

Freud says of 'The Interpretation of Dreams:' 'I learned how
to translate the language of dreams into the forms of expression
of our own thought-language, which can be understood without
further help' (1905c, p. 15). Freud's work at the turn of the
century became hermeneutic. In what Lacan (1977) calls the
three canonical texts of psychoanalysis - the dream book, 'The
Psychopathology of Everyday Life,' and 'Jokes and their Relation
to the Unconscious' - the central concern is with the uncovering
of latent meanings by interpretation. Faulty actions, forgetting
words, slips of the pen and the hundreds of little pathological

acts we commit can be shown, *'if psycho-analytic methods of investigation are applied to them, to have valid motives and to be determined by motives unknown to consciousness'* (Freud, 1901b, p. 239). The psychoanalytic method is interpretation, and its practice depends on the analyst being able to enter into dialogue with the perpetrator of the error in order to uncover the meaning of an action that appears senseless. The error has a meaning, that is, it can be meaningfully interpolated into a person's ongoing life by interpretation.

In the book on jokes, within just over ten pages of each other, are two quotes which vividly demonstrate both the old and the new in Freud's work. First the old:

I am making no attempt to proclaim that the cells and nerve fibres, or the systems of neurons which are taking their place to-day, are these psychical paths, even though it would have to be possible in some manner which cannot yet be indicated to represent such [psychical] paths by organic elements of the nervous system. (1905a, p. 148)

Old dreams never die, but the neurological fantasy of the 'Project' is being replaced by the fact that psychoanalysis as a technique of interpretation works. The revolutionary view is that: 'the unconscious is something we really do not know, but which we are obliged by compelling inferences to supply' (p. 162). The old hope is that psychoanalysis will somehow be grounded in neurology. The new recognizes that psychoanalysis is a method by which the latent, that which is hidden or concealed, may be brought to light by an act of interpretation. We 'supply' by acts of interpretation what must be there so that we can make sense out of an action, a dream, a symptom, or a life. A revolution has taken place in Freud's thought; the 'Freud of the "Project" worried about the confirmation of the magnified eye and the knife...nor did he ever abandon the belief that one day a slide would show the eye a reason; but the Freud who told us the meaning of our slips, jokes, and dreams was a reader and interpreter of texts' (Gass, 1978, p. 238). That is, Freud was engaged in hermeneutics.

New ideas are often presented in old clothes and so Freud's model of the psyche in chapter 7 was cast in the dress of a mechanoenergic system. Such models seem to carry great meaning for inhabitants of the machine age, and volumes have been written discussing the scientific status and validity of Freud's topographic model of the mind. The essential feature of the model is not its mechanical façade and its hidden biological connections. The model's essence is that it structures the psyche within a narrative frame by insisting that psychic processes occur in a chronological order.

The basis of psychoanalysis is in a conversation between two people in which the analysand is charged with the task of giving 'the whole story of his life and illness' (Freud, 1905c, p. 16).

This narrative is broken and at times incoherent, for in the dialogue the analysand is trying to communicate all he or she knows and does not know to the analyst, who in turn is trying to supply by interpretation that which is unknown to the client but which must be active in order to make a coherent story.

Freud's most straightforward description of what happens in dreams, and this could apply to the whole process of psychoanalysis, is presented in a simile, but it is a simile that, unlike the mechanical metaphors of the dream book, comes very close to describing a reality. In dreams it is, 'as though one person who was dependent upon a second person had to make a remark which was bound to be disagreeable in the ears of the second one' (1901a, p. 677). In analysis resistance works to modify one's remarks in order to make them acceptable to oneself and one's conception of what the analyst wants to hear. The analyst must supply what is meant by interpretation of what is said. In the end what is supplied is a story which makes sense of experiences which have been baffling, denied, or simply unknown to the analysand. What is constructed is a history of psychic reality which is 'a special kind of narrative - what may be called the *psychoanalytic life history*' (Schafer, 1978, p. 181). It is the whole lost story constructed along the plot lines of psychoanalysis. It is a story preoccupied with the past which seeks to understand what is by creating the past from what is latent, hidden, or obscure in the present. Psychoanalysis does not excavate; it illuminates.

6 COMPROMISE AND ADVANCEMENT: JUNG'S EARLY CAREER

On 11 December 1900, just a month after receiving his medical degree from Basel University, Jung walked through the doors of the Burghölzli Psychiatric Hospital in Zurich and began practicing his trade as an assistant to Eugen Bleuler. By 1909 Jung had won local and international recognition for his work and become prominent in the psychoanalytic movement. His rapid advancement was built on a series of compromises whereby he put forth his own ideas without antagonizing the reigning authorities in psychiatry. By presenting new ideas within the framework of experimental research and refusing to commit himself to positions which were not supported by his experience Jung pursued a middle path between innovative psychiatric research and advocacy of radical psychoanalytic ideas. An examination of Jung's life while at the Burghölzli, his formulation of a theory of complexes, and his increasing support of Freud's ideas will provide us with a portrait of Jung the empiricist investigating unexplored territories of the mind.

THE BURGHÖLZLI

At the end of the nineteenth century, under the direction of Auguste Forel, the Burghölzli was transformed from a hospital for psychiatric interment into an innovative treatment center for mental illness. A little-known psychiatrist, Eugen Bleuler, was appointed Forel's successor in 1896 and he expanded the hospital's commitment to its patients. Prior to his appointment as chief of the most prestigious mental hospital in Switzerland, Bleuler had been recognized for his devotion to the mentally ill. At Burghölzli he won additional acclaim, because he required of himself and his staff complete dedication to working with the sick.

Newly appointed residents were met by Bleuler, and he, carrying their bags, escorted them to their austere quarters. The work was demanding. Alphonse Maeder, who worked at the hospital at this time and remained a lifelong associate of Jung, says

> The patient was the focus of interest. The student learned to talk with him. Burghölzli was in that time a kind of factory where you worked very much and were poorly paid. Everyone from...[Bleuler] to the young resident was totally absorbed

by his work....Bleuler was kind to all and never played the
role of the chief. (Ellenberger, 1970, p. 667)

As director of the hospital and professor of psychiatry at the
University of Zurich, Bleuler provided both firm direction for
the institution and a setting in which innovative research was
encouraged. He was never dictatorial and often came to residents' rooms to talk with them about new developments in medicine.

Under his direction new programs aimed at treatment were
developed. Bleuler's work in the area of schizophrenia - finally
published in 1911 - led to both a new theory of the disease and
new therapeutic practices. Schizophrenia, then called dementia
praecox, had been seen as a degenerative disease of the brain
progressing on an irreversible course. In a magnificent work of
psychiatric nosological revision Bleuler renamed this disease
schizophrenia and introduced the notion that it could be arrested
or even reversed by therapeutic means. He instituted programs
that, according to some, had miraculous curative effects: he
would often discharge severely ill patients, unexpectedly transfer them to a new ward, or assign them a particular responsibility. He organized supervised work for patients and carefully
structured their leisure time. He instituted out-patient care
and introduced many programs which are now commonplace in
psychiatric practice. He was not the only psychiatrist at this
time 'who strove to introduce psychological understanding and
treatment of mental patients, but he was probably the one whose
efforts...were most successful' (Ellenberger, 1970, p. 288).

Jung's retrospective account of the hospital is at odds with this
picture of a progressive treatment center headed by one of the
great innovators in psychiatry. Jung says,

With my work at Burghölzli, life took on an undivided reality
- all intention, consciousness, duty and responsibility. It was
an entry into the monastery of the world, a submission to the
vow to believe only in what was probable, average, commonplace, barren of meaning, to renounce everything strange and
significant, and reduce anything extraordinary to the banal.
(1973, p. 112)

Jung's retrospective negative assessment shows the change in
a person's evaluation of events that a revolution in consciousness
produces. While at the Burghölzli he was committed to the scientific method and saw experimentation as the hope of psychology,
but a radical change in his thought was to lead to a renunciation
of these views. His contact with Freud and the changes in his
life brought on by his own self-analysis caused a re-evaluation
of his early experimental work in psychiatry. Looking backward
after fifty years of exploring the unconscious, his work at the
Burghölzli must have seemed very constricting. His vow to
science was, in retrospect, a renunciation of mystery and

imagination, and a denial of something which was central to his being. Given the course of Jung's life the Burghölzli seems a strange interlude, a period of nine years when he lived the monastic existence engendered by a commitment to the sterile experimental investigation of the mind and the barrenness of facts.

From 1900 to 1909, however, this world was not empty for him. Only afterwards, only after he committed himself to the powers of the imagination did it become so. In his retrospective account of the years at the hospital we find Jung, as he did with his tales of college life, casting himself as an alien in a culture of narrow-minded materialists. It is questionable whether he was an alien at the time. He did, because of his subsequent revelations, find himself alienated from a life to which he had been totally committed, but judging by his publications from 1902 to 1908, the accounts of others, and his rapid advancement at the hospital, it is clear that Jung was no alien in this worldly monastery of the 'banal;' he passed as a very well-adjusted native.

In his retelling of these times Jung continues his story of the lonely hero's isolation from others. He says for the first six months at the asylum he used all his spare time to read the fifty volumes of the 'Allgemeine Zeitschrift für Psychiatrie.' He did not do this in order to master the essentials of psychiatric practice, but to immerse himself in the psychiatric mentality. He wished to find out how human beings reacted to seeing other human minds fall ill, and so he found his colleagues as interesting as the patients, in whom, he says, the doctors took no interest. He charges that his co-workers had no concern for what went on in the minds of the sick: 'Patients were labeled, rubber-stamped with a diagnosis, and, for the most part, that settled the matter. The psychology of the mental patient played no role whatsoever' (1973b, p. 114). Jung claims that his interests were different and proceeds to tell the stories of several patients all of whom had a profound effect on him.

Although he says that Freud's work was inspirational because it pointed the way to a closer relationship with patients and a more detailed investigation of their minds, he does not mention Bleuler's influence. Bleuler, who fostered a revolution in the psychological treatment of hospitalized patients, who was Jung's chief, who was instrumental in Jung's rapid rise in the hospital, to whom Jung acknowledges a great debt in many of his works between 1902 and 1907, and to whom in a 1936 letter Jung attributes his psychiatric views, is not even mentioned by name in Jung's autobiography. Retrospectively, Bleuler has been excised from Jung's life, and a hospital devoted to innovative forms of treatment has been made into an asylum where patients do not matter. Why? Jung openly declares that his historical account is his fable, his truth, and obviously Bleuler is to play no part in this story. If Jung, in recounting his life, had said that at Burghölzli he was required to work closely with the sick, that Bleuler's whole approach to mental illness strongly shaped his

own thought, and that Bleuler was instrumental in advancing
his career, Jung would have had to forfeit the dramatic scenario
of the young pioneer struggling towards the truth by surmount-
ing the prejudices of his colleagues. Leaving out of a story all
the aid and assistance one has received makes one look so much
more heroic.

About the lonely path he followed while at the hospital he says,
'I need scarcely mention that my concentration and self-imposed
confinement alienated me from my colleagues' (1973b, p. 113).
Given Jung's rapid rise in the hospital administration it is hard
to believe either that he alienated many colleagues or that he
failed to make a good adjustment in his chosen field. In 1902
he completed and published his dissertation. In it he expressed
his 'warmest thanks to my revered teacher, Professor Bleuler,
for his friendly encouragement and the loan of books' (p. 88).
At about this time Bleuler made Jung the director of research on
psychological testing, and Jung began his studies on word association. In 1902 he was promoted from assistant to senior assistant staff physician. In 1905 he was advanced to First Oberarzt,
senior staff physician, and thereby became clinical director of
the hospital and second in command to Bleuler. In addition he
was appointed director of out-patient services where he acceler-
ated the transition from treatment by hypnosis to other forms
of psychotherapy. Capping his accomplishments, in 1905 he
earned the envied title of Privatdozent on the medical faculty of
the University of Zurich. By age thirty Jung had, according to
those acquainted with him at the time, begun 'an unusually
brilliant career as a university psychiatrist' (Ellenberger, 1970,
p. 668).

Although during these early years Jung worked very hard,
he had time both to visit Paris and to get married. In the winter
of 1902-3 he took a leave of absence from the hospital to study
with Pierre Janet at the Salpêtrière in Paris. After Charcot's
death, Janet became the foremost French authority on diseases
of the mind. His work stressed the increase and diminution of
psychic energy in mental illness, the 'abaissement du niveau
mental' (lowering of the level of consciousness) and the loss of
the sense of reality in psychopathic conditions, the role of subconscious fixed ideas in the formation of symptoms, and the differentiation between two types of illness - the hysterical and
psychasthenic. Jung attended Janet's lectures and throughout
Jung's early work Janet's ideas are both used and expanded on.
However, Jung did not make personal contact with Janet, his
sabbatical in Paris is not mentioned in his autobiography, and,
according to Ellenberger, Jung spent much of his time sight-
seeing. While there he escorted his cousin Helene Preiswerk -
the former medium now working as a dressmaker - to the theater
and on an excursion to Versailles.

Upon returning to Zurich Jung married Emma Rauschenbach on
13 February 1903. She was twenty-one, very well educated, the
daughter of a rich industrialist, and a member of an old Swiss

German family. This was the woman whom many years before
Jung had predicted he would marry. He must have been shocked
when Miss Rauschenbach turned down his first proposal; the
second was accepted. Their first residence was at the Burghölzli.
Emma was a great aid to Carl. Marriage meant that his financial
troubles were now over and Emma was careful to neither interfere
with his work nor allow anyone else to do so.

Emma Rauschenbach was a capable mother, housewife, and
social hostess. She won Bleuler's approval. She tolerated, adjusted to, and made the best of Jung's prolonged affair with Antonia
Wolff which began around 1912. Emma helped Carl through periods
of psychic stress and had a strong interest in depth psychology.
She published works of her own on analytic topics and practised
psychotherapy. She was at times not treated with much consideration by her husband, but she persevered through these
crises. That Emma was an aid to Carl in his work from the beginning cannot be doubted. In his first major work on word association, besides thanking Bleuler, he also says, 'We are...parti-
cularly grateful to Mrs. Jung for active help in the repeated
revision of the extensive material' (Jung and Riklin, 1904-5,
p. 192).

THE THEORY OF COMPLEXES

The basis of Jung's later thought can easily be seen in his work
from 1902 to 1907 in which he developed the idea that psychic
complexes play a critical part in both normal and psychopathological mental functioning. The notion of the feeling-toned complex was latent in his dissertation, it was fully developed in
the studies on word association between 1904 and 1906, it was
used in 1907 as part of an explanation of the psychology of
dementia praecox, and from 1905 until the break with Freud in
1913 it was the centerpiece of Jung's psychoanalytic writings.

In chapter 2 we looked at the personal side of Jung's experiences with his cousin Helene Preiswerk. Here we will examine
Jung's psychological explanation of her performances as a medium
in his case study of S.W. 'So-Called Occult Phenomena' combines
a description of somnambulistic states with a theory of psychic
automatisms to account for S.W.'s seance activities. Somnambu-
lism is a state of systematic partial wakefulness, a sleep-like
condition. Impressions received by a person in a somnambulistic
state 'go on working in the subconscious to form independent
growths, and finally reach perception as hallucinations' (Jung,
1902, p. 13). This independent development of trains of association is an automatic phenomenon. An idea, emotion, or stimulus
sets in motion a psychic sequence of ideas, emotions, and small
motor movements. These responses are automatic in that they
occur spontaneously and are not controlled by consciousness.
If the initial stimulus, emotion, or idea sinks below the threshold
of consciousness, or was never conscious at all, then the

automatisms resulting from that stimulus appear as manifestations
independent of ego-consciousness. S.W. engaged in automatic
writing and produced automatic movements of objects such as the
table and glasses. She did not control these movements. While in
a somnambulistic state her subconscious was stimulated by the
questions, suggestions, or movements of seance participants.
These stimuli led to a series of associations below the threshold
of S.W.'s consciousness which included automatic motor movements. These movements were captured in her writing or the
dislocation of objects. She was at best only partially aware of
her actions; she felt that she was directed by forces outside of
her. In a sense she was. Her actions were not under ego control,
but were the expression of powers in her psyche outside of
consciousness.

When S.W. spoke with the voices of the spirits these were
verbal automatisms, and her hallucinations were visual automatisms. Automatisms can be rich in content, because they express
whole groups of associations and have at their disposal a vast
inventory of experiences most of which have never been conscious.

Goethe provided Jung with a good example of a mildly hallucinatory automatism. Goethe says

> I had the gift, when I closed my eyes..., of being able to
> conjure up in my mind's eye the imaginary picture of a
> flower. This flower did not retain its first shape for a single
> instant, but unfolded out of itself new flowers with coloured
> petals and green leaves. They were not natural flowers, but
> fantastic ones....It was impossible to fix the creative images
> that sprang up, yet they lasted as long as I desired them to
> last. (quoted by Jung, 1902, p. 14)

This could very well be a description of what Jung later called
'active imagination,' a therapeutic activity aimed at allowing an
image, thought, or emotion to develop on its own in order to see
where it leads. Goethe retained consciousness of the process of
the automatic unfolding of a series of visual images; mediums,
somnambulists, and hysterics do not. Their fantasies develop
outside of consciousness and appear to them as foreign creations.

S.W. was held in high esteem by some of her family and friends
for her mediumistic abilities and so she and they fostered this
talent. Premonitions, forebodings and mercuric moods were all
in a day's work for her. 'She was happy in the consciousness
of having found her true vocation' and certain of the reality of
her visions. 'She absolutely would not listen to the idea that the
manifestations were a kind of illness' (p. 23). She led a double
life with two personalities existing side by side or in succession.
One S.W. was a normal, if somewhat shy and withdrawn, teenager; the other, the medium S.W., was given to hysterics,
visions, and fainting spells. She told childish stories and created
elaborate fantasy flirtations. Given the encouragement of a

seance, the shy girl was transformed into the medium.

The most striking aspect of S.W.'s mediumistic performances, and the one which Jung discusses in greatest detail, was the presentation of somnambulistic personalities - 'spirits.' These personalities owe their 'existence simply to suggestive questions which strike an answering chord in the medium's own disposition' (p. 53). Mediums are predisposed to dissociation of the ego, thereby releasing previously suppressed partial aspects of their own personality. These seem foreign to the medium, like alien spirits, because they are automatisms acting independently of the will. As the medium feels the automatisms take control she or he is struck by their strangeness and so the split off personality is further dissociated and takes on more of a life of its own. The medium is, of course, also gratified by her or his ability to call up the spirits and is rewarded for doing so, thus dissociation is further encouraged.

S.W.'s spirit personalities were numerous. The dozens of figures each with a different name, however, 'could all be classified under two types, the *serio-religious* and the *gay-hilarious*' (p. 73). S.W.'s grandfather,[1] the first partial personality to appear, was the prototype for the serio-religious figures. These were pompous characters producing 'nothing but sanctimonious twaddle and edifying moral precepts' (p. 77). The prototype for the gay-hilarious spirits was Ulrich von Gerbenstein, an amusing gossip, jokester, and pontificant on the trivial. Another manifestation of this type was Mr P.R., a frivolous ladies' man. These partial personalities had at their disposal all of S.W.'s memory, including events which she was not conscious of in her normal state. They shared her ecstatic visions with her, but knew nothing of her dreams and fantasies while she was in an ecstatic state. These two types of figures were personifications of S.W.'s past - the strictly raised serious, shy, rather religious girl and the frivolous, lively, teenaged gossip. This thematization of fantasy productions into types and seeing the complementary relations between typical figures is highly characteristic of Jung's later work.

The grandfather and Ulrich von Gerbenstein when asked about S.W.'s ecstatic dreams and fantasies always answered '"Ask Ivenes, Ivenes knows"' (p. 32). Ivenes was her somnambulistic ego and expressed S.W.'s dreams of being a mature woman. Ivenes spoke in a dignified language; she was a 'serious, mature person, devout and right-minded, full of womanly tenderness and very modest' (p. 36). This soulful, elegiac character had had many incarnations and presented herself as the ancestral mother of thousands of people down through history. In polar opposition to Ivenes was another spirit whom Ivenes disliked, a woman who was 'a sink of iniquity.' This woman told of countless romances swarming with 'open and secret love-affairs, with illegitimate births and other sexual innuendos' (p. 69).

Jung says these two women figures both fulfilled S.W.'s desires. In Ivenes, S.W. was seeking a 'middle way between

two extremes;' she was creating a sophisticated woman who was
neither too serious nor too gay. In the presence of the ideal
Ivenes, characters like the preachy grandfather and Gerbenstein
faded and a more mature person was present. Ivenes was an aid
to S.W.'s psychic maturation; anticipating his later work Jung
says, 'In view of the difficulties that oppose the future character,
the somnambulisms sometimes have an immanently teleological
significance, in that they give the individual, who would otherwise inevitably succumb, the means of victory' (p. 79). Caught
between a religious upbringing and adolescent flirtatiousness,
S.W.'s dream of Ivenes expressed a future ideal, a personality
which was lived out in the somnambulistic state and which acted
as an exemplar for S.W.'s future conduct of her life. After the
break with Freud, Jung returned to the idea that dreams and
fantasies have a teleological significance and often point the way
for the future development of the individual.

Ivenes's tales of her enormous family, along with Ivenes's
counterpart - the fallen woman - resulted from sexual feelings
aroused in S.W. by puberty. These fantasies were 'nothing but
a dream of sexual wish-fulfillment,' which was spread out over
several months (p. 70). These erotic desires were in part directed
at Jung, who was at various times fantasized by S.W. as one of
Ivenes's grandsons, and also as her son. In another incarnation
Jung had supposedly mourned Ivenes's death by retiring to a
monastery.

S.W. was not ignorant of the major works on somnambulists,
and Jung points out that Ivenes is modeled after Kerner's 'The
Seeress of Prevost.' S.W.'s final great production was a figure
with seven concentric circles. It was a diagram of the relations
between natural and supernatural forces. Having overheard
conversations about Kant's 'Natural History and Theory of the
Heavens,' S.W. presented a cosmological vision of the forces of
attraction and repulsion which bind the universe together.
Although at the time Jung did not label it a mandala figure, it
is the first such figure produced in his work. It is a mystic
vision, reproduced in a circular motif, of the wholeness of the
cosmos and the place of humans within a universal scheme.

'On the Psychology and Pathology of So-Called Occult Phenomena' was Jung's attempt to explain mediumistic experiences
as psychopathological disturbances by using psychological,
and at times physiological, formulations. Within this framework,
spirits were personified automatisms which expressed human
desires. The roots of our own dreams, the medium's spirits and
fantasies, and the hysteric's symptoms are 'feeling-toned ideas'
which may have once been conscious but which sink below the
threshold of consciousness forming chains of associated thoughts
which 'thanks to psychic dissociation...go on working in the
unconscious' (pp. 68-69). Jung felt the impetus for S.W.'s
mediumistic performances, like the problems of many hysterics,
was puberty. The stormy emotions of adolescence caused by the
physiological changes of puberty present serious crises in deve-

lopment for psychologically unstable people.

Three years after publishing S.W.'s case and after investigating seven more mediums, Jung was certain that 'the exact sciences will surely conquer this field [occultism] by experiment and verification, as has happened in every other realm of human experience' (1905c, p. 308). To make this possible one needs an open mind towards occult phenomena, a willingness to investigate them, and in that investigation both exacting observation and careful criticism. At thirty, Jung was dedicated to the scientific method; he saw himself as a psychiatrist and his work as the empirical investigation of pathological phenomena.

Looking back on his study of S.W. many years later, Jung saw in it the first expression of the 'idea of the independence of the unconscious, which distinguishes my views so radically from those of Freud' (1928 [preface written in 1935], p. 123). The unconscious is autonomous, like the automatisms which it produces. It can act independently of consciousness and is often personified in figures who express constellations of feeling-toned complexes. There were other particularly Jungian ideas expressed and used in this work for the first time. We have seen that the notion of active imagination was there, the method of thematizing psychic expressions into types was used, and the teleological significance of fantasies was recognized.

Eight years after the publication of '...Occult Phenomena' Jung saw nothing very Jungian in this work. In summarizing it for a psychoanalytic journal he says that in S.W.'s case, 'The splitting of the personality derives from its infantile tendencies and the fantasy systems are found to be rooted in sexual wish-deliria' (1910d, p. 403). In 1910 Jung was a follower of Freud's, and so he cast this work within the psychoanalytic framework. The distortions he produced in doing this were major. In 1902 he mentioned - in his first published citation to Freud - Freud's work on dreams and wondered if the mechanisms underlying S.W.'s fantasies could be those which Freud postulated for dreams. The influence of Freud is also evident in Jung's assertion that the fantasies about Ivenes's family and the fallen woman's romances are sexual wish-fulfillments. Contrary to his 1910 abstract, he did not find in the original work that all the fantasies were 'rooted in sexual wish-deliria.' As we have seen, the serio-religious and gay-hilarious figures as well as Ivenes were expressions of parts of S.W.'s personality, but not solely sexual fantasy figures. In 1902 Jung did not speak of infantile tendencies in S.W.'s case; in fact he reported absolutely nothing about her early childhood. He traced her problems back to puberty, not infancy.

Jung's 1935 and 1910 accounts of '...Occult Phenomena' illustrate that history shapes the meaning of a scientific work, and in retrospect any study which is important will be reinterpreted. Obviously Jung's hindsight was being shaped by his current preoccupations when in 1910 the case of S.W. was explained psychoanalytically. In 1935 the study was again reinterpreted, and Jung found in it the seeds of his later work in analytical psychology.

Bleuler, in his preface to Jung's 'Diagnostische Assoziations-studien,' briefly highlighted the importance of the word associa-tion test: it provides an 'index of all psychic processes, and we need only decipher it in order to know the whole man' (quoted in Jung, 1910d, p. 407). Bleuler instigated the work on the test, and from 1904 until 1910 many of Jung's publications, as well as the work of other staff at the Burghölzli, dealt with the results of this research. Following work done by Galton, Wundt, Kraepelin, and Aschaffenburg, Jung gave new life to an old psychological procedure. Wundt and others had studied reaction times to stimulus words, but had not been greatly concerned with the meaning of individual responses. Jung and his co-workers took a new look at the test and hypothesized that the responses to stimulus words, the length of reaction times, and failures to respond would tell something about an individual.

After considerable experimentation, Jung (1910 [1909]) standardized the administration of the test. The final list of 100 common words - concrete and abstract nouns, adjectives, verbs, and adverbs - were chosen because over many hundreds of sub-jects these produced the richest yield of information about the person. Before the test is given, the subject is read the follow-ing instructions: 'Answer as quickly as possible with the first word that occurs to you.' The first word on the list is then read, and the subject responds to it. With a stopwatch the experimenter measures the subject's reaction time. The 100 words are read one at a time, and the subject responds to each word before the next is read. If he or she fails to respond in from twenty to thirty seconds, the next word is read. After the entire list has been gone through once the experimenter starts over from the beginning, reading each word to the subject again and asking him or her to reproduce his or her original response to it.

Given the subject's responses, reaction times, perseverations and reproductions the psychic state of the individual at the time of taking the test can be constructed. Grouping associations by thematic content allows one to identify areas of concern to the subject; that is, complexes of ideas. 'The cement that holds the complex together is the *feeling-tone* common to all the indivi-dual ideas' (Jung, 1905d, p. 321).

In the word association test responses are determined by the past history of the subject: '*One associates according to what one is*' (Jung, 1906a, p. 417). Unusual responses, the use of quotations, cliches, or lines from songs, the repetition of the stimulus word, prolonged reaction times, and failure to repro-duce the original response are some of the indicants of the presence of a complex. In everyday life slips of the tongue; for-getting names, words and dates; highly emotional responses; or taking overly long to respond are indicants that a complex is at work. Such deviant reactions, thoughts, and behaviors can be grouped into constellations which share a common thematic

element. A definite feeling-tone - an affective valence - unites
the elements within a complex. The reactions of subjects 'are
thus *constellated by a complex*' (Jung, 1905d, p. 322). The subject produces reactions; Jung interprets these, ordering them
in thematic groups which he calls constellations, and from the
constellations he infers the presence of an underlying complex.
This was his method in this very early and elementary work on
complexes, and he used the same method later in formulating
his most sophisticated and controversial psychological theory
concerning archetypes. As Jung inferred the existence of different complexes from the presence of various constellations, so
he would infer the existence of different archetypes from the
presence of various archetypal images. As constellations are constructed by acts of interpretation - identifying the common theme
in responses, so archetypal images are ascertained by way of
interpretation - finding the common element in a series of imaginative, mythological, and symbolic productions.

In their investigations of normal individuals Jung and Riklin
say that 'an overwhelming number of the complexes we have
discovered...are erotic. In view of the great part played by love
and sexuality in human life, this is not surprising' (1904-5,
p. 137). A year later, in his inaugural lecture at the university,
Jung notes that when speaking about erotic complexes he uses
'the word "erotic" in the noble literary sense as opposed to the
medical' (1906a, p. 422).[2] Jung did not restrict his categorization
of complexes only to the erotic. In women erotic complexes concerned with their husbands, boyfriends, or past romances
dominate. Second in importance are complexes centering on social
questions such as status and earning a living.

The Swiss men whom Jung studied, just after the turn of the
century, had fewer erotic complexes than the women. For them
ambitious concerns were as important as the sexual ones; complexes centered in striving for physical, intellectual, or financial
power played a significant role in their lives.

In labeling and categorizing the different types of complexes,
Jung was carrying on work which he later expanded in his
investigation of archetypes. In his later work we will also see
that Jung was concerned with categorizing individuals into
personality types by assessing the characteristic way in which a
person is oriented toward her or himself and the environment.
Jung's division of subjects into two groups by categorizing their
characteristic ways of responding - into those who produced
subjective, egocentric reactions by reacting to the stimulus words
on the basis of a personal valuation, and those who produced
objective responses which reflect the social meaning or external
qualities of the stimulus words - anticipates his later work in
personality typology.

The establishment of sex differences, educational differences,
personality differences, or any general tendencies concerning
groups was, however, not Jung's major concern. With Riklin he
asserted that in the work on the association tests, 'The most

considerable variations in associations are conditioned by individual differences' (1904-5, p. 190). Jung was interested in the
test, because it provided a quick, fairly standardized, and easy
to administer method for assessing the concerns of individuals.
In any individual assessment the importance of clinical judgment
and interpretative skill is emphasized by Jung:

> Above all it must be stressed that, in addition to the practical
> test, there exists something that cannot be put on paper:
> namely those imponderables of human contact, those innumer-
> able and immeasurable facial expressions which, to a large
> extent, we do not even consciously perceive, which affect
> only our unconscious, but which are most powerfully convinc-
> ing. (1905d, p. 348)

The test can be woefully inadequate if it is not administered with
care and if the investigator uses it as a simple ruler instead of
as an aid to understanding.

Jung's experimental procedures in this work are easily criticized
on methodological grounds: subject recruitment is not the best,
procedures were not precisely standardized on different groups,
and although different experimenters tested different subjects
there is no analysis of what effect this may have had. We must
remember that his major concern was not precise experimental
methodology, but exploration of the uses of a simple test in the
diagnosis of individual cases. Jung's reports are filled with the
profiles of individual subjects to show how in each case the test
in conjunction with interpretation unearths complexes. Jung
relied on conversations with his subjects to find out why they
had difficulties responding to certain words and what the meanings of their responses were. Jung hoped that information gained
from such 'subjective analysis' could be shown to 'have a general
validity' (1905e, p. 263). With people who were not introspective
or who had little psychological acuity Jung hoped that the test
would provide useful 'objective' information where personal subjective insight was lacking.

Looking back on this work, Jung (1957) stresses that it had a
great educational value for him. It aided him to see clearly the
manifestations of unconscious processes. He says that the test
is just like an ordinary conversation with the exception that the
experimental procedures provide the psychologist with more
control than usual. What remained important for him were the
individual cases and the stories which could be constructed using
the test results. Working from idiosyncratic responses, perseverations, and other indicants Jung says you simply have to read
the test of the individual, piecing together its elements, and
then 'you get a nice story' about what is disturbing the person
(1935, p. 51). In 1905 Jung was not stressing the importance of
the individual's story or its construction, but in retrospect it
can be seen that behind all this experimental work on diagnosis
there lies latent a story-teller. Speaking about diagnostic work

Jung, with the perspective of over fifty years, says that diagnosis helps the doctor, not the patient. For the patient, 'The
crucial thing is the story' (1973b, p. 124).

While at the Burghölzli Jung was fully committed to an experimental scientific viewpoint. Chastising the old philosophical
psychology for its dogmatism he casts his lot with science: 'We
are...waiting for enlightenment from experimental psychology
which...is still in its infancy [and] yet can already look back on
a rich harvest' (1906a, p. 408). He stresses the absolute determinism of psychic processes and asserts that responses to the
association test are lawfully related to the operation of feeling-
toned complexes. All psychological events are in fact strictly
determined, because the 'occurrences of everyday life are nothing but association experiments on a major scale.' External
events simply create reactions in us which are strictly determined by 'what we are and have become' (p. 419). Giving his
determinism biological overtones, Jung crowns this pledge to
science: 'We act as our psychological past, i.e., as our cerebral
organization dictates' (p. 420). Within a decade Jung renounced
both experimental psychology and the notion that the present is
completely determined by the past.

In an essay on 'Cryptomnesia' Jung takes his biological determinism one step further claiming that long lost memories can
reappear after the passage of decades in new forms and unexpected ways, because the 'brain never forgets any impression, no
matter how slight; every impression leaves behind it some trace
in memory' (1905a, pp. 103-4). Consciousness operates by
continuously voiding itself of previous impressions; the unconscious is 'everything that is not represented in consciousness,
whether momentarily or permanently' (p. 95). The long-term
storage capacity of the unconscious and the retrieval of memories
years later is made possible, Jung asserts, 'by the physiology
of the brain' (p. 104). In this essay, which makes mincemeat of
distinctions between mental terms - memory, consciousness,
unconsciousness - and physiological terms - the functioning of
the brain - Jung is maintaining an epiphenomenalist, determinist,
and reductionist view of the mind-brain relationship. Psychological functioning, he asserts, is a manifestation of brain processes and can be explained physiologically. Of course, saying
that brain processes account for memory is at too gross a level
of generality to have much significance. The precise mechanisms
must be described or at least speculated on. Jung never did
attempt any detailed physiological explanation. There remained
throughout his later work passages where brain functioning or
structure was enlisted to support his psychological hypotheses,
but he never did go into anatomical detail or construct any
neurological models.

Three years after nearly equating memory with cortical functioning in the 'Cryptomnesia' essay Jung denounced psychiatric
materialism, as if he had never advocated such a position himself,
and attacked the then dominant psychiatric dogma that 'mental

diseases are diseases of the brain.' He held that psychiatry had
forgotten about the psyche. By attempting to reduce mental
functioning to neuroanatomy, 'Modern psychiatry behaves like
someone who thinks he can decipher the meaning and purpose
of a building by a mineralogical analysis of its stones' (Jung,
1908a, p. 160). In the vast majority of cases at the Burghölzli
no anatomical defects could be found when the brains of deceased
patients were autopsied. Jung, in contrast to the thrust of
'Cryptomnesia,' here sees the brain as the 'anatomical substrate'
of the mind, but says 'only beyond the brain...do we reach
what is important for us – the psyche, as indefinable as ever,
still eluding all explanation, no matter how ingenious,' (p. 158).
The psyche is identified with the 'meaning and purpose' of
human existence. Meaning is ascertained by interpretation, not
dissection.

Moving one's attention from the brain to the mind makes mental
illness more understandable. What materialist psychiatry cate-
gorizes as absurdities caused by malfunctioning brain cells take
on meaning if one practices psychical analysis. In attempting to
understand mental illness, 'We understand the method in the
madness, and the insane patient becomes more human to us. Here
is a person like ourselves, beset by common human problems,
no longer a cerebral machine thrown out of gear' (p. 165). Poets
are far better at creating an understanding of madness than are
psychiatrists, and until psychiatry studies the psyche, Jung
feels, the poet and novelist must be our guides.

Jung's work was aimed at creating an empirical conception of
the psyche in order to make it less indefinable and to increase
our understanding of the mental processes operative in mental
illness. The model of the psyche which grew out of his work on
the association experiments was a simple one. The psyche was
a group of feeling-toned complexes. A complex is composed of
sense-perceptions, intellectual material (ideas, memory-images,
judgments), and feeling-tone – an affective state accompanied
by somatic innervations. When a complex is activated by an
internal or external stimulus all three components are expressed.
That is, if I see or recall an old enemy the associations arising
from the hated rival's presence will include sensory sensations –
perhaps tightening of my muscles; cognitive activities – memories
of old combats, judgments concerning current strengths and
weaknesses; and emotional responses – feelings of hate. Complexes are not isolated from each other, and the activation of
one complex may lead to a whole series of responses expressing
many interconnected associative groupings.

Experientially, the ego-complex is the center of our sentient
existence. It is a matrix of associations, which are conscious
or can easily be made conscious, centering around my conception
of who I am. The ego-complex is 'I' and 'me' and its components
can be grouped into what I sense, think and feel. 'The ego is
the psychological expression of the firmly associated combination
of all body sensation' (Jung, 1907, p. 40).

While most of us feel that we are in control of what we experience and so attribute to the ego-complex an exclusive or at least dominant role in the psyche, Jung's experimental work shows that the ego is not the only power in the mind. Although people are fond of saying that they produce associations to stimulus words, responses to environmental stimuli, and thoughts of their own free will, Jung asserts that reactions to the association test:

> are by no means random thoughts but simply symptomatic acts, directed by a psychic factor that can behave like an independent being. The feeling-toned complex, for the time being split off from consciousness, exercises an influence that constantly and successfully competes with the intentions of the ego-complex; in spite of the rejecting and repressing attitude of the ego-complex, it brings about subjective and treacherous reactions and arouses associations the meaning of which is utterly unexpected by the ego-complex. (1905e, pp. 245-6)

Carefully guarded secrets, the most important and yet well-hidden joys and desires, and purposely forgotten events can all be uncovered by the association test, because when stimulus words touch on sensitive psychic areas the ego loses control, reaction times are prolonged, memory is disturbed, and unusual responses are made. All of this points to the existence of an autonomous complex operating outside, but upon, consciousness. The person feels compelled to respond and does not will the response. Overstating his point, Jung says, 'Ego-consciousness is merely the marionette that dances on the stage, moved by a concealed mechanism' (p. 245). The strong affectivity of the complex gives it the motive power to be produced at the slightest provocation, and, when a complex is aroused, ego-control is displaced or at least challenged.

In his first work on schizophrenia, 'The Psychology of Dementia Praecox' (1907), Jung formulates a theory which stresses the role of dissociated complexes and postulates the development of an unspecified metabolic imbalance in the etiology of this disorder. In this work Jung further develops his ideas on the functioning of complexes and the relations between the ego and unconscious complexes.

'Every affective event becomes a complex' (Jung, 1907, p. 67). If an event which arouses an emotional response is of only momentary significance, then the response slowly loses its excitation, fades into memory where the stimulus and affect, which are bound together, lie until a similar event by way of association arouses them. If a stimulus encounters an already existing complex, it both arouses the complex and becomes entangled in its associative web. As long as the emotional charge of a complex is not expressed, the complex retains its constellating power and draws experiences into its sphere of influence.

The formation of a complex is best understood by considering

what happens in frightful or traumatic situations. A situation
threatening danger pushes aside our normal ego-concerns,
activates our bodies, and focuses our attention. A single concern, the threatening situation, dominates our life. By arousing
fright, the event rules our bodily responses, producing somatic
innervations which further dislocate our normal attention and
highlight the dominance of the threatening condition. Normal
ego-functions are diminished; the only relevant event is the
traumatic one.

If we survive the frightful situation, it gradually recedes in
importance. Our knees shake less, our hearts stop pounding
and after a while we are calm. Normal ego-functioning reasserts
itself. That is, until a stimulus or memory recalls the trauma
and there is again a mild to severe upheaval in our emotional
state. Initially our lives are subordinated by a fright, and all
we can do is talk about it. With time the memory of the trauma
fades, but from 'time to time, first at short and then at longer
intervals, the fright-image returns, charged with new associations, and evokes re-echoing waves of affect' (p. 42). This
stretching out over time of the original trauma's effect, coupled
with its persistent emotional importance, increases the number
of associations which constellate around the nucleus of the
original fright. Strong affects, either pleasant or unpleasant,
always produce large complexes, because of their prolonged
and powerful stimulation of the body. Our attention remains
riveted to traumatic events, because our bodies reverberate with
the emotions generated by a fright. Conversely, large complexes
are always strongly feeling-toned, because they contain many
somatic innervations.

A frightful event produces a psychic sore spot, a 'complex-
sensitiveness.' Although the effect of a trauma diminishes over
time, perhaps only to be resurrected in dreams, all complexes
manifest the following characteristic: they reappear almost at
full strength when an event, idea, or stimulus similar to the
original trauma, even though much weaker, presents itself.

Chronic effects of complexes may be produced in two ways.
An occurrence may happen only once, but its emotional effects
are so strong that the event remains forever engraved on the
psyche. We have all had experiences which have changed our
lives, times of tremendous joy or sorrow which remain with us,
consciously or unconsciously, to this day. The event constellates
around itself numerous associations and works to order our lives.
Experiences consonant with the complex are assimilated to it;
dissonant ones are excluded or denied. If the feeling-tone of a
complex is extinguished - if a devotion passes or a trauma is
abreacted - the complex is extinguished with it. One's perspective is expanded for one is no longer dominated by the narrow
focus engendered by a powerful complex.

If the affect associated with a group of constellated ideas is in
a permanent state of excitation, then a complex with chronic
effects will be present. The best example of chronic complexes

are the sexual ones, since unsatisfied erotic desires continuously maintain one in an emotionally aroused state.

The ego's position of dominance is challenged by the existence of complexes; 'the complex occupies a relatively independent position in regard to the ego-complex - a vassal that will not give unqualified allegiance to its ruler' (p. 45). The stronger the feeling-tone of the complex, the more rebellious it is.

Hysterics and schizophrenics are both at the mercy of strong complexes. Their egos have lost exclusive control of their psyches, and so there are extensive distortions in mental functioning. Hysteria, Jung theorized, contains at its core a complex that can never be overcome completely. Psychic development is at a standstill, because all mental activity must cope with the complex. Most associations are directed toward the complex, and desires unfold from wishes associated with it. Bound to the complex, the hysteric is cut off from adaptation to the environment, for his or her responses are determined by the conflicted relations between the complex and the ego, instead of by the ego's relations with the world. Many hysterics regain normal functioning by partially overcoming the complex and avoiding situations which arouse it. According to Jung, hysteria develops because a pathological inheritance fosters the development of psychic traumas. A shock grows into an uncontrollable complex which finds expression in hysterical symptoms.

In dementia praecox, Jung says, the situation is different. There is a genetic predisposition toward this disease, but, unlike hysteria, the causal connection between the complex and illness is not certain. Jung postulates two possible etiologies. The one he favors is that the onset of the disease is caused by the development of a powerful complex, and besides its psychological effects the complex causes the production of 'an unknown quantity, possibly a toxin, which assists the work of destruction' (p. 97). 'It can...easily be imagined that the complex creates a condition in the brain functionally equivalent to an extensive destruction of the cerebrum' (p. 96). The other hypothesis, which he admits as a possibility, is that in individuals predisposed to schizophrenia there may be the physiological production of an unknown toxin, which, when it reaches sufficient levels, acts as a poison in the brain seizing on pre-existing complexes and producing the impression that psychological disturbances connected with the complex are etiologically significant. This latter hypothesis was one put forth by Bleuler.

Either causal scenario leads to the same result. The ego loses control of psychic functioning; the complex seems to be at the helm of the mind, and the prognosis for improvement is poor. Genetic predisposition, biochemical malfunction, and the operation of psychological factors, then, are the three factors in Jung's etiological equations. These three are still the essential ingredients of present-day theories about schizophrenia (Gottesman and Shields, 1972; Meehl, 1972).

In addition to an extensive review of the literature, his

elaboration of the complex theory, and his hypotheses concerning the etiology of dementia praecox, Jung, in his 'Dementia Praecox', also presents a case study of a schizophrenic woman, Babette S. Born in poverty, her father a drunkard and her sister a prostitute, she had a 'severe hereditary taint' and had been hospitalized for over twenty years when Jung began working with her. Babette was ruled by her complexes. She expressed them fairly easily and showed little affect when she did so. This was because her ego had been overthrown by these powerful psychic constellations. On the surface her utterances were bizarre. However, by having her produce all the associations she could to a particular key word in her delusions and then by interpreting and grouping these thematically Jung made sense of Babette's mental world. Her utterances coalesced around three complexes: wish-fulfillments primarily centered in self-aggrandizement, the complex of being wronged by others, and a sexual constellation. She spoke as if in a dream, and so she did not distinguish between logical and analogical connections. The world became an extension of her fantasies. She had been poor all her life and wished to be both rich and famous, so she was: 'I am the master key.' 'I am triple owner of the world.' She had been a dressmaker, but in her wish-filled world she said, 'I was the best dressmaker, never left a bit of cloth on the floor - fine world of art.'

Balancing these pleasant delusions were unpleasant ones. Jung says, 'Ideas of injury are the usual compensation of exaggerated self-esteem, and we seldom find one without the other' (p. 133). Aggrandizing her position, she identified herself with Socrates, but like him she too was persecuted. 'Dreams change metaphors into reality,' and so in her mind, which was always in a dream, Babette was Socrates (p. 113).

The sexual complex was expressed with greater difficulty than the others and with far more affect. Many of Babette's associations were about marriage, and her fantasies contained rich and thinly disguised coitus symbolism. When speaking about sexual matters, there were continual interruptions of Babette's monologue. She blushed and made gestures of embracing. The thoughts were strongly repressed, and there was resistance to their expression. The 'telephone' made several disparaging remarks.

The 'telephone' was the last remnant of her ego-complex and the remains of Babette's self-critical faculties. It manifested itself with intrusions into her speech commenting on what she had just said. After she said that her death would be a great loss to the world, the telephone said, 'It would do no harm.' Babette called herself 'a Switzerland'; Jung laughed, and the phone said to Babette, through Babette, 'That is going a bit too far!' (p. 149). Babette entered into dialogues with the telephone, taking both parts. This is truly a dissociation of personality. Instead of the ego trying to maintain control, Babette's ego had so lost control that it had become a split off complex disturbing her delusional world by making realistic, if somewhat sarcastic, comments.

'The Psychology of Dementia Praecox' was a pioneering study in the psychology of schizophrenia, and Jung foresaw unfavorable critical reactions. He asked his readers' indulgence, but realized 'the critic must be ruthless in the interests of truth' (p. 151). In his autobiography Jung says his 'Dementia Praecox' did not meet with much sympathy: 'In fact, my colleagues laughed at me' (1973b, p. 149). Going back to the reviews, Decker flatly contradicts Jung's account: 'This book was widely and generally favorably reviewed' (1977, p. 143). Attacks on the book were definitely in the minority. Jung's historical fable of his having been an outcast continues, although at the time, 1907, he was receiving recognition as an authority in his field.

SUPPORT FOR PSYCHOANALYSIS

We will return to 'The Psychology of Dementia Praecox,' for in it Jung declares his support for many of Freud's ideas. And yet, in it - and in Freud's reactions to it, and Jung's response to Freud's evaluation - can be found problems that would later lead to the severance of their personal and professional connections. Before taking up this important work again we will trace Jung's growing support for psychoanalysis from 1901 to 1907.

In his autobiography Jung says he read 'The Interpretation of Dreams' in 1900, but failing to grasp it laid it aside and returned to it three years later, when he had gained the personal experience necessary to see how it linked up with his own ideas. In 1901, after Jung had been at Burghölzli for less than two months, Bleuler had him write an extended summary of Freud's 'On Dreams.' This was probably delivered as a report to the professional staff. 'On Dreams' was a somewhat popularized condensation of the dream book, and Jung's (1973a) summary demonstrates a good grasp of the work. Jung's criticisms of it are sympathetic. He chastises Freud for his anthropomorphic description of the censorship and expresses the conviction that some dreams, such as fearful ones, are not wish-fulfillments.

The review is missing one important element of 'On Dreams,' the notion that 'repressed infantile sexual wishes provide the most frequent and strongest motive-forces for the construction of dreams' (Freud, 1901a, p. 682). Nowhere in his review does Jung mention Freud's central thesis: adult dreams are disguised fulfillments of infantile sexual wishes! This creates some problems for Jung in recounting the dynamics of repression and the censorship of the latent dream, but on the whole he gets the mechanics correct even though he leaves out infantile wishes. Although Jung came to support psychoanalysis, he always had a difficult time accepting the importance of infantile sexuality. It is significant that in this first work on psychoanalysis he omits this very important Freudian notion.

Citations to Freud grew steadily in Jung's writing. In 1905 he acknowledged a debt to Breuer and Freud's work as a 'valuable stimulus' to his association studies. In his autobiography Jung says that at this time he underwent great soul-searching in presenting his results on the word association test as supporting Freud's ideas. A few citations and saying a person's work was a valuable stimulus are not a strong commitment. His autobiography continues by saying that his goal was a university career and that at this time Freud was '*persona non grata* in the academic world..., and any connection with him would have been damaging in academic circles' (1973b, p. 148). Jung says he was tempted to publish his conclusions without mentioning Freud, but decided he could not build his life on a lie. He concludes, 'From then on I became an open partisan of Freud's and fought for him' (p. 148).

This account is more of Jung's presentation of his life as a moral struggle fighting against the prejudices of his peers and attempting to follow the path of truth. In 1904 Freud's name was not anathema in academic circles. In 1902 his work had been recognized in Vienna with his promotion to professor extraordinarius at the university. Bleuler, Jung's chief, was professor of psychiatry at the University of Zurich and a supporter of psychoanalysis. As early as 1896 he had written a very positive review of 'Studies on Hysteria.' Bleuler first met Freud in 1904, and they carried on an extensive correspondence. Jung could count on his immediate superior's support of his work on psychoanalysis.

In 1906, as an outgrowth of a debate with another psychiatrist named Aschaffenburg, Jung published a paper defending many of Freud's ideas. In response to this paper Jung, in his autobiography, says that two professors from Germany wrote to him warning that if he continued his advocacy of psychoanalysis he would be endangering his academic career. Jung replied that he '"didn't give a damn for a career if it has to be based on the premise of restricting research and concealing the truth"' (1973b, p. 148). Jung didn't have much to worry about. Two letters do not constitute a serious threat, and Jung's career had not been hurt by his support for Freud. In his inaugural lecture at the university, given in October 1905, Jung, obviously not anticipating academic censure, said modern psychiatry will be 'very much indebted' to Freud's 'far-seeing psychological understanding' (1906b, p. 423).

Like Freud, Jung overexaggerates the opposition to psychoanalysis and to his own work, seeing threats from all quarters aimed at his research. And yet, he received wide recognition and rapid advancement because of his investigations.

In his 1905 papers Jung presents his work as supporting Freud's findings and himself as a proponent of Freud's ideas. In two papers and one review there are declarations concerning the importance of Freud's work; the strongest is that Freud's psychoanalysis 'ranks among the greatest achievements of modern

psychology' (1905d, p. 333). With this accolade came two complaints: Freud's work was not widely enough read or as yet
understood, and criticisms of psychoanalysis had been made by
people who had not tried it. Jung accuses his colleagues of making ex cathedra pronouncements on psychoanalysis and argues
that such tactics have no place in science. He argues that to
make psychoanalytic interpretations and thereby test the fruit-
fulness of the method one must completely assimilate Freud's
ideas. Jung recognizes the possibility that in this type of work
the investigator may interpret into the subject's statements more
than is in them and acknowledges that 'even Freud' has been
accused of doing this (p. 331). He sees that the analytic situation does produce certain typical responses and a uniformity in
the analyst's 'retrospective elucidation' of the material (p. 331).
Although not presented as a criticism here, this point would
later be expanded by Jung into a criticism of psychoanalysis:
Freud's method and his focus create the material he asserts he
is discovering.

In addition to the general declaration of support for psychoanalysis Jung also demonstrated how his researches on word
association provided evidence for it and how Freud's work could
be explained by complex theory. Jung found that repression –
not wanting to remember – operates not only in dreams and
parapraxes, but also in the association test. The test allows one
to diagnose the existence of repressed complexes. The laying
bare of these is of great importance in the therapy of hysteria
because: 'Every hysterical patient has a repressed complex of
causal significance. It is therefore essential for treatment that
the complex be identified, unless one wants to forgo such important psychotherapeutic aids' (Jung, 1905b, p. 273). Freud's
'ingenious' method of free association works to overcome, by
circumventing them, the inhibitions repressing the complex. This
method, however, is time-consuming and requires certain skills
in the patient and analyst. Jung says his association test uncovers the same material and is easier to administer and interpret.

In the above essay, 'Experimental Observations of the Faculty
of Memory,' Jung concludes that the 'theory of our phenomenon
is closely related to the teaching of Freud...' (p. 286). Hysterical
forgetting is motivated by repressing the affect associated with
bad memories and the amnesic blockages on the association test
'are nothing but hysterical amnesias' (p. 286). The production
of an indifferent response after a long delay and the failure to
remember the response are very similar to the hysteric's construction of screen memories, inoffensive scenes which cover
highly charged reminiscences. Hysterics often cannot repeat such
fabrications accurately, just as subjects in the association tests
cannot repeat responses which have been indifferently produced
by them. Screen memories and screen responses are the result
of a compromise. The ego wishes not to be reminded of an unpleasant experience and so represses all material relevant to it, but
a stimulus activates the complex so it pushes for expression.

Delays in reaction time reflect the conflict of conscious and unconscious forces. The result is finally an indifferent response, but it cannot be remembered because during its production and attempted reproduction the ego has been distracted by its attempts not to remember the complex. In the association test repressed unconscious complexes betray themselves in normal subjects by a brief embarrassment or momentary blockage, in hysterical cases by long delays, amnesias, and the production of indifferent associations which are subsequently forgotten.

Jung followed up this work with a paper titled 'Psychoanalysis and Association Experiments.' It opens with the statement that although psychoanalysis has made progress in understanding hysteria, Freud's formulations are still undergoing revision and 'neither Freud nor we, his followers, have gained full knowledge of [hysteria]' (p. 288). We have traced Jung's growing support for and increasing frequency of citations to Freud since 1901; here he commits himself.

Following this declaration of allegiance Jung makes two insightful comments about Freud's approach. The first is that psychoanalytic terms are not clearly defined scientific concepts, but clever 'coinages' from Freud's rich vocabulary. Jung uses this point in an attempt to insulate Freud from criticism, arguing that the debate about analysis should focus on the essential meaning of concepts and not on mere words. Such distinctions, unfortunately, are often very hard to make.

The second point concerns psychoanalytic interpretation. Jung feels that to use Freud's method the practitioner must possess a 'psychological sensitivity' which cannot be taken for granted in either physicians or psychologists. The art of interpretation requires a 'particular way of thinking...that is innate in the poet but is carefully avoided in scientific thought' (Jung, 1906c, p. 289). One must be able to think divergently in flights of ideas, not just convergently in logically linked causal chains.

Obviously inspired by Freud's 'Fragment of an Analysis of a Case of Hysteria,' Jung follows these general remarks with his first psychoanalytic case study. The patient, Miss E., was thirty-seven years old and a teacher. She complained of insomnia, restlessness, irritability toward her family and impatience with other people. E. came to Jung for hypnotic treatment, but he could not hypnotize her so he treated her psychoanalytically. [3]

The history of E.'s problems was hard to obtain. She was vague in her recollections saying only that the illness had started several years ago, she had been to many doctors who did not help her, and she thought she must already be mad. Jung felt E. was talking around her problems; there was something 'she either did not want to or could not say' (p. 292). Here we have the classic psychoanalytic problem: knowing and not knowing.

Making defensive gestures as if to ward off thoughts, blushing and stammering, E. finally divulged some of her troubles. She could not sleep, because if she went to sleep she would die or go mad. Thousands of ideas were running through her head and she was confused. She couldn't tell Jung these thoughts, because if she did he would be contaminated by them. She had already infected a priest and a doctor with her crazy ideas. Jung assured her that he had heard many such thoughts, and they hadn't harmed him. She then confessed, all the while making defensive gestures, that a woman neighbor had recently died without receiving the last sacrament, and it was E.'s fault. Several years ago, a young man who had been her pupil in his childhood had died, and she developed the idea that the beatings that she had occasionally given him had caused his death.

Jung administered an association test in order to identify issues that E. could not speak about freely. By interpreting her responses he identified two complexes. In a 100-word test thoughts related to her alcoholic father accounted for disturbances in reactions to five stimulus words. This minor complex was perhaps related to the dominant erotic complex. The sexual constellation consisted of over twenty disturbed reactions on the test. By grouping these Jung identified three sets of erotic concerns: the dominant one was with masturbation, the other two dealt with her low opinion of her appearance and her hopes and fears about marriage.

Given the results of the test, Jung told E. that 'her obsessional ideas were nothing but excuses and shiftings, that in reality she was tortured by sexual ideas' (p. 304). She denied this and was sincere in her insistence that although she thought about marriage she did not do so any more than most people.

At this point in any treatment Jung says the state of mind and approach of the doctor is crucial. Faced with the neurotic's denials, evasions, and failures of memory, the doctor must be absolutely convinced that if the analytic method is pursued the truth will come forward. If the doctor has reservations, he or she will get lost in 'the snares and traps laid by the complex' and will be of no help to the patient (p. 304). Jung was convinced by the association test that there was a repressed erotic complex operating unconsciously in E. and that only by bringing it to light could she be cured of her obsessions.

The treatment began with E. sitting in an easy chair and Jung sitting down behind her, 'so as not to confuse her.'* He asked her to tell him 'everything that came into her mind, no matter what it was about' (p. 304). After laughing, saying it was impossible, declaring she was wasting his time, asking how he could expect to cure her, moving restlessly about in the chair, exclaiming this was all nonsense, making defensive gestures, gulping, undulating her thorax, claiming that something silly had come into her head, but she could not tell it because he would laugh, and insisting she would leave because she could not face doing this for several weeks the 'following story at last emerged with innumerable stoppages and interruptions...' (p. 306). This is resistance! After an hour and a half the result of the first session was a story about sex. In the household where she had been a governess to the boy there was also a gardener. The gardener

told E. he wanted to sleep with her and had tried to kiss her.
She pushed him away. That night, however, when she went to
bed she listened to try to hear if the gardener was coming to
see her. She thought about what he would do; she then
reproached herself for these thoughts, but the ideas would not
leave her head. Having told this story E. felt somewhat relieved.

That evening, however, while lying in bed she remembered
another story. At the next session she vowed to tell this second
incident and be done with it. It again took her an hour and a
half filled with resistance to tell another sexual tale from the
time when she had been a governess. The third session brought
yet another recollection from her days as a governess of her
fascination with the sexual goings on in the household and her
concurrent reproaches against herself for having an interest in
such matters.

In the analytic sessions sexual remembrances occurred to E.
which she said she had never known before. Jung cautions that
the sexual ideas may have been continuously cultivated by E.,
thus they may not all be relics of the past. Having to speak
about them to someone else, thus focusing her conscious awareness on them, may have caused the blockages in her narrative.
Jung says about E.: 'Her everyday person and her sexual person
are just two different complexes, two different aspects of consciousness that do not want to or must not know anything of one
another' (p. 309). The analytic situation forced the normal E.
to confront and recognize her sexual side, and when she avowed
these interests she felt better.

The reproach that she had caused the death of the boy was a
displacement of her self-reproaches about her sexual fantasies.
Tortured by feelings of inadequacy over not being able to suppress her erotic thoughts she tried to compensate by demanding
more of her teaching. These demands made her think her peda-
gogical techniques were inadequate. She transferred her guilt
from sexuality – which she didn't want to think about – to education, about which she was more willing to be tormented. She was
a bad teacher, not a sex-crazed woman, and her teaching methods
had caused the death of her pupil.

E.'s self-reproaches about failing to obtain the last sacrament
for her neighbor were again displacements of sexual guilt. The
woman neighbor, who had a dubious reputation, and E., who
was a very decent woman from a good family, discussed the
intimate details of all the sexual scandals in the community. E.
felt she had caused the woman's death, because they had shared
sexual stories. Trying to obtain relief from her guilt she consulted a priest and a doctor, but because she had spoken with
them they had become contaminated. Jung concludes, 'Underlying all this is the general idea that she is a horrible creature
who infects everything with her depravity' (p. 311).

E. began to improve at the very beginning of the treatment,
when the sexual stories replaced the obsessive reproaches about
infecting others. The more stories she told the better she felt.

E. 'was so obsessed by the sexual reminiscences that she was
never able to find peace until she had told the story again'
(p. 309). E. was cured by talking: Jung was practicing narrative therapy.

After telling these tales another strong resistance was met.
E. said she had nothing more to say and wanted to leave. There
followed reminiscences about adolescent sexual activity, the
confession that she masturbated and finally the recollection that
at age seven or eight she had often listened to her parents
having sexual intercourse. Jung identifies this last revelation
as the psychic trauma and says that such events leave a strong
emotional charge in a child's mind which is bound to constellate
thoughts and actions for years. E. was interested in finding out
sexual secrets: in spying, overhearing, and gossiping about
sex. Her sexual energies had been perverted; her sexuality had
been identified with the vulgar, the unclean, the secret. Because
E. had to deny any sexual awareness at all there were lacuna
in consciousness. These gaps had to be filled in by producing
ideas which were compatible with consciousness and which would
explain her self-reproaches, inability to sleep, and bad moods.
The obsessive ideas about her student, neighbor, priest, and
former doctor served this purpose.

E. could not acknowledge her interest in sex, had repressed
and denied it, and had, therefore, been unconsciously driven
by it. In the last two sessions she 'produced the choicest selec-
tions of [the] most repulsive obscenities that she had occasionally
heard in the street' (p. 314). Jung says he must be spared
recounting these; 'the number and the extreme vulgarity of these
jokes appeared to me almost incredible for such an educated and
decent lady' (p. 314). No wonder E. could not avow her sexual
side; even her therapist was shocked at her having such
thoughts.

Fortunately E. managed to express the split-off erotic aspect
of her personality. Such dissociated 'contents of the mind are
destroyed by being released from repression through an effort
of will' (p. 317). Jung says that expressing repressed ideas
causes them to lose much of their power, authority, and horror
and, therefore, gives the patient a feeling of once again being
master of her thoughts. He stresses that he puts emphasis 'on
arousing and strengthening...the will and not on mere "abreact-
ing," ' as Freud originally did' (p. 317).

In this, his first psychoanalytic case study, Jung has obviously
committed himself to recounting the sexual history of an obsessive. Although at the beginning of the essay he says Freud sees
hysteria as caused by a series of psychic traumas culminating
in a prepubertal sexual trauma, Jung does not uncover an actual
seduction scene in E.'s case. What Freud did in the case of
Dora, Jung does with E. No pre- or post-pubertal seduction was
found in either case, but the existence of childhood sexual disturbances was established in both cases from the women's reminiscences of childhood sexual activities and events from their

youths related to sex.

Jung stresses the value that the responses to the association test had in bringing forth repressed sexual material. They 'served as signposts among the maze of ever-changing fantasies that at every stage threatened to put the analyst on the wrong track' (p. 316). Jung concludes this essay by saying that Freud's work on obsessional neurosis is 'still consistently ignored' and, therefore, it gives him 'great satisfaction to draw attention to Freud's theories - at the risk of also becoming a victim of persistent amnesia' (p. 317). Neither Freud nor Jung has yet been forgotten.

Jung published another psychoanalytic case study in 1906, 'Association, Dream, and Hysterical Symptom.' The patient was a twenty-four-year-old 'girl' who suffered from various hysterical symptoms. She was troubled by hallucinations of black and white figures, extreme sensations of heat and was afraid of going mad. Several association tests unearthed three complexes: a school, illness, and erotic complex. Besides reporting in detail the test results and his interpretations, Jung also analyzed nine of the patient's dreams. About dreams, he says, 'Nature has an apparatus that makes an extract of the complexes and brings them to consciousness in an unrecognizable form: this is the *dream*' (1906d, p. 383). Jung follows Freud's method of dream-interpretation and presents a more detailed account of his investigations than Freud usually did. Jung records the manifest dream, all the patient's associations, and shows how he has made his interpretations. The presentation is not unreadable, as Freud feared such a report would be, but Jung's study lacks the coherence of Freud's cases. Jung shows that the patient's dreams, responses to the association test, and symptoms all were determined by and point to her complexes. He sees the erotic complex as constituting the core of her difficulties. The analysis was carried back to puberty, but Jung failed to get any further into the past. He hints that the patient, as a girl, might have been seduced by her brother, but admits there is no solid evidence for this.

The woman was not cured, and Jung says the treatment failed because her ego had been greatly weakened by the strongly entrenched sexual complex. Under the domination of this complex and her identification with being ill she had become dedicated to remaining sick. Her symptoms provided a satisfaction of her unconscious sexual desires and an expression, which had become habitual, of her being. To overcome such resistances Jung proposes a 'purposive treatment of hysteria' aimed at strengthening what remains of the normal ego by 'introducing some new complex that liberates the ego from domination by the complex of illness' (p. 407). This strengthening of the ego by the analyst forming a therapeutic alliance with the analysand's healthy ego is stressed by contemporary psychoanalytic ego psychologists as one of their essential treatment strategies. They very seldom credit Jung as one of the pioneers of this idea.

After the break with Freud, Jung found in the numinous fascination of age-old symbols the power needed to dislodge the interest of neurotics from their pathological complexes.

Jung's essays on the word association test, including his case study of Miss E., were collectively republished in 1906 in 'Diagnostische Assoziationsstudien.' In April of that year he sent a copy of this book to Freud. Freud's letter of thanks marks the beginning of their correspondence. He told Jung that in his impatience he had already bought the book. The study that pleased him the most was 'Psychoanalysis and Association Experiments,' because in it Jung argues on the strength of his own experience that 'everything' Freud has said about their common field of work 'is true.' Freud closed, 'I am confident that you will often be in a position to back me up, but I shall also gladly accept correction' (McGuire, 1974, p. 3).

Courtesy did not require a reply from Jung, and so for six months no letters were exchanged. Freud quickly acknowledged the importance of the association experiment work. In a lecture delivered in June 1906. 'Psychoanalysis and the Establishment of Facts in Legal Proceedings,' Freud demonstrated the close ties between psychoanalysis and the work on complexes. His first citation to Jung bestowed his approval and certified the importance of Jung's researches.[5] Freud says that the association experiments 'only became significant and fruitful when Bleuler in Zurich and his pupils, especially Jung, began to turn their attention to...[them]' (1906b, p. 104). Freud then says Jung's paper on 'The Psychological Diagnosis of Evidence' is 'well calculated to make us doubt the occurrence of chance or of what is alleged to be arbitrary in mental events' (p. 104).

Although both Breuer and Freud had used the word 'complex' in 'Studies,' Freud takes up the term in this lecture following Jung's usage of it. Freud is careful to show that the notion of complexes can best be understood within the theoretical framework of psychoanalysis, thereby making the Zurich researches a subset of broader psychoanalytic concerns. He obviously finds the expression 'complexes' congenial. For example, he casts the aim of psychoanalysis in the language of complexes when he says psychoanalysis in every case must uncover 'complexes...which have been repressed because of feelings of unpleasure' (p. 112).

Freud sent Jung a book containing a collection of his essays on psychoanalysis and Jung's letter of thanks, written in October 1906, began a regular exchange which lasted until 1913. 'The Freud/Jung Letters' (McGuire, 1974) record in detail these two men's coming closer to each other both personally and professionally, their united efforts to strengthen the psychoanalytic movement, their agreements and reservations concerning psychological issues, the emotional, intellectual and administrative strains between them, and their final break. Totaling over three hundred letters, with very few missing, this correspondence is a minimally censored account of a significant collaboration and a momentous alienation of affections.

Jung's first letter is concerned with a lively debate he had
with Gustav Aschaffenburg at a congress of psychiatrists in
May 1906. Aschaffenburg was a noted German psychiatrist to
whom Jung had given credit for important work on the association experiments. At the congress and in a later paper (1906)
Aschaffenburg attacked Freud's work, especially his sexual
theories and treatment methods. He found untenable the psychoanalytic proposition that behind every hysteria was a sexual
trauma. In addition he took objection to Freud's discussing sexual
matters with patients for months at a time. Aschaffenburg asserted that Freud found sexual traumas, because his extended
discussions put erotic ideas into his patient's heads (Decker,
1977).

Jung, in his letter to Freud, says his defense was of Freud's
psychological theories, that is the work concerning dreams,
jokes, slips, and psychic mechanisms. Jung felt he did not
understand Freud's therapy well enough to defend it and didn't
yet have the right case material on which to test it. He concludes with a reservation that he expressed throughout the early
letters and which was eventually to play an important part in
the break with Freud: 'it seems to me that though the genesis
of hysteria is predominantly, it is not exclusively, sexual. I take
the same view of your sexual theory' (McGuire, 1974, pp. 4-5).
That is, sexuality is not the single determinant of psychic functioning. In harping on the sexual issue, Jung says Aschaffenburg
missed the essential core of Freud's work - the psychological
theories.

Concerning Jung's defense of psychoanalysis, Freud says to
him: 'Your writings have long led me to suspect that your appre-
ciation of my psychology does not extend to all my views on
hysteria and the problem of sexuality, but I venture to hope
that in the course of the years you will come much closer to me
than you now think possible' (p. 5). He then says Jung's 'splendid analysis' in 'Psychoanalysis and Association Experiments'
shows how the sexual factor can hide and what a therapeutic aid
it is when uncovered.

Focusing as much on the importance of sexuality as Aschaffenburg did, Freud expresses the hope that his investigations
of sexuality 'will prove to be the most significant' (p. 6). Referring to his critic's paper, Freud says Aschaffenburg's attack is
full of 'inanities' and that he fails to understand the simplest
symbolism; 'he is motivated chiefly by an inclination to repress
sexuality, that troublesome factor so unwelcome in good society'
(p. 6). Driving home his attack, Freud asserts 'Here we have
two warring worlds and soon it will be obvious to all which is on
the decline and which is on the ascendant.' The struggle will be
a long one, and Freud believes he will not see the end of it, but
his followers will triumph. His followers, he hopes, will be 'all
those who are able to overcome their own inner resistance to the
truth and...cast off the last vestiges of pusillanimity in their
thinking' (p. 6). Freud was willing to fight for the truth of

sexuality and wanted a few good men with courage to follow him.
Jung, like Breuer ten years earlier, was not prepared to fight
for one truth and especially someone else's. He felt 'alarmed by
the positivism' of Freud's insistence on sexuality (p. 7).

Jung attributed his reservations about sexuality to a lack of
experience, a theme which will recur in subsequent letters. He
asks if Freud does not think that a number of psychopathological
problems may arise through a confluence of the two basic drives
- sex and hunger. Sometimes the hunger drive may be the cause
of problems, at other times sex. Most often the two basic drives
are interwoven, and so one can see in most activities manifestations of both of them. The mouth, for instance, is an organ of
hunger when eating, in sucking hunger predominates although
sexuality may be seen, and in kissing sexuality is dominant.

Freud's reply was understanding, but insistent. He saw no
theoretical objection to the possibility of hunger playing a role,
but says it has never been seen to 'assert itself unmistakably
in the psychoneuroses....For the present I content myself with
pointing out what is glaringly evident, that is, the role of sexuality' (p. 8). Freud closes saying that he is delighted with Jung's
letters.

Jung's reply included a reprint of his 'Freud's Theory of
Hysteria; A Reply to Aschaffenburg.' He says it is tailored to
his own viewpoint, hopes it does not misrepresent Freud, and
says it is written from honest conviction.

The 'Reply' is non-combative. Jung opens saying Aschaffenburg's criticisms of Freud's theories are on the whole moderate.
Jung then separates Freud's work on dreams, slips, and disturbances of thought - the psychological work - from the theories
concerning sexuality and treatment. He says the former have
not been criticized by Aschaffenburg. Jung is trying to isolate
that which he clearly supports in Freud's work, and feels has
won and will win wide approval, from the sexual doctrines.

About sexuality, Jung says it is obvious that it plays an
important role in the psyche, perhaps only rivaled by that of
hunger. Freud's view that sexuality is the causal determinant in
the psychoneuroses can thus claim a high degree of probability,
but the proposition must be limited. This is because Freud has
not examined every hysteric and so his assertion must be 'subject to the general limitation which applies to all empirical axioms'
(1906b, p. 4). That is, the next case may prove him wrong and
thus limit the scope of his theory. Jung presents three empirical
cautions about Freud's work. One, Freud has confirmed his
theory in the cases he has examined, but these are a small frac-
tion of all the cases of hysteria. Two, there might be forms of
hysteria as yet undiscovered. Three, it is possible that 'Freud's
material, under the constellation of his writings, has become
somewhat one-sided.' Given these reservations, Jung modifies
Freud's dictum: 'An indefinitely large number of cases of hysteria
derive from sexual roots' (p. 4).

To disprove this, Jung asserts, the psychoanalytic method

must be used, for without an in-depth psychic exploration one
totally fails to test Freud's ideas. He says that although psychoanalytic investigation is difficult for the beginner, his work on
the association test can be repeated by anyone, and in doing so
one can gain an initial exposure to the processes Freud is describing.

Jung, in his defense of Freud, takes up a position based on
empiricism: try it and find out. He is attempting to avoid a war
by mediating between 'two warring worlds.' He is defending
Freud empirically, which in science should be safe ground. He
proclaims that it is beneath the dignity of science to reject
Freud's work without having thoroughly put it to the test by
using psychoanalytic methods.

Jung separates the question of talking with patients about sex
from the question of the scientific validity of Freud's hypotheses.
Discussions about sex get mixed up with morals, Jung observes,
and the tact of the doctor must be counted on. Jung says in
some cases sexual enlightenment may do good, in others harm –
it is up to the therapist to decide when or when not to discuss
it. Sometimes it is difficult to remain neutral, and this last point
compromises Jung's position that psychoanalysis must be put to
the test by following the psychoanalytic method. The practice of
psychoanalysis depends on a free and open exchange between
analyst and analysand. If the doctor decides in a case that
sexuality will not be discussed then one has made the results of
that case totally irrelevant as a test of psychoanalytic hypotheses.

Freud's reply to Jung's paper defending him is missing, but it
must have been understanding, because in Jung's next letter
he thanks Freud for not taking offense at some of his statements.
He goes on to state his position in the war. He will not attack
the opponents of psychoanalysis, as they deserve to be attacked,
but will leave them 'a line of retreat' so that 'recantation' will
not be difficult for them (McGuire, 1974, p. 10).

The next passage in this 4 December letter is vital, for in it
Jung clearly states his position on his support of Freud's work:

> If I confine myself to advocating the bare minimum, this is
> simply because I can advocate only as much as I myself have
> unquestionably experienced, and that, in comparison with
> your experience, is naturally very little. I am beginning to
> understand many of your formulations and several of them
> are still beyond me, which does not mean by a long shot that
> I think you are wrong. I have gradually learnt to be cautious
> even in disbelief. (pp. 10-11)

His ground rules for collaboration are empirical; he will support
what he has found to be true. The rest he will suspend judgment
on.

Freud's reply evidences a wishful reading of Jung's words:

I am delighted with your promise to trust me for the present
in matters where your experience does not yet enable you to
make up your own mind – though of course only until it does
enable you to do so. Even though I look at myself very critically, I believe I deserve such trust, but I ask it of very few
persons. (p. 13)

Jung did not say he would trust Freud's judgment, but merely
that he would be cautious in his disbelief. Freud has made a
strong bid for Jung's trust and unfortunately assumes he has
it.

Freud's reply also introduced a point which would become a
problem between them. Freud says he sees in Jung's publications
that Jung is modifying his opinions for pedagogic effect. Freud
felt that in Jung's letters his views were obviously in close
accord with Freud's own and, therefore, freer of distortion.
This was not a wise assumption. Jung tailored his views for his
audience. If that audience were hostile to psychoanalysis Jung
tried to win them over by stressing the more palatable – that is
less sexual – aspects of Freud's theories. If the audience was
Freud, Jung stressed his agreements with the fundamental
doctrines of psychoanalysis. To Freud, Jung expressed reservations about the sexual theory, but he usually attributed such
doubts to his own lack of experience.

In reply to Jung's hedgings on talking about sex with patients
Freud stressed the importance of discussing sexuality in therapy
by highlighting the importance of the transference in treatment.
The analyst must talk about sex, because unconscious erotic
attachments are at the center of the analytic relationship. The
analyst exploits and interprets these attachments in order to
make the analysand aware of her or his hidden secrets. The
analyst's task is translation and transference makes translation
possible.

Aschaffenburg behind them and their relationship growing
closer, Freud and Jung found a new crisis at hand. Jung sent
Freud a copy of 'The Psychology of Dementia Praecox,' and
Freud must have written back a rather critical letter. The letter
is missing, but Jung's 29 December 1906, reply opens with his
apologizing to Freud for being a nuisance and saying he understands that Freud 'cannot be anything but dissatisfied with [his]
book, since it treats your researches too ruthlessly' (p. 13).
It did?

In the foreword Jung states, 'Even a superficial glance at my
work will show how much I am indebted to the brilliant discoveries of Freud' (1907, p. 3). Jung restates points he has made
before: Freud's ideas can only be refuted by using the psychoanalytic method, adherence to Freud's ideas does not mean submission to a dogma, and one can respect Freud's work, but still
entertain an independent judgment. Jung, then, states his divergence from Freud. He does not 'attribute to the infantile sexual
trauma the exclusive importance that Freud apparently does'

(p. 4). He admits that sexuality plays an enormous role in psychic life, but he does not grant it psychological universality.
These differences are, he says, trifling given Freud's great
discoveries in psychology. In the text, itself, there are few
critical comments on Freud. Freud's work on dreams is Jung's
central focus and about this work he says Freud put dream analysis on the right track, there has yet to be a refutation of Freud,
and one cannot understand dreams unless one has read Freud.
In a footnote he does qualify Freud's assertion that all dreams
are wish-fulfillments, saying 'Very many dreams are wish-fulfillments' (p. 80). Lacking in Jung's presentation is a recognition
of Freud's view that dreams fulfill infantile wishes.

Jung in his letter of apology to Freud presents several justi-
fications for his 'ruthless' treatment of Freud's researches. His
book was written with German academics in mind, and he was
trying to appease them by demonstrating that he maintained an
independent judgment on psychoanalysis. However, it is true,
that he and Freud do not 'see eye to eye on certain points'
(McGuire, 1974, p. 14). The reasons Jung gives for these differences are interesting, for they are all aimed at appeasing
Freud by downplaying actual disagreements and emphasizing
circumstantial factors: Jung's experience is with uneducated,
hospitalized patients; his upbringing, social mileu, and scientific
training are radically different; his experience is not as extensive as Freud's; Freud has greater talents in this area; and,
because he has not had personal contact with Freud his training
is obviously defective.

Having made his apologies, Jung asserts his fundamental position: 'I speak of things as I understand them and I believe is
right' (p. 15). Jung says he is not trying to differentiate himself
from Freud. Besides, any differentiation 'would come far too
late...since the leading lights in psychiatry have already given
me up for lost' (p. 15). Since this theme is constant in Jung's
early letters to Freud, it is important to restate that Jung's
career was probably not in the least harmed by his association
with Freud. He never had problems publishing, and many reviews
of his work recognized his advocacy of psychoanalysis as being
both important and substantiated by his researches. Besides
nurturing Jung's outsider identification, the complaint may have
had a tactical significance in bringing Freud and him closer
together. Jung is saying that although you, Freud, think we have
major disagreements, our enemies see us as conspirators.

Freud responded quickly to Jung's letter. He told Jung to
abandon the idea that he was not enthusiastic about 'The Psychology of Dementia Praecox.' He offered criticism because he thought
the book was good. He says, 'it would have been most unwise
to offend you, the ablest helper to have joined me thus far.' He
goes on, 'In reality I regard your essay...as the richest and most
significant contribution to my labors that has ever come to my
attention' (p. 17). Each man was highly valued by the other.
Although they both maintained their own views, each went to

some lengths to cultivate the other's support and friendship.
Freud dismisses Jung's self-denigration about his abilities, saying that only one of his Viennese students could match Jung's
understanding of psychoanalysis, and none of them 'is able and
willing to do so much for the cause as you' (p. 17). To his
Viennese followers, who met regularly on Wednesday nights,
Freud said about 'Dementia Praecox' that in it Jung had succeeded in finding the meaning behind the nonsensical talk of
his patients (Nunberg and Federn, 1962). This is a positive,
though brief, evaluation. However, it is nowhere near the praise
given directly to Jung. There were to be problems in the future
when Freud tried to promote Jung's leadership of psychoanalysis
at the expense of his early supporters in Vienna.

Responding to Jung's admission that he tailored his work for
German academic readers, Freud - after asking Jung's pardon -
is straightforward in his advice: 'pay less attention to the opposition that confronts us both and [do] not...let it affect your
writing so much' (McGuire, 1974, p. 18). The future belongs to
us, Freud claims, and although he is still 'ignored by [his]
colleagues and periodically annihilated by some hack' his lectures
are well attended. The young men in the field are on the side of
psychoanalysis. The movement will continue to grow, and Jung
and Bleuler should foster it, each according to his own character.
Bleuler and Jung 'should try to mediate,' Freud says, 'while I
go on playing the intransigent dogmatist who expects the public
to swallow the bitter pill uncoated' (p. 18). Having formulated
this battle plan and suggested Jung's deployment as a mediator
- who, one would assume, tries to 'coat' the pill - Freud reasserts his original piece of advice, this time more strongly: 'But
I beg of you, don't sacrifice anything essential for the sake of
pedagogic tact and affability, and don't deviate too far from me
when you are really so close to me, for if you do, we may one
day be played off against one another' (p. 18). No force alien
to the psychoanalytic movement ever came between Freud and
Jung. The success of the movement was in itself partially responsible for their later troubles. More important, though, was the
identification - so evident in the above passage - of similarities
and differences in psychological viewpoints with personal closeness and distance. In April 1906, in his first letter to Jung,
Freud said he would gladly accept correction of his views; in
January 1907, deviation is seen as a threat. Scientific positions
and emotional investments were becoming inextricably tied
together in their relationship.

Jung's response to Freud's advice and words of warning was
equally fervent: 'I shall never abandon any portion of your
theory that is essential to me, as I am far too committed to it'
(p. 20). But note that he says 'any portion...essential to me.'
Jung would remain master of his own judgment on questions of
theory.

Jung explains that his consideration for his critics comes from
his being young, and his personal 'quirks' about winning

recognition for his research and advancement in his career. By attributing differences in their positions to political consider- ations and his own idiosyncracies Jung deflected attention from real differences in thought. This was unfortunate because it no doubt worked to reassure both Freud and Jung that Jung would come around in time. In fact, he did not come around, because the differences in their views were not founded on Freud's knowledge and experience in conflict with inexperience, oppor- tunism, and ignorance on Jung's part. There were real differ- ences between the two men's observations of and theories about people. Instead of discussing these issues, which might have produced a more open and productive dialogue, each man dis- tracted the other by focusing attention on their opponents.

A good example of this is their discussion about Jung's hypo- thesis that unknown toxins play a role in the causation of demen- tia praecox. Freud questioned Jung's 'inclination to resort to toxins' while he, Freud, would look to sexuality for the cause of dementia praecox (p. 19). Freud admits that neither of their approaches has found much, but he is certain sexuality cannot be ignored. Jung's response is evasive. He says he originally wanted to leave 'material causes entirely out of my psychology,' but included the toxin hypothesis, because he feared misunder- standing 'owing to the notorious dim-wittedness of the esteemed public' (p. 20). He then tries to appease Freud by saying he had thought the toxin might be an endocrine produced by the *'sex glands,'* but he had no proof of this so he dropped the con- jecture. He had no proof that any toxin was involved, but he didn't drop the general hypothesis. The excuse that he included toxins in his theory to please the public is weak. He might have done so in order to please Bleuler who felt that toxins caused schizophrenia. But after Jung no longer had to worry about the approval of the public he still maintained the hypothesis he formulated in 'Dementia Praecox': the etiology of schizophrenia is a dual one. Up to a certain point psychological factors are indispensable in explaining the nature and causes of the initial emotions. These emotions are accompanied by chemical processes - modern toxins - which cause temporary or chronic disturbances, perhaps even lesions (1958c).

The second issue of theoretical interest arising from Freud and Jung's discussion of 'Dementia Praecox' dealt with dreams. In this book Jung analyzed the dream of 'a friend' whose 'personal and family circumstances' were well known to him (p. 57). The dreamer was Jung himself. In his analysis Jung found the expres- sion of an ambition complex and an erotic complex. According to Jung, the dream when interpreted fulfilled the wish that restraints necessitated by marriage, which he wished he could enforce on his nature, had already been imposed, thus saving him the trouble of trying to control himself. This is not the type of wish-fulfill- ment that Freud was talking about. Freud corrects Jung's inter- pretation, saying that the fulfilled wish will not be found until a dream is completely analyzed. The wish 'for reasons of

fundamental theory must be different from what you state'
(McGuire, 1974, p. 18). There would be no reason why a wish
for restraint would undergo censorship since the forces of repression are on the side of control.

Jung again finds causes external to himself for his failing to
produce an analysis which was entirely suitable. He showed his
first interpretation of the dream to Bleuler, who said it was much
too forthright. A censorship was also imposed because his wife
'wrote the whole description' (p. 20). He admits to Freud that
the rationalistic explanation of sexual restraint was simply a
distortion ' hiding an illegitimate sexual wish that had better not
see the light of day' (p. 15).

As for infantile wishes in the dream, Jung says, 'I have been
unable to discover an infantile wish anywhere' (p. 15). The
absence of the theme of infantile sexuality in Jung's work is
becoming marked: in his 1901 review of Freud's 'On Dreams' Jung
had not included Freud's sexual hypothesis – dreams fulfill
infantile wishes; in the current analysis of his first published
dream he could find no infantile wish. Empirically he found
sexuality to be an important factor in the causation of the neuroses, but not the only factor. In his two major psychoanalytic
case studies published in 1906 he definitely stressed sexual etiology, but he was unable to uncover infantile material.

Both in his writings and letters to Freud Jung stresses support
for psychoanalytic discoveries about the psychology of dreams,
neuroses, slips, and mental activities. He explicitly stated that
these discoveries were independent of the sexual theories and
hypotheses about infantile sexuality. While he thought sex played
a vital role in psychic life, he did not attribute to it the position
of a universal causal factor in the psychoneuroses.

Freud's position on sexuality was clear: 'Anyone who knows
how to interpret the language of hysteria will recognize that the
neurosis is concerned only with the patient's repressed sexuality.
The sexual function must...be understood in its true extent,
as it is laid down by disposition in infancy' (1906a, p. 278).
Freud would never separate his psychology from his theories of
sexuality, for he was always speaking of 'psychosexuality.'

Given this fundamental difference in their views, it seems
amazing that the two men came so close together. We must remember that they shared many ideas in common: neuroses have a
psychological causation, neurotics suffer from untold secrets,
behavior is determined by unconscious factors, dreams when
interpreted have a meaning, and through interpretation one can
understand and ameliorate psychological suffering. They also
both saw themselves as outsiders battling against the dogmatism
and hypocrisy of their professional colleagues. They were revo-
lutionaries fighting for the truth. They were winning the war,
which – they assured each other – had to be fought because so
many people condemned what they said. Some people did condemn
their work, but in their letters and their works they fantasized
the opposition as legion.

Prior to his avowal of support for Freud, and in his attempts to experimentally validate Freud's work, we saw Jung developing his own theory of complexes. He had his own findings about the structure of the psyche and had propounded a simple theory about the relations between the ego and dissociated feeling-toned complexes, a theory supported by experimental work and clinical case studies. In the Freud-Jung correspondence there is never any question of Freud changing his views in order to come closer to Jung's formulations. Freud is the professor, Jung the student. Such a relationship is detrimental to an open exchange of ideas. Freud assimilated Jung's work into his, and Jung tried to accommodate his thinking to match Freud's, but they never overcame a basic obstacle - infantile sexuality.

Jung complained that not having personal contact with Freud was perhaps, in part, responsible for the divergence of their ideas. Early in 1907 Jung announced that he had firmly resolved to come to Vienna; their first meeting was to be in March.

7 BINDING TIES: COLLABORATION AND DISCORD

THE FIRST MEETING

Carl and Emma Jung called on the Freuds around noon on Sunday, 3 March 1907. For three hours Jung poured forth his ideas while Freud listened. Freud then outlined what Jung had said and suggested that they proceed in a more systematic fashion. For the next ten hours, with few interruptions, they discussed sexuality, the connotations of the term libido, and their patients. No doubt they also aired their differing views on the etiology of dementia praecox. During the week Freud's consultations and meals were among the few things that interrupted their dialogue; even at dinner Jung never made the slightest attempt to speak with anyone but Sigmund and Carl did all the talking while Freud 'with uncontrolled delight did all the listening' (M. Freud, 1957, p. 109).

At the first meeting Freud asked Jung about his dreams. Jung told him that he had dreamt that 'I saw you walking beside me as a *very, very frail old man*' (McGuire, 1974, p. 96). Binswanger, a colleague of Jung's who also visited Freud at this time, says Freud's interpretation was that 'Jung wished to dethrone him [Freud] and take his place' (1957, p. 23). As this chapter and the next unfold we will see the theme of this dream-interpretation become all too real for both Freud and Jung.

Jung recalls that during this first visit another issue, which worked both to bind the two men together and yet eventually to drive them apart, was raised. Out of the blue, Jung says, Freud asked him what he thought about transference. Jung replied 'with the deepest conviction that it was the alpha and omega of the analytic method, whereupon [Freud] said, "Then you has grasped the main thing"' (1946b, p. 172). Transference, the projection by the analysand on to the analyst of strong emotions of love and hate, is indeed central to analytic therapy. Transference was also the alpha and omega of Freud and Jung's relations, for each man saw in the other an ideal. In Jung, Freud saw an intelligent, hard-working psychiatrist who because of his gift for winning others could spread the psychoanalytic word. In Freud, Jung saw a great man who was courageous, moral, and charismatic. These transference idealizations bound them together, but when this emotional bond was broken, their relationship came apart. Neither man assessed the other realistically. When the transference became negative, idealization gave way to its opposite, denigration.

Before visiting Vienna Jung had complained that his lack of contact with Freud was the cause of many of their misunderstandings. The visit provided the wished-for antidote. His first letter upon returning to Zurich expresses the transformation which had been worked upon him. He says that he is no longer 'plagued by doubts' about Freud's theory of dreams; the 'last shreds were dispelled by my stay in Vienna, which for me was an event of first importance.' Freud made a tremendous impression on him and Jung expressed the hope that 'my work for your cause will show you the depths of my gratitude and veneration' (McGuire, 1974, p. 26).

Under the spell of transference Jung said he could now see that autoeroticism was the essence of dementia praecox, that in this disease the central problem is a withdrawal of libido from the external world and a regression to interest only in one's self. He still had problems with the term libido. He felt that Freud's notion of sexuality and the libido was so broad that it created confusion - especially when he had to explain psychoanalysis to Bleuler. He suggested that they try to accommodate their terminology to generally held notions of what was and was not sexual.

Freud's reply to this suggestion was, as usual, strong. Attack, he said, is the best form of defence. Small concessions would not overcome the massive resistance they were facing: 'We are being asked neither more nor less than to adjure our belief in the sexual drive. The only answer is to profess it openly' (p. 28).

Freud's reaction to Jung's visit was very positive. Jung inspired him with confidence for the future and he hoped Jung would be the man to continue and complete his work. Jung was overwhelmed by this and feared that Freud overestimated his powers. An old pattern of male relations, which we have seen before in Freud's initial overvaluation of his father, Breuer, and Fliess, has been set in motion. Where it will end, of course, is in undervaluation and rejection of Jung as inadequate by Freud.

In his second letter after the visit Jung had more to say about Freud's impact on him. Seeing Freud had helped him to make considerable 'inner progress' and it seemed to him that 'one can never quite understand your [Freud's] science unless one knows you in the flesh. Where so much still remains dark to us outsiders only faith can help; but the best and most effective faith is knowledge of your personality. Hence my visit to Vienna was a genuine confirmation' (p. 30). Here is a resurrection of the religiosity - inner progress, dark, faith, confirmation - so characteristic of Jung's childhood and the transference of these feelings on to Freud.

We have reviewed both Freud's and Jung's immediate reactions to their meeting. Jung had found a man in whom he could believe, and Freud had once again found a man he could overvalue. Both men's historical accounts of this meeting and their initial relations are somewhat negative and therefore at variance with their reactions at the time. This is to be expected because when the

histories were written Jung and Freud were antagonists, not
friends. To correct the biases in the literature about these two
men and their reactions to each other would require several
hundred pages. A good general rule to follow when reading such
accounts is that if a history is written by either a Freudian or
a Jungian - including Freud and Jung - beware. As has been
our practice, we will try to stay on neutral ground. Interpreting their correspondence, works, and events from their lives,
we will be guided by hermeneutic principles in our attempt to
make sense of Freud and Jung's monumental misunderstanding.

A central issue throughout the correspondence was the question of the etiology of dementia praecox. In his second letter
after the visit Jung reverses the position he took in his previous
letter and questions whether there is a regression to infantile
autoeroticism in this disease. He reasserts his previous position
by saying that perhaps a toxic substance is involved and that
sexuality does not provide a totally satisfactory explanation. The
exchange of ideas about the causes of this disease continued
until 1912 and was one of the issues around which Freud and
Jung broke with each other. From 1907 to the break the letters
show Freud's increasing refinement of his position: the etiology
of paranoia - a term he used almost as a synonym for dementia
praecox - lay in a regression to autoeroticism. Paranoia involves
a withdrawal of libidinal cathexes from the external world; as a
consequence of this there is an overinvestment of libido in the
ego. This produces the characteristic megalomania of paranoids
which is accompanied by a strong libidinal interest in themselves
and their bodies (hypochondria) and a lack of interest in others.
In final form these ideas were published in 1911 in 'Psycho-
Analytic Notes on an Autobiographical Account of a Case of
Paranoia,' the Schreber case. Jung's views on Freud's developing position were seldom as positive as those expressed in his
first letter after the visit. At times of personal closeness he
moved nearer to Freud's ideas, but the trend of his thought was
towards the position that dementia praecox involved a general
withdrawal of interest from the external world. This interest was
not specifically sexual. Behind the question of the etiology of
this disease was the issue of the definition of libido. Jung did
not wish to see all interest in the world as being derived from
sexual sources. Therefore he could not endorse Freud's formula
that a withdrawal of libido from the world is necessarily connected with a regression to autoeroticism. Jung fully developed
his objections in 'Wandlungen und Symbole der Libido II' (1912),
the text which marks the break with Freud.

Although Jung had far more experience with dementia praecox
patients, Freud never moved toward Jung's ideas on the causes
of this disease. The only issue was whether Jung would see
things Freud's way. Three months after the visit and after an
exchange of ideas about dementia praecox Jung was again moving
nearer to Freud's position. He requested corrections of his views
and concluded 'My one hope is that [my current views] will bring

me closer to you' (McGuire, 1974, p. 44). Jung's standard of
judgment - for the moment - was not how well his theories described his case material, but whether Freud approved of them.
This is no way to conduct inquiry and Jung, even for Freud,
could not for long renounce his empiricism.

In 1907 this debate was not causing any real strain between
the two men. Jung was trying to find common ground with Freud
and Freud was taking into account Jung's reservations. At this
time Freud published his first interpretation of a work of fiction.
Jung thought Freud's analysis was 'magnificent.' He said, speaking of a revolution in his consciousness, that he could no longer
understand criticisms of Freud's ideas. To do so he had to try
to remember how he saw things 'before the reformation' of his
thought (p. 49). Pre-reformation he feels he was not only intellectually wrong, but morally inferior because he was being dis-
honest with himself.

As we saw in the last chapter, opposition to psychoanalysis
created a bond between Freud and Jung and distracted their
attention from their differences. Jung was to speak in defense of
psychoanalysis in September 1907 at the First International Congress of Psychiatry and Neurology in Amsterdam.

Freud sent a letter to Amsterdam greeting Jung on his arrival.
It was a warm supportive letter encouraging Jung before the
battle. Jung was to be Freud's champion and to prepare him
Freud movingly recounted the tale of his 'long years of honorable but painful solitude.' He recalled his certainty about his
findings and his years of waiting 'until a voice from the unknown
multitude should answer mine. That voice was yours....Thank
you for that, and don't let anything shake your confidence, you
will witness our triumph and share in it' (p. 82). From the
inspirational tone of the letter one would think that Jung was
Henry V's army going to do battle with the French on St Crispin's
day.

Jung's paper 'The Freudian Theory of Hysteria' was similar to
his previous defense of psychoanalysis against Aschaffenburg.
There is more of an emphasis on the sexual etiology of hysteria
and on Freud's 'Three Essays on the Theory of Sexuality.' Jung
encouraged investigation and intoned against decisions made without looking at the facts. The achievements of psychoanalysis 'as
a scientific instrument can be judged only by one who uses it
himself' (1908b, p. 17).

This last assertion was contested. In an issue still being
debated today, one participant argued that an independent test
of psychoanalytic findings is needed because '"faulty methods
give wrong findings, and repeating the faulty method will necessarily produce the same error over and over again"' (Weygandt
quoted in Ellenberger, 1970, p. 798). One's method of investigation shapes and orders one's findings; this is a commonplace
of modern philosophy that some investigators are still unwilling
to accept. Freud never accepted this and Jung did not accept
it until many years after his break with Freud. Freud saw

psychoanalysis as producing fact. The method could not be
faulted for it was scientific. Any questioning or reinterpretation
of the facts of psychoanalysis was simultaneously a rather adolescent questioning of science. Jung's position was similar: objections to the psychoanalytic method 'must be regarded as so many
subterfuges until our opponents come to grips with the facts'
(1913b, p. 102).

Jung's defense at Amsterdam was not a success, but it served
to bring Freud and him closer together. Jung said he realized
he was fighting not only for an important discovery 'but for a
great and honorable man as well' (McGuire, 1974, p. 84). Freud
responded to the attacks on psychoanalysis with joy. He joked
that after only ten years he had begun to fear that his ideas
were being accepted, which would mean something was wrong
with his theories; but given the criticism he could once again
believe in his work.

A token of the men's growing friendship was an exchange of
pictures. Jung had long wanted a photograph of Freud, but saw
this desire as 'almost absurd.' Freud was becoming an idol to
Jung and wanting to have his picture was a symptom of Jung's
growing devotion. Trying to explain to Freud why he had not
written, Jung pleaded overwork, but more importantly he saw
his inability to write as an expression of his inner turmoil over
their relationship. He agreed with Freud's diagnosis that he had
a 'self-preservation complex' and that he was constantly fretting
over his independence from Freud, but the problem was greater:

> Actually - and I confess this to you with a struggle - I have a
> boundless admiration for you both as a man and a researcher.
> . . . so the self-preservation complex does not come from
> there; it is rather that my veneration for you has something
> of the character of a 'religious' crush. Though it does not
> bother me, I still feel it is disgusting and ridiculous because
> of its undeniable erotic undertones. This abominable feeling
> comes from the fact that as a boy I was the victim of a sexual
> assault by a man I once worshipped. (p. 95)

Jung was obviously in great turmoil over this confession: the
crush doesn't 'bother' him, but it is 'disgusting' and 'abominable.'
He closes by saying that he finds intimacy with his colleagues
'downright disgusting' therefore he fears Freud's confidence and
is afraid that Freud also finds such bonds distasteful.

Freud had few objections to close male friendships and in fact
fostered them. His followers were almost all males. Jung's
followers, on the other hand, were to be mostly women. Perhaps
this was an attempt to protect himself from intimacy with men.

Before Freud could respond, Jung wrote to him again. He admitted that he was suffering from all the agonies of a patient in
analysis and was riddled with doubts about the consequences of
his confession. Freud's reply is unfortunately missing. Jung's
response to it, however, was very positive; he said it worked

wonders for him. He agreed with Freud that it was good to keep one's sense of humor about these things; unfortunately his had momentarily failed him. His 'old religiosity had secretly found' a compensatory figure in Freud, but in telling Sigmund about this he thought he had got the better of his troubles (p. 97). Jung had attempted to reveal a deep concern of his. Freud seems to have told him not to worry about it. Jung was only too happy to comply. This is no way to advance insight.

Reassured by this letter from Jung, Freud replied 'a transference on a religious basis would strike me as most disastrous; it could only end in apostasy....I shall do my best to show you that I am unfit to be an object of worship' (p. 98). Freud saw what was to be a final difficulty between them: Jung did apostatize and Freud banished him. However, in November 1907 both men - wishing for the problem to vanish - thought it had been solved by Jung's insight.

THE FIRST CRISIS

Jung's admission of his transference to Freud, the Amsterdam congress, and Freud and Jung's first meeting were the major events in their relationship in 1907. For 1908 they were planning the first psychoanalytic conference which was to be held in Salzburg.

Before considering events at this congress we need to know more about Karl Abraham a man who would be a lifelong disciple of Freud's and a person whom Jung did not like. Abraham's position as a devoted follower is clearly shown in the first paper he sent to Freud. It opens 'According to Freud's theory,' and closes 'the psychological investigation of dementia praecox will have to be based on Freud's theories' (1907, p. 13; p. 20). In response to this paper Freud encouraged Abraham's interest in psychoanalysis and suggested he work on the idea that in dementia praecox and paranoia there is an initial fixation at and subsequent regression to autoeroticism.

Abraham had worked under Jung at the Burghölzli and in response to Freud's inquiries Jung said that he and Abraham did not get along. He characterized Abraham as a loner, intelligent but not original, and lacking in empathy. Freud responded that he was predisposed in his favor because Abraham 'attacks the sexual problem head on' (McGuire, 1974, p. 79). After a first meeting Abraham and Freud became close; Freud considered Abraham his pupil and Abraham responded saying he had long accepted Freud as his teacher. An out of balance triangular relationship had been formed. Freud and Jung had positive feelings towards each other as did Freud and Abraham, but Jung and Abraham did not like each other. Such situations create strain among all three people and we will see that Jung's relations with Freud were made more difficult because of the antipathy between Abraham and him.

The Salzburg congress was held at the end of April 1908. Besides being a tribute to the growing support for Freud's ideas it also produced the first squabble at an international conference between two analysts - Abraham and Jung. Over forty people attended the conference which Jung, with Freud's help, had organized. There were eight lectures including Freud's four-hour presentation of the case of the man with rats and Abraham's and Jung's papers on dementia praecox. Both Freud and Jung felt the conference was a success, but the differences between Abraham's and Jung's views on dementia praecox created difficulties which were not resolved until Freud visited Zurich in September.

Abraham's paper developed the thesis that the pathological manifestations of dementia praecox can be fully explained by the Freudian concept of autoeroticism. This being true, Abraham asserted, 'would render the recently discussed toxin theory unnecessary' (1908, p. 78). This was a direct challenge to Jung.

Only an abstract of Jung's paper has survived. He followed the line of his book on dementia praecox arguing that a pathogenic agent, a toxin, was in part responsible for the disease (1910e [1908]).

Abraham and Jung obviously disagreed about the etiology of dementia praecox, but there was another problem. In reading his paper, Abraham had failed to cite the previous work of Bleuler and Jung. He explained to Freud that in trying to save time he decided to omit their names, but realized it was a symptomatic action: 'They turn aside from the theory of sexuality, therefore I shall not cite them in connection with this' (Abraham and Freud, 1965, p. 36). He did not think this would cause a problem.

It did. Jung was furious. He knew that his paper was not totally to Freud's liking and that Abraham's was. He begged Freud's patience and pointed to his previous work for the cause as a reason why Freud should have confidence in him. Then came the attack, which was in large part directed at Abraham: 'I always have a little more to do than be just a faithful follower. You have no lack of those anyway. But they do not advance the cause, for by faith alone nothing prospers in the long run' (McGuire, 1974, p. 144).

Freud's reply of 3 May 1908, treated Jung's attack as a symptom of Jung's temporary 'negative oscillation' away from psychoanalytic principles. Jung had worked hard in drawing Bleuler closer to psychoanalysis and Freud felt that Jung's Salzburg paper and problems with Abraham were expressions of a temporary reaction to overwork and great dedication. Freud was, however, certain of the bond between them and was sure that Jung, after taking a few steps away, would then go further with him. As for Abraham, Freud requested that Jung do him a favor: make peace. Because there were so few analysts it was necessary for them to stick together. Freud regarded Abraham as a man of great worth, but not as a replacement for Jung. He assured

Jung that Jung had every advantage over Abraham; however,
at Salzburg he had been pleased with Abraham because he had
taken the 'more direct path' to the solution of dementia praecox
'whereas you [Jung] hesitated' (p. 146). Less than a month
before Freud had written to Jung that he was always pleased
when Jung agreed with him, yet never reproached him for deviations. After Salzburg he was not pleased with the stance Jung
had taken on dementia praecox; Abraham's orthodoxy was highlighting Jung's deviancy.

On 3 May Freud also wrote to Abraham. The letter gives a central reason for Freud's willingness to tolerate Jung's independent
attitude. He asked Abraham to make peace with Jung, although
he, Abraham, was in the right. The self-sacrifice was necessary
for the psychoanalytic cause. He closed:

> Please be tolerant and do not forget that it is really easier
> for you than it is for Jung to follow my ideas, for in the first
> place you are completely independent, and then you are clo-
> ser to my intellectual constitution because of racial kinship,
> while he as a Christian and a pastor's son finds his way to
> me only against great inner resistances. His association with
> us is the more valuable for that. I nearly said that it was
> only by his appearance on the scene that psycho-analysis
> escaped the danger of becoming a Jewish national affair.
> (Abraham and Freud, 1965, p. 34)

Jung was to be a bridge to the Gentile world, and therefore
he had great political value, although his Christian heritage was
an obstacle to his understanding psychoanalysis. It does not
occur to Freud that Jung may have a good idea about dementia
praecox. The only good ideas are psychoanalytic ones. Just a
month earlier Freud had written to Jung that either a case could
be explained psychoanalytically or nothing was known about it.

Abraham agreed to make peace, but in July he announced that
Jung still had not replied to his overtures. He had heard that
Jung was retreating to his 'former spiritualistic inclinations'
(p. 44).

Freud's response was one of mediation. He felt he had to hold
on to Zurich and Jung, but realized that Abraham's development
of the autoeroticism idea and dismissal of the toxin theory was
forcing Jung into opposition. On Jung's spiritualism he replied
that it was easier for Jews to accept psychoanalysis 'as we lack
the mystical element.' What attracted him to Abraham was their
common Jewish traits. He suspected that 'the suppressed anti-
Semitism of the Swiss that spares me is deflected in reinforced
form upon you [Abraham]' (p. 46). Here Freud admits that Jung
did not act in an anti-Semitic manner towards him. After the
break he said that for his sake Jung gave 'up certain racial prejudices which he had previously permitted himself' (1914d,
p. 43). There is no evidence from the Freud-Jung letters or
from Jung's work that he was prejudiced. In fact, Freud admitted

to Abraham that although he suspected the Swiss of being anti-
Semitic, their prejudice had not been expressed towards him.
It therefore must have been deflected on to Abraham, but Abraham had said that while he was at Burghölzli Jung evidenced no
prejudice. In Abraham's letters to Freud he does not complain
of any prejudice on Jung's part. There is very little to say about
the charge that Jung or the Swiss were anti-Semitic, but that
they managed to suppress it. Freud has said it all: Jung is anti-
Jew, but it never shows. If it never shows, then why suppose
he was prejudiced? Because as a Christian he must be. Freud's
advice to Abraham was that as a Jew, if he wished to join the
Gentiles, he must develop 'a bit of masochism, be ready to suffer
some wrong' (Abraham and Freud, 1965, p. 46). It was Abraham
who wronged Jung originally by not citing Jung's work. Given
that anti-Semitism does exist, it is unwise to say that Freud or
Abraham did not encounter it, but it does not seem that Jung
expressed religious prejudice against either man.

Freud was sure Jung would not desert the psychoanalytic
cause; after all, he was editor of the 'Jahrbuch' and was bound
by personal ties to Freud. To smooth over troubles, however,
he was going to stop in Zurich on his way home from visiting his
relatives in England. The letters between Freud and Jung during the summer of 1908 show the strain of the Abraham affair,
of the disagreement over the etiology of dementia praecox, and
of Jung's treating a psychoanalytic colleague, Otto Gross.
Although he was learning a great deal about Gross, himself, and
dementia praecox from the analysis, he had little time to write to
Freud. This troubled Sigmund. Jung finally wrote that Gross
was definitely suffering from a regression to autoeroticism. This
news reassured Freud that Jung was coming back to the psychoanalytic view. He confessed that he had feared that Jung had
been alienated from him by some inner problem deriving from his
relations with his father and his Christian beliefs. He now saw
that it was only Jung's continued exposure to Bleuler's ideas
that were producing harmful effects. For Freud Jung's ideas
were not alternative hypotheses requiring serious consideration,
but symptoms.

Jung replied that the Gross case was atypical and only a face-
to-face discussion with Freud would iron out their differing views
on dementia praecox. Freud responded by saying that he was
delighted with the prospect of talking to Jung. He confessed he
needed Jung and in administrative matters did not wish to do
anything of which Jung would disapprove.

Jung now introduced an idea in a letter that was to cause great
difficulties in the future: conflicts in adult life, and not infantile
sexual problems, are the cause of some neuroses. Freud did not
notice the idea. He was full of plans for his Zurich visit, the
foremost of which were to persuade Jung to continue and complete his work by explaining the psychoses psychoanalytically.

The three-day visit in September was a great success. Jung
felt it did him a world of good; Freud said it left him in high

good humor. To Abraham, Freud wrote, 'Jung...has overcome his vacillation..., adheres unreservedly to the cause, and will continue to work energetically on the dementia praecox question on our lines' (Abraham and Freud, 1965, p. 51).

The remainder of the year was spent in harmony. Freud enjoyed Jung's renewed closeness to him and Jung employed the notion of autoeroticism in attempting to explain dementia praecox. In fact, he used the notion of autoeroticism so broadly that Freud had to caution him. Jung's use of the term made it synonymous with a general withdrawal of interest from the world, a process Jung later called introversion.

Towards the end of the year Jung decided to resign his post at the Burghölzli. He was not getting along with Bleuler, was tired of administration, wanted more time to pursue his own research interests, and thought he would have more freedom in private practice. The news thrilled Freud; Jung would no longer be pulled away from him by obligations to Bleuler.

NARRATIVE EXPLANATION: CAUSAL ANALYSIS IN THE RAT MAN CASE

Freud's study of the Rat Man, about whom he had lectured at Salzburg, is of interest to us because in it he enunciates two things which we have been arguing are at the center of psychoanalysis: (1) psychoanalysis provides a causal narrative which makes sense out of a person's life, and (2) that narrative is a retrospective historical reconstruction.

Paul Lorenz, called the Rat Man because of several fantasies about rats and biting, came to Freud with the fear that something might happen to two people he was fond of - his father and a woman friend named Gisela. Freud's case study, as usual, is complex; we will focus on the central scene to which Freud traces Lorenz's problems and Freud's comments on his historical reconstruction.

Following many clues in Lorenz's recounting of his life Freud made a construction. He proposed to Lorenz that as a child he had been guilty of a sexual misdemeanor connected with masturbation and his father had severely punished him for this activity. The punishment had produced a long-standing grudge against his father and had led him to believe that his father was constantly interfering with his sexual life. Lorenz did not confirm this, but told a story that his mother had told him took place when he was between three and four. Paul had bitten someone and his father had given him a beating. Paul was furious and while being punished screamed at his father '"You lamp! You towel! You plate!"' (1909c, p. 205). The child was so enraged he felt he had to revile his father, and not knowing any swear words he used common nouns. After this experience Paul was afraid of his own rage and became a meek child. Lorenz checked with his mother about the details of the story. She confirmed

them. In her account there was no suggestion of a sexual mis-
deed, but Freud says this may have been censored by the mother
in her own memory of the incident.

Lorenz swore he felt only love for his father and so was shaken
by the story of the biting scene. However, he said he could not
remember it himself and therefore doubted it. The scene was
central to Freud's reconstruction of Lorenz's biography and in an
important footnote, which we will consider shortly, he leaves the
question open as to whether it was a fantasy or a reality. First,
we will see how Freud uses this scene to fill in the gaps in
Lorenz's life story.

Unlike the hysteric, the obsessive is not amnesic for the causes
of his illness. The trauma remains conscious, but is simply
deprived of all affect. The obsessive knows, but does not know,
his problems. 'For he knows them in that he has not forgotten
them and he does not know them in that he is unaware of their
significance' (Freud, 1909c, p. 196). Obsessional defense works
by ellipsis. Connecting links in the obsessive's life history are
omitted so that his conscious awareness of his troubles resembles
a distorted telegraph message. Causality having been broken,
uncertainty reigns. The more one doubts experience the further
one withdraws into oneself thus exacerbating the problem.
Thought itself becomes an obsessive activity, a compulsive ritual.
Thoughts become so powerful that the obsessive comes to feel
they are omnipotent.

An example from the case will illustrate these notions. One of
Lorenz's oldest obsessions was that '"If I marry the lady [Gisela],
some misfortune will befall my father."' Lorenz's father was
already dead, so what misfortune could befall him? The analysis
provided the links which had been repressed. The thought, as
restored by Freud, was:

> 'If my father were alive, he would be as furious over my
> design of marrying the lady as he was in the scene of my
> childhood; so that I should fly into a rage once more and
> wish him every possible evil; and thanks to the omnipotence
> of my wishes these evils would be bound to come upon him'
> (p. 226).

Filled in with memories which have been freed from the repression
instituted in childhood, the thought is completed. Its causal
connections in place, it makes sense.

Freud says the problem of translating obsessional ideas, which
are often quite bizarre, is formidable. However, given a deep
enough investigation it is by no means impossible. Freud had
told Lorenz that he 'must say everything that came into his head,
even if it was *unpleasant* to him, or seemed *unimportant* or
irrelevant or *senseless*' (p. 159). With that understood, Freud
gave him leave to begin talking about anything he pleased. The
method of truly free association was used for the first time.
Freud never abandoned free speech, for only via this route

could he obtain the information needed to translate lives made
senseless by distortions and omissions into coherent narratives
with their causal links restored.

One solves the problem of making sense out of isolated obsessional ideas by using information gained from free associations
to make interpretations which serve to bring the obsessions 'into
temporal relationship with the patient's experiences' (p. 186).
Eventually analyst and analysand are able to fill in the ellipses
and thereby construct a coherent story. The omissions in obsessive ideas are filled in with material that was previously unconscious. What is unconscious is unnarrativized. By making it
conscious, it is incorporated into the temporal, or narrative,
sequence of the analysand's autobiography.

In a detailed analysis of the Lorenz case and the logic of
explanation in psychoanalysis, Sherwood finds what I have been
arguing is the essence of Freud's work: 'Psychoanalysis supplies
a context, a narrative about an individual patient within which
isolated pieces of his behavior come to be understood, fitted
together, and organized into a comprehensible whole' (1969,
p. 190). Like the historian, Freud 'is interested in a particular
course of events, namely an individual history' (p. 188). Also,
like the historian, Freud constructs his histories by looking
backward from the present to the past. Unlike the if-then model
of causal prediction adhered to by most natural sciences, the
paradigmatic form of explanation in both psychoanalysis and history is the construction of retrospective causal narratives.
Instead of the form 'if x then y,' the model is 'was-because';
that is x was what occurred because of y.

In connection with the biting scene, Freud enters into a long
discussion about the histories neurotics construct for themselves.
He says, 'in constructing phantasies about his childhood the
[neurotic] individual *sexualizes his memories*; that is, he brings
commonplace experiences into relation with his sexual activity,
and extends his sexual interests to them' (1909c, p. 207). Freud
cautions that if we do not wish to go astray in our judgment of
the historical reality of the neurotic's fantasies then:

> we must above all bear in mind that people's 'childhood mem-
> ories' are only consolidated at a later period, usually at the
> age of puberty; and that this involves a complicated process
> of remodeling, analogous in every way to the process by
> which a nation constructs legends about its early history.
> (p. 206)

In remaking his history the individual 'endeavours to efface the
recollection of his auto-erotic activities' (p. 206). As the historian molds his view of the past from the present, so too does the
neurotic. At puberty love of others is all-important, so the
neurotic remolds his infantile memories constructing scenes of
childhood object-love. This fact explains why neurotics' 'phantasies abound in seductions and assaults, where the facts will

have been confined to auto-erotic activities' (pp. 206-7). It is, Freud is saying, a characteristic of neurotics that they retro- spectively sexualize their early life histories. Childhood seduc- tion is a fantasy.

Jung when he was breaking away from Freud made a very similar argument, but Freud in 1914, and many times later, rejected Jung's claim because he said Jung used it to deny the reality of infantile sexuality. In the Rat Man case Freud says he is not putting foward the above thoughts with the intention of denying the importance which he has given to infantile sexuality by reducing it to nothing more than sexual interest at the age of puberty. He asserts that his 'Analysis of a Phobia in a Five- Year-Old Boy' is proof of the existence of childhood sexuality. One must, however, be careful to differentiate between neurotic fantasies about infancy and the actual content of infantile sexual life: 'The sexual life of infancy consists in auto-erotic activity on the part of the dominant sexual components, in traces of object-love, and in the formation of that complex which deserves to be called the *nuclear complex of the neuroses*' (p. 208). This nuclear complex is the Oedipal situation.

One wonders how Freud could determine what the real con- stituents of infantile sexual life were if his only method of investi- gating infantile sexuality was, as he tells us in 'Three Essays,' through the analysis of the memories of neurotics. Obviously he does not rely on the memories per se, but on his interpretation of them, an interpretation guided by the tenets of psychoanalytic theory. One of the postulates of that theory, never actually observed, is that infants' first sexual activities are autoerotic. In the next chapter we will examine how Freud arrived at that assumption. We will find his method to be the same as he used to establish the existence of latent dreams and primary process (see chapter 5), a method he cautions against in the Rat Man case: he equated the interpretation of adult memories and experi- ences with actual occurrences in infancy and thereby equated material discovered by interpretation in the present with real occurrences in the past.

In the Lorenz case Freud warned that one should realize that neurotics retrospectively sexualize their memories. But in an essay written at the same time 'On the Sexual Theories of Child- ren' he disregards his own advice. Here he explicitly equates adult reminiscences of childhood with actual childhood experi- ences. The paper presents several 'childhood' sexual theories: oral fertilization, anal birth, sadistic parental intercourse, and possession of a penis by both sexes. Also, Freud introduced the idea of the castration complex. Freud says that the material for this work was synthesized from three sources: (1) direct obser- vations of children, (2) the conscious memories of adult neurotics in psychoanalytic treatment, and (3) 'from the inferences and constructions and from the unconscious memories translated into conscious material, which result from the psychoanalysis of neurotics' (1908, p. 209). Freud does not indicate from which of

the three sources a specific sexual idea comes. Although such
a measure would be methodologically desirable, for Freud it is
unnecessary. For him, reconstructions of the adult past that
provide information about childhood are the equivalent of the
actual thoughts and behaviors of children (Jacobsen and Steele,
1979). He commits, and continues to commit, the very error he
warned against in his historical discussion of Rat Man.

Freud's only published analysis of a child was actually carried
out by the father of the boy. Little Hans - Herbert Graf - was
the son of Max Graf, a musicologist who was also a founding
member of the Psychological Wednesday Society and Freud's
friend. On numerous occasions Graf told Freud what Hans had
said or done and Freud suggested to Graf what he in turn should
say to Hans. Freud only talked once with the boy. Although
these were not even close to ideal conditions under which to
pursue a psychoanalytic investigation, Freud felt he learned a
great deal from his analysis of Hans's phobia. The case was a
confirmation that children are sexual creatures. This one case
was used again and again by Freud as proof that actual observation of children confirmed his infantile sexual theories. Actually
Hans's fantasies and behaviors had to be interpreted psychoanalytically before they provided the wished-for confirmation.

Inspired by Freud's analysis of Hans, Jung undertook the
observation of a girl from her third to her fifth year. The child
was his daughter Agatha and he and Emma noted her fantasies
and actions preceding and following the birth of her brother.

Before presenting the case Jung makes an important statement
about his methodology:

> In the report which now follows we shall . . . have to give up
> the idea of a consistent exposition, for it is made up of anec-
> dotes which treat of one isolated experience out of a whole
> cycle of similar ones, and which cannot, therefore, be dealt
> with scientifically and systematically, but must rather take the
> form of a story. We cannot dispense with this mode of exposi-
> tion in the present state of our psychology, for we are still
> a long way from being able in all cases to separate with uner-
> ring certainty what is curious from what is typical (1946a,
> p. 8 [1910a, p. 252]).[1]

A field of investigation dealing with individuals will always have
to deal with both the curious and the typical, the idiographic
and nomothetic, because everyone's life is a synthesis of singular
experiences and common human activities. While science is purely
nomothetic, the story can capture both the general and the
idiographic. Jung here recognizes the need for a story methodology. He fails, however, to see fully its advantages over a scientific approach. This was the third of his Clark University Lectures and no doubt he wished to convince Americans that psychoanalysts did all they could to be scientific.

In this paper there was not only strong support given to

Freud's theories about infantile sexuality, but also the introduction of many new ideas. Jung used the term introversion to describe an inward turning of libido which activates fantasy and introduced ideas about mythology and psychic activity which would be more fully developed during the crisis period of 1912 when he was breaking with Freud. Jung says many of Anna's (Agatha pseudonym) solutions to the riddle of birth were in the form of analogies. Analogical thinking is characteristic of children and in adults 'there is a kind of thinking by analogy which belongs to the stratum lying immediately below consciousness' (1910a, p. 264). This kind of thinking is brought to the surface by dreams and may be observed in cases of dementia praecox. Fairy tales, which seem to be the myths of children, are replete with analogical formations.

During and after the break Jung was formulating his own model for psychological explanation and in the case of Anna we find it in germinal form. The model is analogical and creates understanding by explicating similarities between the mental products of people individually (dreams, fantasies) and collectively (myths, fables). The model takes the form of an 'is-like' statement: that is, dream image x is like mythological image y.

Our discussion branching off from the Lorenz case has led to a deeper consideration of the psychoanalytic construction of life histories, has furthered our inquiry into the nature of both Freud's and Jung's evidence for the existence of infantile sexuality, and has given us a preview of the directions which Jung will take as he separates from Freud. We have also identified three paradigmatic forms of explanation: (1) the scientific 'if-then,' (2) the historical 'was-because' and (3) the analogical 'is-like.' While Freud argued that psychoanalysis was a science, we found in the Rat Man case that his explanatory narratives are historical in nature. We will continue to find this model at the center of psychoanalytic understanding. Jung's method of understanding began in 1909 to depart radically from the predictive natural science model. It was centered in the historical and began to show signs of his later work in explorations of analogical explication.

SPOOKERY AND THE PROMISED LAND

The first quarter of 1909 found Freud and Jung closer together than they had ever been. Freud's visit to Zurich had smoothed the difficulties between them. Jung, feeling that Bleuler's 'passive connivance' had lost him a teaching post at the university, was taking additional pride in his psychoanalytical accomplishments. The most important of these was the publication of the 'Jahrbuch.' The first issue of the first psychoanalytic journal was 'an inexhaustible source of joy' for Freud, and for Jung as editor it was a triumph (McGuire, 1974, p. 211).

With their growing closeness, Jung could admit that in the past he had been rather prudish about sex, but proclaimed 'I don't water down the sexuality any more' (p. 198). A large part of Jung's more active avowal was probably due to an unpleasant experience with a former female patient. In 1907 Jung was treating a severely disturbed female hysteric, Sabina Spielrein, who later became a psychoanalyst. For him, the case was a test of psychoanalytic notions about infantile sexuality and from his brief report it is obvious that he found a wealth of evidence supporting Freud's ideas about infantile masturbation and the pleasures gained in childhood from anal eroticism (1908b). However, Jung failed to terminate the treatment successfully. Spielrein formed a strong erotic attachment to him and Jung realized that he had unconsciously encouraged her. He was innocent of overt misconduct, but he felt guilty because he had not been fully conscious of his actions. Long talks with Emma, a final meeting with Spielrein, and a series of confessional letters to Freud helped him to resolve his difficulties. Jung's letters illustrate the degree to which his emotional transference to Freud had grown. He admitted that as Freud's 'son and heir' he had been reticent about telling Freud the whole problem. He, however, knew it was best to 'confess' everything to Freud 'as my father' (McGuire, 1974, p. 232; p. 236).

Jung's difficulties brought him closer to Freud, but during the first half of 1909 signs of problems emerged which were to become major issues in their final separation. Because of the difficulties with Spielrein, the building of his new house, and finishing up his work at Burghölzli, Jung was not writing as often as Freud wished. Having received a letter from Jung after a two-week wait, Freud said his anxieties were relieved. He realized that his sensitivity 'towards dwindling correspondence' had its genesis in his relations to Fliess (p. 209). Jung replied, 'You may rest assured, not only now but for the future, that nothing Fliess-like is going to happen....Except for moments of infatuation my affection is lasting and reliable' (pp. 211-2). The passage of time often makes such declarations look foolish.

Jung still failed to write often enough to satisfy Freud. A few months later Freud, sounding as if he were writing to Fliess, told Jung that Carl's letters gave him great pleasure, but he did not wish to 'burden' Jung with the 'obligation of a formal correspondence.' The relationship was still relatively sound, but this is a telltale sign. After this Jung never wrote often enough to suit Freud and as the relationship unraveled the frequency of Jung's letters dwindled.

Issues centering on Jung's religious upbringing had previously troubled Freud. A religious tone entered one of Jung's letters about Spielrein when he spoke of the devil and of battles with temptation. Freud commented briefly on this and Jung replied testily 'you mustn't take on about my "theological" style, I just felt that way' (p. 212). This theological style and theological themes began to appear more frequently in his letters. Commenting on a Swiss minister's interest in psychoanalysis, Jung said

that he found a mixture of medicine and theology to his liking.
About another colleague he wrote to Freud, 'Nor does he lack a
certain mystical streak, on which account I set special store
by him, since it guarantees a deepening of thought beyond the
ordinary and a grasp of a far-reaching synthesis' (p. 214). What
he saw in an admired co-worker was something that had lain
dormant in Jung for several years. He was near to fostering his
own tendencies in that direction. The motto over the door of his
new, and quite elegant, house in Küssnacht gave a sign of things
to come. A saying of Delphic origin, inscribed in Latin, it read:
Invoked or not invoked, the god will be present.

At the end of March 1909 Jung left the Burghölzli and on the
first part of their vacation he and his wife visited the Freuds
in Vienna. One evening during this visit two things happened
which had lasting effects: Freud made Jung his heir and the two
men had a strange experience with a bookcase.

After the visit Freud wrote to Jung saying it was 'strange' that
on the same evening that he 'formally' adopted Jung as his
'eldest son and anointed [him]...as my successor and crown
prince' Jung should have 'divested' him of his 'paternal dignity'
(p. 218). Freud noted that Carl seemed to enjoy the latter as
much as he, Sigmund, enjoyed the former. The transference had
peaked with the father adopting the son; such fantasy cannot
be maintained for long.

Freud had been discomposed by what he called the 'poltergeist
business' (p. 218). After Jung's investiture they had been talking about precognition and parapsychology. In his recounting
of the evening's events, which is obviously biased by his later
difficulties with Freud, Jung said he asked Freud what he
thought of such phenomena. Freud's 'materialistic prejudice' and
'shallow positivism' led him to a simplistic denial of the whole
question. While Freud was calling all such phenomena nonsensical, Jung had difficulty 'in checking [a] sharp retort.' He felt
his anger growing. Just then 'there was a loud report in the
bookcase.' Jung said to Freud that this was an example of the
exteriorization of emotion. Freud exclaimed, 'Oh, come, that is
sheer bosh.' Jung replied that it wasn't and to prove his point
he predicted that 'in a moment there will be another such loud
report!' (1973b, p. 155). The bookcase immediately gave another
loud crack. Jung says Freud looked at him aghast and the
incident aroused Sigmund's distrust. He says he never afterward
discussed the incident with Freud.

This is not true. In his first letter to Freud after the visit,
Jung said, 'It seemed to me that my spookery struck you as
altogether too stupid' (McGuire, 1974, p. 216). Freud replied
that his credulity in the poltergeist business vanished with
Jung's departure. His belief in it had been enhanced by the magic
of Jung's presence. He could not deny that Jung's stories and
the bookcase noises 'made a deep impression on [him]' (p. 218).
Freud does not claim to have been quite as disbelieving as Jung in
his autobiography has led us to suspect. After Jung left, Freud

did dismiss the whole business, but not before putting it to the
test. He had noted that since Jung's departure the bookcase had
creaked and moaned on several occasions and these were unrela-
ted to whether or not he was thinking about Jung. The Freud -
who wrote eight years earlier 'I must confess that I am one of
those unworthy people in whose presence spirits suspend their
activity and the supernatural vanishes away, so that I have
never been in a position to experience anything myself which
might arouse a belief in the miraculous' (1901b, p. 261) - reasserted himself: 'I put my fatherly horned rimmed spectacles on
again and warn my dear son to keep a cool head, for it is better
not to understand something than make such great sacrifices to
understand.' Freud closed 'I shall receive further news of your
investigations of the spook complex with the interest one accords
to a charming delusion in which one does not oneself participate'
(McGuire, 1974, pp. 218-19; p. 220).

It took Jung almost a month to reply to Freud's paternal warn-
ings about spookery. He agreed that one must be careful not to
get carried away by such things. Jung obviously still adhered
to psychoanalysis, but fault lines were beginning to appear that
would lead to the schism. He says the visit had done wonders
for him and had 'freed [him] inwardly from the oppressive sense
of [Freud's] paternal authority' (p. 217). His trouble was that
he was 'so eager to discover something' (p. 220). The binding
ties of the teacher-follower, father-son relationship which Freud
and Jung through mutual transference had fostered were becoming for Jung a little too binding.

In his autobiography Jung recounts an incident that must have
occurred during this second visit to Vienna.[2] When Freud spoke
about sexuality, Jung says, his tone became urgent, his manner
almost reverent, and his normal skepticism vanished. Freud
besought: '"My dear Jung, promise me never to abandon the
sexual theory. That is the most essential thing of all. You see,
we must make a dogma of it, an unshakeable bulwark."' Jung
asked, '"A bulwark - against what?"' Freud replied, '"Against
the black tide of mud...of occultism"' (1973b, p. 150).

Jung says this episode struck at the heart of their friendship.
Psychoanalysis had suddenly become a faith; it was no longer a
science. Freud's atheism had been channeled into a religiosity
towards his own creation. Jung says 'I knew that I would never
be able to accept such an attitude' (p. 150). As a child he
wouldn't accept his father's Christianity on faith and as an adult
he wouldn't bow to the dogma of psychoanalysis.

In telling this story forty years later Jung makes it into a
pivotal event in his relations with Freud. If it was so important,
one would expect its occurrence to be mentioned, at least in
passing, in the letters; or to be able to see in retrospect something in the letters that indicates the change in Jung's attitude
towards Freud. There is no sign or mention of it. However, Jung
may have been carefully keeping his thoughts to himself. We will
see that this is exactly what he did with another incident that

shook his confidence in Freud. The second took place during
their visit to America.

Freud, happy with Jung and satisfied with the progress of
psychoanalysis, wrote to Carl, 'We are certainly getting ahead;
if I am Moses, then you are Joshua and will take possession of
the promised land of psychiatry, which I shall only be able to
glimpse from afar' (McGuire, 1974, p. 197). Neither man took
possession of psychiatry, but 1909 produced a triumph for
psychoanalysis. 'Moses' and 'Joshua' lectured at Clark University
in a promised land of sorts - America.

Freud first, and then Jung a few months later, were invited,
independently of one another, to speak at the twenty-fifth
anniversary celebration of Clark. Freud, Jung, and Sandor
Ferenczi, who was an analyst and close friend of Freud's, met
in Bremen and before their ship sailed there was a curious occurrence. Jung was quite interested in the naturally mummified
human bodies which he thought were to be found in the vicinity;
he prosed on about these and Freud asked him why he was so
interested in such things. Finally at dinner the subject came up
again, Jung talking of mummies and Freud asking him why he
was so fascinated with corpses. Suddenly, Freud fainted. Jung
says, 'Afterward he said to me that he was convinced that all
this chatter about corpses meant I had death-wishes towards
him' (1973b, p. 156). Three years later, for apparently the same
reason, Freud was to faint once again in Jung's presence.

At Clark Freud gave five lectures. Gathering his thoughts for
each day's talk during a thirty-minute walk before his presentation, he spoke without notes. He delivered his first extended
introductory synthesis on psychoanalysis. In an address aimed
at the educated lay person he gave a brief history of psychoanalysis - crediting Breuer with its invention; reviewed the
theory of hysteria; summarized the theory of repression; talked
on dreams, emphasizing their importance in uncovering unconscious contents; condemned the critics of psychoanalysis for
resisting the truth; stressed the scientific nature of his findings;
insisted that the causes of psychoneurosis are to be found in
erotic life; and set forth his findings on infantile sexuality and
charged that civilized sexual morality was too restrictive (1910a).

Of special interest to us is what Freud said about causality.
Stressing his conviction that psychic processes are strictly
determined, Freud cited the work of his friend C.G. Jung on
complexes and the association test as proof. The analyst is convinced of the causality of psychic processes, but is prepared
to find many causes for one event. This over-determination may
be hard for some to accept because 'our innate craving for causality' leads us to wish for a single determinant (p. 49). Perhaps
in this phrase we can find the appeal of the psychoanalytic narrative. Although it does not reduce life events to the manifestation of a single cause, something we would probably object to
as absurdly reductionistic, it does reduce the complexity of psychic events by arranging them in a multiply determined causal

framework thus satisfying our desire to order and simplify experience. Adolf Meyer, a leader in American psychiatric reform and one of the many distinguished people in the audience, responded to just this aspect of psychoanalysis. Shortly after the Clark lectures he wrote that Freud appealed to his 'inborn need for causal and dynamic chains' (Hale, 1971, p. 18).

Freud's lectures at Clark were a success. In the 'Nation' Freud's work was called revolutionary and it was said that, 'a growing circle of very vigorous young men in all civilized countries are giving him due recognition and working out his ideas' (p. 20).

Looking back on this experience, Freud wrote that as he stepped to the platform to deliver his first lecture 'it seemed like the realization of some incredible day-dream: psycho-analysis was no longer a product of delusion, it had become a valuable part of reality' (1925b, p. 52). Recognition did mean something to Freud and his first great triumph was in America. It is evident that he never, at least for long, felt that his ideas were a delusion; but still public acceptance of those ideas did provide an important anchorage in social reality.

Jung gave three lectures at Clark. The first was a review of the association test method; the second, 'The Family Constellation,' demonstrated that patterns of responses to the association test showed great similarities within families and among certain members of families. Although referring to Freud in these lectures, Jung was putting forward his own work, stressing the experimental soundness of his method and conceptualizing his findings under the rubric of the complex. His case examples dealt with sexual issues, but he stressed: 'The heuristically important principle of every psychoanalysis runs: *If someone develops a neurosis, this contains the negative aspects of his relationship with the person closest to him*' (1910c, p. 477). The stress on neuroses as compensatory and on current conflicts in patients' lives is typical of Jung's later works.

The third lecture which we have previously reviewed, was Jung's study of his daughter Agatha. In it Jung condemned the prejudice surrounding the rejection of Freud's work because of his focus on sex and implored his audience to suspend judgment until they had heard the evidence. After establishing his status as an independent investigator in his initial talks, he obviously intended this third one to show his support for Freud.

Jung returned many times to America. He says that after his first visit he was fascinated by the US but didn't understand it. From his second visit on he felt that each trip provided new insights into the American psyche. Freud disliked America and never returned. The food didn't agree with him, the pace of life was too fast, and American manners were too informal. However, he did see a porcupine and became very fond of this peculiar creature.

While in America and on the ocean voyages Freud, Jung and Ferenczi analyzed each other's dreams. The dominant theme in

Freud's dreams was care and anxiety about the future of his
children and of psychoanalysis (Jones, 1957). In interpreting
one of them, the content of which Jung does not disclose, Jung
says he asked Freud for additional details about his private life.
Freud looked at Jung with suspicion and said, '"But I cannot
risk my authority!"' In retrospect, Jung says, 'At that moment
he lost it altogether. That sentence burned itself into my memory;
and in it the end of our relationship was already foreshadowed.
Freud was placing personal authority above truth' (1973b,
p. 158). Unlike Jung's story about Freud's insistence that he
pledge an oath to the sexual theory, there is confirmation of
this incident in the letters. However, Jung did not immediately
challenge Freud on the authority issue. He kept his thoughts to
himself - as I suggested he might have done with the Vienna
episode - until their relationship completely deteriorated. It was
not until December 1912 that he challenged Freud with Sigmund's
reticence: 'Our analysis, you may remember, came to a stop with
your remark that you "could not submit to analysis *without losing your authority*." These words are engraved on my memory
as a symbol of everything to come' (McGuire, 1974, p. 526).
     Why didn't Freud and Jung discuss this issue in 1909? Why
couldn't these two men who insisted on complete disclosure from
their patients achieve such an openness in their personal relations? The answer is not profound; they were human. Their letters do not reveal two men with great analytic insight helping
each other to explore their own psychic depths or two great
minds continually grappling with the riddles of human nature.
The letters are the correspondence of two intelligent people trying to stay on the good side of one another, heaping abuse on
their enemies, gossiping about their acquaintance, discussing
their work, speculating on the dynamics of the psyche, admin-
istering the growing psychoanalytic movement, and, sadly, avoiding any revelations to one another that they did not have to
make. In the end each used his insights about the other in order
to attack, not to help. All too human, perhaps; but, 'One admires
as one should only after having understood that there are not
any supermen' (Merleau-Ponty, 1960a, p. 58).
     After telling about Freud's refusal to risk his authority, Jung,
in his autobiography, also reveals his own failures in being open
with Freud. Jung had a dream during the voyage to America
which he told Freud. He dreamed he was on the second story of
a house that he felt was his own. The rooms were decorated in
rococo style. He then went downstairs to the ground floor which
was decorated in a much older medieval style. He descended to
the cellar; it dated from Roman times. In the floor was a stone
slab with a ring. When he pulled it up he saw another staircase.
Descending it he found himself in a cave. There were bones,
broken pottery, and two half-disintegrated human skulls on the
floor.
     Jung says Freud was much taken with the skulls and pressed
to find a wish connected with them. Jung knew Freud wanted

to discover a death wish towards someone, but felt a violent resistance to such an interpretation. He had an idea of what the dream meant, but says he wanted to hear Freud's opinion; 'I wanted to learn from him' (1973b, p. 159). Therefore he submitted to Freud's promptings and said the two skulls were those of his wife and sister-in-law. Jung says Freud was relieved by this. Perhaps Freud was glad to hear that neither of the skulls was his.

In choosing the associations Jung says he had to pick someone whose death was worth wishing, but he 'was newly married at the time and knew perfectly well that there was nothing within [himself] which pointed to such wishes' (p. 160). Jung at the time had been married for six years, had three children, had just been through difficult times with Emma over Sabina Spielrein, and had discovered in himself lustful feelings towards women other than his wife. Unconsciously he might quite possibly have wished for his wife's death.

Jung told Freud a lie about the dream. How can one learn by cheating on one's work? Also, no associations to a dream can be a lie if (as Jung at the time maintained) all associations are strictly determined. Jung admits his actions were not above reproach, 'but *à la guerre, comme à la guerre*!' This was not a war, it was supposed to be a friendship. Jung even says he did not want to put forward his own interpretation of the dream because he knew it would make Sigmund quarrelsome and might endanger their friendship. This point is in part confirmed by a letter written to Emma Jung from America. In it Jung says Freud was 'extremely touchy' about alternative psychological formulations (Jaffé, 1979, p. 47).

Jung says many of the dreams he told Freud at this time had collective contents and were full of symbolic material which Freud did not understand. The house dream foreshadowed his later work and led him towards the concept of the collective unconscious. The second story, rococo style room, was inhabited and represented consciousness. As he descended floor by floor the rooms in the house became older and represented more ancient depths of the psyche. 'In the cave,' Jung says, 'I discovered remains of a primitive culture, that is, the world of primitive man within myself' (1973b, p. 160).

After this interpretation Jung says about dream-interpretation in general, 'I was never able to agree with Freud that the dream is a "façade" behind which its meaning lies hidden' (p. 161). The manifest dream is the dream and must be amplified by interpretation. There is an irony in the fact that Jung writes this when he is recounting events which took place in 1909. For in that very year he wrote - comparing a dream to a house - 'What must we do to get behind the façade into the inside of the house - that is, beyond the manifest content of the dream to the real, secret thought behind it?' (1909, p. 29). This essay fully supported Freud's method of dream-interpretation, although Jung again fails to mention the idea that the wishes fulfilled by dreams are infantile ones.

Jung's view of the psyche was radically altered during and after his break with Freud. Therefore many years later, when writing his autobiography, he probably could not imagine that he ever advocated the psychoanalytic view of dreams. He did, but the changes in his life brought on by the crystalization of his own views altered his recounting of his past beliefs. A revolution in consciousness creates a revision of a person's life history. After Jung's conversion to psychoanalysis he couldn't really understand how he had seen the world in non-psychoanalytic terms. After his own visionary experiences from 1913 to 1918 he could not longer admit that he had seen the world in psychoanalytic terms.

Historically, Jung traces the origin of his difficulties with Freud to 1909, but the Freud-Jung letters from that year show few signs of difficulties between the two men. The pledge supporting sexuality which Freud supposedly demanded of Jung is not mentioned, Freud's fainting at Bremen does not appear, Jung didn't tell Freud that he didn't understand Jung's dreams, and Jung did not challenge Freud's statement about not wishing to risk his authority. In fact one month after the trip Jung wrote to Freud saying he missed him and that the 'analysis on the voyage home had done me a lot of good' (McGuire, 1974, p. 250). Given the drastic change in their relationship, Jung later gave events from 1909 a significance they would not have otherwise had. The import of the present is not set, it is not a fact. Events from the future which will transform the present into the past give new weight to present occurrences. Meanings are not fixed; a text can be revised; a story retold, an event reinterpreted.

STRESSES WITHIN THE MOVEMENT

That Jung and Freud were on very close terms in 1910 cannot be doubted; that both men in recounting events of that year obliterate by silence their bond of friendship is also clear. At the Second Psychoanalytic Meeting in Nuremberg, which took place in March 1910, Freud insisted that Jung be elected the first president of the International Psychoanalytic Association and Jung accepted the post. In his autobiography Jung does not mention this or the faith in him that Freud's act symbolized. In Freud's two histories of psychoanalysis one sentence in each mentions Jung's presidency. Few words, however, are wasted on their friendship while paragraphs are written condemning Jung's work, character, and defection from psychoanalysis.

At the Nuremberg meeting Freud's 'face beamed whenever he spoke of Jung,' and he repeatedly said of him '"This is my beloved son, in whom I am well pleased!"' (Wittels, 1924, p. 138). Freud was determined to establish an international psychoanalytic group with a great deal of power in the president's hands. Jung was to be president. Wittels, who soon after Nuremberg resigned his

membership in the Viennese group, says that Freud, in trying
to push through the plan, 'behaved like the Old Man of the
primitive horde – [he] was simultaneously ruthless and simple-
minded' (p. 139). The Viennese resisted the plan for the International Association. They felt the presidency should go to one
of Freud's long-time followers in Vienna – Adler – and that a
foreigner should not be given so much control. The Viennese
analysts held a private caucus:

> Of a sudden, Freud who had not been invited...put in an
> appearance. Never before had I [Wittels] seen him so greatly
> excited. He said: 'Most of you are Jews, and therefore you
> are incompetent to win friends for the new teaching. Jews
> must be content with the modest role of preparing the ground.
> It is absolutely essential that I should form ties in the world
> of general science. I am getting on in years, and am weary
> of being perpetually attacked. We are all in danger.' Seizing
> his coat by the lapels, he said: 'They won't even leave me a
> coat to my back. The Swiss will save us – will save me, and
> all of you as well.' (p. 140)

Freud's leadership of psychoanalysis was so complete that he
could get away with making such statements.

A compromise was reached. A new journal, the 'Zentralblatt...,'
was established with Freud as the director and the most vocal
Viennese, Adler and Wilhelm Stekel, as the editors. Freud
resigned as president of the Viennese group and Adler took over.
Jung became president of the International and his long-time
co-worker, Riklin, became the secretary. The president's term
was for two years and the offices of the International were in
the home city of the president. Zurich, not Vienna, became at
least officially the center of the psychoanalytic movement.

'There is no doubt that [the conference] was a great success,'
Freud wrote to Ferenczi, the chief architect of the organizational
plans for the meeting. Freud admits that their lack of political
tact probably encouraged some of the problems with the Viennese
and felt that his 'long pent up aversion for [them]' had added to
his clumsy handling of the meetings (Jones, 1955, pp. 70-1).
Freud closes saying he spent an enjoyable day with Jung after
the conference: 'He is at the top of his form, and it is to be
hoped that he will prove himself.' Comparing the Zurichers to
the Viennese he continued, 'The personal relations among the
Zurich people are very much more satisfactory than they are in
Vienna, where one often has to ask what has become of the en-
nobling influence of psychoanalysis on its followers' (p. 71).

Just four months after the conference Freud was troubled. He
felt the plans for the International had been too ambitious and
the Association had been structed too tightly. He complained to
Jung, for the first but by no means last time, about his administration of the movement: 'The first months of your reign, my
dear son and successor, have not turned out brilliantly' (McGuire,

1974, p. 343). Freud felt that Jung must take his new post more seriously, assume the dignity of a president, and cultivate the art of winning people. Jung admitted his failures, said it was difficult to work with Adler and Stekel, and complained that the job of president - which he had never sought - could easily consume all his time. Freud had made Jung president because he wanted to insure a continuance of psychoanalysis after his death, because he wished to be above political issues, and because Jung was a Gentile. However, he was not satisfied with Jung's performance and was continually advising and chastising him.
Because Jung had won Freud's friendship, Freud thought 'all hearts open' to Carl who would therefore make a fine president. But to be a president one must like administrative work. Jung liked it no better than Freud did, and he was not a good administrator.

Freud wanted Jung to handle the Viennese situation which was rapidly deteriorating. Jung declared, 'I am not a politician,' and said he had no personal rapport with Adler (p. 364). Freud's council to him was that both Jung, as president, and he, as Jung's mentor, must compromise. They could humor themselves privately by talking about these 'farts,' but for the good of the Association an accommodation must be reached. Freud, displaying his overvaluation of Jung, wrote to him: 'You are a master of the art of winning people; I should be glad if in the interest of [psychoanalysis] you were to make more use of it' (p. 366). But Adler was not to be won over. One half-year after Nuremberg Freud complained to Jung that Adler was using the 'Zentralblatt' to publish his own 'unintelligible' theories.

In developing his psychological theories concerning the importance of feelings of inferiority and the masculine protest, Adler advanced an extensive critique of psychoanalysis (see Ansbacher and Ansbacher, 1964). He said repression must be seen as the ego's attempt to gain masculine mastery and it usually takes the form of a denial of passivity. The Oedipus complex is a part of the adult neurotic's masculine protest. The complex must be seen symbolically as a compensatory fantasy for current sufferings. The psyche is not, as Freud argues, hopelessly bound to futile attempts to recapture past pleasures. It is, Adler asserts, aimed at obtaining future goals.

Freud's response to this first criticism of his theory from within the psychoanalytic camp was to condemn Adler's views. Adler's theory shows an 'anti-sexual tendency,' but Freud admits these ideas will have an impact: first, because Adler is a persuasive writer, and second, because 'the entire doctrine has a reactionary and retrogressive character' (Nunberg and Federn, 1974, p. 146; p. 147).

More criticisms followed from other members of the Viennese Society and in late February Adler resigned as president because of 'the incompatibility of his scientific attitude with his position in the society' (p. 177). Freud was elected president. The Vienna group was split, with a small number of members, including

Stekel, siding with Adler. By June 1910, Adler had severed all
his ties to psychoanalysis.

There was a warning in all of this for Jung which he did not
heed. Writing to him about Adler's views, Freud says he chided
Adler for his assumption that there was an 'asexual period of
childhood. He denied it, but I showed it to him in print; he had
written presexual, but doesn't *presexual* mean *asexual?*' (McGuire,
1974, p. 404). Freud was adamant about infantile sexuality. In
eighteen months Jung too would argue for the existence of a
presexual period and Freud's response was unchanged. As Adler
had been treated, so Jung was to be rejected.

While Freud was having problems with Adler, Jung was having
trouble with Bleuler. Jung's former chief didn't attend the
Nuremberg conference and balked at joining the Zurich Psychoanalytic Society which was affiliated with the International Association. Jung was facing a total break with Bleuler and admitted
that it aroused his father complex. Freud counseled that this
was the price Jung had to pay for the help he once received
from Bleuler; such help is not free 'any more than the help I
received from Breuer' (p. 320). There is a price to be paid for
severing one's ties to a father-figure. Freud had paid it with
Breuer, Jung was now paying it with Bleuler, and would soon
have to suffer the guilt of breaking with Freud.

The trouble with Bleuler did not come to a crisis. Jung wrote
Freud that he desired a complete separation, but knew that it
might harm psychoanalysis. Bleuler was not a decisive character
and although this kept him from a breach with Jung, it drove
Jung and Freud to distraction. Freud labeled Bleuler 'the
Procrastinator of Burghölzli' (p. 308). Long after the break with
Zurich Freud wrote that Bleuler 'strove too eagerly after an
appearance of impartiality; nor is it a matter of chance that it is
to him that our science owes the valuable concept of *ambivalence*'
(1925b, p. 51). Freud loved to find in the personalities of people
he no longer liked the traits which shaped their psychological
theories. He thereby reduced their work to a symptomatic activity
while insisting that his work retained its universal applicability.

Bleuler was not Jung's only problem in interpersonal relations
in 1910. He wrote to Freud that Emma had made a number of
jealous scenes in reaction to completely groundless rumors about
his conduct. Jung lost his control and the whole situation mush-
roomed. He says when he regained his 'objectivity' 'my wife also
straightened herself out brilliantly.' He continues: 'Analysis of
one's spouse is one of the more difficult things unless mutual
freedom is assured. The prerequisite for a good marriage, it
seems to me, is the license to be unfaithful' (McGuire, 1974,
p. 289). It seems to me that the prerequisite for a good marriage
is equality and Carl and Emma Jung did not achieve this. Emma
Jung was an intelligent, independent woman, who because of
the sexism in her culture and her marriage felt herself to be a
second-class citizen in her relations to her husband. She wrote
to Freud, who thought highly of her,

I am tormented by the conflict about how I can hold my own against Carl. I find I have no friends, all the people who associate with us really only want to see Carl, except for a few boring and to me quite uninteresting persons.

Naturally the women are all in love with him, and with the men I am instantly cordoned off as the wife of the father or friend. Yet I have a strong need for people and Carl too says I should stop concentrating on him and the children, but what on earth am I to do? (p. 467)

What Emma Jung did was become a research assistant for her husband. For his 'Wandlungen und Symbole der Libido' she traced countless etymologies of words. Over the years a circle of women formed around Jung, most of whom furthered his work on analytical psychology. These women made important contributions, but they all lived in Jung's shadow.

Jung announced to Freud that five women from Zurich were going to attend the Third International Psychoanalytic Congress at Weimar to be held in September 1911. They included Spielrein, 'then a new discovery of mine, Frl. Antonia Wolff, a remarkable intellect with an excellent feeling for religion and philosophy, and last but not least my wife' (p. 440). The circle had already begun to form and Wolff was for forty years to be one of the most important members of Jung's coterie. In her early twenties, this woman from an old Zurich family became a patient of Jung's because of difficulties in adjusting to her father's death and in living with her mother. She was shy, proper, feminine, and yet behind this veneer ran deep feelings and a great responsiveness to others. When Jung broke with Freud it was to Antonia, not Emma that he turned for help. She was to become his therapist, 'femme inspiratrice,' and mistress.

The death of Johann Honegger - a friend, colleague, and occasional analysand of Jung's - was yet another crisis with which Jung had to cope. Depth psychology owes two debts to Honegger. His suicide led Jung to advocate a training analysis for all analysts, a practice which became institutionalized. The second is for an observation that Honegger made while on duty at the Burghölzli, an observation that Jung sometimes treated as his own (1931a) and which was one of his favorite examples of an archetypally determined hallucination.

Honegger reported the following hallucination of a schizophrenic patient: 'The patient sees in the sun an 'upright tail' similar to an erected penis. When he moves his head back and forth, then, too, the sun's penis sways back and forth in a like manner, and out of that the wind arises' (Jung, 1916a, p. 109). In an ancient Mythraic liturgy a comparable symbolism of the wind originating from a tube hanging from the sun is also found. Separated by a thousand years and as many miles why was there a match between the Mythraic symbol and the vision of the schizophrenic, who probably had not read a thing about ancient religions? This was one of the questions that drove Jung to investigate symbolism

and the answer to which added another issue that contributed
to his separation from Freud.

At the Weimar Congress Jung spoke on the parallels between
the fantasies of neurotics and psychotics and the myths of both
ancient civilizations and primitive cultures (1911b). Freud presented a 'Postscript to the Analysis of Schreber' in which he
certified the validity of Jung's work on symbolism: 'Jung had
excellent grounds for his assertion [in 'Wandlungen I'] that the
mythopoeic forces of mankind are not extinct, but that to this
very day they give rise in the neuroses to the same psychical
products as in the remotest ages' (1912a, p. 82). Freud called
for the phylogenetic application of psychoanalysis to the psychology of 'primitive man.' Freudian archaeology was born.

The Weimar Congress recaptured the positive feelings that had
made the first conference at Salzburg so successful. The political
intrigues of Nuremberg were absent and Jung was re-elected
president of the International by acclamation. The four days
Freud spent with the Jungs at Küssnacht before the congress,
and the congress itself, were to be the last time that Freud's
and Jung's meetings were a pleasure to them.

In his presidential address at Weimar Jung warned that psychoanalysis must maintain its empiricism, scientific rigor, and watch
within its ranks for unacceptable deviations from the basic
psychoanalytic postulates. 'What fate expects from us is that we
faithfully husband the enormous store of knowledge provided
by Freud's discoveries and pass it on to our fellow men, rather
than pervert it for the gratification of our own ambitions' (1911c,
p. 424). These are the words of a loyal follower and in his warn-
ings Jung anticipated the faults Freud and his followers, within
a little over a year, were to find in Jung himself and in his work.

We have seen the oscillations in Jung's and Freud's personal
relations between their first meeting in Vienna and this eighth
meeting in September 1911. We have traced the growth of the
psychoanalytic movement and seen these two men weather several
administrative storms. We have reviewed their publications up
until 1910, tracing the unfolding of their ideas, and have seen
Jung's advocacy of psychoanalytic theory grow and his defense
of Freud expand. The reservations about infantile sexuality were,
however, still there. We have seen Freud acknowledge the value
of Jung's work, solidify his position on the importance of infantile sexuality, and yet, in the Rat Man case raise the point that
neurotics retrospectively sexualize their memories of childhood.

Before we can understand how disagreements over theoretical
questions along with interpersonal disharmony and administrative
difficulties led to the break between Freud and Jung we must
review their researches in textual interpretation between 1909
and 1911, a time when each man was supportive of the other's
work and curious about what the other would discover.

THE ANALYSIS OF TEXTS

The art or science of hermeneutics was first devoted to Biblical
exegetics and from the eighteenth century on has evolved into a
discipline whose goal is to expand understanding of human forms
of communication - texts, works of art, and interpersonal exchanges - through interpretation. When one interprets a text, one's
goal is to increase one's own and other people's understanding
of that text. Freud's 'Leonardo Da Vinci and a Memory of His
Childhood,' 'Psycho-analytic Notes on an Autobiographical
Account of a Case of Paranoia,' and 'Totem and Taboo,' and
Jung's 'Wandlungen und Symbole der Libido' are hermeneutic
works. They are applications of psychoanalysis to understanding texts. All but the 'Leonardo' analysis are at the center of
the controversy over analytic theory which led to the dissolution
of relations between Jung and Freud. The core of their theoretical disagreements, then, was not over a patient, or how to
conduct therapy, or a scientific hypothesis, but over the analysis of texts. The disagreement was hermeneutic, not scientific.
That is, they did not disagree about alternative hypotheses
which could conceivably be tested by some experiment, but about
the guiding principles of interpretation: what constitutes an
acceptable reading of a text and how is the meaning of human
experience revealed to an interpreter through human communications.

Working from a fragmentary original text, through interpretation, hermeneutics often tries to produce a second text which
completes the first by filling in the gaps. Freud was faced with
precisely this task in writing about Leonardo da Vinci. Only
fragmentary and rather uncertain evidence about Leonardo's
life exists. Working from this Freud used techniques of psychoanalytic interpretation to piece together and supplement these
fragments in order to produce ε more complete life history of this
artist-scientist.

If one does not accept the assumptions of psychoanalysis, works
like Freud's 'Leonardo' are difficult to follow and hard to believe.
Freud's rewrites and elaborations of documents left by da Vinci,
and of biographical information about him seem to be dictated not
so much by Leonardo's life as by Freud's wish to compose a
psychoanalytic biography. One must have a framework of assumptions by which to begin interpreting anything; Freud assumes
that early childhood sexual experiences determine later adult
character. So his study of Leonardo reconstructs the artist's
boyhood sexual history. One must be careful that one's interpretations do not mutilate an original text by giving it meanings
foreign to it. Does Freud's version of da Vinci's life completely
distort his life history? Perhaps, but we do not know. There is
no original life history to which we can compare Freud's version.
All one can do is use the texts Freud used and whatever other
information is available to construct by interpretation another
da Vinci biography. One can also dissect Freud's version to see

how he has perhaps misused information or by sleight of pen
diverted the reader's attention from a troublesome point. In the
next chapter we will do such a dissection of Freud's 'From the
History of an Infantile Neurosis' (1918).

Freud sees that given the paucity of reliable information about
da Vinci his endeavor to construct a psychoanalytic life history
may lead to the charge that he had 'merely written a psychoanalytic novel' (1910b, p. 134). In a letter he said that his
'Leonardo' was, 'as a matter of fact...partly fiction' (1960,
p. 306). One wonders immediately which parts Freud thought
were fiction and which fact. We will probably never know and it
might do us good to be content with asking: did or did not
Freud tell a good story? Stories can be factual or fictional, or a
mixture of both. Unfortunately, Freud himself was not satisfied
with fictions. The problem is that he too often declared fictions
facts when careful examination often shows Freud's facts to be
fictions.

Within a month of congratulating Freud on his 'Leonardo' Jung
was again excited about Freud's investigations. Freud was turning his attention to Daniel Paul Schreber's 'Memoirs of My Nervous Illness.' Jung had made several references to Schreber in
'The Psychology of Dementia Praecox' and it was probably his
work which called the 'Memoirs' to Freud's attention.

Schreber's book provided an ideal vehicle for Freud to test out
his ideas on paranoia and by extension dementia praecox. Freud
did not treat either illness and so could not draw upon his own
cases as Jung could in discussing dementia praecox. The Schreber text provided the case material Freud needed, but first he
had to justify using it. He argues that paranoiac's betray in
distorted form precisely those things which neurotics keep secret.
Paranoiacs are not amenable to therapy because they cannot overcome their resistances to seeing their own motives; 'they only
say what they wish to say, [and so] it follows that this is precisely a disorder in which a written report or a printed case
history can take the place of a personal acquaintance with the
patient' (Freud, 1911b, p. 9). Even to start interpreting the
Schreber case, Freud had to assume that his ideas on paranoia,
which were to be proved by the analysis of the case, were true.
This may sound a little suspicious, but it is not.

It is a commonplace in hermeneutics that one makes assumptions
before one interprets anything. However, one must try to make
implicit assumptions explicit and be able to modify one's assumptions as one enters into an interpretative relationship with a text
or another person. For instance, if you are not amenable to
changing your views upon reading a book then there is little to
be gained from reading it.

Whether we accept Freud's assumption that paranoiacs reveal
their secrets in writing as valid or not will depend on whether
or not he can provide an adequate interpretation of the Schreber
case. To determine whether or not a textual interpretation is
adequate is just what hermeneutics has been studying for

centuries. It is an area where natural science has few tools with which to cope.

Freud is obviously aware that he is entering an area unexplored by science for he says 'It will not be possible to define the proper limits of justifiable interpretation until many experiments have been made and until the subject has become more familiar' (p. 37). Experiments here does not mean laboratory tests, but psycho-analytic endeavors at textual interpretation. He knows that his readers 'will only follow him as their own familiarity with analytic technique will allow them' (p. 37). This is not a bad rule for setting the limits for interpretation: whatever the reader will bear. It is little use writing interpretative works if your inter-pretation will not help others understand a phenomenon. By the time the Schreber analysis was published, Freud had a fairly large following of individuals who would accept what their leader said. Jung, unfortunately, could not bear what Freud did with Schreber's memoirs.

Schreber's fundamental delusion was that he would be emas-culated and turned into a woman. The idea was linked to the notion that he, in the form of a woman, would be God's emissary to the world. The joining together of these two delusions pro-duced a radical change in Schreber. Before his illness he had been inclined to sexual asceticism and had been a doubter of religion; the delusions changed all this. After their onset he spoke of voluptuous sensations and a personal relationship with God. He took up a feminine attitude towards God and felt that he was God's wife.

The danger of any interpretative system is that it might reduce a complex system to a simple formula. Freud came up against these problems when behind Schreber's fantasies about his psychiatrist, God, and the sun he found remnants of a childhood father complex. Schreber's elaborate fantasy about a personal relationship to the sun and battles with it, according to Freud, 'is nothing but another sublimated symbol for the father; and in pointing this out I must disclaim all responsibility for the mono-tony of the solutions provided by psycho-analysis' (p. 54). This is a clever piece of rhetoric. It was one of Freud's great dis-coveries, for which he proudly took credit, that neurotic's fantasies and human fantasy in general are but a resultant of infantile relations to parents, especially the father. Here, by denying responsibility for the answers provided by his interpre-tation, he is trying to convince the reader that they exist independently of hermeneutic activity.

Freud's solution would necessarily be both monotonous and correct if fantasy symbolized in a myriad of ways 'nothing but' childhood relations to parents. The interpretations would be simply monotonous if fantasy had some other reason for its existence or if such an interpretative reduction failed to reveal anything interesting about a text or a person's life.

Freud's position was to become intolerable to Jung. In one of his first lectures given after the break, Jung said that Freud's 'analytic-reductive procedure,' while uncovering the infantile material in Schreber's rich fantasy system, did not do justice to the fantastic symbolism (1914a). Jung claimed that symbolism cannot be reduced to a 'nothing but' equation, for the essence of the symbol is that it is an 'and-or' expression. Symbols can be both retrospectively understood by following the psycho-analytic model of causal historical explanation and prospectively understood by using a constructive method. Prospective under-standing is more important because the symbol carries an as yet to be realized significance for the person. The work of interpre-tation is to create a subjective significance for the symbol and to identify typical symbolic motifs. Jung's critique was a chal-lenge to Freud's reading of the text. As a reader he could not tolerate what he saw as a tremendous loss of information pro-duced by psychoanalytic interpretation. To understand how Jung came to make this criticism we must return to the beginning of his intensive study of mythology.

Just after returning from Clark University Jung announced that he was 'obsessed' with the thought of writing a comprehen-sive account of mythology. He looked forward to years of fact finding and preparation; 'Archaeology or rather mythology has got me in its grip, it's a mine of marvelous material' (McGuire, 1974, p. 252). A month later Jung declared: 'For me there is no longer any doubt what the oldest and most natural myths are trying to say. They speak quite 'naturally' of the nuclear com-plex of neurosis.' Jung in one month had unlocked the secret of myths, finding within them the Oedipal drama of a son's love for the mother. His conclusion was a bit premature, but the letter does suggest another theme that would organize his work on mythology - the story of '"the dying and resurgent god"' (p. 263).

As his study of myth deepened, Jung realized that the field was vast. He saw in mythology a study of the history of the psyche. By the end of 1909 he wrote, 'I have the most marvelous visions, glimpses of far-ranging interconnections which I am at present incapable of grasping' (p. 279). Jung was starting to see beyond the boundaries of science and of psychoanalysis. He was also starting to feel the constriction of his relations to Freud - 'it is a hard lot to have to work alongside the father creator.' He argued that there was a lot more than infantile sexuality expressed in myths. The central problem was with incest and repression, but he was unclear on the interconnections of the two.

Freud was peevish because Jung's work on mythology was mak-ing him an even more dilatory correspondent than usual. His reply to Jung's downplaying infantile sexuality was that he, him-self, had had a flash of inspiration: 'The ultimate basis of man's need for religion is *infantile helplessness*' (pp. 283-4).

For Jung, mythology was his 'coy new love,' revealing and concealing its secrets; 'this "*cour d'amour*" will set me many a test of courage' (p. 285). Like the heroes in myths, Jung was

setting out on a quest, a lifelong exploration of unknown lands.
After a year of intensive study, having just finished the first
part of 'Wandlungen' and looking forward to a study of occultism,
he wrote to Freud:

> There are strange and wondrous things in these lands of
> darkness. Please don't worry about my wanderings in these
> infinitudes. I shall return laden with rich booty for our
> knowledge of the human psyche. For a while longer I must
> intoxicate myself on magic perfumes in order to fathom the
> secrets that lie hidden in the abysses of the unconscious.
> (p. 421).

Jung has certainly captured the spirit of the quest. In his reply
Freud echoed Jung's style; he was supportive, but there was a
paternal warning:

> I am aware that you are drawn by innermost inclination to
> the study of the occult and I am sure you will return home
> richly laden. I cannot argue with that, it is always right to
> go where your impulses lead. You will be accused of mysti-
> cism, but the reputation you won with the *Dementia* will hold
> up for quite some time against that. Just don't stay in the
> tropical colonies too long; you must reign at home. (p. 422)

Jung was to be branded a mystic by Freud and his followers.
Today many still see mysticism as a type of intellectual disease,
but, perhaps, it only seems dangerous to overwrought rationalists.

Some of the insights Jung brought back from the land of myth
were announced at the Weimar Congress. Working a modification
on the Breuer-Freud dictum, Jung said, 'In dementia praecox
the patient suffers from the reminiscences of mankind' (1911b,
p. 446). Myth lives on in the human unconscious and in dementia
praecox this remote heritage is resurrected.

Jung's explorations of myth were to change his views on the
nature of the unconscious. It was no longer to be the unconscious of psychoanalysis filled with instinctual energy and
unacceptable infantile impulses: it was to be the well-spring of
human fantasy and creativity. In a 1910-11 paper on number
symbolism Jung anticipated in an elementary way many of his
later ideas. The unconscious is the matrix of creative and play-
ful fantasy. Musings like numerology, which the modern scientific consciousness finds banal, have occupied the human mind
for thousands of years 'so it would be no wonder if those
tendencies from the distant past gained a hearing in dreams'
(p. 52). The unconscious is the realm of 'free creative fantasy'
and to explore this territory one must rely 'on a broad empiricism.' One must be modest in one's conclusions, but by no means
should one 'pass over in silence what has happened and been
observed, simply from fear of being execrated as unscientific.'

The modern mind has a 'superstition-phobia' against what is called mystical and occult and one should not fall victim to this prejudice, 'for this is one of the means by which the secrets of the unconscious are kept veiled' (p. 53). For Jung, science and its dictates were becoming a restriction to inquiry. He was once again looking beyond the materialist, anti-spiritual orientation of the scientific method, calling for an empiricism that would put no methodological restrictions on investigations which would hinder him in what he wished to explore.

In 'Wandlungen und Symbole der Libido I' Jung carried forward the critique of sciences' prejudice against the study of the prophetic: 'The aversion of the scientific man of to-day to this type of thinking, hardly to be called fantastic, is merely an over-compensation to the very ancient and all too great inclination of mankind to believe in prophecies and superstitions' (1916a, p. 493). Dreams and fantasies, Jung argued, do in a sense fore-tell the future because in them there are often solutions to problems which confront us. Psychoanalysis with its retrospective focus does not reveal this prospective function of dreams because it is concerned with uncovering past determinants. A synthetic, instead of an analytic, approach to the interpretation of products of the unconscious would attempt to explicate the directions to which the unconscious was pointing.

A central thesis of 'Wandlungen' and all of Jung's later work is that: 'Everything psychic has a lower and a higher meaning, as in the profound saying of late classical mysticism: "Heaven above, Heaven below, stars above, stars below, all that is above also is below, know this and rejoice"' (1952b, p. 50).[3] The secret symbolic significance of everything psychic is its dual signific-ance. One does not do justice to a fantasy or dream if one traces it back simply and solely 'to the sexual problem in its narrower sense. That would be only one half of the meaning and the lower half at that. The other half is ideal creation as a substitute for real creation' (p. 50).

If the outward expression of a desire is blocked by the ego or the world, the energy of the wish flows inward, activating the 'historic strata of the unconscious' (1916a, p. 55). Flowing back into the unconscious, the energy moves in a regressive direction reactivating both infantile memories and archaic forms of human thought. The libido finds expression in symbols, the structures of the human psyche which like the objects of the external world can be endlessly transformed. Musings, thoughts, fantasies, and dreams combine and recombine images shifting their shapes in order to find an optimal expression for the libido. No word or symbol is ever entirely new, but the individual, in seeking to find expression for a problem, invests both words and symbols with a new personal significance. These unconscious products often contain a solution to the problem. The solution is an ideal one in that it takes place within the inner subjective world and not in reality. It may point to possible changes in the individual, or reality, or both.

The symbol has a double dual significance. It is retrospective and prospective, individual and collective. When adult conflicts lead to an introversion of libido and an activation of the unconscious, problems in the individual's past, especially childhood difficulties, are reactivated. Obsolete ties to the parents are resurrected, infused with a retrospective significance, and often sexualized beyond the bounds of actual childhood experience. The parents are blown up out of all proportion. Infantile memories of these two central people in an individual's life are recathected and fantasies find in them suitable figures on which to project most difficulties in adulthood and personal relations. Given its historical focus, its was-because model, psychoanalysis tracks down the retrogressive significance of such fantasies. There is more to be done.

Fantasy and dream symbolism is remarkably similar across individuals and Jung began employing analogical interpretation, is-like statements, to explore these similarities. One's actual relations to specific people, for example one's parents, are the seed around which fantasies filled with universal symbolic images crystalize. A person takes on great powers when fantasies become centered around him or her: 'my mother was a saint;' 'he's a devil.' Another example is Schreber's belief that his psychiatrist was the anti-Christ. The individual is powerless to control the projection of unconscious fantasies on to others. The images arising from the unconscious are grouped associations to which the ego reacts as if they were foreign to it. The ego so dissociates itself from them that the images are seen as emanating from another person or an object, but not oneself.

In order to stress the autonomous power of such complexes, to emphasize the similarities across individuals, cultures, and historical periods of the symbolic representation of certain typical situations and relationships, and to clearly differentiate actual relationships from relations infused with fantasy, Jung substituted the word 'imago' for 'complex.' It is not just one's father about whom one has conflicts, it is one's complex of associations which center on the father that produce difficulties. It is the father imago to which one is directing one's rebellion or submission. An imago is a collection of associations expressed in thematically related symbols. Like a complex, the imago is autonomous and gains expression independently of the ego's will. An imago - Jung replaced the term in 1919 with the word 'archetype' - is a group of interrelated images and associations common to humanity. The imago finds expression in symbols.

Just as individuals turn to fantasy to solve problems, so do cultures. Individual symbols partake of societal myths and such myths are built from the collective fantasy of individuals. The path for the development of the individual and culture 'lies in the *mobility of the libido*, and its capacity for transference' (1916a, p. 20). Beginning to use libido to mean psychic energy or interest in general Jung is saying that both cultures and individuals move forward because of a capacity to endlessly transform themselves by transferring their interest from one thing to another. When manipulation of the world fails or a set of cultural beliefs dies, new solutions are found by reallocating libidinal interest. Such movement takes place in creative fantasy. In myths – the creative fantasies of cultures – are to be found solutions, or at least hints to the resolution, of the most difficult questions an individual or culture faces.

Introducing a thesis that was central to all his later work, Jung says, *'There must be typical myths which are really the instruments of a folk-psychological complex treatment'* (p. 40). If a typical mythic pattern parallels the fantasies of a person, or if there are symbolic correspondences between myths and individual dreams, then mythic scenarios may provide a clue to the direction in which the unconscious is headed. Such parallels need to be explored, Jung felt, for it is important in analysis to differentiate between personal, life-historical complexes which have a retrospective significance and impersonal, universal symbolic motifs which have a prospective significance. An imago will contain both, and analyst and client must work together to explore this double significance of symbols.

'Wandlungen' was devoted to illustrating parallels between the fantasies of a young American woman, Miss Frank Miller, and ancient mythology. Jung never met Miller. Her work 'Some Instances of Subconscious Creative Imagination' (in Jung, 1952b) was published in 1906. Miss Miller had a rich imagination, was well educated, and was an accomplished writer. Her report of her dreams and visions is fifteen pages in length; Jung's hermeneutic explication – with long etymological digressions, parallels drawn from Christian, Greek, Egyptian, Hindu, and Mithraic mythology, and comparisons among Miller's work, myths, and the symbols and scenarios of men of letters including Milton, Goethe, Poe and Longfellow – is over four hundred pages in length.

Jung made almost no attempt to speculate on Miller's past or her childhood difficulties. If he had been interested in doing so he could have followed Freud's example in 'Leonardo' and used psychoanalytic theory to help him to interpret her fantasies and construct a childhood history. In 'Wandlungen' there is hardly any psychoanalytic interpretation. Jung takes the Miller work at face value, or nearly so, and draws on his wide reading to demonstrate historical and cultural symbolic parallels. It opens with a tribute to Freud and with acknowledgments to the work of other psychoanalysts, but the work is not so much Freudian as it is Jungian. It developed a new approach to the psychology of the unconscious.

Jung's goal was not to trace back Miller's fantasies to their childhood origin or explore their erotic significance. It was to show that mythopoeic forces did not die with the Greeks nor perish with the dawning of the Enlightenment; it was to show that a modern young woman was a myth-maker and that in our fantasies and dreams we are still making myths, or at least

producing symbolic motifs which have striking similarities to
classical and primitive mythologems. Jung's method for establishing correspondences was interpretation. He says that modern
individuals have forgotten their common bond with ancient
humanity, but that 'there is an identity of elementary human
conflicts existing independent of time and place' (p. 5). Finding
in ourselves the same age-old conflicts which are the central
concern of myths produces in us an 'inner sympathy' with, and
an 'intellectual comprehension' of, ancient cultures (1916a,
p. 5). This position is similar to statements of Dilthey, the
nineteenth-century founder of modern hermeneutics, on how
understanding is reached through empathy. We understand an
author by finding in ourselves an inner resonance to his or her
words. In this first work of analytical psychology Jung, although
he does not mention hermeneutics or Dilthey by name, is advocating an essentially hermeneutic methodology.

Miss Miller was sexually attracted to a man, but this erotic
desire could not be expressed towards him. The impulse, however, did find expression in sublimated form in fantasies. These
were centered on the theme of love and spiritual-fulfillment. Jung
explored the idea that both erotic and spiritual desire arise from
libidinal interest. Their source is the same; it is their object
that changes. Miss Miller's fantasies show a progressive detachment of the libido from flesh and blood people and a concomitant
investment of energy in fantastic, poetic, mythological images.
She turned away from the real young man towards a mythic hero.
Her fantasies 'uncovered an old buried idol, the youthful, beautiful, fire-encircled and halo-crowned sun-hero, who, forever
unattainable to the mortal, wanders upon the earth, causing
night to follow day; winter, summer; death, life; and who returns
again in rejuvenated splendor and gives light to new generations'
(p. 116). Miss Miller's hero was an Aztec named Chiwantopel.
He performed many heroic feats.

Miller in some associations to her fantasy points out similarities
to the works of Shakespeare, Samuel Johnson's 'Rasselas,' Longfellow's 'Hiawatha,' and the legend of Siegfried and Brunhild.
In addition to exploring these parallels, Jung presents a vast
array of other mythic material from which he extracts the motif
of the journey of the hero. This mythologem is universal; it is
the story of the individual's quest for spiritual perfection. It
is one of the greatest stories ever told, elaborating the trials of
the individual in a search for the unattainable; the perfection
of the self, unification with God, enlightenment. It is a story
told in many different ways by American Indians, Africans, and
Polynesians; by the ancient Greeks, Egyptians, and Sumerians;
by Hindus, Jews, Christians, Moslems, Bhuddists, and worship-
pers of Mithras; by Gnostics and alchemists; it is told in the
American Western novel and epics set in outer space.

Miller's fantasies were a solution in imagination to a problem
which in reality did not have a solution. She could not express
love towards the real man so her erotic desire found an alter-

native expression in the fantasy constructed around Chiwantopel.
What Miller did individually, religion does collectively. Religion
and its myths provide a compensation for erotic desire. Numinous
religious symbols lead desire away from the carnal to the spiritual. For the parents who are unacceptable erotic objects, religion
substitutes mythic figures towards whom erotic desire transformed into spiritual fervor can be expressed. Religion provides
a collective solution to problems which, if they were left to the
individual, might lead to neurosis. Ritual and myth capitalize on
forbidden desire, deflecting it towards the gods. The energy is
utilized, the problem is symbolically dealt with, and the libido
is expressed.

The symbol is the transformer of energy for it expresses both
the upper spiritual and lower carnal side of human longing. The
symbol leads the individual out of conflict by providing an ideal
solution, not a real one. The carnal, material solution is one possible way to resolve life's problems. It is the one favored by
moderns, celebrated in the scientific method, implemented by
technology, and advocated by psychoanalysis with its canonization of the reality principle. The spiritual solution is an alternative, one that has long given comfort to humanity and one
that Jung was resurrecting and outfitting in the language of
modern psychology.

Jung advised Freud about reading 'Wandlungen I:' let it
'unleash your associations and/or fantasies: I am sure you will
hit upon strange things if you do.' He felt that they were living
in a 'time full of marvels' and that if he was not deceived by
'the auguries' Freud's discoveries had put them 'on the threshold
of something sensational, which I scarcely know how to describe
except with the Gnostic concept of σοφια [Sophia, wisdom],
an Alexandrian term particularly suited to the reincarnation of
ancient wisdom in the shape of ΨA [psychoanalysis]' (McGuire,
1974, p. 439). Style matching content, Jung is expressing a
pivotal reorientation of his thought and trying in vain to convince Freud that psychoanalysis is at the heart of it. The fusion
of ancient wisdom with psychoanalysis was Jung's own synthesis
– analytical psychology. Years before, Jung had said that
analysts had to be able to think in 'flights of ideas'; 'Wandlungen,' with its analogical methodology, extensive quotes from
poetry and recapitulation of myths, achieved this goal. To read
it successfully one must read it associatively, letting the imagination wander, for in it Jung's style is more mythopoeic and
analogical than it is directed and logical.

Freud's response revealed a new interest. He too was exploring the origin of religion. He had read 'Wandlungen I' once,
knew he would have to reread it, and saw in it that his own
conclusions about religion had been anticipated. His rather narrow reading saw that Jung was also 'aware that the Oedipus
complex is at the root of religious feeling. Bravo!' (p. 441).
The Oedipal theme did appear in 'Wandlungen I,' but in
'Wandlungen II' Jung found the significance of the Oedipal motif

to be far different from Freud's findings in his work on the
origin of religion - 'Totem and Taboo.'

EMERGING DIFFERENCES IN TWO SYSTEMS OF THOUGHT

Significant differences between Freud's and Jung's conceptualiz-
ations of psychic functioning were beginning to emerge in 1911.
Given our knowledge that these differences helped to foster the
dissolution of their collaboration, we can retrospectively highlight the significance of them. It is important to realize, however,
that at the time neither man was emphasizing the divergence of
his views from the other's.

Both men agreed that there was a difference between conscious
and unconscious ways of thinking. Both also agreed that conscious thought is tied to language, is causal, and that in the
development of consciousness there is a weaning of thought from
subjective modes of representation towards communal objective
sign systems. It was in their concepts of the unconscious and
the significance of the difference between conscious and unconscious modes of thought that they differed.

Freud (1911a) saw conscious secondary process functioning
as being ruled by the reality principle, which delays action until
a maximum of pleasure with a minimum of pain can be achieved
through manipulation of the external world. Unconscious primary
process functioning is ruled by the pleasure principle's drive
to obtain immediate satisfaction even if such pleasure is only
hallucinatory. The ego instincts (i.e. hunger), because they
are object-related from the beginning, form the core around
which the reality principle operates. The sexual instincts,
because they can be satisfied autoerotically, retain their primary
process functioning longer and are resistant to the demands of
the reality principle. Likewise, fantasying, which begins in
children's play and develops into daydreaming, is ruled by the
pleasure principle. Neurosis arises when one turns away from
reality and the pleasure principle dominates sexuality once again.

Jung's view of conscious functioning was similar to Freud's.
Where he disagreed, and would continue to disagree, was over
the nature of the unconscious. The unconscious for him was not
only ontogenetically prior to consciousness, as it was for Freud,
but also a phylogenetic precursor of directed thinking. The
unconscious is characterized by mythopoeic forms of thought,
the mental activity found in dreams, fantasies, play, and myths.
The poet is the master of this type of thinking, the madman its
victim.

While the vehicle for directed thinking is ordered speech
attempting to file and categorize the world, subjective associational mythopoeic thought is different: 'Image crowds upon
image, feeling upon feeling; more and more clearly one sees a
tendency which creates a make believe, not as it truly is, but as
one indeed might wish it to be' (Jung, 1916a, p. 21). The

material for this thought arises from our memories of the past.
When our interest turns away from the world, and directed
thinking is exhausted, psychic energy involutes and energy
flows into old memories, reactivating them. Jung says Freud's
work shows that infantile reminiscences are initially resurrected.
Behind these, reached by a further regression, a stronger
introversion, 'There come to light pronounced traits of an archaic
mental kind which...might go as far as the re-echo of a once
manifest, archaic mental product.' The 'soul possesses in some
degree historical strata, the oldest stratum of which would
correspond to the unconscious' (p. 37). Jung in later work
designated the first level, characterized by infantile memories,
the personal unconscious. The second level of archaic mental
products he called the collective unconscious. For us, myths are
the artifacts of the deepest stratum of the soul. We are capable
of returning to mythopoeic thought, for within us are sedimented
remnants of the long evolution of human consciousness.

Style and content in these two essays – Freud's 'Two Principles
of Mental Functioning' and Jung's second chapter in 'Wandlungen'
'Concerning the Two Kinds of Thinking' – also evidence striking
differences. Freud's essay was a forerunner to a series of metapsychological papers and is a return to questions raised in
chapter 7 of 'The Interpretation of Dreams.' He is again taking
up the topic of psychic dynamics and his language is energic,
quasi-mechanical, and quasi-biological. Cathexes, bound and
unbound energy, instincts, and memory traces are the words
with which Freud operates. The style is one of scientific speculation. Jung is introducing a style which is new to his published
writings (although we have seen it in his letters) and which will
be characteristic of analytical psychology. It is philosophical,
if not theological. Citations to medieval philosophers are present,
contemporary philosophical positions on language are discussed,
and there is a synthesis of ideas ranging from Abélard through
Nietzsche to Freud. The soul is frequently mentioned and the
style certainly is not scientific. It is an eclectic mixture – which
can best be called Jungian – of history, mythology, theology,
science and philosophy.

The most important difference between the essays is the
philosophical position towards religion and science taken up by
each man. Freud states his position as follows. Religious myths
of an afterlife capitalize on the development of the reality principle in order to suppress the pleasure principle. Pleasure is
promised after death if one renounces carnal satisfactions in life.
Religion provides an illusory triumph over the pleasure principle,
but science does better since it provides intellectual pleasure
and 'promises practical gain in the end' (1911a, p. 224). It marks
the highest development of the reality principle. Freud's world-
view is beginning to take shape in this essay: individual health
resides in the domination of the reality principle over the pleasure principle and cultural advancement in the triumph of
science over religion.

For Jung myth and religion were no illusion. They provide a
psychological solution to typical human problems. Modern scientific thought eliminates subjectivity, directing all interest towards
objectivity. Jung rejects the notion that directed, rational,
modern thought is in any way superior to ancient mythopoeic
thought: 'our knowledge has increased but not our wisdom.'
Modern interest 'is displaced wholly into material reality; antiquity preferred a mode of thought which was more closely related
to the fantastic type....We see the antique spirit create not
science but mythology' (1916a, p. 24). Here is the foundation of
Jung's position that the soul is healed by reestablishing an individual's connection with myth and ago-old psychological truths.
It is modern civilization itself which often causes the self-
alienation of neurosis. It is the soul's return to the psychological truths of mythology which facilitates healing.

These differences in the evaluation of the modern versus the
ancient, of science versus mythology, and of reality versus
fantasy are divergences which will come to radically differentiate
the psychological theories of Freud and Jung.

A good example of their divergence at this time can be found
in papers which they wrote for the Australian Medical Congress,
articles which were written in 1911 when they were still on
good terms, but which were published after the break. Each
man's paper praises the other's work, but the fundamental
issues which were to divide them are clearly present. Freud
(1913 [1911]) stressed the importance of infantile experience,
sexuality, and repression in understanding neurosis. Jung focused on the etiological significance of adult conflicts and the
parallels between the fantasies of schizophrenics and ancient
myths. The study of this parallelism, Jung announced, is the
province of a 'special science, a science which may be called
"Analytical Psychology"' (1913a, [1911], p. 603). Jung's own
science had been christened.

The Weimar Congress and Freud's visit to the Jungs in September 1911 came after the two Australian papers were written, and
after the publication of 'Wandlungen I,' 'Two Principles' and
the Schreber case. The Weimar Congress was a success and we
have seen Freud's endorsement at it of Jung's work on mythology.
On the surface the two men were still close and in their letters
it is not until the end of 1911 that signs of the break emerge.

A letter written by Emma Jung to Freud in October 1911
announces the coming of the end. She as an outsider saw the
signs of strain which both men, still blinded by their mutual
transference, were failing to acknowledge. She says that ever
since Freud's visit to Küssnacht she had sensed that relations
between the two men were not as they should be. She wanted
to do what she could to help. Worried that she might be deceiving herself, she felt that Sigmund and Carl were not in agreement over 'Wandlungen I.' She continued, 'You didn't speak of
it at all and yet I think it would do you both so much good if
you got down to a thorough discussion of it' (McGuire, 1974,

p. 452). A thorough discussion never took place and the publication of 'Wandlungen II' played a large part in the termination of Freud and Jung's six-year collaboration.

8   THE BREAK AND ITS RAMIFICATIONS

Emma Jung's next letter to Freud elaborated points in her
October letter, highlighting issues her husband and Sigmund
were failing to confront. She questioned Freud about whether
his desire to have Carl complete his work was not exaggerated.
The father-son relationship was becoming restrictive for Carl
and in 'Wandlungen' he was not only exploring mythology, but
also himself and his relations with Freud. Emma Jung advised
Freud: do not let your fantasies of a successor and heir lead
you to demand too great an allegiance from Carl. She told Freud
to analyze and abandon his paternal relation to Jung, setting in
its place a non-authoritarian egalitarian bond. Freud's reply
to her letter must have been negative because Emma's next letter opens, 'You were really annoyed by my letter, weren't you?'
(McGuire, 1974, p. 462).

In November Freud did write to Jung about 'Wandlungen I;'
his review of it was mixed. The book was 'one of the nicest'
works he had read in preparing to write his own book on religion.
Ideas in it were 'well-expressed,' but Jung had read too widely
and included too many thoughts of other people. Freud also felt
that in places Jung's horizon had been 'too narrowed by Christianity' (p. 459).

Because he and Jung were both working on the topic of religion, Freud was tormented by the thought that ideas he came up
with were being taken away from Jung. He wished to suggest
various leads to Carl, but could not do so for fear of influencing
Jung's work. He was paralyzed in his researches for fear of
offending Jung and uttered a presentient cry which foreshadowed
the grief the two men would come to over the question of religion,
'Why in God's name did I allow myself to follow you into this
field?' (p. 459). He consoles himself with the thought that his
explorative 'tunnels will be far more subterranean than your
shafts and we shall pass each other by' (p. 459). This wish did
not come true; their tunnels collided over the issue of sexuality.

Jung's reply was a quietly phrased declaration of independence.
He said the outlook was 'very gloomy' for him if Freud began
the study of religion: 'You are a dangerous rival - if one has to
speak of rivalry' (p. 460). Rivalry was, of course, a salient
topic. Their relations had never been free from Jung's comparing
himself with Freud. Freud found the son's wish to overcome the
father in the first dream of Jung's that he analyzed. Emma had
just pointed out the rivalry to Freud and suggested that his
paternal identification encouraged it. Jung tried to depotentiate

potential conflict by declaring 'our personal differences will make
our work different' (p. 460). There are no longer any apologies
for his background or training producing deviations from Freud's
views; there is the mature realization that each man's work will
be shaped by who he is. Jung follows this with an apt characterization of Freud's and his own style:

> You dig up the precious stones, but I have the 'degree of
> extension.' As you know, I always have to proceed from the
> outside to the inside and from the whole to the part. I would
> find it too upsetting to let large tracts of human knowledge
> lie there neglected. (p. 460)

Freud deplored Jung's wide reading for 'Wandlungen' and the
work's extensive citations. He once joked that he invented
psychoanalysis because it did not have a literature which he
would have to review (Roazen, 1971). He disliked doing the
literature search for 'The Interpretation of Dreams,' and says
he avoided reading Nietzsche because he did not want his own
thoughts influenced. Freud saw himself as the lone explorer
discovering truth empirically through his observations and their
refinement. He sifted through vast amounts of experience in
order to extract those causal core elements with which all psychic
phenomena could be explained. He reduced myriads of material
to an interwoven nexus of findings which constitute the central
theses of psychoanalysis. Jung worked synthetically. He read
widely and enjoyed citing everyone he read, thereby connecting
his thought to his contemporaries and ancient predecessors. He
grouped, categorized, and typed, producing a superordinate
system which co-ordinated vast amounts of human observation
and speculation on psychic functioning.

In examining the issues which brought the dissolution of
relations between these two we will see that personal, administrative, and intellectual disagreements worked in concert to
destroy the six-year collaboration. Disputes over psychological
issues concerning religion, mythology, and science will produce
the seemingly antithetical and irreconcilable tenets of two
psychological systems. Before considering these theoretical
issues we will explore the personal and administrative difficulties
which ended the exchange of letters between Freud and Jung.

ALIENATION OF AFFECTIONS AND ADMINISTRATIVE TURMOIL

Freud's hope in his relations with Jung was that in Carl he had
found the person to whom he could leave psychoanalysis. Prior
to the last months of 1911 and the fateful year of 1912 Freud
had sought to diminish their interpersonal and theoretical differences in order to insure the succession. Jung complied in this.
For Jung, Freud was someone who could teach him, offer him
guidance, and foster his dreams of fame. But Freud's need of

Jung as a successor gradually diminished. The psychoanalytic movement grew, and by 1911 the International Association could boast of branch societies in several countries. Jung became expendable. Freud had men like Abraham who would adhere faithfully to psychoanalytic principles, and Jung's growing deviations no longer had to be tolerated.

Jung after a half-decade of work in psychoanalysis felt he had sufficient experience to publish his own ideas. The reservations about infantile sexuality, the libido theory, and the sexual causation of neurosis which he had had since the beginning of his relations with Freud were now to be expressed openly by him. For almost six years their relations had been sustained by tolerance and an avoidance of conflict. That changed. Now they amplified their differences, dwelt on their emotional conflicts, and exaggerated their difficulties. This reversal meant that what had been sustained by compromise for years disintegrated within twelve months.

While still maintaining that he wished to leave psychoanalysis to Jung, Freud found more and more to criticize in his heir. While Freud had explicitly encouraged the father-son transference, he wrote to Jung, 'The trouble with you younger men seems to be a lack of understanding in dealing with your father-complexes.' Some of Freud's followers accepted this sort of chastisement relatively well. Ferenczi, for example, had complained that Freud had been cold and rejecting, but when Freud analyzed his complaints Ferenczi capitulated, admitting that he was wrong and that Sigmund's conduct had been correct. Some of Freud's own unanalyzed identification with the father is shown in the conclusion he draws from this for Jung: 'I don't deny that I like to be right. All in all, that is a sad privilege, since it is conferred by age' (McGuire, 1974, p. 476).

Jung responded that he had never complained of any lack of affection on Freud's part, a statement that is substantiated by the letters. It was Freud who groused about Jung's failing to write and who worried over Jung's tie to him. Freud's complaints about Jung's failures as a correspondent were now intensified. Freud said he derived no 'triumph' from breaking his habit of writing to Jung, but realized Carl did not have an interest in writing because his work was so absorbing. Under this testiness was another difficulty. Freud said that he had wanted to see Jung's work represented in the new psychoanalytic journal 'Imago,' but this had not occurred because 'you [Jung] hide behind your religious-libidinal cloud' (p. 485).

It was Jung's work on 'Wandlungen' that was alienating Freud from him and specifically the religiosity of that work. Jung replied to Freud's charge with a statement that fueled Sigmund's criticisms: he said, in essence, don't be peeved, for I am in the realm of the mothers. He had invested his energy in his investigations of maternal symbolism in mythology. He had found that the significance of unconscious incestuous ties to the mother and the need to overcome them by a descent into the realm of the mothers - an exploration of the unconscious - had long been recognized by the poets, for example in Goethe's 'Faust,' and in mythology. A great danger in every quest is in being captured by the regressive longing for the mother and the hero must fight to free himself from maternal captivity, that is, becoming lost in unconscious fantasies. Jung did admit that he had been remiss in writing and asked for Freud's tolerance.

Freud's letter of reply, dated 29 February 1912, marks a vital point in their relations. Freud says that in the past he had been a demanding correspondent, but now he had himself under control. The end of years of overvaluation of Jung was announced: 'I took myself in hand and quickly turned off my excess libido. I was sorry to do so, yet glad to see how quickly I managed it. Since then I have become undemanding' (p. 488).

With this withdrawal of affection, Freud felt less need to believe that things were going well. He accused Jung of neglecting his presidential duties. Freud listed several complaints saying he only brought these matters up because in the future he wanted things to operate smoothly so psychoanalysis could be safely put in Jung's hands. Emma Jung had pointed out just a few months earlier that Freud should analyze this façade of wanting psychoanalysis to run smoothly not for his own benefit, but for the future and Jung's good.

Freud's playing the parental role produced its complement in Jung's replies. He became the rebellious son: 'I would never have sided with you in the first place had not heresy run in my blood.' Quoting Nietzsche, he continued, 'One repays a teacher badly if one remains only a pupil.' Jung concluded saying that psychoanalysis had taught him the importance of developing his own ideas and that as 'one who is truly your [Freud's] follower [he] must be stout-hearted, not least towards you' (p. 492).

Responding to Jung's heretical remarks, Freud said he was in full agreement with them. He then, however, denies that agreement by assuming an analytic stance: 'But if a third party were to read this passage [in Jung's letter], he would ask when I had tried to tyrannize you intellectually, and I should have to say: I don't know. I don't believe I ever did' (p. 492). In the original German Freud wrote 'warum,' 'why;' instead of 'wenn,' 'when.' This slip was not analyzed by Jung but one might well have asked why Freud tried to intellectually dominate Jung.[1] Freud's assumption that he could take the stance of an impartial third party in commenting on his relations to others was his tyranny. He insisted he was objective and treated all evidence to the contrary as the emotional outpourings of his troubled acquaintances. Freud says Adler had 'made similar complaints [to those of Jung's], but I am convinced that his neurosis was speaking for him' (p. 492). It does not seem to have crossed Freud's mind that Adler's objections to psychoanalysis could have been made on reasonable grounds and that he had resented Freud's failure to recognize that his views had merit. No, for Freud other men's ideas and their problems in getting along with him were a manifestation of their psychopathology.

Just a year before his current problems with Jung Freud wrote to Ferenczi: 'I *no longer* have any need to uncover my personality completely....Since Fliess' case...that need had been extinguished' (Jones, 1955, p. 83). No person should ever place himself beyond continuing self-analysis, for in doing so he creates the illusion of complete self-knowledge. Given Freud's certainty that his motives were known and that psychoanalysis uncovered the reasons behind other people's problems he created a despotism which he could not see, the despotism of the self-righteous man who has the truth which others, because of their problems, will not or cannot see. Given Freud's unshakeable self-assurance and perfected ability to find fault in others, Jung was doomed to be yet another victim of the truth.

Freud's letter proclaiming he did not know of any time he had tyrannized over Jung continues with his saying that he was not looking for anyone to replace Carl as his 'friend...helper and... heir' (McGuire, 1974, p. 483). Expecting one man to be all these things is quite a burden. Personal intimacy, administrative competence, and intellectual stewardship were what Freud expected of Jung. A failure in any one of these areas threatened the other two. Freud saw failures in affection and administration and was certainly wondering about Jung's revisions of psychoanalytic theory.

Jung's reply assured Freud that he had not 'the slightest intention of imitating Adler' (p. 493). He apologized, called himself 'empty-headed,' and said when he was no longer so involved in work he would try to gather his wits together.

They had approached a precipice and had for the moment drawn back, but their relationship had been shaken. There was a month of calm; then Freud raised the libido question. He said that he imagined Jung's 'Declaration of Independence' had been fostered by the new concept of libido that Jung was proposing in 'Wandlungen II.' He assured Jung that he was capable of listening to and accepting new ideas or of waiting until a new formulation was made clear to him. In reality, Freud seldom changed his views to match another's and in the six years of their collaboration Freud had never yet moderated his opinions in order to accommodate Jung's criticisms. He was not about to start.

Several letters by each man were given over to a discussion of incest and the libido theory. Jung sketched the ideas he was developing in 'Wandlungen II.' If incest were an actual biologically based fear, then father-daughter incest, as well as mother-son incest would be strongly prohibited. It is not. The importance of the mother in mythology goes far beyond the son's biological ties to her. Adult dread concerning all sorts of unknowns regressively reactivates infantile longing for the mother and retrospectively sexualizes memories of this early bond. The actual wish to commit incest, incest taboos, and the role of the mother in mythology have a significance 'far outweighing the biological incest problem - a significance that amounts to pure fantasy'

(p. 502). Although myths and rituals build on the raw materials of a seemingly important incest wish, the meaning of mother myths can no more be understood by reducing them to their infantile elements than a temple can be understood by analyzing the composition of the stones from which it is built. Incest myths and rituals built around incest have as their goal the consolidation of the community by severing one's ties to the mother and engendering a wider identification with the entire tribe.

Jung tied his revolutionary ideas on incest to a critique of the real trauma theory of hysteria. Freud had been in error when he thought actual seduction caused hysteria and Jung cautioned that one should avoid the same mistake by thinking that just because primitive societies outlaw incest, actual incest wishes of any significance must exist in children. Jung argued that in psychoanalysis the notion of an incest wish and its prohibition in the Oedipal situation had replaced the seduction theory. Like seduction, however, whether children actually have incest wishes is immaterial. The etiological significance of the Oedipus complex lay in the fact that adult neurotics and primitives retrogressively fantasize incestuous wishes towards the mother. Jung, here, is questioning the actual existence of the Oedipus complex in children and like Adler just a year earlier, and to some extent like Freud in the Rat Man case, is asserting that adults rewrite their childhood histories in response to difficulties in coping with current conflicts.

Freud responded that he really did not understand what Jung was trying to do or why Jung had made such modifications. He said he had a 'strong antipathy' towards Jung's innovations for two reasons. First they were regressive: Jung's views sounded like those put forward 'before the days of psychoanalysis.' Second, Jung's views had 'a disastrous similarity to a theorem of Adler's.' Freud still thought that Adler's idea that the adult retrospectively creates an incestuous wish for the mother was fanciful and was 'based on utter incomprehension of the unconscious' (p. 507).

If one's two most promising followers proposed similar modifications in theory, one might be tempted to alter one's views, especially if one had previously made the error which a follower had warned against making again. Freud thanked Jung for reminding him of his 'first big error, when [he] mistook [seduction] fantasies for realities' (p. 507). He promised to guard against repeating it. However, he never abandoned his search in either ontogenetic or phylogenetic history for an actual wish or real event of a sexual or aggressive nature to which he could trace the origins of fantasy. The discussion of the libido and incest question was closed by Freud's saying the nature of Jung's changes were unclear to him and he had no understanding of why Jung felt the need for revisions. Jung had actually explained his views fairly well, but it would have been foolish to believe that Freud, the man who resisted all criticism of his work, could have given his ideas a fair hearing. The problem over the

psychological issues of libido and incest worked to renew and
worsen their interpersonal difficulties.

In his 23 May letter criticizing Jung's views Freud announced
that on the 24th he would be leaving for Kreuzlingen to visit
Binswanger and, therefore, would be near Jung geographically.
Freud visited Binswanger, who was seriously ill, from 25-8 May.
On 25 May Jung wrote to Vienna asking Freud why there had
been such a delay in Freud's response to his previous letter.
Jung then took revenge on Freud by saying that he would not
make exorbitant demands on his time by expecting him to write.
Obviously Jung had not received Freud's 23 May letter.

Jung's next letter complained that Freud's failure to visit
Zurich when he had come as far as Kreuzlingen was obviously
a sign of Freud's displeasure over Jung's revisions of libido
theory. He said the comparison of his work to Adler's was a
bitter pill, but he would 'swallow it without a murmur. Evidently
that is my fate' (p. 509). Although he had set out with every
expectation of corroborating Freud's views, there was overwhelming evidence set forth in 'Wandlungen II' for his revisions.
He closed by saying he was prepared to go his own way and
Freud should know 'how obstinate we Swiss are' (p. 509).

Freud's reply explained the visit to Kreuzlingen. He had not
specifically asked Jung to travel there to meet him because it
would be an imposition to ask anyone to leave his family on Whit-
sun holiday. 'But I should have been pleased,' Freud added,
'if you yourself had thought of it' (p. 510). After sending this
letter in June Freud did not write to Jung again until the following November. This was the longest time by far that Freud had
gone without corresponding with Jung since the beginning of
their friendship. Jung took over a month in responding to
Freud's June letter and his response was brief: 'Now I can only
say: I understand the Kreuzlingen gesture' (p. 511). He closed,
'I have always kept my distance, and this will guard against
any imitation of Adler's disloyalty' (p. 511).

Jung's next letter announced that the lectures he was to give
in America were finished and in them he would put forward some
tentative suggestions for modifications in psychoanalytic theory.
He again dissociated himself from Adler saying that he would
not 'follow Adler's recipe for overcoming the father, as you
[Freud] seem to imagine' (p. 512).

The summer of 1912, with Freud's not writing to Jung and
Jung's letters referring to the Kreuzlingen gesture and avowal
that he would follow his own path, marked the informal break in
the two men's relations. It would take another two years to
formalize the severance of the association.

In July Freud wrote to Binswanger about Jung. He said he was
disappointed in Jung's personal behavior, but did not wish a
break with him over scientific issues. He was currently 'completely indifferent' towards Jung (Binswanger, 1957, p. 45). The
withdrawal of his affectional ties was easy because he could
reinvest his emotions in a host of friends and followers including

Ferenczi, Rank, Sachs, Abraham and Jones.

These five men, with Freud, formed a group known as the Committee. Ernest Jones, distressed by the 'defections' of Adler and Stekel and worried that Freud's relations with Jung were showing signs of strain, proposed first to Ferenczi, then to Freud, that a group of loyal followers join together to protect Freud and insure psychoanalytic orthodoxy. Among members of the Committee there 'would be only one definite obligation...if anyone wished to depart from any of the fundamental tenets of psychoanalytic theory...he would promise not to do so publicly before first discussing his views with the rest' (Jones, 1955, p. 152).

One would think that such a 'Star Chamber' had no place in science and that as a scientist Freud would have rejected the notion. On the contrary, Freud was enthusiastic about it. For him there was a boyish and romantic element in the whole idea and he let his fantasy play freely about it. The most important thing to him was that the Committee 'would have to be *strictly secret* in its existence and in its actions' (p. 153).

The Committee first assembled as a body the next summer. Freud celebrated the event by presenting each of the five members with an antique Greek intaglio which each man had mounted in a gold ring, much like the one Freud wore. Later, when Eitington joined the Committee, it became the secret society of the 'Seven Rings' (Sachs, 1944). Freud the man of reason, who with his followers on the Committee condemned Jung for mysticism, founded a secret society whose purpose was to investigate possible deviations from psychoanalytic doctrine. Jung, whom Freud after the break accused of aspiring to be a prophet, never formed a group sworn to preserve orthodoxy.

While Freud's loyal followers were gathering around him and agreeing with him that Jung's objections to psychoanalysis were unfounded, Jung was refining his criticisms. In September 1912 'Wandlungen II' was published and Emma Jung immediately sent a copy to Freud. Jung, in America, gave a series of lectures at Fordham University which criticized some very central psychoanalytic doctrines. In both works Jung questioned the etiological significance of infantile sexuality and suggested that there was a presexual period in childhood. He stressed the importance of current adult conflicts as the significant causitive factor in psychoneurosis and maintained that a side effect of such conflict was the reactivation and sexualization of memories from childhood. He criticized the narrow identification of the libido with sexuality and called for an expansion of the definition to mean psychic energy in general.

In the preface to the published version of the Fordham Lectures, 'The Theory of Psychoanalysis,' Jung said he did not view his 'modest and temperate criticism as a "falling away" or a schism; on the contrary I hope thereby to promote the continued flowering and fructification of the psychoanalytic movement' (1913b, p. 86). Brill, the most prominent American analyst in the early days of psychoanalysis, confirms what Jung wrote: 'I can definitely state that Jung would have preferred to have remained in the psychoanalytic fold' (1942, p. 547).

Writing to Freud after returning home, Jung said that he was favorably received in America and therefore he 'was able to do a very great deal for the spread of the movement' (McGuire, 1974, p. 515). Jung felt that many people who had been 'put off by the problem of sexuality in neurosis' were won over to psychoanalysis by the modifications he had made. He was sorry if Freud thought the changes in the libido theory were prompted solely by personal resistances: 'I can only assure you that there is no resistance on my side, unless it be my refusal to be treated like a fool riddled with complexes' (p. 516). Jung argued that he was fighting for what he held to be true and that personal regard for Freud would not restrain him. He was still angry over Freud's 'Kreuzlingen gesture' because he felt Freud had purposely avoided a direct confrontation with him. He asserted that he had done more for the psychoanalytic movement than all of Freud's other followers put together.

Jung's conduct in the three areas which constituted the core of their relationship was questioned by Freud in his November reply. He talked again of his decreased personal affection for Jung, found fault with Jung's administration of psychoanalysis, and questioned the modifications of analytic theory. He found Jung's 'harping on the "Kreuzlingen gesture" both incomprehensible and insulting' (p. 517). He felt they could not resolve this difficulty through the mails. The misunderstanding over their failing to meet at Kreuzlingen was to be settled that very month in Munich when they met to discuss problems concerning Stekel. Freud chastised Jung's failure to leave someone in charge of the International Association before he departed for America. But the most serious problem was the problem over theory. Freud felt Jung had reduced much of the resistance to psychoanalysis with his modifications, but this should not be entered in 'the credit column because...the farther you remove yourself from what is new in psychoanalysis, the more certain you will be of applause and the less resistance you will meet' (p. 517).

At about this time Stekel had broken with Freud but insisted on his right to remain editor of the 'Zentralblatt.' Freud's plan of leaving the 'Zentralblatt' to Stekel and starting a new journal required a meeting. This was held in late November at the Park Hotel in Munich. Freud's motion was approved and thus one problem was solved. The misunderstanding between Freud and Jung over Kreuzlingen was also finally settled. Jung told Freud that he had been offended by Sigmund's notifying him of his visit to Kreuzlingen at too late a date for them to get together. Freud said he had sent the letters to Binswanger and Jung on the same day and that Carl should have had one day's notice prior to the visit. Jung suddenly recalled that he had been away from home both the day and the day after Freud's letter arrived and

therefore he had been mistaken about when the letter came.
Freud asked him why he hadn't looked at the postmark, and
chastised him for making so much trouble over the Kreuzlingen
affair. He gave Jung a fatherly lecture; Jung was contrite,
apologized, and promised to reform (Jones, 1955).

The Munich meeting was marked by an incident which would,
because of Jung's insistence on its significance, contribute to
the final break. After resolving the Kreuzlingen problem, the
two men joined the other analysts for lunch. There was a discussion of Abraham's paper on Amenophis IV (Akhenaton) and
the significance of this ruler's actions in destroying his father's
cartouches. Freud argued that this demonstrated that behind
Akhenaton's creation of a monotheistic religion there lay a hatred
of his father. Jung replied that Akhenaton was a profoundly
creative man and that the founding of a religion could not be
reduced to a father complex. Besides, it was common practice
among Egyptian kings to replace the inscriptions on their father's
monuments with their own names.

The theme of obliterating the father's name was then made more
personal. Freud, who had just a few months before criticized
Jung for citing him too extensively, asked Jung why recent Swiss
articles about psychoanalysis had omitted his name. Jung, in
fact, had rarely omitted references to Freud. Suddenly, Freud
fainted. Jung picked him up and carried him to a couch. Jung
recalls, 'I shall never forget the look he cast at me [when he
came to]. In his weakness he looked at me as if I were his father'
(1973b, p. 157).

The fainting aside, Freud felt the meeting had been a success.
He wrote to a friend that his and Jung's talk 'had swept away a
number of unnecessary personal irritations,' but he was sure
he would not accept Jung's modifications of libido theory because
all his experience contradicted Jung's views (Hale, 1971, p. 150).

Jung's first letter to Freud after the meeting was almost con-
descending in tone. He said he now had a radically different
attitude towards Freud, asked Sigmund's forgiveness for his past
mistakes, and said he hoped to guide his future conduct in order
not to cause Freud any further distress. He was worried about
Freud's health and hoped the journey from Munich to Vienna
had not been too great a strain.

Freud was buoyed by Jung's letter. He expressed a hope that
they would continue to collaborate, but realized controversy
was inevitable between two people who insisted on their own
viewpoints. For him their relations would always 'retain an echo
of past intimacy' (McGuire, 1974, p. 523).

Freud next raised the issue of his fainting. His diagnosis was
that it was due to migraine 'not without a psychic factor which
unfortunately I haven't time to track down now.' The Park Hotel
held a certain 'fatality' for him. It and Munich had strong
associations with Fliess, and Freud had on two previous occasions
suffered milder attacks there. He called his troubles a 'bit of
neurosis that I ought really to look into' (p. 524).

This admission and Freud's statement that in 'Wandlungen II' Jung had unintentionally produced a great revelation by showing that mystic symbolism is derived from complexes which have outlived their function unleashed Carl's fury. Jung replied that this view demonstrated to him that Freud vastly underestimated 'Wandlungen.' The insight about complexes was very elementary. He said the thrust of his book had been to show how symbols helped to transform an individual's life.

In this letter of early December 1912 Jung warned Freud to look out because he was adopting a new style. He was going to be completely honest. Freud's brief review of 'Wandlungen II' had infuriated him because he 'occasionally,' as he sarcastically puts it, had 'the purely human desire to be understood *intellectually* and not be measured by the yardstick of neurosis' (p. 526). Jung obviously felt that Freud's reference to the relationship between mysticism and complexes hinted that Jung's ideas were being shaped by his own psychic difficulties. Jung used this reading of Freud's intention to launch a highly emotional attack on Freud and his followers. He said he had suffered at the hands of Freud's 'bit of neurosis' and that Freud's neurotic problems had kept Sigmund from understanding 'Wandlungen II.' He advised Freud to analyze the problem and reminded him that their mutual analysis had been terminated when Freud had insisted that he could not risk losing his authority. Jung warned: do not belittle my advice with insinuations that it is neurotically caused by a father complex. Psychoanalysts, he charged, too often misuse analysis 'for the purpose of devaluing others and their progress by insinuations about complexes (as though that explained anything. A wretched theory!).' 'Anything,' Jung concluded, 'that might make them think is written off as a complex' (pp. 526-7).

Freud's reply was aloof. He said he did not take Jung's style amiss and agreed that relations between analysts should be frank. He too recognized that analysts often use psychoanalysis to attack new ideas. His remedy: 'let each of us pay more attention to his own than his neighbor's neurosis' (p. 529). Contrary to Jung's belief, Freud asserted, Carl had never been injured by his neurosis.

Eleven days later Freud violated his own prescription. Jung wrote that his views did not mean he was moving over to Adler's position: 'Even Adler's cronies do not regard me as one of theirs' (p. 533). For 'theirs' instead of 'ihrigen' Jung had written 'Ihrigen' which means 'yours.' Freud seized on this slip in retaliation for Jung's analytic comments about his neurosis. Freud asked if Jung was '"objective" enough to consider the following slip without anger? "Even Adler's cronies do not regard me as one of *yours*"' (p. 534). In Freud's letters to Jung he had made significant slips which Jung did not point out, but now all reticence in their relations was gone. Freud was obviously baiting Jung. Analysis had become a weapon.

Jung responded, 'Your technique of treating your pupils like patients is a *blunder*.' He continued:

> You go around sniffing out all the symptomatic actions in
> your vicinity, thus reducing everyone to the level of sons
> and daughters who blushingly admit the existence of their
> faults. Meanwhile you remain on top as the father, sitting
> pretty. For sheer obsequiousness nobody dares to pluck the
> prophet by the beard and inquire for once what you would
> say to a patient with a tendency to analyze the analyst
> instead of himself. You would certainly ask him: 'Who's got
> the neurosis?' (p. 535)

Jung charged Freud with having the neurosis and said that
Freud had got nowhere with self-analysis. If he, Freud, ever
analyzed his complexes and stopped playing the father then
Jung said he would mend his own ways. Jung closed assuring
Freud of his public support, but said that privately he would
continue telling Freud what he thought of him.

Freud said Jung's allegation that he treated his followers like
patients was 'demonstrably untrue' (p. 538). In fact, he said,
in Vienna he was reproached for the exact opposite. As with the
Kreuzlingen episode Freud charged that Jung was making an
immense issue out of a trivial matter. There followed a counter
accusation: 'One who while behaving abnormally keeps shouting
that he is normal gives ground for the suspicion that he lacks
insight into his illness' (p. 539). Given their difficulties, Freud
proposed that they abandon their personal relations.

Jung acceded to Freud's wish, saying that he did not thrust
his friendship on anyone. Borrowing a line from Hamlet he closed,
'"The rest is silence"' (p. 540).

In January 1913 the seven-year friendship was at an end. Both
men had withdrawn from each other and in the course of this
change had abused analysis by using it to attack the other. Each
man tried to find in the other's actions the reasons for their
mutual difficulties. Such reasons are not to be found in a single
incident or a neurotic trait, but within the entirety of each
man's past life and his hopes for the future. The reasons cannot
be given in the form of a causal explanation, but are to be found
in the stories, reaching from childhood to middle age which
constitute each man's biography. For example, let us look at
Freud's fainting in Munich. It goes back to his relations with
Fliess and farther. He wrote to Jones that it had to do with an
unruly piece of homosexual libido which he had not yet mastered.
In a letter to Ferenczi he carried it back to his earliest childhood.
Before he was two he had wished for the death of his baby brother and rival, Julius. Julius died; young Sigmund got his wish,
but this event left in him tremendous guilt over his aggressive
desires. Having triumphed over Jung by having Carl admit he
was wrong about Kreuzlingen may have produced guilt in Freud,
the atonement for which was a symbolic death. When he came to
he said, 'How sweet it must be to die' (Jones, 1953, p. 317).

Another explanation, not contradicting this first one, can also be constructed. For Freud, victory meant completely defeating one's opponent and also surviving him. Jung's interest in the peat bog corpses of Bremen in 1909 and the discussion in 1912 of Akhenaton and of the Swiss failing to cite Freud aroused Freud's belief, going back to their first meeting, that Jung harbored death wishes against him. The fainting could have been a compliance with this wish perhaps with the underlying motive of exposing to Jung his patricidal desires and instilling in him a guilty conscience. Given his own relations to his father and Paul Jung's timely death, Jung may have wished that Freud, whom Jung also called father, would die so that he would be free from Freud's oppressive authority.

Superordinate to these two interpretations is the fact that Freud invented psychoanalysis and explained his own and other people's lives in terms of it. For him, all sons harbor death wishes against their fathers, a fainting attack can have psychological causes, and a dominant motive in human relations is aggression. In that psychoanalysis was used by Freud to understand his life and the actions of others, and in that we too look to psychoanalysis for an explanation of human actions it is perhaps not too absurd to say that Freud fainted because of a theory, the very theory that explains his fainting.

A substantial part of this book can be seen as an attempt to explain the break. We have discussed the proximal reasons for it which can be found in the areas of personal affection, administration, and the construction of theory. The deterioration in their personal relations can be seen in the Kreuzlingen episode, the Munich fainting, Jung's analytic attacks, and Freud's interpretation of the slip of the pen. Concomitant with the alienation of affections, Freud became increasingly dissatisfied with Jung's administration of the psychoanalytic movement and Jung focused more of his energy on his own work. There were also the conflicts over theory - the libido question, the role of sexuality in the causation of neurosis, and the meaning of myths.

Beyond these immediate problems, many lines of strain can be traced back through the seven years of their relations. There was Jung's fear of becoming Freud's disciple and losing his independence. There was Freud's belief that Jung had death wishes towards him. There were the failures to openly discuss theoretical disagreements or air emotional issues. Abraham's orthodoxy highlighting Jung's deviancy and Freud and Jung's failure to agree on the etiology of dementia praecox must also be seen as a factor in the eventual break.

Beyond their first exchange of letters, we recall Freud's troubled relations with Fliess and his treatment of Breuer. For Jung, we remember his picture of himself as an outcast, and advocacy of anti-materialist philosophy. For Freud there was the strong belief in materialism and the certainty that any opposition to his sexual theories was a sign of resistance to psychoanalysis. Further back are Jung's fights with his father and

Freud's self-analysis which focused on his relations with Jakob.
Still further back are the two childhoods which were so radically
different. There is Freud's heritage as a Jew and Jung's as a
Protestant and the strains that religion put on their relations.
    The break is a focal point of many lines of stress from the past
and was the origin for innumerable future events. All was not
silence after January 1913, for the termination of Freud and
Jung's personal relations produced, and is still producing, countless ramifications - from Freud's replacing Jung's picture on his
wall with Abraham's to the identification of analysts today as
Freudians and Jungians.

RAMIFICATIONS OF THE BREAK

The break with Freud was one of the incidents which precipitated
Jung's intensive self-analysis. Jung's five-year period of introspection formed the experiential basis for his later psychological
work. Jung's self-investigation will be considered in detail in
chapter 9.
    Freud's reaction to the break was mild in comparison with
Jung's. He had been through severe crises before with Breuer
and Fliess and had already dealt with the defections of Adler
and Stekel. As he had commiserated with Jung about Adler, so
Freud turned to members of the Committee over his troubles with
Jung. He complained to Jones about Jung's insolence and to both
Abraham and Ferenczi Freud reasserted his conviction that 'We
possess the truth; I am as sure of it as fifteen years ago' (Jones,
1955, p. 148). He 'was struck by the complete analogy that can
be drawn between the first running away from the discovery of
sexuality behind the neurosis by Breuer and the latest one by
Jung. That makes it more certain that this is the core of psychoanalysis' (Abraham and Freud, 1965, p. 151). Not only did
critics' attacks convince Freud of the truth of his views, but now
the desertions from psychoanalysis by experienced analysts were
also taken as confirmation. Nothing shook Freud's faith; in fact
those things which might cause a lesser man some moments of
doubt were used by him to fortify his convictions. Jung had
renewed the opposition to sexuality and this rejuvenated Freud's
sense of mission.
    Although all personal relations between the two men came to an
end in early 1913, the break was not made officially until April
1914 when Jung resigned as president of the International
Psychoanalytic Association.
    The papers delivered by Jung and Freud at the Fourth Private
Psychoanalytic Meeting which was held in Munich in September
1913 demonstrate the discordance in their theoretical positions.
Anticipating his later work on psychological types, Jung pre-
sumed to analyze psychoanalysis, putting forward the thesis
that Freudian and Adlerian theories are complementary. Freud's
system with its emphasis on striving to gain pleasure from others

and its reductive, causal and sensualistic focus is an extraverted psychology; Adler's focus on personal supremacy, the masculine protest, and life-guiding fictions created an introverted psychology. Jung (1913c) had completely relativized psychoanalysis by putting Freud's work on the same plane as Adler's.

The assurance that nothing has changed because of Jung's criticism can be seen as the message Freud delivered at Munich. By example and by statement he asserted that psychoanalysis is concerned with discovering the causation of adult neurosis in infantile sexuality. His paper, 'The Disposition to Obsessional Neurosis' (1913c), is an excellent example of the fruits of the paradigm he created. Freud's method of constructing the infantile past from the adult present and then using that past as a cause of the present is vividly illustrated in this work (Jacobsen and Steele, 1979).

Freud, who called the Fourth Congress 'fatiguing and unedifying,' says that at Munich he found it necessary to clear up the confusion caused by Jung's modifications of psychoanalysis. He did so by 'declaring that [he] did not recognize the innovations of [Jung] as legitimate continuations and further developments of the psycho-analysis that originated with [him]' (1914d, p. 60). This statement makes the criterion of validity for analytic research obvious: if Freud accepts it, then it is psychoanalysis; if Freud rejects it, then it is not. No field of inquiry should ever be founded on this basis, but we can see in it a canonization of Freud's fundamental stance towards the world: either you are for me or against me.

Given Freud's and the Committee's opposition to Jung it is surprising that he was re-elected as president of the International. When Jung stood for re-election, thirty participants voted for him and twenty-two abstained. The Association was clearly divided, but the majority obviously did not feel that Jung's ideas put him outside of psychoanalysis.

In November 1913 Jung resigned as editor of the 'Jahrbuch' citing reasons of a personal nature and in April 1914 he sent a letter to all the branch presidents of the International Association resigning his presidency. With this the break was formal and complete. It is in Freud's letters to Abraham, who replaced Jung as President of the International, that we find Freud's reactions to the break. Freud found in the Committee the political guidance he needed. He said his confidence in his political judgment had greatly declined 'since being taken in by Jung' (Abraham and Freud, 1965, p. 157). Jung has fallen to the level of a shady character who had 'taken in' the innocent Freud.

The Committee also filled another gap left by Jung; its members praised Freud's work. They were unanimous in their approval of 'Totem and Taboo' and in his response to their praise Freud was explicit in what he treasured in his followers: 'The way in which all of you try to show me the value of the work by supplementing and drawing conclusions from it is of course quite marvelous' (p. 142). Freud did not want an egalitarian give and

take of ideas; he wanted disciples. Jung was never comfortable
in this role, but Abraham was ideal.

By the summer of 1914 Freud had managed to completely alter
his valuation of Jung. The man he once declared his heir became
'the brutal sanctimonious Jung' and Freud was glad to be rid
of him. A decade after the break Freud was certain that Jung
had 'used his first independent experiences to shake himself
free of analysis' and that Jung had 'strong neurotic and selfish
motives' which distorted his discoveries (p. 352). As he did with
Adler, so Freud did with Jung, he found a neurosis at the base
of Jung's revisions of psychoanalytic theory.

During the break Jung accused Freud of 'sniffing out' the
problems of his followers while he remained on top as the father.
Freud did abuse psychoanalytic theory by using it to condemn
the work of others as neurotically motivated and thereby insulate
himself and his work from criticism. This does not deny that
Jung's discoveries had their origins in his character and even
that they were grounded in neurotic difficulties. It argues that
this is no more a reason for dismissing Jung's work than it is
for rejecting psychoanalysis because of its clear linkages with
Freud's self-analysis and his neurotic difficulties.

CONFLICTS OVER THEORY

The meaning of myth and religion plus the libido question –
issues which had long been sources of irritation between Freud
and Jung – were the center of their theoretical conflicts both
during and after the break. How one defines libido and what is
to be seen as the essence of religion are not questions that can
be answered by natural or social science. They are answered by
interpretation and the answers given by Freud and Jung were
founded upon fundamentally different assumptions arising from
dissimilar world-views. Is the libido specifically sexual or is it
psychic energy in general? No experiment will answer this, but
the answer itself will shape empirical observation. Is religion an
illusion, a mass neurosis seeking to expiate Oedipal guilt by
glorifying the father or is it an attempt through symbolic transformation to free one from regressive longing for the parents?
Freud's and Jung's answers were arrived at by interpretation
and an evaluation of their answers is not a task for which one
could design a series of crucial experiments. It is in hermeneutic
criteria that we will find the techniques of evaluation by which
to judge their works on religion.

The question of the etiological significance of sexuality in the
causation of dementia praecox was the issue around which Freud
and Jung's disagreements over the libido theory focused. In his
analysis of the Schreber case Freud asked if a detachment of
libido from the world explained the paranoid dement's loss of
interest in other people or if the ego's non-sexual interest in
the world would be sufficient to maintain rapport with reality

(1911b, p. 74). He admitted that such questions were difficult
to answer, wished that psychoanalysis knew more about the
instincts, and reasserted the position he took in 'Three Essays'
that he accepted the popular differentiation between ego-
instincts, like hunger, which are aimed at self-preservation and
the libidinal sexual instincts whose ultimate aim is preservation
of the species.

In 'Wandlungen II' Jung seized on Freud's questions, saying,
'It affords me especial satisfaction that our teacher also, when
he laid his hand on the delicate material of paranoiac psychology,
was forced to doubt the applicability of the conception of libido
held by him at that time' (1916a, p. 144). Jung admits that he
had 'surreptitiously introduced' into 'Wandlungen I' a broader
conception of the libido using the term to mean psychic energy
in general. 'The explanation of this harmless deceit,' Jung says,
has been 'saved until' the publication of 'Wandlungen II' (p. 151).
Jung knew that his attempts to broaden and desexualize the
notion of libido would arouse Freud's wrath so he did not overtly
change the definition until he had to and until Freud's own
questioning of the relation between libido and interest in the
world had justified, at least in Jung's own eyes, the modifications
he was making.

Returning to the broad conception of psychic energy he used
in 'The Psychology of Dementia Praecox' Jung asserted that while
the neuroses could be explained by a withdrawal of sexual
interest from others, the psychoses which are characterized
by an almost total alienation from the world could not be. There
is a profound schism between the psychotic and reality which,
unlike the neurotic's difficulties, cannot be bridged by a transference relationship to the analyst. Jung asserts that the 'sexual
character of this [break with the world] must be disputed absolutely, for reality is not to be understood as a sexual function'
(p. 143).

Psychological relations to reality are founded upon a 'primal
libido,' an undifferentiated psychic energy, which is invested
in specific patterns of interaction with the world. In 'The Theory
of Psychoanalysis' Jung detailed the developmental unfolding
of psychic energy. He identified 'The Three Phases of Life'
(p. 117): (1) the presexual stage ending between the third and
fifth year is taken up almost exclusively with the functions of
nutrition and growth. There are 'signs of interest and activity
which may fairly be called sexual' during this period, but 'these
indications still have the infantile characteristics of harmlessness
and naïveté.' (2) The prepubertal stage from about five to
puberty in which the 'germination of sexuality takes place.'
(3) The adult period from puberty on where sexuality proper
comes into being. With this genetic sequence Jung expressed a
reservation that had existed from the beginning of his psychoanalytic work. He has disavowed infantile sexuality, postulating
instead a presexual predominantly nutritionally oriented infantile
phase. One can hear Freud's comment to Jung about Adler,

'Doesn't *presexual* mean *asexual*?' It does, and Jung was explicit
in his formulation that although one can, by analogy with adult
sexual activity, see a host of infantile behaviors as precursors
of later sexual functioning, doing so overextends the concept of
sexuality and distorts one's view of childhood.

It is true that neurotics recall infantile sexual experience, but
Jung argues that this is no proof of the existence of infantile
sexuality. It is proof that neurotics withdraw from adult sexual
activities and this detachment of libido accompanied by its psychic
introversion regressively reactivates parental imagos. These
redintegrated memories are retrospectively sexualized as the
neurotic recreates a history to explain current adult difficulties
which are primarily sexual. In making this argument Jung was
only extending the point about neurotics rewriting their histories
which Freud had previously made in the Rat Man case.

While the neurotic reactivates memories of parental relations,
the regression in dementia praecox patients is deeper. Their
libidinal interest introverts to such a degree that reality is lost
and in its place an elaborate internal fantasy world is constructed.
The inward libidinal flow reactivates archaic modes of mental
functioning, producing images analogous to those of mythological
systems. To speak of autoeroticism in neurotic regression is
correct, but Jung condemns Abraham's - and by extension Freud's
- view that in dementia praecox a sexual regression is taking
place. He agrees with Bleuler that the schizophrenic is more than
simply autoerotic. Such patients shun the world, 'building up
an intra-psychic equivalent for reality' (1916a, p. 152).

This and more, including a brief philosophical recapitulation
and etymology of the uses of the words energy, libido, will,
desire, and eros, then, was Jung's answer to the questions
Freud raised about the libido theory. Freud said he did not
understand or agree with Jung's revisions and wrote to Abraham
that he had asked the libido question purely rhetorically in order
to answer it in the negative. One should not ask questions if
one does not wish to open debate, but within a page of questioning the libido theory Freud indicated the answer, saying that
it was far more probable that the paranoid's or schizophrenic's
altered relation to the world 'is to be explained entirely or in the
main by the loss of his [sexual] libidinal interest' (1911b, p. 75).
Jung could not have been so foolish as to mistake a rhetorical
for an actual question or such a poor reader that he failed to
see the thrust of Freud's answer. He was driven by his observation of the striking similarities between myths and the fantasies
of schizophrenics to modify the libido theory and perhaps
dominated by a wish that Freud would now, confronted by the
problems of explaining psychosis, see things his way. He felt
he finally had the analytic experience necessary to challenge
Freud's formulations and, after all, he had maintained from the
beginning that when one had sufficient empirical evidence one
could question psychoanalysis.

Jung had treated far more psychotics than Freud and so had

more observational evidence about this class of diseases, but the definition of libido as sexual or psychic energy is not an empirical question. Observation is irrelevant to a decision in favor of one definition or the other. Although Freud, early in his work and at some points throughout his writing, tries to anchor the libido to sexual metabolism, libido for him is fundamentally an unmeasurable quantitative sexual factor in psychic functioning. Its existence is inferred not observed. Jung says, 'By libido I mean *psychic energy*. Psychic energy is the *intensity* of psychic process' (1921, p. 455). Psyches are not directly observable and certainly the energy metaphorically circulating through them is not measurable. Deciding whether libido is sexual or libido is psychic energy in general is a commitment to a definition which one will use to conceptualize the energic essence of psychological life. To be a psychoanalyst (and Freud in response to Jung's ideas said he had the right to decide what was and was not psychoanalysis), one had to commit oneself to Freud's definition. In proposing his own, Jung was establishing an alternative framework of definitions for the practice of analysis. Freud's response to Jung's revisions of libido theory will be taken up shortly in our consideration of his work on narcissism.

How one defines the basics of any system will of course have ramifications throughout that system. Are infants or are they not sexual creatures? Looked at psychoanalytically, they are; from the perspective of analytical psychology they are not. Were Schreber's fantasies fundamentally sexual? Freud said yes, Jung no. Is religion a manifestation of infantile sexual desire or a system of symbols aiding psychological maturation? The first was Freud's conclusion, the second Jung's. If one feels compelled to decide between these alternatives, and many still feel the compulsion although it may not be a necessity to choose sides, how does one evaluate the relative worth of Freud's and Jung's answers? By examining the texts in which they put forward their arguments and judging the merits of their interpretative efforts.

We will focus on two texts, 'Totem and Taboo' and 'Wandlungen,' to assess these men's analyses of myths and religion. Since the texts were written at the same time, one has a built-in control for access to anthropological, archaeological, and mythological material. Both men could have read and used the same books. It is significant that they did not. Their answers were shaped by this, by their methods of working, and by their theoretical presuppositions. Jung read widely for 'Wandlungen' and it is full of long quotes from myths, poets, and philosophers. Freud, as usual, ignored most outside sources and focused on a few contemporary anthropological accounts. Jung's work rambles, tries to create a mood, and mixes psychological theory with esoteric quotations from medieval philosophers; Freud focuses one's attention on a single hypothesis and shapes his evidence in support of it. Jung works by comparison, speaking tentatively about causes; Freud founds his essay on an analogy, but produces a causal analysis.

Freud's method of transporting observations made in the present to the past is carried a step further in 'Totem and Taboo.' We have seen him construct an ontogenetic history from the reminiscences of neurotics about their childhood. Now he will construct a phylogenetic history using as a starting point his study of twentieth-century neurotics. By interpreting the secondary sources he read, Freud found striking similarities between obsessional symptoms and primitive taboos. He set out, with only rhetorical reservations, to 'reconstruct the history of taboo...on the model of obsessional prohibitions' (1913a, p. 31). His first archaeological study then proceeds by the analogical method. As in obsessional sanctions, the basis of taboo is a prohibited action for the performance of which there is a strong impulse in the unconscious. The primitive is in a state of ambivalence over the taboo object just as the obsessive is towards prohibited actions. Both are simultaneously drawn towards and repulsed by certain objects and practices.

Reducing the multiplicity of anthropological evidence to its bare essentials, Freud found the 'most ancient and important taboo prohibitions are the two basic laws of totemism;' not to kill the totem animal and the avoidance of sexual intercourse with opposite sex members of one's totem clan (p. 31). Given these two prohibitions plus the observation that 'a savage's attitude towards his ruler is derived from a child's infantile attitude to his father,' Freud had the material necessary to explain the totemic origins of religion. He has got these basic facts through a good deal of interpretation and in establishing them has relied heavily on his psychoanalytic conception of childhood which as we know was constructed speculatively from his observations of adult neurotics. In that Freud compares primitives to neurotics, Freud's picture of primitive culture must be a portrait of primal neurotics, hordes of savages afflicted with a mass obsessional neurosis.

From his strongly focused interpretation of anthropological accounts and an obvious psychoanalytic substitution, Freud finds:

> If the totem animal is the father, then the two principal ordinances of totemism...coincide in their content with the two crimes of Oedipus...as well as with the two primal wishes of children, the insufficient repression or the re-awakening of which forms the nucleus of every psychoneurosis. (p. 132)

Freud has found in the primeval past what he found in himself in 1897, incestuous wishes towards the mother and ambivalence towards the father.

Trying to uncover the primal arrangements of human existence which would contain the germs of all future developments, Freud found a Victorian family structure – a powerful father with wife, daughters, and female servants under his control and sons struggling for independence and envying the father's power. In a magnificent synthesis of speculation built on his previous interpretations and on Darwin's scenario of the primal horde - 'a violent and jealous father who keeps all the females for himself and drives away his sons' (p. 141) - Freud constructs a 'just so' story about man in the beginning.

His narrative begins with the timeless fairytale words 'One day....' He tells of the sons' banding together. They kill, then devour the father; they rape their mother and sisters. Although their hatred caused them to kill the father, the sons also loved him. After the primal crime they felt guilty and to atone for their actions they deified the father and put into effect his sanctions against sexual intercourse within the family unit. Freud concludes that totemic religion arose from this filial sense of guilt and from the attempt to expiate bad conscience and appease the father by a delayed obedience to him. 'All later religions are seen to be attempts at solving the same problem,' Freud concludes, and 'all have the same end in view and are reactions to the same great event with which civilization began and which, since it occurred, has not allowed mankind a moment's rest' (p. 145). The brothers' primal crime which was constructed by Freud in an obviously mythic form, and the psychological state of mind of totemic primitives which was established by analogy with modern obsessional neurosis and which necessitated the story of the primal crime, has been transformed into a causal point of origin for all religion. Admitting he cannot explain female deities, Freud announces, 'God is nothing other than an exalted father' (p. 146). In supposing he had discovered the origin of religion, Freud thought he had explained it. For Freud, the most ancient, be it in an individual's past or a species' past, was always the most real. It is as if historical evolution did nothing to modify the human condition.

Jung said in 'Wandlungen' that 'an important...development of the human mind is due to the impulse towards the discovery of analogy' (1916a, p. 156). Freud, using analogy, created a psychological profile of the primitive mind by comparing primitives to neurotics. While himself condemning analogical thinking as immature and preaching the necessity of its replacement by logical causal analysis, he magically transformed his own analogical thought into a causal explanation. Refusing to admit that he too was engaged in the art of myth-making, of writing a psychoanalytic historical scenario about the origins of man, he did what good story-tellers do. He insisted that this was what happened and because it did things today are the way they are.

In finding the Oedipus complex at the birth of civilization, Freud engaged in the mythic art of creating in the past an event which for him and his followers was the essential structuring principle of human relations. The Oedipus complex is thereby glorified, universalized, and made fundamental. It was there in the beginning. Merleau-Ponty passes judgment on Freud for this act: 'When Freudianism has deteriorated to this degree it is no

longer an interpretation of the Oedipus myth but one of its
variants [;] it is neither true nor false but [itself] a myth'
(1960b, p. 122). Freud's myth was of classic dimensions.

The power of Freud's 'Totem and Taboo' is immense; its merits
are still being debated today (see Neu, 1974). It presents a
compellingly simple hypothesis in a style which establishes strong
causal linkages. Its appeal is that it is a masterpiece of scientific
fiction. It extols the virtues of science while denigrating as
infantile other modes of enquiry. What more could a godless culture want than evidence that religion is just a step above primitive animism, that God is nothing but a glorified father, and
that our modern scientific way of doing things is superior to all
other forms of enquiry?

'Totem and Taboo,' however, is not a scientific work. It is a
work of interpretation and evaluated by hermeneutic criteria it
is fatally flawed. A central tenet of hermeneutics is the assumption that human communications have an integrity and are
attempting to say something. As an interpreter, one must
seriously engage the text as someone who is trying to communicate
and needs assistance. One must make attempts to be aware of
one's own biases and identify how one's presuppositions might
be distorting one's interpretations. These are, as we will see in
chapter 11, also fundamental tenets of psychoanalytic therapy.
In 'Totem and Taboo' Freud violated all these principles. His
method betrays this. In this work he says he will 'submit the
recorded [anthropological] facts to analysis, as though they
formed a part of the symptoms presented by a neurosis'
(pp. 48-9). By analyzing taboos as if they were neurotic symptoms he will, of course, find that they are just like neurotic
symptoms. But, and here is the central fault of this work, he
does not analyze the mythic stories of primitive societies, but
western anthropologists' accounts of totemic cultures. Strictly
speaking, he is analyzing a few anthropologists' conceptions of
totemism and finding that their views of it are similar to his views
on neurosis. To say that Freud is analyzing primitive cultures
would be to equate what a parent says about a child with the
actual observation of the child. Of course, Freud made this error
in his analysis of Little Hans.

Freud's great distance from the people he was analyzing (not
once did he cite even a fragment from a primitive myth) means
that he really never confronted the communications which he is
purportedly interpreting. This is a hermeneutic crime of the
first magnitude and a gross violation of psychoanalytic principles.
The distance, of course, means that Freud's psychoanalytic
assumptions are not challenged by contact with what he is
attempting to understand. The actual texts are absent so no
dialectical exchange between the interpreter and the text takes
place. Freud finds what he set out to create: the Oedipus complex is at the core of human experience. After a month of reading in mythology Jung also found this, but a deeper immersion in
the material greatly altered his hasty initial conclusions.

The anthropologists' accounts, of course, are not taken at face value. Freud interprets these accounts, in the belief that he is thereby getting even closer to the mentality of primitives. Generalizing the distinction between latent and manifest dreams to textual analysis, he justifies his supposed interpretation of primitive taboos by saying behind any system of thought are at least two reasons - manifest and latent - which explain its content: 'a [manifest] reason based upon the premises of the system (a reason, then which may be delusional) and a concealed [latent] reason, which we must judge to be truly operative and the real one' (pp. 95-6). Nothing is what it seems; no text, except perhaps scientific ones, has the meaning it purports to carry. This single assumption justifies innumerable interpretative modifications of any document. The text is but a cipher to be deciphered by analysis. This principle of interpretation, if it is indeed universal, undercuts the very text that Freud has written.

Let us see what is latent in 'Totem and Taboo.' Freud says that magical acts mistake 'an ideal connection for a real one' (p. 79). That is, magic projects into nature a connection, usually based on analogy, which men wish to find and attempt to produce by ritual activities. Such connections are seen as real and causally efficacious but are actually ideal mental constructions. Through the ritual activity of psychoanalytic interpretation Freud commits verbal magic in 'Totem and Taboo.' He transforms a mental construction into a real event. Asserting that as children neurotics actually harbored evil impulses towards their parents, he says that the analogy between primitives and neurotics would be complete if 'primitive men actually *did* what all the evidence shows they intended to do' (p. 161). Taboo practices show that primitive men psychologically behave as if the primal crime took place: the crime is a psychic reality. But Freud was not satisfied with an 'ideal' solution, with the notion of the reality of mental events. He pushed farther, looking for an actual historical reality. In the last paragraph he creates this by making just one more assumption: primitives are uninhibited so for them thought passes directly into action. If there is evidence that they thought it then they must have done it. Freud concludes, 'I think that in the case before us it may safely be assumed that "in the beginning was the Deed"' (p. 161). The primal crime actually occurred. Freud has found as real something which he established as possible by analogy, interpretation, and speculation. He has transformed an ideal mental construction built by using the principles of his psychoanalytic system into a real event with causal historical significance for mankind; this fits his own definition of a magical act. What is latent in 'Totem and Taboo' is that Freud's method is mythic. He uses magical transformations to establish what he calls real events. He created the real by moving observations made in the present to the ontogenetic and phylogenetic past by comparing infants and primitives to modern neurotics. Freud's real past is a myth of

origins, a causal scenario created by analogy which like all myths
makes sense of the present.

Calling some of Jung's interpretations of myth a 'surface translation,' Freud implicitly condemns them (p. 150). Freud thought
the surface, manifest content was illusion and that in his 'Totem
and Taboo' he had penetrated beyond the façade to the real
meaning of myths. But the value of Jung's work is that it is a
'surface' reading. In taking myths seriously, in believing that
they were trying to communicate a meaning, in attempting to
understand them, and in extensively quoting them, Jung avoided
the hermeneutic crimes that Freud committed. Jung submerged
himself in mythic texts, while Freud read anthropological
accounts. It is Freud who did a superficial reading, not Jung.

In his reading of both ancient and modern myths, of poets,
philosophers and Miss Miller's fantasies, Jung found endless
symbolic transformations which analogize human psychic functioning. Gradually reducing this wealth of material by finding
thematic threads common to all of it, Jung argued that mythopoeic
symbol systems express in colorful, forceful, and emotionally
meaningful ways the transformative processes undergone by
human creative energy. Symbols give expression in a multiplicity
of forms to human psychic reality. Projected into the world
through myths, humans find reality mirroring their desires
because they know the world through the symbol systems which
they create in interaction with the environment. We find in the
outside world to be actual what in our inner world of imagination
is possible.

According to Jung there is a central primal story being told
again and again in the myths of the dying and resurrected god,
of death and rebirth, of the sun's eclipse in setting and resur-
gence in rising, and of winter decay and spring's return to life.
The story analogized in modern psychological language is of the
transformation of energy which is neither created nor destroyed,
but endlessly changing its form, shifting its shape in image after
image, seeking expressions for human desires.

Jung speculates that there is in all symbol systems an attempt
to express 'the pairs of opposites which are hidden in the will of
life; the will for life and for death' (1916a, p. 464). Libido is
bifurcated; it finds expression in both progressive and regressive forms. This dialectic in human desire is seen most simply
in our longing for growth and for what is new, and yet our fear
of change. Where Freud saw the Oedipus complex in the male's
relation to his parents, Jung saw the quintessential expression
of libidinal conflict. The child at about five is on the threshold
of the future; the wider world beckons, promising growth and
the fulfillment of dreams of growing up. However, all the child
has previously known - the world of the family and especially
the mother - pulls the libido backward. The mother's and maternal goddesses' powers of attraction symbolize this regressive
longing. The mother is an immense figure in the child's early
years and her gravitational pull is strong. In mythological

systems the realm of the mothers is a symbol for the draw of the primordial unconscious, for the desire to forsake progression and return to the womb of maternal symbiosis. Development, however, requires that the child sacrifice his or her tie to the mother and commit him or herself to the world.

All passages in human development - puberty, graduation, marriage, the 'crise de quarante,' retirement - require for their successful navigation a departure from old ways with a commitment to new directions. Mythologies provide symbolic scenarios to guide human interest out of the old channels and into new ones. Jung's explanation of taboos against incest illustrate this point. Neither the primitive nor the child carnally desires the mother. The 'incest barrier' forces libido away from its investment in the mother, the past, the unconscious, and infancy. The libido freed by this detachment is made available for expenditure in the world; 'mother libido' must be sacrificed in order to enter the world. Freed libido, however, does not invest itself immediately in reality, but in fantasies which regressively reactivate the maternal and progressively, through directed thought, create wished for future ideals. Thinking is a way station between the past and the future. Magical thought, myths, and even modern goal setting are ways of preparing for the future by wrapping oneself in the strengths of the past and thereby marshaling one's forces for a confrontation with stern reality.

Neurotics and schizophrenics out of fear fail to sacrifice old ties. They cling to the past and try to resurrect old patterns of adaptation. Met by a seemingly insurmountable problem in adult life - almost always concerned with sexuality - the neurotic shrinks from it. Energy instead of moving outward flows inward. Fantasies abound and libido regressively reactivates reminiscences. These memories become colored by current difficulties so that they are almost always sexualized in retrospect. For the neurotic, the Oedipus complex is symbolic. It expresses the regressive longing for the parents. In retrospectively sexualizing childhood memories, the adult expresses in fantasies of love for the mother and hate for the father the child's wish to stay forever at the maternal bosom and avoid the father's world outside the home.

While neurotics avoid sexuality by regressing in fantasy to childhood, schizophrenics in attempting to avoid all of reality regress even further. Their refusal to venture into the world frees libido from that commitment and this energy flows inward creating an internal psychic world in place of external reality. Regressing beyond ontogenetic memory traces the libido resurrects deeply buried archaic modes of mental functioning. The thought of schizophrenics is filled with symbols which are homologous with primitive mythologies because mythopoeic forms of thought are resurrected by the deep regression. The schizophrenic gets lost in the realm of the mothers and is overwhelmed by visions. Only with a sacrifice of the libido invested in overpowering fantasies can reality be regained. In myths the hero

must make a sacrifice, die and be reborn, to escape the dangerous realm of the mothers and come back with the fruits of his
trials - with the fantastic visions engendered by a sojourn in the
unconscious.

Jung spoke in his letters about being lost in the realm of the
mothers and about being overwhelmed by the mythological material
he was investigating. His research for 'Wandlungen' was a pre-
lude to his own heroic quest and visionary experiences. 'Totem
and Taboo' is flawed because Freud was so distanced from what
he was analyzing. 'Wandlungen' suffers because Jung was not
distanced enough from the texts he was reading. Being immersed
in myth, Jung immerses his reader in it also. The analysis of the
Miller fantasies which was Jung's thread through a labyrinthine
study of mythology is too often broken by long digressions on
tree, horse, snake, and moon symbols. Whereas Freud stays
firmly anchored in psychoanalysis, Jung's analysis drifts. The
interpreter and the reader become lost in the twists and turns
of that which is to be interpreted. Jung argues that myths are
representations of psychic reality and few references are made
to material reality, those cultural conditions surrounding various
mythic traditions. As Jung presents them, one gets the idea that
the Greeks did nothing but think mythopoeically. One begins to
wonder if anything is real, if all is not simply psychic reality.
The realm of the imagination is the whole world between the
covers of this book.

The analysis of symbols in 'Totem and Taboo' and 'Wandlungen'
captures the essential interpretative conflict between psychoanalysis and analytical psychology. The symbol for Freud has
at base a single significance. It stands for an event or events in
the past which, because they are unacceptable to consciousness,
must be disguised. The symbol is a sign pointing backwards to
the reality of infantile and primitive sexual desires. For Jung,
the symbol captures the dualities inherent in a psyche which is
part unconscious and part conscious. Symbols point backward to
infancy and primitive forms of thought and forward to yet-to-be-
realized future possibilities. They capture in an image the carnal
and the spiritual, the real and the ideal, the material and the
imaginary, and the base and the noble. Jung's analyses of symbols, however, usually fail to capture their carnal, base, and
material referents. His focus is on the spiritual. In 'Wandlungen'
we find out very little about Miss Miller's actual life because
Jung's interest is in her fantasies, not in her realities.

PSYCHOANALYTIC RESPONSES TO JUNG'S VIEWS

Jung's modifications of psychoanalytic theory in 'Wandlungen'
and 'The Theory of Psychoanalysis' met with immediate condemnation from Freud, Abraham, Ferenczi, and Jones. The Committee
came together in its opposition to Jung. Admitting that Jung's
knowledge of classical literature and myth was remarkable,

Ferenczi (1913) faulted 'Wandlungen' as unfocused because of Jung's ramblings and he criticized Jung's revisions of libido theory. Abraham (1914) and Jones found mystical and theological tendencies in Jung's work which they abhorred. Jones's (1916) on the whole reasonable criticism of Jung's work found that in abandoning a strict adherence to causality and determinism Jung had forsaken the canons of science. This meant that he and psychoanalysts had parted company for they no longer 'adhere to one universe of discourse' (p. 179). Jones has, assuming that psychoanalysis is a science, correctly identified the breach. Jung found a causal reductionist viewpoint inadequate for a description of psychic functioning; therefore he renounced a strictly scientific philosophy. We have been arguing that psychoanalysis is not a natural science because although it uses causal narrative explanation its causality was retrospective, like history's, and not predictive. There is between psychoanalysis and analytical psychology a conflict, but it is not between a scientific and an unscientific system. It is between two hermeneutic systems which are founded on fundamentally different world-views.

Jones also criticized Jung's view that there is an inheritance of ideas. In 'Wandlungen' Jung does speak about inheritance of ideas, a position he was soon to reject firmly. Freud, too, spoke of inherited ideas in 'Totem and Taboo,' and he never abandoned this notion.

As a therapeutic expression, Freud's 'The History of the Psycho-Analytic Movement' must have helped him to relieve his rage and disappointment over Jung's defection; as a work of history it is tendentious. Written during the break, it is a bitter attack on both Jung and Adler. The essay opens with Freud's proclaiming his right to declare what is and is not psychoanalysis. This he must be granted if he insists on it, but later in the essay he says the 'stress on arbitrary personal views in scientific matters is bad; it is clearly an attempt to dispute the right of psychoanalysis to be valued as a science' (1914d, p. 59). If psychoanalysis was a science and its founder lived by what he preached one would not expect him to proclaim the right of authority and would expect a sound critique of Jung's findings. Instead, Freud produces an essay filled with personal attacks on Jung and criticisms which demonstrate a serious misunderstanding of Jung's work.

Jung is introduced in Freud's biased history as a man who had to give up 'certain racial prejudices' to work with Freud, as an individual incapable of either tolerating or wielding authority, and as a person solely interested in advancing his own career (p. 43). The first charge is groundless, the second we have seen as a difficulty for which both men were responsible, and the third is exaggerated. As he had done before, Freud was making difficulties in interpersonal affairs solely the other person's fault.

Jung's theoretical modifications are dismissed as an expression of 'the historic right of youth to throw off the fetters in which

tyrannical age with its hidebound views seeks to bind it' (p. 58).
One must suppose that Freud here is referring to 'Wandlungen,'
but this summary is so distorted by a self-referential miscon-
struction of Jung's work that it bears little connection to the
thrust of Jung's thought. Freud saw 'Wandlungen' as nothing
but a symptom of Jung's revolt against his authority and so for
him this came to be the theme of the work.

Although he said that focusing on arbitrary personal views
denigrates analysis as a science, Freud felt the need to emphasize
that the 'theological prehistory of the Swiss' helps to explain
their theories (p. 61). His science was objective; however, the
views of his opponents were determined by their life histories.
It is hard to believe that someone whose self-analysis was supposed to have produced a 'benign and imperturbable' man could
be so blind and so angry that he would publish an essay which
contained such violent contradictions.

In one of his works on narcissism and in the Wolf Man case
Freud did make two rational attempts to respond to Jung's ideas.
Steele and Jacobsen (1978) have traced in detail the evolution
of the narcissism concept in Freud's work: the term was introduced in 1909 to explain the object choices of male homosexuals
(that is, they choose men like themselves), and ended up as a
description of the earliest, most primitive form of mental life.
The mid-point in Freud's use of the concept was an essay
inappropriately titled 'On Narcissism: An Introduction' (1914c).
It was written in part as a refutation of Jung's critique of the
libido theory and was an important link in Freud's chain of papers
which led to his identification of all interest in the world as
sexual. Freud's response to Jung's dictum that reality is not
constituted solely by sexual interest was to show that it was. In
'Wandlungen' Jung emphasized that Freud's 'Three Essays' differentiated between ego instincts and sexual instincts, and that
in the infantile anaclitic stage it was hunger which lead the
infant's sexuality to the mother's breast. Technically, then,
there is a presexual stage dominated by nutritional needs. In
his revisions Freud eradicated this possibility by subsuming
under sexuality all that he had previously viewed as self-
preservative functions. The role of the ego instincts was eliminated. Freud's portrait of the infant initially having strong
nutritional then sexual ties to the mother was modified as his
theorizing became more involuted. Narcissism became identified
with autoeroticism and primary process as Freud (1915) came to
see infants as self-enclosed sexual monads.

Let us see what evidence there is in 'On Narcissism...' to
confirm Freud's argument for the existence of infantile narcissism. If there is evidence, then Jung's claim that the libido is
neither originally nor solely sexual would have been refuted.
Narcissism, Freud says, was introduced into psychoanalysis in
order to explain homosexual object choice and its meaning has
been expanded to explain two characteristics of paranoia: megalomania and withdrawal of interest from people and things.

Freud reiterates that megalomania develops from the libido's being withdrawn from the world and directed towards the ego. In the scheme he proposes in this essay this is called secondary narcissism and it is observed in adults. Not surprisingly, in light of what we know about his method of theorizing, Freud hypothesizes an original event underlying - but clearly derived by speculation from - 'secondary' observable events; 'This leads us to look upon the narcissism which arises through the drawing in of object-cathexes as a secondary one, superimposed upon a primary narcissism that is obscured by a number of influences' (1914c, p. 75).

Freud admits that primary narcissism is 'obscured' from direct observation: 'The primary narcissism of children which we have assumed and which forms one of the postulates of our theories of the libido, is less easy to grasp by direct observation than to confirm by inference from elsewhere' (p. 90). Freud will confirm his postulate of primary narcissism by using observations which are examples of secondary narcissism. Observing adult homosexuals, he developed the notion of narcissism. Moving backwards from this, he postulated an original infantile primary narcissism which he will in turn confirm by inference from observations of adults. The infantile past was for Freud a speculative reconstruction unconfirmable by direct observation. Freud's best piece of evidence to prove the existence of primary narcissism in infants is found in another observation of adults: 'If we look at the attitude of affectionate parents towards their children, we have to recognize that it is a revival and reproduction of their own narcissism, which they have long abandoned' (pp. 90-1). Laplanche points out that the only observable situation here is 'the narcissistic object-choice or *relation* of parents to children' (1976, p. 78). That is, parents love their children because their children remind them of themselves, just as male homosexuals love men because men remind them of themselves. This is a good example of narcissism, or in Freud's new scheme an example of secondary narcissism, but not of primary narcissism. In primary narcissism libidinal cathexes are supposed to be entirely invested in the infant's developing ego. Freud feels he has proved the existence of this infantile non-object related state by inference from one of the most intense adult object relations in our culture! We cannot support him in his inference (see also Balint, 1937; Bowlby, 1969).

As with primary process, we have another example of Freud's confusing interpreted and original events. Freud has once again postulated an original infantile state (primary narcissism) by interpreting adult activities (megalomania) to be recreations of previous experiences. He has then used interpretation of observations of adults (their love for their children) to prove the existence of primary narcissism. What led him to his postulate could just as well have been proof; what was his proof could have been the observation creating the postulate.

Freud has provided observational evidence only for the

existence of secondary narcissism. Only if one accepts the psychoanalytic view that all adult behavior is a 'revival and reproduction' of early infantile activities will Freud's evidence be
plausible. In 'On Narcissism...' Freud attempted to refute Jung's
criticism that neurotics retrospectively sexualize their past
histories by following his usual method: moving from present
to past, Freud retrospectively created a picture of infancy by
inference from observations of adults. This is the very tactic
Jung was criticizing.

While theorizing about narcissism Freud, in 'Instincts and Their
Vicissitudes' (1915), did away with the role that the ego instincts
played in development when he eliminated anaclisis by postulating a primary autoerotic narcissistic stage in infancy. With this
change Freud's dualism between the self-preservative ego
instincts and the sexual instincts was effectively put to an end.
However, Freud waited five years to revise his instinct theory.
Why did it take him so long to realize that the old dualism no
longer held? There are remarks in a number of essays (1914c;
1915; 1916-7) to the effect that the old instinct theory might have
to be re-evaluated in the light of new theoretical developments.
Yet only when Freud believed he could offer a new instinctual
dualism between Eros and the death instincts would he discard
the earlier theory. His only possible systematic formulation of
instinct theory between 1914 and 1920 would have been a one-
instinct model with libido as a generalized energy encompassing
both the ego instincts and the sexual instincts. This would have
been an embarrassing capitulation to Jung whose modifications
of libido theory produced a notion of a generalized energy
manifest in both sexual and self-preservative drives. Developed
in part to refute Jung's claim that non-libidinal factors entered
into individual's relations with the world, narcissism created
the notion that the ego too is cathected with libido and this
dealt a fatal blow to any distinction between ego and sexual
instincts. Freud, rather than abandon the position that sexuality
is at the center of psychic functioning, amalgamated the ego
instincts with the sexual instincts in the notion of Eros - the life
instincts.

Freud's final instinctual duality was between the life instincts
whose aim is creating and maintaining ever greater unities, and
the death instincts which tend towards the destruction of unities,
the absolute equalization of tensions, and a return to a position
of rest. Eight years after Jung wrote about the two great pairs
of opposites, 'the will for life and for death,' Freud (1920) himself, while condemning Jung's instinctual monism, placed a
similar dichotomy at the center of psychoanalytic theory. Jung's
comment on this was that in rejecting 'Wandlungen' Freud had
particularly attacked the idea 'that the libido has a contradictory
character, wanting life as much as death....later he brought
the whole thing out as his own discovery' (Adler, 1973, p. 73).

We have seen that Freud's work on narcissism produced
speculation and involuted theorizing in response to Jung's

criticisms, but very little observational evidence. There was, however, a case study written in 1914 which was designed, in part, to provide objective, observational proof that would refute 'the twisted re-interpretations which C.G. Jung and Alfred Adler were endeavoring to give to the findings of psychoanalysis' (Freud, 1918, p. 7). The study was 'From the History of an Infantile Neurosis' (the Wolf Man case) and in it, for Freud, there was proof that infantile factors contributed to the formation of a neurosis because the illness analyzed was a childhood obsessional neurosis. In such a case all the conflicts of adult life and the possibility of retrospective fantasy distorting recollections are eliminated, leaving only infantile history as the etiologically significant factor. The Wolf Man case is seen by Jones (1955) as Freud's best; Strachey (1955) says it is the most important of all Freud's case histories; and A. Freud (1971) calls it a paradigmatic case for psychoanalysis. At stake in this text is Freud's method of explaining psychopathology; this is his evidence against Jung's assertions that adult neurotics retrospectively sexualize their childhood histories and sexuality is not a vital force in early childhood.

Although the case was written in an attempt to refute Jung and Adler and near the end of it Freud assures us that they have been bested, he warns that 'analyses such as this are not published in order to produce conviction in the minds of those whose attitude has hitherto been recusant and skeptical. The intention is only to bring forward some new facts for investigators who have already been convinced by their own clinical experiences' (1918, p. 13). The case then only refutes Jung's and Adler's views for people already convinced of the truth of psychoanalysis, but such people would have already rejected the defectors' unorthodox theories.

Why is Freud unsure about the refutational power of this case? Let us find out by examining the 'facts' which Freud brings forward in it and the rhetorical manipulations he uses in establishing these facts.

Freud admits that the case is characterized by 'a number of peculiarities' (p. 7). First of all, the patient is not a child but a young man who begins treatment at age twenty-three following a mental breakdown at seventeen. In the course of the therapy Freud uncovered a childhood obsessional neurosis, the onset of which was at about age four, and the termination between ages eight and ten. Freud is thus examining the neurosis approximately fifteen years after its disappearance. This method of investigating 'the History of an Infantile Neurosis' is clearly anything but direct, since he reaches the infantile material by a very circuitous route leading from the adult present to the infantile past. He cannot thus rule out the effect that post-pubertal experiences might have had in retrospectively shaping memories from childhood (Jacobsen and Steele, 1979).

Another reservation which Freud had about the case was that its explanation involved a seduction. In chapters 4 and 5 we

have seen that although he once believed that childhood seduction was the cause of later adult neurosis he came to view it as
a fantasy constructed after puberty and retrospectively projected
back into childhood. In the letters Jung reminded Freud of the
error of taking fantasies of seduction as realities and Jung
(1913b) had emphasized that childhood seduction was a prime
example of adult neurotics' sexualizing their pasts.

Interpreting two of Wolf Man's screen memories, Freud proposed that Wolf Man's English governess had, when he was about
three-and-a-half, threatened him with castration and thus had
been responsible for his falling ill. This was not confirmed by
Wolf Man, but several dreams followed this construction. Their
content was of aggressive actions towards his governess and his
sister Anna. The dreams' contents were treated by Freud as a
retrospective fantasy formed at puberty and projected back into
childhood. There was, however, a real event hidden within the
dreams. Wolf Man soon reversed the direction of the aggression;
it was his sister, Anna, who acted upon him; he was seduced
by her when he was three-and-a-quarter years old. One partial
and one fairly complete seduction scene were recalled by him.
As Freud so often did with his earlier cases of hysteria, he
accepted these seductions as real events. They had been the
impetus for the formation of the retrospective fantasies which
Wolf Man had developed after puberty in order to transform his
status as victim into that of aggressor. Concerned about convincing the reader of the reality of the seduction, Freud declares,
'But his seduction by his sister was certainly not a phantasy'
(p. 21). Freud assures us of the credibility of the seduction by
saying that Wolf Man recalled that when he was a young man an
older cousin had told him that he, the cousin, had had his penis
fondled by Anna when she was four or five. Just seven pages
earlier Freud had warned his readers about the unreliability of
information gained from relatives of a patient, and advised
against seeking it. It is unclear, then, what evidential value
there is to the testimony of a relative which Freud gets through
a recollection by the patient. Certainly it would have to be as
suspect as the actual words of the relative.

The assurance to the reader that the seduction scene was a
reality and was supported by other information is, then, one
technique which Freud uses to still doubts. In his construction
of another scene, the Grusha episode, his rhetorical techniques
are more subtle.

Wolf Man recalled a dream he had at age four of a number of
wolves sitting in a large tree. In an elaborate interpretation of
the dream, in which Freud displays his mastery of transforming
manifest thoughts into their latent content, he uncovers a scene
which occurred when the patient was one-and-a-half. Wolf Man
had observed his parents copulating 'a tergo.' This scene was
not initially traumatic. Its effects were deferred until age four
when, after his supposed seduction by Anna, the event's meaning was understood and expressed in the dream. The wolf phobia

which developed after the dream was a displacement of the Wolf Man's fear of castration by his father. To be passive as he had been when he was seduced by Anna was to be like his mother had been in coitus; like his mother, then, it also meant not having a penis. This dynamic of deferred action is familiar to us from Freud's seduction theory, but here that theory has been integrated with the work on infantile sexuality and moved back to the first four years of life.

Did the year-and-one-half child really observe his parents copulating, or was it a fantasy retrospectively constructed at age four or at puberty, or perhaps by Freud to make sense of the case?

The construction of the primal scene was necessitated by other interpretations in the case which created a causal web into which the scene was woven as a point of origin. About it, Freud says, 'it is indispensable to a comprehensive solution of all the conundrums that are set us by the symptoms of the infantile disorder' (p. 55). It is the lynchpin of the narrative, that puzzle piece which brings the whole case together. For Wolf Man too, the scene was vital, it 'had become transformed into the necessary condition for his recovery' (p. 101). Just because belief in it is necessary to the narrative or to the patient does not mean it really happened. In his discussion Freud seemed apprehensive about making the same mistake he had made once before in accepting fantasies as real events. A draft of the Wolf Man case was completed in 1914, but between 1914 and its publication in 1918 Freud became deeply concerned about the reality of the scenes he had constructed, notably the primal scene. Evidence for this can be found in two additions he made to the initial drafts of the case.

In his first addition Freud attempts to show how the primal scene could have been a retrospective fantasy built on a fusion of events from Wolf Man's childhood. However, he cautions us to temporarily postpone judgment on the reality of the primal scene until we have considered another additional piece of evidence.

The evidence is a scene with the nursery maid, Grusha, and in its construction Freud's skills at creating a convincing narrative are put to the test. Wolf Man recollects: 'a scene, incomplete, but, so far as it was preserved, definite. Grusha was kneeling on the floor, and beside her a pail and a short broom made of a bundle of twigs; he was also there, and she was teasing him or scolding him' (p. 91). Freud interpolates two pieces of evidence taken from other parts of the analysis between Wolf Man's recollection and Freud's construction. These were Wolf Man's compulsion as an adult for falling in love with servant girls, and his feeling of compassion when he heard the story of John Huss being burned at the stake. This information, coming just after Wolf Man's recollection, creates the impression that these were associations by Wolf Man to the scene. They were not. The juxtaposition is created by Freud. The interpolation also

separates Freud's construction of the scene from Wolf Man's
recollection making a comparison of the two less likely. From
Wolf Man's recollection, the two interpolated pieces of evidence,
and other material in the case Freud constructs the Grusha
scene: 'This material fitted together spontaneously and served
to fill in the gaps in the patient's memory of the scene with
Grusha. When he saw the girl scrubbing the floor he had micturated in the room and she had rejoined, no doubt jokingly,
with a threat of castration' (p. 92). The only mention of an
association by Wolf Man to this construction was between the
firewood used to execute Huss and Grusha's broom of twigs. It
is clear that the 'material fitted together spontaneously' for
Freud, but it is important to compare what Wolf Man recollected
and what Freud constructed. By interpretation Freud adds to
the recollection both urination and the threat of castration. The
'no doubt jokingly' is an inspired inclusion for it distracts one's
questioning from whether or not a threat of castration was
uttered to whether it was voiced seriously, or as a joke. Castration and micturation are inserted into the recollection, because
they articulate with Freud's other constructions in the case. The
threat of castration relates forward to the wolf dream at age four
and via that dream back to the primal scene. It is also connected
with Wolf Man's fears after the dream of castration by his father.
Micturation is added because of Freud's notion that people who
suffer from eneuresis often admire Huss and because urination
provides a link to the primal scene. Grusha when scrubbing the
floor was in a position similar to Wolf Man's mother when she was
copulating with his father. Wolf Man's urinating when he was
two-and-a-half was a recapitulation based on a child's understanding of the father's act which the infant had supposedly
observed a year earlier.

Freud, just four pages later, uses 'the fact that the boy
micturated' in Grusha's presence to go on to make further interpretative constructions. Is it a 'fact' that Wolf Man urinated in
the room with Grusha? Freud says about the scene: 'the action
of the two-and-a-half-year-old boy in the scene with Grusha is
the earliest effect of the primal scene which has come to our
knowledge' (p. 94); it is 'the first experience that he [Wolf Man]
could really remember' (p. 94); 'The Grusha scene emerged in
the patient's memory spontaneously and through no effort of
mine' (p. 95). What Wolf Man recollected spontaneously was
Grusha kneeling beside a pail and a broom, and teasing him.
This is the Grusha recollection, and it is certainly not directly
related to the primal scene. What is related to the primal scene
is Freud's construction of the Grusha scene which has added
both urination and castration to Wolf Man's recollection. The
fabrication of the Grusha scene was necessitated by the primal
scene and other events in the case. Freud equates his construction with Wolf Man's recollection. Later in the text, Freud notes,
'The gaps in it [Wolf Man's Grusha recollection] were filled up
by the analysis in a fashion which must be regarded as unexcep-

tionable, if any value at all is attached to the analytic method of work' (p. 112). At stake in this case, if it is to be seen as a refutation of Jung, is the value of the analytic method. Freud has done a fine job of analysis. He has constructed a psycho-analytic reality which fills in the amnesic holes in Wolf Man's recollections. However, one may attach great value to the analytic method without forfeiting one's ability to differentiate between a patient's recollection and the analyst's construction, or abrogating the distinction between a remembered event and a scene built around that event in order to provide coherence to an historical reconstruction of someone's life.

Our dissection of the Wolf Man case has extracted scenes from their context within a tightly constructed narrative, thereby highlighting the degree to which Freud molds his evidence in order to present a coherent, plausible case history. That Freud can construct a psychoanalytic biography is not in question. It is testimony to his brilliance that one must read with a keen eye to uncover the points at which his rhetorical skill masks difficulties and incongruities in the case material. Where such a careful dissection might be misguided in questioning a biographer, it is to the point in reading Freud. For in this case he proclaims he has refuted Jung and Adler: 'All the alleviations which the theories of Jung and Adler seek to afford us come to grief, alas upon such unimpeachable facts as these' (p. 102). The unim-peachable facts are: (1) the wolf dream at age four which brought on the childhood neurosis; (2) the fact that the dream was insti-gated by Wolf Man's grandfather's story of the tailor and the wolf; and (3) 'the interpretation of which [points 1 and 2] neces-sitates the assumption of...[the] primal scene' (p. 102). An interpretation is not a fact so number three is hardly unim-peachable. The other two are not facts, but are dependent upon the psychoanalytic method for their establishment and Freud's interpretative and narrative skills for their organization and meaning. The wolf dream underwent elaborate interpretation and to establish its etiological significance Freud had to rely both on the deferred trauma theory, which he had in part previously abandoned, and a multitude of other assumptions including an actual seduction. Although trivial, even the time at which the grandfather told the story was not established with factual cer-tainty. At the end of the case Freud says Wolf Man's dream was 'instigated' by the grandfather's story but in his original pre-sentation of the material Freud says Wolf Man 'could not remember whether it [the story] was before or after the dream, but its subject is a decisive argument in favor of the former' (p. 30). Even this small point is established by interpretation.

As a scientist defending his theories Freud needed facts to refute the 'twisted re-interpretations' of Jung, and as a writer Freud possessed the narrative skills to create very plausible fictions which he proclaimed provided such facts. Freud's search for the real event and his conviction that psychoanalysis led to the truth surely convinced him that what he constructed was historical reality. In chapter 10 we will return to Freud's search for real events in a discussion of his and Jung's views on reality and fantasy.

In conclusion let us listen to a former patient of Freud's, the Wolf Man, on the nature of the psychoanalytic method's construction of facts:

> When one tries to reconstruct a childhood neurosis after twenty or thirty or more years, one must depend on circumstantial evidence. From legal practice one knows how often circumstantial evidence can lead to false conclusions, since one is forced to deduce causes from results. But the same facts could lead back to various causes, or, respectively, arise from various circumstances, which people are all too prone to forget. (Gardiner, 1971, p. 344)

What holds for the law is also true of other hermeneutic disciplines: history, literary interpretation and psychoanalysis. Each tries to construct the best case possible from the information available and the information it can uncover through investigation and interpretation.

That Jung questioned Freud's method or reinterpreted psychoanalytic findings is not necessarily a twisted act of a crazy man, but simply evidence that he was capable of formulating another interpretative matrix which he felt better explained 'the facts.' It is unfortunate that both Freud and Jung were so intractable, each so convinced that the other was crazed, and so good at using interpretation to rouse the other's anger. If they could have remained in dialogue, or perhaps we should say, if they could ever have achieved a true dialogue, and continued to argue their cases we might have benefited greatly from such an exchange. A synthesis of Freud's dedication to the real with Jung's devotion to the reality of imagination might have enriched our understanding of depth psychology more than either work alone has done.

9 ARCHETYPAL VISIONS AND ANALYTICAL PSYCHOLOGY

Archetypal visions are wordless occurrences needing no substitutes; they do, however, demand to be 'individually shaped in and by each man's life and work' (Jung, 1943, p. 79). Jung's consciousness and vocation underwent a revolution after his break with Freud and this change created a new psychology through which Jung tried to find words for the unspoken, attempted to give form to the transcendental, and sought to reproduce that which is not replicable. His work and life became one when he found that only through the critical introspection of self-analysis could he write a psychology that was true to experience. He says, 'Philosophical criticism has helped me to see that every psychology – my own included – has the character of a subjective confession' (1929b, p. 336). In 1912 he took his first steps on a quest that was to occupy his whole life. His mission was to legitimate his own and others' spiritual experiences by ordering the transcendental within the framework of analytical psychology.

THE QUEST: VISIONS AND ANALYSIS

By Christmas 1912 Jung had finished 'Wandlungen und Symbole der Libido,' his American lectures criticizing psychoanalysis had been delivered, and the emotional and intellectual separation from Freud was nearly complete. Fantasies which were to alter his being irrevocably now began. What he had written about he now experienced. From 1913 to 1918 the mythologem of the hero's death and rebirth became part of Jung's life story.

Before the hero is reborn as a new spiritual being he must die. Dreams and visions of death nearly overwhelmed Jung as his 'Confrontation with the Unconscious' began. He dreamed of a messenger who communicated with the twelve dead, of corpses with life still in them, and of mummified knights who still moved as he walked among them. He tried to psychoanalyze these dreams, but says he got nowhere with this method. Not knowing what to do, he resolved to do whatever occurred to him. He began to play, building small villages from stone as he did in his youth. The play steadied him, but more importantly it allowed expression in a material form of his fantasies. Play and fantasy are the wellsprings of creativity and Jung found in his building games a way to articulate and reproduce urges which he could not yet understand.

The assault by his unconscious continued. In the autumn of

1913 an overpowering vision of a flood covering Europe and
rising towards Switzerland seized him. As the rubble of civilization and thousands of corpses floated past him the water turned
to blood.

Saying he was driven by fate and commanded by a higher
authority, Jung resolved to descend into the land of the dead,
immersing himself in the unconscious. He conceived of his
'voluntary confrontation with the unconscious as a scientific
experiment' which he was conducting on himself, but in retrospect he felt that one could say he was being experimented upon
by forces outside of his ego's control (1973b, p. 178). What
emerged from this experiment was a science which, like Freud's,
was based upon introspection and self-analysis, a science in
which a modicum of objectivity is gained only through an exhaustive exploration of one's own subjectivity. Jung fought to find
images to express the strong emotions he could barely control
and then struggled to find ways to make sense of these images.

His resolve to descend into the unconscious was actuated when
sitting at his desk he decided to let himself go. He felt that he
was plunging downward into dark depths. What he saw after
squeezing past a mummified dwarf, who stood before the cave he
entered, was a red glowing crystal. As he picked up the crystal
he saw the corpse of a youth with blond hair and a wound in
his head float by in a stream. The boy was followed by a black
scarab and a new sun rising out of the stream. Dazzled by the
sun, Jung attempted to put down the crystal, but from where it
had rested a river of blood rushed forth. With this vision Jung's
passive role in his fantasy came to an end. There are hints of
rebirth following death here - the scarab and the sun rising
after the corpse - but the vision ending in the nauseating sight
of blood indicates that Jung had not yet experienced the full
impact of spiritual death.

Just six days later and just a year after his dreams filled with
death and destruction began, Jung took an active part in his
dreams and thereby took his first step towards rebirth. He
dreamed he was in the mountains accompanied by a small brown-
skinned savage. They heard Siegfried's horn and knew they
would have to kill him. Siegfried, illuminated by the first rays
of dawn, appeared at the crest. He drove down the slope on a
chariot made from the bones of the dead, and as he turned the
corner Jung and the savage shot at him. Siegfried was struck
dead. Fearful of being captured and filled with remorse for
having killed someone so beautiful, Jung fled. A rainstorm began.
Jung knew this would wipe out all traces of the crime, but he
still felt unbearably guilty. He woke up. A voice within him said
he had to understand the dream at once because if he did not he
would be forced to shoot himself.

This dream was a climax to the first phase of Jung's psychic
adventures. As the alchemist begins the opus with the nigredo,
as Odysseus journeys to the land of the Dead, and as the shaman
in his initiation must undergo a ritual death, so Jung began his

odyssey by a confrontation with the dead. In myths the old must die before the new can be born. In the language of analytical psychology death means the destruction and dislodgement of ego-consciousness. Old ego desires must die before one's personality can be changed. This is accomplished by exposing consciousness to the unconscious - the land of the dead.

Jung saw the Siegfried dream as his act of self-sacrifice, his ritual death. With Siegfried's death Jung felt he himself had been shot and he awoke hearing the command that if he failed to understand the dream he would commit suicide. For Jung, the dream showed that 'the attitude embodied by Siegfried, the hero, no longer suited me. Therefore it had to be killed' (p. 180). His ego's desire to consciously control destiny and inflict its dreams on the world in the name of heroic idealism had to be abandoned 'for there are higher things than the ego's will, and to these one must bow' (p. 181). The ego had been displaced when Siegfried was killed and Jung found in the rain which washed away the marks of the confrontation a sign that the conflict between the conscious and the unconscious was beginning to be resolved.

Before pursuing this resolution we must ask one question: where is Freud in all this? In Jung's autobiography the chapter preceding his report of these fantasies is about Freud and the break, but in analyzing the dreams of death, his guilt, and his strong negative emotions the name of Freud is nowhere to be found. Jung's analysis draws parallels between his psychic state and the turmoil in Europe before the First World War and focuses on the mythological nature of his experiences. But what of the feelings of loss over separating from his teacher and the remorse over the death of their friendship? Could the dwarf who was standing before the cave, past whom Jung had to squeeze to see the sunrise, be Freud? Could Freud, who was five-feet-seven and swarthy be the dark-skinned primitive who Jung says took the initiative in killing Siegfried with whom Jung was identified? It was Freud who stood at the entrance to the dark abyss of the unconscious and helped to destroy Jung's idealism, opening his eyes to the unconscious 'shadow' side of humanity. It was Freud who was blocking, and trying to kill off with his demands for orthodoxy, Jung's explorations of hero myths. Could not all the corpses reflect in part the realization of death wishes against Freud, who from the beginning insisted that Jung harbored murderous fantasies against him? The above questions are asked neither coyly nor rhetorically, but because they are possibilities. No answers are given here because the information by which to make even tentative assertions is not available. Letters tracing the course of Jung's analysis - if any were written - have not been published. Those which might have been an aid, his letters to Antonia Wolff, were burned by him. Jung, in 'Memories, Dreams, Reflections,' has told us almost all we know about his internal struggles and he has either chosen to leave Freud out of the retrospective account of his psychic difficulties by design, or because in 1913 he failed to analyze the role Freud

had in his fantasies or because after fifty years whatever part
Freud played was no longer important to him.

Just as Freud's name was omitted from Jung's account of the
first phase of his quest, Antonia Wolff's is not present in the
second. Rebirth requires intercourse. In myths the hero encounters mysterious female figures; in alchemy the nigredo is followed by the mixing of masculine and feminine elements in the
coniunctio phase; and in Jung's exploration he began speaking
with anima figures, that is, the personifications of the unconscious feminine side of a man's personality. While Jung describes
the process of amplifying his fantasies by voicing, in a partially
dissociated state of consciousness, the sentiments of his unconscious, he nowhere mentions the role that Antonia Wolff must
have played in shaping his exteriorization of his feminine side.
After Wolff had been in treatment with Jung for three years,
they tried to separate, but it did not work. She was depressed,
and he was making life difficult for all those around him. He
finally turned to Wolff for help with his distress. Behind what
Jung tells in his autobiography about some of his anima figures
is Wolff and as we review what Jung says about these spiritual
females we will speculate on the role that his passion for Antonia
Wolff played in his analysis.

As the first phase of Jung's descent into the unconscious came
to a close, he found himself unsure of what he believed in and
uncertain about his psychological theories. In 1913 he resigned
his teaching post at the University because he felt he was incapable of professing anything. He was also cut off from his psychoanalytic colleagues and missed his exchanges with Freud. He
felt isolated. However, his close associates, Riklin, Maeder and
the women in his circle, especially Emma and Antonia, stood
beside him and encouraged him in his work.

To facilitate his self-exploration, Jung began to practice what
he would later elaborate as a therapeutic technique - active
imagination. This method attempts to give expression to unconscious ideas and emotions by allowing fantasy images to unfold
on their own. Jung would conjure up a steep slope which he
descended in imagination. He would then experience as fully as
possible the adventures and personalities he met along the way.
On one such journey, feeling he was in the land of the dead, he
saw an old man accompanied by a young blind girl. The man said
he was the prophet Elijah and gave a speech which Jung did not
understand, Elijah's companion was Salome.

This combination of a wise man and beautiful young woman
together is a common motif in both myths and mystic texts. The
male, in this case Elijah, usually represents the wisdom of the
ages; he is Logos incarnate. The female represents the erotic
element; she is Eros in the flesh.

Elijah was a substitute for Freud, who had been Jung's first
guide. Freud, like Elijah, was an older man, a Jew, and a prophet. Both were representatives of Logos - reason and the word.
However, there was more in Jung's relations with Freud. Jung

also had a deep affection for him and Freud's work stressed the importance of sexuality. Salome takes on Jung's libidinal interest as a representative of Eros.

In Jung's affectional life Freud was replaced by Antonia Wolff and Salome may be an anima image whose inspiration comes from Wolff. Salome was the fashionable daughter of a queen; Antonia was aristocratic and a fashionable dresser. In the Biblical story Salome was not blind, but in Jung's tale she is. Wolff was blind in a sense. She could not do active imagination; she was not adept at letting her fantasies unfold on their own (Hannah, 1976). She became a capable therapist and was a great aid to Jung and others in helping them achieve self-insight, but had difficulties in doing this for herself. For Jung she seems to have been a screen on to which he could project his fantasies, exteriorizing them into the world. He could then by way of actual perception and with Wolff's interpretative help disentangle the actual from the projected.

That Wolff was closely identified with projections from Jung's own unconscious is supported by a passage from a paper written during his analysis. The paper is a searching questioning of a man's right to follow his own path and not capitulate to the demands of society. Through his analysis he was following a course of inner spiritual development - individuation - and in his relations with Wolff he was defying conventional morality. He writes that if a man's love 'goes to a human being, and it is a true love, then it is the same as if the libido went direct to the unconscious, so very much is the other person a representative of the unconscious, though only if this other person is truly loved' (1970, [1916], p. 454). If Carl truly loved Antonia then she served as a transference figure for his unconscious fantasies and was essential to him, not only because of his sexual attraction to her but also because she was a complement to his own psychic being - a representative of his unconscious.

We have seen before Jung's propensity for forming strong attachments to women. His relations with Wolff culminated this emotional tendency in his life and his conceptualization of the anima expressed this trend in psychological terms. Anima figures exist because: males have strong attachments to their mothers and must repress feminine elements in their personalities; there is a biological complementarity between male and female; and throughout history men have found women to be both terrifying and terribly attractive. The archetype of the anima is a psychic predisposition in males to form similar images of women. It is an unconscious structuring element which directs men's erotic interests, creates projections of great fascination around women, and leads to enthrallment.

Wolff's presence helped Jung to exteriorize, and therefore see, the feminine aspects of his personality which he had heretofore not expressed. The other by her presence as therapist, friend, or guide provides a counterpole to the subject thereby engendering dialogue. The give and take of questioning, interpretation and analysis is essential for individual development. Such exchanges are supposedly possible even if another living person is not present. Because no references to Wolff are made in his autobiography Jung was forced to represent the process of coming to insight through dialogue as a work of self-discovery made possible by conversations with imaginary therapeutic guides.

Elijah was replaced by a more active spiritual leader, whom Jung named Philemon. Jung held long conversations with him and Philemon took the part of an outsider with an independent view of experience. He taught Jung psychic objectivity, that is, that the psyche is not merely the subjective province of the ego, but has within it forces which cannot be identified with the 'I.' Philemon was an emanation of these unconscious forces and a representative of the other within Jung's own psyche.

To encourage the development of his fantasies Jung wrote them down in 'The Red Book.' In Gothic script and a bombastic language he tried to capture the emotional and intellectual style which best characterized his unconscious. He also painted. In bright vibrant colors and highly symbolic motifs he expressed in visual images the contents of the unconscious, those affects, sentiments, and stirrings which he was trying to understand. Philemon was painted as a white-haired, bearded man in long robes. He had the wings of a kingfisher and was accompanied by a snake. Jung's use of symbolism in his paintings and writings in 'The Red Book' is not naive. His previous research had given him a wide exposure to traditional symbolic motifs. In his analysis he exploited this intellectual preparation by using it as a medium through which to express his inner agitation.

Jung's considerable gifts as a painter and his creative expression of his fantasies in writing led him to question himself about what he was doing: 'Whereupon a voice within...said, "It is art"' (1973b, p. 185).[1] He insisted it was not; the voice - a woman's - insisted that it was. Jung cultivated this 'woman within,' encouraging her to speak through him. She was another anima figure and in his exchanges with her Jung explored the question of whether his work were art or science. Part of him, represented by the anima, insisted that it was art and, therefore, that it could not be science. He agreed that his own analysis was certainly not science, but balked at seeing his products as artistic. To see them as the latter he felt would diminish his work's imperative moral quality and lead him to a further dissociation from reality by encouraging him to identify himself as a misunderstood artist.

The debate was an important one for Jung: was his work art or science? He was trained as a scientist and called his self-analysis a scientific experiment, but this analysis led to paintings and written works which were artistic in nature. His visionary experiments changed his life and work. To express what he saw he had to go beyond the methodological confines of science and locate his work within the broad boundaries of hermeneutics - the art or science of interpretation. His analysis was an

interpretative activity, an attempt to give form to the strong
but wordless forces of the unconscious. Such creative efforts
have traditionally been called art. The science lay in attempting,
again through interpretation, to order or classify the images he
produced.

In recounting this debate Jung speaks of the anima figure as
if she were a real person. Art actualizes the imaginary and Jung
feels analysis must do the same. S.W., Jung's cousin who was
a medium, had been called pathological by him a decade earlier
because in her trance state she brought the spirits of the dead
to life. Jung was now engaged in a similar activity, but with one
important difference. He sought to remain conscious of what he
was doing and explore the significance of the spirits as manifestations of his own being. Spirits are personifications of
unconscious contents. Such contents are autonomous; they
coalesce in complexes around certain themes and because of this
they are easily personified. They are the others within oneself
and to achieve greater self unity one must, through dialogue,
become familiar with them. Only by finding expression for unconscious urges and then confronting them does one strip them of
their power. The known is usually less frightening than the
unknown.

Jung was so involved in his dialogues with his internal others
that one must search for the presence of real people in his life
at this time. He stresses, however, that it was external commitments that provided an anchor for him in the stormy turbulence
of his own fantasies. Submerged in the depths, he kept his
orientation by thinking of his family and his commitments to his
patients. Nowhere in his extant published writings does Jung
acknowledge Antonia Wolff's role in helping him to maintain his
sanity in this difficult middle phase of his analysis. Emma Jung
did acknowledge this debt. She said of Wolff, 'I shall always
be grateful to Toni for doing for my husband what I or anyone
else could not have done for him at a most critical time' (van der
Post, 1975, p. 177).

For many years Jung spent frequent weekends with Wolff at
Bollingen, a medieval-type dwelling he built from stone. She went
to conferences with him and became a prominent administrator
of the small, yet growing, group of people practicing analytical
psychology. Emma Jung and Wolff, with great difficulty, reached
an understanding and so for many decades Jung achieved what
he had sought in 1914; he got to keep both Emma and Antonia.
When Wolff was in her late fifties there were occasions when Jung
purposely avoided her and times when he expressed the hope
that her visits would not last long. She died in 1952. Carl Jung
did not attend her funeral, but Emma did. Perhaps he withdrew
from Wolff late in life in an attempt to expiate his guilt over
having so strongly insisted in his late thirties that he could not
live without her.

Wolff's effect on Jung's autobiography even though she is not
mentioned, was probably greater than that of any other person.

To keep her name out Jung was forced to treat his story as a
record of his own internal psychic development. In comparison
to his inner numinous experiences Jung says, 'All other memories
of travels, people and my surroundings have paled' (1973b,
p. 5). However, Jung does describe his travels and his environs;
it is people, and particularly Antonia Wolff, who are not accounted
for. The paucity of other humans in this work may have been
motivated by the necessity not to mention this one particular
person. Concern for his family and Wolff's relatives was probably
the prime motive for the omission of her name, but also there was
Jung's concern for propagating his legend as a man dedicated
to the exploration of the spirit. A prolonged extramarital love
affair would have necessitated some explanation and perhaps
required a consideration of the physical, material side of human
experience. Given that the stated purpose of his autobiography
was to tell a story of inner experience rather than interpersonal
relationships, Jung may have been technically honest with his
readers in omitting any references to Wolff, but one wonders if
he was honest with himself.

The third and last phase of Jung's analysis had its beginnings
in 1916 when he wrote 'Seven Sermons to the Dead' and painted
his first mandalas. Mandalas, usually balanced circular designs,
are symbols of the whole psyche. In the gradual evolution of his
mandalas over the course of the next three years Jung found
that he was achieving inner stability. This third phase of his
analysis, like the third and last stage in the alchemical opus - the
unus mundus, lasted a lifetime. It is the never-ending quest for
oneness and wholeness; the search for the unification of soul
and body, spirit and matter. The mandala is a symbol of the self,
the center of the personality. It is to the self that individuation
leads. Although seldom achieved, the self is that point where
the unity and balance of the conscious and unconscious is attained; it is the god within. Jung's life and work became dedicated
to mapping the symbols which across cultures and through time
have directed individuals on the spiritual road to selfhood. His
work became an extension of his analysis; his analysis an
ancillary to his work. After a near-fatal heart attack in 1944,
facing his own death, he experienced visions of magnificent proportion. With Emma's death in 1955 his visions and dreams were
again renewed, assuring him that his life's researches into the
mysteries of the spirit had had an objective basis. That base
lies in the union of the spiritual and the material, a coniunctio
achieved when both fantasy and reality shape the course of an
individual's life.

Looking back on his analysis, Jung says, 'All my works, all
my creative activity, has come from those initial fantasies and
dreams which began in 1912....Everything that I have accomplished in later life was already contained in them, although at
first only in the form of emotions and images' (p. 192). His
archetypal visions were the prima materia for a lifetime's work
of interpretation. It was by endless rerepresentation, exploration,

and collation of such symbols that he shaped them into a roughly
hewn system known as analytical psychology.

THE THEORY

Mystic in style and content, 'Seven Sermons to the Dead' was a
forerunner of analytical psychological theory. We noted that in
'Wandlungen' Jung made reference to gnostic writings. After
finishing 'Wandlungen,' and during the course of his own self-
analysis, he read extensively in gnostic texts searching for
further ancient symbolic parallels to modern fantasies. In
gnosticism Jung found works which were highly symbolic, which
stressed man's search for redemption through intuitively gained
knowledge, which deviated significantly from Christian doctrine,
and which had a dualistic structure stressing the interplay of
opposing forces. The gnostics confirmed for him that other people
had ordered the world within a symbolic frame which was analogous to the one he was developing. The parallels between ancient
gnostic writings, the works of Goethe and other poets, noble
literature, and the fantasies of his patients were numerous.
    Not only did Jung interpret gnostic texts, but these writers
helped Jung to articulate his own experiences. Interpretation,
if it is to be a hermeneutic endeavor, must be reciprocal. Ideally,
the text transforms the reader as much as the reader, through
interpretation, reshapes the text. In his 'Septem Sermones ad
Mortuos' Jung completely enveloped himself in the gnostic style.
    'Seven Sermons' marked the end of the second phase of his
analysis and put an end to a strange episode during which Jung
and his family seemed to be haunted. An ominous atmosphere
hung around Jung, as if 'the air was filled with ghostly entities'
(1973b, p. 190). His daughter Agatha saw a white figure passing
through the room and her sister had had her blanket snatched
away during the night. Jung's son had an anxiety dream in
which a fisherman and an angel were struggling with the devil.
The next day, Sunday, the doorbell rang frantically. No one was
at the door, but Jung, who was sitting near it, saw the doorbell
moving. His family stared at one another. The atmosphere was
thick. 'The whole house was filled as if there were a crowd
present, crammed full of spirits.' Jung 'was all a-quiver with the
question: "For God's sake, what in the world is this?" Then they
cried out in chorus, "We have come back from Jerusalem where
we found not what we sought"' (1973b, pp. 190-1). This is the
opening of 'Seven Sermons,' which Jung immediately began to
write. As soon as he picked up his pen 'the whole ghostly as-
semblage evaporated....The haunting was over' (p. 191).
    Using the name of a second-century gnostic, Basilides, Jung's
message to the dead was that the world of human existence is
constituted by 'PAIRS OF OPPOSITES,' which are qualities such
as living and dead, light and darkness, force and matter, good
and evil (1916c, p. 381). Within the Pleroma - a term borrowed

from the gnostics - all the opposites exist in an undifferentiated
state. The Pleroma is nothingness or fullness, good and evil,
and although all qualities are within it and it pervades everything, it itself has no qualities. For their existence to be apprehended, qualities require differentiation and it is Creatura, born
out of the Pleroma, who does this; 'man discriminateth because
his nature is distinctiveness. Wherefore also he distinguisheth
qualities of the Pleroma which are not. He distinguisheth them
out of his own nature.' The essence of man, of human consciousness, is a striving towards differentiation and away from same-
ness; this is called the 'PRINCIPIUM INDIVIDUATIONIS' (p. 380).
The essay continues in this archaic style, which Jung says was
the language of his spiritual guide Philemon, to speak of the one
god Abraxas who is effect, the effective itself.

The Pleroma would be integrated later into analytical psychology under the notion of the psychoid, a term used to describe
processes beyond human consciousness and therefore outside of
space and time. In this state, the opposites differentiated by
consciousness exist in an undifferentiated form (1954d). This is
the realm of the psycho-physical, the spiritual-material, and the
all inclusive region of the undifferentiated unconscious. Abraxas
- another term borrowed from the gnostics - as personification
of the force of the Pleroma (the psychoid, the unconscious) is
equivalent to Jung's conception of psychic energy which 'is
something that has an effect' (1914a, p. 190). Jung finds consciousness is that which characterizes humans and differentiates
them from the unconsciousness of the Pleroma. The goal of being
is to become increasingly conscious of the qualities which as
humans we 'distinguisheth' out of our own nature.

In 'Seven Sermons' Jung uses the diacritical distinctions of
language to establish a dualistic system founded upon the recognition that human consciousness is a faculty of discrimination.
Basilides - Jung says, 'Everything that discrimination taketh out
of the pleroma is a pair of opposites. To God, therefore, always
belongeth the devil.' They 'stand one against the other as effective opposites. We need no proof of their existence. It is enough
that we must always be speaking of them' (1916c, p. 382). That
is, in the language of analytical psychology, they are psychic
realities, enduring concerns of humanity through which we give
expression to ourselves. Some other opposites on which Jung
expostulates are spirituality and sexuality, masculinity and
femininity, singleness and communality. To understand clearly
what he says in 'Seven Sermons' would require translation into
other terms and the best translation to be found is analytical
psychology. Jung's later work is, for the most part, outlined in
'Seven Sermons' but without his later work the sermons would
be difficult to understand, except perhaps for a second-century
gnostic.

This twentieth-century gnostic text was privately published
by Jung, and he gave copies of it to his friends. He says it was
an initial attempt by him to respond to the dead whose voices

are those of the 'Unanswered, Unresolved, and Unredeemed'
(1973b, p. 191). One might add to these the Unconscious and
the Unnarrativized. Jung sought to give form to chaos by constructing a narrative which would order his emotional life and
put an end to the doubts which were haunting him.

'Seven Sermons' is to analytical psychology what 'The Project'
is to psychoanalysis. Both were written at a time of emotional
strain for their authors, both were attempts to capture in a single essay what would become the psychological work of a lifetime;
and both were written in styles which were later abandoned by
their authors. Jung's choosing the ancient, religious style of
gnostic mystics to write about the unconscious, consciousness,
sexuality, and symbolism and Freud's using the language of
modern neurobiology to speak about some of the same topics
capture the difference between these two men perhaps better
than any other example could. The styles by which they communicated their theories and the theoretical positions they adopted retain the vestiges of these two 'primal' essays, which in
their exaggerations - Freud's phi, psi, and omega neurons;
Jung's Pleroma, Abraxas, and Creatura - illustrate vividly the
conflict between Freud's and Jung's modes of representation and
their ways of seeing and ordering the world.

The style of 'Seven Sermons' would not gain a writer a wide
audience in the modern world. In comparing the visions of psychiatric patients to philosophers, Jung saw the former as
embryonic, reaching expression only in a private or not widely
understood form. A philospher may begin with the same inspiration, but he transmutes it by 'translating it into a universally
valid language' (1916b, p. 272). 'The Structure of the Unconscious' written in the same year as 'Sermons' did just this for
Jung's work. Taking ideas expressed in mystical terms and combining them with his own self-insights and his clinical experiences Jung formulated in modern psychological terms a theory
of the mind. Although he did not manage successfully to communicate his thought to a vast throng, he did succeed in transmuting his vision by translating it into a language within the
boundaries of twentieth-century discourse.

'On Psychological Understanding' and 'The Structure of the
Unconscious' contain important statements about Jung's methodology. In the first he threw off the shackles of science, proclaiming that all investigations of psychological processes are grounded
in subjectivity and therefore should not be considered scientific.
Objective sciences stress causal explanation and reduce phenomena to their lowest common denominator. In that Freud's method
stresses causality and attempts to reduce the unknown to the
known, transforming the complicated into the simple, and seeks
to understand events retrospectively by their prior determinants,
his 'method of psychological explanation is strictly scientific'
(Jung, 1914a, p. 181). Jung's description is correct except that
these characteristics do not make psychoanalysis a science. They
do make it a causally based reductive historical method.

Jung continues his attack: although psychoanalytic explanation 'is undoubtedly scientific it misses the point. This is true of psychology in general' (p. 183). Retrospective causal analyses of a text can clearly show its psychological origins, but such analyses do not lead to an understanding of the 'living meaning' of such works. Resurrecting an old favorite, Jung asserts '*Faust* is understood only when it is apprehended as something that becomes alive and creative again and again in our own experience' (p. 183). He is calling for a vital engagement with the text, a commitment which is essential to any interpretative activity and fundamental in all hermeneutics.

To achieve this Jung advocates a constructive-synthetic method as a necessary complement to analytic-reductive practices. A Gothic cathedral can be partially understood by researching its history and the technology of its construction, but Jung asks what about its meaning. The vital questions are, 'What goal of redemption did the Gothic man seek in his work, and how have we to understand his work subjectively, in and through ourselves?' (p. 182).

The cathedral, 'Faust,' Schreber's memoirs, or the human psyche can all be understood retrospectively as things that are, but if they are granted a living existence, if one wishes to find meaning in them, then they must be seen as things having a future, phenomena directed towards an unknown goal, and entities in the process of becoming. The future, the teleology of life, necessarily must be grasped synthetically and constructively. The 'constructive standpoint asks how, out of the present psyche, a bridge can be built into the future?' (p. 183). The psyche with its past, present, and future is thus a narrative ever unfolding to a resolution which in the present is but a dream. For Jung, the dream, the vision, the goal which humans seek to realize in their buildings, works of art, religious rituals, books, myths, sciences, and fantasies was what needed to be understood.

An individual practicing the constructive method, Jung cautions, should make no claims to universal validity for the results of such speculation. The goal in interpreting a text or a patient's fantasies is to try to understand how the author or patient is trying to find self-expression or redemption through creative activities. The subjective world of the patient or another person can be analyzed objectively, but any such endeavor will be inadequate: 'The subjective can only be understood and judged subjectively, that is, constructively' through an empathetic process whereby the interpreter tries to find her or his way into another's meanings (p. 187).

This emphasis on subjectivity, Jung realizes, is an 'utter violation of reason' to the scientific mind, but he locates his method outside of science, carefully stating that he recognizes its subjective status. He now presents the method he has been using since 'Wandlungen' and will use for the rest of his work:

constructive understanding...*analyzes* but it does not
reduce. It breaks...[a] system down into *typical* components.
What is to be regarded as a 'type' at any given time is dependent on the scope of our experience and knowledge. Even the
most individual systems are not absolutely unique, but offer
striking and unmistakable analogies with other systems. From
the comparative analysis of many systems the typical formations can be discovered. If one can speak of reduction at all,
it is simply reduction to general types....This paralleling
with other typical formations serves...to widen the basis on
which the construction is to rest. (p. 187)

Jung in identifying typical symbols and then categorizing these
fantasy images into archetypal groupings used this method, and
in his work on psychological types he again followed the principles laid down in this quintessential statement of his methodology.

Finding parallels to any one fantasy system is important, for
in doing so one creates a cross-referenced matrix which will aid
exchanges between interpreters. The interpreter's task is to
facilitate communication through interpretation, thereby creating
a shared basis of understanding. Such communication can be
objective if the interpreter, with minimum bias, reports the
material that has been found and details the method used in constructing parallels. But, a person practicing the constructive
method must realize that it 'does not produce anything that could
be called a scientific theory. It traces, rather, the psychological
path of development' in a given text or individual. The method
is older than science, going back far beyond the Greeks. It is
a method which has been used for thousands of years by human
beings seeking to understand themselves. To claim that this
method 'resulted in a scientific theory...would be a relapse into
the darkest superstition' (p. 193). This is because it would be
to claim that an understanding of human psychic processes
reached subjectively was actually the resultant of objective forces in the world.

Jung has been accused by many of relapsing into superstition
with his studies of gnosticism, alchemy, and the occult. In these
areas he was attempting to find in each system parallels with the
others, with the fantasies of his patients, with literature, and
with his own visions. He felt that only by demonstrating that
the types he found in one place were also to be found in many
others could he begin to demonstrate the validity of his theories
on an objective basis. If ones does not accept his evidence, or
by fiat rules out that anything can be learned about the psyche
from the 'I Ching' or fairy tales, then Jung's work will indeed
be - as it was for one of his more obtuse critics - 'a mishmash of
Oriental philosophy with bowdlerized psychobiology' (Glover,
1950, p. 134).

We spent almost all of chapter 5 uncovering the latent hermeneutic method which was embedded in Freud's façade of science,
but Jung saves us a good deal of effort. In 'The Structure of

the Unconscious' he expands on what he has said in 'On Psychological Understanding' and in one page he clearly articulates the
method he was to follow for the next half-century. Talking about
fantasy, Jung says taking it literally is worthless and interpreting it semiotically as a sign or substitute for latent realities, as
Freud does, is interesting only from the scientific point of view.
However, if fantasy 'is understood *hermeneutically*, as an authentic symbol, it acts as a signpost, providing the clues we need in
order to carry on our lives in harmony with ourselves' (1916b,
p. 291). Arguing that symbols are not disguises or codes for
basic drives and that to interpret them by Freudian methods
reduces their value, Jung says that the symbol's meaning
'resides in the fact that it is an attempt to elucidate, by a more
or less apt analogy, something that is still unknown or still in
the process of formation.' To attribute 'hermeneutic significance'
to the symbol is to recognize 'its value and meaning' (p. 291).
Jung now outlines his hermeneutic method:

> The essence of hermeneutics, an art widely practiced in for-
> mer times, consists in adding further analogies to the one
> already supplied by the symbol: in the first place subjective
> analogies produced...by the patient, then objective analogies
> provided by the analyst out of his general knowledge. (p. 291)

The patient through active imagination, associations, or paintings
produces images, fantasies, ideas and emotions which like those
of the symbol are an expression of a mixture of unconscious and
conscious activities. This is subjective amplification. Objective
amplification can be done by the patient - after all Jung did it
for himself - but the therapist with his or her wide reading in
mythology, study of symbolism, and analytic experience is initially responsible for this work.
      Notice Jung's introduction of 'objectivity' into his constructive
method. Just two years before he had balked at this word, but
he had said that when his work had established a wide range of
parallels among fantasy products then a science would be possible. Two years is hardly enough time to do this, but if he and
others could demonstrate that myths, literary works, etc., all
contain similar elements in structurally consistent patterns then
he could call such patternings objective. This work took Jung
fifty years and has consumed the interest of many other researchers.
      The hermeneutic amplification 'widens and enriches the initial
symbol, and the final outcome is an infinitely complex and varie-
gated picture the elements of which can be reduced to their
respective *tertia comparationis*.' This analysis of typical motifs
brings into relief certain 'lines of psychological development...
that are at once individual and collective' (p. 291). Jung, in
discussing these developmental patterns, argues for the subjective validity of such psychological motifs. He says correctly that
there 'is no science on earth by which these lines could be

proved "right": on the contrary, rationalism could very easily prove them wrong. Their validity is proved by their intense value for life.' Here he has again renounced scientific criteria in favor of subjective valuation. In treatment what matters is 'that human beings should get a hold on their lives, not that the principles by which they live should be proved rationally to be "right"' (p. 291). In that both experience and symbols are in part irrational, that is, they are determined by unconscious forces, they cannot be subsumed under rational systems like science.

Jung continues his renunciation of a science of individual treatment, saying the construction of 'life-lines' reveals the ever-changing direction of psychic interest; the 'life-line constructed by the hermeneutic method is...temporary, for life does not follow straight lines whose course can be predicted far in advance. "All truth is crooked," says Nietzsche' (p. 294). Jung has ruled out the possibility of causal prediction in individual cases and has, therefore, moved outside of a scientific framework for conceptualizing his therapeutic work.

Freud argued to the end that psychoanalysis and its therapy were scientific; Jung, in building his own psychology, disavowed the possibility of scientifically based therapeutics. Therapy, he asserts, must first deal with the individual as a unique entity and must be directed initially to helping that person find his or her life path. Science, Jung argues, must waive its claims in regard to individual psychology because to 'speak of a science of individual psychology is already a contradiction in terms.' Jung, however, has not rejected the possibility of a psychological science: 'It is only the collective element in the psychology of the individual that constitutes an object for science; for the individual is by definition something unique that cannot be compared with anything else' (p. 289). Jung is somewhat confusing here and such passages understandably give many of his readers difficulties. One can, of course, compare individuals; we do it all the time and hermeneutics as well as science is built upon an analysis of the typical as it is manifest in the individual case. What Jung is trying to say is that each individual in his or her life uniquely combines universal traits, behaviors, emotions, and modes of thought. How the person has done this in the past can be demonstrated; just how he or she will do this in the future cannot be predicted with certainty. However, Jung wishes to maintain, as he did when stating the tenets of hermeneutics, that there are typical symbols and patterns of fantasy which can be established by interpretation. A hermeneutic science can systematically and with some degree of objectivity identify these patterns. Jung's science was dedicated to a search for these schemata which he used as an aid in helping individuals understand the course of their psychic development.

Although an outline of Jung's hermeneutic science is present in 'On the Structure of the Unconscious,' we will not review the essay in detail. Instead, we will use it as a starting point from

which to develop an understanding of analytical psychology.
Jung's theory is much easier to summarize than Freud's because,
unlike Freud, Jung never systematically altered the basic outline which he introduced in this essay. He modified, elaborated,
honed, and expanded points. In presenting his work we will try
to capture the essence of what he said about: character types,
fantasy and symbols, the structure of the psyche and the process of individuation, psychopathology, and Freud.

Although Jung speaks about extraversion and introversion in
'The Structure of the Unconscious,' his thought on these was
still in transition. His definitive statement on them was in
'Psychological Types' (1921), Jung's first major work after the
break and his own analysis. 'Types' is a study of character differences in the history of thought. Using the comparative method,
Jung identifies two typical attitudes towards human experience –
the extraverted and the introverted – which he used to classify
the opposing positions in several major philosophical disputes.

Using the dualistic distinction between object and subject,
external and internal, Jung says that from the observation of
his patients, he has identified two primary modes of psychological orientation. The extraverted type is oriented towards
the object, that is, the extravert's interests are external; 'the
object works like a magnet upon the subject,' determining
activities and alienating these people from considerations of their
own motives (p. 4). The introverted type is primarily oriented
towards the subject, interest is directed inward. Introverts
draw the world into themselves, trying to resist external influences to the point of alienating themselves from reality. External
controls and situational factors dominate the extravert; internal
controls and experiences dominate the introvert. It is important
to realize that every human being possesses both mechanisms
and uses them both in the varied experiences and occupations
of life. Psychic energy flows outward as the person is involved
in the world and inward as interest returns to the self.

In intellectual controversies these two opposites solidify into
antithetical world-views. Jung traces type differences in gnostic
and early Christian theological disputes, in classical and medieval
thought, and in the dispute over communion between Luther and
Zwingli.

Jung then discusses works by Schiller, Spitteler, and Nietzsche,
showing how typological differentiations in their works can be
assimilated to his system. An analysis of Friedrich Schiller's
'On the Aesthetic Education of Man' established strong parallels
between Jung's typology and the eighteenth-century German
poet's work. Schiller's text also allows us to consider the compensatory relation between introversion and extraversion. The
introvert abstracts from the world, but this long-standing inter-
nality is exaggerated by an explosion back into reality. Schiller
captures this extraverted movement which compensates the chronic introverted attitude in his discussion of two types of poets.
Speaking about the sentimental poet, Schiller says, 'he must

impart form to matter: he must externalize all within, and shape
everything without' (1795, p. 65). The naive poet, on the other
hand, expends himself in the world until an imploding reversal
takes place. This introverted movement compensating character-
ological extraversion leads to an internalization of everything
from without, thereby shaping all that is within.

Schiller recognized a remarkable 'psychological antagonism
among men' which, based on their natures, blocked any hope of
writing poetry with a universal appeal. The differentiation
between sentimental and naive poets was found in the antipathy
between the idealist and realist. The differentiation is at least
as old as recorded culture with the realist (extravert) focused
on observation and the evidence of the senses, the idealist
(introvert) on speculation and the coming into existence of the
absolute through acts of human will.

Nietzsche's differentiation, in 'The Birth of Tragedy,' between
the Apollonian and Dionysian provided Jung with another parallel for the distinction between introverted and extraverted types.
The antagonism in Greek culture between the Apollonian spirit
of contemplation, refinement, and repose; and the Dionysian
excesses of intoxication, lewdness, and ecstasy were bridged by
tragedy: 'An Apollonian embodiment of the Dionysiac insight
and power' (1872, pp. 56-7). The Dionysiac chorus again and
again discharges itself in Apollonian images. This dialogue, this
continual oscillation between passion and aesthetic contemplation,
is the vehicle of mediation between the two antithetical positions.
Nietzsche calls tragedy 'a metaphysical miracle of the Hellenic
"will."' Jung, translating into the terms of modern psychology,
says this creative synthesis found in tragedy is, metaphorically,
the consensus product of a dialogue between introverted and
extraverted tendencies. If the exchange between the two is
terminated by a belief that only subjectivity or objectivity provides the truth then dialogue breaks down and dogmatism sets
in. Each side, then, insists it has the truth.

Jung had observed the break between Freud and Adler and we
saw him characterizing their respective psychologies as extraverted and introverted. He returned to this analysis in 'Psychological Types.' But what of the differences between Freud and
Jung? Their dialogue also broke down and each man thought
his system was at odds with the other's.

In establishing parallels between his system and other contemporary philosophical and psychological typologies Jung found in
James's (1907) differentiation between the tender-minded and
the tough-minded another system congruent with his introvert-
extravert dichotomy. James's distinctions also apply fairly well
to Jung and Freud. From James's list of traits it is clear that
Jung - who went by 'principles,' was oriented towards the
intellect, was idealistic, optimistic, religious, and a free-willist
- was tender-minded. His own evaluation matches the one produced by the James typology for he called himself an introvert.
Jung categorized Freud as an extravert, and this is congruent

with Jamesian traits of the tough-minded type; Freud went by
'facts,' was oriented towards the sensations of the body, was
materialistic, pessimistic, irreligious, and fatalistic. Their psychological theories can also be differentiated on the extraverted,
tough-minded/introverted, tender-minded dimensions. Freud
stressed the instinct's drive towards the object, the formation
of character by copying significant others through identification
and internalization, the chaotic nature of the internal world of
the unconscious and the goal of development as adaptation to the
external world through the functioning of the reality principle
with the concomitant renunciation of fantasy. Natural science
was his ideal. Jung saw the unconscious as being highly structured, the archetypes providing an inherent formative patterning of the internal world. He warned against an uncritical accommodation of oneself to social reality. The goal of development
was to shape one's life by finding a middle path between the
external and the internal. It was through fantasy that such a
mediation was to be found. Fantasy is the transcendent function
uniting the opposites through symbolic activity. Jung rejected
science, finding his ideal in interpretation, which is itself
mediation.

Returning to 'The Structure of the Unconscious,' let us examine the mediators of psychic functioning: fantasies and symbols.
About fantasy, Jung says, 'It is in *creative fantasies* that we
find the unifying function we seek;' fantasy 'remains the creative
matrix of everything that has made progress possible for humanity;...[it] has its own irreducible value, for it is a psychic
function that has its roots in the conscious and the unconscious
alike' (p. 290). The union of conscious and unconscious contents
produces the transcendent function or symbol. This product is
an irrational conjoining of thesis and antithesis to form a media-
tory synthesis: the 'shuttling to and fro of arguments and affects
represents the transcendant function of opposites' (1958b [1916],
p. 90). The confrontation of two positions, like consciousness
and the unconscious, generates a tension-charged energic situation which 'creates a living, third thing...a living birth that
leads to a new level of being, a new situation' (p. 90). If the
existence of the unconscious or its creative function is denied or
if consciousness is obliterated by the unconscious then the com-
pensational dialogue between the opposites, which is necessary
for the creation of living symbols, is impossible.

The stance of the interpreter or of consciousness towards the
symbol is vital; 'the unconscious has a symbol-creating function
only when we are willing to recognize in it a symbolic element'
(Jung, 1918, p. 23). Christ can be a man who was crucified as
a troublemaker; or, seen symbolically, he is the god-man linking
heaven and earth while suspended on the tree of life in the throes
of spiritual rebirth. Dreams can be nonsensical, or elaborate
disguises for infantile wishes, or symbolic products of the unconscious; what they are depends on the presuppositions of an interpreter, for only through interpretation do they become what they

are supposed to be.

Jung rejects the view of dreams that he had held while working with Freud. He states that the dream is a product of the
unconscious and although its symbolism is often foreign and
arcane it contains no purposeful distortion. Dreams have a meaning and purpose in that they provide a compensatory viewpoint
to that of the ego. Consciousness must confront the dream,
recognizing that its view requires consideration.

Besides dream-interpretation, there is another and often better
way to enter into dialogue with the unconscious; this is active
imagination. While awake one allows spontaneous fantasies to
unfold. Such fantasies are often much easier to interpret than
dreams because of their more coherent narratives. In an essay
written in 1916, 'The Transcendent Function,' Jung describes
in detail the cultivation and analysis of spontaneous fantasies,
obviously trying to systematize the method which he used in his
own analysis. The starting point for such fantasies should be
any powerful affect, mood, emotion, or unarticulated feeling.
While concentrating one suspends conscious criticism and lets
the mind unfold a scenario. The method is not free association,
because its goal is the enrichment and clarification of a specific
affect. It is a form of interpretation with criticism left in abeyance by which the affect is amplified and made clearer to consciousness. The process is the initial step of the transcendent
function, of the collaboration of the conscious and the unconscious.

Painting, drawing, automatic writing - 'Often the hands know
how to solve a riddle with which the intellect has wrestled in
vain' - and hallucinations may all be used, depending on personal
predisposition, to bring unconscious moods and contents into
consciousness by giving them expression (1958b, p. 86). Once
one has the material, which has been allowed to develop on its
own, then one re-engages one's critical faculties in interpreting
it. There is a rhythm to working with such material. There
should be an alternation of creation and interpretation. Understanding is not achieved unless both are done. If one tries to
analyze too quickly, then one blocks the fantasies which produce
the material necessary for analysis. If one suspends all interpretation, then one achieves a creative product which may not
contribute to increased understanding.

The process of making the unconscious known is dialectical.
The unconscious must be encouraged to express itself, ego-
consciousness must take heed of what is being said, and from
this dialogue, which is filled with conflict, there will arise a
synthesis - a point of mediation, the transcendent function, the
symbol. This sets the stage for further interpretation, further
development of unconscious fantasies, ego-confrontation, and
another synthesis. The process of self-discovery is never-ending; it is a dialectical hermeneutic task which takes a lifetime.

The dialogue widens the boundaries of consciousness, reducing
the egocentric subjectivism produced by clinging to one point

of view and denying all others. The capacity 'for inner dialogue is a touchstone for outer objectivity' (p. 89). To achieve this one must take the unconscious seriously, but by no means literally. The symbol is not a sign standing for something real to which it must be reduced. The symbol is pure fantasy and one must experience it by placing oneself within its drama. Thereby the fantasy becomes more real and you create by criticism of it an effective counterbalance to its tendency to get out of hand. In that fantasy exists experientially, it is real and as a lived reality it is worthy of our critical attention.

The majority of Jung's published work was occupied with describing the symbolic contents of the psyche as they are manifest in human communications: myths, religious and mystical texts, fictions, poetry, and scientific speculation. Through this work he developed not only a hermeneutic history of human thought, but also a theory concerning the dynamics and structure of the human psyche.

Jung's psychic dynamics stress that psychic energy, libido, is the life force. It is pure energy without form, but is only experienced when it is expressed in forms. To give shape to this force has been a task which has occupied humans for millennia. Insisting that one form is *the* form that all energy takes and attempting to dam the flow of libido by channeling it into rigid dogmatic expressions have also been human occupations for thousands of years. Jung felt it was a necessity to free psychic energy from the bonds of personal and institutional dogmatism in order to experience its ever-shifting manifestations in a multitude of forms.

With the dualism characteristic of his thought, Jung says the unconscious is compensatory to consciousness 'because it adds to consciousness everything that has been excluded by the drying up of the springs of intuition and by the fixed pursuit of one goal' (1918, p. 19). It is the complement of consciousness because it contains everything that is needed in order to make a whole, everything required to describe completely the psychic situation. The complementary-compensatory dynamic relation between the conscious and unconscious exists because: (1) consciousness possesses an energy threshold and if psychic contents do not have the intensity necessary to cross this line they remain unconscious. (2) Consciousness, because it is intentional, exercises an inhibition on all incompatible material. As a result of this, such material sinks into the unconscious. (3) Consciousness is always in the present, it is a process of continuous momentary adaptation. The unconscious is timeless; it contains all the forgotten material of the individual's past and the inherited behavioral and perceptual predispositions which constitute the structure of the mind. (4) In the creative matrix of the unconscious are all the fantasies yet to be realized by consciousness. These imaginative products are forever changing, moving towards an energic form which achieves the threshold intensity necessary to enter the life of consciousness.

The unconscious is the forgotten, unknown and yet to be known. It is the internal horizon of our being, that boundary beyond which, at the moment, we cannot see. The area inhabited by consciousness is not set. One may establish its perimeter very narrowly, restricting its territory, or widen it by the exploration of unknown lands.

Point three above introduced the idea that unconscious structures patterning both perception and behavior are inherited. Jung (1919) introduced the term archetype as a complement to the notion of instinct. Instincts are species-typical behavioral predispositions; archetypes are species-typical perceptual predispositions. The schema of the instinct is the archetype; the actualization of an archetypal pattern is instinctual behavior. The archetype is to the mind, what instinct is to the body; archetypes are 'instincts' of the soul, instincts are 'archetypes' of the flesh.

Archetypes, Jung points out again and again, are not inherited ideas, but predispositions to the formation of typical ideas. The archetype is a structure inferred from the fact that across individuals, throughout history, and in diverse cultures remarkable similarities in fantasy products are evident.

The notion of archetypes is a very old one and Jung traces its history in several places (1919; 1954a). It is also an idea which evolved gradually in his own work. Complexes were inferred from the association test and Jung found similarities in complexes from patient to patient. From this grew the transitional idea of the imago which expressed the notion that one's childhood interactions, both imaginary and actual, sediment stereotyped ways of perceiving and interacting with other people in later life. Similar cultures produce similar imagos. The archetype is a universal complex, an imago produced by the continual repetition of certain typical experiences in human prehistory and history. Like complexes or instincts, the archetype is an inferred psychological structure. No one has ever seen an archetype. One must not confuse - as Jung in too many places does - the archetype with the archetypal image. What one sees of the complex is a pattern of responses on the word association test; what one sees of the instinct is its behavioral manifestation; and what one sees of the archetype is the archetypal image, that is, the symbol, the fantasy form, the sacred object, or the visual image which deeply moves one. The archetype is numinous; its manifestation in an image is a profound spiritual experience. It is as if one were under a spell, possessed, in the grip of a demon or in the presence of a god. Archetypal images evoke ecstasy, despair, joy, fright, elation and depression, but never indifference.

The archetypal image is never a pure manifestation of the archetype. The image is the product of an amalgamation of many diverse elements. It is always an individual product, but in its components it manifests typical features. The image is an alloy of the individual's manner of expression; the individual's proximal and distal emotional state; the person's life history; the

subculture, culture, and era in which the person lives; the
cultural heritage of the individual; and the inherited predisposition. The archetype is the predisposition; to infer its existence
from the image one must partial out all the other contributing
factors.

Jung felt he did this when he saw in the fantasies of his modern
European patients elements 'which did not correspond to any
events or experiences of personal life, but only to myths' (1918,
p. 9). He asked, 'Where do these mythological fantasies come
from?' and answered from the 'inherited brain-structure itself'
(pp. 9-10). Jung, engaging in biological speculation which leaves
physiological empiricism far behind, says that we 'receive along
with our body a highly differentiated brain which brings with it
its entire [evolutionary] history, and when it becomes creative
it creates a history - out of the history of mankind.' This is not
a recounting of actual historical events, but 'that age-old
natural history which has been transmitted in living form since
the remotest times, namely, the history of the brain-structure'
(p. 10).

This cerebral reductionism, which considerably outdistances
any of Freud's biologizing, is not a one-time materialist aberration in Jung's work, but is found in several places in his writing (1928; 1958c).

We have argued that the psyche has a narrative structure;
Jung asserts that the brain does also; 'This [brain] structure
tells its own story, which is the story of mankind: the unending
myth of death and rebirth, and of the multitudinous figures
who weave in and out of this mystery' (1918, p. 10). No anatomical or neurophysiological techniques were available in 1918
or are yet in sight by which to test this hypothesis. It is doubtful, even in the distant future, that someone will isolate a neuro-
chemical combination which is a physiological concomitant to the
myth of the hero.

Fortunately, for Jung, his argument does not rest on this
brain speculation. The psyche is connected with the brain for
him, but most of the time he deals with it as an experiential
given and not as an epiphenomenal emanation of biological processes. Although he says that the unconscious is 'buried in the
structure of the brain,' just five pages later he writes, 'The
unconscious is, first and foremost, the world of the past which
is activated by the one-sidedness of the conscious attitude'
(p. 10; p. 15). Since Jung's methodology stressed dialogue,
interpretation, and historical study, and he did no biological
experimentation, let us examine the psyche and its contents as
a structure which tells a story. The plot of this tale is the mythologem of the hero's journey towards individuation. The characters
are the archetypal images in which the archetypes of the collective unconscious are manifest. The story has been told throughout time and in every land; Jung was translating it into twentieth-
century psychological language.

The process of defining oneself, of reconciling the opposites

in one's nature, cannot take place until there is an internal
necessity to do so. This necessity arises out of the exigencies
of life created by the dualistic development of the psyche, usually at around age forty, which is co-incidentally the age at which
Jung began his self-analysis.

Jung (1931b) speaks about four stages of life: childhood,
youth, middle age, and old age. About childhood, which extends
from birth to puberty, Jung says that although a child's psychic
life is a problem to parents and educators, 'when normal the
child has no real problems of its own' (p. 392). This certainly
is a rejection of the psychoanalytic focus, but Jung was not
interested in child psychology. His interest was the problems
of adults. Although he recognized that some problems of maturity
could be traced back to childhood, he thought that such analysis
was a simple preparation for the harder task of establishing a
spiritual reorientation.

Out of the primordial state of being ruled by instincts and
archetypes of the inherited collective unconscious the child's
consciousness develops and slowly coalesces around a central
complex – the ego. The ego is the center of consciousness and
is all those things one calls 'I' and avows as 'me.' The development of the ego requires a disavowal of certain activities and
ideas and these, often seen as bad, become the nucleus of the
personal unconscious. The first duality of the psyche, ego/
personal unconscious, is the legacy of childhood.

The hormonal influences of puberty and the cultural expectations associated with maturation make the second stage of development more difficult. Problems do arise here even in normal
development. Difficulties of childhood are resurrected and retrospectively sexualized when individuals avoid the necessary
sacrifice of differentiating themselves from their parents. The
differentiation, which can extend from puberty to the end of
this stage between one's third and fourth decade, involves a
further solidification of the ego's identity. The goal is to be
someone, to make one's place in the world. Seeking the good,
the ego represses all that does not articulate with its vision of
itself. The gulf between it and the personal unconscious is
widened.

Youth is also a time of adaptation to society, an age in which
one tries on various social roles, rejecting some and forming part
of one's conscious identity out of others. Roles are like masks,
the individual has several and can change from one to another
at a moment's notice. The persona for Jung is an omnibus term
which signifies all the roles which a person uses to constitute
his or her social identity. The persona mediates between the ego
and society. The task of youth is extraverted: establishing social
ties outside the family, marriage, founding one's own family,
finding and advancing in a career.

Masculine and feminine roles become extremely salient at
puberty. Expanding upon biological differences, cultures elaborate vital diacritical definitions of what is male and what is

female; people are divided into two non-overlapping classes
primarily because of a difference in genital structure. The differences between the sex roles which are learned in childhood
become important at puberty. One must develop a persona and
ego identity which is non-ambiguous in this area. Males must
purge their mannerisms and thoughts of anything feminine;
females, to a lesser extent, must rid themselves of male traits.
What is excluded from the persona falls into the unconscious. A
second duality is formed, one which is more pronounced than
the first: the opposition of persona and soul image.

As the persona mediates externally between the ego and
present-day social reality, the soul image is in an intermediate
position between the personal unconscious and the archaic,
timeless internal world of the collective unconscious. The dichotomy between persona and soul image is illustrated by the language which people use in describing the necessities which
govern their actions. The individual enveloped in his persona
and in his social role commitments, will plead that he did something because of his family, business, social duties, etc. The
person with an internal orientation will talk of being driven by
the muse, inspiration, and necessity of the soul, etc. The second
despises the materialism, opportunism, and shallowness of the
first; the first condemns the second as a dreamer, a narcissist,
and as not being in touch with reality.

The sex-role stereotyping of the persona is complemented by
archetypal complementarity in the soul images of males and
females. Taking the traditions of his day and of ages of patri-
archy as natural and deducing from these what is masculine and
feminine, Jung saw the woman's inevitable place as being in the
home and the man's in the world. Women, in fulfilling their social
roles, are the helpmates of men; they are the man's inspiration;
they are fecund, erotic, connected to the earth, and dominated
by Eros. The internal complement to the cultural and 'biologically
determined' woman's role is the animus, the masculine soul image
of the female. Animus images are multiple figures complementing
the narrow focus of women's conscious interest. They appear
as intellectually opinionated pontificants, compensating a woman's
'essentially' feeling nature. They represent Logos.

The masculine social role requires agentic as opposed to communal actions. The man strives. With his focus narrowed on
worldly success he is dominated by his intellect and committed
to the building of society. He values reason over feeling, his
god is Logos. His soul image, the anima, complements the orientation of the persona. The anima image is an erotic figure usually
clothed in ancient costume. She inspires, seduces, and beguiles.
She is the quintessence of the feminine.

Compensating the exclusively externally focused development
of consciousness in childhood and youth, the unconscious has
also been developing. Silently the psychic split between conscious and unconscious - ego/personal unconscious, persona/
soul image - has been widening. Around the age of forty, as

middle age begins, a crisis develops for a few individuals. The
lustre of external achievements pales, life loses meaning. A
change of attitude is necessary. One needs to invert ones focus,
turning away from worldly success and concentrating on the
inner self. There is a necessity to give up the identity which
has been bestowed upon one by the societal collectivity and find
another person within. Socialization is adaptation to the world,
individuation is adaptation to inner reality and it is a more difficult task because there are few supports for such an activity.

What Jung says about individuation is closely paralleled by
events in his own life. At age thirty-five he was president of
the International Psychoanalytic Association, an internationally
known psychologist, he had a beautiful new house, several
children, and could look forward to the good life. But he had
lost touch with himself. In working on 'Wandlungen' he began to
explore the world of fantasy which he had been dealing with in
his psychoanalytic practice, but had not confronted in himself.
His confrontation with the unconscious was a turning inward,
a renunciation for several years of worldly advancement and an
exploration of things that he had forgotten or had never known.

In reviewing Jung's analysis we have already talked about a
particular case of individuation. Here we will review the scenario
of this developmental process which Jung saw as the issue to be
confronted in psychic life. Jung's model of the psyche is a
distillation of the central features of individuation. The antinomies of the psyche: (1) ego/personal unconscious, (2) persona/
soul image, and (3) societal collective conscious/archaic collective
unconscious are the very sets of opposites which individuation
progressively reconciles. Individuation is born of conflict within
oneself. The process of self-discovery is a process of finding
within all that one has denied, ignored and avoided.

'We walk through ourselves, meeting robbers, ghosts, giants,
old men, young men, wives, widows, brothers-in-love. But
always meeting ourselves' (Joyce, 1914, p. 213). The path of
individuation is a journey into oneself and any summary of Jung's
writing on this topic is like saying that 'Ulysses' is about a walk
through Dublin. Rich in metaphor and filled with images from
poetry, Christianity, eastern philosophy, etc., Jung's description of the archetypes by way of their manifestations in a myriad
of archetypal images attempts to evoke their numinous quality.

> The meeting with oneself is, at first, the meeting with one's
> own shadow. The shadow is a tight passage, a narrow door,
> whose painful constriction no one is spared who goes down to
> the deep well. But one must learn to know oneself in order to
> know who one is. For what comes after the door is surprisingly
> enough, a boundless expanse full of unprecedented uncertain-
> ties. (Jung, 1954a, p. 21)

The shadow is the complement of the ego.[2] It is the archetype of
the personal unconscious. The personal unconscious is all those

things which have been repressed because they are incompatible
with the ego. It is the ontogenetic unconscious and its contents
come from a person's life experiences. It is roughly equivalent
to Freud's notion of the repressed unconscious. Perversion,
licentiousness and evil reign here. Since everyone has a personal
unconscious, the confrontation with the dark side is represented
in myths and Jung groups these mythologems within the archetype of the shadow. In myths the hero's shadow is represented
in his sojourn in dens of iniquity, in his struggle with the snake,
in pacts made with the devil, and by the dark brother whom he
must confront.

If the person neither retreats from nor is engulfed by images
of strange and dark powers pouring from himself then he comes
to recognize the 'evil' within himself. This realization widens
consciousness for it engenders a dialogue with shadow figures.
Not all these figures are bad, it is thinking they are that makes
them so. Often recognizing their rights transforms them into
helpers and guides who lead the hero onward.

The anima or anima figures are the next to be met. They tempt
and instruct. Often they introduce the hero to sexuality and try
to enslave him with their charms. Translating, the anima introduces a man to his own femininity and sensuality. She recalls the
mother in fantasies of womb-like security. In myths this is the
devouring female monster Circe who detains Odysseus, and the
Indian maiden who tempts the cowboy to live the life of the
savage. Sexuality and spirituality tend to fuse in myths and the
unconscious. The hero's quest is often undertaken on behalf of
a fabulously beautiful and yet spiritual female, or the hero meets
along the way a ravishing woman dressed in white with the wisdom of the ages in her violet eyes. His task is to learn from her,
to make her wisdom his own.

Psychologically the lesson to be learned is that a man for his
own good must come to recognize his emotions, his spiritual
ecstasies, and the subtleties of sexual attraction. If he denies
them he will continue to see them as either great gifts or defects
within the other sex. If he is overwhelmed by the anima he will
lose his masculine orientation towards the world, putting in its
place an exaggerated undeveloped femininity. It is through
recognition and dialogue that the anima is understood and when
an accord is reached the doors to the collective unconscious
are open.

'The collective unconscious contains, or is, an historical mirror-
image of the world. It too is a world, but a world of images'
(Jung, 1916b, p. 298). Compensating the social truths of the
day, which for consciousness are the facts and laws of reality,
are the age-old truths of the imagination. These are images of
great power and experiencing them gives a sense of coming to
know eternal wisdom. When an accord is reached with the shadow
and anima consciousness is greatly expanded, if the ego then
asserts that it now commands magnificent truths the individual
has fallen prey to the mana-personality and been consumed by

the archetype of meaning. The man becomes a prophet in his own eyes, declaring his possession of eternal wisdom; this can lead either to his becoming a tyrant, using his powers for the sake of his own needs; or conversely the individual is stricken by his pitifulness in the face of the almighty and aggrandizes himself as the most degraded being alive.

Great courage and powers of self-criticism are needed as one confronts the god, the magician, and eternal truths. Conscious realization of the meaning of the mysteries of the unconscious, without, however, claiming their possession as an individual acquisition, leads to an entry into the spirit and a renewal of life. It is a reconnection with mankind's spiritual heritage and creates a new bond to the world. The path to individuation is a profound exploration of one's inner subjectivity which in the end binds one to all of humanity.

The hero is reborn, the ego is recentered. The submersion in the sea, baptism, the divine child, all represent this penultimate stage. Mandala figures, golden perfect flowers, lush green trees represent the new centering of the personality. The rule of an exclusively externally focused consciousness is overthrown. The self is now the center; it is a transcendental point of infinite circumference by which the ego feels itself directed. It is god incarnate in man, the spirit materialized in the body.

Jung (1955-6), in his last major work on alchemy, in which he explored the parallels between the alchemical opus and individuation, concluded that the goal of the philosophically minded alchemist was this unification of spirit and matter. The 'unio mystica' was long sought and never achieved. It is the 'tao,' the content of 'samadhi,' the kingdom of heaven, and the experience of 'satori.' Jung bows before the ineffable when after fifty years of writing about such experiences, he says, 'Not unnaturally, we are at a loss to see how a physic experience of this kind... can be formulated as a rational concept' (pp. 539-40). He did not try. He was willing in work after work to evoke through his writing, pictures, and quotations from others a sense of what the experience might be. It is an experience which has been recorded throughout history and Jung recognized it as such - an experience which is a psychic reality.

However, the self is rarely, if ever, achieved. Archetypal images of the self and rebirth 'are naturally only anticipations of a wholeness which is, in principle, always just beyond our reach.' Such images always point to the self, 'the container and organizer of all opposites,' promising wholeness and a deliverance from internal division (Jung, 1946b, p. 319). But the 'unconscious...can never be "done with" once and for all;' what one hopes for is progress in a life-long quest: 'The more numerous and the more significant the unconscious contents which are assimilated to the ego, the closer the approximation of the ego to the self, even though this approximation must be a never-ending process' (Jung, 1951, pp. 20, 23).

The change in personality created by self-discovery, with its

continual conscious realization of unconscious fantasies coupled
with an active participation in imagination, is a transformation
of the general attitude of the person. The horizon of consciousness is extended, there is a gradual diminution of the feeling
of being driven by unknown influences and of being trapped
in the flow of external events, and finally one lives at ease with
oneself for the internal gulf dividing the psyche has been bridged.

The road towards individuation is not well traveled. Neither
necessity nor moral decision are enough to force one to under-
take the perilous journey. In the end it is fate; it is a calling,
a vocation; 'an irrational factor that destines a man to emanci-
pate himself from the herd and from its well-worn paths' (Jung,
1934a, p. 175). Few are chosen and Jung saw himself as one
of the elect.

If this whole process and Jung's psychology are so esoteric
then why does he claim to be talking about the human psyche in
general? Analytical psychology is a general psychology because
as an interpretative system it increases our understanding of
fantasy. To some degree all people fantasize. Human beings are,
as far as we know, the only animals who fantasize, who create
fictions, and who, through imagination, envisage worlds in
which to live. Jung's analyses of myth provide an anatomy of
imagination.

The primary method by which the unconscious manifests itself
is by projection. What has its origins within us is seen as being
in the world around us. 'The country... [primitive man] inhabits
is at the same time the topography of his unconscious' (Jung,
1918, p. 26). For the Greeks the mountains at the horizon housed
their gods; here again the unconscious was projected outward
just beyond the perceptual grasp of consciousness. Religious
dogmas capture the numinous, distilling it in texts, symbols and
rituals through which they bind their believers to a reality created by faith and experience. In medioval times, when the material
world was a mystery, alchemists naively (by the standards of
today) projected into matter unconscious psychic products. For
us today to understand what our ancestors were doing requires
interpretation, for our trees are no longer inhabited by spirits,
the mountains are no longer the scene of heavenly battles, and
mercury is something in our thermometers and not a manifestation of Hermes in matter. Reality has changed; we no longer
hear angels. To understand the reality of our ancestors we must
postulate that they projected internal psychic states onto the
world or accept the less palatable alternative that the material
world has substantially altered its form.

Jungian hermeneutics identifies typical ways in which humans
invest their world and their existence with psychic significance.
Looking at Jung's method, and for the moment putting aside
his metaphysics, we can see that by identifying similar themes
in narratives and imaginative products from different times and
places he identified enduring concerns of human thought. He

also said that we moderns still think in these ways and are just
as blind to our own projections as were our ancestors. In fiction,
art, and science we still find the motifs which are found in
mythologies, mystic texts, and religious works. It is in fiction
where we now find the numinous and at the movies our fantasies
are literally projected. We, too, still find the gods at the horizon.
Now they are aliens from outer space and speculation about what
they are like is necessarily filled with unconscious projection.
Flying saucers are usually circular in shape, paralleling the
structure of mandala figures, and they promise either salvation
or doom. They are literally numinous in that they light up the
sky. They are definitely a psychic reality, be they material or
not (Jung, 1958a). We also hear from the science of cosmology
about black holes in which light and matter are captured within
an unknown 'X' and about white singularities from which matter
spews forth into the universe. The black death and the shining
creation live on in mankind's sophisticated science.

Interpretation by finding parallels allows one to see the con-
tinuities in human thought and to situate oneself within a world
from which we have been alienated by the cant of modernity.
Freud charged that Jung's psychology was reactionary; it certainly was. It was so reactionary in finding its roots in myth and
in alchemy that it might, in a society devoted to the 'au courant,'
be revolutionary.

Jung's therapy was a treatment method aimed at ameliorating
alienation from oneself and the world. He never deviated from
his position - first put forward in a 1912(b) case study - that
'Neurosis is self-division' and its etiology must be found in the
current conflicts of the patient's life (p. 261). 'The true reason
for a neurosis always lies in the present...[and] it is only in
the today, not in our yesterdays, that the neurosis can be
"cured"' (Jung, 1934b, p. 171). Modern society with its mass
movements, mass consciousness, and scientific rationalism was
seen by Jung as a large part of the problem. For thousands of
years before the rise of nineteenth-century psychotherapy as
a medical treatment humans were concerned with the sick soul;
'Religions are psychotherapeutic systems in the truest sense
of the word....they express the whole range of the psychic problems in mighty images; they are the avowal and recognition of
the soul, and at the same time the revelation of the soul's
nature.' The loss of religion, our separation from mystery - 'is
the prime evil of neurosis' (p. 172). Jung's psychotherapy was
a method for rejoining people to their souls. It was a reunion
he sought to create by guiding individuals in explorations of
the numinous images of the unconscious. Grounded in myth his
therapy sought to re-root moderns in mythopoeic experience.

For Jung, neurosis was primarily a moral, not a medical,
problem. It was self-betrayal. Faced with difficult choices, the
neurotic seeks safety either in conventionality or in what has
now become conventional - blaming current problems on past
relations with parents. Faced with the alien within, with moods

and emotions that are contrary to the conscious will, the mentally troubled individual either denies them or is overwhelmed. 'The mentally unbalanced person tries to defend himself against his own unconscious...; he fights against his own compensating influences' (Jung, 1914b, p. 208). The counterbalancing contents which break through ever growing conscious resistance should begin a 'healing process,' but they do not. This is because in struggling past ego-opposition they become distorted, and are therefore perceived as dangerous. The material having been unconscious is uncultivated and so it appears in primitive forms. The ego in fright attempts to flee, or is overwhelmed, or tries to erect more defenses. Even if the unconscious is not acknowledged it still gains expression. The forces within become so strong and are so violently denied by the ego that they are seen as threats from the outside world. The unconscious material is projected into reality. The religious fanatic sees sin everywhere, but not in himself. The devoted scientist, failing to acknowledge his own materialist orthodoxy, sees people of faith as deluded and dangerous.

The denial of the power of the unconscious amounts to a 're-gressive restoration of the persona.' Frightened by the unconscious, one acts as if one had never seen such a thing. One insures that one never will do so again by circumscribing life, shoring up one's conscious identity as a holder of a social position, and explaining away anomalies of experience by proclaiming them to be 'nothing but' manifestations of something already known. This retreat from possibilities produces a general malaise, but some find this far preferable to the frightening prospect of finding out who they might be.

In contrast to this extraverted reaction, there may be an exaggerated introverted response. One is overwhelmed by the unconscious; conscious criticism is displaced, the ego is shattered, and archetypal contents flow freely into the world. One comes to live in a dream. Archaic fantasies are grafted on to current perceptions and reality becomes a manifestation of the collective unconscious. This is the psychotic reaction characteristic of schizophrenia.

Between psychosis and conventionality there are two other reactions which are not ideal. One may 'either become an eccentric with a taste for prophesy or...revert to an infantile attitude and become cut off from human society' (1928, p. 163). Both reactions have in common a failure of self-criticism and moral integrity. The reversion to an infantile dependence on others is fostered by the infantile nature of fantasies arising from the personal unconscious. The individual submits to these, sees them as a real expression of his or her nature, and so acts them out in life. The prophet succumbs to a vision and identifies himself - his ego - with an archetypal image. His persona becomes that of the messiah when an archetypal role replaces a social role. Both roles are stereotypes, the former arising from the internal world and the latter from the external. The prophet, the psychotic, the infantile neurotic, and the person who clings to his or her profession have all sacrificed an individual to a collective identity.

To doubt and yet to listen is for Jung the ideal way by which to resolve the difficulty of self-division and maintain psychic balance. One must make the taxing moral decision to listen to one's own inner urges and also to criticize what one hears. One must neither submit to or deny the unconscious; one must enter into a dialogue with it. To the man who gives over his identity to his social role and the prophet who finds that he is an emanation of the divine Jung says, 'One could wish both of them a *sense of humour*, that...truly "divine" attribute of man which alone befits him to maintain his soul in freedom' (p. 154). The distance from one's passion that humor requires is a concomitant of the ideal reaction to facing the unconscious: critical understanding.

Jung preached the gospel of the individual: 'in reality only a change in the attitude of the individual can bring about a renewal in the spirit of the nations. Everything begins with the individual' (1918, p. 27). This is probably not as true as Jung fervently believed it to be, but it is more than right-wing idealism. It may be truer than the modern advocates of societism could, in their advocacy of the power of mass consciousness, admit.

Although highly honored in his day, Jung saw his work as antithetical to the spirit of his age. He was renewing for our times a world-view which, while always having had its adherents, has never been pre-eminent in Western culture. We are rarely taught in school about the gnostics or alchemists, nor do most of us read 'Faust' or study Nietzsche's 'Zarathustra.' Jung's work is difficult to read because our schools - those purveyors of the Zeitgeist - simply do not prepare us to read texts born of a tradition which has been outside the central current of Western thought. Philosophies stressing individual insight and the solitary pursuit of knowledge will by necessity always remain on the fringes of society for they do not engender mass movements.

Jung denounced orthodoxy and wrote, 'I am not in the habit of interfering with my pupils. I have neither the right nor the might to do that. They can draw such conclusions as seem right to them and must accept full responsibility for it' (Adler, 1973, p. 518). Such a position makes apostasy difficult.

In the four years immediately following the break Freud wrote several extended works which were in part criticisms of Jung's ideas. But, after 1918 his references to Jung were criticisms in passing and by no means extensive. After the break almost all of Jung's essays contained criticism of Freud and from 1920 on the majority of his writings devoted at least a paragraph to critical comments on psychoanalysis. Like Freud's criticisms of Jung's work, Jung's criticisms of Freud are at times personal and in general are aimed at showing psychoanalytic truths to be only partial descriptions of the facts.

The main thrust of all Jung's criticism is found in his obituary to Freud: 'Freud's psychology moves within the narrow confines of nineteenth-century scientific materialism. It's philosophical premises were never examined, thanks obviously to the Master's insufficient philosophical equipment' (1939, p. 47). Freud's work, Jung tells us, was a necessary, understandable, and brilliant critique of the idealism, romanticism, sentimentality, and prudishness of Victorian society; Freud 'is a great destroyer who breaks the fetters of the past' (1932, p. 36). With the unerring eye of the physician trained to spot disease, Freud exposed the sexual hypocrisy and denial of man's natural, baser side which so characterized the Victorian consciousness. However, his genius was also his flaw for he saw all religion, art, and philosophy as a façade and reduced it to a manifestation of infantile sexuality. To find religion as nothing but an expression of a child's longing for the father may be a valid criticism of Victorian piety, but not of all religions.

Freud's attempt to reduce psychic activity to its origins in infantile events and instinctual causes was for Jung far too reductive. Jung charged that instincts, especially sexuality, had become a fixed idea for Freud; a dogmatic well-ordered cognitive system - psychoanalysis - was founded upon the notion that anti-cognitive instinctual forces dominate psychic life. This is ironic, but given the dynamics of compensation, understandable. Following this same compensatory formula we can see in Freud's deep concern for the future of the psychoanalytic movement a counterbalance for his theoretical views in which everything was oriented towards the past.

From Jung's earliest works and letters we saw his reservations about Freud's emphasis on sexuality. His critique of the sexual theory is strongly stated when he charges that 'an excursis into the thousand and one possibilities of obscene fantasy and unfulfillable infantile wishes is just a pretext for avoiding the essential question,' which is how is a person going to face present life dilemmas. Jung continues, saying that Freud made two errors in his work on the neuroses. First in looking to the past Freud followed the neurotic's wish to avoid the future and second, like neurotics, Freud fell into the trap of euphemistic disparagement: 'He undervalued the neurosis and thereby won the applause of patients and doctors alike, who want nothing better than to hear that neurosis is "nothing but..."' (1934b, p. 171). This attack on Freud is an exaggeration of Jung's more reasoned criticism of Freud's exclusive emphasis on reductionistic, causal-historical explanation. Such a focus does obscure important questions: what purpose does an action serve? What is being expressed about an individual's current life by a dream? And, what are the multiple meanings of any experience?

Freud, for all his focus on sexuality, did not discuss adult sexual problems. Such problems do have their infantile roots, but they are also problems of adjustment to sexual situations

which adults and not children must face. Given his view that
infantile sexuality was primarily a retrospective sexualization of
the past by adults, Jung could be excused for not exploring
childhood eroticism, but his writings also avoid any discussion
of adult sexuality. If sexual intercourse is discussed at all it is
as a metaphoric expression of spiritual union, the mysterium
coniunctionis. It is important to see, as Jung is supposed to
have once said, that 'the penis is a phallic symbol,' but - and
one loses sight of this in Jung's work with its elaborate embroi-
dery of symbols - a penis is also a penis and is often employed
in extremely carnal activities.

It is true that Freud did not read widely in philosophy, but
like many scientists he felt that his method was not to be faulted.
The trouble is that there are grave problems in applying the
scientific method to the study of reflexive objects, the prime
example of which is people. If the object knows it is being
observed then it can alter its behavior, either to fulfill the
observer's expectations or to defy them. Freud, in insisting
that only by using the psychoanalytic method could his findings
be tested, also sealed his system into a framework which resists
potentially fruitful exchanges with other methods of inquiry.
Finally, if Freud had read more widely in philosophy he might
not have felt the need to cling so desperately to his claim that
psychoanalysis was a natural science, when it is not. Jung
(1929b) also charges that Freud failed to rigorously criticize
his own thought. This is not true and the several major revisions
which psychoanalysis underwent at his hands show him to be a
man of sufficient intellectual honesty to discard a position when,
after an internal critical dialogue, he found it no longer tenable.
It was Jung's psychology that never underwent major revisions,
but this is not because he lacked an ability for questioning his
own ideas. Jung's initial postulates were so broad that he could
easily accommodate any of his findings within them.

That Freud did not see or admit that his psychology was predicated on his own personality was another fault that Jung found
in psychoanalysis. Freud did insist that psychoanalysis was
objective, although he did concede that 'The Interpretation of
Dreams' was part of his own self-analysis. Jung, however,
insisted that psychologists must recognize and proclaim that
their theories are an expression of their own subjectivity. Jung
confessed this time and time again, 'I consider my contribution
to psychology to be my subjective confession. It is my personal
psychology, my prejudice that I see psychological facts as I
do.' But, just as frequently, he turned this confession around
saying, 'So far as we admit our personal prejudice, we are
really contributing towards an objective psychology' (1935,
p. 125). Jung comes perilously close to assuming that one can
clearly identify all of the prejudices which might influence one's
work and thereby achieve objectivity. This is as dangerous as
the myth of the perfectly analyzed analyst. Jung's revolt against
Freud's dogmatism, which Jung does not seem to have analyzed,

definitely shaped his own absolutist position on the relativity of all psychological theories.

Why did Jung in essay after essay, year after year, keep criticizing Freud? First, because Freud and his ideas greatly influenced Jung's thought and in detaching himself from psychoanalysis Jung was reacting to something he had once avowed. Second, because psychoanalysis continues to be the benchmark to which all theories of the unconscious are compared. In his attempts to promulgate his own views Jung, in order to make sure he was understood, had to keep insisting that his ideas were different from Freud's and that psychoanalytic theory was limited. An incident at a lecture-discussion over twenty years after the break illustrates the battle he had. After Jung had reviewed his conception of the unconscious a psychoanalyst charged, as though discovering a mistake in Jung's work, that 'Jung refuses to recognize the word "unconscious" in the meaning Freud gives to it.' Jung's reply: 'The word "unconscious" is not Freud's invention' (1935, p. 62). It has a long history and Freud did not discover THE unconscious.

Freud and Jung broke because they did not agree on what constituted the unconscious. Of course, Jung refused to recognize the meaning which Freud gave to the word; his whole theory is built on a different view. Failing to realize that there may be several ways to interpret a phenomenon so enigmatic as the unconscious is a sign of dogmatism. It is a blindness born of the conviction that there is a truth, an unfortunate aberration carried over into science by individuals still searching for a religion. It is difficult for the orthodox to see that conflicts of interpretation are a natural product of the never-ending search for understanding.

10 CONFLICTS OF INTERPRETATION

The extravert and introvert, the realist and idealist, the scientist and philosopher, the man who found himself by refinding his life history and the individual who discovered his being in fantasy, these are the differences between Freud and Jung. Although they collaborated with each other they lived in different realities and psychoanalysis and analytical psychology are two world-views in collision. Freud believed in external reality, Jung in psychic reality. Believe, here, is too weak a word. Their belief went beyond belief to utter commitment, and beyond commitment to the conviction for Freud that the external is what exists and for Jung that the internal is the real. Such fundamental differences in experiential orientation and phenomenological presuppositions have profound effects and their ramifications are evident in the conflicts of interpretation produced by the two men's systems. We will explore the most important of these as we critically compare Freud's and Jung's ideas on reality, on religion and science, on mythology, mysticism, and fiction, on biology and history, and on women. A comparison of their case studies and textual analyses will show that their differing valuations of reality and fantasy greatly affected the evidence that they presented for their own theories.

In Freud's writings we have seen the lengths to which he went in trying to establish first the reality of seduction, then of latent dreams, primary process, infantile sexuality, primary narcissism and primal scenes. But what of the notion of psychic reality in his work? After all, he did establish a hermeneutics of the psyche. Freud says that in analytic treatment, 'It will be a long time before he [the analysand] can take in our proposal that we should equate fantasy and reality and not bother to begin with whether the childhood experiences under examination are one or the other.' He continued, 'The fantasies possess *psychical* as contrasted with *material* reality, and we gradually learn to understand that *in the world of the neuroses it is psychical reality which is the decisive kind*' (1916-17, p. 368). With this phenomenological reduction - suspending within the analytic session all reality judgments - it seems that Freud has committed himself to psychic reality.

However, Freud does not maintain this position long, the requirements of science being different from those of the analytic encounter. Following this statement, Freud reasserts his commitment to the actual event. He says it would be a mistake to suppose that occurrences such as the observation of parental

314

intercourse, seduction by an adult, and castration threats were 'never characterized by material reality' (p. 369); such events, he argues, can be corroborated by asking the patient's family. But remember that Freud in the Wolf Man case warned strongly against such evidence: 'Any stories that may be told by relatives in reply to enquiries and requests are at the mercy of every critical misgiving that can come into play. One invariably regrets having made oneself dependent upon such information' (1918, p. 14). For the analysis such questions are bad and one must be skeptical about answers given to them; yet to establish that such events do occur, in order to provide evidence to make a theoretical point, the enquiries are acceptable. Evidence not fit for the analysis is accepted as scientific proof!

Following this point that such events can at times be characterized by material reality, Freud argues that actual experience and fantasy form a complemental relationship: 'If they [childhood traumatic events] have occurred in reality, so much to the good; but if they have been witheld by reality, they are put together from hints and supplemented by phantasy.' He then asks, 'Whence comes the need for these phantasies and the material for them?' (1916-17, p. 370). He answers that primal scenes, seductions, castration threats and a few others are primal phantasies and are a phylogenetic endowment. Although such events are 'told to us to-day in analysis as phantasy... [they] were once real occurrences in the primaeval times of the human family' (p. 371). Behind the psychic reality of the analytic session lies the real event in the history of the species. The real has simply been moved, in a familiar fashion, from the present to the past. For Freud, if something was in the mind it had to be in the senses first, even if the actual experience occurred eons ago.

Jung saw this view as typically Western and woefully inadequate. He admits that restricting the real to '*material* reality carves an exceedingly large chunk out of reality as a whole, but it nevertheless remains a fragment only, and all round it is a dark penumbra which one would have to call unreal or surreal' (1933, p. 382). In a materialist frame from which one must view everything as the result of sensate physical causes the psyche must be seen as epiphenomenal, as some form of 'secretion of the brain.' Jung rejects this view, committing himself to the position that, 'The psychic alone has immediate reality, and this includes all forms of the psychic, even "unreal" ideas and thoughts which refer to nothing "external."' He concludes, 'Between the unknown essences of spirit and matter stands the reality of the psychic - psychic reality, the only reality we can experience immediately' (p. 384).

Experientially we are not aware of the complex physiological processes by which the material world comes into being for us. Consciousness has no direct relation to any material objects, but lives in a world of psychic images. A complicated process of

which consciousness is not aware transforms physical sensations
into perceivable psychic events. The physiological nature of
these processes can be known and science has made immense
progress in their exploration. But in order to even approximately
determine the nature of material things we need the elaborate
apparatus and complicated procedures of the natural sciences.
'These disciplines are really tools which help the human intellect
to cast a glance behind the deceptive veil of images into a
non-psychic world. ...Far, therefore, from being a material
world, this is a psychic world, which allows us to make only
indirect and hypothetical inferences about the real nature of
matter' (Jung, 1933, p. 384).

Material reality was a hypothesis for Jung; experiential psychic events were real. Freud's view was the opposite and his
epistemology was materialistic and empirical, 'correspondence
with the real external world we call "truth"' (1933a, p. 170). If
two people cannot agree on what constitutes the real they will
not agree on very many issues. It is difficult to decide which
man's position on reality is superior for only personal prejudice
or a superordinate framework would help us to decide, and such
prejudices and paradigms are themselves usually divided by
the positions which they adopt on epistemological and ontological
issues.

RELIGION AND SCIENCE

The antithetical positions on the real constitute the basic difference in Freud's and Jung's world-views. This difference even
affects how they define Weltanschauung (world-view) and is of
major importance in their differing valuations of religion and
science. For Freud, a Weltanschauung exists as an external
social set of beliefs, it is 'an intellectual construction which
solves all the problems of our existence uniformly on the basis
of one overriding hypothesis' and to possess one 'is among the
ideal wishes of human beings' (p. 158). A Weltanschauung,
according to Jung, is an individual construction; 'We can only
speak of a Weltanschauung when a person has at least made a
serious attempt to formulate his attitude in conceptual or concrete form, so that it becomes clear to him why and to what
purpose he acts and lives as he does' (1931c, p. 361). Developing a world-view, which Jung advises should be done, and
constantly revising that view in light of experience, which Jung
advocates as a necessity, produces a widening and deepening
of consciousness. In defining Weltanschauung Freud has charac-
teristically stressed the external, while Jung has emphasized the
internal. This divergence in their definitions is amplified in their
analyses of religion and science as world-views.

When Freud speaks of religion he means Western Judeo-
Christianity in its most dogmatic forms: 'Religious ideas are
teachings and assertions about facts and conditions of external

(or internal) reality which tell one something one has not discovered for oneself and which lay claim to one's belief' (1927,
p. 25). In stark contrast, Jung says, 'Religion appears to me
to be a peculiar attitude of mind which could be formulated in
accordance with the original use of the word 'religio,' which
means a careful consideration and observation of certain dynamic
factors that are conceived of as "powers"' (1940, p. 8). Given
Freud's definition, he will find religion to be a system of authority which stultifies the mind and blinds individuals to external
realities. Jung will find it to be a psychic reality, an attitude
peculiar to a consciousness which has been changed by a deeply
moving spiritual experience.

Definitions are predispositions for finding certain conclusions.
We will not be surprised that Freud and Jung disagree about
the value of religion given that they do not agree on what constitutes the real, do not agree on what a 'Weltanschauung' is,
and disagree on what religion is. They do agree that religious
systems serve a protective function. Jung sees this as positive,
Freud negative.

Realizing that what he calls a creed is what is ordinarily called
religion, Jung felt it necessary to determine what functions
organized religions perform. They 'have the obvious purpose of
replacing "immediate experience" by a choice of suitable symbols
tricked out with an organized dogma and ritual' (p. 43). They
function as buffers between potentially overwhelming influences
from the unconscious and the individual. Their symbol systems,
capitalizing on belief, provide a structure in which the person
can find meaning for what he or she does not understand.
Through its devotional exercises a religious system provides an
approved mode of expression for experiences which threaten,
either by fear or ecstasy, individual consciousness. Far from
denigrating organized religion, Jung recognizes that it can have
immense psychological value.

However, developments in Western history have made it impossible for many modern individuals to submit to a dogma and
therefore Jung says that in order to understand religion, probably all that is left to many of us is the psychological approach.
Without a creed, individuals must face the numinous on their
own and this is a forbidding task requiring great courage. Jung
did this in his own analysis, and analytical psychology is an
attempt to express in psychological terms the drama of the
individual's confrontation with unknown internal psychic powers.
It is a system of guidance providing a conceptual framework in
which to understand potentially overwhelming spiritual events.
'Look not outward, the truth lies within' is the gospel of religion
and Jung saw religious experience as a confrontation with oneself, an intense introspective self-criticism which is indispensable
in any attempt to understand one's own psychology.

Ruling out the possibility of individual religiosity either in the
form of a moving personal experience or a philosophical formulation about the nature of the divine, Freud finds religion to be a

societal neurosis, and sees no value in it. He asserts that none
of its teachings are grounded upon empirical fact and that it
provides only wishful solutions to life's most difficult problems.
For Freud, religion was illusion and the foe of science. Science
was his safeguard against illusion; 'No, our science is no illusion.
But an illusion it would be to suppose that what science cannot
give us we can get elsewhere' (1927, p. 56). A scientific world-
view, Freud says, 'has, apart from its emphasis on the real
external world, mainly negative traits, such as submission to
the truth and rejection of illusions' (1933a, p. 182). Of course,
we know that truth is 'correspondence with the external world,'
and if we cling to our unscientific prejudices, we are preferring
the solace of falsehoods and wishful fabrications to the facts.
Freud's rejection of religion and his scientific fervor reminds
one of James's brilliant characterization of the modern intellect:
'our esteem for facts has not neutralized in us all religiousness.
It is itself almost religious. Our scientific temper is devout'
(1907, p. 23).

Since science gives us the truth let us hear what 'the judgment
of science on the religious "Weltanschauung" is': religion is a
wishful attempt to master the sensory world; it is a transitional
stage in human developmer.t analogous to the Oedipal neurosis
which individuals pass through on their way from childhood to
maturity; it was born during the 'ignorant times of the childhood
of humanity' and its 'consolations deserve no trust' (Freud,
1933a, p. 168). 'Science tells us...' is a modern equivalent of
'the Bible tells me so' and Freud has used it in an attempt to
legitimate his very suspect findings about religion. Chemistry,
physics, and biology tell us little about religion. Their research
techniques are not designed to investigate human social structures. However, according to Freud, psychoanalysis has extended scientific investigation into the mental realm and has shown
that many of the claims that people make about the world are
based upon emotion and that while the irrational basis of such
beliefs can be understood science has no reason to regard such
claims as justified. Freud continues, 'On the contrary it sees this
as a warning carefully to separate from knowledge everything
that is illusion and an outcome of emotional demands' (p. 159).
Both science and psychoanalysis accomplish this by a continuous
process of research: forming hypotheses, testing these by
observations, revising the hypotheses, and again putting one's
ideas before reality, that great arbiter of truth.

Freud reminds us that an essential of science is that one 'must
renounce early convictions so as not to be led by them into
overlooking unexpected factors' (p. 174). Belying all of his
glorious rhetoric about the objectivity and nobility of science,
he says that although in his analysis of religion he has only
been considering Western systems he is certain that 'the most
careful working-over of the material of the problem of religion
would not shake our conclusions' (p. 169). Certainly Jung's
careful work did not disturb Freud's views on religion, ideas

that were never put to the test but were elaborate psychoanalytic criticisms based on his materialistic and atheistic prejudices. Freud's position on religion was both so dogmatic and
ill-informed that he could claim that religious systems are 'complete in all essential respects' and are incapable of improvement
(p. 174). There is a history of religion and like the sciences
religions have their revolutions, their debates, their schisms,
and their canons of evidence.

There is a gross asymmetry in Freud's comparison of science
and religion, an imbalance which is tendentious. Freud simplifies
religion's complexities to the point of absurdity and considers
it in its institutional forms and as a folk belief system. He does
not view science as an institution nor does he consider that
faith in science often develops as a suitable substitute for religion. Jung is more realistic about science when he says: 'For a
certain type of intellectual mediocrity characterized by enlight-
ened rationalism, a scientific theory that simplifies matters is a
very good means of defense because of the tremendous faith
modern man has in anything which bears the label "scientific"'
(1940, p. 45).

For Freud, faith in science was not enough; the last vestiges
of religion had to be obliterated. The problem with religion was
the 'prohibition against thought' which it sets up in order to
preserve itself. This is a problem of all dogmatism, not just
religion. Freud proposed to abolish this prohibition by establishing his own: 'Our best hope for the future is that intellect –
the scientific spirit, reason – may in process of time establish
a dictatorship in the mental life of man' (1933a, p. 171). He
assures us that 'the nature of reason' insures that once the
scientific revolution is complete emotional impulses will bo given
'the position they deserve.' But revolutionary governments cannot always be trusted to deal justly with the opposition, especially when that government is a dictatorship!

Science as a method of inquiry is a powerful tool, but it suffers from typical institutional problems. Modern science cannot
be separated from technology and the many problems of Western
civilization. Its unfortunate, though understandable, propensity
towards dogmatism and pontification cannot be overlooked. The
people cry out for answers and their tax money supports an
elaborate system of welfare scholarship which we call government funding for research. This very support of the search for
knowledge is a problem. Inquiry is not free when it costs money,
and science as institutional practice has been perverted by
Mammon and the people's worship of the expert.

Freud so trusted science that he could not see the difficulties
of which it was a part and overlooked for the sake of argument
the supposed scientific prejudice his work met. Jung, the
idealist, reather naively refused to see science as Weltanschauung.
He insisted that it was a tool to be employed with others in constructing world-views, but that it should not turn people into
instruments of observation. Jung saw in the growth of scientific

devotion the problem that if 'science is an end in itself, man's
raison d'être lies in being a mere intellect' (1931c, p. 377).
Freud's dream of a rule of intellect, like his insistence on psychoanalytic orthodoxy, was a nightmare to Jung. In contrast
to Freud's unabashed boosterism of science, Jung saw that the
'marvelous development of science and technics is counter-
balanced by an apalling lack of wisdom and introspection' (1940,
p. 17).

Freud was determined that psychoanalysis be seen as a science
and argued in several places for its scientific status (1913d;
1914d; 1933a; 1940a). That he and his followers have felt the
necessity to do so warns us, on the principle of protesting too
much, that there may be reasons for debating whether or not
psychoanalysis is a science on the model of the natural sciences.[1]
The outcome of such debates, grossly simplified, is that analysts
either find psychoanalysis to be a science or they find that it
could be made scientific with a bit more rigor; neutral parties
find its status as a science problematic; and philosophers of
science find it to be unscientific. Few seem unconcerned about
the question and this has much to do with the unfortunate fact
that being a science confers status and such accoutrements of
rank as higher fees, government funding, and public respect.

Although criteria of what is and is not science are almost as
uncertain as those for art it is easily shown that psychoanalysis
as practiced by Freud does not meet the criteria of two of the
most important and liberal philosophies of science. Popper's
criterion of falsifiability for solving the problem of demarcation
between the scientific and unscientific clearly positions psychoanalysis as a pseudo-science. The falsification criterion holds
that 'statements or systems of statements, in order to be ranked
as scientific, must be capable of conflicting with possible or
conceivable observations' (1963, p. 39). About psychoanalysis
Popper says that its theories are 'simply non-testable, irrefutable. There ... is no conceivable human behavior which could
contradict them' (pp. 37-8). Popper does not deny that psychoanalysis is based on observation or that it contains useful
information about people or that some day it may be a science.
The power of non-falsifiable theories is immense. Psychoanalysis
can, in the human sphere, explain the most bizarre actions by
putting them into a coherent framework of retrospective casual
explanation. Any such system will engender strong support
and violent opposition.

By the criteria of Feyerabend (1970), psychoanalysis is not
a science. He holds that science for its existence requires two
things: proliferation of ideas and tenacity in their pursuit.
Proliferation means that '*everyone may follow his inclinations*
and science, conceived as a critical enterprise, will profit from
such an activity. Tenacity: this means that one is encouraged
not just to follow one's inclinations but to develop them further,
to raise them, with the help of criticism (which involves a comparison of alternatives) to a higher level of articulation and

thereby to raise their defense to a higher level of consciousness'
(p. 210). In science there is a constant interplay between proliferation and tenacity. Although Freud was tenacious in the
defense of his ideas, he was not amenable to a critical comparison
of his thought with other hypotheses. He said, 'There is a
common saying that we should learn from our enemies. I confess
I have never succeeded in doing so' (1933a, p. 139). This coupled with the fact that a proliferation of ideas within psychoanalysis was not allowed by Freud, much less encouraged,
brands his work as unscientific.

About psychoanalytic dissidents Freud says that when the
differences of opinion between him and them had gone beyond
a certain point the most sensible thing to do was to part company, 'especially when the theoretical divergences involved a
change in practical procedure' (p. 143). Almost all scientific discoveries require some modifications in method. One does not
discover something by looking in the same way into the same old
places. Feyerabend's quite modest criteria for science, which are
also essentials for hermeneutics, would have been achieved by
psychoanalysis if the banishment of Adler and Jung had not been
instigated by Freud. Freud's articles of faith, strictures on
method, and refusal to openly confront competing hypotheses
deprived psychoanalysis of the proliferation of thought essential
to all critical enquiry. They also retarded its establishment of
canons of proof. The early analysts did not wrestle with the
problem of what to accept and reject as evidence because Freud
simply declared what was and was not psychoanalysis.

Since Freud's death psychoanalysis has been more open to a
multiplicity of ideas, but this does not mean that a certain
objectionable orthodoxy does not remain.[2] There is a more important difficulty in psychoanalysis and this too can be traced back
to Freud's dogmatism. He once confidently asserted 'applications
of analysis [in other fields] are always confirmations of it as
well' (1933a, p. 146). Speaking of the spirit of pseudo-science
versus science, Popper says, 'the dogmatic attitude is clearly
related to the tendency to verify our laws and schemata by seeking to apply them and to confirm them, even to the point of
neglecting refutations, whereas the critical attitude is one of
readiness to change them - to test them; to refute them; to
falsify them if possible' (1963, p. 50). Psychoanalysis is as yet
too eager to confirm and still recalcitrant in recognizing refutations.

MYSTICISM, MYTH AND FICTION

In his essay on Weltanschauung Freud maintains that the
scientific world-view proclaims that 'no knowledge' is derived
from 'revelation, intuition or divination' (1933a, p. 159). Knowledge is only gained by careful research and the intellectual
working-over of carefully scrutinized observations. Why Freud

wishes to rule out individual revelation as a source of knowledge is made clear by the following question: 'If one man has gained an unshakeable conviction of the true reality of religious doctrines from a state of ecstasy which has deeply moved him, of what significance is that to others?' (1927, p. 28). Such experiences, while always individual, have happened to a vast number of individuals throughout history - including Freud while he was undergoing his own self-analysis - but he now maintains that one cannot insist that something which 'exists only for a few' need bind the majority. What one may insist on from every man is that he 'use the gift of reason he possesses' (p. 28). It seems strange for Freud to expect this of people since he saw the fundamental state of humanity as irrational and ideal development as the cultivation of reason and reality testing. However, he is arguing against religion and when he does so he is often unreasonable. Freud's argument is aimed at the declaration: 'There is no appeal to a court above that of reason' (p. 28). Religious devotion which depends on inner experience and which is almost always irrational cannot therefore be binding on the majority. Only confirmation by careful observation with appeal to reason as the arbiter of experience should be acceptable as evidence for or against the validity of events.

Speaking of mystical experience, Freud says a close and respected friend of his had written to him in response to the ideas expressed above which were taken from 'The Future of an Illusion.' The friend had said that he was never without a certain feeling which he had found confirmed by others and which he supposed that millions had experienced, a 'feeling which he would like to call a sensation of "eternity" a feeling of something limitless, unbounded - as it were "oceanic"' (Freud, 1930, p. 64). Jung, who also had such experiences, describes them better. He says that the collective unconscious is "as wide as the world and open to all the world. ... There I am utterly one with the world, so much a part of it that I forget all too easily who I really am. "Lost in oneself" is a good way of describing this state' (1954a, p. 22).

Oceanic feelings, as psychoanalysis calls them, are for analytical psychology archetypal visions and for Jung they were fundamental in his own experience and universals of human existence. Freud says, 'I cannot discover this "oceanic" feeling in myself' (1930, p. 65). For a man who understood others by finding in himself a resonance with them and who depended on careful self-scrutiny as a source and validation of his theories this creates a formidable obstacle for his understanding of mystical experience.

What is the meaning of oceanic experience? Freud agrees that it exists; 'The only question is whether it is being correctly interpreted and whether it ought to be regarded as the *fons et origio* of the whole need for religion' (p. 65). The question then is hermeneutic, it is one of interpretation and the interpretative framework one uses will shape one's answer. Using psycho-

analytic speculation about infantile psychic life, Freud predictably finds the origin of such experiences in infancy. The infant's
ego is not well-developed and the boundaries between itself and
the world are not clearly drawn. Oceanic experiences in which
unconscious id experiences dominate are a regression to and
revivification of this primordial state. Since the ego owes its
origin as well as its most important acquired characteristics to
reality psychoanalysis is forced to assume that 'the ego's pathological states, in which it most approximates once again to the
id, are founded on a cessation or slackening of that relation to
the world' (Freud, 1940a, p. 201). For Freud, the domination of
psychical reality over external reality oriented functioning is a
sign of sickness and the wellspring of all illusion.

Jung does not disagree that oceanic feelings are achieved by
dislodging the ego's control; he does, however, violently oppose
the idea that such experiences are inherently pathological. He
accepts revelation as a form of knowledge and as necessary for
psychological insight. Revelation is an '"unveiling" of the depths
of the human soul' (1940, p. 74). That it is a psychological
experience is certain and its psychology can be investigated
systematically. Whether or not revelation points to a higher
being or another reality is not a question within the province
of science. Jung's position is that people experience intuitions,
revelations, and flashes of insight; therefore these exist. Such
experiences are very powerful, carry absolute conviction, and
are difficult to dispute. 'You can only say that you have never
had such an experience, whereupon your opponent will reply:
"Sorry, I have"' (Jung, 1940, p. 105). Such mystical experiences
transform consciousness, changing the ego's view of the world,
and are often an aid in therapy. Responding to Freud, Jung says
mystical experience 'must be a very real illusion, if you want to
put it pessimistically' (p. 105).

It was not that Freud wished to be pessimistic, he wished to
be rational and under the rule of reason irrational experiences
must be interpreted in order to make sense of them within a
system of logic. Reason, not experience, was the absolute
authority in Freud's hermeneutic. Experience for Jung was
primary and although he recognized the necessity for interpretation he would not deny the integrity of experience. Jung's
credo was 'I believe only what I know' and to know for him meant
to experience (p. 44).

Living within a culture which so highly values reason and
causality, it is difficult to realize that they are schemata of
interpretation. Causality is not inherent in nature and there is
no scientific evidence - for certainly the reasonable person would
insist on the best evidence available - that reason is an inherent
human faculty. Causality and reason are powerful hermeneutic
tools for ordering human experience and natural phenomena and
with them we weave a coherent narrative which situates us
within a reasonable world governed by causality. But there are
other forms of understanding, for example immediate experience,

argument by analogy, proof by religious testimony, and conviction by participation. We, of course, in our wisdom denigrate
these, but in doing so we limit the experiential world in which
we live. Freud argued that this is how it should be; after all
reality calls and we cannot remain forever both primitive and
infantile. Jung saw rationalistic materialism - the belief that reason, causality, and external verification determine truth - as an
obsession of modern consciousness which helps alienate individuals from themselves. For Jung, Freud's work was the premier
example of rationalistic materialism, about which he says,
'Materialism and mysticism are a psychological pair of opposites,
just like atheism and theism. They are hostile brothers, two
different methods of grappling with...powerful influences from
the unconscious, the one [materialism] by denying, the other
by recognizing them' (1931c, p. 370).

Mysticism need not be mysterious. It is a direct experience of
life's mysteries, an immediate perception of unconscious psychic
forces. As a practice, it attempts to amplify and articulate these
experiences by shaping them into a communicable form. The form
chosen will depend on individual predisposition and cultural
preferences. The communications products used extend from
cave paintings to motion pictures, from tribal dances to ballet,
from gnostic texts to modern psychological theories, and from
mythologies to scientific speculation.

The challenge of experience, and especially numinous experience, is to communicate it by translating it into a form which
can be understood by and shared with others. An experience
only happens once and in order to make it known one attempts
something like a scientific replication, by producing a verbal
or plastic reproduction. Reproduction is always an interpretation
and an attempt at communication.

On the issue of replication of experience, hermeneutics and
the natural sciences or experimentally oriented social sciences
take opposite positions. Science fulfills the human wish for
certainty in the face of an ambiguous world. Social science promises that human activity is understandable and that experience
is predictable. With its doctrine of replication - somebody else
must see what you have seen or you must see it again - science
limits experience by insisting it must be repeatable. We can dam
the ever-changing flow of experience by so restricting the
parameters of permissable observation that we force events into
fixed forms.

Hermeneutics recognizes that each experience has certain
unique and certain typical qualities, but that unless one severely
limits events by methodological fiat, every experience will be
different. Science's problem is replication, hermeneutics' is reproduction. How does one communicate unique events to another?
How does one translate experiences of a person, epic, or culture
into a form which will be understood by another person from
another time and another place?

Freud and Jung were translators. Freud's translations transformed accounts of mystical experiences, which he himself had never had, into a dialect of causality and reason which to him and many others is the language of reality. He saw mysticism as 'the obscure self-perception of the realm outside the ego, of the id' (1941, p. 300). For both him and Jung, mysticism was a perception of unconscious forces. Freud traced these back to childhood and primitive mental factors still operating in the psyche. With this he thought he had explained them scientifically. He had not; he had explained them psychoanalytically, within a historical, causal, narrative scheme.

For Jung, revelation was anything but obscure. Mystical experience was immediate and overwhelming. However, to make such experience understood by rationalists he felt he had to translate the insights which had been produced by humankind about the unconscious, the transcendental, and the mystical into a contemporary language. He could not accept either causality or reason as the givens of explication, for he saw them and the world-view they created as antithetical to what he was attempting to reproduce. Analytical psychology works to a great extent by analogy because only through analogy did Jung feel he could reliably reproduce the sense of the systems he was trying to understand.

One learns a great deal more from Jung on mysticism than from Freud. This is because Jung had extensively studied mystical texts and had had numerous mystical experiences. For the modern reader he can be hard to follow at times because to create an understanding of mysticism he sometimes adopts a rather archaic, mystifying style. Freud's pronouncements on religion, mysticism, and the occult – although hermeneutically inadequate because they are nearly barren of confrontation with the texts of these traditions – are easy to read because they are in harmony with the whole thrust of modern rational discourse.

Myths for both Freud and Jung were projections of unconscious psychic contents into the world. Freud (1901b) saw his psychology of the unconscious as providing an explanation of the origins of mythologies. Jung saw his as a translation of mythologems into modern language. Because of Jung's conviction that myths express truths about psychic reality his investigation of them was extensive and his presentation of this material involves comparatively little distortion. Myths for Freud were illusions; they contained a truth but in distorted form. In his work there is little close textual interpretation of myth. He writes broad summaries shaped by his psychoanalytic focus. This is nowhere more forcibly shown than in his rendition of the Oedipus story. From but one version, Sophocles' tragedy, he found a single theme: lust for the mother and hate of the father. What of the other elements: the blind prophet, dual parentage, exposure of the infant king, self-blinding producing insight, the heroic search, and the unheeded oracle? In myths Freud sought to find the manifestations of actual life conflicts. He found them, first because he was an adept interpreter and

second because they are there. After all, myths are forms of
human communication and will therefore be infused with human
drama.

Myths are structures for organizing experience that are no
longer perceptual givens for the critical consciousness that
views them as fictions. When we discovered we could create fictions, an event which drastically altered consciousness, we
created the modern conception of reality by attempting to clearly
demarcate the real from the mythic. Science took reality; art
took fiction. Its products restricted by the criterion of correspondence with reality, science's creativity is both focused and
limited. Since fictions may be either reproductions of the real,
or purely fictive, or a combination of the two, art has a broader
range in which to create but less focus in its researches. Fictive
constructions in science - its 'as if' hypotheses - must be tested
by an observable correspondence with reality or a reality which
can be built by methodological practice. The fictions of art have
no such limitations: their eventual success depends on their
ability to communicate and thereby create a shared understanding of experience.

There is a unity in the programs of both art and science and
this is in giving form to what exists. Both are finding that
expressing what exists is an endless task. A myth that has died
by ossification is no longer a living fiction which endlessly
recreates the truth. A dead myth 'operates within the diagrams
of ritual, which presupposes total and adequate explanations
of things as they are and were; it is a sequence of radically
unchangeable gestures.' Living myths are fictions 'for finding
things out, and they change as the needs of sense-making
change' (Kermode, 1967, p. 39). A moribund myth is a dogmatism, and such myths call for absolute assent. They are agents
of stability. Fictions are agents of change requiring only condi-
tional assent.

Attacking the fictions of religion, with an attack which would
have to apply to all fictions, Freud tells a story:

> I am reminded of one of my children who was distinguished...
> by a ... marked matter-of-factness. When the children were
> being told a fairy story and were listening to it with rapt
> attention, he would come up and ask: 'Is that a true story?'
> When he was told that it was not, he would turn away with a
> look of disdain. We may expect that people will soon behave
> in the same way towards the fairy tales of religion. (1927,
> p. 29)

The truth criterion of reality correspondence is crippling to
fiction and the matter-of-factness of dogmatic rational materialism
destroys the beauty of ideal creation. To insist on finding the
real at the root of all fiction is the activity of a childish mind
uncomfortable with the ambiguities of existence. Outlawing fiction would seriously damage psychoanalysis and would abolish

analytical psychology.

Hypotheses - scientific fictions - are killed by dogmatism, by statements like 'we possess the truth.' The power of science lies in its ability to overthrow its operating premises and replace them with fresh hypotheses in a continual cycle of discovery, elaboration, certainty, questioning, and rediscovery. If reality were knowable then the scientific task would be finite, but it appears that the realization of the scientific program lies in an infinite future of research. It is the essence of a fruitful myth, fiction, or science to leave an enormous amount open and to produce constant new inventions from within itself.

The development of critical consciousness, of being able to live within the 'as if,' is a necessity for modern individuals. The spirit of inquiry is at the heart of our age. Living in the heritage of Freud, we are all philosophers of suspicion and Jung, in questioning Freud's orthodoxy and rebelling against analytic dogmatism, simply carried forward the critical dialogue of the twentieth century. Freud found in his fictions scientific truths for he required them to correspond with a reality which he in part created through interpretation. Jung found in his fictions a myth which he assumed we are all living within. Neither attained that true critical attitude, described by Stevens, which provides for the continuous renewal of consciousness: 'The final belief is to believe in a fiction, which you know to be a fiction, there being nothing else. The exquisite truth is to know that it is a fiction and that you believe in it willingly' (1975, p. 163).

BIOLOGY AND HISTORY

With his devotion to reality and materialist sensibility, Freud grounded his hermeneutics in biology. Psychoanalytic biology, however, is not a natural science, but a mode of discourse within which Freud speculates on cultural and historical processes. Jung recognized that analytical psychology was a historical discipline concerned with the evolution of the psyche. His attempts to link his history with biology were superfluous speculations. An examination of Freud's and Jung's writings on instincts, archetypes, and psychic structures will uncover the interplay of biology and history in their theories and an examination of their ideas on feminity will serve to show the effects of a historical change in consciousness on both men's work.

Instincts are both the biological base on which psychoanalysis is built and the pinnacle of Freudian speculation. Freud needed the instincts as a source of biological drives which provide the impetus for psychic functioning, and yet instincts must be inferred from their behavioral and psychic manifestations. Freud hoped for biological confirmation of his instinct theory; however, in the end he turned to mythology and folk psychology to justify his dualism between Eros and the death instincts.

What could be more fundamental than life and death, love and hate? Realizing that instinct theory is psychoanalysis' mythology (1933b) - an 'as if' which functions as a working hypothesis - Freud used the parallels between his theory and Plato's myth of the androgyne, and the story of creation in the Upanishads to bolster his hypothesis that instincts seek to *'restore an earlier state of things'* (1920, p. 57). In the beginning there was a unity, but this was torn asunder and ever since the instincts have been trying to reestablish the primal order. Eros - love, the impetus to create binding unities - moves by continuous combination to restore oneness. Death instincts, by destroying everything and leading life back to a quiescent state, try to achieve the same end which was the state of things in the beginning. Freud's final instinctual dualism is homologous with typical stories of the origins of life and therefore an archetypal variant, phrased in biological terms, of an age-old myth.

Archetypes are perceptual predispositions to order experience in certain typical patterns. Freud in finding the mythological parallels for his biological speculation was engaged in what Jung saw as the primary activity of analytical psychology. Jung felt that analogies with the ancient put his psychological observations into their historical setting.

Instinct and archetype are terms of mediation between the collective and the individual. 'We regard instinct,' Freud says, 'as being the concept on the frontier-line between the somatic and the mental, and see in it the psychic representative of organic forces' (1911b, p. 74). Freud bridged the Cartesian chasm between body and mind with a concept that has its origins in species-typical biological processes but its manifestation in individual psychic functioning. Instinct is a causal mechanism of transmission linking the individual to the species and the present to the past. Instinct and archetype are antonyms because the term instinct belongs within a materialist, scientific frame and archetypes within a historical, artistic field of signification. Archetypes mediate between culture, spirit, or history and the individual. They represent within the individual psyche the heritage of eons of symbolic activity on the part of our species.

Using Haeckel's formula for phylogenetic causality - ontogeny recapitulates phylogeny, and his own scheme of developmental determinism - the child is father to the man, Freud seemingly produces a causal, biologically based explanation, grounded in instinct theory, of adult behavior and modern civilization; although, as we have seen, Freud's evidence concerning the folkways of our remote ancestry and infantile mental life was drawn primarily from observations made on present-day adults in psychotherapy. In addition to instincts, Freud also felt that memory traces of endlessly repeated traumatic events in human history - observation of parental intercourse, seduction by an adult, and castration threats - were inherited. He says the individual 'fills in the gaps in individual truth with prehistoric truth, he replaces occurrences in his own life by occurrences

in the life of his ancestors. I fully agree with Jung in recognizing the existence of this phylogenetic heritage' (1918, p. 97).
By 1919 Jung had renounced the theory of inherited ideas.
Freud never did and the inheritance of traumatic memory traces
is central to one of his last works, 'Moses and Monotheism'
(1939).

With the notions of instinctual inheritance and primal fantasies
being a phylogenetic endowment, Freud fused his search for
historical origins with biology; the phylogenetic memory trace is
the biological recorder of historical trauma. Psychoanalytic
biology is far removed from the speculative neurophysiology of
the 'Project.' It is a biology constructed from psychoanalytic
observations and it provides a framework for psychoanalytic
interpretation. Like Freud's history, its origins are in the verbal exchanges between analyst and analysand.

Primitives killed their fathers, seduced their children, and
castrated their sons. After all, they had to because this would
explain the existence of phylogenetic memory traces of these
events in the psyches of modern people. Unable to find the
real event within the patient's life history, Freud created it in
the past and saw it recreated in the present because of a biological predisposition. We have seen this same tactic used in
Freud's development of his two fundamental 'biological concepts'
- primary process and primary narcissism. It is Freud's technique
of establishing causality speculatively and retrospectively.

A common characteristic appears in the points of origin in
psychoanalysis: primary process, primary narcissism, and primal
fantasies. None of them are actual events; they are all fictions.
Freud, in discovering the past, creates it. He cannot with
certainty uncover the original forgotten event in his therapeutic
practice, nor does he describe verifiable origins of life in his
developmental scenarios. What Laplanche and Pontalis say about
the primal scene applies to all the primaries and primals of
psychoanalysis, 'Since it has proved impossible to determine
whether the primal scene is something truly experienced by the
subject, or a fiction, we must in the last resort seek a foundation
in something which transcends both individual experience and
what is imagined.' They conclude that Freud uses primal scenes
'less in order to provide a reality which escapes him in individual
history, than to assign limits to the "imaginary" which cannot
contain its own principles of organization' (1968, p. 9). This is
giving Freud more credit than he deserves. Freud was looking
for and discovering what he considered to be real events.
Laplanche and Pontalis are, however, correct in that Freud's
achievement is not in discovering real events, but in creating
structures for the understanding of experience. Primal fantasies
or archetypes are not realities, they are guidelines for the
construction of reality.

Freudian biology is a morphology of the psyche. Instincts are
psychical representatives of somatic forces; phylogenetic memory
traces are not engrams in the brain but psychic precipitates of

primal traumas. Both instincts and primal fantasies as unconscious structures can only be known through interpretation.
Their explanation is not found in natural history, but in the
interpretation of the analysand's life history. 'Freud, the biologist, hungry and impatient for sound laboratory data on which
to hang the most profound speculations on human behavior,
reached the end of that known world [of biology] early in his
studies' (Stoller, 1972, p. 246). Biology came to furnish for
Freud a language in which to articulate his discoveries. Freud's
use of biological concepts, however, cuts them off from what
is essential to biology - reference to material objects. Instincts,
the bridges between biology and psychoanalysis, are psychical.
Something psychic is not material; 'What is psychical is something so unique and peculiar to itself that no one comparison
can reflect its nature' (Freud, 1919, p. 161). Freud employs
biological concepts in instinct theory and metapsychological
speculation in order to provide something seemingly solid by
which to represent the unique psyche he is describing. 'But
such is Freud's genius that, in order to describe imaginary
structures, he makes use - with exemplary indifference - of
an imaginary anatomy' (Laplanche, 1976, p. 141). When Freud
uses biological terms there is a slippage in their meaning which
parallels a change in what is being described; the alteration
severs them from what is materially signified by them and
thereby breaks the connection to the fundamental referent of all
biology. Psychoanalytic fiction is created by this disjunction.
Primal occurrences, Eros, and the death instincts in order to be
imagined are transposed into terms borrowed from biology. Their
legitimation will not be found in biology or in reference to the
material world but in the practice of psychoanalysis and the
world of the psyche. The fusion of biology and history in Freud's
search for origins creates a psychoanalytic vision of humans in
nature and history.

Freud's use of Haekel's formula nicely demonstrates the transformation he works on biological concepts when he uses them
for psychoanalytic purposes. Haekel's law - for it was once felt
to be a near scientific certainty - is that the development of
anatomical structures and to some extent functions in individual
members of a species parallels the evolutionary development of
the same organs in the history of the species. The law was a
mainstay of embryology, comparative anatomy, and evolutionary
theory. Freud simply transferred Haekel's formula to the psychic
sphere and employed it as justification for his premise that
psychic ontogeny recapitulates the mental history of homo sapiens.
There is of course no biological justification for this move.
Natural history is not noted for its investigation of human communication, which produces artifacts of the mind. Biology provided Freud with a convenient formula to use as a justification
for psychoanalytic speculation about infantile and primitive
mental life. Of course, in his use of Haekel's law, Freud presents
no material evidence demonstrating similarities between primitive

thought and infantile mentation. Freud showed, working backwards from adult mental functioning, that he could construct a model of primitive and infantile mental functioning. If, like Jung did, Freud had made a more thorough use of the texts and other products of communication created by our ancestors he could have demonstrated parallels in psychic functioning between primitives and moderns. This would not have established a causal connection, but at least it would have shown an analogical coupling.

Freud felt that natural science had produced a solid collection of discoveries on which it would build in the future. One of these was Haekel's hypothesis which Freud took as a given. Biologists no longer abide by Haekel's law. The current view is that both embryological development and evolutionary history are very complex and cannot be easily analogized and certainly not causally linked with such a simple formula, and that Haekel's law is at best a useful metaphor. If this biological given is overthrown then it would seem that havoc would be created for psychoanalysis which conceptualizes human functioning as a progressive unfolding in the individual of the past history of the species. However, this is not necessarily the case. Haekel's law was from the beginning used by Freud in a metaphoric way, although he did not see this himself. In psychic functioning, Freud is saying, there is a recapitulation just as in biological functioning. The slippage in the transfer of the formula from biology to psychoanalysis which severs the connection from the material saves psychoanalysis from problems which might arise out of the current dismissal of Haekel. Of course, in saving Freud's formula - psychic ontogeny recapitulates mental phylogeny - we must recognize that he used it retrospectively, creating a non-material ontogeny and phylogeny by analogy with observations made on adult neurotics.

Evolutionary biology is currently confronting the historical problem of the present's shaping our view of the past. It is coming to see that its constructions of what proto-humans must have been like are clearly influenced by contemporary cultural values. Victorian biologists, in their society of competition, saw our progenitors as savage competitors engaged in the survival of the fittest; twentieth-century biologists, immersed in a technological society, see our anthropoid ancestors as tool-using animals. Dominated by male researchers, biology has until recently primarily emphasized the male's role in evolution, but feminist researchers have now begun to explore the part played by females in our evolutionary past. Certainly our ancestors have not changed so we must have. As science develops a history it will, like the arts, philosophy, and social and political history, come to realize the importance that ideological influences have on its findings. When it does this and enters into a critical examination of itself as well as nature it will come closer to being a hermeneutic discipline.

Although Jung makes passing references to Haekel's formula

and speaks of an inherited brain structure predisposing individuals to reproduce similar fantasy motifs, such arguments are
sheer speculation on his part and detract from the actual evidence which he has for the existence of archetypes. His evidence
is that imaginative and cultural products of the ancients and of
non-Western societies are strikingly similar to those of modern
Western Europeans. The evidence is hermeneutic and is based
on textual exegesis. He needs no other evidence. He has shown
that we have carried forward a cultural heritage of symbols.
He accomplished this by using an analogical method and demonstrating that our dreams and fantasies are like those of our
progenitors.

His biologizing takes the form of postulating that this correspondence is caused by a similarity of brain structures or by
some genetic mechanism, for example, his statement that the
'anima is presumably a psychic representation of the minority
of female genes in a man's body' (1940, p. 30). This speculation,
for which he has no biological evidence, is harmful to his hermeneutic proof for two reasons. The first is that it leads him to
speak of archetypes as causal agents in biological functioning.
His methodology does not establish causality, but his supposition that if archetypes could be shown to be localized in certain
regions of the brain, then it would be possible to understand
the production of a toxin in schizophrenia as an aberrant biological defense against an archetypal seizure is clearly causal
(1958c). This is a reshaping of his original theory of dementia
praecox into archetypal form, but there is not much change: a
psychological complex in interaction with a toxin causes schizophrenia. He had no more evidence for the existence of a toxin
in 1958 than he had in 1907 and he certainly had no evidence
that archetypes invaded the body and acted as causal physiological forces. Jung realizes this is all speculation, but it is
imprudent. Archetypes cannot be used as physiological agents
because to do so Jung must transform a psychic structure into
a material force, he must transmute that which is found by introspection and interpretation into an object. Early in his work
(1914a) he realized that such alchemy was a mistake for it was
analogous to the error the ancients made of projecting into matter what were psychic realities. Jung has made this same error
by projecting the archetypes into the gray matter.

The second harmful effect of such speculation is that we
modern scientific materialists take it far too seriously. We know
that all genetic material is not divided up along masculine and
feminine lines, we know that there is no biological evidence for
the inheritance of a predisposition to form similar symbols, and
we wonder how a predisposition could ever seize the brain. We
can use all this to dismiss Jung's work as scientifically unsound
(see Kline, 1972). Jung's speculation is not supported by modern
neurophysiology or genetics, but these fields are not at a stage
of sophistication where they would want to rule out too many
things as impossible. The more important point is that Jung's

work does not require any natural scientific support. He never claimed his work was natural science and he has provided hermeneutic evidence in support of his interpretative psychology.

Jung usually links the notion that individuals have archetypal perceptual predispositions to similarities in brain structures, but in one passage he moved from this cephalo-centric view towards a much more viable hypothesis: 'The whole anatomy of man is an inherited system identical with the ancestral constitution, which will unfailingly function in the same way' (1931c, p. 371). The brain does not live by itself. Our bodies are quite similar to those of our ancestors and we live in a world that in its essentials has not drastically changed. An ecological psychology would hold that similar organisms in similar environments produce similar products – behaviors, fantasies, houses, rituals, etc.[3] As environments and organisms change, variations will be worked on the fundamental pattern. Human environments differ not only because of geographic variations but also because of cultural differences. Archetypal images are shaped and molded by cultures and individuals so they are not equivalent, but there are fundamental human concerns which are represented in remarkably similar symbolic forms across cultures and down through history.

We are all born into cultures and the *'origin* of the unconscious must be sought in the process that introduces the subject into a symbolic universe' (Laplanche and Leclaire, 1966, p. 161). What transforms us from a natural state to cultural beings is a natural human process of acculturation. The unconscious is the unknown background out of which consciousness arises and into which consciousness can only penetrate with the light cast by interpretation. Symbol systems are diacritical and like figure and ground the symbol defines itself against all that it is not. And so consciousness, as a sign for the known, the cultural, the light, and the present, defines itself against the unknown, the natural, the darkness, and the past. Freud defined human consciousness against the background of natural biological processes, Jung against historical symbolic processes. Each man's work was devoted to making the unconscious conscious, to showing how the backgrounds they constructed were forces in human psychic development.

Freud came to house all his background events – instincts, primary process, primary narcissism, latent dreams, and primal fantasies in the id. An imaginary structure, the id is a psychic agency which is on the border between the somatic and the mental. True to his biological determinism, Freud says the id is inherited; true to his methodology, this basic structure is the culmination of his speculation on psychical topography. In the id Freud managed to merge under the rubric of the death instincts all those processes that he had inferred as existing from the beginning, but could never observe. The notion of the death instincts holds that life moves towards death by trying to restore a quiescent state undisturbed by the demands of life itself.

This, of course, is what primary process, the pleasure principle, and primary narcissism were all pointing towards, a non-object-related state where any disturbance was quelled as quickly as possible. What were once the primary states of sexuality came to be the manifestations of the death instincts. The id is the null-background to which all life returns and from which everything develops, for under the aegis of Eros culture-building moves forward guided by the libidinal drives, secondary process, the binding of energy, and the development of the ego.

With the id (das Es) Freud created the ultimate in psychic structures, an internal 'it' which was in all its manifestations foreign to the I, the ego (das Ich). But, the unconscious becomes progressively known by interpretation and so the alien takes on form. If the id is inherited it must contain phylogenetic memories which, if they function like other memory traces, bind energy and thereby channel thought. Just a year before his death Freud noted, 'The hypothesis of there being inherited vestiges in the id alters... our views about it' (1941, p. 299). Was another revision of psychoanalytic theory at hand? If the id contained memory traces it would not only be a biological structure but a historical-cultural one as well. It would contain more than mere predispositions to form similar fantasies; it would carry their actual inscription; it would be a collective unconscious which contained the real events for which Freud had so diligently searched in the life histories of his patients and in human pre-history. Biology would indeed become destiny for our past, which for Freud was the only determinant of the present and future, would be engraved within us from birth. History would be obliterated because life would simply be an ontogenetic repetition compulsion of phylogenetic events. Freud's methodology of finding the past by speculations based on observations made in the present would be totally inverted as he found in the present nothing but transcriptions of the past.

Where Freud saw the past made present through biological inheritance, Jung saw it made present in the heritage of symbols which are the cultural background into which each new being is born. He wrote of the inherited unconscious, but his methodology speaks clearly to the fact that he was exploring our collective unconscious heritage; that is, through interpretations of ancient texts he was renewing their meaning for modern individuals, and through the interpretation of the fantasies of his patients he was showing them that they shared in imagination a great deal with their ancestors.

A historical methodology like Jung's must speak of heritage and not inheritance. His descriptions of the archetypes of the collective unconscious are of figures from the past, dramatis personae clothed in antique costume: the anima, the animus, the wise old man, the magician, magna mater. Although Jung speculates that there is a biological predisposition to form fantasy images such as these, we know that there is a social predisposition sedimented in our language, our myths, our stories, and our dreams which forms a heritage that molds the mind of each individual from the day he or she is born into the symbolic universe that we call culture.

Historical distance provides perspective on some of Freud's and Jung's difficulties with the interplay between culture and biology. At some point in the future what they were saying may be as obscure as alchemical texts are to us today, but for now the passage of time allows us to see in their writing the ideological imprint of their age. Nowhere is this stamp more pronounced than in their theories about women. Cultural consciousness about women and the relations between the sexes has changed significantly since Freud and Jung wrote. Around the issue of feminity we can gain an analytic distance on their theories, finding in them a bias we no longer share. This does not argue that the essence, if there is one, of feminity and masculinity is known; it does assert that it can be shown that Freud's and Jung's views evidence the sexism of patriarchal prejudice. Both men used their theories to speak about the nature of women. The further development of the twentieth-century feminist movement has thrown into doubt much of what they said. What we have come to see as female traits and behaviors created by the subjugation of women, Freud, using arguments based on biological determinism, and Jung, using historical determinism, explained as natural.

Both Freud and Jung could have listened to the feminists of their day, and if they had read Adler's work - 'The archevil of our culture...[is] the excessive pre-eminence of manliness' (1910, p. 88) - they could have gained some insight into their overvaluation of masculinity. Both men rejected feminism. Freud was direct; he said that individuals with feminist sympathies would disagree with his psychoanalytic theories about women by arguing that his view was shaped by a masculinity complex. He dismissed the objection, maintaining condescendingly that it was understandable that feminists should reject views which stand in the way of their desire to achieve equality with men (1931). Freud held that his position was objective. He did not see that it might be understandable for him to accept the ideology of male superiority which pervaded his culture. He felt so secure in his beliefs that he was able to dismiss the possibility that he had accepted them for self-serving reasons.

Freud bases his theories about women on biological arguments, but his 'biology' is wrong and is not even really biology. The most blatant error he makes is the assertion that in their development girls must give up 'phallic like' clitoral eroticism, putting in its place vaginal pleasure. This is, of course, a way of gaining no physical pleasure at all since the clitoris is the female genital organ most sensitive to stimulation.

If he is wrong about physiology, Freud, by his own criterion, is wrong about women for he says he has 'only been describing women insofar as their nature is determined by their sexual function' (1933a, p. 135). His argument, which he feels applies

to all women, and rests on biology, comes down to the statement
that for women in analysis:

> We often have the impression that with the wish for a penis
> and the masculine protest we have penetrated through all the
> psychological strata and have reached bedrock, and that our
> activities are at an end. This is probably true, since for the
> psychical field, the biological field does in fact play the part
> of underlying bedrock. (1937a, p. 252)

A 'wish' and a 'protest' are not very close to any form of biological statement. *People* wish and dream, not material objects.
A wish is a desire voiced in words or by the body in symptoms.
Explanation of these desires is not to be found in biology, but
in the interpretation of the analysand's life history which must
take into account cultural forces influencing maturation.

Biologically the penis is the male organ of copulation and in
mammals it is composed of three columns of erectile tissues. It
is, as a material object, prosaic. When Freud says that with the
discovery of the wish for a penis he has reached biological bedrock, he is not really saying that his female patients' desire
for a cylindrical tube of erectile tissue explains their difficulties.
Although he tries to treat the penis as a physical entity, he is
clearly influenced by all its social connotations. Here again the
sliding of meaning from the material object to its psychical
representative has taken place. The body is infused with meaning and the penis is a very significant object in our culture.
Its psychical significance is both biological and cultural, but
Freud is nearly oblivious to the ways in which cultural attitudes
towards the penis have affected his opinion of its biological
significance.

Those who argue that in his works on female psychology Freud
correctly observed the plight of women and was using the penis
as a metaphor for masculine power have failed to realize that
he rarely used the penis as a metaphor for anything. For him
the penis was not a phallic symbol; it was the central biological
object to which metaphors refer. Biological determinism for him
meant that masculine social power was a manifestation of having
a penis and female inferiority a symptom of being without one.

From his supposed objective biological distinction of penis/no
penis Freud sets out to consider the psychical significance of
this anatomical difference. However, the difference, as he
phrases it, is not anatomical. Having a clitoris is not a condition
of not-having-a-penis. A clitoris is a perfectly respectable organ
and as such it is neither inferior nor superior to a penis. It is
inferior only in a theory which values the possession of a penis
above all else.

From penis/no penis it is not far to masculine/feminine, and
Freud (1913) claims that the differentiation of masculinity and
feminity is one of the psychoanalytic links to biology. With these
terms Freud smuggles more cultural presuppositions into his

'biological' determinism. One of the forms in which masochism is observed, Freud says, is 'as an expression of the feminine nature' (1924, p. 161). He continues: there are three forms of masochism and 'Feminine masochism... is the one that is the most accessible to our observation and least problematical... we have sufficient acquaintance with this kind of masochism in men' (p. 161). What? Masochism in men is evidence for feminine masochism? In fact, Freud's case examples for feminine masochism are all drawn from the fantasies of men! These include such ideas as being castrated.

Freud has moved far beyond biology when men's fears of castration are seen as evidence for the existence of feminine masochism. He provides a quasi-biological scenario which attempts to justify, by explaining in natural instead of cultural terms, his society's misogyny. The story goes like this: a little girl when she discovers she does not have a penis, or in other words that she is castrated, renounces her own clitoris as inferior, rejects her mother as the cause of her genital deformity, and lusts after her father who possesses the valued organ. Her genital wound is at the root of her narcissism and masochism. A fantastic tale, perhaps, but according to Freud, it is supported by observation and involves almost no speculation (1933a). The observations come from the analyses of adult women in therapy and for Freud there was little speculation involved in reconstruct-ing the childhood past from the adult present. Given Freud's account we are encouraged to believe that decades of living within a culture which restricted their activities, told them they were inferior, and idolized masculinity had not affected these women's recollection of girlhood - a girlhood, moreover, in which they had already been subjected to these same cultural forces. Culture's power is its invisibility, its ability to create the illusion that what humans do within it is natural. Freud was culture-blind and historically naive in failing to see that his reconstruc-tions of women's pasts were symptomatic of his and his milieu's prejudices against females.

The significance of male and female goes far beyond anatomical differences. The words are antonyms standing for two worlds developed and sustained by culture. Jung surveyed the history of these lands and found the women's world to be that of Eros: fertile, dark, and rich in feeling. This is a land that men find mysterious, dominated as they are by Logos: reason, the spirit, and dry intellect. Jung admits that what men see in women is influenced by their own projections. Masculine consciousness is balanced by a feminine unconscious, the anima, which is moody, emotional and mysterious; women's consciousness is compensated by a masculine unconscious, the animus, which is opinionated, rationalistic, and argumentative. Each sex projects the unknown in itself on to the other sex. That Jung's description of female character is nearly equivalent to his description of the uncon-scious in males is consonant with his theory of complementarity, but it exposes a fault in his method. Rooted as he was in his

own male-dominated culture and immersed in the texts of
patriarchal societies, he inferred what was natural from cultural
evidence. The distinction male/female exists in all societies and
every group elaborates around this dichotomy typical fantasies.
Jung inferred from these that a natural difference, going beyond
genital anatomy, exists between men and women. Historically,
he can assert that men have identified themselves with Logos
and women have been identified with Eros. Whether or not women
themselves hold such an identification is hard to ascertain
because men controlled the cultures from which Jung took his
evidence. We do know that men have traditionally identified
women as mysterious, emotional, intuitive, and irrational. To
claim that this is woman's nature because she has for so long
seemed this way to men is to deny women a voice in describing
their own psychology and to deny the possibility and desirability
of change.

One of the instruments of change in a culture is education,
and the founding of women's colleges was an important step in
improving women's place in society. About such institutions Jung
says, 'You know there are peculiar institutions in America called
universities and colleges for women; in our technical language
we call them animus incubators, and they turn out annually a
large number of fearful persons' (1935, p. 147). It does not do
to take what Jung intended partially as a joke too seriously, but
this is nevertheless an excellent example of his prejudice. He
felt that women's colleges encourage women to develop their intellect, that is their unconscious masculine side, their animus.
Thus, college-educated females are unnatural creatures dominated
by the unconscious.

Jung was not joking when in speaking of a woman patient he
said that her mentality 'had that peculiarly protesting quality
such as is unfortunately often encountered in intellectual women'
(1928, pp. 158-9). Such animus-possessed women, dominated
as they are by their intellects, are always trying to point out
faults in others, are extremely critical, are far too personal in
their attacks, and always want to be considered objective; 'This
invariably makes a man bad tempered' (p. 159). It is interesting
that Jung presents this as an objective portrait of intellectual
women and is very critical of *their* personal faults. Is Jung himself animus-possessed? Or is all this pontification on women's
psychological nature simply personal animosity on his part?
Denigration of women's powers of reason has long been a bastion
of male claims to superiority.

Jung, however, valued women highly. He felt that their inherent psychological acuity, emotional sophistication, sensitivity to
others, and intuitive gifts were greatly undervalued by our culture and that women should lead the way in developing these
qualities in both themselves and men (1927). He acknowledged
the contribution that women had made to his work both as
patients and as analytical psychologists. These women accepted
their 'feminity,' as the title of Harding's book, 'Women's

Mysteries' (1955), shows. In this now standard analytical psychological work on female psychology Harding carried forward and
elaborated the myth of women as dark, feeling, mysterious creatures. Jung's introduction to it warns that feminism may be
dangerous because when 'a woman develops too masculine an
attitude - something that may very easily happen owing to the
social emancipation of woman today - the unconscious compensates this one-sidedness by a symptomatic accentuation of certain
feminine traits' (1948b, p. 520). The example Jung gives of
these symptoms is a woman alienating herself from her husband
by always insisting she is right.

Jung's message to women is clear: do not become masculine.
That is, do not be intellectual or dogmatic or insist on your
rights. If you do you will alienate men. Your own powers are
great; develop them. The doctrine of separate but equal all too
readily becomes discriminatory. A positive valuation of women
may be as sexist as a negative one if it leads to the assertion that
women are incapable of doing what men do and to the warning
that they had better not try for if they do they will make men
cranky.

Unless the equality of women is acknowledged, unless their
abilities and opportunities to do whatever they wish to do are
not questioned, we will never know what women are like. For
ages men have controlled the means of production in society,
have dominated the academy, and monopolized the ideological
machinery of culture. How can men find out what women are like
unless they listen to women and enter into dialogue with them?

If a woman must fear that her intellectual capabilities will make
a man 'bad tempered' then she dare not speak her mind, at least
to men. Jung's prejudice against intellectual women probably
hampered him in really talking to any woman, because if a
woman became critical, or tried to argue intellectually, or insisted
on her rights, he saw her as stepping out of her natural role.
Having her reason belittled as a symptomatic expression of her
unconscious would lead her to an emotional protest that she
really was being reasonable, just as anyone protests if his or
her arguments are being undercut by psychological interpretations. Certainly Jung protested in a very emotional way when
Freud questioned the objectivity of his theories and assessed
them as neurotic symptoms.

It has been amply demonstrated that women are able to exercise
intellect. Reason is not a masculine trait, nor is intellectual
ability some natural gift bestowed upon men at birth. Emotionality
may be encouraged in women by men who are afraid to recognize
it in themselves, but if they cultivate it men will find that feelings come as easily as reasons.

Women's studies as an academic discipline is fairly new and that
a special field must be created for the study of women is a testimony to the sexism of our culture. Women are finding their own
voice and what they are saying about themselves and about men
is radically different from what either Freud or Jung said about

males and females (see Dinnerstein, 1977; Miller, 1976). The
conditions which make genuine dialogue possible between the
sexes are just coming into being. To find out what women want,
dream, think and feel one should talk with women, read their
books, see their art exhibits, and live with them in equality.
Until this happens, psychological theories about women, even if
supposedly based on biology, are liable to be mostly a statement
of cultural values.

CASE AND TEXT

Freud's case studies have become historical documents recording
what drove people mad around the turn of the century. Each of
his studies contains carefully drawn portraits of supporting
characters, a detailed biography of the protagonist, and a narrative of great complexity which weaves together the intricacies
of interpersonal interactions. Most important, he has created
people we remember - Lucy, Dora, Little Hans, Rat Man, and
Wolf Man. We have seen Freud's use of fictional techniques. The
greatest fiction one can create is the illusion that as one turns
the pages of a book a life unfolds before the eyes. Freud achieves
this illusion because his cases are so relentlessly referenced to
the real. Through words he creates a world which we all know:
illicit love affairs, tyrannical fathers, beautiful mothers, fears
of this and ecstasies over that.

Novels are used as resources for historical studies because
the writer in creating a good fiction must draw heavily upon
reality. Be they factual case histories using fictional techniques
or fictions based on real life, Freud's cases bring us into contact with the experiences of his characters. Unlike most fictions
or histories, where the author's character remains unknown and
therefore those prejudices which shape his or her account remain
hidden, Freud's texts open easily to a deeper understanding.
Not only do Freud's case stories contain their own analysis,
but his analyses lend themselves to further interpretation because
their author is so well known to us. This makes his work so
much more interesting because it is not the product of some
unknown being called the researcher or the historian, but is the
work of someone we are familiar with and since we know him we
know how he is prone to exaggerate some points while leaving
others out. The façade of absolute truth is created by works
which have become divorced from life because we know nothing
of their authors who live as disembodied observers. The truth
of psychoanalysis which is so vitally alive in Freud's cases is
the presentation of analyst and analysand trying to make sense
out of experience.

Freud's cases exploit our sense-making propensities for he
gives us a complex causal narrative about mothers, fathers,
brothers and sisters all of whom, we feel certain, must play some
part in life's drama. Jung's case studies fail because they are

cut off from life. He does not create memorable characters; in
fact the lives of his analysands remain unknown to us. When he
gave up the analytic-reductive method he sacrificed a report of
the details of life which are so necessary in engaging the reader's
sympathy. While under Freud's influence, Jung's histories were
captivating because the lives of his patients were presented to
us - for example, his analysis of a woman suffering from an
hysterical attack because of her secret love for a friend's husband
(1912b). After breaking with Freud, Jung attempted to demonstrate the inadequacies of the reductive interpretation of dreams.
But his analysis shows the technique's strengths for instead of
an elaborate exegesis relating dream symbols to ancient mythologems we learn of the dreamer's relations to real people (1958b).

The synthetic-constructive method which Jung first used in
analyzing Miss Miller's fantasies dominated his analytical psychological case histories, and this method, as we saw with Miller,
tells us little about the analysand's actual life. In one major case
study, 'A Study in the Process of Individuation' (1950), the
analysand is forgettably named 'Miss X.' We learn that she
greatly admired her father, did not like her mother, was well
educated, and began working with Jung when she was in her
fifties. In a sixty-page case, one-and-a-half pages are about
Miss X's actual life. The rest is devoted to an analysis of the
development of mandala images in a series of her paintings and
to establishing the symbolic parallels between these and alchemy.
In Jung's only other extended case study, 'Individual Dream
Symbolism in Relation to Alchemy' (1936), we find out even less
about the person whose dreams are being interpreted. The
analysand is simply named 'the dreamer.' Wishing to rule out
any personal influence he might have on 'the dreamer,' Jung
had the man work with another therapist and keep a careful
record of his dreams. These dreams are rich in symbolic content
and Jung beautifully illustrates their detailed symbolic similarity
to alchemical images and the progressive development in the
dreams of mandala symbols. However, we find out far more about
alchemy than we do about 'the dreamer.' Jung declares that he
has purposely removed the dreams from the context of the man's
life. He is using them as a modern text in which he will demonstrate parallels to ancient thought.

As examples of textual interpretation, and not case studies,
Jung's analyses are exceptional. He is careful to reproduce the
original material - Miller's fantasies, Miss X's paintings, and
'the dreamer's' dreams; and the parallels he draws with the
symbolic arts - mythology, mysticism, gnosticism, alchemy -
and Christianity are nearly overwhelming. There is in his
hermeneutics a concern for the old texts and a willingness to
explore in detail the symbolic worlds they create. An entire
volume of his collected works, 'Aion' (1951), is given over to
an exploration of the psychological significance of Christian
symbolism and by the time his studies of alchemy were complete
he had written over 1500 pages on that mystical art. Jung's

textual analyses succeeded in demonstrating that there are detailed correspondences between the fantasies of modern individuals and ancient texts. Reading Jung's works, one learns a great deal about our symbolic heritage and his great success is that he brings the mystical into the realm of modern comprehension by treating it as a psychic reality, an attempt by humans to come to an understanding of their own being.

Analytical psychology is a synthesis of ancient wisdom and modern critical consciousness. Jung's analyses do not intrude on the texts he is analysing, but rather renew those works for the modern reader. Where Jung succeeds in bringing the interpreted to life, Freud fails. Works like his analysis of Michelangelo's Moses (1914b) or Goethe's recollection from 'Dichtung und Wahrheit' (1917a) nicely illustrate Freud's method of starting with pieces and from these constructing a meaning for the whole. Such works provide fine examples of his technique of interpretation, which is often hard to follow in case studies, and usually provide the reader with new insights about the interpreted work. However, they fulfill our psychoanalytic expectations; the interpreted recedes into the background and we realize we have learned more about psychoanalysis than about the work which Freud was interpreting.

This is certainly evident in 'Totem and Taboo,' where far more space is given to psychoanalytic theory than to a review of either totems or taboos. It is also evident in Freud's last work on religion - 'Moses and Monotheism' (1939). Both of these works show that Freudian interpretative methods can be used to construct psychoanalytic histories. Their evaluation must necessarily be done hermeneutically and both Jung (1939) and Ricoeur (1974) fault 'Moses and Monotheism' for essentially the same hermeneutic problem we found in 'Totem and Taboo:' Freud did not try to check his interpretations against the texts available to him. He found what he knew before undertaking the analysis - a personal god who is a transfigured father. If Freud had exposed psychoanalysis to a real encounter with religious works he might have discovered something new. Instead, in 'Moses and Monotheism,' a work which Freud called a historical novel, we have the scenario of 'Totem and Taboo' slightly altered and moved from its primeval setting to the middle east circa 1300 B.C. Freud's method of telling the story of Moses and the founding of Judaism is yet another example of how by analogy with his ideas on psychopathology he constructs fictional events in human history and transforms these into causal factors in phylogenetic and ontogenetic development (Jacobsen and Steele, 1979).

Late in his life Jung also confronted his religious heritage and his textual analysis is as original as Freud's is redundant. Jung's 'Answer to Job' (1952a) is a personal essay, a reaction on Jung's part to the beastly way in which Yahweh treats Job. The study is textually well-grounded and traces the evolution in God's character from a primitive tyrant through various transformations to His humanization as He suffers with the sacrifice of His son.

Jung succeeded in his textual analyses in bringing God to life, in making alchemy sensible to the modern mind, and much more. Phenomena he analyses be they the Mass (1954c), the Trinity (1948a), astrology or UFOs (1958a) become accessible to non-believers because he does not insist on their existence as a reality or even as a sign pointing to a reality, but as the expression through symbols of archetypal human concerns.

The people in Jung's cases do not come to life because they too are treated as psychic realities. We only know their fantasies and never their real lives. Freud's cases come alive because they are filled with reality, whereas his textual and artistic interpretations are nearly moribund because what he seeks in art, religion, and literature is the actual event underlying ideal creation. If humans lived by real events alone they would not have created fictions. Fiction goes beyond the real to express a mixture of the actual and the fantastic and the alloy is best appreciated as a psychic reality.

Two literary genres are carried forward in the works of Freud and Jung. Freud is an author in the 'base' tradition. He glorifies the intricacies of everyday life, delves into the seamy side of his characters' lives, and reduces the high flown and noble to the fevered imagination of souls suffering from sexual dysfunction. Jung's province is the 'noble' tradition. He finds in the daydreams of his patients images drawn from the symbolic arts, shows that popular fiction contains a recapitulation of classical myths, and demonstrates that even science must live by numinous symbols. Freud's case studies succeed because our lives are quite base and we find in his characters people like ourselves. His textual analyses fail because the noble is reduced to the base and therefore one no longer feels ennobled by it. Jung's cases fail because no baseness is left in his characters, who are all heroes and heroines, living out some mythic fate. His textual analyses succeed because he provides a bridge from our daily lives and our occasional moments of illumination to the world of the idealistic imagination made real because within his work one comes to abide in fantasy.

Paralleling the base and noble in literature are the scientific and artistic modes of inquiry. The former explores the material reality in all that exists, the latter seeks to create the ideal from all that is real. Freud infused his science with artistic gifts and Jung brought order and classification to the symbolic arts. Freud found the real in the ideal through the creation of fictions and Jung found in fictions expressions of the ideal, of human fantasies which are psychic realities. Each system is a combination of science and art – a systematic interpretative method whose goal is the creation of understanding – and as such both are hermeneutic disciplines.

11 HERMENEUTICS AND INTERPRETATIVE PSYCHOLOGY

We are born into a world of words and seek to articulate an account of ourselves, our history, and nature through words, those non-material atoms of culture. The psyche is the spoken and the unspeakable and its existence is coextensive with human dialogue. This history of the psyche is a narrative because the mind itself tells stories in its attempts to understand our individual and collective being. In the word, or its plastic equivalent, the image, the past, present, and future are endlessly reproduced and reinterpreted.

Freud, in the mechanistic style of his theorizing, and Jung, in his own way, make the point that we are both subject and object in explorations of the mind. Freud (1940a) points out that all scientific observation is made through the medium of our own 'psychical apparatus' and that psychoanalysis differs from all other sciences because the medium itself is the subject of analytic investigation. 'Although the mind cannot apprehend its own form of existence, owing to the lack of an Archimedean point outside [itself],' Jung says, 'it nevertheless exists. Not only does the psyche exist, it is existence itself' (1940, p. 12). It is through the many forms of dialogue that we explore ourselves, the world, and others. Natural science puts questions to nature, in introspection one questions oneself, and in conversation we discover the dimensions of another person's experience. This a priori of communication - humans talk with each other - is the sole presupposition of hermeneutics. This is also the methodological base of psychoanalysis and analytical psychology for both maintain that understanding is achieved through dialogue between analyst and analysand, and between interpreter and text, painting, sculpture, poem, scientific treatise, primitive myth, religious ritual, etc. After establishing what hermeneutics is, we will show that analytical psychology and psychoanalysis are hermeneutic disciplines and then we will explore the outlines of a psychology based on an interpretative instead of an experimental methodology. Only within such a psychology will the value of the works of both Jung and Freud be fully appreciated.

HERMENEUTICS

'Hermeios' referred to the priest at the Delphic oracle. The roots of the word hermeneutics lie in the Greek verb 'hermeneuein,' to interpret, and the noun 'hermeneia,' interpretations. These

344

words all point to Hermes, the messenger god, who is associated
with transmuting what is beyond human understanding into a
shape amenable to human comprehension. The forms of the word
suggest a general process of bringing the unintelligible to
understanding.

In the eighteenth and nineteenth centuries the work of Ernesti,
Schleiermacher, and Dilthey gradually dissolved the traditional
association between hermeneutics and scriptural interpretation.
Wilhelm Dilthey, 1833-1911, viewed hermeneutics as the methodological foundation of the Geisteswissenschaften. Dilthey's differentiation between the interpretative sciences, which explore
human cultural products 'from the inside,' and the natural
sciences, which investigate objects 'from the outside,' has been
preserved in the modern empirical differentiation between the
two disciplines. The distinction is between methods investigating
*'entities with which the enquirer can establish communication and
may at least in principle enter into a dialogue* [Geisteswissen-
schaften] and those with which this is not possible [natural
sciences]' (Radnitzky, 1973, p. 213). The domain of the interpretative sciences is human existence and their goal is the understanding of people and their creations.

The hermeneutic task is to aid communication in order to
facilitate understanding. Communication occurs between subjects,
not objects. Texts, works of art, human lives need not be seen
as objects; all of them are resources of communication carrying
meaning for anyone interested in them. All are capable of dialogue. The text, like a human being, must be aided in speaking,
and providing such assistance is one of the jobs of an interpreter. To treat texts or other humans as objects is to deny that
they can help us in comprehending them. It is to make them
needlessly opaque and to deny the possibility of an alliance with
them.

This does not deny that a text or a person can be studied as
an object. A book's pages may be counted, its sentences parsed,
its word frequencies quantified; a person's body may be measured, dissected and classified, her or his use of certain phrases
can be noted. All of this can be done without reference to the
meaning of a book or the significance an individual attaches to
his or her existence. However, if texts or people are viewed as
carriers of meaning then they are subjects capable of answering
our questions.

Control in the natural scientific investigation of objects is
achieved by observing them in empirical situations. For texts,
or other human products, including people themselves, *'one of
the main control mechanisms is the "answers" which the texts
themselves provide*' (p. 213). Objects speak only in a meta-
phorical sense; humans and their constructions radiate meaning
and speak the language of their creation. Their existence is
dependent upon the significance they carry. Texts, art works,
historical events, and people are lost, misplaced, or forgotten
when they lose their meaning; we speak of discovering a book,

of understanding an event or knowing a person when their meaning becomes important to us.

Understanding and language, meaning and method, history, and self-reflection are all interwoven in the creation of comprehension and to explore in detail what hermeneutics is we will examine its ideas on each of these.

For Heidegger, understanding is a condition of human existence. It is situational and historical. Understanding arises in dialectical, linguistic interactions with other people and the world; it is always 'in terms of' and 'in relation to.' Past experience, current intentions, and future expectations all shape understanding. The primary repository of the past is language and language is the medium through which we come to understand. Experience flows past with no need for words and without questions looking for answers. When we question experience we ask for understanding in terms of language. When our experience questions us we find our answers in language. Only when we commit the human action of questioning does our experience require interpretation, that is representation and re-representation in the multiple linguistic and imagistic forms through which humans seek to know.

The methodological goals of the interpretative sciences are radically different from those of the natural sciences. The latter seek to explain by manipulation and control. Hermeneutics tries to understand through participation and openness. Objects and methods used to investigate them cannot be separated because methods delimit what we shall see. The scientific method tells us that what is to be examined is an object and so defines a relationship to the observed. Every method is already interpretation, and a phenomenon seen through a different method will be another thing. Natural science with its objective method, doctrine of replication, and controlled situations which require causal explanation determines what it will find: objects in causal relationships which are stable over repeated observations. Gadamer counters this fixated notion of experience by saying, 'Every experience worthy of the name runs counter to our expectation' (1975, p. 319). Insight emerges from the negativity of experience and insight 'always involves an escape from something that had deceived us and held us captive' (p. 320). To be human is to question experience and to have counter-expectational experiences question us. Answers are always provisional. Only if we methodically limit life do we make replication possible. If we listen, experience and interpretation will teach us about internal and external reality; methodologies stressing control protect us from ourselves and nature.

The method of the interpretative sciences is consonant with the hermeneutic view of understanding experience. The method is simple: it is dialogue. We come to understanding, we establish meaning - mutual co-understanding - by the age-old dialectic method of question and answer. Meaning is not something locked up in the solitary person; it is established through language in

relationship to people, to their products, and to the universe.
Dialectic as the art of conducting conversation is an ongoing
process of questioning and answering. It leads to the formation
of concepts through the working out of a shared meaning. Dialogue is asking and answering, giving and taking, arguing and
agreeing, talking at cross purposes and coming to see the other's
point.

Dialogue is not always easy to achieve. The thrust of interpretation is to aid communication. Seeing a text as only words on
a page renders it mute. People are also made dumb by treating
them as objects or metaphoricizing them as machines. It is not a
metaphor to say hermeneutics helps a text to communicate because
an object is transformed into a subject if it has meaning for us
and if we aid it in speaking by asking questions, answering
questions, and listening.

The process of reaching understanding by establishing shared
meanings through dialogue can be represented in the image of a
circle. Concepts derive their meaning from a context, horizon
or circle in which they stand. And yet, the horizon is composed
of the interconnections of all the elements to which it as the
situating context gives meaning. Through dialectical exchange
between the whole and its parts each gives the other significance.
Understanding, then, is circular because in the complex inter-
relatedness of part and whole meaning comes to exist. This is
the hermeneutic circle. In relation to this 'thought figure,'
several key notions of the interpretative method can be presented.

First, the hermeneutic postulate says that there is no pre-
suppositionless knowledge and no unprejudiced inquiry. Meanings
are derived from prior meanings and we cannot ask fruitful questions unless we already know something about a topic.

Second, in attempting to understand texts or other people we
must try to do so on their own terms. One strives to understand
what a text says about the phenomena about which it talks by
listening to it and learning to see the things of which the text
speaks in its own language.

Our third point combines the first and second. The interpreter
has presuppositions, but tries to meet and understand texts or
other persons on their own ground. This sets up the dialectics
of exchange and the movement towards greater understanding
through successively revised interpretations. Prejudices must
give way upon exposure. If they do not then one's effort as an
interpreter has failed because conjectures must be continuously
checked against what the text itself says. If one is blinded by
dogmatism such checking operations will be a sham for one will
not be open to correction from one's partner in dialogue. The
main checking operation is the test of the part against the
whole, that is, seeing that each new interpretation of an element
fits with an emerging conception of the whole. If it does, then
a wider understanding is emerging. If it does not, then revisions
are needed in the partial interpretations or the emerging holistic
view made up of past partial constructions, or both. An

interpreter should not get so carried away with interpretations that he or she coerces the other into agreement or fails to see the corrections the partner or text provides.

The fourth point is that coming to understand involves a continuous movement back and forth from the part to the whole and back again from the whole to its parts. To capture this movement Radnitzky (1973) uses the image of different viewing altitudes. In looking at an object from various heights we gain different perspectives on it. Observation from a high altitude gives us a view of the whole object and perhaps some of its horizon. Lower level viewing eliminates an object's contextual horizon; its details come into view with the object itself forming the horizon. A detailed picture means giving up a view of the whole, a generalized portrait means giving up detail. A complete picture combines both specificity and abstraction.

The fifth point combines the third and fourth. The goal of interpretation is to arrive at a set of meanings which maximize the understanding of the parts in terms of the whole. Such constructions are evaluated by their consistency, coherency and configuration – the harmony of the parts with the whole. One moves towards a consensus within the interpretative circle, constituted by interpreter and partner, that increases shared meaning.

The circle is a rather static image and to discuss historical interpretation we need to slightly modify our figure of thought. The hermeneutic circle captures the synchronic aspects of comprehension. Understanding of a given time is broadened by interpretations which include more and more contemporary events. Synchronically, understanding expands in ever-growing concentric circles. We need an image that layers circles on top of one another in order to capture both the synchronic and diachronic dimensions. Such a figure is the hermeneutic spiral. If we visualize a spiral as a stack of circles with each opening into the one above and below it we will have an aid to help us see several points about history and hermeneutic methodology. The vertical dimension of the spiral represents time, with each new understanding being built upon and replacing an older circle of meaning. Our sixth point, then, is that understanding is open at both ends. We can always improve upon it. No matter how complete each circle is, it will eventually be an old, superseded meaning. Each new turn of the spiral brings into the open something new about a text or person and exposes some previous misunderstanding, misdirected presupposition, or hidden prejudice. The goal of interpretation is to make meanings manifest that have been unarticulated, unseen, or hidden by misunderstanding disguised as comprehension. The passage of time brings reflection on experience and reflection should bring new understanding. Historical perspective shows us that the past determines who we are and, in that understanding is retrospective, we see that the present determines who we were.

While synchronic interpretation broadens our comprehension

of contemporary material, diachronic explication situates the
material in reference to past and future. Our seventh point is
that through interpretation we can know more about a text than
the author knew, or more about an event in a person's life than
the person knew at the time of the episode or may know before
reaching an understanding of it with the interpreter. A text
reaches a point where it is no longer revised by the author; at
this point the work is revised by interpretation. The passage
of time, itself, changes the meaning of a work. Often commentary
tries to establish what a book would have meant to the author's
contemporaries. Such a reading usually radically alters our
present-day understanding of the work. An author writes in
order to communicate with contemporaries and with future generations. We can see the effect a book has had; it is hard for the
author to do so. We can know more about a text than the author
because his or her future is our past and hindsight, although
not perfect, is usually better than foresight.

To view a text as finished, to lock it away as having spoken
once and for all is to dismiss it. The same is true of an episode
in one's life. To declare that it is done with is to blind oneself
to its subtle manifestations in one's present and future activities.
Orthodoxy attempts to preserve unchanged the words of a text
and idolatry sanctifies a life thereby removing it from examination. Integration into the present, not preservation of the
past, is the work of hermeneutics. Through interpretation texts
and lives are saved from ossification and are renewed as living
creations.

While attempting to renew the past in light of present understanding the interpreter must also try to minimize his or her
distortions of the past. The eighth point is about checking
operations within the historical dimension. Taking a text as our
example, one must check interpretations by investigating parallel texts by the same author and texts from the same tradition,
and by examining the historical period of the text's creation.

Our ninth and final point is that as historical and cultural
differences between an interpreter and that which is interpreted
increase, the need for rigorous application of hermeneutics also
increases. Communicating with what is foreign, either because
of cultural or temporal distance, is more difficult than with what
is familiar. The hermeneut must become, especially with foreign
partners, acutely aware of his or her own historical and cultural
position. If one assumes that present-day Western knowledge is
incontestable, then dialogue is impossible, or at least extremely
difficult. Only through open dialogue, through the exploration
of one's own as well as the other's presuppositions, can understanding be improved. This is not easy.

To aid another person in understanding him or herself one
must be aware that the need for interpretation and the difficulty
of establishing communication will increase as an individual's
alienation from his or her peers, present actions, and the past
and future increases. In working with another person the

interpreter's goal is to establish co-understanding and aid the
individual in comprehending both the past and present in hopes
of making his or her future more viable. Just as interpretation
of a text is never finished, so coming to self-comprehension is
never complete; reflection is always open. 'In hermeneutical
theory, man is seen as dependent on constant interpretation of
the past, and thus it could almost be said that man is the
"hermeneutical animal" who understands himself in terms of
interpreting a heritage and shared world bequeathed him from
the past, a heritage constantly present and active in all his
actions and decisions' (Palmer, 1969, p. 118). Understandings
of the past and past understandings are always undergoing
revision in the present and future.

Hermeneutics is concerned with self-reflection and its methods
assume that people individually and collectively carry on a
continuous dialogue, called thought, about themselves and can
by thinking reach provisional understandings of themselves.
Since Nietzsche, Freud, and Jung, however, we can no longer
put our faith in the evidence of conscious reflection. 'Reflection
and consciousness,' Ricoeur declared, 'no longer coincide'
(1974, p. 172). Interpretation has become a process of getting
behind the surface of what is meant. Within the language that
constitutes us we all have an unknown partner in dialogue.
Consciousness can no longer be satisfied that its conversations
with itself produce total comprehension of being. There is
another speaking below the surface; the process of introspection
has become a hermeneutic situation. Even in ourselves we must
now try to help the other speak, to understand the foreign
language of the unconscious and look at conscious reflection
with an eye to seeing what it does not see. We have become
distorted texts in need of interpretation and although we can
never escape ourselves, we are capable of thought and reflection
and so we can take up different analytic perspectives on ourselves.

An interpreter who claims complete self-understanding and
objectivity puts him or herself outside the vicissitudes of time
and of the world and cannot practice hermeneutics. Such an
individual has become dissociated from what is being interpreted
by denying that his or her own understanding is linguistic,
historical, and dialectical, and is therefore provisional. Hermeneutics is a never-ending labor. Only through engagement with
another – a text, an event, another person, or the other within
ourselves – in an attempt to understand do we confront our
self-deceptions. Finding how one misunderstood is the origin of
new meaning.

Hermeneutics as a discipline is reflexive; its method encourages
examination of itself. The hermeneutic practitioner must be self-
reflexive, coming to know him or herself through encounters
with others. The horizon of the interpreter meets the horizon
of a text or another person and if the engagement is dialectical
both will be changed. Few, if any, absolute truths arise from

interpretation, for hermeneutics realizes that it is a human occupation and is therefore subject to history. Interpretation is a process not a product and self-reflection never ends. As Merleau-Ponty says,

> my confidence in reflection amounts in the last resort to my accepting and acting on the fact of temporality, and the fact of the world as the invariable framework of all illusion and all disillusion: I know myself only in so far as I am inherent in time and in the world, that is, I know myself only in my ambiguity. (1962, p. 345)

THE THERAPEUTIC AND TEXTUAL DIALOGUE

A novice at interpretation can see that Freud and Jung did not have a viable relationship. In their relationship they both violated repeatedly nearly all the hermeneutic guidelines for reaching co-understanding through dialogue. The gravity of their own experiences, the utterly convincing nature of their scientific visions, and each man's view of inquiry as competition blocked the co-operation necessary in any hermeneutic enterprise. In response to Freud's tenacity in defense of psychoanalysis, Jung became equally dogmatic in asserting his own position. Neither man, in the end, encouraged the proliferation of the other's thoughts.

They wrote better than they lived and each constructed a hermeneutic science. Although they failed in practicing with each other what they preached, and although Freud, in his conviction that psychoanalysis had the truth, failed to encourage the diversity of thought necessary in any discipline, they did establish hermeneutics as a method of investigation in psychology. The therapeutic dialogue and its analogue, textual interpretation, are the methodological core of both psychoanalysis and analytical psychology.

Before we synthesize our demonstration that psychoanalysis is an interpretative, and not a natural, science let us examine Jung's work. It is easy to show that hermeneutics is the method of analytical psychology because Jung correctly saw that his investigations were part of the interpretative sciences.

Like Dilthey, Jung stressed the role which empathy plays in interpretation. One feels a bond to a text or another person based on an intersubjective sympathetic resonance. Neither empathetic nor intuitive understanding, which are so little understood by rationalism, can be ruled out as sources of knowledge. They exist. However, they must be supplemented by a great deal of interpretative work in order to make one's insights clear to oneself and to another. Dilthey proposed several hermeneutic procedures by which to explicate an initial empathetic understanding and Jung's life work was an exegetics of a personal sense of connection with the texts of the symbolic arts. The sources of Jung's empathetic response are easily seen in the Preiswerks' interest in the occult, in his own religious experiences as a youth, in his adolescent admiration of Goethe, in his work with his cousin the medium, and in his own confrontations with the unconscious. These and many other experiences gave Jung a feeling of being connected with the gnostics, alchemists, and spiritualists. Although analytical psychology had its roots in Jung's sympathetic response to occult and Christian texts its evidence for a correspondence between these and the fantasies of modern individuals is developed in careful textual research. We have examined this effort in previous chapters and found Jung's textual hermeneutics to be satisfactory.

His hermeneutics is good, in part, because he clearly conceptualized what was involved in the activity of interpretation. He recognized that the interpreter and interpreted – the unconscious, a patient, or a text – must enter into a genuine dialogue and that from this exchange there arises a synthetic understanding. The unconscious for Jung was not an absolute unknown, but something constituted in relation to consciousness. The analytic process attempts to make the unknown known through a 'dialectical discussion between the conscious mind and the unconscious' (Jung, 1944, p. 4). Jung compares this intrapersonal conversation between the conscious and unconscious to an interpersonal exchange:

> It is exactly as if a dialogue were taking place between two human beings with equal rights, each of whom gives the other credit for a valid argument and considers it worth while to modify the conflicting standpoints by means of thorough comparison and discussion or else to distinguish them clearly from one another. Since the way to agreement seldom stands open, in most cases a long conflict will have to be borne, demanding sacrifices from both sides. (1958b, p. 89)

The role of the other in psychotherapy is taken by the analyst who provides another viewpoint either to the analysand's living out of unconscious fantasies by offering conscious criticism of them, or to the analysand's too critical consciousness by serving as either an advocate for the rights of the unconscious or as an embodiment of unconscious forces which have been projected on to the therapist by the analysand. Therapy is dialogue between analyst and analysand and Jung, realizing that dialogue requires interaction between two subjects, was careful to emphasize that the therapist cannot conceive of him or herself as an objective observer. Jung never tired of saying to analysts: 'Never forget that the analysis of a patient analyzes yourself, as you are just as much in it as he is' (1968, p. 439).

Because Jung's case studies focus on the establishment of symbolic parallels to the analysand's fantasies they fail to capture the interpersonal exchanges in the therapeutic setting. This is unfortunate, because in doing therapy one is all too

prone to seek refuge in objectivity as a defense against the
continual muddle of trying to create order out of chaos. One
magnificent passage in Jung's work will have to stand for the
thousands of unrecorded therapeutic exchanges in which neither
he nor the analysand were quite sure of what was taking place
but were engaged in talking with and trying to understand each
other. Jung reports that in response to his interpretation that
the analysand was projecting her own unconscious animus fantasies on to him, she said:

'What, so I am a man, and a sinister, fascinating man at that,
a wicked magician or demon? Not on your life! I cannot accept
that, its all nonsense. I'd sooner believe this of you!' She is
right: it is preposterous to transfer such things to her. She
cannot accept being turned into a demon any more than the
doctor can. Her eyes flash, an evil expression creeps across
her face. ... In her glance there lurks something of the
beast of prey, something really demoniacal. Is she a demon
after all? Or am I the beast of prey, the demon, and is this
a terrified victim sitting before me, trying to defend herself
with the brute strength of despair against my wicked spells?
All this must surely be nonsense - fantastic delusion. What
have I touched? ... Yet it is only a passing moment. (1943,
p. 92)

Jung saw psychotherapy as a process involving four stages:
(1) catharsis, the analysand's confession of secrets; (2) elucidation, the linking together of fantasies with life's experiences;
(3) education, the formulation of what can be done to change
one's life; and (4) transformation. The last stage refers to the
revolution in personality that effective interpersonal interaction
produces. In therapy both analysand and analyst are changed.
Speaking again to analysts, Jung says, 'You can exert no
influence if you are not susceptible to influence' (1929a, p. 71).
To practice either hermeneutics or analytical therapy, one must
be open to experience and be amenable to the transformations
which another person or text can work upon one's soul. To think
that one no longer has anything to learn or that one's illusions
have been forever dispelled is to put oneself beyond life, history,
and the possibility of change.

We have seen the centrality of dialogue and interpretation in
Jung's views on introspection and therapy; we now turn to an
examination of the role of hermeneutics in his textual analyses
and work in general. About the interpretation of ancient texts he
said,

The importance of hermeneutics should not be underestimated:
it has a beneficial effect on the psyche by linking the distant
past, the ancestral heritage which is still alive in the unconscious, with the present, thus establishing the vitally important connection between consciousness oriented to the present

moment only and the historical psyche which extends over
infinitely long periods of time. (1955-6, p. 336)

Archaic texts are the material memory traces of our heritage
and contain a view of the world which has been lost to modern
consciousness. Reading such texts transforms one's vision of
life because one comes to see experience in a different way.
Jung's goal in interpreting symbolic works was to keep our
Western spiritual heritage alive in an age when consciousness
has seriously capitulated to materialism. The spiritual vitality of
any myth, world-view, or fiction depends on its continuity and
this, Jung felt, could 'be preserved only if each age translates
the myth into its own language and makes it an essential content
of its view of the world' (p. 336). Myth is preserved by orthodoxy, but in the end dogmatism kills myth by protecting it
from an encounter with history. Living myths, true fictions,
are constantly undergoing change because they are continually
exposed to experience. Jung renewed the ancient by locating it
within the unconscious of every person and thereby making a
confrontation with it a necessity for the development of self-
knowledge. To know oneself became a process of discovering
one's symbolic heritage. The old myths were transformed by him
into a modern discourse on human psychology. Analytical psychology bears the stamp of the mythic and this is a mark of its
success as an interpretative science, for Jung's work was transformed by his encounters with the symbolic arts.
   Jung's conviction that knowledge depends on self-reflection,
his declarations that the analyst must not be an objective observer in therapy, his fiat that the interpreter must let the text
work its magic on him, and his repeated assertion that all truth
is transitory and must be continually renewed through translation puts his work within hermeneutics and outside of the
natural sciences.
   A discussion of whether or not analytical psychology is a
natural science is contained in an exchange of letters between
Jung and Bennet - a psychotherapist, friend, and biographer
of Jung. In a review of one of Jung's works, Bennet (1960) said
that the hypothesis of the collective unconscious was useful in
explaining psychological phenomena, but it lacked a scientific
foundation. Jung wrote to him that this hypothesis was useful
in explaining things and so it was scientific. Bennet responded
that applicability was not the sole criterion of science; natural
scientific proof claims that for certain phenomena there is 'an
invariable order in nature' (1961, p. 96). Scientific proof means
that a phenomenon is 'capable of being checked and observed by
others and found to possess an unchanging predictable order'
(p. 98). Bennet and most people see chemistry and physics as
having achieved this sort of proof and think that psychology in
its present state cannot reach this plateau. This is because
there is so little agreement in psychology about fundamentals and
whether or not certain forms of evidence are acceptable.

Jung responded that all proof need not be material. In law courts where proof may decide someone's death the jury must rely on facts which are often of a non-material sort. He says, 'It would be too much to expect chemical proof in a murder case, yet the case can be proved by legal methods quite satisfactorily. Why should psychology be measured against physics - if one is not a member of the Leningrad Academy?' (Adler, 1975, p. 566). Jung claimed that his work was scientific because he observed, classified, established relations among observed data, and even tried to show how predictions could be made. He felt the difficulty over understanding his theories as scientific was that in Anglo-Saxon countries what is meant by 'scientific' is 'physical, chemical, and mathematical evidence. On the continent, however, any kind of adequate logical or systematic approach is called "scientific"; thus historical and comparative methods are scientific' (p. 567).' Jung places his work with history, anthropology, ethnology, and mythology, all of which are disciplines of the Geisteswissenschaften, the human or interpretative sciences. Within these, the canons of evidence are hermeneutic, not material or hypothetical-deductive.

While Jung located his work within hermeneutics, we must show that psychoanalysis is an interpretative science because Freud mistakenly conceptualized his work as a natural science. Having just said that psychoanalysis is a part of psychology and equating, in his usual way, the methods of psychology, psychoanalysis, and physics, Freud wrote 'Psychology, too, is a natural science. What else can it be?' (1940a, p. 282). The question is obviously rhetorical, but one should not ask questions if one does not mean to start a discussion. Freud opens the discussion for us with another comparison between psychoanalysis and physics; this time he finds them dissimilar. He notes that a physicist does not need a patient in order to study X-rays, 'But the only subject-matter of psycho-analysis is the mental processes of human beings and it is only in human beings that it can be studied' (1926, p. 254). At the level of observation, and Freud explicitly states that for any science there is a single foundation and 'that foundation is observation alone' (1914c, p. 77), the natural sciences and psychoanalysis are radically different. The analytic investigator enters into dialogue with what is being investigated; the physicist does not. Apel (1972) and Radnitzky (1973) use the simple fact that the analyst's observations are made in relation to an 'object' which can communicate to make the psychoanalytic therapeutic dialogue paradigmatic for the Geisteswissenschaften.

Not only is therapy hermeneutic, Freud's entire work establishes an interpretative science. There are great similarities between Freud's and hermeneutics' conceptions of understanding, language, meaning, method, and self-reflection. Freud's interwoven ideas concerning these issues remained stable over the course of his work and constitute the hermeneutic center of psychoanalysis. We will proceed by first investigating Freud's interlocking formulations concerning understanding, self-reflection and language. Next we will see the concurrence of psychoanalytic verification procedures and hermeneutic checking operations when we examine Freud's work on meaning and method and then we will deal with Freud's misconstruing of psychoanalysis as a natural science.

Understanding between analyst and analysand takes place in language; 'Nothing takes place between them except that they talk to each other' (Freud, 1926, p. 187). However, they converse under very special conditions, those laid down by the fundamental rule of psychoanalysis which holds that the analysand must report whatever comes to mind without criticizing it. The rule is fundamental because it confronts the analysand with the demand that not only are secrets to be told, but that even thoughts kept secret from him or herself are to be divulged.

The analysand's difficulty is one of knowing and not knowing his or her problem. This paradox for a psychology of consciousness is not a mystery for psychoanalysis because of its formulations concerning unconscious mental processes. For the analysand, the difficulty of understanding him or herself becomes the problem of making the unknown, known; the unconscious, conscious; of having the 'I' (ego) come to be where the 'it' (id) was. The problem is one of avowing that which has been disavowed or unrecognized. The analysand comes to self-understanding by attempting to follow the fundamental rule and by listening to and working with the analyst's interpretations. Psychoanalytic explanations provide plausible reasons for the analysand's thoughts and actions and if the interpretations are correct the analysand will - at least ideally - come to agree with them in the long run (Mischel, 1965). Freud says, 'The patient may say: *"Now I feel as though I had known it all the time."* With this the work of analysis has been completed' (1914a, p. 207).

The client's coming to self-understanding depends on the aid provided by the analyst's interpretations and constructions. In order to understand the analysand, the analyst must have reached some understanding of him or herself. Self-reflection is indispensable in analytic practice. While the analysand is pledged to follow the fundamental rule, the analyst must make a similar commitment to open communication. Freud recommends to any physician practicing psychoanalysis that he 'must put himself in a position to make use of everything he is told...without substituting a censorship of his own for the selection that the patient has forgone' (1912c, p. 115). The analyst must be receptive to experience. As an analyst, one must not be selective in one's listening or have one's discernment biased by warps in one's own personality. The analyst is the measuring instrument in analysis and so must be as free as possible from prejudice. The analyst, Freud cautions, 'may not tolerate any resistances in himself;' resistance creates distortions and hence the recommendation that all analysts 'should have undergone a psychoanalytic purification' through a self-analysis or a training analysis (p. 116). Twenty-five years later this recommendation was stronger: every analyst must have a training analysis; he should use this as the basis of a continuing self-analysis; and because his analytic work in its preoccupation with unconscious material will create biases in him, 'every analyst should periodically - at intervals of five years or so - submit himself to an analysis once more' (1937a, p. 249). This makes the analyst's analysis interminable and requires a commitment to an ongoing process of introspection. Psychoanalysis and analytical psychology are two of the very few disciplines which demand methodical self-reflection. A picture is forming of the interlocking circles of interpretation, understanding, and reflection required for analytic insight to be achieved. The analysand's self-understanding is dependent on the analyst's own self-comprehension and as an analyst one is always either the analysand of oneself or another analyst. Understanding in psychoanalysis is based on the existence of a community of individuals devoted to the ongoing activity of self-examination. This commitment to self reflection, and not instinct theory or infantile sexuality, is the foundation of psychoanalysis.

Freud was fond of saying that 'the analytic relationship is based on love of truth - that is, on a recognition of reality - and that it precludes any kind of sham or deceit' (p. 248). This is not the material reality of the natural sciences nor the truth of a scientific law. The truth of analytic dialogue is that of shared experience formulated in language and the reality revealed is the one that lies behind the daily deceits of our lives. This is not 'truth understood as the correct statement, the historical fact - only in need of discovery to be brought to the surface;' it is 'truth as the emergent, the construction of something that makes sense and that therefore permits one to rely on it and continue living' (Loch, 1977, pp. 220-1). An insight emerges and illumination comes when we escape from the darkness of a self-deception which has debilitated us. The reality which comes into being does not last forever. Reality is not given, but created and recreated. Its continual renewal depends on individuals pledging themselves to dismantle their shams and build on more solid ground. New truth is constructed within the ever expanding circles of psychoanalytic dialogue.

Psychoanalytic understanding is intimately tied to language. From the inception to the end of his work Freud realized the power words have in both enslaving and freeing humankind. In investigating how we deceive ourselves by the distortions which language helps us create, Freud was employed in the hermeneutic endeavor of the critique of ideology or false consciousness (Apel, 1972). This is the task of using language to free ourselves from the false gods and misunderstandings we have created. The technique of free association frees speech from conscious intention. When that intention is self-deception then this liberation is a first movement towards emancipation from false consciousness. The interpretation of dreams, parapraxes, and symptoms requires the use of free association because the associations allow one to reveal the wish that has been disguised by the censor - the agent of false consciousness.

Freud equates speech with all expressions of mental activity including gestures and writing and says psychoanalytic inter-pretations 'are first and foremost translations from an alien method of expression into the one which is familiar to us' (1913d, p. 176). Hermeneutically, 'Neurotic symptoms ... are the scars of a corrupt text that confronts the author as incomprehensible' (Habermas, 1971, p. 219). Psychoanalysis and hermeneutics work to replace the incomprehensible by the understandable through interpretation.

Dream-interpretation is the foundation of psychoanalytic work and we know that for Freud 'All dreams have a meaning' (1913d, p. 170). Like dreams 'Parapraxes are full-blown psychical pheno-mena and always have a meaning and an intention' (p. 167). Meaning and intention are words singular to the human order and when Freud speaks of interpretation, translation, meaning, and intention he is using a human, hermeneutic language. This is not Freud's only language; he also uses the discourse of the natural sciences. In the same essay in which he speaks of the meaning and intention of dreams and parapraxes he says that 'psycho-analytic research has introduced law, order and con-nection' into the study of what was previously considered unpredictable (p. 174). Law, order, and connection, words used to describe the relations of objects in the natural sphere could roughly be replaced by understanding, intention, and meaning - words of the human sphere. To do so, however, would rob Freud of his own language of understanding: the discourse of the science of objects.

Let us recall the hermeneutic postulates: there is no presup-positionless knowledge. Freud came to understand people, in part, by using the conceptual system of his nineteenth-century scientific training, but we saw in chapters 3, 4 and 5 that because of his contacts with Breuer, Charcot and Bernheim, his interactions with patients, and his own self-analysis, this language and his understanding were modified. The conceptual scheme of natural science as the 'Project for a Scientific Psycho-logy' showed was not broad enough to bring coherence to the multifaceted objects he was investigating.

Throughout Freud's work there were two forces operating: the hermeneutic and the natural scientific. He was never satis-fied with interpretation alone. He always sought to go beyond it by constructing causes and explanations in the natural scien-tific language of his day for what had been observed and trans-lated. It is no irony that Freud's hermeneutic principles remained constant throughout his work while metapsychology, which was to anchor these principles to biological science, was forever changing. In psychoanalysis observation and interpretation pre-cede metapsychological speculation. Hermeneutics is prior to and the base for Freud's causal model-building, just as the chapters interpreting dreams come before the construction of the mental apparatus in 'The Interpretation of Dreams.'

In any system one needs different perspectives from which to check one's ideas. Metapsychology with its mechanistic, scientific language and its different points of view - economic, dynamic, and topographic - provided the perspective from which Freud checked his observations and interpretations. Metapsychological theory supports what Apel and Radnitzky call the quasi-naturalistic phase in therapy. It provides a language of objects which the analyst can use to order in the simple terms of machines, agencies, forces, and causal history the very complex events of human action. Psychoanalysis contains its own dialectic because by moving between hermeneutics and naturalistic explanation it improves the insights gained by each.

There is, however, a problem. Freud's metapsychological explanations are not naturalistic - they are quasi-naturalistic. Such explanations are both quasi-causal and quasi-naturalistic because Freud cannot avoid the use of intentional concepts. By calling quantitative considerations economic, Freud freed himself from purely Newtonian concepts of energy and thereby broke any connection with physicalistic physiology. The topographic point of view was freed from anatomy and so the mental apparatus was liberated from the confines of the cranial cavity. Natural science with its purely extensional language was too restrictive to allow Freud an adequate framework in which to articulate and check his observations. He maintains the general form of this language, but because it is coupled dialectically with his hermeneutics the language is expanded to accommodate intentional concepts and is thereby divorced from material referents. Naturalism becomes quasi-naturalistic explanation when it no longer serves to explain relations in nature, when it cannot be checked by observations made on objects, when it is put to use in understanding human beings as subjects with intentions, and when it must be checked through dialogue.

In chapter 5 we saw how Freud freed his language and thought from the confines of natural science to create psychoanalysis, 'a procedure *sui generis*, something novel and special, which can only be understood with the help of *new insights*' (Freud, 1926, pp. 189-90). And, we might add, a new language. Language became for Freud a medium for the construction of imaginary structures: topographical and structural maps of the mind. Derrida (1972) has shown that Freud's models of the mind move from brain analogues, to mechanical apparatuses, and culminate in a representation of the psychic system in terms of the relations among inscriptions on a Mystic Writing-Pad (Freud, 1925a). The mind, for Freud, came to reside not in the brain, but in language. Given his methods of investigation this is the proper place for it.

The canonical works of psychoanalysis - 'The Interpretation of Dreams,' 'The Psychopathology of Everyday Life,' and

'Jokes and Their Relation to the Unconscious' - all have a
hermeneutic theme, the bringing forth by interpretation of latent
meanings. In the dream book Lacan says there is 'absolute
coherence between his [Freud's] technique and his discovery'
(1977, p. 163). Using the methods of free association and interpretation, Freud discovered that dreams could be seen as a
distorted language which when translated was understandable.
If analyzing a description of a dream is the best way to understand the unconscious then it is a small step from Freud's ideas
to Lacan's: *'the structure of the unconscious is the structure of
language'* (Miel, 1966, p. 98). Hermeneutically, the unconscious
becomes 'a fragment of discourse that must find its place in the
discourse as a whole' (Laplanche and Leclaire, 1966, p. 126).
Meaning resides in the text of the analysand's speech in a latent
state. The analyst's job is to make it manifest. As was shown in
chapter 5, Freud's technique of dream-interpretation makes it
evident that the meaning of a dream does not reside in some prior
latent dream, but in the manifest dream and the analysand's
associations to it. Interpretation brings coherence to the dream
and associations by formulating a causal narrative that analyst
and analysand can agree on.

For the analyst, the analytic dialogue has two purposes: to aid
the analysand and to advance psychoanalytic knowledge in
general. Although Freud (1912c) at times felt that the goals of
therapy and science might be incompatible and although many
reject the case study as scientific evidence (Fisher and Greenberg, 1977), there is no conflict between therapy and research
in a hermeneutic discipline. Essential to any interpretative
science is the fusion of theory and practice. One simply cannot
separate one's method from one's speculations and findings.
Freud realizes this and states again and again that the findings
of psychoanalysis must be tested by the psychoanalytic method.
He also realized that this would be a cause for skepticism and
lead to questions about the scientific validity of his work and
yet he remained committed to the position that psychoanalytic
knowledge and psychoanalytic therapy are fused.

Unfortunately, Freud's belief that his work was science, and
as such discovered the truth, and his stance that either someone
was for or against him created a dogmatic system. He had not
developed the critical consciousness necessary to see that psychoanalysis was a method which constructed a causal historical
narrative, but that other methods, like Jung's, could formulate
different and yet equally plausible scenarios. His insistence
on orthodoxy kept his approach to enquiry from being either
truly scientific or truly hermeneutic. The inquiry itself, however, was hermeneutic. This is further demonstrated by Freud's
ideas on the establishment of shared meaning between analyst
and analysand, on what constitutes a psychoanalytic interpretation, and on how interpretations are checked.

To make known to the analysand that part of him or herself
which was unknown was the goal of psychoanalytic interpretation

from the beginning to the end of Freud's work. The effort of transforming the unknown into the known begins when understanding between analyst and client breaks down, when there are lacunae in the text of speech, and when there are gaps in the analysand's memory. It begins when 'He [the client] says something to you [the analyst] which at first means as little to you as it does to him' (Freud, 1926, p. 219). Given this failure of dialogue, the analyst, guided by analytic theory, his or her own self-analysis and previous analytic experience searches through all that has been said looking for the elements which form connections from which a meaningful interpretation can be built. The analyst, because he or she is listening with undivided attention, that is, not selectively listening in order to confirm or disconfirm hypotheses, has a wealth of material out of which to build interpretations. This material is gained through open communication, it is all linguistic as broadly defined by Freud, and it is used to create greater co-understanding.

Freud insists that the material of analysis, be it memories, associations or dreams, 'has first to be *interpreted*' before it is usable (p. 219). After this statement in 'The Question of Lay Analysis,' the 'Impartial Person' to whom Freud is explaining psychoanalysis objects. Similar objections are heard today from all those who think knowledge is gained only through controlled experience. The Impartial Person exclaims, '"Interpret!" A nasty word! I dislike the sound of it; it robs me of all certainty. If everything depends on my interpretation who can guarantee that I interpret right?' (p. 219). Opposed to this concern with security, fixity, and objectivity is the hermeneutic view that events will affect us, that we will misunderstand and have to interpret as best we can, and only provisionally, what is happening to us. Life comes with no guarantees. Freud has gone to the heart of fears about interpretation and his response to these is reason. The analyst's training, self-discipline, and analytic knowledge will help him or her make interpretations that will be independent of personal idiosyncrasies. After all, psychoanalysis does provide guidelines for interpretation and a standardized context in which observations are made. Also, the training analysis and self-examination of the analyst should free her or him from personal resistances which would distort interpretations. Freud concedes that 'This individual factor [the analyst's personality] will always play a larger part in psychoanalysis than elsewhere,' but agreements are still possible and much can be learned from 'the interpretative art of analysis' (p. 220).

Once the analyst formulates the interpretation, he or she finds out if it is correct by telling it to the analysand. In hermeneutics and psychoanalysis the main control on interpretation is the answers which texts or clients themselves provide. The analyst, of course, must be careful about when and how an interpretation is made. Part of the analysand does not want to know and resists any increase in understanding. The analyst must be ready for

resistance. An interpretation is made when the analysand is so
close to the knowledge that only one more step is needed for
him or her to make a decisive synthesis.

If resistance to an interpretation is met one does not argue it
down, but either interprets it or notes it for future reference.
Freud says his early view, that simply providing a patient with
knowledge about his or her symptoms would lead to improvement,
was mistaken; treatment only deserves the name of psychoanalysis 'if the intensity of the transference has been utilized
for the overcoming of resistance' (1913b, p. 143). The importance of the transference and its interpretation was commented
on by Freud as early as the 'Dora' case and remained a central
issue to the end of his work. Transference and resistance are
so vital because when transference serves the resistance the
analysand 'produces before us with plastic clarity an important
part of his life-story, of which he would otherwise have probably
given us only an insufficient account. He acts it before us, as
it were, instead of reporting it to us' (Freud, 1940a, p. 176).
The problematic real events of the analysand's past, which we
have frequently commented on, become unproblematic actual
events within the psychoanalytic session. The unknowing repetition of behaviors in the transference becomes the focal point for
interpretation. The analyst interprets these to the client so
that he or she may come to know them consciously, recollecting
and working through them, rather than repeating them. Freud's
search for the real event could stop here. About transference,
he says, it takes 'over all the features of the illness....It is a
piece of real experience' (1914f, p. 154). In transference the
analysand is showing the analyst 'the kernel of his intimate life
history: *he is reproducing it tangibly, as though it were actually
happening*' (Freud, 1926, p. 226).

Reality thus comes to reside in the ever-expanding circle of
meaning constructed by analysand and analyst. Freud (1918)
insures the sanctity of this shared experience and its explication
by saying there should be no court of appeals outside the analysis. This putting to the side of questions of outside or material
reality maintains the integrity of the analytic dialogue. If Freud
(1916-17) could maintain for all of psychoanalysis his position
that in the analytic situation it makes no difference if childhood
scenes are fantasy or reality and that for the neuroses what is
important is psychical reality, then psychoanalysis would be on
sound phenomenological and hermeneutic ground. The foundation
of all analytic knowledge could be the therapeutic session. In
practice this is indeed the case. Freud asked where evidence for
the etiological significance of sexuality in the psychoneuroses
is found; he replied 'the psycho-analytic examination of neurotics
is the source from which this disputed conviction of mine is
derived' (1906a, p. 278).

Methods and findings merge. Belying his claims that his work
was scientific, Freud states that a therapeutic procedure cannot
be conducted in the same way as a scientific investigation:

Cases which are devoted from the first to scientific purposes
and are treated accordingly suffer in their outcome; while
the most successful cases are those in which one proceeds,
as it were, without any purpose in view, allows oneself to be
taken by surprise by any new turn in them, and always meets
them with an open mind, free from any presuppositions.
(1912c, p. 114)

This is a clear and simple statement of what has been identified
as the hermeneutic approach to inquiry. If Freud had not been
so singleminded in his attempts to have psychoanalysis be seen
as a natural science he could easily have defended his work
on hermeneutic grounds. There are more efficient ways of checking analytic formulations than by the scientific method which
treats all data sources as objects incapable of entering into
an extended conversation. If the data source is a person who
can provide the investigator with information when asked, it is
inefficient to treat her or him as a mute object. The checking
operations Freud established assume that the analysand is a
partner in communication.

Freud reviews the analysand's possible responses to an interpretation (a formulation dealing with a single piece of material)
or construction (an interpretative account of an episode in the
analysand's history) and the most likely meanings of such
reactions. These responses provide specific checks on an interpretation. An analysis is made up of many constructions and
many checks upon them. The important point is 'Only the further
course of the analysis enables us to decide whether our constructions are correct or unserviceable' (Freud, 1937b, p. 265). The
parts, interpretations and constructions, must be checked
against the emerging whole. About dream-interpretation, Freud
says it is both possible and advisable to incompletely interpret
a dream and often the 'whole analysis is needed to explain it'
(1911c, p. 93). Dreams and symptoms are similar in that one
endeavors to lay hold first of this, then of that, fragment of
meaning 'one after another, until they can all be pieced together'
(p. 93). The dialectical relationship between analyst and analysand in the assembling process is nicely described by Freud:

The analyst finishes a piece of construction and communicates
it to the subject of the analysis so that it may work upon him;
he then constructs a further piece out of the fresh material
pouring in upon him, deals with it in the same way and proceeds in this alternating fashion until the end. (1937b,
pp. 260-1)

The end either to a dream-interpretation or, to add to Freud's
thoughts in the following quote, to the analysis as a whole comes
when analyst and analysand overcome doubt. The analyst, like
the client, may and perhaps should remain in doubt about some
interpretations and constructions:

What makes him certain in the end is precisely the complication of the problem before him, which is like the solution of
a jig-saw puzzle....If one succeeds in arranging the confused
heap of [puzzle] fragments, each of which bears upon it an
unintelligible piece of drawing, so that the picture acquires
a meaning, so that there is no gap anywhere in the design
and so that the whole fits into the frame - if all these conditions are fulfilled, then one knows that one has solved the
puzzle and that there is no alternative solution. (1923b,
p. 116)

The jigsaw puzzle is an image which is equivalent to the hermeneutic circle. Analysis is complete when the circle of meaning is
constructed. Meaning resides in the articulation of the parts with
each other and the whole. It is vital that the puzzle should fit
together precisely because any incongruities create doubt. Meaning resides in the scenario which answers the riddles of the
analysand's life. The solution is reached by the slow assembly
through interpretation and construction of narrative segments
and by the fitting together of these pieces to form a picture, a
narrative history, of the analysand's life agreed upon by both
partners in the dialogue.

Freud's jigsaw puzzle image demonstrates the similarities of
psychoanalytic and hermeneutic checking operations. There is,
however, something troublesome about the puzzle analogy and
it is the same problem which was pointed out in Freud's analogy
comparing the interpretation of dreams to the solution of a
rebus (see chapter 5). A rebus and a jigsaw puzzle are designed
by a puzzle-maker. For the rebus, we can compare our solution
to the one provided by the rebus-maker. In putting together
a jigsaw puzzle we often check our progress against the completed
picture on the cover of the box. Where is the answer for the
solution of the dream-rebus or the prototype for reconstructing
a person's puzzling life? The original text of the dream - its
solution, the latent meaning - exists solely as a product of interpretation; just as the analysand's life story with its gaps filled
in and its distortions corrected is a product of analytic therapy.
There simply is not a master with which to compare one's analytic puzzle solutions.

Freud, the master to many, would disagree. He asserts that
evidence is to be found in places other than treatment which
supports psychoanalytic hypotheses (1910c). This evidence is
primarily historical and comes from speculation on childhood and
the mental life of primitives. In chapters 5, 7, 8, and 11 we
have thoroughly examined the evidence from both these sources
and have found it to be unacceptable. We have shown that starting from observation of adults, Freud by analogy transfers his
insights to the past thereby constructing infantile and primitive
histories. He then treats these as causal determinants of the
adult present. In his historical studies Freud is not unearthing
real events but creating a world in which his explanations of

neuroses make sense. He is saying that adult neurotics behave as they do because civilization creates discontent and our primitive ancestors actually lived out the Oedipal drama. His studies of history are hermeneutically unsound because his reading of historical texts was superficial; he found in the past what he set out to find. His presuppositions were never challenged; the past was a recreation of the present.

In trying to convince his readers that there is evidence supporting his speculations on childhood, Freud endangers the credibility of the hermeneutic discoveries made within the analytic session by making false claims. He says 'We have become quite generally convinced from the direct analytic examination of children that we were right in our interpretation of what adults told us about their childhoods' (1926, p. 216). Brody (1970) has shown that Freud treated very few adolescents and only one child. When Freud made this overly strong claim child analysis was not widely practiced. The case of 'Little Hans' does not meet Freud's own methodological requirements for psychoanalysis. Freud's constructions about children were historical and he had no unequivocal evidence from the observation of childhood which validated his speculation.

Freud would again disagree. He asserts that analytic constructions about childhood have been confirmed by parents and nurses who have 'provided irrefutable evidence that these occurrences...really did take place' (1926, p. 216). But, we have seen Freud proclaim that such evidence must always be doubted and that one should not put one's trust in it. Also, only a systematic study of both confirmations and failures to confirm such constructions would produce acceptable evidence. Freud's theories about infancy and childhood have been put to the test by direct observation and treatment of children. The results are mixed. Our point, however, is that Freud systematically treats speculation as proof and this creates doubt about all his evidential claims.

Having stated that both direct observation of children and corroboration by adults confirms psychoanalytic views on childhood, Freud says, 'The correct reconstruction...of such forgotten experiences of childhood has a great therapeutic effect, whether they permit of objective confirmation or not' (p. 216). The first and last line of defense for him was evidence from psychoanalytic treatment. This is as it should be for all of Freud's findings and speculations came from the therapeutic encounter. Correctness here must be evaluated by the hermeneutic methods which constitute psychoanalytic checking procedures: the articulation of the parts with the whole, the arrival at shared meanings between analyst and analysand, and the maximal freeing from distortion of the analysand's life story.

Seeking an understanding of the present and future in terms of the past is a fundamental of human consciousness; 'We can say in a very general way that an understanding of consciousness always moves backwards' (Ricoeur, 1974, p. 113). The

key to the Freudian dialectic between consciousness and unconsciousness is that the unconscious is the unknown of childhood,
primitive, and biological experience out of which through interpretation present understanding is created. The meaning of
this unconscious background is created by the act of interpretation which makes the unknown known. Interpretation does not
reveal something biologically or historically real. It speaks of
desires which are themselves referents to a whole trail of wishes
and the derivatives of wishes caught in an infinite self-symbol-
izing system. The reflexiveness of consciousness is its ability
to backtrack along this trail of derivatives. Reading the signs
of its own development in history, consciousness attempts to
follow these pathmarkers of desire back to its origins.

Psychoanalytic case histories are narratives linking the life
of the individual to a general historical scheme. This scheme does
not uncover deterministic causes, but develops a framework of
general story elements – paradigmatic puzzle solutions – which
can be used for guidance in the reconstruction of individual life
histories. Psychoanalysis does what we all do: 'we look backwards, from the later to the earlier, in order to understand
the present as a lightly or heavily disguised re-enacting of the
problems of the past' (Hampshire, 1962, pp. 129-30). Looking
backwards into our past we can always find causes for what we
have become. Jahoda is correct when she says, 'analysis can
recognize causality retrospectively with certainty, whereas
prediction is impossible' (1977, p. 15). This is historical determinism and none of us would disagree that we can find the
influences of the past in the present. But, Jahoda and others
argue that Freud's retrospective causality makes his work a
natural science. If Freud's causality were strictly deterministic,
then it should allow prediction, but psychoanalysis is not predictive. Within the hypothetical-deductive paradigm of natural
science determining causality retrospectively is post hoc interpretation and is not accepted as proof for a hypothesis. Freud's
reconstructions were causal narrative explanations; they were
historical not scientific. They were reasonable interpretations
that helped make the past intelligible.

The slippage of Freudian terminology from the biological to
the psychical which severs any reference to material objects,
the fusion of biology and history in Freud's search for the
original conditions of human life, and the fact that his causality
is retrospective requires a shift in the criteria of success for
analytic explanation from those of the natural, or naturalistically
oriented social, sciences to those of hermeneutics. Given its
method and the language it has created, one robs psychoanalysis
of its uniqueness if one tries to fit it within the confines of
natural science from which Freud freed it in its creation.

But Freud constantly sought the certification that his work
was scientific because science was his faith, his bulwark against
illusion; science 'has given us evidence by its numerous and
important successes that it is no illusion' (Freud, 1927, p. 55).

In psychoanalysis, a field unsure of its successes, dependent
on the uncertainties of human interaction and misunderstanding,
and immersed in the investigation of madness, the value to its
practitioners of an assurance that one is practicing science cannot be underestimated. Such an assurance may, however, be
an illusion. Certainly the proclamation that science is no illusion
cannot be assessed scientifically and it defies history. For the
present science is no illusion, just as every current understanding and new insight is seen as revealing truth hidden by previous misunderstandings. Nineteenth-century science overthrew
the claims to absolute truth put forward by religion and unfortunately substituted its own dogmatism. As we move towards
the twenty-first century we are beginning to see science for
what it is, a human endeavor trying to make sense out of the
world. As such it exists in history and is therefore subject to
human reflection. Unless a dictatorship of reason, science, and
technology is established science too will someday be seen as
illusory. The history of human thought is the chronicle of
people overthrowing illusions to establish new truths, with which
in time they become disillusioned.

The improvement of thought requires reflection, formation of
ideas about ideas, interpretation, investigation, and critical
consciousness. While natural science does not include in its
method reflection upon itself, both hermeneutics and psychoanalysis do. Freud is all too aware that his cases read like fictions, that instinct theory is psychoanalysis' mythology, that
the analyst's constructions are similar to the patient's delusions
(1937b) and of other points that could shake any investigator's
certainty. We cannot grudge Freud, the great destroyer of illusions, the solace that the self-awarded stamp of science provided him; and yet, we cannot afford to sustain 'the scientific
self-misunderstanding of psychoanalysis inagurated by Freud
himself' (Habermas, 1971, p. 214). We have seen too much. We
have seen that psychoanalysis is a hermeneutic discipline because
for it therapy and research are unified; the analyst and analysand are partners in communication; the goal of the analytic
encounter is greater understanding reached by the analyst aiding
the client through interpretation to fill in the gaps in the client's
life story; the analysand's reactions are vital in assessing the
value of a construction; the analyst's personality always plays
a role in analysis; and, every analyst must be analysed because
he or she is the psychoanalytic measuring instrument. We have
seen the effects that Freud's own self-analysis, his personality,
and his conflicts with Jung had on psychoanalysis. We have seen
that: the work of psychoanalysis takes place in language; the
language of psychoanalysis describes the psychic not the material;
and that Freud constructs meaningful causal narrative histories
employing fictional techniques. We have seen that psychoanalysis
as a method functions by observation and interpretation in the
therapeutic situation, that reality resides in the analytic encounter and truth is founded upon co-understanding between

therapist and patient.

INTERPRETATIVE PSYCHOLOGY

Experience and interpretation are the dynamic complements of
human existence. If one controls experience by specifying what
is to be observed, by limiting the parameters in which observation is to take place, by assuring that all observation is standardized, and by training observers to be objective or in other
words not to let their own being influence what they see, then
one reduces, but does not eliminate, the necessity of interpretation in order to establish consensus about what has happened.
If experience is not limited, if the only parameters set on observation are the presuppositions of the experiencer, if one encourages individual confrontation with life, and recognizes the value
of subjectivity, then one expands the possibilities of experience
and increases the need of interpretation in order to reach agreement about what has occurred. The first approach is that of
the natural sciences and of the naturalistically oriented social
sciences; the second is that of hermeneutics.

Continually worried about its respectability as a discipline,
psychology has in large part opted for the first approach. The
procedures of this orientation when applied to interpretative
sciences like psychoanalysis or analytical psychology severely
limit the information which can be gained from them and disre-
gard a wealth of evidence for their validity. Fisher and Greenberg's massive study investigating 'The Scientific Credibility
of Freud's Theories and Therapy' (1977) illustrates this point.
In reviewing over a thousand studies on psychoanalysis they
felt the necessity to make rules about what was and was not
acceptable evidence. The way they formulated their criteria is
typical of psychologists who have abdicated their personal
responsibility for evaluating research and put in its place a
faith in experimentalism. They say that in citing evidence for
or against a Freudian hypothesis they did not 'rule out studies
that had defects in their experimental designs or that were
based on oversimplistic notions concerning Freud's models.' They
assure us that they cite only information gained by 'procedures
which are repeatable' and in which one can check on the 'objectivity of the reporting observer' (p. 15). Any study that meets
those scientific pillars of faith – repeatability and objectivity –
is acceptable even if it is badly designed and shows an obvious
misunderstanding of psychoanalysis. They rejected all case
studies. Allowing that these may contain interesting and important information, they assert that 'there is no way to separate
the good from the bad' (p. 15). Of course, they accepted both
good and bad experimental studies, but those have the advantage of appearing scientific. About case histories, Fisher and
Greenberg say that there is no way to tell if their authors
actually report what has happened or if the report has been

distorted to match the investigator's theory. They do not seem
to realize that their own massive review has been warped by their
supposition that experimental evidence, good or bad, is the
only acceptable proof. In their attempt to be scientific they have
so severely restricted their view that they have denied the
relevance of reports taken from the major investigative tool of
psychoanalysis - the psychoanalytic encounter.

In questioning the integrity of clinicians' case reports, Fisher
and Greenberg fail to see that the same questions can be asked
about all research work. How does one know that an experimenter has not shaped data to fit his or her hypothesis in some
way ranging from the innocent subtleties of experimenter bias
to the deliberate fraud occasionally perpetrated by a researcher
desperate to achieve some specific outcome? Because of the massive amount of interpretation required in summarizing and
grouping hundreds of studies, one can question whether Fisher
and Greenberg have in all cases reported exactly what a study
has found. Of course, one can check on an experiment by
repeating it, but, being a replication, that study itself has
been shaped in a way that the original was not. One can check
on Fisher and Greenberg by reading the original experimental
reports. One can check on the findings of a case study by
seeing if they are applicable in one's own clinical work or seeing
if they help one to understand oneself and other people.

Scientific techniques and hermeneutic methods can both be
misused. The only checks on misuse of any method are the
investigator's integrity and the community of investigators who
employ the technique. Objectivity in science is assured not only
because of method, but also because scientists can use agreed-on
checking procedures to evaluate the work of other researchers.
Open dialogue between analyst and analysand or interpreter
and text, which is the prerequisite for the practice of the
interpretative sciences, is insured by adhering to the principles
of hermeneutics and because the efforts of psychoanalysts,
analytical psychologists and hermeneuts can be checked by
other workers in these disciplines.

The fundamental tenets of these three fields are that understanding comes through dialogue and that to insure this we,
as interpreters, must be continually assessing ourselves and our
work. The hermeneutic principles presented in the first part
of this chapter provide an idea of how to do this and are methodological guidelines for the practice of a humanistic interpretative
psychology. Case studies or textual analyses can be read and
evaluated on the basis of coherency, logical consistency, agreement of the parts with the whole, openness of the investigator
to anomalies, and for the contribution they make to shared
understanding within a discipline. Any judgment depends on
educated subjectivity, on the study of how we come to understand ourselves and others. Analytical psychology, hermeneutics,
and psychoanalysis are all involved in this inquiry.

Interpreters, in their work and their evaluations of the work

of others, cannot rely on formulae. They must rely on themselves and on other people engaged in attempts to create co-
understanding. To do this they need to recognize that experience, as both Jung and Freud so often stressed, provides the
best evidence. The case study or analysis of a text attempts to
recreate for the reader the experience of understanding between
analyst and analysand, interpreter and text. To comprehend
another person, a case study, or a text one needs to be open,
to listen, and to see in another way. Case studies do not disclose
facts about objects, they construct life stories. To understand
a story we do not quantify it, we participate in it and reflect
upon it.

'Therapy is a restorying of life' (Hillman, 1975, p. 18). We
have seen how Freud's self-analysis formed his life story and
was part of the work necessary in establishing psychoanalysis.
We have seen his defense of his theories against Jung's criticisms
and have noted that their debate was over more than just their
theories; it was over the explanation of their own lives. Jung's
life story in turn was drastically altered by his visions during
and after the break with Freud and he recognized the degree to
which his confrontation with the unconscious shaped his life's
work. Their theories about the unconscious were in part so different because their experiences of this inner unknown were of
two different worlds. Freud in his self-analysis felt constricted,
sensed he was driven by forces from his past, and was sure
that his analysis had, when it was completed, put to rest many
of his difficulties. He turned outward again with relief and
enthusiasm. Jung, however, turned inward not against resistance,
but eagerly, and felt that his analysis opened up a new world
for him. He sensed a boundless expanse and a timeless internal
history which it would take him years to explore. We have
uncovered experiences the men did not report and have questioned their interpretations of what occurred to them, but their
experiences remain the radically different foundations of two
hermeneutic systems.

Psychoanalysis with its emphasis on biological determinism -
although our analysis has shown that determinism to be historical
and narrative rather than predictive - by necessity must speak
of adjustment for there is nothing else within this world-view
than to tune the machine to the demands of reality. Freud's goal
in therapy remained what it had been in 'Studies on Hysteria:'
to transform neurotic suffering into common unhappiness. This
is what he succeeded in doing with his own life. Jung's goal in
his therapeutic work was what he had sought in freeing himself
from Freud, attained in his own analysis, and provided a model
for achieving in his theoretical writing: 'We moderns are faced
with the necessity of rediscovering the life of the spirit, we must
experience it anew for ourselves. It is the only way in which
to break the spell that binds us to biological events' (1929b,
p. 339).

Body and mind, matter and spirit, reality and imagination,

instinct and archetype, are the great antinomies that divide the
work of Freud and Jung. Freud, committed to the real, constructed a hermeneutic grounded in the body, materialism, and
instincts. Jung, devoted to the realities of imagination, talked
of mind, spirituality, and archetypes. We must understand that
these words are antonyms of reflection and not of experience.
Experientially there is a bond between body and mind and
between these other pairs of opposites. Disembodied minds feel
nothing, mindless bodies know nothing. Matter and spirit, body
and mind are abstractions of reflective consciousness. The words
posit a difference for the purpose of analysis. What is posited
then becomes lived, as experience responds to reflection. The
notion of body highlights the sensate, material and corporeal,
that of mind the abstract, spiritual, fleeting. Consciousness,
immersing itself in the sensate frame, finds mind to be mysterious, or an odd emanation of physiological processes, or a ghost
in the machine. Submerging itself in the mental, consciousness
feels the body to be an illusory material manifestation of itself,
or a foreign object which can only be known through careful
observation, or a demon which must be denied by ascetic practices.

The duality of being is not between body and mind, but
between experience and reflection and this duality vanishes
when we realize that our existence will always be a narrative to
us, an unfolding story which we live and tell at the same time.
Experiences differ and so do interpretative systems which seek
to order experience. If we could give up the notion of right or
wrong solutions to life and see life as stories either well or
poorly lived and as a history which is relatively well understood
or in need of more investigation we would open ourselves to a
better understanding of our own and other people's narratives.

We might also free ourselves from the distinction between fact
and fiction which has haunted our being far too long and seems
to have been exaggerated lately by scientism and the 'cult of
the fact' (Hudson, 1972). The psyche mythologizes: it creates
narrative worlds which transform facts into fictions and fictions
into facts. Behind Freud's factual claims we have found fictions
and in Jung's study of the structures of imagination we have
found not the facts of reality, but the reality of psychic fictions.
We found Jung constructing a model of the psyche which recapitulated mythological themes and we found Freud creating biological fictions, imaginary psychic structures in which he ordered
experience. Experience cannot order itself and myths, fictions,
and hypotheses have always been used by people as coordinates
for orienting reflection.

Fact and fiction are yet another opposition born of the rhyth-
mic alteration of experience and interpretation. Experience is
always of the real, be it psychic or material, and is a factual
given. In experience we live in a single reality that is utterly
convincing. Reflection and interpretation create fictions as they
loosen being from the bondage of the fact and free consciousness,

allowing it to speculate. The world-creating powers of fantasy mold future experience as they shape our realities.

We need as many fictions as we can create for without fiction there is no plasticity in molding either our pasts or futures. Based on experience and reflection, Freud and Jung created systems that structure events through interpretation, that allow us to restory our lives, and that guide us into the future as maps direct us in unknown lands. For both men the unconscious was not this or that thing, but an internal unknown as it is perceived by us. That the two men mapped this land so differently is understandable given their lives, their self-analyses, and their philosophical presuppositions. The exploration of the unconscious requires both experience and interpretation. The word, itself, stands for what lies just beyond consciousness; it is the horizon towards which self-reflection is continuously moving. When we move beyond the boundary of the known we travel by speculation which comes to shape what we will discover with the next step of experience.

Let us not be bound in our explorations by the notion that all we can know lies without and by the naive empiricism of the nineteenth century which idolized direct observation of objects in the external world. Introspection is the fundament of true empiricism because it is a combination of internal and external perception, and of reflection upon what is experienced. Both Freud and Jung were empiricists in that their work began with and returned to experience. However, they practiced anything but naive empiricism because neither took what was given by perception as what was. They sought through interpretation, which is always reflection upon experience or upon reflection itself, to explicate the possibilities in being - to create fictions of what might have been and what might be.

Over the years one adopts and abandons many interpretative schemes as experience calls for this and then that point of view. As one uses psychoanalysis and analytical psychology to order one's own life and the lives of others an evidence accumulates for both theories, but this is not the proof - the hard facts - of the natural sciences. It is the far more convincing evidence of subjectivity, of experience ordered by reflection. The practice of the interpretative sciences requires a tolerance for ambiguity, an ability to live with partial understandings, and a willingness to accept a case formulated on circumstantial evidence. All cases remain open to appeal - life cannot be relived, but it can be retold - and this is as it should be. For the findings of all hermeneutic disciplines and the disciplines themselves must be endlessly reexamined. Without systematic self-reflection, the fate of both individuals and interpretative systems is to live in the illusion that present understanding is true forever.

Experience and interpretation open being to countless possibilities.

NOTES

2 RECOLLECTIONS

1 Page numbers not preceded by a date refer to the previous dated citation.
2 'According to Pestalozzi (1956) the real author of the essay was G.O. Tobler, a Swiss writer' (Strachey, 1959, p. 8). The ideas were Goethe's, but were recorded by Tobler after a conversation with him. Goethe then included Tobler's essay in his own works (Trosman, 1973).
3 Freud's explanation, fifty years after his change of plans, seems convincing; as a young man he had a great respect for Goethe and was happy to identify himself with the poet. The story of being moved to change one's career plans by a beautiful lecture also matches the romantic spirit of the essay. The letters to Fluss announcing Freud's decision to study science, however, do not mention this lecture and Grinstein (1968) could find no newspaper records of any such lecture having been given by Brühl. When we consider Freud's self-analysis we will return to his change of interest from law and politics to natural science.

3 JOSEF BREUER: FREUD'S LAST FATHER

1 In an excellent psychoanalytic reconstruction of the case Pollock (1968) has carried Freud's interpretations further and in a sympathetic investigation has shown that Breuer's feelings for his mother, who died when he was very young, colored his entire relationship with Bertha Pappenheim.
2 Roazen (1971) points out that Freud in his earlier work on psychoanalysis, up until 1910, often used Breuer's name to avoid taking full responsibility for developing psychoanalysis.

4 THE IMMACULATE ANALYSIS

1 According to Bonaparte et al. (1954, p. xi) 'Fliess's letters to Freud have not been found.'
2 'Bartlos' in the original German is translated as 'clean-shaven' (p. 107). A better word is beardless; it suggests M. has lost his full beard (Erikson, 1954).
3 The term Oedipus complex was first used by Freud in 1910. It is of some interest to note that Freud gives credit to Jung and Bleuler for elaborating the notion of complexes in a lecture published the same year (1910a). So Jung shares part of the honor for this phrase which has become a part of our vocabulary.

5 THE WHOLE LOST STORY: THE PSYCHOANALYTIC NARRATIVE

1 Many of the ideas expressed here come from conversations with Paul B. Jacobsen and an unpublished paper of his 'The Problem of Quality

and the Failure of the "Project"' (1975).
2 Symbolism became an important aspect of dream-interpretation for Freud, but since his major work on this was done after 1914 and the break with Jung, we will take up this topic in chapter 8.

6 COMPROMISE AND ADVANCEMENT: JUNG'S EARLY CAREER

1 This was Samuel Preiswerk who was also Jung's grandfather.
2 The meanings of words connected with love and sexuality were later to cause difficulties between Jung and Freud. Jung's refusal to limit sexuality to an exclusive linkage with biological functioning or psychological eroticism led Freud to charge that Jung was taking the sting out of the sexual theory in order to make psychoanalysis more palatable.
3 Jung practiced hypnotic treatment in the outpatient clinic. When he began practicing psychoanalysis he gave up hypnosis with the majority of patients, feeling that it did not allow him the control he wanted in the therapeutic situation.
4 Already Jung is modifying Freud's method. Freud had patients lie down on a couch - a holdover from hypnotic treatment - and he sat behind them.
5 Because Freud's initial citation to the work of Alfred Adler is also here the names of the triumvirate of depth psychology - Freud, Jung, and Adler - come together for the first time in this essay.

7 BINDING TIES: COLLABORATION AND DISCORD

1 This essay was revised by Jung in 1946 in order to de-emphasize its Freudian perspective. The passage from the 1946 version only differs from the 1910 version because of translation. The 1946 text is quoted here because it reads better.
2 Jung says the incident occurred on a visit to Vienna in 1910, but Jung's last meeting with Freud in Vienna was in March 1909.
3 'Wandlungen I and II' (1911a; 1912a) was first translated into English as 'The Psychology of the Unconscious' (1916a). 'Wandlungen' was extensively revised by Jung and this revised version was translated as 'Symbols of Transformation' (1952b). The 1952 version is cited here because its meaning is equivalent to the 1911 version, but it is expressed more clearly. The 1916 translation will be our primary source for what Jung said in 'Wandlungen,' but at some points in 'The Psychology of the Unconscious' the translation is confusing and in those instances 'Symbols of Transformation' will be used.

8 THE BREAK AND ITS RAMIFICATIONS

1 Below, we will see that Freud later used a slip of the pen in a letter by Jung to belittle Jung's attempts at questioning Freud's paternal attitude towards other analysts.

9 ARCHETYPAL VISIONS AND ANALYTICAL PSYCHOLOGY

1 Jaffé's (1979) work contains several reproductions of Jung's paintings.
2 The journey of the hero is a male myth and Jung uses it as a parallel to the individuation process in men. We will here follow the hero's journey for it is well documented by parallels with mythologies from patriarchal societies. Jung's minimal development of the female version is a simple adaptation of the hero's story, replacing male figures with female ones. Since the texts he used to establish mythological parallels

for it were in large part produced by men it is questionable whether
these documents provide corroborating evidence for his psychology of
women. What the similarities do demonstrate is that Jung's view of women's
mysteries is consonant with the fantasies of his forefathers.

10 CONFLICTS OF INTERPRETATION

1 Collections of articles concerned with the issue of psychoanalysis as
science are numerous, see for example Pumpian-Mindlin (1952), Hook
(1959), Wollheim (1974), and Mujeeb-ur-Rahmann (1977).
2 In the 1950's Lacan, Lagache and others were banished from the International Psychoanalytic Association. The Lagache-Lacan group was
chastised by Anna Freud, and Heinz Hartmann - a staunch defender
of the scientific status of psychoanalysis - presided over their dismissal.
3 Rhoades (1979) has shown that the Swiss and Nepalese, two cultures
that have come into contact only recently, have remarkably similar
habitats and evidence striking similarities in everything from agricultural
practices to religious beliefs.

11 HERMENEUTICS AND INTERPRETATIVE PSYCHOLOGY

1 For a similar distinction see Radnitzky's (1973) work on Anglo-Saxon
and Continental schools of meta-science.

BIBLIOGRAPHY

Abraham, H. (ed.) (1955), 'Clinical Papers and Essays on Psycho-Analysis,'
London: Hogarth.
Abraham, H., and Freud, E. (eds) (1965), 'A Psycho-Analytic Dialogue:
The Letters of Sigmund Freud and Karl Abraham, 1907-1926,' trans.
B. Marsh and H. Abraham, New York: Basic Books.
Abraham, K. (1907), On the significance of sexual trauma in childhood for
the symptomatology of dementia praecox, in H. Abraham (1955).
—(1908), The psycho-sexual differences between hysteria and dementia
praecox, in 'K. Abraham: Selected Papers on Psycho-Analysis,' London:
Hogarth, 1927.
—(1914), Review of C.G. Jung's 'Versuch einer Darstellung der Psycho-
analytischen Theorie... [The Theory of Psychoanalysis],' in H. Abraham
(ed.) (1955).
Adler, A. (1910), Trotz und Gehorsam, in A. Adler and C. Furtmüller
(eds), 'Heilen und Bilden,' Munich: Reinhardt, 1914.
Adler, G. (ed.) (1973), 'C.G. Jung Letters 1: 1906-1950,' Princeton
University Press.
—(1975), 'C.G. Jung Letters 2: 1951-1961,' Princeton University Press.
Amacher, P. (1965), 'Freud's Neurological Education and Its Influence on
Psychoanalytic Theory,' Psychological Issues, Monograph 16, New York:
International Universities Press.
Ansbacher, H., and Ansbacher, R. (eds) (1964), 'The Individual Psycho-
logy of Alfred Adler: A Systematic Presentation from His Writings,' New
York: Harper & Row.
Anzieu, D. (1959), 'L'Auto-Analyse. Sa Rôle dans la découverte de la
psychanalyse par Freud,' Paris: Presses Universitaires de France.
Apel, K.-O. (1972), Communication and the foundations of the humanities,
'Acta Sociologica,' 15, pp. 7-26.
Aschaffenburg, G. (1906), Die Beziehungen des sexuellen Lebens zur
Entstehung der Nerven- und Geisteskrankheiten, 'Münchener medizinische
Wochenschrift,' 53, pp. 1793-8.
Balint, M. (1937), Early developmental states of the ego. Primary object-love,
in 'Primary Love and Psycho-Analytic Technique,' New York: Liveright,
1965.
Bennet, E. (1960), Archetype and 'Aion', 'British Medical Journal,' 1.
—(1961), 'C.G. Jung,' London: Barrie & Rockliff.
Bernfeld, S. (1944), Freud's earliest theories and the school of Helmholtz,
'Psychoanalytic Quarterly,' 13, pp. 341-62.
Bernfeld, S., and Bernfeld, S.C. (1952), Freud's first year in practice,
1886-1887, in Ruitenbeek (1973).
Binswanger, L. (1957), 'Sigmund Freud: Reminiscences of a Friendship,'
New York: Grune & Stratton.
Bleuler, E. (1950 [1911]), 'Dementia Praecox, or the Group of Schizophrenias,'
trans. J. Zinkin, New York: International Universities Press.
Bonaparte, M., Freud, A., and Kris, E. (eds) (1954), 'Sigmund Freud:
The Origins of Psycho-Analysis: Letters to Wilhelm Fliess, Drafts and
Notes,' trans. E. Mosbacher and J. Strachey, New York: Basic Books.
Boring, E. (1950), 'A History of Experimental Psychology,' 2nd edn,
New York: Appleton-Century-Crofts.

Bowlby, J. (1969), 'Attachment,' New York: Basic Books.
Breuer, J., and Freud, S. (1893), On the Psychical Mechanism of Hysterical Phenomena: Preliminary Communication, 'The Standard Edition [SE] of the Complete Psychological Works of Sigmund Freud,' vol. 2.
—(1895), 'Studies on Hysteria,' SE 2.
Brill, A. (1942), A psychoanalyst scans his past, 'Journal of Nervous and Mental Disease,' 95.
Brody, B. (1970), Freud's case-load, in Ruitenbeek (1973).
Brome, V. (1968), 'Freud and His Early Circle,' New York: William Morrow.
Bry, I., and Rifkin, A. (1962), Freud and the history of ideas: primary sources, 1886-1910, in Masserman (1962).
Campbell, J. (1956), 'The Hero with a Thousand Faces,' New York: World Publishing.
Cioffi, F. (1974), Was Freud a liar? 'The Listener,' 91, no. 2341, February 7, pp. 172-4.
Collingwood, R.G. (1956), 'The Idea of History', ed. T.M. Knox, New York: Oxford University Press.
Crites, S. (1971), The narrative quality of experience, 'Journal of the American Academy of Religion,' 39, pp. 291-311.
—(1978), The demiurgic imagination in art and experience, 'boundary 2,' Winter.
Decker, H. (1977), 'Freud in Germany: Revolution and Reaction in Science, 1893-1907, Psychological Issues,' Monograph 41, New York: International Universities Press.
Derrida, J. (1972), Freud and the scene of writing, in Mehlman (1976).
Dinnerstein, D. (1977), 'The Mermaid and the Minotaur: Sexual Arrangements and Human Malaise,' New York: Harper.
Dodds, E. (1968), 'The Greeks and the Irrational,' Berkeley: University of California Press.
Donoghue, A., and Hillman, J. (eds) (1963), 'The Cocaine Papers,' Vienna: Dunquin Press.
Ehrman, J. (ed.) (1970), 'Structuralism,' Garden City, New York: Anchor.
Eissler, K. (1951), An unknown autobiographical letter by Freud and a short commentary, 'International Journal of Psycho-Analysis,' 32, pp. 319-24.
Ellenberger, H. (1970), 'The Discovery of the Unconscious,' New York: Basic Books.
Erikson, E. (1954), The dream specimen of psychoanalysis, in Knight and Friedman (1954).
—(1955), A historic friendship: Freud's letters to Fliess, in E. Erikson, 'Life History and the Historical Moment.' New York: Norton, 1975.
Ferenczi, S. (1913), Review of C.G. Jung's 'Wandlungen und Symbole der Libido,' 'Internationale Zeitschrift für ärztliche Psychoanalyse,' 1, pp. 301 403.
Feyerabend, P. (1970), Consolations for the specialist, in T. Lakotos and A. Musgrave (eds), 'Criticism and the Growth of Knowledge,' London: Cambridge University Press.
Fisher, S., and Greenberg, R. (1977), 'The Scientific Credibility of Freud's Theories and Therapy,' New York: Basic Books.
Freud, A. (1971), Foreword to Gardiner (1971).
Freud, M. (1957), 'Glory Reflected: Sigmund Freud, Man and Father,' London: Angus & Robertson.
Freud, S. (1884), On Coca, in Donoghue and Hillman (1963).
—(1885a), Contribution to the knowledge of the effect of cocaine, in Donoghue and Hillman (1963).
—(1885b), Coca, abbreviated translation by S. Pollak of On Coca with a note added by Freud. In Donoghue and Hillman (1963).
—(1886), Observations on a Severe Case of Hemianaesthesia in a Hysterical Male, 'The Standard Edition [SE] of the Complete Psychological Works of Sigmund Freud,' vol. 1, trans. and ed. J. Strachey, London: Hogarth.
—(1887), Craving for and fear of cocaine, in Donoghue and Hillman (1963).
—(1888), Preface to the translation of Bernheim's 'Suggestion,' SE 1.

Freud, S. (1890), Psychical (or Mental) Treatment, SE 7.
—(1892-3), A Case of Successful Treatment by Hypnotism, SE 1.
—(1893a), Some Points for a Comparative Study of Organic and Hysterical Motor Paralyses, SE 1.
—(1893b), Charcot, SE 3.
—(1894), The Neuro-Psychoses of Defence, SE 3.
—(1895), On the Grounds for Detaching a Particular Syndrome from Neurasthenia under the Description of 'Anxiety Neurosis', SE 3.
—(1896a), Heredity and the Aetiology of the Neuroses, SE 3.
—(1896b), Further Remarks on the Neuro-Psychoses of Defence, SE 3.
—(1896c), The Aetiology of Hysteria, SE 3.
—(1899), Screen Memories, SE 3.
—(1900), 'The Interpretation of Dreams,' SE 4-5.
—(1901a), 'On Dreams,' SE 5.
—(1901b), 'The Psychopathology of Everyday Life,' SE 6.
—(1905a), 'Jokes and their Relation to the Unconscious,' SE 8.
—(1905b), 'Three Essays on the Theory of Sexuality,' SE 7.
—(1905c [1901]), Fragment of an Analysis of a Case of Hysteria, SE 7.
—(1906a), My Views on the Part Played by Sexuality in the Aetiology of the Neurosis, SE 7.
—(1906b), Psycho-Analysis and the Establishment of Facts in Legal Proceedings, SE 9.
—(1907), Obsessive Actions and Religious Practices, SE 9.
—(1908), On the Sexual Theories of Children, SE 9.
—(1909a), Analysis of a Phobia in a Five-Year-Old Boy, SE 10.
—(1909b), Family Romances, SE 9.
—(1909c), Notes Upon a Case of Obsessional Neurosis, SE 10.
—(1910a [1909]), Five Lectures on Psycho-Analysis, SE 11.
—(1910b), 'Leonardo da Vinci and a Memory of his Childhood,' SE 11.
—(1910c), The Future Prospects of Psycho-Analytic Therapy, SE 11.
—(1910d), A Special Type of Choice of Object Made by Men, SE 11.
—(1911a), Formulations on the Two Principles of Mental Functioning, SE 12.
—(1911b), Psycho-Analytic Notes on an Autobiographical Account of a Case of Paranoia (Dementia Paranoides), SE 12.
—(1911c), The Handling of Dream-Interpretation in Psycho-Analysis, SE 12.
—(1912a), Postscript to the Case of Paranoia, SE 12.
—(1912b), The Dynamics of Transference, SE 12.
—(1912c), Recommendations to Physicians Practising Psycho-Analysis, SE 12.
—(1913a), 'Totem and Taboo,' SE 13.
—(1913b), On Beginning Treatment, SE 12.
—(1913c), The Disposition to Obsessional Neurosis, SE 12.
—(1913d), The Claims of Psycho-Analysis to Scientific Interest, SE 13.
—(1913e [1911]), On Psycho-Analysis, SE 12.
—(1914a), Fausse reconnaissance ('déjà raconté') in psycho-analytic treatment, SE 13.
—(1914b), The Moses of Michelangelo, SE 13.
—(1914c), On Narcissism: an Introduction, SE 14.
—(1914d), On the History of the Psycho-Analytic Movement, SE 14.
—(1914e), Some Reflections on Schoolboy Psychology, SE 13.
—(1914f), Remembering, Repeating, and Working-Through, SE 12.
—(1915), Instincts and their Vicissitudes, SE 14.
—(1916-17), 'Introductory Lectures on Psycho-Analysis,' SE 15-16.
—(1917a), A Childhood Recollection, from 'Dichtung und Wahrheit,' SE 17.
—(1917b), A Metapsychological Supplement to the Theory of Dreams, SE 14.
—(1918 [1914]), From the History of an Infantile Neurosis, SE 17.
—(1919), Lines of Advance in Psycho-Analytic Therapy, SE 17.
—(1920), 'Beyond the Pleasure Principle,' SE 18.
—(1922), Some Neurotic Mechanisms in Jealousy, Paranoia and Homosexuality, SE 18.
—(1923a), 'The Ego and the Id,' SE 19.

Freud, S. (1923b), Remarks on the Theory and Practice of Dream-Interpretation, SE 19.
—(1924), The Economic Problem of Masochism, SE 19.
—(1925a), A note upon the 'Mystic Writing-Pad,' SE 19.
—(1925b), 'An Autobiographical Study,' SE 20.
—(1925c), Josef Breuer, SE 19.
—(1925d), Negation, SE 19.
—(1926), 'The Question of Lay Analysis,' SE 20.
—(1927), 'The Future of an Illusion,' SE 21.
—(1930), 'Civilization and its Discontents,' SE 21.
—(1931), Female Sexuality, SE 21.
—(1932), My Contact with Josef Popper-Lynkeus, SE 22.
—(1933a), 'New Introductory Lectures on Psycho-Analysis,' SE 22.
—(1933b), Why War? SE 22.
—(1936), A Disturbance of Memory on the Acropolis, SE 22.
—(1937a), Analysis Terminable and Interminable, SE 23.
—(1937b), Constructions in Analysis, SE 23.
—(1939 [1937-1939]), 'Moses and Monotheism: Three Essays,' SE 23.
—(1940a [1938]), 'An Outline of Psycho-Analysis,' SE 23.
—(1940b), Some Elementary Lessons in Psycho-Analysis, SE 23.
—(1941 [1938]) Findings, Ideas, Problems, SE 23.
—(1950a [1892-1899]), Extracts from the Fliess Papers, SE 1.
—(1950b [1895]), Project for a Scientific Psychology, SE 1.
—(1954 [1887-1902]), 'The Origins of Psycho-Analysis: Letters to Wilhelm Fliess, Drafts and Notes,' eds M. Bonaparte, A. Freud and E. Kris, trans. E. Mosbacher and J. Strachey, New York: Basic Books.
—(1956 [1886]), Report on My Studies in Paris and Berlin, SE 1.
—(1957 [1891]), Psycho-Physical Parallelism, SE 14.
—(1960), 'The Letters of Sigmund Freud,' ed. E. Freud, trans. T. and J. Stern, New York: Basic Books.
—(1969), Some Early Unpublished Letters of Freud, 'International Journal of Psycho-Analysis,' 50, pp. 419-27.
Gadamer, H.-G. (1975), 'Truth and Method,' New York: Seabury Press.
Gardiner, M. (ed.) (1971), 'The Wolf-Man,' New York: Basic Books.
Gass, W. (1978), 'The World Within the Word,' New York: Knopf.
Gedo, J., and Pollock, G. (eds) (1976), 'Freud: The Fusion of Science and Humanism, Psychological Issues,' Monograph 34/35, New York: International Universities Press.
Gedo, J., and Wolf, E. (1970), The 'Ich Letters,' in Gedo and Pollock (1976).
—(1976), From the history of introspective psychology: the humanist strain, in Gedo and Pollock (1976).
Gittelson, B. (1976), 'Biorhythm: A Personal Science,' New York: Arco Publishing.
Glover, E. (1950), 'Freud and Jung,' New York: Norton.
Goethe, J. (1893 [1780]), 'The Maxims and Reflections of Goethe,' trans. B. Saunders, New York: MacMillan.
Gottesman, I., and Shields, J. (1972), 'Schizophrenia and Genetics,' New York: Academic Press.
Greenfield, N. and Lewis, W. (eds) (1965), 'Psychoanalysis and Current Biological Thought,' Madison, Wisconsin: University of Wisconsin Press.
Grinstein, A. (1968), 'On Sigmund Freud's Dreams,' Detroit: Wayne State University Press.
Habermas, J. (1971), 'Knowledge and Human Interests,' trans. J. Shapiro, Boston: Beacon Press.
Hale, N., Jr (1971a), 'Freud and the Americans: The Beginnings of Psychoanalysis in the United States, 1876-1917,' New York: Oxford University Press.
Hale, N., Jr (ed.) (1971b), 'James Jackson Putnam and Psychoanalysis,' Cambridge, Mass: Harvard University Press.
Hampshire, S. (1962), Disposition and memory, in Wollheim (1974).
Hannah, B. (1976), 'Jung: His Life and Work,' New York: G.P. Putnam's Sons.

Harding, M.E. (1955), 'Woman's Mysteries: Ancient and Modern,' reprinted
  New York: Bantam, 1973.
Hillman, J. (1975), The fiction of case history: a round, in Wiggins (1975).
Holt, R. (1965), A review of Freud's biological assumptions and their influence
  on his theories, in Greenfield and Lewis (1965).
Hook, S. (ed.) (1959), 'Psychoanalysis, Scientific Method and Philosophy,'
  New York: New York University Press.
Hudson, L. (1972), 'The Cult of the Fact,' London: Jonathan Cape.
Jacobsen, P. (1975), The problem of quality and the failure of the 'Project,'
  Unpublished paper, Wesleyan University.
Jacobsen, P., and Steele, R. (1979), From present to past: Freudian
  archaeology, 'International Review of Psycho-Analysis,' 6, pp. 349-62.
Jaffé, A. (1968), 'From the Life and Work of C.G. Jung,' trans. R.F.C. Hull,
  reprinted New York: Harper & Row, 1971.
Jaffé, A. (ed.) (1979), 'C.G. Jung: Word and Image,' trans. K. Winston,
  Princeton University Press.
Jahoda, M. (1977), 'Freud and the Dilemmas of Psychology,' New York:
  Basic Books.
James, W. (1907), 'Pragmatism,' New York: Meridan, 1955.
Jones, E. (1914), The unconscious and its significance for psychopathology,
  in 'Papers on Psycho-Analysis,' 2nd edn, London: Balliere, Tindall & Cox,
  1918.
—(1916), The theory of symbolism, in 'Papers on Psycho-Analysis,' 2nd edn,
  London: Balliere, Tindall & Cox, 1918.
—(1953), 'The Life and Work of Sigmund Freud,' vol. 1, New York: Basic
  Books.
—(1955), 'The Life and Work of Sigmund Freud,' vol. 2, New York: Basic
  Books.
—(1957), 'The Life and Work of Sigmund Freud,' vol. 3, New York: Basic
  Books.
Joyce, J. (1914), 'Ulysses,' reprinted New York: Random, 1961.
Jung, C.G. (1902), 'On the Psychology and Pathology of So-Called Occult
  Phenomena,' 'The Collected Works [CW] of C.G. Jung,' vol. 1, trans.
  R.F.C. Hull, Princeton University Press.
—(1905a), Cryptomnesia, CW 1.
—(1905b), Experimental Observations on the Faculty of Memory, CW 2.
—(1905c), On Spiritualistic Phenomena, CW 18.
—(1905d), The Psychological Diagnosis of Evidence, CW 2.
—(1905e), The Reaction-Time Ratio in the Association Experiment, CW 2.
—(1906a [1905]), The Psychopathological Significance of the Association
  Experiment, CW 2.
—(1906b), Freud's Theory of Hysteria: A Reply to Aschaffenburg, CW 4.
—(1906c), Psychoanalysis and Association Experiments, CW 2.
—(1906d), Association, Dream, and Hysterical Symptom, CW 2.
—(1907), 'The Psychology of Dementia Praecox,' CW 3.
—(1908a), The Content of the Psychoses, CW 3.
—(1908b), The Freudian Theory of Hysteria, CW 4.
—(1909), The Analysis of Dreams, CW 4.
—(1910a), The Association Method, trans. A. Brill, 'American Journal of
  Psychology,' 21, pp. 219-69.
—(1910b [1909]), The Association Method, CW 2.
—(1910c), The Family Constellation, CW 2.
—(1910d), Abstracts of the Psychological Works of Swiss Authors, CW 18.
—(1910e [1908]), On Dementia Praecox, CW 18.
—(1910-11), On the Significance of Number Dreams, CW 4.
—(1911a), Wandlungen und Symbole der Libido, pt I, 'Jahrbuch für
  psychoanalytische und psychopathologische Forschungen,' III, pp. 120-227.
—(1911b), Contributions to symbolism, CW 18.
—(1911c), Annual report by the president of the International Psychoanalytic Association, CW 18.
—(1911-12), 'Wandlungen und Symbole der Libido,' Leipzig and Vienna:

Franz Deuticke.
Jung, C.G. (1912a), 'Wandlungen und Symbole der Libido,' pt II, 'Jahrbuch für
  psychoanalytische und psychopathologische Forscnungen, IV,' pp. 162-464.
—(1912b), New Paths in Psychology, CW 7.
—(1913a [1911]), On the Doctrine of Complexes, CW 2.
—(1913b), The Theory of Psychoanalysis, CW 4.
—(1913c), A Contribution to the Study of Psychological Types, CW 6.
—(1914a), On Psychological Understanding, CW 3.
—(1914b), On the Importance of the Unconscious in Psychopathology, CW 3.
—(1916a), 'Psychology of the Unconscious. A Study of the Transformations
  of the Libido. A Contribution to the History of the Evolution of Thought,'
  trans. B. Hinkle, New York: Moffat, Yard & Co.
—(1916b), The Structure of the Unconscious, CW 7.
—(1916c), 'The Seven Sermons to the Dead Written by Basilides in Alexandria,
  the City Where the East Toucheth the West,' trans. H.G. Baynes, in
  Jung (1973b).
—(1918), The Role of the Unconscious, CW 10.
—(1919), Instinct and the Unconscious, CW 8.
—(1921), 'Psychological types,' CW 6.
—(1927), Woman in Europe, CW 10.
—(1928), The Relations Between the Ego and the Unconscious, CW 7.
—(1929a), Problems of Modern Psychotherapy, CW 16.
—(1929b), Freud and Jung: Contrasts, CW 4.
—(1931a), The Structure of the Psyche, CW 8.
—(1931b), The Stages of Life, CW 8.
—(1931c), Analytical Psychology and *Weltanschauung*, CW 8.
—(1932), Sigmund Freud in his Historical Setting, CW 15.
—(1933), The Real and the Surreal, CW 8.
—(1934a), The Development of Personality, CW 17.
—(1934b), The State of Psychotherapy Today, CW 10.
—(1935), The Tavistock Lectures: On the Theory and Practice of Analytical
  Psychology, CW 18.
—(1936), Individual Dream Symbolism in Relation to Alchemy, CW 12.
—(1939), In Memory of Sigmund Freud, CW 15.
—(1940), 'Psychology and Religion,' CW 11.
—(1943), On the Psychology of the Unconscious, CW 7.
—(1944), 'Psychology and Alchemy,' CW 12.
—(1946a [1909]), Psychic Conflicts in a Child, CW 17.
—(1946b), 'The Psychology of the Transference,' CW 16.
—(1948a), A Psychological Approach to the Dogma of the Trinity, CW 11.
—(1948b), Foreword to Harding, 'Woman's Mysteries,' CW 18.
—(1949 [1909]), The Significance of the Father in the Destiny of the
  Individual, CW 4
—(1950), A Study in the Process of Individuation, CW 9.1.
—(1951), 'Aion: Researches into the Phenomenology of the Self,' CW 9.2.
—(1952a), 'Answer to Job,' CW 11.
—(1952b), 'Symbols of Transformation,' CW 5.
—(1954a), Archetypes of the Collective Unconscious, CW 9.1.
—(1954b), Psychological Aspects of the Mother Archetype, CW 9.1.
—(1954c), Transformation Symbolism in the Mass, CW 11.
—(1954d), On the Nature of the Psyche, CW 8.
—(1955-6), 'Mysterium Coniunctionis: an Inquiry into the Separation and
  Synthesis of Psychic Opposites in Alchemy,' CW 14.
—(1957), The Houston films, in McGuire and Hull (1977).
—(1958a), 'Flying Saucers: a Modern Myth,' CW 10.
—(1958b [1916]), The Transcendent Function, CW 8.
—(1958c), Schizophrenia, CW 3.
—(1968 [1953]), Answers to Questions on Freud, CW 18.
—(1970 [1916]), Adaptation, Individuation, Collectivity, CW 18.
—(1973a [1901]), Sigmund Freud: 'On Dreams,' CW 18.
—(1973b), 'Memories, Dreams, Reflections,' revised edition, ed. A. Jaffé,

trans. R. and C. Winston, New York: Pantheon.

Jung, C.G., and Riklin, F. (1904-5), The Associations of Normal Subjects, CW 2.

Kermode, F. (1967), 'The Sense of an Ending: Studies in the Theory of Fiction,' New York: Oxford University Press.

Kline, P. (1972), 'Fact and Fantasy in Freudian Theory,' London: Methuen.

Knight, R., and Friedman, C. (eds) (1954), 'Psychoanalytic Psychiatry and Psychology: Clinical and Theoretical Papers,' vol. 1, New York: International Universities Press.

Kohut, H. (1976), Creativeness, charisma, group psychology: reflections on the self-analysis of Freud, in Gedo & Pollock (1976).

Kris, E. (1954), Introduction, in Bonaparte, Freud and Kris (1954).

Lacan, J. (1977), 'Ecrits: A Selection,' trans. A. Sheridan, New York: Norton.

Laplanche, J. (1976), 'Life and Death in Psychoanalysis,' trans. J. Mehlman, Baltimore: Johns Hopkins University Press.

Laplanche, J., and Leclaire, S. (1966), The unconscious: a psychoanalytic study, in Mehlman (ed.) (1976).

Laplanche, J., and Pontalis, J.-B. (1968), Fantasy and the origins of sexuality, 'International Journal of Psycho-Analysis,' 49, pp. 1-18.

—(1973), 'The Language of Psychoanalysis,' trans. D. Nicholson-Smith, New York: Norton.

Loch, W. (1977), Some comments on the subject of psychoanalysis and truth, in Smith (1977).

Lowenstein, R., Newman, L., Schur, M., and Solint, A. (eds) (1966), 'Psychoanalysis - a General Psychology: Essays in Honor of Heinz Hartmann,' New York: International Universities Press.

McGuire, W. (ed.) (1974), 'The Freud/Jung Letters: The Correspondence between Sigmund Freud and C.G. Jung,' Princeton University Press.

McGuire, W., and Hull, R.F.C. (eds) (1977), 'C.G. Jung Speaking: Interviews and Encounters,' Princeton University Press.

Marcus, S. (1974), Freud and Dora: story, history, case history, 'Partisan Review,' 41, pp. 12-23; 89-108.

—(1977), Introductory essay in Bonaparte, Freud and Kris (1954).

Masserman, J. (ed.) (1962), 'Psychoanalytic Education,' vol. 5 in the series 'Science and Psychoanalysis,' New York: Grune & Stratton.

Meehl, P. (1972), A critical afterword, in Gottesman and Shields (1972).

Mehlman, J. (ed.) (1976), 'French Freud: Structural Studies in Psychoanalysis,' Millwood, New York: Kraus Reprint Co.

Meng, H., and Freud, E. (eds) (1963), 'Psychoanalysis and Faith: The Letters of Sigmund Freud and Oskar Pfister,' trans. E. Mosbacher, New York: Basic Books.

Merleau-Ponty, M. (1960a), Indirect Language and the Voices of Silence, in 'Signs,' trans. R. McCleary, Evanston, Ill.: Northwestern University Press, 1964.

—(1960b), From Mauss to Claude Lévi-Strauss, in 'Signs,' trans. R. McCleary, Evanston, Ill.: Northwestern University Press, 1964.

—(1962), 'Phenomenology of Perception,' trans. C. Smith, London: Routledge & Kegan Paul.

Miel, J. (1966), Jacques Lacan and the structure of the unconscious, in Ehrman (1970).

Miller, J.B. (1976), 'Toward a New Psychology of Women,' Boston: Beacon.

Mink, L.O. (1972), 'Collingwood's historicism: a dialectic of process,' in M. Krauz (ed.), 'Critical Essays in the Philosophy of R.G. Collingwood,' New York: Oxford University Press.

Mischel, T. (1965), Concerning rational behavior and psychoanalytic explanation, in Wollheim (1974).

Montaigne, M. (1965), 'The Complete Essays of Montaigne,' trans. D. Frame, Palo Alto: Stanford University Press.

Mujeeb-ur-Rahman, M. (ed.) (1977), 'The Freudian Paradigm,' Chicago: Nelson-Hall.

Neu, J. (1974), Genetic explanation in 'Totem and Taboo,' in Wollheim (1974).
Niederland, W. (1971), Freud's literary styles: some observations, 'American Imago,' 28, pp. 17-23.
Nietzsche, F. (1872), 'The Birth of Tragedy and The Genealogy of Morals,' trans. F. Golffing, Garden City, New York: Doubleday-Anchor, 1956.
—(1878), 'Human All-Too-Human,' trans. H. Zimmern, Edinburgh: T.N. Foulis, 1909.
Nunberg, H., and Federn, E. (eds) (1962), 'Minutes of the Vienna Psychoanalytic Society. Vol. 1, 1906-1908,' trans. M. Nunberg, New York: International Universities Press.
—(1974), 'Minutes of the Vienna Psychoanalytic Society. Vol. 3, 1910-1911,' trans. M. Nunberg, New York: International Universities Press.
Oeri, A. (1935), Some youthful memories, in McGuire and Hull (1977).
Palmer, R. (1969), 'Hermeneutics: Interpretation Theory in Schleiermacher, Dilthey, Heidegger, and Gadamer,' Evanston, Ill.: Northwestern University Press.
Pestalozzi, R. (1956), Article in 'Neue Zürcher Zeitung,' July 1.
Pollock, G. (1968), Josef Breuer, in Gedo and Pollock (1976).
Popper, K. (1963), 'Conjectures and Refutations: The Growth of Scientific Knowledge,' New York: Harper.
Post, L. van der (1976), 'Jung and the Story of Our Time,' New York: Pantheon.
Pribram, K., and Gill, M. (1976), 'Freud's "Project" Re-assessed,' New York: Basic Books.
Pumpian-Mindlin, E. (ed.) (1952), 'Psychoanalysis as Science,' New York: Basic Books.
Radnitzky, G. (1973), 'Contemporary Schools of Metascience,' Chicago: Henry Regnery.
Rhoades, R.E. (1979), Cultural echoes across the mountains, 'Natural History,' 88, no. 1, pp. 46-57.
Ricoeur, P. (1970), 'Freud and Philosophy: An Essay on Interpretation,' New Haven: Yale University Press.
—(1974), 'The Conflict of Interpretations: Essays in Hermeneutics,' ed. D. Inde, Evanston, Ill.: Northwestern University Press.
Roazen, P. (1971), 'Freud and His Followers,' New York: New American Library.
Robert, M. (1966), 'The Psychoanalytic Revolution,' trans. K. Morgan, New York: Harcourt, Brace & World.
—(1976), 'From Oedipus to Moses: Freud's Jewish Identity,' trans. R. Manheim, Garden City, New York: Anchor Books.
Ruitenbeek, H. (ed.) (1973), 'Freud as We Knew Him,' Detroit: Wayne State University Press.
Sachs, H. (1944), 'Freud, Master and Friend,' Cambridge, Mass.: Harvard University Press.
Sadow, L., Gedo, J., Miller, J., Pollock, G., Sabshin, M., and Schlessinger, N. (1968), The process of hypothesis change in three early psychoanalytic concepts, in Gedo and Pollock (1976).
Schafer, R. (1978), 'Language and Insight,' New Haven: Yale University Press.
Scheibe, K.E. (1978), The psychologist's advantage and its nullification: limits of human predictability, 'American Psychologist,' 33, pp. 869-81.
Schiller, J.C.F. von (1795), 'On the Aesthetic Education of Man, in a Series of Letters,' trans. R. Snell, New Haven: Yale University Press, 1954.
Schlessinger, N., Gedo, J., Miller, J., Pollock, G., Sabshin, M., and Sadow, L. (1967), The scientific styles of Breuer and Freud in the origins of psychoanalysis, in Gedo and Pollock (1976).
Schorske, C. (1973), Politics and patricide in Freud's 'Interpretation of Dreams,' 'American Historical Review,' 78, pp. 328-47.
Schur, M. (1966), Some additional 'day residues' of 'the specimen dream of psychoanalyses,' in Lowenstein, Newman, Schur and Solint (1966).

Schur, M. (1972), 'Freud: Living and Dying,' New York: International Universities Press.

Schwaber, P. (1976), Scientific art: 'The Interpretation of Dreams,' 'Psychoanalytic Study of the Child,' 31, New Haven: Yale University Press.

Shakow, D., and Rapaport, D. (1964), 'The Influence of Freud on American Psychology,' Psychological Issues, Monograph 13, New York: International Universities Press.

Sherwood, M. (1969), 'The Logic of Explanation in Psychoanalysis,' New York: Academic Press.

Smith, J. (ed.) (1977), 'Thought, Consciousness, and Reality,' New Haven: Yale University Press.

Steele, R. (1979), Psychoanalysis and hermeneutics, 'International Review of Psycho-Analysis,' 6, pp. 389–411.

Steele, R., and Jacobsen, P. (1978), From present to past: the development of Freudian theory, 'International Review of Psycho-Analysis,' 5, pp. 393–411.

Steele, R., and Swinney, S. (1978), Zane Grey, Carl Jung and the journey of the hero, 'Journal of Analytical Psychology,' 23, pp. 63–89.

Steiner, G. (1965), Errinnerungen an Carl Gustav Jung, 'Basler Stadtbuch,' pp. 117–63.

Stevens, W. (1975), 'Opus Posthumous,' New York: Knopf.

Stoller, R. (1972), The 'bedrock' of masculinity and feminity: bisexuality, in J. Miller (ed.), 'Psychoanalysis and Women,' New York: Bruner/Mazel, 1973.

Strachey, J. (1955), Editor's note, SE 17.

—(1959), Footnote to Freud's 'An Autobiographical Study,' SE 20.

—(1962), Editor's note to Charcot, SE 3.

—(1966), Editor's introduction to the Project for a Scientific Psychology, SE 1.

Strümpell, A. (1895), Review of Breuer and Freud's 'Studien über Hysterie,' 'Deutsche Zeitschrift für Nervenheilkunde,' 8, pp. 159–61.

Swinney, S. (1978), Freud and Dora, Lecture given to class on Personality and Interpretation, Wesleyan University.

Trosman, H. (1973), Freud's cultural background, in Gedo and Pollock (1976).

Waelder, R. (1962), Psychoanalysis, scientific method, and philosophy, 'Journal of the American Psychoanalytic Association,' 10, pp. 617–37.

Wiggins, J. (ed.) (1975), 'Religion as Story,' New York: Harper & Row.

Wittels, F. (1924), 'Sigmund Freud: His Personality, His Teaching, & His School,' New York: Dodd, Mead.

Wolf, E. (1971), 'Saxa Loquuntur:' artistic aspect of Freud's 'The Aetiology of Hysteria,' in Gedo and Pollock (1976).

Wollheim, R. (ed.) (1974), 'Freud: A Collection of Critical Essays,' Garden City, New York: Anchor.

INDEX